S0-AZJ-439

THE YEARS OF
MacArthur

Volume II

1941–1945

By D. Clayton James

The Years of MacArthur
Volume I, 1880–1941

The Years of MacArthur
Volume II, 1941–1945

THE YEARS OF
MacArthur

Volume II

☆ ☆

1941–1945

D. Clayton James

*Illustrated with photographs
and with maps by Samuel H. Bryant*

HOUGHTON MIFFLIN COMPANY

19 · *Boston* · 75

FIRST PRINTING C

COPYRIGHT © 1975 BY D. CLAYTON JAMES
ALL RIGHTS RESERVED. NO PART OF THIS WORK
MAY BE REPRODUCED OR TRANSMITTED IN ANY FORM
BY ANY MEANS, ELECTRONIC OR MECHANICAL, INCLUDING
PHOTOCOPYING AND RECORDING, OR BY ANY INFORMATION
STORAGE OR RETRIEVAL SYSTEM, WITHOUT PERMISSION
IN WRITING FROM THE PUBLISHER.

Library of Congress Cataloging in Publication Data (Revised)

James, Dorris Clayton, 1931–
The years of MacArthur.

Includes bibliographical references and index.
CONTENTS: v. 1. 1880–1941. — v. 2. 1941–1945.
1. MacArthur, Douglas, 1880–1964. I. Title.
E745.M3J3   355.3'31'0924 [B]   76–108685
ISBN 0–395–20446–1 (v. 2)

PRINTED IN THE UNITED STATES OF AMERICA

The author is grateful for permission to quote from the works listed below:
Daniel E. Barbey, *MacArthur's Amphibious Navy: Seventh Amphibious Force Operations 1943–1945,* © 1969, United States Naval Institute. Robert L. Eichelberger and Milton MacKaye, *Our Jungle Road to Tokyo,* copyright 1951 by Robert L. Eichelberger. Reprinted by permission of The Viking Press, Inc. Edward M. Flanagan, Jr., *The Old Breed: A History of the First Marine Division in World War II,* Infantry Journal Press, 1949. George C. Kenney, *General Kenney Reports: A Personal History of the Pacific War* and *The MacArthur I Knew.* Reprinted by permission of the author. Jay Luvaas (editor), *Dear Miss Em: General Eichelberger's War in the Pacific 1942–1945.* Reprinted by permission of the publisher, Greenwood Press. Gavin M. Long, *The Final Campaigns (Australia in the War of 1939–1945),* copyright © 1963 by Australian War Memorial. Douglas MacArthur, *Reminiscences,* McGraw-Hill Book Company. Copyright © 1964 Time Inc. Reprinted with permission. Dudley McCarthy, *South-West Pacific Area — First Year: Kokoda to Wau* (Australia in the War of 1939–1945), copyright © 1961 by Australian War Memorial. Louis Morton, *Strategy and Command: The First Two Years (U.S. Army in World War II: The War in the Pacific).* Reprinted by permission of Center of Military History, Department of the Army. Samuel I. Rosenman, *Working with Roosevelt.* Reprinted by permission of Harper & Row, Publishers, Inc. Robert R. Smith, *Triumph in the Philippines (U.S. Army in World War II: The War in the Pacific.* Reprinted by permission of Center of Military History, Department of the Army. Henry L. Stimson, "Henry L. Stimson Diary," Yale University Library. Arthur Vandenberg, Jr., *The Private Papers of Senator Vandenberg,* copyright 1952 by Arthur Vandenberg, Jr. Reprinted by permission of the publisher, Houghton Mifflin Company. Various MacArthur documents. Reprinted by permission of the MacArthur Memorial. Charles A. Willoughby, *Reports of General MacArthur,* U.S. Government Printing Office, 1966. *A complete listing of source material is given in the Bibliographical Note, p. 811.*

To Erlene

Foreword

THIS PROJECT began as a two-volume biography of General of the Army Douglas MacArthur, but it has been expanded to three volumes, the last of which will cover the years 1945–64. As was true of the treatment of his career to 1941, excessive adulation or cruel disparagement has characterized nearly all biographical and other unofficial writings about MacArthur's role in the war against Japan. On the other hand, the American and Australian official histories of that conflict generally have been fair, if sometimes severely frank, in their evaluations of him as a theater commander. I have endeavored in my research and writing to strive toward the level of objectivity, as well as of thoroughness, achieved by the official historians. They, however, were dealing largely with impersonal matters of strategy, logistics, and operations, whereas I, though employing a life-and-times approach that encompasses a considerable coverage of the Southwest Pacific war, was primarily concerned with the person and position of the theater commander himself, who, in this case, happened to be one of the most controversial figures in American military annals. Thus, while I tried earnestly to be objective, I am quite aware that some of my judgments will appear far from neutral to certain readers.

Like me, you the reader will probably find yourself alternately admiring and despising MacArthur as the story of his wartime decisions and actions unfolds. Most of his colleagues interviewed in the research for this volume readily asserted that no one will ever probe fully the complex personality and character of MacArthur. Never was his contradictory nature more vividly apparent than during the Second World War. In the following pages you will find him engaged in acts of rare courage, yet at other times refusing to visit combat areas for long periods; he will gain both the Medal of Honor and the scurrilous nickname of "Dugout Doug." He will decide and act on strategic moves with brilliance and boldness on some occasions, yet display inexplicable hesitancy at other times. He will shrewdly bypass enemy strong points, but later demand their seizure despite their uselessness. He will achieve remarkable military results with relatively meager logistical support, while misusing and wasting his resources when they were later augmented. He will show intense concern over keeping his forces' casualties as low as possible, yet will relentlessly compel his field commanders to assault some objectives which could have been enveloped. He will develop cordial, harmonious relations with certain admirals at the same time that he will charge the Navy's leadership with conspiring against him and his theater's interests. He will display amazing flexibility in his thinking on the uses of air, naval, and amphibious forces, but will remain within the narrow, conventional bounds of the "old Army" thinking on some matters of strategy, tactics, and logistics. He will adjust to and work effectively with the socialist leaders of the Australian Labor ministry while himself remaining a political conservative as staunch in his convictions as Hoover. He will be extremely sensitive about his public image, but will blunder repeatedly in press and public relations. He will prove to be a skilled administrator who can organize and inspire his headquarters personnel to maximum efforts, yet at the same time coddle some inept staff officers and permit Sutherland to become a virtual Rasputin. He will diligently endeavor to turn over civil affairs to the Commonwealth officials as rapidly as Philippine areas are liberated, but will become thoroughly embroiled in the cauldron of Philippine politics. A firm believer and expounder of spiritual and moral values, he will avoid formal religious services and will engage in mendacious, face-saving schemes. He will demand the utmost loyalty and obedience from his subordinates, yet will be continuously critical of the decisions of his superiors, the President and the Joint Chiefs of Staff, and will sometimes defy their directives. The reader of this volume will not find it difficult to understand that after the high degree of success MacArthur enjoyed in his bold, sometimes impertinent relations with his superiors of 1941–45 he would feel confident that similar techniques would work later during the Korean War.

Surely MacArthur must rank as one of the most famous, colorful, and controversial commanders of World War II. Whether he was a great, if not the greatest, commander in that war, as some distinguished authorities have claimed, is a judgment that should be deferred until definitive studies of all the potential nominees have been published. If and when such an evaluation can be fairly made, it will have to be made in comparison only to the other theater commanders of World War II. It is inconceivable that criteria can be formulated for comparing his leadership with that of officers in totally dissimilar positions, such as Marshall and Patton. At this stage of scholarly research on that war, the complicated relations of the Combined Chiefs, Joint Chiefs, and theater headquarters have not been fully analyzed. It is not now clear, for example, exactly how much of the decision-making on Pacific strategy can be attributed to MacArthur's influence. Moreover, both popular and professional historians of the war still tend to categorize virtually all Anglo-American officers from the level of army commanders to the Combined Chiefs as "great" leaders. The attention devoted in this volume to Southwest Pacific strategy, logistics, and operations was deemed essential for relating MacArthur's decisions and actions to their context, particularly in view of the general reader's lack of knowledge of that theater in comparison to the European and Central Pacific theaters.

Through his first two campaigns especially — the defeat in the Philippines and the prolonged, bloody Papuan operation — MacArthur appears to be a commander who made an ample number of blunders. But were his mistakes actually worse than those of other theater commanders who may have been operating under less extenuating circumstances? If his relations with the Australian high command were sometimes poor, how badly did he handle the situation in comparison to the dealings of Stilwell or Eisenhower with their Allied colleagues? If MacArthur's key headquarters leaders were predominantly American Army officers, did he exhibit any more of a bias than Nimitz in his staff selections? If MacArthur ordered some operations that in retrospect appear needless, how many operations in the Central Pacific or in Italy were of little or no military value? It is doubtful that when the full, honest story is known of the leadership of the other major commanders of World War II MacArthur's reputation will suffer in comparison. Regardless of history's ultimate verdict on his greatness as a military commander, I remain convinced at this stage of my research that in the long run MacArthur's most significant contributions were made when he served as an administrator during the Japanese occupation. The proof of this thesis must await the concluding volume of the study.

Many officers who knew MacArthur or served under his command, as well as numerous laymen and professional scholars interested in this project, have contributed generously of their time and primary materials to assist me. I have listed them in the section on interviews and correspondence in the Bibliographical Note as well as in the chapter notes. Valuable assistance was provided by the staffs of the MacArthur Memorial Bureau of Archives, the Manuscripts Division of the Library of Congress, the Modern Military Records Division of the National Archives, the Washington National Records Center, the Center of Military History, the U.S. Military Academy Archives, the U.S. Army Military History Research Collection at Carlisle Barracks, the Albert F. Simpson Historical Research Center of the Air University, the Naval History Division, the U.S. Marine Corps Historical Division, the Franklin D. Roosevelt Library, the Harry S. Truman Library, the Dwight D. Eisenhower Library, the Australian War Memorial, the Oral History Office of Columbia University, and the manuscripts and archives departments of Duke University, the University of North Carolina, Yale University, and the Hoover Institution on War, Revolution, and Peace of Stanford University.

The administration of Mississippi State University has provided generous support and personal encouragement, particularly President William L. Giles and Vice President J. Chester McKee, Jr. The staff of the university's Mitchell Memorial Library has given splendid cooperation, especially George R. Lewis, director; Miss Margarete Peebles, acquisitions head; and Mrs. Martha B. Irby, interlibrary loan head. Secretaries who assisted in the transcription of interviews included Mrs. Judy R. Hotard, Mrs. Anna L. Kinton, Mrs. Nancy J. Upchurch, Mrs. Suzanne H. Sorrells, Mrs. Sally K. Richardson, and Mrs. Sherry S. Jackson. Mrs. Hotard has also served in the indispensable roles of secretary and research assistant; among her many tasks were the typing of the manuscript and the compiling of the basic data used in the Appendixes. Mrs. Helen J. Thompson, as part-time secretary, proved invaluable in performing countless chores, including proofreading the manuscript. Miss Anne S. Wells was a most helpful and able research assistant in the late stages of the project. The editorial guidance of Philip Rich and Grant Ujifusa of Houghton Mifflin Company and Frances L. Apt has been excellent. For their encouragment, advice, and patience, I am especially indebted to Erlene, Sherrie, Ned, Judy, and Allie James and Miss Dorris Bankston.

Mississippi State University   D. Clayton James
August 1974

Contents

Part III. Cartwheel Operations

Part IV. Advance to the Philippines

Part V. The Last Campaigns

Illustrations

Observes Australian operations at Balikpapan, Borneo, July 1, 1945. *U.S. Office of War Information*

Addressing the Philippine Congress, Manila, July 9, 1945. *U.S. Army Signal Corps*

With Lord Mountbatten at Manila, July 13, 1945. *Acme*

The first meeting of Generals MacArthur and Derevyanko, at Manila, August 26, 1945. *MacArthur Memorial*

Arrival in Japan, August 30, 1945. *MacArthur Memorial*

An emotional reunion at Yokohama, August 31, 1945. *U.S. Army Signal Corps*

General MacArthur and Colonel Egeberg in front of the New Grand Hotel, Yokohama, August 31, 1945. *International News Photos*

MacArthur signs the Japanese surrender document aboard the U.S.S. *Missouri*, September 2, 1945. *U.S. Army Signal Corps and D. N. Diedrich*

Maps

PART I

Defeat in the Philippines

CHAPTER I

Desperate Withdrawal

1. Nine Hours to Disaster

IT WAS ABOUT 12:20 P.M., December 8, 1941 (December 7, Honolulu time), at Clark Field, the large American air base lying in the Central Luzon Plain northwest of Manila. Nine hours had passed since news of the attack on Pearl Harbor had been received, yet the Clark Field planes had not been attacked or ordered to attack the enemy. Lieutenant W. Dupont Strong, a bomber pilot, had finished lunch and was walking to his quarters when he heard "a low moaning sound" and looked up to see "a whole crowd of airplanes" approaching from the northwest. The air-raid sirens began screaming just as the aircraft were directly overhead. Strong ran for a nearby slit trench: "By the time I hit the trench, the bombs had begun to hit the ground." Apparently everyone at Clark was as surprised as Strong when the first wave of Japanese bombers attacked.

A second flight, like the first, of about twenty-seven planes flying at nearly 25,000 feet, delivered its bombs with devastating accuracy soon after. Then came the attack most destructive to parked aircraft — a wave of thirty-four Zero fighters that strafed the field for over an hour. Four P-40 fighters managed to get into the air and give battle, but the rest of the Clark aircraft were destroyed on the ground, including the two squadrons of B-17 heavy bombers that were supposed to have been flown to Mindanao several days earlier. "With complete disregard for their lives," Captain Allison Ind said later, the bomber crews "rushed out in a futile attempt to take the big machines off . . . One after another, these vitally needed, expensive, irreplaceable bombers collapsed in bullet-ridden heaps, or sagged to the ravenous flames that were consuming them." Late that afternoon Captain William E. Dyess, a P-40 pilot from Manila's Nichols Field, flew over Clark and reported that planes, oil dumps, and hangars were still "blazing fiercely . . . It was a mess." [1]

Meanwhile, shortly after 12:30 P.M. that day a formation of fifty-four Japanese bombers and fifty Zeros caught the defenders off guard at Iba Field, forty miles west of Clark, and annihilated that fighter base's facilities and its P-40 squadron, which had unfortunately just returned from a patrol over the South China Sea, nearly out of fuel. By midafternoon of December 8 the strength in modern combat planes of Lieutenant General Douglas MacArthur's air arm had been reduced by more than half: the seventeen B-17's that were on Mindanao when the Luzon raids occurred were all that remained of the original thirty-five heavy bombers, and at least fifty-five of the seventy-two P-40's were lost. Another twenty-five to thirty-three older military aircraft of various types were destroyed. Only seven Japanese planes had been downed. Compared to personnel losses at Pearl Harbor, casualties had been moderate: about eighty killed and 150 wounded at Clark and Iba. But the Far East Air Force (FEAF), which MacArthur had counted on heavily in his plans for defense of the Philippines, had been eliminated as an effective combat force on the first day of war.[2]

Although the Pearl Harbor attack was the subject of several lengthy investigations resulting in the removal of the top commanders in Hawaii, the Clark-Iba fiasco did not produce even one official inquiry. It would not have been feasible, of course, during the ensuing months of combat in the Philippines, but some persons assumed that a later inquiry would be conducted. Francis B. Sayre, the Philippine high commissioner, said, "We supposed that an official investigation would follow. But the war was on then, and minds were immersed in the immediate problems of resistance." After the war Lieutenant General Claire L. Chennault castigated the War Department for failing to punish the Army Air Corps commanders of December, 1941: "If I had been caught with my planes on the ground . . . I could never again have looked my fellow officers squarely in the eye. The lightness with which this cardinal military sin was excused by the American high command . . . has always seemed to me one of the more shocking defects of the war."

Lieutenant Edgar D. Whitcomb, a B-17 navigator at Clark that first day of war, was still convinced many years later that "our generals and leaders committed one of the greatest errors possible to military men — that of letting themselves be taken by surprise. That error can be exceeded only by treason." Other than mentioning that "General MacArthur, having the Magic [code-breaking] intercepts, was in a better position to judge the situation than was Admiral [Husband E.] Kimmel" at Pearl Harbor, the U.S. Senate's joint committee, which in 1946 investigated the attack on Hawaii, dismissed the situation in the Philippines as beyond the scope of its inquiry.[3]

Charges and recriminations among the Philippine high command were nonexistent in the aftermath of the Clark-Iba raids, perhaps because of the preoccupation with continuing enemy attacks or a consensus that Washington's inadequate reinforcements to the islands was the underlying reason for the catastrophe. In their conversations most of the pilots and other air personnel on Luzon tended to blame MacArthur, the overall American Army commander in the Philippines, rather than

Major General Lewis H. Brereton, the FEAF commanding general, for the postponement of a planned raid against Formosa on the morning of December 8. The only commander in the Philippines to be reprimanded by a Pentagon superior, however, was Brereton, who received a blistering call on the afternoon of the 8th from General Henry H. Arnold, chief of the Army Air Forces, in which he demanded to know "how in hell" a veteran airman like Brereton could have been caught by surprise after having nine hours' advance notice of the Pearl Harbor raid. General George C. Marshall, the Army's chief of staff, did not rebuke MacArthur, although he did comment to a correspondent two weeks later, "It's all clear to me now except one thing. I just don't know how MacArthur happened to let his planes get caught on the ground." In his first wartime press conference on December 9 President Franklin D. Roosevelt responded to a reporter's query about the Clark Field disaster by saying that he had no new information on it and moving quickly to another topic.[4]

Arnold later stated that he was never satisfied with the explanations unofficially offered by the principal figures in the affair — Brereton, MacArthur, and Major General Richard K. Sutherland, MacArthur's chief of staff. Although in the following years oral and written apologias by the key participants in the decision-making at Manila were added to the few surviving official documents on the affair, Army and Air Force historians who have undertaken research on the subject frankly admit that gaps and contradictions in the available evidence make it impossible to explain fully the reasons for the Clark-Iba tragedy or to determine definitively who was at fault.

The following reconstruction of the key developments on Luzon during the critical morning hours of December 8, 1941, must be read with the above limitations in mind. At 2:00 A.M., December 8, a 27th Bombardment Group party at the Manila Hotel began to break up; it had been given in Brereton's honor and was a gala affair, considered by some veterans of Manila night life to be "the best entertainment this side of 'Minsky's.' " At 3:40, about an hour after Asiatic Fleet headquarters in Manila had received the news, Sutherland learned from a commercial radio broadcast of the Pearl Harbor attack. He immediately notified MacArthur, and by 4:00 Brereton's headquarters at nearby Nielson Field had the news. The War Department's message officially confirming the existence of war with Japan and ordering the execution of the war plan, Rainbow-5, was not received by MacArthur's general headquarters until 5:30. A half-hour earlier, according to Brereton, he went to Mac-Arthur's office, but Sutherland insisted that the general was busy and could not see him. Brereton then requested permission through Sutherland to launch a B-17 raid shortly after daylight against Japanese shipping at Takao harbor, Formosa. Sutherland responded that he could start preparations for the mission but that MacArthur would decide later when to begin offensive operations. According to Sutherland's account, he told Brereton that a photoreconnaissance mission should precede the raid because of the lack of data on possible Formosan targets and Brereton agreed. Several versions state that Brereton came back at 7:15 but again found MacArthur too occupied to receive him and had to return to his disappointed air staff with Sutherland's instructions to stand by for orders.

Within an hour after Brereton's second meeting with Sutherland the Iba radar began to track a formation of aircraft over the South China Sea headed for Luzon. While fighter squadrons were scrambled to intercept sectors from Lingayen to Manila, the B-17's at Clark were sent aloft without bomb loads to escape destruction on the ground. The Japanese attackers managed to avoid detection by the fighters, and shortly before 9:30 reports of bombings of Baguio, the Philippine summer capital, and of Tuguegarao, eastward in the Cagayan Valley, reached FEAF headquarters at Nielson Field. Again Brereton called Sutherland to get permission to launch an offensive strike but was refused. About ten minutes later, however, Sutherland telephoned Brereton and said that the photoreconnaissance mission had been approved.

Some accounts say that between 10:14 and 11:00 MacArthur called Brereton and stated that the matter of offensive air action would now be left to his discretion as air commander. Brereton told him that he planned to send three B-17's on a reconnaissance flight to Formosa immediately and would decide the time of the two-squadron B-17 raid after the photo mission's report was studied. If the photo planes had not returned by late afternoon, however, Brereton said that he would go ahead and send the bombing force to Formosa. He also planned to have the two other squadrons of B-17's that were on Mindanao fly to Clark that night and stage from there the next morning for another raid on Formosa, probably this time against airfields.

On several occasions in later years MacArthur emphatically denied that Brereton ever discussed a proposed Formosan raid with him, yet a radiogram bearing MacArthur's name went to Marshall that day mentioning the attack on Formosa planned for the 9th (but later canceled). Perhaps Sutherland sent the message without MacArthur's knowledge, but even so the discrepancy between the alleged MacArthur-Brereton telephone conversation and MacArthur's later denial of any knowledge of the projected mission of the 8th remains unresolved.

The B-17's that had been marking time aloft were recalled to Clark, three of them to be readied for the reconnaissance mission and the others prepared for the afternoon raid. By 11:30 all but two of the B-17's had landed, and the P-40's of the 20th Pursuit Squadron had also returned to Clark to refuel before resuming their patrols. About that time Iba's air warning service sent word to Nielson headquarters of new flights of enemy aircraft bearing in from the sea. Three fighter squadrons were sent up to intercept sectors over the South China Sea, Bataan, and Corregidor, while the fighters at Del Carmen Field, between Clark and Manila, were to cover Clark as the 20th's planes completed their refuel below. Because of communications difficulties and other problems that slowed preparations for take-off, including unusually thick clouds of dust sweeping the field, the Del Carmen fighters did not take their assigned cover position over Clark Field.

The chief of the air warning service at Nielson maintained later that his message to Clark telling of the Japanese formations bearing down on Central Luzon was acknowledged. But the head of the bomber command, who was at Clark, countered that he had never received the warning — another conflict that, for want of conclusive evidence, cannot be resolved.

The photo planes had been delayed in taking off for Formosa because additional cameras had to be flown up from Nichols Field at Manila; the plane carrying them arrived at Clark Field about ten minutes before the enemy bombers appeared overhead. One of the first buildings demolished by Japanese bombs in the Clark attack was the communications center. Iba's communications equipment and radar were also destroyed during the first minutes of the raid there. Meanwhile, unaware of the raids, the three pursuit squadrons, which could have wrought considerable damage on the attackers at Clark and Iba, continued patrolling their assigned sectors to the south and west. The Del Carmen fighters finally arrived over Clark but were too late to engage the Japanese aircraft, which by then were returning northward. No contact with the attacking formations was made by these squadrons except for Iba's fighters, which, as earlier stated, landed at their base just in time to be destroyed on the ground.

The fog of war seemed to settle permanently over the Clark-Iba catastrophe, and even now the inadequate or contradictory evidence leaves moot many questions about the actual attacks as well as the prelude. Accounts of the start of the Clark attack, for example, give various times, ranging from 12:10 to 12:35. Moreover, even the matter of dispersal, one that seems easy to settle, is confused since some versions allege that the Clark planes were parked wing to wing in long lines while other accounts indicate that they were well dispersed.[5]

Brereton, MacArthur, and Sutherland have each tended to stress different basic reasons for the disaster. Brereton argued that the deferment of the Formosan raid by Sutherland and MacArthur was the main reason the aircraft were caught on the ground, to which Sutherland responded that reconnaissance was necessary first and was delayed too long by the FEAF, and MacArthur steadfastly denied knowledge of the proposed raid. Japanese records studied after the war showed that over 500 aircraft were stationed at twenty-five or more bases on Formosa at the time. Without long-range fighter escort the two B-17 squadrons would have had little chance of success and surely would have suffered such heavy losses as to preclude further raids. Moreover, the Japanese on Formosa were expecting an attack and their air defenses were on alert all that day. It is doubtful that the FEAF leaders would have been as enthusiastic for the attack had they known the strength and readiness of the Japanese air power on Formosa.[6]

Thus, while Sutherland seems correct in having proposed reconnaisance to precede the attack and in criticizing the airmen's slowness in readying the photo planes, MacArthur said that if he had known about the projected attack he would have disapproved of it because of the certainty of a disastrous outcome. MacArthur's most extensive remarks on the subject were given in reply to a query from an Army historian after the war:

> My orders were explicit not to initiate hostilities against the Japanese. The Philippines while a possession of the U.S. had, so far as war was concerned, a somewhat indeterminate international position in many minds, especially the Filipinos and

their government. While I personally had not the slightest doubt we would be attacked, great local hope existed that this would not be the case. Instructions from Washington were very definite to wait until the Japanese made the first "overt" move. Even without such a directive, practical limitations made it [un]feasible to take the offensive. The only possibility lay in striking from the air but the relative weakness of our air force precluded any chance of success for such an operation. Our only aggressive potential consisted of about thirty-six B-17's. Their only possible target was the enemy's fields on Formosa. Our advance fields in Luzon were still incomplete and our fighters from our other fields in Luzon were too far away from Formosa to protect our bombers in a Formosa attack. They did not have the necessary radius of action. The enemy's air force based on excellent fields outnumbered ours many times. In addition, he had a mobile force on carriers which we entirely lacked. Our basic mission directive had confined our operations to our own national waters so no outside reconnaissance had been possible. The exact location of enemy targets was therefore not known. Our air force was in process of integration, radar defenses not yet operative, and personnel raw and inexperienced. An attack under such conditions would have been doomed to total failure. As a matter of fact, I had for safety reasons ordered the bombers to withdraw from Luzon to Mindanao to be out of enemy range. This was in process of accomplishment when the enemy's air attacked. I did not know it at the time, but later understood that General Brereton had suggested to the Chief of Staff, General Sutherland, that we should initiate operations by an attempted "strike" at Formosa. Had such a suggestion been made to me, I would have unequivocally disapproved. In my opinion it would have been suicidal as well as in direct defiance of my basic directive.[7]

In his statements about the Clark incident, Sutherland chose to stress not the decisions of December 8 but rather an alleged disobedience of orders by Brereton before that day as the underlying reason for the Clark tragedy. On at least three occasions during the previous five days MacArthur, through Sutherland, had ordered Brereton to transfer the Clark B-17's to the

Del Monte base on Mindanao. Only two of the four squadrons had been moved by the 8th, Brereton's excuse being that he was shortly expecting another B-17 group to arrive at Del Monte and that the field would be too crowded to handle the remaining Clark B-17's. According to Brereton, on the other hand, the idea of the movement of two squadrons to Del Monte was his own, and Sutherland had insisted that they be returned to Clark as soon as possible. The evidence, however, seems to favor Sutherland's version.

In late November MacArthur had told Marshall of his concern over the B-17's exposed so far northward at Clark and had, indeed, ordered their transfer to the safer confines of Del Monte.[8] Holding them in reserve there to await the main Japanese amphibious operations or, even better, sending them to Java or Australia to be employed later against long-range strategic stationary targets would have been more sensible, if not as daring as Brereton's idea of expending them in one hopeless raid on Formosa. Any of these three possibilities, of course, would have been preferable to the fate they suffered — being caught helpless on the ground.

In addition to emphasizing, like Sutherland, the tardiness in moving the heavy bombers to the south, MacArthur also stressed the responsibility of the War Department in the disaster by its failure to provide adequate reinforcements for the Philippine defenses:

> Our air forces in the Philippines containing many antiquated models were hardly more than a token force with insufficient equipment, incompleted fields and inadequate maintenance. They were hopelessly outnumbered and never had a chance of winning. They were completely overwhelmed by the enemy's superior forces. They did everything possible within their limited resources. I attach no blame to General Brereton or other members of the command for the incidents of the battle. Nothing could have saved the day for them.[9]

It was true that the United States had never provided the personnel or matériel adequate for a successful defense of the Philippines despite the acceptance since the early 1920's of a war plan (Orange) that, through many revisions, consistently called for a defense of four to six months by the Philippines garrison in case of a Japanese attack, at the end of which the Pacific Fleet was expected to achieve a breakthrough to the islands with reinforcements. Arnold and his air staff in Washington must also bear some of the blame because of the exaggerated significance they attached to the role that the B-17's could play in the defense of the islands. What possessed them to send the Army Air Forces' largest force of B-17's there without adequate radar equipment, antiaircraft defenses, and fighter protection is not known. Nor is it clear what role they envisaged the B-17's could perform if, as actually happened, the Japanese preceded their main landings with two weeks of devastating air assaults. The loss of the B-17's was regrettable, but their assignment to the Philippines without sufficient protection and without clearly formulated plans as to their proper employment was equally lamentable.

Nevertheless, when all the evidence is sifted, however contradictory and incomplete it may be, MacArthur still emerges as the officer who was in overall command in the Philippines that fateful day, and he must therefore bear a large measure of the blame. Nor was his chief of staff guiltless. Sutherland had a reputation, to be sustained during the next four years, of arrogantly refusing to permit high-ranking officers to see MacArthur promptly. He also was known for interfering particularly with orders and plans of air commanders. According to General George C. Kenney, who would be MacArthur's air commander in 1942–45, Sutherland had some limited flying experience and considered himself an authority on air matters. Kenney and Sutherland often clashed, and the former became convinced in later years that Brereton, though not free of blame for the events of December 8, was effectively cowed and thwarted by Sutherland that morning and was never able to discuss his plans with MacArthur.[10]

As later incidents in this volume will reveal, Sutherland, although able and efficient, sometimes intervened in the plans of air, naval, and ground commanders without the knowledge of MacArthur. Some generals and admirals would find it virtually impossible to communicate personally with MacArthur because of Sutherland's obstructions. If Brereton's reasoning on the significance of his proposed attack is valid, then his early morning talks with Sutherland assume extreme importance in indicting the chief of staff and at least partially absolving MacArthur. But if MacArthur, the commander of United States Army Forces in the Far East (USAFFE), delegated such a large measure of authority to his chief of staff, regardless of Sutherland's alleged brilliance, then he assuredly does not escape criticism himself as overall chief of Philippine defenses. Moreover, MacArthur's remoteness lessened the opportunity for personal communication with his top-level officers, as is evidenced by the fact that the air commander, probably the most important individual in his chain of command, did not have free access to him.

If, as some accounts indicate, MacArthur did telephone Brereton about 11:00 and tell him that the execution of offensive air action would be left to his discretion, the nagging question that remains is why MacArthur hesitated nearly eight hours in reaching that decision. Brereton later surmised that MacArthur may have been uncertain, in view of the War Department's earlier insistence on refraining from hostile moves until the Japanese actually attacked, whether a state of war existed, since reports on the Pearl Harbor incident were still fragmentary. But the War Department's official confirmation of war had reached MacArthur at 5:30, and he knew of the early attacks on Davao, Baguio, and Tuguegarao. Rear Admiral John D. Bulkeley, then a young PT boat squadron commander but unusually close to MacArthur, without hesitation blamed Philippine Commonwealth President Manuel L. Quezon for deferring offensive action not only by the bombers but also by his naval craft: "He was not convinced that the Japanese were actually making war. He was the one who insisted on the three-mile limit until the Japs actually dropped their bombs. It was Quezon who put the clamp on things."

On the other hand, when C. L. Sulzberger of the *New York Times* interviewed General Dwight D. Eisenhower in Paris in 1951, Eisenhower stated that in Washington in 1942 Quezon had told him that "when the Japanese attacked Pearl Harbor MacArthur was convinced for some strange reason that the Philippines would remain neutral and would not be attacked by the Japanese. For that reason, MacArthur refused permission to General Brereton to bomb Japanese bases on Formosa immediately after the attack on Pearl Harbor." [11]

In retrospect, if Sutherland had not blocked Brereton from seeing MacArthur, a conference of the two commanders, in view of MacArthur's opposition to a raid on Formosa, would probably have concluded with the decision to send the heavy bombers at Clark down to Mindanao that morning. As attested to by Captain Chihaya Takahashi of the Japanese Navy's 11th Air Fleet staff, that action would have been what the attackers dreaded: "We did not expect to destroy all of them [on December 8] because it was thought that many of them would seek refuge in southern areas. The Japanese feared mostly that, at the time of the first attack, the American planes would take refuge in the southern areas, therefore making the campaign very difficult." [12] The helpless position of the American heavy bombers on the ground was therefore an exhilarating sight to the attackers and resulted in the one fact about which no researchers disagree: the destruction on the first day of war of one of the most formidable obstacles to the Japanese conquest of the Philippines.

2. *Farewell to Brereton and Hart*

For another three weeks Brereton tried frantically, but to little avail, to reorganize and revitalize his tattered air units in
order to challenge the enemy's supremacy in the skies over the
Philippines. On December 10, despite brave efforts by FEAF
fighters, vastly superior Japanese formations bombed at will
Nichols Field and the Cavite Naval Station, south of Manila,
with devastating results. That same day minor Japanese amphibious landings were made at Aparri and Vigan on the
northern coast of Luzon, again in spite of valiant efforts by
FEAF aircraft. By the 12th when another small Japanese
force landed at Legaspi on the southern end of Luzon, the
Japanese had conducted fourteen major air raids against strategic points around the Manila and Clark military complexes
and the Olongapo and Cavite naval facilities. Each raid cost the
dwindling FEAF units more planes as they rose in vain attempts
to deflect the attackers. On the 15th Brereton obtained Mac-
Arthur's permission to move the remaining B-17's and some
other combat aircraft to Darwin, Australia, which was none too
soon since the first heavy attack on Del Monte Field occurred
four days later.

On the 24th MacArthur reluctantly ordered Brereton to
move to Australia with his FEAF headquarters: "Your mission
is to organize advanced operating bases from which, with the
Far East Air Force, you can protect the lines of communications, secure bases in Mindanao, and support the defense of
the Philippines by the U.S. Army Forces in the Far East." [13]
Brereton describes their farewell meeting:

On the afternoon of Christmas Eve I was called by General
MacArthur for a conference. He expressed his extreme grati-
fication over the part the Far East Air Force had taken in the
battles of Luzon and told me that I was being ordered to pro-

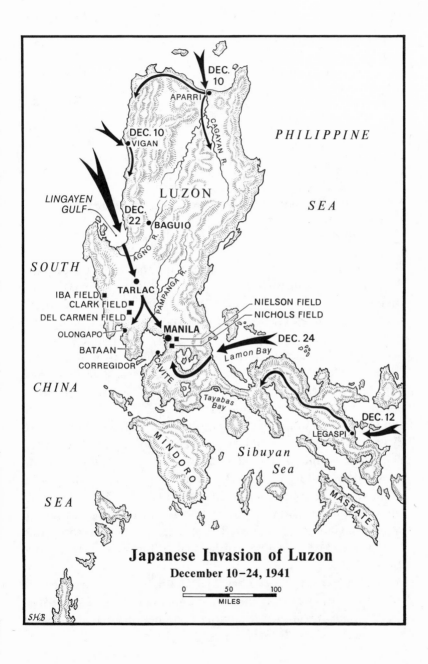

DEC.
10

APARRI

CAGAYAN R.

PHILIPPINE

DEC. 10
VIGAN

LUZON

SEA

LINGAYEN
GULF

DEC.
22 • BAGUIO

AGNO R.

SOUTH

IBA FIELD
CLARK FIELD
DEL CARMEN FIELD

OLONGAPO

BATAAN

CORREGIDOR

TARLAC

PAMPANGA R.

MANILA

CAVITE

NIELSON FIELD
NICHOLS FIELD

DEC. 24

Lamon Bay

CHINA

Tayabas
Bay

DEC. 12

LEGASPI

MINDORO

Sibuyan

Sea

MASBATE

SEA

Japanese Invasion of Luzon
December 10–24, 1941

0   50   100
MILES

SHB

ceed south with my headquarters. I asked to remain on his staff
in any capacity in which he could use me.

"No, Lewis," he said. "You go on south. You can do me
more good with the bombers you have left and those you should
be receiving soon than you can here. Since communications
over that distance are practically impossible now, I must depend to the greatest extent upon your own initiative to support our forces here."

I rose and prepared to leave, and General MacArthur said, "I
hope that you will tell the people outside what we have done
and protect my reputation as a fighter."

As I shook hands with him I said, "General, your reputation
will never need any protection."

Those were the last words I had with him.[14]

Departing on a Navy PBY patrol bomber because his own
bombers had left earlier, Brereton traveled to Darwin and
managed to launch a few B-17 attacks against enemy positions
in the Philippines, especially against Davao on Mindanao, which
the Japanese seized on December 20. By mid-January, despite
attempts to get air reinforcements into the Philippines and to
mount strikes from Darwin, Brereton's efforts proved ineffectual, and his primary mission was changed to assisting the Allied
forces of ABDACOM (American, British, Dutch, and Australian Command) in the defense of the Malay Barrier. Meanwhile,
Brigadier General Harold H. George, head of the FEAF inter-
ceptor command that remained on Luzon, continued to send
up his diminishing force of P-40's and P-35's against the hordes
of Japanese aircraft daily raiding the islands. Most of the airmen became infantrymen after Christmas, although as late as
March 2 George's last four P-40's, each carrying a 500-pound
bomb, attacked Japanese shipping at Subic Bay, northwest of
Bataan.[15]

Almost daily in December MacArthur sent messages to the
War Department describing the mounting enemy air offensive:
"The enemy has an overwhelming preponderance of air strength

. . . The crescendo of the enemy air offensive is rapidly rising." As early as the 12th he reported that the FEAF fighters were being conserved mainly for reconnaissance: "Pilots have been ordered to avoid direct combat." Never, however, did he give up hope that air reinforcements to the islands were possible, even arguing in his communications to Washington that fighters could be brought in by aircraft carriers. He also rushed to completion nine all-weather fields on Mindanao and four in the Visayas suitable for fighter use.

Nor did Roosevelt, Marshall, Arnold, and their war planners abandon hope during the first few weeks. A convoy of eight transports and freighters led by the cruiser *Pensacola,* which was en route from Honolulu to Manila when war erupted, was detoured to Brisbane, Australia, with the intention of transshipping the aircraft it carried to the Philippines although Navy leaders had wanted the convoy returned to Hawaii. With the tightening Japanese blockade around the islands and the enemy's seizure of Davao and Jolo, the aircraft had to be assigned to Australian bases rather than be sent on the suicidal trip northward.

As late as December 22 Arnold told his British counterpart, Air Vice Marshal Charles F. Portal, at the Arcadia Conference in Washington that he was convinced that if eighty heavy bombers and about 200 fighters could be gotten to MacArthur, "we could regain superiority of the air in that theater." Although every possible effort was made to accomplish this end, only three P-40's and a trickle of other types of equipment and supplies ever reached the beleaguered USAFFE forces.[16]

On the surface at least, MacArthur and Brereton maintained a polite if not cordial relationship despite the FEAF's collapse, but relations between MacArthur and Rear Admiral Thomas C. Hart, the Asiatic Fleet commander, were strained as early as September, worsened during the crisis of December, and in later years erupted in invective. Before the Japanese attack the

two differed sharply about jurisdiction over offshore air patrolling, with Hart claiming his plan was "strongly rebuffed" by
the general; movement of the main part of the fleet south of
Luzon, which Hart undertook on Navy Department orders in
late October; Hart's handling of incidents between American
sailors and soldiers at Shanghai and Hongkong, which MacArthur called "dictatorial"; and MacArthur's defense plan for the
islands, which the admiral termed "grandiose." The situation
became so fraught with pettiness that before one of President
Quezon's parties Sutherland told Colonel James V. Collier to
"go over and talk to Quezon's aide. Tell him General MacArthur will accept, but he's to sit on Quezon's right, not Admiral
Hart. Make that very clear. If MacArthur should go over and
find that he was seated on the left, he isn't staying." [17]

The war aggravated an already tense relationship between
the two commanders. The Navy suffered a serious setback
when its base at Cavite was "practically wiped out" on the 10th
by Japanese bombers. Twelve days later as the main invasion
began at Lingayen Gulf, the twenty-nine submarines of the
Asiatic Fleet, Hart's main striking force, proved shockingly
ineffectual because of heavy destroyer screens, dangerously shallow waters, and defective torpedoes. MacArthur's criticism increased after he urged Hart to use his surface craft to escort the
Pensacola convoy from Australia to the Philippines, but Hart
"seemed to be of the opinion that the islands were ultimately
doomed," said MacArthur in reporting the matter to Marshall.
Hart commenced to send the submarines south by Christmas,
leaving only some PBY's, six motor torpedo boats, and a few
old gunboats and auxiliary craft as the naval defenses of Luzon.
In the meantime, MacArthur was sending vigorous protests to
Washington about the "inactivity" of the Asiatic Fleet and the
Japanese Navy's "complete freedom of action" in Philippine
waters.[18]

The regrettable inability of MacArthur and Hart to communicate and cooperate during this critical period is evident in Hart's account of their final two conversations:

> On about 18 December, MacArthur called and talked at length concerning the PENSACOLA's convoy, then bound for Brisbane. As usual, he talked very well, bringing in many theoretical considerations . . .
> I knew the General was coming and had ready in my office the location chart showing where all submarines were, with the exception of the eight which were off enemy ports . . . He barely glanced at the chart and, after I had gotten off one or two sentences, again launched forth into one of his characteristic "speeches" about his own side of the war. It was only by using some sharpness and repeatedly interrupting him in turn that I was able to tell him anything of the Navy situation at all. He asked no questions whatever, evinced no curiosity and, as has too often been the case, the interview was quite futile as far as furthering any meeting of minds between us.
> On 22 December, A.M., I called on MacArthur, incidentally to congratulate him on his promotion [to full general], but with plenty of time for as much discussion of our situation here as might come forth. The General also seemed to have plenty of time, but the conversation for ten minutes was entirely inconsequential and the two leads which I took to turn the interview into useful channels were altogether without results.
> At this date [December 23], looking back over the short period since hostilities began, it is clear that as far as MacArthur and I are personally concerned there has been very little get-together.[19]

Having lost his air force, MacArthur felt that the Asiatic Fleet should have tried to assist in the defense of the islands. Indeed, the only contribution of Hart's force in December that even Admiral Ernest J. King, the chief of naval operations, could praise was the escape of a large number of Allied ships from Manila Bay, which upon getting to the southern Philippines were then escorted by Hart's vessels "under what amounted to cover" until they safely reached Australia.

On Christmas Day Hart himself departed for the Malay Barrier, where his ships joined the British and Dutch naval forces. Even on his final day in Manila there was a misunderstanding with MacArthur, the admiral insisting that his headquarters had not been given adequate notice that MacArthur was going to declare Manila an open city on the 26th. Recriminations continued in ensuing weeks as MacArthur tried to get Hart, operating off Java, to send submarines with supplies to Corregidor, which the admiral was reluctant to chance.[20]

Three days after Hart left, MacArthur, obviously irritated, proposed that "Washington employ counter propaganda especially with reference to [the] activity [of] our Navy to offset a crescendo of enemy propaganda which has appeared in all elements of society, claiming U.S. inactivity in support." Later MacArthur told Marshall that what was most needed was an "American sea thrust" which "would immediately relieve the pressure on the south" and would reopen supply lines to the Philippines. "A great naval victory on our part is not necessary to accomplish this mission," he continued, emphasizing that if the Navy would merely make an effort at offensive action in the Western Pacific it would help.

With the Asiatic and Pacific fleets undoubtedly in mind, MacArthur warned Washington that unless the Navy moved to the attack, the Southwest Pacific would be lost: "The war will be indefinitely prolonged and its final outcome will be jeopardized. Counsels of timidity based upon theories of safety first will not win against such an aggressive and audacious adversary as Japan." Although the Asiatic Fleet was soon fighting for survival in the Java Sea, MacArthur was convinced to his death that Hart "made no effort to keep open our lines of supply" and that the Pacific Fleet, staggering from the Pearl Harbor catastrophe, "might well have cut through to relieve our hard-pressed forces." His outspokenness on what he considered to be the Navy's desertion of the Philippines was returned in kind by many of the admirals.[21] It would be a long while before Mac-Arthur and the Navy brass developed an appreciation of each other.

When Hart left the islands, Rear Admiral Francis W. Rockwell, commandant of the 16th Naval District with headquarters at Cavite, took charge of the remaining naval forces, about 4300 officers and men, including the 4th Marine Regiment. Rockwell and Bulkeley, who led the torpedo boat squadron, got along well with MacArthur, although the Marines did not appreciate the omission of any mention of their activities in USAFFE communiqués, a minor matter compared to the Hart-MacArthur differences. Like Brereton's remaining airmen, most of the sailors who stayed under Rockwell eventually fought as infantry. These sailors and marines were transferred under USAFFE's control, and since they had remained to fight, MacArthur came to regard them proudly as an important part of his forces.[22] It is unfortunate that the positive aspect of MacArthur's relations with the Navy in the Philippines never seemed to become part of the scuttlebutt in Honolulu or Washington.

3. A Change in Plans

With the collapse of his air and naval defenses, MacArthur faced a bleak prospect when, at dawn on December 22, Lieutenant General Masaharu Homma's Fourteenth Army began landing along the beaches of Lingayen Gulf. Bothered by rain squalls, high seas, landings at the wrong sites, confusion in getting men and equipment ashore, and brief but ineffectual appearances by a few American planes and submarines, Homma fretted unduly about his chances of successfully establishing a beachhead. A Philippine Scout cavalry regiment and three Philippine Army infantry divisions were in the Lingayen area,

but, except for a valiant fight by the Scouts, the Filipinos made
short-lived stands and then retreated from the beaches, often
in pell-mell confusion. By noon three Japanese regiments and
a considerable number of tanks and artillery pieces were moving inland, easily securing Homma's first-day objectives. In a
few days more than 43,000 troops of the Fourteenth Army
would be ashore and poised for the push toward Manila.

On the 24th the other arm of Homma's pincer, the 16th Division, numbering about 7000 combat troops (besides service
and supporting personnel), landed against slight opposition at
three locations along Lamon Bay, about seventy miles southeast of Manila. Like the Lingayen forces, the 16th Division
easily secured its early objectives in spite of the efforts of the
Philippine Army's 51st Division. The next morning the Japanese crossed the narrow peninsula to Tayabas Bay, while the
northernmost unit struck inland toward Laguna de Bay, the
large lake whose northwest corner lay only ten miles from
Manila. Shortly, however, the 16th Division's advance slowed
as it confronted mountainous terrain and increasing though
sporadic defensive efforts.

For the most part, MacArthur held his reserves intact, but the
few reinforcements that were committed to action were sent to
the Lingayen front. It was obvious to him that, although the
Lingayen invaders were over 100 miles northwest of Manila,
they had the most direct route to the capital and the only one
with relatively good roads across open country, and since the
invasion force was more than six times the size of the Lamon
Bay force, Homma's northern pincer was the most serious
menace. Reports reaching MacArthur's headquarters from the
panicky defenders in the Lingayen region estimated the enemy
troops there at over 80,000, which magnified even more the
threat posed by the northern arm of the pincer.

The USAFFE units that faced Homma's well-trained and
highly disciplined Fourteenth Army consisted mainly of the

26th Cavalry Regiment, a regular United States Army unit of Philippine Scouts, and the 11th, 21st, 71st, and 91st divisions of the Philippine Army. The main Japanese thrust on December 23 was along the principal highway to Manila, Route 3, which was defended by Brigadier Clyde A. Selleck's 71st Division. As soon as the battle began to develop along the highway, the 71st collapsed as an organized fighting force. With their flanks exposed and some of their units already disintegrating, the other Philippine Army divisions and the Scouts also retreated after brief fire fights. Meanwhile, other Japanese units were astride the key highway leading to Baguio in the hills to the north where the defenders of that sector were also fleeing in disorganized fashion after offering only little resistance.[23]

The scene was virtually the same from one end of the Lingayen front to the other as the defenders fell back, some fleeing to the hills never to return to their units and others regrouping later to resume the futile, uneven struggle. Highly trained Filipino soldiers, such as the Scouts, fought well, but their numbers were few. American Army officers were completely frustrated in their desperate efforts to make combat troops overnight out of the recently mobilized Filipinos constituting the three infantry divisions. Two of the three regiments of each of these divisions had been in training a month or less and some of the men had never fired their rifles.

Selleck, who was later reduced to colonel because of the disintegration of his 71st Division, commented, "The division was never organized, was never adequately equipped, and the training was so meager that when attacked by veteran troops, bombed and confronted by tanks, it had a minimum of stability." Another American general, speaking of the recent Filipino recruits, which were the majority of the defenders facing Homma, said simply, "They were a mob." Major General Jonathan M. Wainwright, commander of the North Luzon Force, confirmed the shocking unpreparedness of almost all of

the Philippine Army: "Few units of any force had been completely mobilized and all lacked training and equipment. No
division or force had been assembled or trained in unit maneuvers; staffs lacked organization and trained personnel." He
added that the Filipino troops "did not have steel helmets,
intrenching tools, or in many cases, blankets or raincoats,"
possessed "no modern arms," and "lacked even obsolete equipment." [24]

By late afternoon of December 23, it was obvious to Wainwright that such a ragtag force could not stop Homma's offensive unless some time could be gained to get reinforcements and
prepare a defensive line. The first natural obstacle to the south
was the Agno River, which runs parallel to the Lingayen
beaches about twenty miles inland. So Wainwright called Sutherland and obtained permission to withdraw to the river and
prepare a defense line there. Astonishingly, in view of the pitiful condition of the Philipine Army, Wainwright and Sutherland contemplated a counterattack for the next day, although
Wainwright was unsuccessful in getting the Philippine Division, a regular American Army unit in reserve to the south, sent
to the Agno for the action.

While Wainwright pondered his plight and the rejection of
his request for the additional division, MacArthur called him
on the night of the 23rd and announced that he was to withdraw
to Bataan, that War Plan Orange-3 was being put into effect immediately. Similar word was sent to Major General
George M. Parker, Jr., the South Luzon Force commander, as
well as to the rest of the USAFFE field officers. The reactiva-
tion of WPO-3 was a move that most officers of the American
Army in the Philippines had long felt would have to be made
when the main invasion occurred. In November, as explained
in the first volume of this work, MacArthur had persuaded the
War Department to allow him to drop the decades-old Orange
Plan, which he called "defeatist," in favor of a beach defense

plan to be effected throughout the major islands of the archipelago. His proposal, as well as Marshall's sanction, was predicated on the assumption that the Philippine Army could be developed into a potent combat force, supplied with modern arms and equipment by the United States, before the spring of 1942, when, MacArthur confidently argued, the Japanese attack would come. This illusion of MacArthur's was accepted by the War Department, which forsook its earlier, more realistic assessment of Philippine defenses and began a last-minute rush of reinforcements to the islands.

Since no significant ground fighting occurred during the first two weeks of the Philippine campaign, the illusion lasted until it was quickly punctured by the troops' performance on the 22nd and 23rd. But the facts that the war had come earlier than expected and the Filipino forces were still very much in need of training and matériel should have been evident to all concerned from the 8th on. Many regular American Army officers in the field, especially with the North Luzon Force, were fully cognizant of the situation and were not surprised when the Filipinos could not stop the Japanese at the beaches, but these officers, mostly of the former Philippine Department, had been unable to convince USAFFE headquarters of their view. Brigadier General Clifford Bluemel probably expressed the sentiment of most of the regular officers in describing the Mac-Arthur Plan as "a terrible thing." [25]

Since the 8th MacArthur had not been living in a dream world of great expectations about his beach defense plan. According to Sutherland, MacArthur told him privately on the day the war began that they would have to "remove immediately to Bataan." Four days later MacArthur confided to Quezon, who had been doubtful about the beach defense scheme and had been engaged in "a running argument" with him for weeks about its feasibility, that, though the situation was not yet serious enough to warrant the move, he might have to declare Manila an open city and eventually withdraw his forces into Bataan. At least MacArthur correctly predicted that the small Japanese landings at Aparri, Vigan, and Legaspi on the 10th and 12th were diversionary efforts and that the main thrust would come from the Lingayen Gulf. But he was too sure of his own plan at first or simply too busy to be concerned about the possible failure of his defense scheme.

In his operations (G-3) section some officers were already concerned about the need to stock Bataan with provisions for that eventual day of withdrawal. Colonel Collier of G-3 said that at one staff meeting at USAFFE headquarters this proposal was made as "a safety measure," but "MacArthur said, 'Oh, no!' He wouldn't even listen to the suggestion. He didn't want any divided thought on it." Many of his high-ranking staff and field officers and Quezon were opposed to the MacArthur Plan; Sutherland and Brigadier General Charles A. Willoughby, chief of the intelligence (G-2) section, seem to have been the only key officers who supported MacArthur in this instance.[26] Why he hesitated until the 23rd to renounce his cherished beach defense plan, especially after the ruin of his air and naval defense plans, continues to be a mystery.

For forty long and critical hours after Homma's troops came ashore at Lingayen Gulf MacArthur stubbornly clung to his beach defense scheme, perhaps because reports from the front about the effectiveness of the Philippine Army's defense were confusing and contradictory. But by the evening of the 23rd when he made the fateful decision to revert to WPO-3, the frantic messages from front-line officers had assumed a consistent pattern and pointed to one shocking fact: the Philippine Army, about which MacArthur had spoken proudly for so long, had collapsed in its first two days of fighting. In later remarks about the events of the 22nd and 23rd, however, he never alluded to the failure of the Filipino units, but insisted that "the imminent menace of encirclement by greatly superior numbers forced me to act instantly."

Reversion to WPO-3 meant going back to a war plan that was familiar to all of the regular American Army officers. Besides calling for an orderly withdrawal of Luzon forces into prepared defensive positions on Bataan, WPO-3 stipulated that all civilians were to be evacuated from the peninsula beforehand, ample supplies were to be provided, and field hospitals, communications lines, and other facilities were to be readied on Bataan for the incoming troops. Since the War Department's decision in November favoring the MacArthur Plan, little had been done toward furthering preparations on the peninsula. During the two weeks after the first enemy air attacks some supplies had been sent to Corregidor but virtually none to Bataan. In order to permit time to transport supplies and prepare positions on the peninsula and to gain time for the South Luzon Force to cross the vital bridges at Calumpit and escape into Bataan, MacArthur ordered Wainwright to withdraw slowly down through the Central Luzon Plain along a series of five delaying lines. Each delaying position was to be held long enough to force the Japanese to undertake a time-consuming deployment, the necessary prelude to a major assault, while Wainwright's troops retreated to the next defensive line just before the enemy attacked in force.

The entire retrograde operation depended on split-second timing and coordination by the North and South Luzon forces as well as the engineer, quartermaster, and other service troops who would be endeavoring to hasten preparations on Bataan. According to MacArthur's new plan, the withdrawal was to be completed by January 8, or two weeks from its inception. If Homma pushed his offensive aggressively and forced Wainwright southward too rapidly, the South Luzon Force would be cut off and destroyed. If supplies and preparations on Bataan were not readied in time, the American and Filipino forces would move onto a malaria-infested jungle peninsula, which would be a trap affording the men little opportunity to live off the countryside.[27] As it turned out, the escape to Bataan was executed brilliantly, but the preparation of Bataan failed miserably. The latter situation will be considered first; it ranks as surely the cardinal blunder of the entire campaign.

While MacArthur and most of his headquarters staff, along with Quezon, Sayre, and some of their subordinates, were moving to Corregidor on Christmas Eve, Brigadier General Richard J. Marshall, the USAFFE deputy chief of staff, remained in Manila with a few headquarters officers to oversee the final evacuation of troops and matériel from the city. That morning Marshall met with Brigadier General Charles C. Drake, quartermaster, and Colonel Lewis C. Beebe, supply chief (G-4), to draw up a new supply plan. Many of the supplies formerly scheduled under the Orange Plan to go to Bataan had been shipped to depots near the beaches after the MacArthur Plan had been approved. When the reversion to WPO-3 was ordered on the 23rd, the officers faced the almost insurmountable problem of garnering the scattered supplies and transporting them to Bataan and Corregidor despite enemy control of the skies, only 1300 quartermaster troops to provide for 80,000 or more incoming troops, an inadequate number of motor vehicles, no rail lines, and enemy advances that were overrunning the forward supply depots.

Disregarding the menace of Japanese aircraft, about 300 barges and commercial vessels of all types made numerous trips from the Manila piers to docks at Corregidor and Bataan. For some reason priority was given to Corregidor, which was soon stocked with supplies for 10,000 men for six months; about 30,000 tons of supplies were successively sent across the bay in the next week. Although Manila was declared an open city on the 26th, it was the center of feverish activities for the next five days as Marshall, Drake, and Beebe attempted to evacuate all conceivable supplies that might be of use to the USAFFE defenders and to destroy other stocks that the Japanese could use.

At the same time Japanese planes continued to bomb and

strafe Manila, disregarding the open-city proclamation, perhaps because of the continuing USAFFE activity there. Nearly ten million gallons of gasoline in commercial storage tanks in Manila were set afire by USAFFE troops to keep the fuel from enemy seizure. When the USAFFE rear echelon staff closed out its operations in Manila on New Year's Eve and hastily departed for Corregidor as enemy forces neared the city, large quantities of food prepared for shipment to Corregidor and Bataan had to be left behind and were looted by thousands of desperate Filipinos.[28]

Robert W. Levering, a civilian employed by the USAFFE engineers in Manila, described the final scene:

> By this time the erstwhile neat Port Area was an ugly mess — pockmarked with scores of bomb-craters. All the piers from 1 to 7, and vacant lots opposite the piers, were piled high with a conglomeration of cargo hastily discharged from ships that had made a run for safety. This unsightly myriad included everything from personal Christmas parcels from the States to the servicemen in the Islands, to uncrated grand pianos. One lot opposite pier 7 was almost completely filled with 100-lb. bags of wheat flour and canned cherries.
>
> These goods were now being looted right and left, and nobody seemed to care. Beggars and priests, children and wrinkled old men preyed on the heaps like flies on a dung hill. Filipinos who had never owned more than a loin-cloth and a bolo in all their lives, suddenly saw laid before them a fortune in worldly goods.[29]

The Japanese occupation of the capital two days later, of course, terminated supply shipments from Manila, which had been the principal source of the last-minute provisioning of Corregidor and Bataan.

The new supply plan worked less successfully in the rich agricultural regions of the Central Luzon Plain. At Fort Stotsenburg, near Clark Field, huge amounts of gasoline, fresh beef, dry rations, clothing, ammunition, and various types of military equipment were stored. For unexplained reasons the base was evacuated well ahead of the advancing Japanese, and several reports, including Drake's, state that an inexcusably small amount of supplies was removed before the evacuation. The post quartermaster claimed that most items of value were sent to Bataan or issued to troops in the vicinity of the base, but the evidence indicates that little of Stotsenburg's stores ever reached Bataan. There were other incidents of premature evacuations of sectors containing depots brimming with supplies, but in some cases regimental quartermaster officers were able to get matériel of value aboard their units' vehicles. The front line was changing so fast in many areas that, especially with the confusion of thousands of fleeing soldiers and refugees, orderly evacuation of advance depots was difficult or impossible.

A critical blow to quartermaster plans was the loss of use of the Manila Railroad north to Tarlac; it had been counted on as the main artery for transporting supplies from the forward depots between Tarlac and Lingayen where some of the largest food stocks had been concentrated. As early as the 15th, crews on the rail line had started deserting their jobs because of mounting enemy air attacks, and by Christmas not one locomotive was operating. USAFFE transport officers wanted to have American Army personnel take over the operation of the line, but because of Quezon's opposition USAFFE headquarters decided to depend on the Philippine Constabulary to run the trains. With the coming of the main invasion, however, most of the constabulary troops were withdrawn from their home districts to form the 2nd Division, a combat unit assembled near Manila. So the Manila Railroad was left without crews, proved useless in evacuating supplies to Bataan, and was soon overrun by the advancing Japanese.[30]

Quezon objected so strenuously when USAFFE field commanders proposed confiscating food stocks in commercial warehouses, even of Japanese-owned firms, that MacArthur ordered his unit commanders not to commandeer food that might be used by the Filipino civilians later. Sutherland told an American colonel in charge of Tarlac's supply depot that he would be court-martialed if he confiscated 2000 cases of canned fish and corned beef and a large quantity of clothing in the warehouses of Japanese firms. The USAFFE quartermaster officers proposed purchasing as much rice as possible from local sources, but USAFFE headquarters, under pressure from Quezon, responded that rice could not be transported from the province in which it had been bought. This prohibition also applied to sugar, of which there were vast quantities in storage on Luzon.

Most deplorable was the situation at the large Cabanatuan rice central, where about fifty million bushels of rice were stored. Even if only a fifth of this rice had been transported to Bataan, according to the official Army history, it would have been "enough to have fed the troops on Bataan for almost a year." Colonel Ernest B. Miller, a tank battalion commander operating in the Cabanatuan area, claimed that the grain could have been moved to Bataan: "A vast number of commercial trucks were available, as were many military trucks, not only in the Quartermaster Pool, but those on hand with troops, and not being used." But because of Quezon's prohibition on the movement of rice outside the local province, which MacArthur apparently did not try to get lifted, Drake's quartermaster troops were unable to make a move at Cabanatuan. Miller was livid with rage: "Not one grain of the rice at Cabanatuan was touched! Although a vital part of the war plan, none of it reached Bataan! The warehouses at Cabanatuan were bombed, and most of the rice was burned by the Japs — but not until the very last of December!" Deeply embittered by such experiences, Miller later commented. "Perhaps it was fortunate that, as we bivouacked amid the smoking ruins of Clark Field on that first day of war, we could not see these things that were yet to come — food and materiel of war sabotaged by that same mismanagement and indecision which had destroyed our air power." [31]

In the southern Philippines the temporary adoption of the MacArthur Plan had also spelled problems. If the Orange objective of defending only the entrance to Manila Bay had been retained, virtually all of the forces in the Visayas and Mindanao would have been transported to Luzon before the start of the war. Instead, troops and supplies were scattered at various locations on the main southern islands of Panay, Negros, Cebu, Leyte, Samar, Palawan, and Mindanao. By the 23rd, when MacArthur changed back to WPO-3, the Japanese Navy had interdicted sea traffic from the south and the USAFFE forces that were there could not possibly reach Luzon. Moreover, no supplies could reach the southern forces. Fortunately some of the units were in areas where they could live off the countryside.

Brigadier General Bradford G. Chynoweth, who headed the Visayan forces, found the supply situation chaotic and could do little to remedy the conditions because of the "over-centralized" organization of USAFFE. Chynoweth said that "in Cebu when I got there everything was on the docks. There were ten million rounds of ammunition held for the quartermaster in Manila . . . I ran around to the commander of troops, [Colonel Irvine C.] Scudder. I said, 'How much ammunition have your men got?' Some had ten rounds to a man. Yet ten million rounds on the Cebu dock! It was a nightmare." For want of authorization from USAFFE headquarters, the ammunition supply could not be moved into the hills as Chynoweth wanted. On orders from Manila on the 15th, the Visayan and Mindanao commanders were told to "ensure that preparations are complete for destruction . . . prior to any definite threatened enemy occupation [of] all useful military supplies including transportation and oil equipments." Later, however, MacArthur decided that guerrilla operations should be conducted in the southern islands even if Luzon fell, so the supplies and equipment were to be removed to the hills, but by then some local commanders had already destroyed the stocks.[32]

When the North and South Luzon forces began to enter Bataan during the first week of January, they soon found the food supply there alarmingly low. The stocks would have provided on normal ration a 20-day supply of rice, a 30-day supply of flour and canned vegetables, a 40-day supply of canned milk, and a 50-day supply of canned meat and fish. Very small stocks of salt, lard, and sugar were present, and such items as potatoes, fresh and canned fruits, onions, cereals, and other foods necessary for a balanced diet were almost nonexistent. In addition, an unexpected 26,000 Filipino refugees followed the 80,000 troops into the peninsula. On January 5 MacArthur had to order all USAFFE forces placed on half ration. In the following weeks the ration would be reduced several times, until the desperate search for food would become more important to the soldiers than the presence of the enemy nearby. Shipment of medical supplies and hospital equipment had lagged behind even that of foodstuffs. Quinine, which should have taken a high priority, was in short supply from the first day on Bataan. Other matériel, such as equipment required by the engineers, was also seriously lacking. In the hurried withdrawal much of the engineers' stocks had to be destroyed or left behind.

Colonel Lloyd E. Mielenz of the engineers later stated that "many supplies could have been saved and the troops finally retreating into Bataan would have been much more adequately provided for" if WPO-3 had not been temporarily discarded for the MacArthur Plan. Colonel Glen R. Townsend led his regiment into Bataan expecting to occupy well-prepared defensive positions, "but no work was ever done on these positions," he remarked, "until the troops arrived and staked them out in the untrod jungles." The only encouraging discovery about the stocking of Bataan was that ammunition stores for most weapons seemed reasonably adequate.[33] But the defenders would need more than bullets and shells to hold out for six months, as they were expected to do under WPO-3.

MacArthur later said of his decision to withdraw to Bataan:

I have always regarded it as the not only most vital decision of
the Philippine Campaign but in its corollary consequences one
of the most decisive of the war. This view was confirmed later
from the Japanese records. Imperial Japanese Headquarters
stated, "It was a great strategic move." The Japanese 14th
Army Headquarters ". . . never planned for or expected a withdrawal to Bataan. The decisive battle had been expected in
Manila. The Japanese commanders could not adjust to the new
situation." And, "Politically, it stood as a symbol — there was
a spiritual influence exerted by the American resistance on
Bataan." [34]

It is true that his decision to reactivate WPO-3 compelled the
Japanese to fight a costly four-month campaign to secure the
use of Manila Bay, about four times longer than Imperial General Headquarters in Tokyo anticipated. Had he stayed with
his beach defense plan, the Japanese pincers on Luzon would
have closed on Wainwright's and Parker's forces and quickly
annihilated them, probably before mid-January. It is to Mac-
Arthur's credit that, in spite of his great pride and his strong
belief in his own defense plan, he changed his mind in time to
save the North and South Luzon forces from immediate destruction. But neither plan could spare them from ultimate
capitulation.

Although the withdrawal to Bataan was the wiser move in
this situation, one that was truly a dilemma, MacArthur's unexplained delay in ordering the reversion to WPO-3 hastened
the downfall of the American and Filipino defenders of Bataan
more than did any subsequent action by Homma's troops. General Harold K. Johnson, then a lieutenant with the 57th Infantry Regiment and later chief of staff of the United States
Army, expressed the consensus of nearly all survivors of that
campaign in maintaining that the beach defense plan was "a
tragic error" in judgment that should have been corrected much
earlier: "The supplies that could have been moved in that two-
week period probably meant the difference between another
three or four weeks' delay on Bataan. It wasn't the enemy that

licked us; it was disease and absence of food that really licked us." This is confirmed also in the official Army accounts, one of which puts it succinctly: "Lack of food probably more than any other single factor forced the end of resistance on Bataan." [35] Unlike the Clark-Iba disaster, for which the blame cannot be firmly fixed, there is little doubt among authorities that MacArthur's hesitation in reverting to WPO-3 during the first two weeks and Quezon's obstructionism during the following week were the main reasons for the lack of supplies on Bataan.

4. Destination Bataan

With the start of the incredibly difficult series of movements on December 24 that was supposed to result in the escape of the USAFFE forces into Bataan, MacArthur spent much of his time on Corregidor in a mood of tense anxiety, "like a caged lion," eager to be in the action himself. Poring over every message from the field and nervously pacing around his desk as he conferred with subordinates, he realized that he had now entered that strange interlude of helplessness which commanders of armies throughout history have experienced as a battle began. Having developed the plan of withdrawal in detail and studied it again and again, as well as having carefully selected the commanders, the participating units, and those to be held in reserve, he now faced two weeks of waiting before he would know finally whether his decisions had been sound.

Until January 8, by which time the last USAFFE forces were due into Bataan, MacArthur, the general who possessed supreme authority over all defending forces in the islands, was restricted to sending messages to his field commanders prodding them to move faster, urging them to hold a little longer here, or warning them of a threat to their flank there. Now the outcome of his risky plan depended on other men far removed from Corregidor: bewildered but brave Filipino privates who hesitantly chose to stay with their comrades in arms, young inexperienced American lieutenants who could not speak the dialects of many of their troops, division commanders who never before had led units above regimental size, and, above all, Wainwright, the tough, wiry, heavy-drinking, hard-driving cavalryman who headed the North Luzon Force.

The problems in executing the complicated maneuver of withdrawal into the peninsula would be so formidable that the plan was, indeed, a bold gamble. Somehow the troops on two fronts, originally over 160 miles apart, would have to be supplied, while the undermanned service units would try simultaneously to get provisions into Bataan depots. Somehow divisions with only a third of their authorized strength would have to hold critical positions for long hours. Somehow companies and regiments that had collapsed during the first days of fighting, many of whose men were now wandering in rear areas, would have to be reorganized quickly and sent back to fill gaps in the front lines. Somehow commercial buses and trucks, along with private vehicles, would have to be found, commandeered, and promptly gotten to the numerous units that lacked military transportation. Somehow, despite enemy air supremacy, vital bridges would have to be protected until the USAFFE troops were across, and then be demolished before the arrival of enemy forces who often were close behind. Somehow the North Luzon Force, with its thinly manned lines stretched across the wide Central Luzon Plain, would have to guard its flanks from envelopment while also slowing the Japanese offensive from Lingayen long enough for the South Luzon Force to complete its arduous movement from Tayabas Bay to Bataan. And finally, somehow Wainwright's force would then have to disengage itself and back into Bataan in a danger-laden rearguard maneuver dependent upon precise timing. A more difficult operation than the planned retreat into Bataan, or one beset by more disastrous contingencies, had seldom been attempted in military history.

On the 24th General Parker was transferred to Bataan where he was to take command of the three reserve divisions that were moving there to prepare defensive positions. This left three divisions, a cavalry regiment, and a tank group as the main units of the North Luzon Force, while the South Luzon Force, now commanded by Brigadier General Albert M. Jones, comprised a division plus an infantry regiment. In the delaying lines of the North Luzon Force, the center position was held by the 11th Division of Brigadier General William E. Brougher, with Brigadier General Mateo Capinpin's 21st Division on the left flank and Brigadier General Luther Stevens' 91st Division on the right. The main supporting forces were the 26th Cavalry Regiment, led by Brigadier General Clinton A. Pierce, and the Provisional Tank Group, commanded by Brigadier General James R. N. Weaver. Jones's force consisted of the 51st Division, his former command, which he retained while heading the South Luzon Force, and two infantry regiments, the 1st and 42nd.

Except for the Scouts of the 26th Cavalry and Weaver's tank crews, plus some field artillery forces, the units involved in the precarious withdrawal were of the Philippine Army, with Filipino enlisted men and a sprinkling of American officers in each outfit. Some of MacArthur's best combat regiments, including the American Army's 43rd Infantry, the Scouts' 57th Infantry, and the 4th Marines, had been kept in reserve and were already en route to Bataan. Although criticized by some for withholding these forces, he was wise to save them for the crucial battles that lay ahead rather than risking their destruction in a retrograde maneuver that was not intended to produce major engagements.[36]

The first scheduled delaying line (D-1) was really nonexistent by the time the withdrawal plan went into effect. On paper it

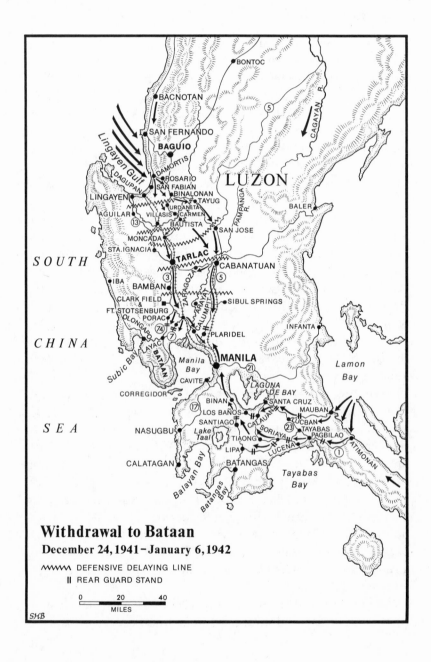

Withdrawal to Bataan
December 24, 1941–January 6, 1942

∿∿∿∿ DEFENSIVE DELAYING LINE

‖ REAR GUARD STAND

```
0        20        40
   MILES
```

SHB

was about halfway between the Lingayen beaches and the Agno River. The troops were expected to form their first real line of resistance on the south bank of the Agno and hold it until December 26. The Japanese concentrated on the right, or northern, flank on Christmas, but failed to disrupt the withdrawal. By that evening all USAFFE units were in position on the second delaying line (D-2), considering themselves lucky that no outfits, despite much confusion, had been trapped north of the Agno. On the 26th the Japanese drove the exhausted 26th Cavalry out of Tayug, a key road junction on the right flank, and another enemy force broke through the center of the USAFFE positions at Villasis on Route 3, temporarily cutting off the 11th Division's escape route down that major highway.

Brougher quickly took some troops to Tarlac, where he got a train under way and successfully rescued the trapped forces by rail. Weaver's tanks caught by surprise and defeated an enemy armored column that was racing to Moncada where the rail line crossed Route 3. This brief taste of victory was marred a few hours later by the forced abandonment of one tank company when engineers, thinking all USAFFE forces had already moved south, demolished the bridge below Moncada. Most of the crews made it to safety, but fifteen valuable tanks were left behind.

When the American and Filipino forces reached the D-3 line on the 27th, they were on the least defensible and widest of the delaying positions, stretching from Santa Ignacia on the west to San Jose on the east. Some forces had barely escaped being overwhelmed in the withdrawal from D-2. According to Brougher, "The 11th Infantry was the only one of the three Infantry Regiments of the 11th Division that was still intact and remotely to be considered a fighting unit . . . and for the next two days were the only troops of the 11th Division holding the entire division front." Fortunately, as in the case of the other divisions, Brougher's 11th Division was augmented on the D-3

line by large groups of USAFFE stragglers who had been making their way from the Lingayen beaches and Cagayan Valley
in disorganized fashion since the opening engagements.

Had Homma pursued aggressively on the 27th, the exhausted
and still poorly organized USAFFE forces might well have been
routed from their D-3 positions. But he decided to slow down
the Fourteenth Army's advance in order to bring up supplies
and reinforcements. So, in spite of occasional rumors of an
impending attack, the USAFFE troops manned the D-3 line
without significant fighting on the 27th. That night they began
pulling out for the fourth delaying line (D-4), which extended
from Tarlac about twenty-five miles east to Cabanatuan and
the Pampanga River.[37]

On the 29th, while the main body of the Japanese 48th Division was starting southward, enemy tank regiments attacked
the 91st Division at Cabanatuan and seized the town that night.
Instead of halting to await the arrival of the 48th Division, the
Japanese tanks, followed by infantry and artillery units that had
also moved rapidly along the eastern fringe of the plain, continued down Route 5 toward that highway's junction with
Route 3. Another column of tanks, supported by infantry,
turned west at Cabanatuan and attacked the 11th Division's
positions in the center of the D-4 line. A company of bicycle-
mounted Japanese infantry, moving incautiously ahead of the
tanks toward Zaragoza, was turned back by point-blank fire
from American tanks drawn up along the road into the town.
As enemy reinforcements arrived, the USAFFE tanks withdrew
across the Zalagot River into Zaragoza. The bridge was then
dynamited prematurely, leaving a battalion of USAFFE infantry on the east side facing the oncoming Japanese. The troops
were caught by heavy enemy fire as they tried to ford the river
and lost nearly 400 of 550 men. On the western end of the
D-4 line the Japanese attack came on the 30th, with the 21st
Division soon yielding Tarlac.

Although Wainwright had hoped his forces could hold the

D-4 line a few hours longer, he was compelled to order a withdrawal to the final delaying line. By December 31 the battered soldiers of the 21st, 11th, and 91st divisions were on the D-5 line. Now there could be no further retreat until the South Luzon Force had crossed the Calumpit bridges, and the danger was very real that the enemy tanks moving down Route 5 might interdict Jones's movement at the intersection with Route 3 near Plaridel. The USAFFE withdrawal had reached its most critical stage.[38]

But luck was with the beleaguered defenders on several counts: Homma, though aware by then of MacArthur's plan to abandon Manila and withdraw into Bataan, did not press the advance of either of his flanking forces. If the 48th Division had pushed quickly down Route 3 on the west or if the tank regiments had continued at a swift pace down Route 5 on the east, the withdrawal would have been disrupted. But the Japanese flanking movements strangely slowed in pace, perhaps because Homma and his staff were still debating whether to push on to Manila or shift the bulk of the Fourteenth Army toward Bataan. Whatever the reason, the brief pause was time enough for Jones. In an unexpectedly rapid manner the South Luzon Force had extricated itself from difficult situations south of Manila and was hastening northward. With comparatively light losses, Jones's two main units, the 51st Division and the 1st Infantry Regiment, had fought a series of savage rear-guard actions, escaped several envelopments, and had moved so fast that the Japanese 16th Division was unable to maintain contact. At dawn on the 31st, the advance South Luzon Force troops started crossing the Calumpit bridges while the 16th Division was far to the south, still struggling to ford countless streams where bridges had been destroyed by USAFFE engineers.

As Jones's men reached Calumpit, Wainwright's forces were blocking the Japanese effectively to the north along the D-5 line, which extended from Bamban on the west to Sibul Springs

on the east. Despite some confusion in orders, the North Luzon
Force tanks and an infantry regiment detained the Japanese
near Plaridel, northeast of the Calumpit bridges, long enough
for the last of the South Luzon Force troops to cross the spans
on New Year's Day. Amazingly, the Japanese air forces, despite
their nearly complete control of the skies, made no effort to
bomb the bridges. As the USAFFE covering force withdrew
westward across the Pampanga River at Calumpit, the engineers
exploded the spans with the pursuing Japanese only minutes
away. Meanwhile, to the north on the D-5 line the 21st and
11th divisions repelled several Japanese assaults and, with the
good news that the South Luzon Force had passed Calumpit,
began withdrawing toward Bataan. The blocking tactics had
worked, but the road to Bataan was still a dangerous one.[39]

During the period of January 2–6 the North and South Luzon forces jammed the two main roads into Bataan, Route 7
from San Fernando and Route 74 from Porac. The traffic was
often bumper to bumper with gaudily decorated commercial
buses, antique American automobiles, Army trucks, and peasant
carts, while miles-long columns of weary, hungry soldiers
marched beside the crowded roads. The congestion would have
made ideal targets for Japanese bombers and Zeros. Some did
attack but, by not following the wide-ranging patterns that had
proved devastating in previous raids, the enemy air forces
missed an excellent opportunity to destroy a sizable part of
MacArthur's army on the final road to Bataan. Homma and
the bulk of the Fourteenth Army moved on to Manila and
only two reinforced regiments were sent to put pressure on the
USAFFE forces entering Bataan. Relentless, rapid pursuit and
heavy air attacks could have badly crippled the defenders, who
were especially vulnerable at this stage of the withdrawal.

The last divisions to enter Bataan were Capinpin's 21st and
Brougher's 11th, which held covering positions respectively on
Routes 74 and 7. When Wainwright ordered their move into
Bataan on January 5, the 11th Division's line of retreat was cut

off by a sudden thrust by the Japanese. To get his main force back on Route 7, Brougher had to send the troops by commercial buses on a fourteen-hour trip on a side road to the west, then down Route 74, and finally back to Route 7. Again the Japanese could have exploited the situation to achieve a major breakthrough down Route 7 to Layac, the junction of the two routes at the entrance to Bataan. But probably because of ignorance of the 11th Division's unusual maneuver and Homma's overly cautious disposition, no enemy attack was launched. On the 6th the two last divisions crossed the Culo River at Layac and moved into Bataan, the engineers blowing their final bridge of the withdrawal early that morning. While the main USAFFE forces were moving down to the first prepared defensive line on Bataan, a small covering force, led by Selleck, conducted a costly delaying action, finally retreating when the Japanese resorted to heavy artillery fire.[40]

In the long and harrowing withdrawal no major USAFFE units had been lost, and the 91st Division's failure at Cabanatuan marked the only time one of the divisions had to yield a critical position before the scheduled pullback to the next line. The North Luzon Force had about 28,000 troops when the withdrawal began and about 16,000 when it entered Bataan, although many of the losses were Filipino desertions rather than combat casualties. The South Luzon Force managed to get 14,000 of its original 15,000 men into Bataan. Japanese losses in killed, wounded, and missing during the two weeks amounted to between 2000 and 4500. In the words of the official Army history of the campaign, "The success of this complicated and difficult movement, made with ill-equipped and inadequately trained Filipinos, is a tribute to the generalship of MacArthur, Wainwright, and Jones and to American leadership on the field of battle." [41] MacArthur's plan, as well as his choice of leaders and units in the withdrawal, had proven wise, although Homma's failure to pursue rapidly and relentlessly was an unexpected stroke of good fortune.

CHAPTER II

Nowhere to Retreat

1. Last Line on Bataan

POINTING LIKE A SWOLLEN THUMB toward Corregidor, Bataan is a rugged peninsula which, had adequate preparations been made, would have been well suited for MacArthur's final stand on Luzon. It is twenty-nine miles from Olongapo, at the northwest corner of Bataan, down to Mariveles, the port at the tip of the peninsula. MacArthur's first defensive line, however, extended from Mauban, eleven miles south of Olongapo, to Mabatang, six miles south of the eastern entrance to Bataan, so the upper third of the peninsula was forfeited at the start of operations in January, 1942. A chain of jungle-clad mountains stretches along the spine of Bataan, dominated by two extinct volcanoes, Mount Natib (4200 feet), splitting the first defensive line, and Mount Bataan (4700 feet), fourteen miles south. On the northeast side of Bataan lies a swampy coastal plain, but mountains extend almost to the sea along the rest of the shoreline, with high cliffs and jagged promontories covered by dense jungle on the western coast. Numerous mountain streams and steep ravines cut the interior landscape. A road runs the entire length of the eastern coast and as far up

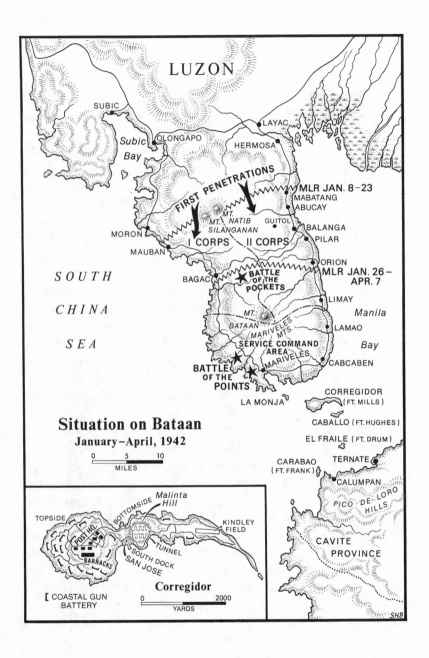

LUZON

SUBIC

Subic
Bay

OLONGAPO

LAYAC

HERMOSA

FIRST PENETRATIONS

MLR JAN. 8–23

MABATANG

ABUCAY

MT.
NATIB

MT.
SILANGANAN

GUITOL

BALANGA

MORON

PILAR

MAUBAN

I CORPS   II CORPS

SOUTH

CHINA

SEA

BAGAC

ORION

MLR JAN. 26–
APR. 7

BATTLE
OF THE
POCKETS

LIMAY

MT.
BATAAN

Manila

MARIVELES
MTS.

LAMAO

SERVICE COMMAND
AREA

Bay

MARIVELES

CABCABEN

BATTLE
OF THE
POINTS

CORREGIDOR
(FT. MILLS)

LA MONJA

CABALLO (FT. HUGHES)

Situation on Bataan
January–April, 1942

EL FRAILE (FT. DRUM)

CARABAO
(FT. FRANK)

TERNATE

0   5   10
MILES

CALUMPAN

*PICO DE LORO
HILLS*

*Malinta
Hill*

TOPSIDE

BOTTOMSIDE

KINDLEY
FIELD

CAVITE
PROVINCE

POST HQ

BARRACKS

TUNNEL

SOUTH DOCK

SAN JOSE

[COASTAL GUN
BATTERY

0   2000
YARDS

Corregidor

SHB

the western shoreline as Moron, just above Mauban, and another road crosses the middle of the peninsula from Bagac to Pilar. Aside from their attacks on roads and clearings, the Japanese air forces' activity would be sharply curtailed in the Bataan campaign because thick jungle concealed most of the defenders' positions from air observation.

On January 7 MacArthur reorganized the command on Bataan, placing Wainwright in charge of the I Philippine Corps on the west side of the Mauban-Mabatang line and Parker in command of the II Philippine Corps on the east side. The I Corps' main forces comprised the 1st and 91st Philippine Army divisions, as well as the 26th Cavalry and several field artillery regiments — about 23,000 troops in all. Parker's corps, which was east of Mount Natib, had approximately 25,000 soldiers, principally of the 11th, 21st, 41st, and 51st divisions of the Philippine Army, the 57th Infantry (Scouts), and supporting artillery. The 31st and Philippine divisions (less a regiment of each which were at the front), along with tank and artillery outfits, were in reserve behind the Mauban-Mabatang line. No defensive positions were established for about two miles on either side of Mount Natib, although MacArthur had ordered the corps commanders to close the gap. Patrols were sent out in vain by both corps to make contact, but most officers at the front were convinced that the enemy could not penetrate the inhospitable region around Mount Natib.

Other troop dispositions included various regiments that manned coastal watches along the eastern and western shores, and Brigadier General Allan C. McBride headed the Service Command Area, a sector at the southern end of the peninsula that held an assortment of troops ranging from American and Filipino regulars to constabulary troops, some of the 4th Marines, and airmen and sailors now functioning as infantry. MacArthur hoped that the Mauban-Mabatang line could be held until a potentially stronger defensive line was prepared south of the Bagac-Pilar road, about midway between Mounts Natib and Bataan.[1]

As the Bataan campaign began, neither MacArthur nor Homma had accurate information about the strength of his enemy's forces. The former thought that 80,000 to 100,000 enemy troops were on Luzon, although, in reality, Homma had used only two divisions and some supporting units thus far. On January 2 Tokyo ordered his better division, the 48th, and most of the air group that had supported his operations to join the offensive against the Malay Barrier. In return, Homma got Lieutenant General Akira Nara's inexperienced 65th Brigade, about 6500 troops. But since his intelligence reported only 25,000 USAFFE troops on Bataan, and those in poor condition, Homma assigned the 65th Brigade and a regiment of the 16th Division the task of seizing the peninsula where, in fact, about 80,000 American and Filipino soldiers were entrenched.[2]

Meanwhile, on Corregidor MacArthur continued to cling to the illusion that massive reinforcements would be sent to him. At that time he knew nothing of the Anglo-American strategic talks under way in Washington or the latest developments in the thinking of the War Department's planners, and he had good reason to be bolstered by the statements reaching him from Washington. On December 28 in a special broadcast to the Philippine nation, President Roosevelt sounded optimistic in proclaiming that "the resources of the United States, of the British Empire, of the Netherlands East Indies, and of the Chinese Republic have been dedicated by their people to the utter and complete defeat of the Japanese war lords." That same day a Navy Department communiqué announced that "the United States Navy is following an intensive and well-planned campaign against Japanese forces which will result in positive assistance to the defense of the Philippine Islands."

In a message to Marshall on New Year's Day MacArthur re-

minded him that "our soldiers at the front and the Filipino
people in general have placed their trust in this indispensable
help coming from America, especially after the proclamation of
the President and the announcement made by the Navy which
gave them the impression that help is forthcoming." Stressing
that "the question of time is paramount," MacArthur argued
that the Philippines could be saved by "the immediate combined effort of all resources of the United States and her allies
by land, sea and air, beginning with the securing of air supremacy in the NEI and Mindanao, the landing of an expeditionary force on that island to secure bases and the reopening of the line of communications, followed by a drive to the
north." [3]

As unrealistic as that proposal was, Marshall sent a reply,
received by MacArthur on the 4th, that must have sounded
encouraging to the trapped, desperate USAFFE commander:

> Replying to your no. 23, January 1st. There is here a keen
> appreciation of your situation. The President and Prime Min-
> ister, Colonel Stimson and Colonel Knox, the British chiefs of
> staff and our corresponding officials have been surveying every
> possibility looking toward the quick development of strength in
> the Far East so as to break the enemy's hold on the Philippines.
> Previous losses in capital ships seriously reduce the capacity of
> the Navy to carry on indispensable tasks including convoys for
> heavy reinforcements for the Far East and protection of vital
> supplies for 600,000 men in the Near East and to [the] British
> Isles. The net result is a marked insufficiency of forces for any
> powerful naval concentration in the Western Pacific at this
> time. Our great hope is that the rapid development of an over-
> whelming air power on the Malay Barrier will cut the Japanese
> communications south of Borneo and permit an assault in the
> Southern Philippines. A stream of four-engine bombers, previ-
> ously delayed by foul weather, is en route with the head of the
> column having crossed Africa. Another stream of similar
> bombers started today from Hawaii staging at new island fields.
> Two groups of powerful medium bombers of long range and

heavy bomb-load capacity leave next week. Pursuit planes are coming on every ship we can use. Our definitely allocated air reinforcements together with British [reinforcements to Singapore] should give us an early superiority in the Southwestern Pacific. Our strength is to be concentrated and it should exert a decisive effect on Japanese shipping and force a withdrawal northward. These measures provide the only speedy intervention now possible unless naval carrier raids may be managed. We are searching our resources to develop means to disrupt the present Japanese operations. Every day of time you gain is vital to the concentration of the overwhelming power necessary for our purpose. Furthermore the current conferences in Washington between all anti-Axis nations are developing a unity of purpose, plans and execution which are [sic] extremely encouraging in respect to accelerating speed of ultimate success.[4]

Yet as early as December 14 Brigadier General Dwight D. Eisenhower, deputy chief of the War Plans Division, had told Marshall, "It will be a long time before major reinforcements can go to the Philippines, longer than the garrison can hold out with any driblet assistance, if the enemy commits major forces to their reduction." At the Arcadia Conference Roosevelt had already reaffirmed the United States' commitment to the defeat of Germany first and the relegation of the Pacific theater to a secondary priority, much to Prime Minister Churchill's satisfaction. Marshall must have been aware of the Philippines study under way in the War Plans Division, the conclusions of which were reported to him on January 3. The planners' consensus was that the relief of the Philippine garrison could not be effected soon, and, besides, so vast a force as would be essential to try it would be "an entirely unjustifiable diversion of forces from the principal theater — the Atlantic." [5]

Like the false encouragement given by some physicians to dying patients, the hopeful words of Roosevelt and Marshall perhaps were intended to brace MacArthur and his men to fight longer than they would have if told the truth. If so, these words were an insult to the garrison's bravery and determination. Moreover, such misleading messages deepened the final disillusionment of both the USAFFE troops and the Filipino populace. They also prompted MacArthur, who at first sincerely believed these statements, to spread the news that help was on the way. Ironically, in the end the Americans in the Philippines who felt deceived would turn their resentment against MacArthur rather than against the leaders in Washington.

Brimming with renewed confidence, MacArthur told Quezon on the 6th that he planned to visit the troops on Bataan. After getting a report from Willoughby, his intelligence chief (G-2), that a major enemy attack could be expected about the 11th, MacArthur sent instructions to Wainwright and Parker on the evening of the 9th to assemble their general officers the next day for conferences with him. At dawn on January 10 MacArthur and Sutherland crossed by torpedo boat from Corregidor to Mariveles, from where they drove in a Ford sedan up the dusty east road to Balanga, stopping on the way to visit briefly at field hospitals and rear command posts. At Balanga they conferred with Parker and his II Corps commanders, assuring them that reinforcements from the States were coming soon. Then they journeyed to Abucay where they talked to officers and men of the crack 57th Infantry. At the time Nara's 65th Brigade was beginning to probe the Scouts' outpost line four miles north of Abucay, and sporadic shelling of the 57th's main line had begun. The Abucay churchyard, where MacArthur met with the assembled officers of the 57th, had earlier received some artillery rounds, but luckily no shelling occurred during his visit.

Later in the day MacArthur and Sutherland traveled west to Wainwright's sector and met with him and his top officers, besides making side tours to divisional and regimental command posts. Sutherland saw enough of the I Corps' exposed right flank near Mount Natib to warn Wainwright that the gap between the two corps should be closed. Bluemel of the 31st Division recalled MacArthur's words to his group of officers: "Help is definitely on the way. We must hold out until it arrives." When MacArthur asked if the officers had any questions, a young captain inquired if he and others who had savings in the Philippine Trust Company in Manila were going to lose their money. MacArthur assured him that they would be recompensed after the war (though they had great difficulty in securing reimbursements in the postwar years).

MacArthur was effusive in his praise of Wainwright's withdrawal from Lingayen, calling the operation "as fine as anything in history." He also promised to nominate Wainwright for promotion from temporary to permanent major general. When MacArthur inquired about the I Corps' 155-mm. guns, Wainwright offered to take him to see two that were within walking distance. But MacArthur responded, "Jonathan, I don't want to see them. I want to hear them!" After an all-day trip on Bataan, including about ten hours spent in conferences and inspections, MacArthur and Sutherland returned to Corregidor.[6]

The next day MacArthur buoyantly described his observations of the journey to Quezon, reassuring the Philippine president that "there was no reason for immediate worry." According to Quezon, MacArthur "felt confident that he could hold Bataan and Corregidor for several months without outside help; that the morale of our forces was high." Especially pleasing to Quezon was the USAFFE commander's assessment "that those Filipino reservists who had only five and a half months' training had become veterans in less than one month [of] actual fighting against a determined and superior force." Ominously, MacArthur's visit to Bataan on the 10th had coincided with the first surrender ultimatum issued by Homma. Copies of the message were dropped by planes in a number of areas he visited.

MacArthur made no reply to Homma, and about three weeks later copies of the same leaflets were dropped by Japanese aircraft with an additional statement about the stupidity of MacArthur.[7]

Wainwright and a number of other USAFFE officers later asserted that the trip of January 10 was the only one MacArthur made to Bataan. However, Brigadier General Milton A. Hill, who was the inspector general and spent much time at USAFFE advance headquarters on southern Bataan, recalled a later visit by MacArthur "to one of the corps headquarters." Among the stories about MacArthur's absence that made the rounds on Bataan was one that he had been stricken with a "serious heart condition," another that he was "forbidden" to leave Corregidor, and a malicious tale with several versions that told of his newly developed fear of leaving "the vicinity of the protecting tunnel" on the island fortress.[8]

Captain Ind offered this rambling but more rational explanation of MacArthur's absence from Bataan:

> The facts are that, through bombing and shelling alike, he has lived "topside" in a house [on Corregidor]. Frequently he has gone up to observe during enemy shellings. During duty, he must be in the tunnel. Every communication nerve fiber in this whole setup terminates right there in the Administration-Operations lateral of Malinta Tunnel. General MacArthur runs this show through General Sutherland. He knows every minute what the situation is at all points. If he is in any doubt, he fires an order over to USAFFE Advance here on Bataan. Then his subordinate generals — yes, generals, not junior officers — paddle off to find out exactly what the score is. Immediately they determine that, they signal back to the Rock. Thus, through a tight chain, all vital information is relayed back by the experts who observed it. Orders are issued accordingly. Not only is there no need for his presence over here, but there is every need for his presence almost continuously in that tunnel — the focus point of this nasty little war really.[9]

Apparently this interpretation was not widespread on the peninsula. In view of the bitterness of some soldiers toward the USAFFE chief that was a consequence, in part, of his failure to make appearances on Bataan, it would seem that a commander as brilliant and as sensitive about his image as MacArthur would have assessed more wisely the value to his soldiers and his own reputation of such visits. On the other hand, he was often seen in exposed areas on Corregidor during bombardments, setting a courageous and inspiring example. MacArthur explained that "it was simply my duty. The gunners at the batteries, the men in the foxholes, they too were in the open. They liked to see me with them at such moments." [10] Why he mingled with the soldiers during action on the island but stayed away from the Bataan front has never been satisfactorily explained. Ind's justification is the most plausible, yet no amount of business on Corregidor warranted his persistent dissociation from the exhausted, starving men on Bataan whose morale he could so easily have boosted by an occasional appearance. Even stranger was his later practice of naming his personal planes *Bataan* — a phenomenon that will be left to psychologists to explain.

The first major Japanese attack against Parker's II Corps came on January 11, the day after MacArthur's visit. Initially forced to fall back in the coastal area north of Abucay, the 57th Infantry rallied, regained most of the lost ground by the next dawn, and inflicted heavy casualties on the enemy. Releasing the 21st Infantry from reserve to aid the 57th, Parker ordered another counterattack the following day, which pushed the Japanese farther away from Abucay. By January 16 the principal action had shifted to the left side of the II Corps where Nara's 65th Brigade struck the 41st and 51st divisions. Following several days of fierce fighting, many of the 51st's Filipinos panicked, dropped their weapons and equipment, and "melted into the jungle." The division ceased to exist. USAFFE reserves, including units of the 31st and Philippine divisions, were rushed into the sector in a futile effort to restore the left, or west, flank of the II Corps. Meanwhile, another Japanese force had moved through supposedly impenetrable jungle east of Mount Natib and threatened to envelop the II Corps. After advancing nearly five miles behind the corps' main line, the column was stopped near Guitol. By that time, however, the entire left side of Parker's front was giving way despite savage resistance by the USAFFE reserves. On January 21 the enemy advance slowed on the left flank, but Nara seemed to be massing his forces for an all-out assault.

On Wainwright's front, west of Mount Natib, Japanese forces moved through Moron from Olongapo and started attacks on January 19 against the coastal and central sectors of the I Corps line, held by units of the 1st and 91st divisions and the 26th Cavalry. In the meantime, an enemy column advanced through the foothills west of Mount Silanganan, part of the Natib mountain massif, and infiltrated the right flank of the I Corps. Though only of battalion size, the Japanese unit pushed through to the Mauban-Mariveles road, a mile behind the main line, and set up a road block, cutting the corps' line of communications. Despite attacks by Wainwright's troops, the small enemy force staunchly held the block, and moreover, by January 21, pressure against the I Corps' main positions to the north was intensifying. One USAFFE battalion fled without firing a gun when attacked. Wainwright's and Parker's corps were in desperate situations, the enemy having outflanked each of them through the undefended areas on either side of Mount Natib.[11]

As the fighting had begun to mount on Parker's front, MacArthur issued a proclamation on the 15th to be read to all troops on Bataan. Desperately trying to bolster their fighting spirit, he employed hyperbole in much the same manner as the men in Washington had in communicating with him: "Thousands of troops and hundreds of planes are being dispatched.

The exact time of arrival of reinforcements is unknown . . .
No further retreat is possible . . . If we fight we will win;
if we retreat we will be destroyed." The next day he sent a
message in a different tone to all unit commanders on Bataan,
saying that he was "very much displeased at continuous reports
stating that troops are tired and need relief"; he wanted "such
reports to cease." He also told them that he "deprecated most
severely loose talk tending to aggrandize the potentialities of
the enemy" and directed "all commanding officers to deal
harshly with every man who spreads such enemy propaganda."
In closing, he called upon all officers to remember "that demeanor of confidence, self-reliance and assurance which is the
birthright of all cultured gentlemen and the special trademark
of the Army Officer." [12] How these messages were received on
the front lines is not fully known, but the fact that renewed
enemy assaults would shortly crumble both corps fronts was
becoming apparent even on Corregidor.

On January 22 MacArthur sent Sutherland to the front lines
to check on the combat situation. After talks with Wainwright
and Parker, both of whom favored pulling back to the shorter,
stronger position to the south, Sutherland recommended withdrawal to the Bagac-Orion line, which MacArthur quickly approved. The decision was wise and timely and probably averted
a rout. The next day MacArthur notified Marshall of the withdrawal, assuring him that he was determined "to fight it out to
complete destruction" on the new line. Obviously shocked and
depressed by the enemy's breakthroughs, MacArthur seemed to
be forewarning the Army chief of staff of impending doom
when he asked Marshall to be sure that the glorious service of
the Bataan forces was "duly recorded by their countrymen,"
for "no troops have ever done so much with so little." He
gloomily requested that in case of his death Sutherland be
appointed as his successor since "of all my general officers he
has the most comprehensive grasp of the situation."

At a staff conference on Corregidor on the 24th, MacArthur

appeared discouraged and implied that the fall of Bataan was imminent. He ordered Major General George F. Moore, the harbor defense commander, to start withdrawing food stocks from the peninsula to Corregidor in the hope that at least the island fortress could hold out until reinforcements arrived. He also informed Moore that he planned to transfer the Philippine Division to Corregidor before Bataan fell.[13]

The two embattled corps undertook the withdrawal to the Bagac-Orion line on January 24–26. A great amount of confusion attended the move, not unlike the earlier chaotic situation in the Lingayen area: some Filipino units were disintegrating rapidly as organized combat forces, many troops simply abandoned their weapons and gear as they pulled back, and a welter of confusing orders transferring units from one corps to the other resulted in temporary gaps in the new line. Colonel Ernest Miller, a tank battalion commander, commented that "bringing out the Philippine Army was like herding a flock of sheep . . . Units intermingled with other units and became hopelessly lost in the mob." USAFFE headquarters contributed to the mix-up by ordering the Philippine Division into reserve, probably preparatory to transferring it to Corregidor, but then Sutherland reversed the order and permitted the corps commanders to retain the Division's three regiments of infantry. In a rare episode during the disorderly withdrawal General Bluemel, after having one of his regiments suddenly transferred to the other corps' front, somehow managed to rally enough of his 31st Division troops to hurl back a Japanese attack shortly after getting to the Bagac-Orion line. If Nara had pushed his forces in more assertive pursuit, the USAFFE retreat undoubtedly would have turned into a disastrous rout. Even so, the withdrawal, remarked Miller, "was a nightmare while it lasted." [14]

During the last week in January only intermittent, piecemeal attacks were made against the new defensive line south of the

Bagac-Pilar road. With one exception the assaults against the main line were quickly repulsed by the USAFFE defenders, whose commanders had performed near-miracles in reorganizing units and buttressing weak points in their positions. The 1st Division, however, was late in taking its place near the center of the I Corps front, and a Japanese regiment sneaked through the opening amid dense jungle along the Tuol River. The enemy soldiers were not spotted until the next day, January 29, by which time they had split into two groups. I Corps units, mainly of the 1st and 11th divisions, soon surrounded the infiltrators in the so-called "Little Pocket" and "Big Pocket." Lacking reliable maps and handicapped by rugged terrain and thick vegetation, the American and Filipino troops, led by Generals Jones and Brougher, tried in vain to reduce the pockets. In early February a Japanese relief column thrust a deep salient into the main line north of the pockets in an effort to reach the entrapped but still battling regiment. This advance was thwarted, but it took the forces of Jones and Brougher until February 17 to eliminate the pockets and the salient.

Japanese losses in the engagements were severe; in the Big Pocket alone over 450 enemy bodies were later found. USAFFE casualties were also heavy, and some participating officers blamed the drawn-out action on "the lack of suitable weapons" for close jungle fighting. Colonel Townsend commented that "more than anything else we needed mortars." They had employed obsolete Stokes mortars, "but the only ammo available had been stored in the Islands since World War I and had greatly deteriorated." Townsend observed that "on one occasion in the Tuol [Big] Pocket we fired 70 rounds and got only 14 bursts . . . No wonder the Japs once set up a captured Stokes mortar between the lines and scoffingly draped it with flowers." [15]

While the action at the pockets was under way, another

threat loomed when Japanese forces landed at Longoskawayan and Quinauan points on the southwest corner of the peninsula. On February 1, about a week later, other enemy troops seized Anyasan and Silaim points, just north of the previous landings. The Japanese on these four points made up only several battalions in all, but they still posed a serious threat to the Service Command Area. The 45th and 57th infantry regiments, together with a conglomeration of Filipino soldiers and American marines, sailors, and airmen, contained the enemy on the points but had great difficulty in wiping them out. The battle of the points raged for three weeks, with the final Japanese resistance ending on February 13.[16]

The operations against the pockets and the points marked the bloodiest fighting yet seen on Luzon, but both terminated in costly Japanese defeats. MacArthur reported that the enemy was "badly mauled" in these engagements. He particularly praised the Igorots, hardy recruits from the North Luzon mountains, who boldly rode on the fronts of tanks in attacking the pockets: "For sheer, breath-taking and heart-stopping desperation, I have never known the equal of those Igorots riding the tanks." Wainwright later cited several units for distinguished roles in the fighting, especially the Scouts of the 45th and 57th infantries. "It was the teamwork of all," he remarked, "that insured success." In a letter to General Chynoweth in the Visayas, Sutherland jubilantly wrote, "We have stopped the Japs cold on Bataan, inflicting very heavy casualties . . . The Jap is going to have to put in a lot more troops up here to push us around any."

Homma and Nara would have agreed with Sutherland's assessment, for they were facing a critical and somewhat humiliating situation. Imperial General Headquarters in Tokyo had scheduled the Philippines operations to be completed by the end of January. But the Japanese high command on Luzon, alarmed by its army's serious depletions from transfers, combat losses, and disease, was reluctant to launch another attack soon.

Homma later claimed that his forces were "in very bad shape. If the USAFFE took the counter-offensive, I thought they could walk to Manila without encountering much resistance on our part." On February 8 he ordered Nara to pull his troops back to a line several miles north of the Bagac-Pilar road. Homma planned to appeal to Tokyo for reinforcements and to postpone further offensive action until they arrived.[17]

According to Townsend, "Jap pressure on our lines almost ceased" after early February. From then until the end of March an unnerving lull existed on the front except for completion of the pockets and points operations, patrol skirmishes, and occasional exchanges of artillery fire. MacArthur reported to the War Department on February 26, "The enemy has definitely recoiled . . . His attitude is so passive as to discount any immediate threat of attack." During the lull both sides were busy preparing positions, training, and evaluating the mistakes made in earlier operations. Along the USAFFE positions miles of telephone wire were strung connecting command posts, fields of fire were blasted out of the jungle in front of carefully concealed machine-gun nests, new and more accurate maps were prepared, and intricate systems of tunnels, trenches, barbed-wire entanglements, mine fields, and tank traps were constructed.

Brigadier General Hugh J. Casey, the able, energetic Irishman who headed the USAFFE engineers, often inspected the various engineer projects under way on Bataan. On his last visit to the front, during the first week of March, Casey reported back to MacArthur that, although the men were exhausted, hungry, and disease-ridden, much excellent work had been accomplished in constructing and organizing defensive positions. He mentioned a number of weaknesses that still needed correction, particularly the lack of a mobile reserve force, but Casey emphasized that he had refrained from criticizing the men at the front, "knowing full well that morale and a determination to fight it out were of paramount importance." [18]

Casey was undoubtedly aware, as was every other officer on

the front, that by then the defenders' ability to stop the next enemy offensive would be determined less by the quality of their breastworks than by their morale and alarmingly increasing rates of disease and malnutrition. Every day the emaciated defenders could see and hear growing activity along the enemy lines as troop reinforcements, stocks of munitions, and large amounts of provisions began to arrive north of the Bagac-Pilar road. Declining morale was apparent in some outfits, but an amazingly large number of the troops continued to be hopeful. "Day after day," said Captain Amado N. Bautista of the 11th Engineers, "the boys would scan the skies for the long awaited Allied planes that would help us win over the enemy; lookouts never tired of watching for the convoy of ships that would bring us supplies and reinforcements." [19] Creating fantasies had become easy for the soldiers who manned the last line on Bataan.

The food situation had been serious on Bataan in January; by early March it was critical. Colonel Richard C. Mallonée of the 21st Division described the half ration his men started receiving in early January: "3.7 oz. rice — 1.8 oz. sugar — 1.2 oz. canned milk — 2.44 oz. canned fish, salmon or sardines — tomatoes when available, basis 10 men per can." On March 2 MacArthur ordered the Bataan ration reduced to three-eighths of a regular ration despite protests from Wainwright and Parker. Major Calvin E. Chunn said that he and his 45th Infantry Scouts had become "so weak that we could hardly crawl from the fox holes and aim our rifles." Capinpin, the 21st Division commander, tried to prohibit "food patrols" of volunteers from foraging "too far inside enemy territories," but finally had to ignore the practice: "The thought was current among the 21st Division men that it was better to die from an enemy bullet than by hunger and disease. Many were instances when patrols fought with a carcass of a dead carabao or the fruits of the cashew trees." Lieutenant Henry G. Lee of the 57th Infantry said that through such "foraging parties" his soldiers' diet "was augmented by monkey meat, iguana, wild chicken or pig, papaya, edible roots, edible leaves and bread fruit. However, even with these additions, hunger was with us constantly." [20]

Mounting hospital lists and rolls of troops "incapacitated for combat" resulted from the reduced ration, lack of adequate shelter and clothing, poor sanitation conditions, prevalence of jungle diseases, and shortage of medical supplies and equipment. On February 18 the USAFFE surgeon general's report showed only 55 per cent of the Bataan troops listed as "combat efficient," the reasons being "debilities due to malaria, dysentery, and general malnutrition." By March 12, according to Wainwright's estimate, "at least 75% of the command was incapacitated to some extent." The field hospitals were reporting 500 to 700 daily admissions of malaria victims, although Lieutenant Juanita Redmond, a nurse, stated that "there were many days when we were out of quinine." Avitaminosis, diarrhea, beriberi, dengue, hookworm, and dysentery accounted for many other patients. The water supply on Bataan was "totally inadequate," commented Army surgeon Alfred A. Weinstein. "Thirst-crazed men drank water they knew to be polluted, from carabao wallows and stagnant mountain pools," thus adding to the rising disease rate, especially of bacillary and amoebic dysentery.[21]

From officers and enlisted men who had occasion to visit rear areas, the soldiers on the front lines gradually became aware that provisions were distributed inequitably and that the rear echelons were living on more generous rations of food, clothing, and other subsistence items severely lacking in the combat areas. By early March the food ration of the Harbor Defense Command's troops, mainly on Corregidor, was forty-eight to fifty-five ounces, while that of the Bataan combat soldiers was only fourteen to seventeen ounces. Lieutenant Harold Johnson of the 57th Infantry noted the contrast when he was sent occa-

sionally to the tip of Bataan. There he and other soldiers from
the front visited the submarine tender *Canopus,* anchored in
Mariveles harbor, and indulged in "a great amount of trading
of captured enemy material in return for cigarettes and canned
rations from the Navy." Johnson observed that "it was only a
few days before the end of the war [on Bataan] that they ran
out of ice cream at Mariveles." Many of the combat troops
naturally resented the unequal distribution of supplies, but
Colonel Collier accepted the situation stoically: "To try to
feed all of us would have been impossible. We on Bataan would
have taken everything they had [on Corregidor] in a week's
time."

Since Corregidor had been adequately stocked with supplies
for 10,000 men for six months in late December, it is difficult
to understand why MacArthur felt it necessary to order Moore
on January 24, when the harbor forts' population was only
9000, to remove food stocks from Bataan, especially since the
planned transfer of the Philippine Division was canceled. Yet
the removals from Bataan depots continued until subsistence
reserves on Corregidor were built up to provide for 20,000
men through July 1, although not over 12,000 were on the
island that spring. It is little wonder that many soldiers at the
front resented the "favored ones" who enjoyed a ration three
or four times larger than theirs and could eat their meals in the
comparative safety of Corregidor's tunnels. Eventually much
of their criticism centered on MacArthur and rightly so, for
this was one inexcusably unfair situation that he could have
tried to correct. It is difficult to believe that he was ignorant
of the inequitable condition. If his failure to remedy this injustice can be explained, it would probably be on the grounds
that he still hoped to get some of the Bataan units to Corregidor
before the peninsula was lost.[22]

Besides problems of health, food, clothing, and shelter, the
Bataan defenders also had to cope with Japanese propaganda.

Every day enemy loudspeakers on the front lines and Japanese-controlled radio stations in Manila broadcast appeals to the troops to surrender, and enemy aircraft continued to drop thousands of propaganda leaflets. MacArthur countered by issuing a daily news sheet to keep the troops informed of the brighter happenings of the war, usually elsewhere than in the Philippines, and he appointed Colonel Carlos P. Romulo, a former Manila editor, to direct the "Voice of Freedom," a radio station on Corregidor that beamed comforting music and more favorable news to the soldiers. There is little indication that the USAFFE combat troops were significantly influenced by the propaganda barrages of either side. Affecting them far more was a radio broadcast of a "fireside chat" by Roosevelt on February 22, in which he analyzed the global predicament of the Allies and emphasized the many demands upon American men and matériel by the far-flung theaters of war. The President reiterated his commitment to defeating Germany first, and no hope of relief for the Philippines could be inferred from any of his remarks. Colonel Mallonée commented, "The President had — with regret — wiped us off the page and closed the book." [23]

Despite disease, starvation, and enemy efforts to undermine their morale, the Bataan troops generally maintained a strong *esprit de corps* and a dogged determination to give a good account in the final round of fighting. MacArthur's reputation remained untarnished among virtually all the Filipino soldiers and probably among a large majority of the Americans. But some of the American soldiers on Bataan lost faith in him, although officers tended to refrain from caustic comments about him at least until their later period in Japanese prison camps. The situation that was developing on Bataan portended the worst disaster ever suffered by an American army, and it was to be expected, especially in view of their physical deterioration, that some men would seek a scapegoat.[24]

Sometime in February a ballad, set to the tune of "The Battle Hymn of the Republic," began to appear in camps at the front. Colonel Miller first saw a copy when he walked into tank headquarters and found the men "laughing quite heartily" over the anonymous verses. He claimed that the ballad depicted "with clarity, just what went on in the minds of the men on Bataan." A less prejudiced observer would conclude that it represented the thinking of some men but, on any count, was malicious and grossly unfair to MacArthur. Several versions of the anonymous ballad were circulated, the one below being that which Miller obtained:

USAFFE Cry of Freedom

Dugout Doug MacArthur lies ashaking on the Rock
Safe from all the bombers and from any sudden shock
Dugout Doug is eating of the best food on Bataan
And his troops go starving on.

Dugout Doug's not timid, he's just cautious, not afraid
He's protecting carefully the stars that Franklin made
Four-star generals are rare as good food on Bataan
And his troops go starving on.

Dugout Doug is ready in his Kris Craft [sic] for the flee
Over bounding billows and the wildly raging sea
For the Japs are pounding on the gates of Old Bataan
And his troops go starving on.

We've fought the war the hard way since they said the fight was on
All the way from Lingayen to the hills of Old Bataan
And we'll continue fighting after Dugout Doug is gone
And still go starving on.

Chorus:
Dugout Doug, come out from hiding
Dugout Doug, come out from hiding
Send to Franklin the glad tidings
That his troops go starving on! [25]

Other examples of vicious doggerel assailing MacArthur circulated on Bataan as conditions worsened. According to Lieutenant Lee of the 57th Infantry, even his Scouts, whose fighting ability was unquestioned and whose morale was generally high, succumbed gradually to the temptation to make MacArthur the scapegoat of their difficulties. In a long poem entitled "Abucay Withdrawal" Lee recalled the 57th's gallant stand at Abucay, the false hopes his men held at first, and their subsequent disillusionment with MacArthur:

> . . . Four days fighting at Layac Ridge
> And ten on the Hacienda Ridge.
>> And they swing along in a happy mood
>> With visions of rest and baths and food,
> Their first engagement, well-fought behind
> And MacArthur's promise in every mind.
>> "The time is secret but I can say
>> That swift relief ships are on the way.
> Thousands of men and hundreds of planes —
> Back in Manila before the rains!
>> With decorations and honors, too."
>> MacArthur said it, it must be true.
> And the future broods like a living thing —
> A hooded beast that is crouched to spring . . .
> Rifles spatter, machine guns spray
>> As the weary doughboys take up the fray.
>> Bataan is saved for another day —
> Saved for hunger and wounds and heat
> For slow exhaustion and grim retreat
>> For a wasted hope and a sure defeat.
>> "MacArthur's Forces," home papers whine —
> "Strategic Withdrawal" — a better line
> "The rear displacement proceeds as planned
>> And the situation is well in hand." [26]

Perhaps an inkling that such attitudes existed on Bataan, even if only among a minority of his men, was a primary reason why the proud, sensitive USAFFE commander refused to make more visits to the peninsula. The official Army history of the campaign states that, nevertheless, most of the defenders continued to hold him in esteem: "His prestige among the Filipinos can hardly be exaggerated. Among American officers, to many of whom he was already a legend, his reputation placed him on a lofty eminence with the great captains of history." If judged by the postwar literature of the various Bataan-Corregidor veterans' societies, however, his stature among the American combatants on Bataan never matched Wainwright's. Of course, it must be remembered that Wainwright endured the surrender and prison experiences with those veterans. The existing evidence indicates that as of early March, 1942, most of the men on Bataan still believed, or wanted to believe, that somehow, as Mallonée phrased it, MacArthur "would reach down and pull the rabbit out of the hat." [27]

2. Life on "The Rock"

Between Bataan and the Pico de Loro Hills of Cavite Province is the twelve-mile-wide mouth of Manila Bay. Five islands dot the bay entrance, and all but one were fortified. Corregidor, or Fort Mills, is the largest in size (2.74 square miles), had most of the harbor defense firepower, and contained over 90 per cent of the personnel on the islands. From the air it looks like a tadpole with a large bulbous head facing the South China Sea and a long, slightly twisting tail extending eastward into Manila Bay. From the Bataan shore, two miles to the north, Corregidor more nearly resembles a legendary sea monster, its 628-foot-high head tapering down to sea level near the neck, then rising abruptly 390 feet in a rugged hump, with lower irregular ridges sloping along the lower spine and out to the end of the tail. The island's chief construction features included the post headquarters, a huge barracks, and the principal coastal batteries on "Topside," the high ground on the west end; the barrio of San Jose and dock area at "Bottomside," the neck area; a vast tunnel complex deep in Malinta Hill, the second highest ground; and Kindley Field, an air strip near the extremity of the tail. The administrative and operational heart of the island fortress was Malinta Tunnel, whose main shaft extended 1400 feet in length and thirty feet in width, with twenty-five 400-foot laterals branching from it.

Built into the rocky cliffs and steep ravines, particularly on Topside, were batteries containing a formidable array of eighteen twelve-inch and ten-inch coastal rifles and twenty-four twelve-inch mortars. Some of these huge coastal artillery guns could hurl shells up to eleven miles. In addition, the island bristled with antiaircraft and machine-gun positions, usually situated in well-protected areas. Many of the island's larger guns, however, had been emplaced two decades or more before the war, and all of the antiaircraft weapons, though newer, were obsolescent. Most critical for the future, both nearby shorelines had hills that towered several thousand feet higher than Corregidor and would provide the enemy artillery with excellent positions for observation, firing, and protection. Despite these liabilities, the troops of Fort Mills could effectively keep the Japanese fleet from using Manila Bay, which was their basic mission according to War Plan Orange. "In some ways Corregidor's sobriquet, 'the Gibraltar of the Far East,' " one authority says, "was an understatement rather than an exaggeration." [28]

On an average day in the early spring of 1942 about 11,500 persons were crowded onto Corregidor's 1735 acres, yet the coast artillery batteries were undermanned and the beach defenses had less than half the number of defenders needed. This was because over half of the persons on the island were not trained combatants: they included about 2000 civilians and 4000 military personnel in noncombatant supporting functions. Besides MacArthur's headquarters staff, there were the staffs brought to

Corregidor by President Quezon, High Commissioner Sayre, and Admiral Rockwell. Also there were engineer, quartermaster, and other troops of the technical services, many sailors not yet assigned to infantry or artillery roles, numerous civilian employees of USAFFE, and an unfortunately large number of supernumeraries, including some officers whose duties had terminated when their offices in Manila and Cavite had to be abandoned. This last group, it has been charged, spent much of its time "eating precious food, contributing little, administering paper commands that no longer existed." If short of men, the crews of the gun batteries were well trained, and Colonel Samuel L. Howard's 4th Marines provided a powerful nucleus for the beach defenses. These trained fighters were the exception, however, for the bulk of the population of the fortress was more like that of a sprawling Philippine version of the Pentagon.[29]

The first large-scale air attack against Corregidor occurred on December 29, four days after MacArthur had arrived and established his headquarters on Topside. Shortly before noon eighteen twin-engine bombers, escorted by nineteen Zeros, hit Fort Mills, followed in a half-hour by twenty-two medium and eighteen dive bombers. At 1:00 sixty Japanese Navy bombers completed the day's devastation, leaving the island covered with fires, debris, and heavy casualties. MacArthur hastily moved with his family and staff to Malinta Tunnel. The air raids continued daily during the next week, but casualties and property damage were relatively lighter because the defenders had concealed much matériel that had been exposed earlier and had reacted more quickly to air-raid alarms. The USAFFE antiaircraft batteries scored some "kills," but the three-inch guns were short on ammunition, too many of the shells were duds, and often the attackers flew above the limited range of the guns. After January 6, except for occasional nuisance raids, the aerial bombardment virtually ceased as most of Homma's 5th Air Group was transferred to Thailand. The massive air attacks against Corregidor would not resume until March 24, but then they would come almost daily until the surrender in May and would far exceed the bomb tonnage of the earlier phase.

The artillery bombardments of Corregidor were also conducted in two distinct stages. In mid-January the Kondo Detachment moved into the Pico de Loro hills, south of Corregidor, and started preparing artillery emplacements, mostly around the town of Ternate. For two weeks MacArthur prohibited the harbor defense guns from firing on the area because Quezon heatedly protested that the barrages would kill large numbers of Filipino residents. Finally, on January 31 the gun crews on the fortified islands received permission to open fire, but by then the Kondo Detachment was entrenched and most of its artillery concealed or well protected. On the morning of February 8 the Kondo batteries of 105-mm. and 150-mm. guns began shelling Corregidor and the three smaller fortified islands. The bombardments reached a zenith of intensity during the period of February 15–20, causing much more damage that week than the total of all previous air bombings.

The artillery fire from Cavite Province began to slacken after the 20th until by the end of February it amounted to only sporadic shelling. But more enemy guns were on the way to the Ternate vicinity, including huge 240-mm. howitzers. On March 15 the second phase began with a devastating bombardment of the islands. The barrages would mount as the end neared for the defenders in later weeks, particularly after additional artillery was positioned on the hills of southern Bataan when the peninsula fell. Often air and artillery bombardments would occur at the same time. The worst periods while MacArthur was on Corregidor were the aerial attacks of December 29–January 6 and the artillery barrages of February 8–20. But for the men who remained on the island until the surrender these earlier bombardments were like "chicken feed," said one of the officers, compared to the havoc after mid-March.[30]

Nevertheless, some of the older officers who had served in

France in 1918 testified that the February shellings were reminiscent of the terrifying barrages they had experienced in World
War I. Men who were afraid to leave Malinta Tunnel and
"used all sorts of excuses to stay there" possessed "tunnelitis"
fever, claimed the soldiers whose duties left them exposed to the
bombs and shells. But even some of the bravest, who valiantly
stayed by their guns during heavy attacks, often were reluctant
to leave the underground laterals when they had a chance to
go to them briefly. The shrill whistling of the shells from Cavite
Province was especially unnerving to those who had never heard
the sound, but Colonel William C. Braly, a veteran of World
War I, pointed out that at least the "whiz-bangs" provided "a
warning whistle which permitted you to hit the dirt" before
the detonations.

Major John M. Wright, Jr., the commander of a coastal battery, said that later, when he was a prisoner, the Japanese officers
were interested in learning his reaction to the bombardments
and "wanted to know which had frightened me most, artillery
or bombs." Wright's response was probably typical of most
persons on Corregidor: "I suppose it all depended on which
burst closer, and when they burst close enough, either one is unpleasant." By late February Corregidor was already, in Robert
Levering's words, a "sunburned, God-cursed land, where bombs
and shells made life a Hell, with death on every hand." [31]

From the first Japanese bombing of Corregidor until his departure, MacArthur and his wife displayed extraordinary coolness and courage and often toured defensive positions on the
island to chat with gun crews and offer words of encouragement.
Lieutenant Colonel Sidney L. Huff, an aide to the general, was
with the MacArthurs when the air attack of December 29 struck
Topside and recalled their reactions:

Jean MacArthur grabbed young Arthur and ran to a little
command post not far from the house. Just as they reached it

an enlisted man, who had been taking a bath in the open nearby, ran madly up, grabbed a blanket in lieu of his clothes and dropped down into the protection of the dugout. The protection wasn't much. The dugout had iron doors which were old and wouldn't close. Every time a stick of bombs hit the hill the doors swung madly in and out, clanging like a four-alarm fire. Jean held Arthur in her arms and crouched back against the wall. Occasionally, when there was a lull in the bombing, she sent someone to the house to find out how the General was getting along.

The General was fine except that he was building up a towering anger against the enemy, to relieve his own feelings of frustration at our inability to fight back. When the first enemy flight appeared, he walked out in the yard to count the number of planes. He stayed throughout the bombing, "protected" only by a thick hedge around the yard. Once a direct hit went through the house, landing in his bedroom and shattering the whole building. Then a near miss sent fragments flying across the yard and MacArthur ducked behind the hedge while his orderly, Sergeant Domingo Adversario, took off his own helmet and held it over the General's head. A piece of steel hit the helmet and wounded Domingo in the hand as they crouched there. When the raid was over, there was nothing but rubble left on Topside of Corregidor.[32]

The MacArthurs moved to a crowded, poorly ventilated lateral of Malinta Tunnel after this raid, but the general continued to walk outside during bombings and shellings, to the alarm of his staff. General Hill observed that the detonations "didn't faze him at all," MacArthur remaining "very cool" through the worst attacks. High Commissioner Sayre was walking with MacArthur one afternoon when the enemy started shelling the island. Sayre and the officers with them dropped to the ground, but MacArthur remained standing. "Anyone who saw us," Sayre remarked, "must have had a good laugh — at the General erect and at ease while the High Commissioner lay prone in the dust. I have often wondered whether he was as amused as I. In any event, his expression never changed."

This scene was re-enacted many times when the general visited batteries during attacks and refused to seek cover. On January 6, to cite another example, he was at Battery Chicago when enemy bombers appeared overhead. The battery commander urged him to get down as the gun crews dived for shelter, but MacArthur "stayed up, watching through his binoculars, counting off the attacking planes, and remarking calmly that the bombs would fall close." Sayre said that MacArthur told him "he believed that death would take him only at the ordained time" — a conviction that he had voiced ever since his days with the 42nd Division in World War I. Even if he was a confirmed fatalist, the USAFFE commander demonstrated such bravery, boldness, and sometimes foolhardiness under fire that his exploits became widely known on the island. Few Corregidor survivors cannot relate an instance in which they personally witnessed MacArthur courageously exposing himself to enemy fire. It is unfortunate that the Bataan soldiers did not have an opportunity to see this side of Dugout Doug.

The men on Corregidor were impressed by the inspiring conduct not only of the USAFFE chief but also of his wife. Leaving her four-year-old son with his nurse in the tunnel, Jean MacArthur frequently visited gun crews to chat amiably and sometimes eat lunch with them. At least one officer said that he saw her visiting the troops nearly as often as he saw his own battery commander, who seemed to have much business in the tunnel, apparently a victim of tunnelitis. Clark Lee, a correspondent, recalled meeting her one day during an air raid when he was caught a long distance from the tunnel. As he ran down the road, Mrs. MacArthur drove up and invited him to ride with her. "By stopping," Lee observed, "she had spent the precious couple of minutes that might have meant the difference between her being killed on the road, and reaching a place of safety." At other times she could be seen with Arthur as they visited the hospital lateral or talked cheerfully with all levels of soldiers and civilians in the tunnel. One of her favorite places was a canvas shelter at the entrance to Malinta Tunnel, which served as the officers' mess; there she often sat knitting and talking to whoever came over to converse. Lee commented, "Like the general, Mrs. MacArthur never let down. She always had a word of cheer and encouragement. She was one of MacArthur's finest soldiers."

Young Arthur seemed to adjust well to the restricted, noisy, and smelly life of Malinta Tunnel. His parents did not often allow him to go outside the crowded tunnel, so he spent much of his time playing with Ah Cheu, his Chinese nurse, and with soldiers and nurses who happened along with a few minutes to spare. He became a favorite with the tunnel personnel, who nicknamed him "The Sergeant," a title he preferred to a higher rank. Sometimes passers-by would give him souvenirs; Hill, for example, presented him with a bloodstained Japanese battle flag, which delighted him. On February 21, his fourth birthday, the MacArthurs gave a small party in his honor. The Quezons, the Sayres, and a few staff officers were present, but only one non-adult, the Sayre's teen-age son; there were no children of Arthur's age on the island. Someone had baked a small cake for him, and he received a few simple, makeshift gifts. Using a twig, Arthur was often seen mimicking his father's cigarette smoking, so Huff gave him a cigarette holder, which the boy prized.[33] The party was probably not an exciting one for Arthur, but at least he appeared grateful to the adults, who must have had difficulty in finding anything on embattled Corregidor for a four-year-old's birthday celebration.

MacArthur spent many long hours in damp, dimly lit Lateral No. 3 of Malinta Tunnel, where USAFFE General Headquarters was situated. The lateral was bare except for a row of desks and a minimum of other office equipment, over which hung drop lights that glowed and dimmed intermittently and swung crazily when shells burst on the surface above. Pieces

of cardboard had to be placed over documents lying on desks
to keep off the seepage that occasionally dripped through the
rock ceilings. Despite the dampness of the walls and ceiling,
the lateral, like the rest of the tunnel, had a dusty squalor that
made house-cleaning an impossible chore. Lateral No. 3 was
closed to all but authorized personnel, but the fetid odors of
thousands of persons living in Malinta Tunnel and the echoing
sounds of vehicles and persons moving along the main shaft
pervaded MacArthur's domain with no respect for rank.

Like the persons elsewhere in this foul-smelling underworld,
the USAFFE staff officers always enjoyed taking a walk outside
the tunnel during lulls in the aerial and artillery bombardments. Whenever possible in the evenings, usually around 7:00,
MacArthur would leave Lateral No. 3 and stroll arm in arm
with his wife around the hill outside. Sayre and his wife, who
were staying in a nearby lateral, also found such outdoor excursions during peaceful moments to be welcome breaks from the
"fetid atmosphere and oppressive sights of the tunnel" and its
germs and dust, which the high commissioner considered more
dangerous, physically and mentally, than the bombs and shells.

Headquarters officers were compelled to keep unusual hours
because MacArthur himself worked seven days a week and
often until late at night. Although MacArthur never expressly
ordered his staff to maintain a work schedule like his, he sometimes became impatient or irritated when he wanted a particular section chief or report and neither could be found. The
key members of his staff, therefore, found it easier, if more
exhausting, to be present when their commander was. Willoughby, the G-2, found the pace that MacArthur kept "difficult
to match day after day," but the intelligence officer, like his
colleagues, "preferred" to be around when MacArthur called
for him, whether at 8:00 A.M or 11:00 P.M. Sundays were like
any other workday at headquarters: MacArthur did not attend
worship services and neither did most of his main staff officers,
who apparently judged it wiser to stay on the job.

MacArthur displayed the same air of confidence in his head-quarters that he manifested to the troops on his tours of the island. "He always swung into the USAFFE lateral as if bring-ing great news," said Colonel Romulo. Often he would stop at the desk of a staff officer as he went by, offering some comment or advice which, though seldom humorous, was usually opti-mistic. When on rare occasions he appeared depressed, his spirit rebounded quickly and in a few hours his self-confidence was apparent to everyone around him. He jested infrequently, but he did so when a report came in that Santa Barbara had been shelled by an enemy submarine. MacArthur chuckled and told his staff, "I think I'll send a wire to the California commander and tell him if he can hold out for thirty more days I'll be able to send him help."

Captain Steve M. Mellnik, a coast artilleryman on duty with the headquarters staff, observed, however, that MacArthur usu-ally "wrapped himself in a cloak of dignified aloofness" when it came to personal matters and never "tried to be 'one of the boys.' He talked pleasantly, calmly, but always formally. Al-though he called everyone by his first name, no one dreamed of calling him anything but 'General.' " Most of his personal re-marks and private reservations he limited to his conversations with Sutherland, his chief of staff and trusted confidant. Typi-cally, after a dramatic entry and a display of supreme confidence to the staff at large, he would go over and talk somberly and in a hushed voice to Sutherland. Then MacArthur would some-times walk alone to the darker end of the lateral where beds were set up for off-duty officers. There he would pace back and forth in the shadows for long periods, deep in thought and often frowning.[34]

In addition to his devoted wife, Jean, and his long-time friend, Quezon, a handful of staff officers made up the small cir-cle of MacArthur's close companions. Foremost in that group was Sutherland, the "hatchet man" of the staff, who was con-temptuous of mediocrity and inefficiency and ruthlessly de-nounced subordinates found guilty of such cardinal sins. He once explained to Marshall, his deputy, "Well, Dick, somebody around here has got to be the S.O.B. General MacArthur is not going to be, and you certainly aren't going to be, so I guess I'm it." In recommending him later for promotion, MacArthur described Sutherland as an officer who has "demonstrated outstanding strategical and tactical judgment, command and executive ability, and great personal courage and leadership in actual combat. While not so designated officially, he has actually performed all the functions of deputy commander." In early 1942 Sutherland was not lacking recognition: MacArthur bestowed on him the Distinguished Service Medal and the Silver Star. The USAFFE commander trusted his judgment implicitly in dealing with the staff and, according to some observers, too much so in strategic and operational matters. Nearly all officers who worked with Sutherland came to respect his devotion to MacArthur, his mental sharpness, dedication to his job, and ability to get the maximum effort from his staff. But ultimately almost everyone was antagonized by his nasty temper, brusqueness, and autocratic manner. Seldom did anyone try to argue a point with him, so positive were his opinions.

A superb golf player in prewar Manila and a dashing gentleman in the presence of ladies, Sutherland was such a loner among the officers that few, other than his aides and Marshall, knew much about his personal life. Indeed, most officers were so offended by his egotism and haughtiness that they did not care to know him better. The immediate headquarters staff accepted his faults and considered him an efficient chief of staff "who got the job done no matter what it took," but some who tangled with him would have agreed with a later evaluation by an Australian: "Sutherland was the wrong kind of chief of staff for MacArthur, whose foibles he would not offset but nourish." [35]

Brigadier General Richard Marshall, the quiet-spoken deputy

chief of staff, ranked next in MacArthur's hierarchy of staff relations and friendships. Lacking the dash and brilliance of MacArthur and Sutherland, Marshall, nevertheless, was an invaluable catalyst in producing staff teamwork. Quiet and amiable, he placated many an officer whom Sutherland had infuriated. "A calm and methodical Quartermaster," Mellnik said of him, "he had long since mastered the technique of finding a path through the jungle of Army supply regulations. Attacking problems with simplicity, he selected experienced project officers, gave them mission directives, and sent them to the field with the means and authority to do the job." While they may not have been adequate, whatever supplies were gotten to Bataan and Corregidor during the hectic days after the reversion to WPO-3 were there largely because of Marshall's vigorous, often ingenious efforts. Since January much of his time had been spent on Bataan, where he ably headed the advance headquarters of USAFFE. Of the top three in the high command, Marshall seemed to be the background figure in comparison to the spectacular personalities of his two superiors, but his ability to harmonize staff relations and his broad knowledge of logistics made him indispensable.

Colonel Charles Willoughby, the intelligence chief, could run the gamut of emotional extremes during the course of one day, ranging from long periods of brooding over someone's caustic reception of an idea of his, to loud, hot-tempered displays when an officer of another section meddled in his bailiwick, to abject sorrow over a G-2 estimate that proved erroneous. An avid student of military history, Willoughby considered himself an authority on strategy and did have a great familiarity with the makers of strategy through the centuries, which gave him an excellent opening for informal talks with MacArthur, also an ardent reader of military history. Willoughby tried to be careful and meticulous in his intelligence work but was often handicapped in the Philippine campaign by limited means for gathering G-2 data. His nemesis was Sutherland, with whom he sometimes crossed swords, because both men possessed sharp tongues and enlarged egos. Headquarters personnel secretly called Willoughby "Sir Charles," but his demeanor was more like that of one of Count H. C. B. von Moltke's Prussian Guard officers. A colleague of his commented that Willoughby seemed to be "always looking out over a high board fence." Marshall learned to like him but said that he "was, until you got to know him, very reserved, dignified, and formal . . . very correct in his bearing." Like the others who would someday be dubbed the "Bataan Gang," he was devoted to MacArthur. Willoughby would be the only one of the group to serve his commander continuously from 1941 to 1951.

Next in closeness to MacArthur were Brigadier Generals Hugh Casey, chief engineer officer; William F. Marquat, chief antiaircraft officer; Harold George, head of the remnant of the Far East Air Force in the Philippines; Milton Hill, inspector general; Spencer B. Akin, chief signal officer; and Colonel Charles P. Stivers, personnel officer (G-1). George would be killed later that spring in Australia in an aircraft mishap, and Hill, who was suffering from malaria and other jungle diseases, later had to be evacuated to the States and never returned to MacArthur's command. Casey, Marquat, Akin, and Stivers would be mainstays of the MacArthur coterie throughout the war against Japan. Two others who shared a close personal relationship with MacArthur were Lieutenant Colonels Le-Grande A. Diller and Sidney Huff, both aides to the general. Diller also served as public relations officer, later to be a much-maligned role. Huff, a former naval officer, would gradually be relegated to the position of aide, or escort, to Mrs. MacArthur. Major General George Moore, who commanded the harbor defenses, was described as "one of those rare persons who had no enemies," which was fortunate because, as Corregidor commander, he was sometimes in an awkward position in relation to MacArthur, not dissimilar to the plight of a cruiser captain who has the fleet commander aboard during a battle. Moore and MacArthur maintained a harmonious relationship, but the two were never close friends.

Similarly, though MacArthur called each by his first name, neither Wainwright nor Parker was an intimate of the USAFFE chief. Wainwright, whose peers nicknamed him "Skinny," said that MacArthur was "the only man in the world who calls me 'Jonathan.'" But, like everyone in the hierarchy from Sutherland down, Wainwright addressed him as "General MacArthur." In fact, in the presence of others Mrs. MacArthur usually referred to her husband by his title. MacArthur's close friendships were few, and even those were narrowly circumscribed by certain formalities. No one was permitted to forget that he was both warrior and aristocrat.[36]

3. In the Name of the Philippines

By the end of February, 1942, Japanese offensives south and west of the Philippines were racing along ahead of schedule. British pride and expectations of the empire's forces in Malaya and at the touted bastion of Singapore had led to the illusion of a protracted struggle there against the invaders, however overwhelming their numbers. The Japanese advance down the Malayan peninsula, nevertheless, had been shockingly rapid. "When all our hearts hardened on fighting it out at Singapore," said Churchill, "the only chance of success, and indeed of gaining time, which was all we could hope for, was to give imperative orders to fight in desperation to the end." But the conclusion had been something less than a desperate clash to the finish: after two weeks of confused defensive efforts the 70,000-man Singapore garrison had surrendered on February 15 to a smaller

Japanese force. Roosevelt commented that Singapore's fall "gives the well-known back-seat driver a field day." [37]

On the Burma front British troops were yielding too fast to suit the chiefs of staff in London; enemy soldiers would enter Rangoon in early March. Another Allied disappointment was the six-week-old ABDA command in the East Indies, which collapsed in late February. During the last days of the month Japanese naval forces totally destroyed the ABDA fleet and enemy ground units landed on Java. By the second week of March the Japanese conquest of the Netherlands East Indies, which had begun with landings on Borneo and Celebes in January, would be nearly completed. Threatening the line of communications between the United States and Australia in the meantime were enemy thrusts into Northeast New Guinea, the Bismarck Archipelago, and Bougainville in the Solomons.

East of the Philippines lay the Japanese-controlled Caroline, Marianas, Marshall, and Gilbert islands; Guam and Wake had fallen early in the war. The British garrison at Hongkong, the only other Allied strength near the Philippines, had surrendered on Christmas Day. The USAFFE defenders seemed like persons trapped on a crumbling bit of high ground as a raging flood swirled about them on all sides. There was no route of retreat or relief left, and the flood had not yet crested.

In spite of the hopeless plight of the Philippines, Roosevelt and the War Department's leaders did everything possible to get reinforcements and supplies to MacArthur. In mid-January Secretary of War Henry L. Stimson authorized Brereton, then in Australia, to spend $10 million to hire ships and crews to make supply runs to the Philippines. Other funds were allocated to MacArthur and commanders in the southern Philippines and in the East Indies for the same purpose. To head the blockade-running program from Australia, Marshall sent Brigadier General Patrick J. Hurley, an old friend of MacArthur's and former Secretary of War. Hurley did not arrive in

Australia until February 8, by which time three vessels had gotten their cargoes to the southern Philippines. Two other ships, while en route, were sunk by enemy planes. Despite his tremendous promotional efforts and handsome pay offers to captains and crews, Hurley was unable to get any more ships to make the dangerous trip. Moreover, transporting supplies from Mindanao and Cebu to Corregidor was difficult and hazardous; fast inter-island vessels were employed, but few escaped enemy aircraft and shore batteries.

About 10,000 tons of supplies reached the southern Philippines by ship, but only a tenth of it, or about a four-day supply for the Bataan and Corregidor troops, was delivered to the Manila Bay area. The captain of the *Legaspi,* a small craft that made the run to Corregidor, later recounted to Chynoweth on Cebu how MacArthur "spoke to him as though he were his son . . . He left General MacArthur 'crying like a baby,' " so moved was the commander by this Filipino's "risking his life for his country." [38]

MacArthur wrote to Marshall on February 22 criticizing the organization of the blockade-running and proposing that cargo ships be sent directly to the Philippines from the States. He stated that "this revised effort should center in Washington and not in Australia or the N.E.I." since the latter "have neither the resources nor the means at their disposal properly to accomplish this mission . . . If it is left as a subsidiary effort, it will never be accomplished." He added that "careful consideration should also be given as to troop replacements by this means; even if losses occur, they will be small compared to the loss out here if we do not have success." On March 4 Hurley and Lieutenant General George H. Brett, commander of United States Army Forces in Australia (USAFIA), sent a joint message to Marshall stating that their disappointing relief program was "no longer justified" and that direct cargo shipping across the Pacific should be tried. A plan was hastily developed in Wash-

ington to convert six obsolete destroyers to cargo vessels and
send them from the States, but the new program, which seems
absurdly unrealistic in retrospect, ran into delays and the ships
never got to the Philippines.[39] If they had, Japanese naval and
air forces undoubtedly would have disposed of them in short
order.

Other efforts to get provisions and ammunition to MacArthur included at least seven trips by five different submarines to
Corregidor by March 1. They brought in less than 130 tons of
food, medicine, and ammunition, and carried out about 220
select personnel, some official records, and a portion of the Philippine Treasury's gold and silver bullion (as ballast). Several
planes made it safely to Mindanao's Del Monte Field with limited cargoes, mostly medical supplies, but, again, it proved exceedingly difficult to transship the items north to Corregidor.
After late January no more was heard from Washington of the
"streams of bombers" and troop reinforcements that previously
had been promised to MacArthur.

Indicative of the increasing impatience of War Department
leaders to accelerate operations against Germany was a reminder
to himself which Eisenhower noted on his desk pad on January
22: "We've got to go to Europe and fight, and we've got to quit
wasting resources all over the world — and still worse — wasting time." The sundry attempts to relieve the Philippines had
consumed large amounts of time and energy of key war planners and many other persons, along with great expenditures of
funds and matériel, but had resulted in only negligible tonnages
of supplies reaching MacArthur's forces. Regardless of their
Europe-first commitment, however, Roosevelt, Stimson, Marshall, and Eisenhower, who succeeded Brigadier General Leonard T. Gerow as chief of the War Plans Division in February,
all realized that the Philippine quandary required them to continue endeavors, no matter how futile, to break the blockade.
The blockade-running program, in the words of one authority,

"was doomed at the outset by geography, short-sighted pre-war planning, and the overwhelming might of the Japanese offensive." Nevertheless, they had to try. The official Army history states well their predicament: "The gallant stand of the Philippine garrison required it; MacArthur demanded it; and the American people supported it." [40]

One day in early February Captain Ind delivered to Sutherland a fervent plea from General George that a greater effort be made to get aircraft for his pilots, some of whom were now serving as infantry. Sutherland pulled out a large file of radio-grams and said, "Just in case you have some idea that we are not trying, look at this — and this — and this!" Ind, who apparently was not fully aware of the way in which MacArthur was bombarding Washington with pleas for aid, described his reaction: "My heart sinks with each new tissue thumbed over before my eyes. Appeal after appeal has gone forward; but a war-engulfed world is powerless even to approach satisfying the endless, frantic demands from Polar Circle to Equator, from Greenwich time line all the way round to Greenwich time line again." Not many on Corregidor grasped the global picture as quickly as Ind. General Hill was one of the few USAFFE head-quarters officers who appreciated the many demands being made on Marshall, whom he later called "the outstanding general in winning the war." Hill said, in appraising Marshall's view of the Philippine predicament, "You have to determine from the whole thing, not just one part of it."

MacArthur and most of his chief lieutenants, on the other hand, had become convinced that the basic strategy of the Allies, with its priority on the European theater, was a blunder and that the preponderance of Allied resources should go to the war against Japan. Willoughby claimed that the intention of relegating the Pacific theater to a secondary status "was not known by MacArthur. He never could understand the defeatist Far Eastern military strategy pursued in those early days of 1942 by the high command, both military and diplomatic, in Washington." But MacArthur was thoroughly familiar with Rainbow-5 and knew that both it and WPO-3 were based on the assumption that the Philippines would probably be conquered before the Allies could launch a counteroffensive in the Pacific. It is true that MacArthur did not have the details of the Arcadia decisions, but they reaffirmed the priorities stated in existing war plans. Some of MacArthur's strongly worded demands for a drastic change in grand strategy could have been interpreted by Roosevelt and Marshall as arrogance bordering on insubordination, but both men were sympathetic and understanding in their responses to the USAFFE commander.[41]

MacArthur and some of his staff officers also were convinced that "the leaders in Washington" were "against MacArthur" personally, and that Roosevelt, Marshall, and Eisenhower were leaders of a clique that was maliciously trying to undermine his career. This almost paranoid outlook may have been natural and even excusable for men caught in the Corregidor trap, but the charge had no basis in fact at that time. Although the two men had differed often when MacArthur was Army chief of staff in the years 1933–35, Roosevelt was sincerely concerned about the general's ever-worsening plight. Brigadier General Louis J. Fortier, who was on the Joint Intelligence Committee, brought intelligence summaries to the President each morning while he ate breakfast. Fortier said that the first documents Roosevelt wanted to see each day were those concerning MacArthur.

The President had consistently urged the War and Navy departments to exert every effort to help the USAFFE forces, and it was Roosevelt who proposed MacArthur for the ABDA command, a post that ultimately went to General Archibald Wavell in a move to placate the British chiefs. At a presidential press conference on February 24, by which time MacArthur was expressing utter exasperation over Washington's relief failures, a correspondent asked about rumors that "perhaps General Mac-Arthur is a little at odds with the high command here as to the possibility of reinforcing him."

If Roosevelt had chosen to, he could have tossed out a few barbed remarks, at which he was a master, about MacArthur's implications of halfhearted efforts on his garrison's behalf. Instead the President put up a smoke screen: "I wouldn't do any — well, I wouldn't — I am trying to take a leaf out of my own notebook. I think it would be well for others to do it. I — not knowing enough about it — I try not to speculate myself." He must have looked foolish to the reporters, but, despite the temptation, Roosevelt had not derided his general.[42]

Generals Thomas T. Handy and John E. Hull, both of whom were in the War Plans Division in 1942 and each of whom later served as chief of its successor, the Operations Division, denied emphatically that Marshall or Eisenhower was biased against MacArthur during the Philippine relief program. According to Handy, when the Anglo-American chiefs of staff were considering the problem of unity of command for the Pacific theater, Marshall commented, "If one commander were designated out there, it couldn't be anybody but MacArthur, on the basis of pure competence alone." Eisenhower maintained that the notion of an anti-MacArthur faction in the War Department "was an illusion of General MacArthur or of his staff." Actually no one in Washington tried harder than Eisenhower to get help to the Philippines, where he had served in 1935–39 and had many close friends. As late as March 13 Eisenhower made this notation on his desk pad: "For many weeks — it seems years — I've been searching everywhere to find any feasible way of giving real help to the P.I. . . . I'll go on trying, but daily the situation grows more desperate." And all along Eisenhower was aware that the disproportionate amount of time he was spending on that problem was compromising his dedication to the Europe-first strategy.[43]

Unhappily, just as some men on Bataan could never be persuaded that MacArthur was sincere in proclaiming that help was forthcoming, so the USAFFE chief became embittered toward his Washington superiors who had assured him of assistance. Over a year after the fall of the Philippines, MacArthur was mulling over that tragedy when he replied to a letter from Brigadier General Bonner F. Fellers, one of the few men to whom MacArthur would express his personal sentiments:

> It has been a desperate time for me ever since the war started, always the underdog, and always fighting with destruction just around the corner. I could have held Bataan if I had not been so completely deserted. I take some comfort from Stonewall Jackson's creed, "that if necessary we will fight them with sticks and stones." But I find that sticks break in our hands and stones can't go very far. A merciful God has miraculously brought me through so far, but I am sick at heart at the mistakes and lost opportunities that are so prevalent.[44]

If MacArthur failed to appreciate the earnestness of those heading the relief program, they, in turn, were far from the dangers of war and could not fully comprehend his alarmed concern for his family, friends, troops, and the Philippine nation. One measure of his desperation was the fact that he called for the entry of the Soviet Union in the Pacific war, although ever since the Hoover presidency he had been outspoken in denouncing Communists and a "soft" policy toward the Russians. In December, 1941, MacArthur advised Marshall that Soviet participation in the Pacific conflict was Japan's "greatest fear" and "a golden opportunity exists for a master stroke" if Stalin could be persuaded to attack in North Asia. On the Red Army's anniversary in February he sent a glowing message: "The world situation at the present time indicates that the hopes of civilization rest on the worthy banners of the courageous Russian Army." "The scale and grandeur" of that army's recent "smashing counterattack," driving the Germans away from Moscow's gates, "marks it as the greatest military achievement in all history." The Tass news agency in Moscow broadcast his words widely, and, according to Robert E. Sherwood of Roosevelt's staff, "From then on, the Russian propagandists were much more favorably disposed toward American fighting men."

Later in the spring, when Stalin was demanding an Anglo-American "second front" in Europe, MacArthur told the War Department, "That front should be in the Pacific theater." He argued that "nowhere else can it be so successfully launched and nowhere else will it so assist the Russians." He claimed it would pull Japanese forces out of Manchuria and Korea, which the Soviets could then easily conquer.[45] What MacArthur advised made good sense and Stalin's help in almost any form in the Pacific would have delighted Washington, but such statements emanating from an old anti-Communist crusader served to indicate how desperate the general was.

The credibility gaps between Washington and MacArthur and between the general and his Bataan troops were widened by the egotistic, often erroneous communiqués issued by the USAFFE public relations office. At first MacArthur had pledged daily press conferences with the handful of American, Filipino, and other correspondents who hovered about his headquarters in Manila and later on Corregidor. But, as the battle reports worsened, MacArthur clamped a tight censorship on these reporters, and for a while almost all the news of the campaign that reached the American public came from his daily communiqués or headquarters releases to the press. Of 142 such communiqués issued between December 8, 1941, and March 11, 1942, 109 mentioned only one individual, MacArthur. The Marines, traditionally used to more than their share of publicity, were especialy incensed, but seldom were any USAFFE units cited. When an action was described, it was "MacArthur's right flank on Bataan" or "MacArthur's men"; the communiqués, with rare exceptions, omitted the names of combat units, commanders, and individuals who had performed exceptional exploits.

Not only did the communiqués seem like blatant self-advertising, but they were also frequently inaccurate; for example, they mentioned glorious victories in several battles that never occurred and inevitably referred to "MacArthur's army" as "greatly outnumbered." Captain Colin P. Kelly was one of the few other individuals cited, and that communiqué erred in stating that his B-17 had sunk the battleship *Haruna.* Among the worst blunders were those in the communiqués of March 8–9, which announced Homma's suicide in MacArthur's former Manila Hotel suite and the arrival of General Tomoyuki Yamashita as his successor. In fact, Homma was quite vigorous, and Yamashita, then in Singapore, would not take command in the Philippines until the autumn of 1944.

The Bataan soldiers were "terribly annoyed," said one of them, by the vainglorious, inaccurate communiqués, and Washington officials found them repulsive, amusing, pitiable, or inspiring, depending on the reader's knowledge of the true situation. The releases were usually vividly written, and some Army officers who were ardent admirers of MacArthur were impressed by the communiqués, one praising them as "gems of battle reporting." For the most part, the American press and public gullibly and enthusiastically accepted them during that dark period when the nation was in need of heroes and news of glory and gallantry. Colonel "Pick" Diller, who headed the USAFFE public relations office, later asserted that MacArthur himself wrote many of the communiqués and closely edited many of the others. What MacArthur hoped to accomplish with releases that were really propaganda is not certain, but his communiqués surely did not lessen the misunderstandings between him and his troops or official Washington.[46]

Some of MacArthur's reactions and behavior in early 1942 are hard to comprehend apart from the context of his personal ties and devotion to the Philippine nation and its president, Quezon. MacArthur yielded to Quezon on several critical occasions, as already seen, when the welfare of the USAFFE forces seemed to be sacrificed to that of the Filipino populace. Instances were the prohibition on rice and sugar removals and the postponement of the shelling of Ternate. Both MacArthur and Quezon were greatly concerned about the loyalty of the Filipinos, who were thought to be given to instability and highly emotional responses. Captain Jesus A. Villamor, a Filipino pilot with the FEAF, remarked of his people, "It really isn't so much the collapse of the Philippine defenses that has hurt the Filipinos; rather they were hurt because the resources of the United States, in which they had such great hopes, never came through." He continued, "I would not be surprised in the least to find quite a number believing Japanese propaganda and even perhaps hostile to the Allied cause." Bulkeley, who was shot at by some Filipinos, pessimistically estimated that by the spring of 1942 "about 80% of the Filipinos were against us or were neutral; only 20% were for us."

But MacArthur was counting on a strong guerrilla movement to pave the way for his reconquest of the islands someday. Moreover, he had an understanding with Quezon that he would resume his high-salaried post of Philippine military adviser after the war. Quezon, of course, expected to continue in power when the postwar republic was established. A violent anti-American swing in Filipino public opinion could upset the future plans of both men. At the current stage of the military campaign, strong pro-American support by the people could have little effect on events, but a widespread anti-American reaction among the Filipino civilians could assist Homma in a number of ways. Not the least of these would be undermining the morale of the Filipino soldiers, who constituted the bulk of the USAFFE defenders.[47]

The Japanese lost no time in saturating the occupied areas of the archipelago with the "good news" that they had come to free the Filipinos from the rule of the "American imperialists." A Japanese-controlled provisional government was soon organized with the widely publicized understanding that Japan would grant the Philippines independence within the "Greater East Asia Co-Prosperity Sphere" as soon as possible. On January 23 Homma set up a puppet cabinet called the Philippine Executive Commission; it consisted of six departments headed by prominent Filipinos, with Jorge B. Vargas, Quezon's former secretary, as commission chairman. An advisory body, the Council of State, was also established and included a number of leading Filipino politicians. Quezon had instructed the political leaders left behind in Manila to cooperate with the enemy for the sake of the people, but never publicly to denounce him or the United States or take an "oath of allegiance" to Japan.

Soon, however, the actions of Vargas and other collaborators brought consternation to Quezon. On February 6 propaganda leaflets bearing Vargas' signature were dropped behind the USAFFE lines. In them Vargas told the Filipino soldiers that America's "greed for power is insatiable," but Japan would help the Filipinos "shake off the yoke of white domination forever." Emilio Aguinaldo, the old but respected leader of the insurrection against the Americans at the turn of the century, was enlisted by Homma to make a radio appeal to MacArthur to surrender, which the USAFFE commander admitted "disturbed me greatly." Eventually, about 75 per cent of the prewar Philippine Senate and 30 per cent of the House yielded to Japanese persuasion and accepted positions in the puppet regime, most believing that they had no other recourse but some avowing that the Japanese overlordship was preferable to the American. Most of the peasantry seemed to have retained its allegiance to the Quezon government and the United States, but in early 1942 most of the reports that MacArthur and Quezon were getting concerned the influential leaders of the upper class in Manila, who were among their long-time friends and seemed to be turning to collaboration with astonishing rapidity.[48]

MacArthur frequently visited Quezon on Corregidor to encourage him during his periods of depression and serious illness. Quezon's tubercular condition worsened in the damp Malinta lateral, and sometimes his temperature soared to 105°. Aurora, his wife, remarked that MacArthur and her husband were "like brothers" and that the latter was deeply appreciative of the kindness and attention the busy USAFFE chief gave him. Increasingly, both men felt a sense of abandonment by Washington, and, though MacArthur may have been troubled by some of his old friend's ideas about returning to Manila or making a "separate deal" with the Japanese, the two leaders were bound by a common disillusionment, especially about Roosevelt. In December Quezon and Roosevelt had exchanged a number of mutually complimentary messages, each pledging support to the other. The message the American President sent, for example, on the occasion of Quezon's second inauguration on December 30 spoke of the Filipino's "loyal and effective cooperation," and in his inaugural address Quezon pledged that the Filipinos would "stand by America with undaunted spirit."

By the middle of January, however, with no reinforcements in sight, Quezon wrote to Roosevelt in exasperation: "We decided to fight by your side and we have done the best we could . . . But how long are we going to be left alone?" He added ominously, "I want to know, because I have my responsibility to my countrymen . . . I want to decide in my own mind whether there is justification for allowing all these men to be killed when for the final outcome of the war the shedding of their blood may be wholly unnecessary." Two weeks later Quezon told Roosevelt bluntly, "It seems to me questionable whether any government has the right to demand loyalty from its citizens beyond its willingness or ability to render actual protection." In a note appended to this message MacArthur stated cryptically, "I urge most earnestly that no effort be spared adequately to meet this situation." In his memoirs MacArthur wrote, "It was the Atlantic war, not the Japanese, that was bothering Washington in those days, and Quezon felt the Philippines were being given, in the slang of the day, the 'brush-off.'" Yet those words echo the theme of MacArthur's own messages to the War Department in December and January.[49]

Distressed by a possible collapse of morale in the Philippine Army, Quezon sent a memorandum to MacArthur on February 7 which concluded: "If those men knew that help is not coming within a reasonable time and that they are only being used to gain time in other fronts, I wonder . . . how long their morale and will to fight would last." MacArthur's response is not known, but the next day Quezon sent a message through Army channels to Roosevelt in which he proposed that, since further armed resistance in the Philippines was useless, the United States should grant immediate independence to the islands, the Philippines should be neutralized, and Japanese and American forces should be withdrawn by mutual consent, with the Philippine Army being disbanded. "The situation of my country," said Quezon, "has become so desperate that I feel that positive action is demanded." His neutralization proposal, he argued, offers "a solution that will not reduce the delaying effect of our resistance here but which will save my country from further devastation as the battleground of two great powers." [50]

Quezon's message was accompanied by a supporting one from MacArthur to Marshall, which is printed in full:

> I took the liberty of presenting this message [of Quezon] to High Commissioner Sayre for a general expression of his views. He states as follows: "If the premise of President Quezon is correct that American help cannot or will not arrive here in time to be availing, I believe his proposal for *immediate* independence and neutralization of [the] Philippines is the sound course to follow."

My estimate of the military situation here is as follows: The troops have sustained practically 50% casualties from their original strength. Divisions are reduced to the size of regiments, regiments to battalions, battalions to companies. Some units have entirely disappeared. The men have been in constant action and are badly battle worn. They are desperately in need of rest and refitting. Their spirit is good, but they are capable now of nothing but fighting in place on a fixed position. All our supplies are scant, and the command has been on half rations for the past month.

It is possible for the time being that the present enemy force might temporarily be held, but any addition to his present strength will insure the destruction of our whole force. We have pulled through a number of menacing situations, but there is no denying the fact that we are near done. Corregidor itself is extremely vulnerable. This type of fortress, built prior to the days of air power, when isolated is impossible of prolonged defense. Any heavy air bombardment or the location of siege guns on Bataan or even on the Cavite side would definitely limit the life of the fortress. My water supply is extremely vulnerable and may go at any time. Every other vital installation can be readily taken out.

Since I have no air or sea protection, you must be prepared at any time to figure on the complete destruction of this command. You must determine whether the mission of delay would be better furthered by the temporizing plan of Quezon or by my continued battle effort. The temper of the Filipinos is one of almost violent resentment against the United States. Every one of them expected help, and when it has not been forthcoming, they believe they have been betrayed in favor of others. It must be remembered they are hostile to Great Britain on account of the latter's colonial policy. In spite of my great prestige with them, I have had the utmost difficulty during the last few days in keeping them in line. If help does not arrive shortly, nothing, in my opinion, can prevent their utter collapse and their complete absorption by the enemy. The Japanese made a powerful impression upon Philippine public imagination in promising independence.

So far as the military angle is concerned, the problem presents itself as to whether the plan of President Quezon might offer the best possible solution of what is about to be a disastrous debacle. It would not affect the ultimate situation in the Philippines, for that would be determined by the results in other theatres. If the Japanese Government rejects President Quezon's proposition, it would psychologically strengthen our hold because of their Prime Minister's public statement offering independence. If it accepts, we lose no military advantage because we would still secure at least equal delay. Please instruct me.

MacArthur[51]

Stimson found the Quezon-MacArthur messages "most disappointing" and "wholly unreal"; he was shocked that MacArthur would go "more than half way towards supporting Quezon's position." Roosevelt's responses to the two men were prompt, lucid, and emphatic. He told Quezon that he was "not lacking in understanding of or sympathy with the situation of yourself and the Commonwealth Government," but that his proposal could not be accepted by the United States. He did assure the Philippine leader, however, that "so long as the flag of the United States flies on Filipino soil as a pledge of our duty to your people, it will be defended by our own men to the death."

In his message to MacArthur the President authorized him "to arrange for the capitulation of the Filipino elements of the defending forces, when and if in your opinion that course appears necessary." But he stressed that "American forces will continue to keep our flag flying in the Philippines so long as there remains any possibility of resistance . . . The duty and the necessity of resisting Japanese aggression to the last transcends in importance any other obligation now facing us in the Philippines." Roosevelt went on to discuss the possible evacuation of the Quezons and Sayres, as well as MacArthur's own family, suggesting that Jean and Arthur "should be given this opportunity if you consider it advisable." A week earlier Marshall had asked for MacArthur's opinion on his own evacuation, concluding that such would be effected only "by direct order of the President." At the time MacArthur had not responded to Marshall.[52]

In his reply to Roosevelt, Quezon assured him that he would abide by his decision. MacArthur's answer to the President, printed in its entirety below, represented his response to Roosevelt's "no surrender" dictum as well as to Marshall's request for his own evacuation:

For President Roosevelt. I have delivered your message to President Quezon and have shown yourad [your radiogram] 1029 to High Commissioner Sayre. If opportunity presents and it can be done with reasonable safety and, of course, with their own consent, I will evacuate the members of the Commonwealth Government, the High Commissioner, Mrs. Sayre, and their son. I am deeply appreciative of the inclusion of my own family in this list, but they and I have decided that they will share the fate of the garrison. My plans have already been outlined in previous radios; they consist in fighting [on] my present battle position in Bataan to destruction and then holding Corregidor in a similar manner. I have not the slightest intention in the world of surrendering or capitulating the Filipino elements of my command. Apparently my message gave a false impression or was garbled with reference to Filipinos. My statements regarding collapse applied only to the civilian population, including Commonwealth officials, the puppet government, and the general populace. There has never been the slightest wavering among the troops. I count upon them equally with the Americans to hold steadfast to the end.

MacArthur[53]

Marshall immediately sent him a radiogram expressing concern over his decision to remain on Corregidor to the end. MacArthur ignored the matter of his evacuation in his next message to the Army chief of staff, which he sent on February 15, the day Singapore fell. Instead, he renewed his appeal for a Pacific counteroffensive: "The opportunities still exist for a complete reversal of the situation. It will soon, however, be too late for such a movement." In the following days MacArthur cooperated fully in arranging the evacuation by submarine of the Quezons and Sayres, which took place in the third week of February, but he himself gave no indication of a readiness to depart.

Finally, on February 22 Roosevelt sent him a definite order to leave Corregidor for Australia where he would assume command of a new Southwest Pacific theater, as yet not formally established. He was instructed to go first to Mindanao to check on preparations there for "a prolonged defense" but was to stay no more than a week before journeying on to Australia. MacArthur said that at first he considered disobeying the order, "even to the extent of resigning my commission and joining the Bataan force as a simple volunteer." But Sutherland and other senior staff officers persuaded him that he could be of more value to the Allied cause in the new command position. On February 24 MacArthur replied to the President, agreeing to leave but requesting that he be allowed to decide the right "psychological time" of departure: "I know the situation here in the Philippines and unless the right moment is chosen for so delicate an operation a sudden collapse might result." Marshall quickly informed him that Roosevelt said he could decide the date of his exit.[54]

The lull in combat activity on Bataan and Corregidor continued day after day for the next two weeks. MacArthur left no record of his thoughts during that period, but he must have pondered the intelligence estimates on Homma's next major assault, the impact of his departure on the troops, the odds against a safe trip through the enemy blockade, and the future command in Australia. Suddenly, on the morning of March 10 he called for Wainwright and told him that he planned to leave the next night. They discussed the new command arrangements: MacArthur planned to retain overall command in the

Philippines and to divide USAFFE into four separate field commands, with Wainwright heading the Bataan forces. MacArthur gave Wainwright a box of cigars and two jars of shaving cream and tried to appear cheerful. Then he said with determination, "If I get through to Australia you know I'll come back as soon as I can with as much as I can. In the meantime you've got to hold."

Wainwright later wrote: "The sudden note in his voice communicated his spirit to me. For the moment we both felt that, as dim as the outlook now was, at least he would soon be in a place where he could establish a base, build up a force." Both men were realistic about the doom that awaited the Philippine garrison. "Perhaps it was that thought," Wainwright observed, "that kept both of us from speculating aloud on how long it would take him to come back with a force . . . and of just how much longer Bataan and then Corregidor would last."

The professional careers of Wainwright and thousands of other American and Filipino soldiers would soon end in the squalor of prison camps, but MacArthur would be given another chance to succeed. Long afterward he commented with deep sadness, "I was to come back, but it would be too late — too late for those battling men in the foxholes of Bataan, too late for the valiant gunners at the batteries of Corregidor." [55]

CHAPTER III

A Beginning and an End

1. Journey from Disaster to Disappointment

TIRED, AND TWENTY-FIVE POUNDS under his normal weight, Mac-Arthur bade an emotional farewell to Wainwright, Moore, and a few other soldiers at the south dock of Corregidor's Bottomside. He, his family, their Cantonese amah, fifteen Army officers, two Navy officers, and an Army sergeant boarded four battle-worn patrol torpedo boats, each passenger having been allowed one hand bag. The Army officers included the eight whom MacArthur counted on to form the nucleus of his new headquarters in Australia: Sutherland (chief of staff), Marshall (deputy chief of staff), Stivers (G-1), Willoughby (G-2), Casey (engineer), Marquat (antiaircraft), Akin (signal), and George (air). Intermittent enemy shelling had occurred during the day, March 11, 1942, but the bay entrance was relatively quiet when MacArthur and his carefully selected group departed shortly before 8:00 P.M.

As the small craft roared away in the darkness, both rain and sea spray soon drenched the travelers, most of whom were making their first journey on a PT boat. Although slowed by engines long in need of overhauling and by ten fifty-gallon drums of extra gasoline secured on each vessel's deck, the boats made their way westward into the South China Sea without being detected by Japanese shore batteries or surface craft. Fortunately rain clouds hid the moon, but the frequent squalls meant rough seas and nearly all of the landlubbers eventually succumbed to seasickness.

Lieutenant John Bulkeley's PT-41, with the MacArthurs aboard, took the lead as the four craft traveled in a diamond formation. They successfuly eluded the enemy naval blockade during the night, but became separated from each other because of engine difficulties, stormy weather, and lack of navigational aids. "It was a bad night for everyone," said MacArthur, who compared the battering by the "towering waves" to "a trip in a concrete mixer." Admiral Rockwell, a passenger on the trailing vessel, was astounded to see the young skipper sighting with his fingers as they raced by small islands. Rockwell asked how he could navigate without the proper instruments. "By guess and by God, sir," the lieutenant replied with a smile.[1]

The prearranged plan, in case the boats became scattered, was to rendezvous at Tagauayan in the Cuyo Islands at the north end of the Sulu Sea. As one PT boat entered the island group, its captain thought he saw an enemy destroyer bearing down on them through the early morning fog. He ordered the extra fuel drums jettisoned and the torpedo tubes readied for action, but Generals Akin and Casey persuaded him to wait a few moments before firing. The pursuing craft turned out to be PT-41, which was carrying MacArthur. Later that day, March 12, three of the four vessels met at Tagauayan. By then young Arthur, who had been extremely nauseated during the night, was happily getting to know the cook's monkey, "General Tojo." After discussing with Rockwell whether to wait for the fourth boat, MacArthur ordered the expedition to move on at dusk. The boat that had dumped its spare fuel was abandoned, and its passengers and crew were transferred to the other two craft. The PT boat that had been delayed arrived at Tagauayan two hours later and followed the others toward Mindanao. A submarine was supposed to meet MacArthur at Tagauayan in case he wished to change his mode of travel by that point, but it did not reach the island until after he had departed.

As the travelers continued south through the Sulu Sea during the night of March 12–13, the weather became calmer, but Mrs. MacArthur still spent much of her time with Arthur and Ah Cheu, both of whom continued to suffer from nausea. Not long after leaving the Cuyos, Bulkeley had to cut his speed suddenly to avoid crossing the path of a Japanese warship — Bulkeley and Huff said it was a cruiser, MacArthur and Willoughby a battleship. The enemy moved on without noticing the PT boats. As everyone's nerves began to relax, Mrs. MacArthur decided to turn over the wet mattress on which she and her family were reclining. She had turned on her flashlight so that her husband and Huff could see to move the mattress when Bulkeley, in "a roar of indignation," shouted from the bridge, "Put out that damn light!" The MacArthurs obeyed as promptly and silently as buck privates. Another narrow escape from the enemy occurred later in the night as they neared the coastline of Negros at the entrance to the Mindanao Sea. Apparently the Japanese at a base on shore mistook the roar of the boat engines for aircraft. They flashed searchlights into the sky but none onto the dark waters as the PT boats hurried on undetected.[2]

By then Mrs. MacArthur had lost her hand bag overboard and possessed only a compact, lipstick, and comb. Bulkeley stated, "The General had only what he wore . . . He did not even bring a razor; in fact, he borrowed mine." The crew thought the experience must have been an extremely depressing one for the former military head of the United States Army. In the early, black hours of morning as the passengers on PT-41 tried to sleep, MacArthur sat up on his mattress and called softly to Huff. He told the aide he could not sleep and wanted to talk. Huff asked what he wanted to discuss, and the general replied, "Oh, anything. I just want to talk." For two hours he went over the Philippine campaign, "trying to analyze it and get it all straight in his mind." Huff remarked, "It was all a little uncanny . . . and gravely sad." The general's "voice choked up as he expressed his chagrin at being ordered to leave Corregidor." But he was already determined to return to the Philippines. Huff stated, "He meant it, and he was already planning how he would do it."

The two leading boats arrived at the port of Cagayan on the north coast of Mindanao at 7:00 A.M., March 13, the third craft joining them an hour or so later. A colonel waiting on the dock saw MacArthur's tall figure near the bow of the first boat and commented that he looked "like Washington crossing the Delaware." Brigadier General William F. Sharp, the commander on Mindanao, met the group and rode with them to the large Del Monte pineapple plantation, less than an hour's ride into the interior. Adjoining the plantation was Del Monte Field, the FEAF base where four B-17's from Australia were scheduled to pick up MacArthur's party. Only one had arrived, however, and Sharp had sent it back to Australia because it was "dangerously decrepit," as MacArthur maintained, or "the plane couldn't remain there during daylight hours because enemy planes were all over the place," as Huff stated.

Whatever the reason, MacArthur was upset and sent demands to Brett and the War Department for "the best three planes in the United States or Hawaii," which were to be manned by "completely adequate, experienced crews." He told Chief of Staff Marshall, "To attempt such a desperate and important trip with inadequate equipment would amount to consigning the whole party to death and I could not accept such a responsibility." Unknown to MacArthur, Brett had earlier requested the use of four new B-17's that had been assigned to

Rear Admiral Herbert F. Leary, the Allied naval commander in Australia, but the admiral had turned him down. Now, when Brett asked again, Leary relented and three B-17's were released for the trip.[3]

Since the air base had never been completed and the housing facilities were primitive, the members of the MacArthur party secluded themselves in the clubhouse and nearby guest lodges of the Del Monte plantation. Neal Crawford, the manager, played the role of the unseen host, busily making arrangements for their meals and other necessities. Sharp placed a strong guard around the compound since Japanese forces were reported to be moving north from Davao and some enemy patrols had been sighted within thirty miles of the airfield. One Filipino lady who had somehow learned of the sojourners walked twenty-five miles to inquire about her family on Luzon. She got to talk briefly to Mrs. MacArthur, who knew nothing of the family's fate, but nervous security guards then took her away under arrest. The "extremely angry" woman was promptly released after the brass departed for Australia.

Unintentionally, the MacArthurs also offended their host: a friend of the plantation manager stated that "neither the general himself nor any member of his staff had the courtesy to say 'thank you' to the Crawfords even by telephone." In another incident Captain Ind, who had come to Mindanao before MacArthur, encountered the USAFFE commander in an unlikely location. While strolling outside the guard line one night, Ind saw two dark figures on a rise just above him. He had his rifle aimed at the taller figure when he suddenly recognized MacArthur's voice as the general stood talking to his wife. Ind gasped and yelled to the couple, "I almost shot your ears off." MacArthur laughed and said, "Well, you better come up here and we'll decide who's going to escort whom back to the compound."

Roosevelt's orders had stipulated that MacArthur was to stay on Mindanao only long enough "to insure a prolonged defense" by Sharp's forces. Earlier MacArthur had described Sharp as "a big man who never had a chance," so he had given him his opportunity with the Mindanao-Visayan command. Just before leaving Corregidor, MacArthur had split the southern command, retaining Sharp as head of the Mindanao Force and appointing Chynoweth as Visayan commander. He directed both of them to resort to guerrilla warfare if the Luzon troops should finally be defeated, and he depended on making his return to the archipelago through the southern islands. During their talks at Del Monte on March 13–16, Sharp was "warm and gracious" and "charmed" the USAFFE chief. He assured MacArthur that "his plans for intensified guerrilla warfare were well advanced."

MacArthur nominated Sharp for promotion to major general because he "believed that here was one commander who would carry on guerrilla warfare to the end," according to Chynoweth. Actually, the Visayan commander said, "General Sharp, at the age of fifty-five, had lost physical agility, and even more important, the mental agility to adjust himself to unforeseen conditions. He was simply unfit for that job. It was pathetic to give him the responsibility" of commanding combat or guerrilla operations on Mindanao. The collapse and surrender of Sharp's command later would be a keen disappointment to MacArthur.[4]

Late in the evening of March 16 two B-17's landed at Del Monte, the third having turned back to Australia with engine trouble. The Corregidor passengers were each limited to thirty-five pounds of luggage as they boarded the bombers. The only extra item that the MacArthurs carried was a mattress, needed mainly for Arthur who was still in poor condition and might, it was feared, suffer a recurrence of nausea on the long flight to Darwin. The mattress was the cause of several wild stories around Del Monte that did not take long to get back to the States: one was that MacArthur had his furniture loaded aboard and the mattress was filled with gold coins.

Having just flown 900 miles, Lieutenant Frank P. Bostrom, the pilot of the B-17 that would carry the MacArthurs, needed eight cups of coffee to revive himself during the brief stop at Del Monte. "With one engine sputtering and missing before it finally took hold," his B-17, followed by the second bomber, took off for Australia at 1:30 A.M., March 17. Bostrom said he was already "terribly tired" before starting the return trip, but he would be even more exhausted on this run since the automatic pilot broke shortly after takeoff. Moreover, because there was not enough oxygen equipment for all passengers and crew, the planes flew at altitudes of 8000 feet and lower. The necessity of flying low and the possibility of interception by enemy fighters over the East Indies kept Bostrom and the other airmen in "considerable suspense," but no Japanese aircraft were encountered.

MacArthur impressed Bostrom as "a pretty tough Joe" who was surprisingly fresh and relaxed. During most of the flight the general sat in the radio operator's seat and that crewman took a gun position near him since they were on radio silence. When a box of apples was opened for the passengers, Sergeant Sheldon D. Beaton, the radio operator, figured out a way to join the feast. According to another crewman, Beaton "kept staring with his mouth hanging open, looking as hungry as possible, while the General munched on an apple, until finally they broke down and gave him one." When they neared the northwest coast of Australia, an enemy air raid was reported to be under way at Darwin, so the B-17's flew on to Batchelor Field, about forty miles to the south, landing at 9:30 A.M., March 17. MacArthur shook hands with Bostrom, thanked him and his crew for a "good trip," and, as he had done with the PT boat crews at Cagayan, awarded Silver Stars to the airmen of both bombers. Of more immediate value to Bostrom, the general also gave him his mattress.[5]

Mrs. MacArthur commented to Huff as they got off the plane at Batchelor, "Never, never again will anybody get me into an airplane! Not for any reason! Sid, please find some way that we can get to Melbourne without getting off the ground." No sooner had the aide begun checking on other means of travel than a report came in that Japanese bombers were headed toward Batchelor Field. A C-47 transport plane was ready to go, so MacArthur, with his wife agreeing reluctantly, hurried everyone from Corregidor aboard for the next leg of the long journey, to Alice Springs. Landing at the isolated town in the center of Australia after four more hours of flying, the Mac-Arthur party debarked, totally exhausted, to find themselves in "a flat, arid and uninviting region of scrub and sand." They had just missed the weekly train that went south, so a special train was called up from Adelaide. Since it would not arrive until the next afternoon, the haggard travelers spent the night at an old frontier-style hotel that was overcrowded with people and with bugs of "various kinds."

That evening MacArthur and several officers tried to relax at the local theater, which was showing a double feature of American Westerns, MacArthur's favorite type of movie. The first one was so bad, or MacArthur was so tired, that they left before the end of the film. Huff commented, "It was one of the very few times I ever saw him walk out on a movie, even a double feature." All night and the next morning the distinguished visitors at the hotel were plagued by flies, which, Huff claimed, "swarmed around us by the hundreds. If you weren't careful they would crawl right into your nose or mouth." Mrs. MacArthur was particularly upset by the flies. "It's almost a phobia with her and she will chase a single fly all over her house under ordinary circumstances," said Huff. At a meal she put a morsel of food into her mouth, then looked horror-stricken as she realized a fly had been perched on it. MacArthur grinned and said, "It's all right, Jeannie. Just swallow it. A fly won't kill you." There is no record of when her next swallow occurred.[6]

On the morning of the 18th Hurley flew to Alice Springs to

greet MacArthur and report that in the United States the general's reputation as a national hero had reached the levels of acclaim accorded to Charles A. Lindbergh, General John J. Pershing, and Admiral George Dewey. Hurley wanted the MacArthurs to return to Melbourne in his aircraft, but, with Arthur again ill from the flight, Mrs. MacArthur adamantly refused. Most of the USAFFE officers flew the rest of the way, but the MacArthurs, Sutherland, Huff, and Major Charles H. Morhouse, the FEAF medical officer who had accompanied them from Corregidor, departed by train on the afternoon of March 18. The trip to Adelaide on the south coast was an uncomfortable one: the weather was stifling in the late Australian summer, the countryside was desolate, the coach seats were hard benches along the walls, and the train was unimaginably slow. Besides stopping at sidings to let freight trains pass, the train also halted at one small rural station where a group of persons was gathered. At first it was thought the people had come to see MacArthur, but it turned out that they had heard a physician was aboard, and MacArthur was persuaded to delay the journey while Morhouse operated on a rancher who had a steel splinter in his eye.

MacArthur took all of the interruptions with graceful forbearance, even when the train had to stop at each mealtime so that the passengers could walk back to the dining car because there was no passage from one car to another. Sitting on an uncomfortable bench in a day coach, MacArthur spent part of the time talking about his plans for leading an army back to the Philippines and another part sleeping soundly with his head on Jean's shoulder. She commented softly to Huff during his four-hour nap, "That's the first time he's really slept since Pearl Harbor."

Met at the Adelaide railroad station by a group of reporters who were anxious for a statement, MacArthur explained that President Roosevelt had ordered him to proceed to Australia "for the purpose, as I understand it, of organizing the American offensive against Japan, a primary object of which is the relief of the Philippines. I came through and I shall return." Whether that statement squared with the strategic plans of the Joint Chiefs of Staff did not seem to matter at the time. His last sentence quickly caught the headlines all through the free world. While a large crowd at the Adelaide station shouted "Welcome to Australia," the MacArthur group transferred to another train and into a special private car sent by the Australian government. Brigadier General Richard J. Marshall, the USAFFE deputy chief of staff, who had flown ahead to Melbourne, joined them for the final leg of the journey from Adelaide to Melbourne. He brought news that shocked MacArthur: the American forces in Australia numbered only about 25,000 and had fewer than 250 combat aircraft, while the Australian Army had only one regular division on the continent, the rest being engaged in the Middle East conflict. "God have mercy on us!" MacArthur exclaimed. It was said that he spent the night pacing back and forth in his private coach.[7]

At 10:00 A.M., March 21, the express train pulled into the Spencer Street Station at Melbourne. A crowd of 4000 to 6000 Australians was waiting and cheered him enthusiastically when he stepped from the coach. A 360-man honor guard of American soldiers, sixty correspondents, and a large delegation of Australian officials, headed by Army Minister Francis M. Forde, were in the forefront of the welcoming throng. MacArthur "had on his jaunty garrison cap, glinting in the sun with golden oak leaves," observed a reporter who was there. "He had on, instead of a severe tunic, just an old bush jacket, like a windbreaker, open at the throat and bare of his four shiny stars. He had on neatly pressed khaki trousers, and black and white checked stockings, and tan civilian shoes with little decorative holes in them. He carried his cane. Among the braid-horses and stovepipes he looked like business." [8]

After shaking all official hands in sight, he was guided to a microphone. Because of the earlier briefing by Marshall on the shocking inadequacy of the forces in Australia, he was ready with a short message that seemed to be directed not only to the Australians but also to his superiors in Washington. He drew a crumpled sheet of paper from his pocket and slowly, somberly read it to the crowd:

> I am glad indeed to be in immediate cooperation with the Australian soldier. I know him well from World War days and admire him greatly. I have every confidence in the ultimate success of our joint cause; but success in modern war requires something more than courage and a willingness to die: it requires careful preparation. This means the furnishing of sufficient troops and sufficient material to meet the known strength of a potential enemy. No general can make something out of nothing. My success or failure will depend primarily upon the resources which the respective governments place at my disposal. My faith in them is complete. In any event I shall do my best. I shall keep the soldier's faith.[9]

"Smiling frequently," in contrast to the general's demeanor, Mrs. MacArthur told the reporters that her three principal problems at the moment were "rest, some clothes, and a home for my family." Later, as the MacArthurs were escorted to a limousine, the general stopped in front of some soldiers of the honor guard: they were seven Filipinos who had been wounded on Luzon and evacuated. "He looked at them wistfully," said an observer, and then he moved on to the automobile, which took the tired MacArthur family to the Menzies Hotel for their first extended rest and relaxation after eleven days and nearly 3000 miles of arduous traveling.[10]

2. *A New Challenge*

While Jean and Arthur were busy shopping for winter clothes, exploring Melbourne, and making new acquaintances, General MacArthur, after only one day's rest at the Menzies Hotel, plunged into a busy schedule of conferences on defense plans with Australian and American civilian and military leaders. On March 26 he journeyed by automobile to Canberra, the nation's capital, where he met with the Australian Advisory War Council and attended a lavish dinner given in his honor by Prime Minister John Curtin at the imposing Government House. Nelson T. Johnson, the American minister to Australia, read to the dinner group a message he had just received from Roosevelt announcing the award to MacArthur of the Congressional Medal of Honor. MacArthur offered a toast to the Australians and made a short speech in which he reiterated his determination to defeat Japan: "I have come as a soldier in a great crusade of personal liberty as opposed to perpetual slavery. My faith in our ultimate victory is invincible, and I bring you tonight the unbreakable spirit of the free man's military code in support of our joint cause."

Correspondent Robert Sherrod, who was observing from the balcony, was as impressed as the Australians were by MacArthur's dramatic earnestness: "He was terrific as he said slowly and emotionally, 'There can be no compromise. We shall win or we shall die.'" Another American reporter in Canberra commented that whatever defense proposals MacArthur offers "he can look forward to the acquiescence of Australia's leaders" and that his new command will be inaugurated "in circumstances indicating that he can have anything he asks for" from the Curtin ministry. The *Times* of London, summarizing "Aussie" journalistic reactions to MacArthur, stated:

"Australian newspapers welcome the appointment of General MacArthur not only for his renown as a fighter but also as proof of the prime importance which the United States Government attaches to the task of holding Australia and its willingness to undertake commitments to this end." [11]

Other than the fiery Quezon, who arrived in Australia on March 27 and departed for the United States three weeks later (sharply critical of Washington's failure to reinforce both the Philippines and Australia), MacArthur could not have wished for leaders more in accord with his own Pacific-first views than Curtin and his Labour Party leaders. The Curtin ministry had come into power in the fall of 1941 and from the start had been assailing the British government for its neglect of Australia's safety and its opposition to equality of status for Australia in the higher echelons of Allied decision-making. In a strongly worded message to the Australian people on December 27, Curtin declared: "We refuse to accept the dictum that the Pacific struggle must be treated as a subordinate segment of the general conflict . . . The Australian Government, therefore, regards the Pacific struggle as primarily one in which the United States and Australia must have the fullest say in the direction of the democracies' fighting plan." With boldness (and hyperbole) that shocked Churchill, the Australian prime minister announced: "Without any inhibitions of any kind, I make it quite clear that Australia looks to America, free of any pangs as to our traditional links or kinship with the United Kingdom."

Curtin had no intention of severing ties with the British government, but rather was proclaiming closer collaboration with America and putting pressure on London for a voice in British and Allied councils. Nevertheless, his "no pangs" assertion set off a tempest of indignation and misunderstanding in London. The next five months were marked by the worst relations yet between London and Canberra, one authority characterizing the exchanges of messages between Churchill and Curtin as "acid and embarrassing." [12]

As the Japanese advanced to Java, Timor, New Guinea, New Britain, and the Solomons, the Australian government and people became increasingly fearful of an enemy invasion of their continent. Reluctantly responding to Curtin's demands, the British chiefs of staff finally agreed to return two of the Australian divisions that were in the Mediterranean theater but then antagonized Australian officials further by trying to detour some of these troops to Ceylon and Burma. While London authorities discounted the threat of a Japanese invasion of Australia, Curtin and his military leaders claimed that twenty-five divisions would be needed to repel the enemy assault, which they expected soon. Largely because of pressure from the Australian and New Zealand governments, Churchill created a Pacific war council in London in February and Roosevelt established a second Pacific war council two months later in Washington, with representation by both aggrieved nations. Neither council, however, became much more than a sounding board, and the American and British heads of state and chiefs of staff continued to determine strategy, logistics, and operations in the Pacific as well as in the South Asian and Mediterranean theaters.

Dr. H. V. Evatt, the Australian minister for external affairs, journeyed to Washington in March to plead Australia's case, which he said was "a desperate one" requiring "the entire United Kingdom allocation" of American munitions shipments for at least the next six weeks. As late as May 28, Evatt cabled Curtin the text of the Arcadia agreement between Roosevelt and Churchill expressing the Europe-first strategy. In anger and frustration he told Curtin that "the existence of this written agreement came as a great surprise to myself and, I have no doubt, to you. We were not consulted about the matter." It is difficult to believe that they knew nothing of the "beat Hitler first" policy, but it was substantiated in Evatt's mind by the runaround he encountered in Washington and London when he tried to get increased allocations of troops and equipment for the Southwest Pacific theater.[13]

A USAFIA G-2 estimate on "the attitude of the people" in Australia in mid-March stated:

> The indicated weaknesses of the Australian people and their Government, faced with Japanese invasion, appear to be, first, a deep-rooted complacency and a feeling that "it can't happen here." Second, a lack of realism and a tendency to avoid unpleasant issues. Third, some tendency to panic when suddenly faced by reality. Fourth, a certain lack of individual self-reliance, resourcefulness and initiative, due principally to the fact that traditionally they have looked to England for detailed direction . . . Faced by reality, self-confidence may seriously weaken.
>
> Strong, forceful leadership is required to maintain morale in the event of an invasion. The people need to be continuously spurred on to an effectual war effort. They appear to be too willing to lay the burden of responsibility on someone else and, lacking prospects of effectual direction and support from England, they were turning to the United States to assume that responsibility.[14]

Hurley wrote Marshall that Australia was "very vulnerable" and that "our own forces and those of our Allies were inclined to be casual and carefree." He added: "The static defense concept appears to permeate all planning in Australia." Some USAFIA officers, as well as the incoming USAFFE staff, were persuaded that the Australian high command planned to yield most of Australia in case of invasion and defend only the so-called "Brisbane Line," a defensive position said to run from Adelaide to Brisbane in the southeast corner of the continent. Australian leaders, as well as the official Australian war histories, have persistently denied the existence of such a plan. But most Australian authorities would agree with Lieutenant General Edmund F. Herring's observation that MacArthur "played a large part in restoring the morale of the Australian people, which was at its lowest ebb at the time of his arrival." [15]

Just as MacArthur was pleased to find in Australia leaders who were sympathetic to his conviction that the Allies were neglecting the Pacific war, so Curtin and his colleagues were delighted with the arrival of so influential a commander as MacArthur. They hoped that his "direct channel to Washington" would prove in the future to be "the most effective way of influencing American opinion to respond to Australia's wartime needs." MacArthur and Curtin felt their appeals could be more fruitful if they were made together, although some of the early joint techniques they tried were not productive. In April, for instance, Churchill received a message from Curtin purporting to forward MacArthur's latest requests: he wanted, pending the return of the last Australian division from the Middle East, two British divisions, an aircraft carrier, and a large increase in the number of British ships assigned to the Australia–United States supply run.

Convinced that Curtin was "using General MacArthur" (while Washington was probably thinking the influence was in reverse order), Churchill inquired of Roosevelt "whether General MacArthur has any authority from the United States for taking such a line." Roosevelt assured him that MacArthur would be instructed to send his future requests solely through War Department channels, whereupon Churchill sent a firm refusal to Curtin. MacArthur responded weakly to Marshall that he should not be held liable for the use to which Curtin put the remarks he made at informal conferences with the Australian prime minister.

All in all, however, the weeks following MacArthur's arrival in Australia coincided with a substantial increase in reinforcements to that continent. The decisions in Washington to divert these men and matériel largely preceded MacArthur's move to Australia, but they included the shipments of two American infantry divisions and several groups of bombers and fighters, the air commitment representing "the largest projected concentration of American air power outside the Western Hemisphere" at the time, despite Washington's dedication to the Europe-first concept.[16]

The dispatch of MacArthur to Australia and the gradual build-up there of American forces since December did not result, as has sometimes been alleged, principally from Australian demands. It is true that in February Curtin, with New Zealand's concurrence, asked Roosevelt that an American general be appointed supreme commander in the Southwest Pacific as the ABDA organization collapsed. Also the War Department released a statement that MacArthur went to Australia "in accordance with the request of the Australian Government." But Curtin did not know of the general's arrival or his assignment until Brett informed him on March 17 and, on Roosevelt's instructions, proposed that the prime minister nominate MacArthur to command the Southwest Pacific theater. Curtin was "enthusiastic" and offered the nomination at once. But the development of Australia as a primary base for later offensive operations against the Japanese, rather than merely as a supply depot for the Philippines, had begun earlier and not basically because of Curtin's or MacArthur's entreaties.

The impending loss of the Malay Barrier forced the Joint Chiefs in Washington to turn to Australia in desperation as the anchor of the Allied defense line in the Southwest Pacific. This, in turn, promoted the expansion of bases in the islands along the line of communications from Hawaii to Australia. Thus the Australian build-up stemmed not from plan but from circumstance. The American chiefs, states one authority, "accepted Australia as a base before they had any clear idea of her strength as an ally; in fact her strength was one of the most rewarding surprises the Americans had in the Pacific war." [17] In the spring of 1942, however, Australia's strength was still largely in the potential state.

On March 24 the Anglo-American Combined Chiefs of Staff reached agreement on a worldwide division of strategic responsibilities, assigning the United States the chief responsibility for the direction of the war in the Pacific. The American Joint Chiefs of Staff then set to work on dividing the area into theaters, which were determined by a number of factors not the least of which was the chiefs' decision to forgo unity of command in the Pacific. As advantageous as a single commander might have been, they could not appoint the outstanding commander already in the Pacific, MacArthur, despite support for him from the President, key leaders in the War Department, influential congressmen, perhaps a majority of the American people, and the Australian government and public.

Admiral King, chief of naval operations, and his colleagues in the Navy Department staunchly argued that the Navy did not have sufficient confidence in him — or in any other Army officer — to entrust the Pacific to his command. In addition, the Navy leaders pointed out that the Pacific conflict would be mainly a war of naval and amphibious operations over huge expanses of ocean and therefore should be directed by an admiral. King's nominee was Admiral Chester W. Nimitz, commander of the Pacific Fleet, but Nimitz was not yet well known outside Navy circles and he was far below MacArthur in seniority and length of service. So the Joint Chiefs decided to place MacArthur in command of the Southwest Pacific Area (SWPA) and Nimitz in charge of virtually the rest of the Pacific, a vast theater to be known as the Pacific Ocean Areas (POA).[18]

While the Joint Chiefs wrestled with the exact wording of the directives to be issued to the two commanders, MacArthur occupied an anomalous position in Australia. He was USAFFE commander, but he officially commanded neither the USAFIA nor the Australian forces on the continent. Nevertheless, with full cooperation from Australian authorities, who already

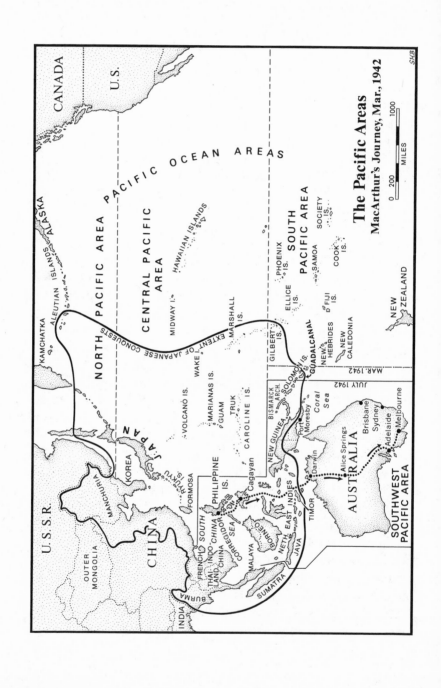

The Pacific Areas
MacArthur's Journey, Mar., 1942

SHB

looked on him as Southwest Pacific commander, he began working toward "placing the country in as secure a position of defense as the means available allowed." Brett had thought MacArthur would assume his USAFIA command, but Marshall forbade this on the grounds that MacArthur's impending international command of the Southwest Pacific theater would make him ineligible "to retain direct command of any national force."

MacArthur was allowed, however, to select several of the commanders for his future command and he began planning with them. He chose Brett to head the air forces and Leary to command the naval forces. Major General Julian F. Barnes, who had headed the forces on the *Pensacola* convoy which had arrived in Australia before Christmas, was selected to command the service forces. The War Department insisted that command of the Allied ground forces should go to an Australian. General Thomas Blamey, commander of Australian Military Forces, had just returned from the Middle East and was later designated to command the Southwest Pacific land forces.[19]

The directives to MacArthur and Nimitz were drafted by the Joint Chiefs, approved by the President, and issued on March 30. MacArthur's theater included Australia, the Bismarck Archipelago, the Solomon Islands, New Guinea, and the Netherlands East Indies, except Sumatra. The British, Dutch (in exile), Australian, and New Zealand governments had to concur, and it took nearly three more weeks before the Southwest Pacific Area command was formally set up on April 18. Curtin's government was the last to concur on the SWPA directive: it worked out some unclear points with the Joint Chiefs about the right of its commanders to communicate freely with the Australian government and the movement of its troops outside Australian territory. The SWPA directive would basically determine MacArthur's command duties, relations, and general objectives for the next three years of the struggle against Japan.[20]

The first part of it defined the geographical limits of the theater; the other nine parts of the directive were as follows:

2. You are designated as the Supreme Commander of the SOUTHWEST PACIFIC Area, and of all armed forces which the governments concerned have assigned, or may assign to this area.

3. As Supreme Commander you are not eligible to command directly any national force.

4. In consonance with the basic strategic policy of the governments concerned your operations will be designed to accomplish the following:

a. Hold the key military regions of Australia as bases for future offensive action against Japan, and in order to check the Japanese conquest of the SOUTHWEST PACIFIC Area.

b. Check the enemy advance toward Australia and its essential lines of communication by the destruction of enemy combatant, troop, and supply ships, aircraft, and bases in Eastern Malaysia and the New Guinea–Bismarck–Solomon Islands Region.

c. Exert economic pressure on the enemy by destroying vessels transporting raw materials from the recently acquired conquered territories to Japan.

d. Maintain our position in the Philippine Islands.

e. Protect land, sea, and air communications within the SOUTHWEST PACIFIC Area and its close approaches.

f. Route shipping in the SOUTHWEST PACIFIC Area.

g. Support the operations of friendly forces in the PACIFIC OCEAN Area and in the INDIAN Theater.

h. Prepare to take the offensive.

5. You will not be responsible for the internal administration of the respective forces under your command, but you are authorized to direct and coordinate the creation and development of administrative facilities and the broad allocation of war materials.

6. You are authorized to control the issue of all communiques concerning the forces under your command.

7. When task forces of your command operate outside the SOUTHWEST PACIFIC Area, coordination with forces assigned to the areas in which operating will be effected by the Joint Chiefs of Staff, or the Combined Chiefs of Staff, as appropriate.

8. Commanders of all armed forces within your Area will be immediately informed by their respective governments that, from a date to be notified, all orders and instructions issued by you in conformity with this directive will be considered by such commanders as emanating from their respective governments.

9. Your staff will include officers assigned by the respective governments concerned, based upon requests made directly to the national commanders of the various forces in your Area.

10. The governments concerned will exercise direction of operations in the SOUTHWEST PACIFIC Area as follows:

a. The Combined Chiefs of Staff will exercise general jurisdiction over grand strategic policy and over such related factors as are necessary for proper implementation, including the allocation of forces and war materials.

b. The Joint U.S. Chiefs of Staff will exercise jurisdiction over all matters pertaining to operational strategy. The Chief of Staff, U.S. Army will act as the Executive Agency for the Joint U.S. Chiefs of Staff. All instructions to you will be issued by or through him.[21]

On the 18th MacArthur formally established Allied Land Forces (Blamey), Allied Naval Forces (Leary), and Allied Air Forces (Brett) and incorporated into the SWPA command structure the Philippine forces as well as USAFIA, which was to be commanded by Barnes and was to function largely as a service command. Despite an admonition from Marshall that he should include a fair representation of Australian and Dutch officers in the higher staff positions of his general headquarters, MacArthur's staff appointments, announced on April 19, consisted, except for three men, of officers who had served on his USAFFE staff on Corregidor: Sutherland, chief of staff; Marshall, deputy chief of staff; Stivers, G-1; Willoughby, G-2; Brigadier General Stephen J. Chamberlin, G-3; Colonel Lester

J. Whitlock, G-4; Akin, signal officer; Casey, engineer officer; Marquat, antiaircraft officer; Colonel Burdette M. Fitch, adjutant general; and Diller, aide and public relations officer. Chamberlin had been Brett's chief of staff, while Whitlock and Fitch had also served on the USAFIA staff.

MacArthur later informed the War Department that there were no "qualified" Dutch officers available in Australia to sere as senior members of his staff. "There is no prospect of obtaining senior staff officers from the Australians," he said, because the Australian Army was growing so rapidly that it did not have enough staff officers to meet its own needs. Although generally overlooked amid the euphoria surrounding the creation of the new command, the failure to include other Allied officers in key positions on MacArthur's headquarters staff would become a sore point later, especially with the Australian Army.[22]

MacArthur also received a copy of the directive sent to Nimitz authorizing the establishment of his Pacific Ocean Areas command. He undoubtedly noticed the differences in the directives immediately. Nimitz would command mostly American forces, but he was not restricted from directly commanding other national forces or interfering with their internal administration. Nimitz also retained command of the Pacific Fleet. Moreover, Nimitz's directive instructed him to "prepare for the execution of major amphibious offensives against positions held by Japan, the initial offensives to be launched from the South Pacific Area [a sub-theater under Nimitz] and Southwest Pacific Area," implying that the admiral might command offensives in MacArthur's theater as well.

The SWPA directive emphasized the defensive aspect of MacArthur's role and merely stated that he was to "prepare to take the offensive." At the time the only objection MacArthur raised was to his title, which he arbitrarily changed from "Supreme Commander" to "Commander in Chief," partly because the latter was the title given to Nimitz.[23] In later years, however, MacArthur became convinced that the Joint Chiefs erred in not designating a single commander for the Pacific war:

> Of all the faulty decisions of the war perhaps the most inexplicable one was the failure to unify the command in the Pacific. The principle involved is perhaps the most fundamental one in the doctrine and tradition of command. In this instance it did not involve an international problem. It was accepted and entirely successful in the other great theaters.
>
> The failure to do so in the Pacific cannot be defended in logic, in theory or even in common sense. Other motives must be ascribed.
>
> It resulted in divided effort, the waste of diffusion and duplication of force, undue extension of the war with added casualties and cost.
>
> The generally excellent cooperation between the two commands in the Pacific, supported by the good will, good nature and high professional qualifications of the numerous personnel involved was no substitute for the essential unity of direction of centralized authority.
>
> The hardships and hazards increasingly resulting were unnecessary indeed.[24]

Actually, MacArthur's operations would be restricted not so much by the terms of the directive as by the War Department's policy governing the deployment of its forces in the Pacific. Shortly after his arrival in Australia, MacArthur received word from Marshall that Army commitments to the Southwest Pacific would be limited to the eight air groups and two infantry divisions already in Australia or en route there. With the war against Germany ever in mind as the top priority, Marshall explained that the SWPA limits were "fixed by shortages in shipping, which is of the utmost seriousness, and by critical situations elsewhere." Also there would be little hope in the near future of getting sufficient elements of the Pacific Fleet into the Southwest Pacific to enable MacArthur to undertake offensive

operations. For a long time to come he would have to rely on
the Australian Army as the strongest part of his combat forces.
But at least that prospect was improving: newly formed Australian units, together with the ones returning from the Middle
East, totaled nine divisions and twenty-eight brigades within
two months after MacArthur's move to Australia.[25]

If the Joint Chiefs were not thinking in terms of a major
offensive effort in the Southwest Pacific, MacArthur and Curtin
surely were from the start of their cooperation. Several days
before the general formally assumed command of the new theater, Curtin enthusiastically wrote to him:

> This is a momentous occasion for the peoples of the United
> Nations. You have received a charter as Supreme Commander
> not from your own Government alone but also from the Gov-
> ernments of the United Kingdom, Australia, New Zealand, and
> the Netherlands. You have come to Australia to lead a crusade,
> the result of which means everything to the future of the world
> and mankind . . .
>
> Your directive, amongst other things, instructs you to pre-
> pare to take the offensive. I would assure you of every possible
> support that can be given you by the Government and people
> of Australia in making Australia secure as a base of operations,
> in assisting you to marshal the strength required to wrest the
> initiative from the enemy and, in joining with you in the ulti-
> mate offensive, to bring about the total destruction of the com-
> mon foe.[26]

Thanks to the able performances of Australian combat units,
the unexpected manpower and industrial resources that the
Australian nation would provide, and the energetic supportive
leadership of the Curtin ministry, MacArthur and his Southwest Pacific forces would play a far greater role in the future
war against Japan than the Joint Chiefs or the Navy envisioned
in early 1942. Although the relationship would not be without
vexations, the teaming of MacArthur and the Australians would

be mutually beneficial in giving a new surge to the fortunes of both the general and Australia. With heavy reliance on Australian veterans, especially during the first phases of the later advance northward, and on Australian supplies and services, which would more than offset the value of American lend-lease shipments to that country, MacArthur would put together a string of victories that would carry him back in triumph to the Philippines.

For Australia, the "Curtin-MacArthur era" would mark a turning point in its dependence on Great Britain and its comparative insignificance in international affairs, and a movement toward close collaboration with the United States and toward its emergence as a power in the Pacific world. Thus the spring of 1942 signaled a new beginning for both the tired, defeated general and the insecure, frustrated Australian nation. It was, indeed, a fortunate union of interests not only for MacArthur and Australia but also for the Allied cause.

3. The Making of a Hero

On the morning after MacArthur's departure from Corregidor, Wainwright broke the news to his general officers. He observed that "they were all at first depressed by the news . . . But I soon saw that they understood just as I understood. They realized as well as I what the score was." Colonel James D. Carter did not notice "any real reactions" among his men; he himself thought "it was a good thing because MacArthur would be a valuable man in the place he was going." Collier believed that "to capture MacArthur was to them [the Japanese] next to winning the war. I think it would have been terrible. Besides, in those last days he couldn't do us any good." Hill agreed that "he did the right thing because he was no good there" to the Allied effort. Among the gun crews on Corregidor, remarked

Captain Benson Guyton, "there were certainly many individuals who expressed disappointment or bitterness, but I don't think as a whole it damaged them" in their determination to fight to the end. Johnson found "mixed reactions" and "some cells of bitterness" among the officers and men of the 57th Infantry.[27]

Most of the men on Bataan were probably too exhausted or disease-ridden to exhibit a strong reaction either way to Mac-Arthur's leaving, but among some who responded negatively the feeling ran deep. And there were those who maintained that his departure seriously affected the spirit of the troops. The parents of a USAFFE soldier from Texas wrote to Roosevelt, "Nothing you could have done would have broken their morale and that of their parents at home so thoroughly as removal of General MacArthur from their direct command." In the 31st Division the news "hurt morale all the way down to the front-line people," according to Bluemel. With enemy loudspeakers broadcasting pleas to the Filipino soldiers to desert, Bluemel told his troops, " 'Help is going to come. He's going to bring it back.' I had to lie a little bit." In one regiment on Bataan it became "standard practice" to say on the appropriate occasion, "I am going to the latrine, but I shall return." [28]

Of the known writings by USAFFE soldiers that contain references to MacArthur's departure, most are filled with bitterness. One of the most savage indictments of him is a poem by a Bataan veteran composed when he was in an enemy prison camp in June, 1943:

Ang Puno Nanwala
(The Lost Leader)

"Just for a handful of silver he left us,
Just for a ribband to stick in his coat . . ."

Blockaded, unaided, we fight to the last,
Though we now realize that all hope is past.

Our leader has vanished like last summer's rose.
　　"Gone to get help," he would have us suppose.
May his medallion grow tarnished with tears,
　　Now that his honor is built on our fears.
May the ghosts glimmering in nebulous mist,
　　Ghouls of thirty thousand tombs haunt him and list
To his excuses of why he forsook us;
　　Heedlessly hear his historical census:
"Bonaparte, Witold, King Bela and Rommel,
　　Orlof, Benhadad, Toktamish and Wavell;
All of these soldiers — to save their own lives —
　　Raced from the field of arms home to their wives."

Let him go, let him go, we are the braver,
　　Stain his hands with our blood, dye them forever.
Recall, oh ye kinsmen, how he left us to die,
　　Starved and insulted by his infamous lie;
How he seduced us with boasts of defense;
　　How he traduced us with plans of offense.
When his publicity chairman presides,
　　Vaunts his fame as high as the Bay of Fundy tides —
Recollects bonus boys gassed out by him;
　　Remember Bataan boys sacrificed for him.
Try him, Tribunal of Public Opinion;
　　Brothers, condemn him through our dominion.
Then when he stands before Judges Olympian,
　　Quakes at his final court-martial: oblivion! [29]

About three weeks after the Bataan surrender, while at Camp
O'Donnell on Luzon with prisoners by the hundreds ill and
dying around him, Brougher wrote the following conclusion to
the 11th Division operations report which he submitted to
Wainwright, a fellow prisoner:

Who had the right to say that 20,000 Americans should be
sentenced without their consent and for no fault of their own to
an enterprise that would involve for them endless suffering,
cruel handicap, death, or a hopeless future that could end only
in a Japanese Prisoner of War Camp in the Philippines? Who
took the responsibility for saying that some other possibility was

[not] in prospect? And whoever did, was he not an arch-deceiver, traitor and criminal rather than a great soldier? . . . A foul trick of deception has been played on a large group of Americans by a Commander in Chief and small staff who are now eating steak and eggs in Australia. God damn them! [30]

Just as the response among the Philippine defenders was varied, so the mail to the White House on the evacuation of MacArthur came from citizens who were delighted with the news and others who were irate over it. In a public statement on the day of the general's arrival in Australia the President said that "every man and woman in the United States admires with me General MacArthur's determination to fight to the finish with his men in the Philippines." But "all important decisions must be made with a view toward the successful termination of the war," so that is why, Roosevelt explained, he and "every American, if faced individually with the question as to where General MacArthur could best serve his country, could come to only one answer." That evening, March 17, at a White House dinner a lady at the table asked him to tell the guests how MacArthur escaped. "I told her," as Roosevelt related the story to reporters a few days later, "that he had taken a rowboat, which was the only safe way, had disguised himself as a Filipino fisherman . . . [and] had rowed all the way down there — right past the Japs. Perfectly simple. It was only a matter of 2500 miles." The reporters and the President laughed when he remarked, "She really believed it! . . . And I think that several people at the table believed it."

This tale received much more attention in the press than did his earlier statement that day, with Roosevelt detractors exploiting the rowboat story to show the President's disdain for the general. Dr. Ross T. McIntire, the President's physician, remarked, however, that Roosevelt "may have smiled now and then at some of the General's purple communiqués, but always there was appreciation of him as a military genius who had worked miracles in the face of heart-breaking odds." The President held a "sincere admiration" for MacArthur, McIntire maintained, "and it was out of his feelings that the General was too valuable to be endangered that he had ordered him to leave the Philippines." A correspondent-friend of the President's later lamented that the nation's press had "in the excitement of joy at the happy solution of the General MacArthur problem failed to give credit to the mastermind that planned it — the brain of Mr. Roosevelt." There is some indication that Roosevelt was sensitive for a while about the neglect of his role in the matter and that he probably agreed with reporter Raymond G. Carroll's assessment: "The real story was the action of the President and not the MacArthur angle." [31]

Japanese newspapers and radio broadcasts in the home islands, as well as in the Philippines and other occupied territories of Asia, emphasized the cowardice of MacArthur and the desertion of the Filipinos and Indonesians by their white supporters. The *Japan Times and Advertiser* in Tokyo announced that MacArthur "fled from his post" and that he and the War Department "admitted the futility of further resisting Japanese pressure in the southern extremity of the Bataan Peninsula." Marshall had anticipated this propaganda barrage and decided that one countermove would be to award the Medal of Honor to MacArthur. He discussed the idea with Stimson and Eisenhower. The latter argued that neither MacArthur nor any other full general was so closely involved with actual battle as to perform the acts of valor that warranted the award, but Marshall pointed out that a precedent was set in 1927 when the medal was given to Lindbergh after his trans-Atlantic flight. Besides, MacArthur already had every major decoration other than the Medal of Honor (and had been nominated twice for it). There was also the need to try "to offset any propaganda by the enemy directed against his leaving his command."

Marshall persuaded Stimson that "this action will meet with

popular approval, both within and without the armed forces, and will have a constructive morale value." In addition, bills were introduced in Congress in January and February by Republican Representatives J. Parnell Thomas of New Jersey and James E. Van Zandt of Pennsylvania to authorize the awarding of the Medal of Honor to MacArthur. Marshall felt that it would be more proper and meaningful if the award came from the President and the War Department rather than from Congress.

On January 31 Marshall sent a radiogram to Sutherland: "The Secretary of War is extremely anxious that no opportunity be overlooked to recognize General MacArthur's gallant and conspicuous leadership by award of the Medal of Honor." He added: "I desire you to transmit at the proper time your recommendations and supporting statement with appropriate description of any act believed sufficient to warrant this award. Acknowledge." [32] Sutherland, undoubtedly in consultation with MacArthur, who may have preferred congressional action, took his time in replying, waiting until March 16 to provide the following information to the Army Chief of Staff:

> I am sure, in the opinion of every officer and man here, no officer has ever more richly deserved the award of the Medal of Honor than General MacArthur. No more appropriate occasion could be found for its award to the General than the time of his arrival in Australia. Such an award would receive the enthusiastic and unanimous approval of both the U.S. Army Forces in the Far East and of the entire Filipino people.
> I would suggest the possibility of the citation being written in Washington due to the certainty of compromising the only code available to us en route if I send a citation before our arrival in Australia. It is suggested that such a citation written in Washington be based upon his utter contempt of danger under terrific bombardments during one of which a two hundred kilogram bomb exploded within thirty feet of him in the open except for momentary shelter taken in a shallow drain beside a sidewalk. His refusal to take cover and his complete calm

on this and many other occasions had a tremendous effect upon the morale of his troops among whom his personal valor was the subject of constant comment; and upon the magnificent leadership and vision that enabled the General to conduct a defense with a partially mobilized and equipped citizen Army that has merited the acclaim of the world and that enabled him to galvanize the spirit of resistance of sixteen million Filipinos.[33]

Marshall thereupon wrote the citation himself, probably relying largely on Sutherland's message. He may also have referred to an earlier message from the Combined Chiefs of Staff to MacArthur in which they told the USAFFE commander that they were "watching with admiration and gratitude your magnificent resistance against overwhelming numbers. Your successful and resolute leadership, and the gallantry of your troops, both United States and Philippine, are an inspiration to us." (The illusion that MacArthur's defense of the Philippines was conducted against massive enemy superiority would persist for some time after the war, until Army historians began to investigate Japanese military records.) Eisenhower may have begrudgingly contributed the idea of including in the citation a tribute to the formation of the Philippine Army, in which he had a major part in 1935–39 when he was MacArthur's chief of staff in Manila. Marshall sent the draft citation to Stimson on March 24, recommending its approval on grounds of its probable beneficial effect on morale at home and abroad and also "because I am certain General MacArthur is deserving of the honor."[34] With Stimson's concurrence, it went to Roosevelt, who was agreeable and announced the awarding of the medal to MacArthur on March 25.

The citation, apparently approved by the President just as Marshall worded it, mentions Bataan but not Corregidor, although the latter was the locale where MacArthur had been under fire:

For conspicuous leadership in preparing the Philippine Islands to resist conquest, for gallantry and intrepidity above and beyond the call of duty in action against invading Japanese forces, and for the heroic conduct of defensive and offensive operations on the Bataan Peninsula. He mobilized, trained, and led an army which has received world acclaim in men and arms. His utter disregard of personal danger under heavy fire and aerial bombardment, his calm judgment in each crisis, inspired his troops, galvanized the spirit of resistance of the Filipino people, and confirmed the faith of the American people in their armed forces.[35]

Somehow the telegram notifying MacArthur of the award was missent and ended up in the hands of the room clerk at the Canberra hotel where MacArthur was staying briefly during his first sessions with the Australian Advisory War Council. The clerk turned it over to correspondent Robert Sherrod, who gave it to the general on the steps of the Parliament building. On Roosevelt's request and as previously mentioned, the American minister in Canberra presided at the hastily arranged and simple ceremony honoring the recipient. MacArthur sent a reply to Marshall and Roosevelt expressing his gratitude for the medal and stating that he was sure "this award was intended not so much for me personally as it is a recognition of the indomitable courage of the gallant army which it was my honor to command." Reporter Frazier Hunt, as well as other MacArthur disciples, later asserted that "Congress openly prodded" the President to bestow the medal, which MacArthur may also have believed. But if Roosevelt was primarily responsible for MacArthur's being in Australia, Marshall deserves the chief credit for introducing the idea of the award. It is regrettable that MacArthur was never fully informed of the roles of Roosevelt and Marshall during this critical period of his career.[36]

When Admiral William H. Standley, the American ambassador to the Soviet Union, returned to Washington in mid-March, he found that "the War Department was worried about the press release and public reaction to MacArthur leaving his command." It is not difficult to understand why Marshall would have considered "popular approval" a factor in recommending the Medal of Honor for MacArthur when the public craze over the USAFFE chief is examined. Beginning about January, and fed by many anti-Roosevelt newspapers and periodicals, the excitement swept the hero-hungry nation throughout the spring of 1942, sometimes manifesting itself in ludicrous extremes.

A *New York Times* reporter discovered that thirteen babies born in the city between March 1 and April 8 were given first and middle names of "Douglas MacArthur," and Josephus Daniels, a veteran Raleigh, North Carolina, journalist who had served as Wilson's Secretary of the Navy, wrote to MacArthur that the naming of newborn infants after the general was spreading like a contagion through the Carolinas also. A state horticultural society announced a new "MacArthur Narcissus," and a council of dancing masters introduced the "MacArthur Glide," a new ballroom dance "not too difficult to learn." The board of commissioners of San Juan, Puerto Rico, changed the name of one of the city's streets to "General MacArthur Street" and directed the city schools to set aside a day "to pay homage to General Douglas MacArthur." Conduit Road in Washington, Belle Isle Bridge in Detroit, and Douglas Dam in Tennessee were among a number of roads and structures renamed "MacArthur." The city fathers of Little Rock joined those who were rededicating sites: City Park, the area around the old arsenal building where he was born, was renamed "MacArthur Park." MacArthur, North Carolina, which had long borne that name, profited from the craze when the Postmaster General announced that the village would at last have its own post office; the first letter canceled at the new post office the next month was a ceremonial message from Stimson and Secretary of the Navy Frank Knox to MacArthur. For a time it seemed that every street and building in the nation would bear the MacArthur

name. Even Corregidor, which was withstanding enemy bombs
and shells, was in danger: Senator W. Lee O'Daniel, a Democrat from Texas, wrote to the President on January 30, "Permit
me to suggest that if practical and possible that you advise him
[MacArthur] on this your birthday that hereafter all American
citizens will refer to the island he and his brave patriotic men
are defending as MacArthur Island." [37]

That spring MacArthur was given as many honorary mem-
berships and awards as a candidate for the presidency garners
on a campaign tour. The Blackfeet Indians of Montana adopted
him as a member of their tribe, naming him Mo-Kahki-Peta,
"Chief Wise Eagle"; a United Press correspondent reported
that "the ceremonial rites were performed before a large portrait of the hero of the Philippines." The general was elected
an honorary member of the Union League Club of Chicago,
the New York Southern Society, the Society of Tammany, and
the Tennessee Society, among other groups. Herbert C.
Hoover, Charles Evans Hughes, Pershing, and other distinguished members of the Union League Club sent congratulatory
messages on his election to that exclusive group. The Tammany
Hall motion, which carried by a unanimous vote, was offered
by Representative Michael J. Kennedy, the head of that powerful Democratic organization. When the National Father's Day
Committee chose him as "Number One Father for 1942," Mac-
Arthur, who managed to find time to answer nearly all of the
various groups and individuals who wrote to him, replied that
"nothing has touched me more deeply." He continued, "It is
my hope that my son when I am gone will remember me not
from the battle but in the home repeating with him our simple
daily prayer, 'Our Father, who art in Heaven.' " [38]

Other distinctions that were bestowed on MacArthur that
spring included medals from Prime Minister Wladyslaw Si-
korski's Polish government-in-exile and the Cuban regime of
President Fulgencio Batista. At the University of Wisconsin's

spring commencement exercises the honorary degree of Doctor of Laws was conferred on MacArthur *in absentia*. Major General George Grunert, whom MacArthur had dismissed as Philippine Department commander in the fall of 1941, accepted the degree in his behalf, and Governor Julius P. Heil delivered an address praising MacArthur as "the ideal of American manhood" for the graduating class.[39] Even after the surrenders of Bataan and Corregidor, the momentum of the popular expressions of hero worship of MacArthur did not lessen. It was reported that mothers were using MacArthur's name to coax their children to eat spinach. An Atlanta junior high school teacher asked his class to name an American possession in the Far East, and one pupil responded "General MacArthur" — a tale that the news services widely publicized. The craze was profitable, too: lapel buttons bearing MacArthur's image sold well in New York City, and Castle Films produced a lucrative home movie on him entitled *America's First Soldier.*

To a lesser extent, Australians also joined the adulation: an Australian fighter pilot asked MacArthur to be the godfather of his newborn son (the general consented), and a lady in Brisbane presented the SWPA commander with a flag that had once belonged to General Stonewall Jackson and somehow had ended up in a seamen's mission chapel in Australia. Down in Panama his heroic image was exploited in another manner: the San Blas Indians made an ornate likeness of the general to ward off evil spirits after an epidemic spread through one of their villages. According to an American missionary who eventually obtained the hand-carved wooden statue, the image was attired in a green cap decorated with a pink band and a white star, a blue coat with pink pockets, a black bow tie, black trousers, and "below the left pocket was what appears to be a German Iron Cross." [40]

Colonel George W. Cocheu, who had been MacArthur's roommate at West Point, wrote to him in May, "In the past few months I have been literally besieged by writers of all kinds regarding information about you." Francis T. Miller's *General Douglas MacArthur, Fighter for Freedom,* the first of a spate of poorly researched, "quickie" biographies of the general, was published on March 25 and quickly became a best seller. The publisher said that Warner Brothers was anxious to make a movie based on the book. Viking Press offered Mac-Arthur a $35,000 advance for his autobiography, pointing out that "the film rights alone to the book would be worth a half million dollars to the General." MacArthur refused to evince interest in any such offers on the grounds that he was "too busy fighting a war." [41]

The nation-wide excitement over MacArthur was fanned and sustained by the highly favorable notices of his exploits as reported in the newspapers and magazines of his old friends William Randolph Hearst, Roy W. Howard, Colonel Robert R. McCormick, and Henry R. Luce. They were not only sympathetic to MacArthur but hostile toward Roosevelt, and sometimes their publications' articles were by implication as vitriolic toward the President as was Father Charles E. Coughlin's *Social Justice,* which stated bluntly that MacArthur had been "thrown to the dogs" by Roosevelt. Journalists of nearly every persuasion outdid themselves in superlatives to describe MacArthur in their headlines: "Destiny's Child," "Lion of Luzon," "Hero of the Pacific," "Incredible Warrior," and so on. The descriptions soared like the advance publicity for a Hollywood extravaganza. The rather staid *New York Times* and the *Times* of London seemed to be competing for the slightest tidbit of news about the general, the latter devoting an article, for instance, to a message that MacArthur sent to the Church of Christ in Little Rock, where he had been christened as an infant.

Even liberal journalists were in support when the 6000-member New York Newspaper Guild voted to award him its most esteemed honor, the "Column One, Page One Plaque," and the Philadelphia Pen and Pencil Club, the oldest newspapermen's organization in the nation, passed a resolution praising his leadership in the war. Walter Lippmann, normally not known for extolling generals, called him "a great commander" with "vast and profound conceptions" who "knows how to find the right men" to command his troops. *The Nation* observed that a "wave of optimism" was sweeping the Allied world "as a result of General MacArthur's assumption of supreme command in the Pacific" (a slight error) and that "psychologically" the people had hungered for the emergence of a military leader with "fighting qualities" like MacArthur. The fact that the dramatic SWPA commander's words and deeds were ready-made for sensational reporting which, in turn, boosted sales, was not emphasized by the newspaper and magazine writers.[42]

Politicians, who are seldom slow to catch the pulse of their constituents, contributed laudatory speeches and resolutions to the MacArthur excitement. Several state legislatures, including those of such politically disparate communities as New York and Mississippi, and some governors and large-city mayors, including Governor Coke Stevenson of Texas and Mayor Fiorello H. LaGuardia of New York, sponsored resolutions or messages of praise honoring the commander. MacArthur's known Republican sympathies and his close ties with Hoover and other Republican party leaders did not deter some Democrats in Congress from uttering paeans that spring, the addresses on MacArthur including ones by Democrats John W. McCormack, John E. Rankin, and Luther Patrick in the House and Elbert D. Thomas and Theodore G. Bilbo in the Senate. Senator Robert M. LaFollette, Jr., son of the great Wisconsin Progressive, sponsored a joint congressional resolution setting aside June 13 as "Douglas MacArthur Day." The date would be the forty-third anniversary of his induction into the Army as a West Point cadet. The resolution won easy passage in both houses on Capitol Hill and was signed by the President, who was probably tiring of the craze; he waited until June 10 to add his signature.[43]

The rapid growth of the MacArthur boom was reflected in various public opinion polls. The National Opinion Research Center conducted a survey in early January in which one of the questions was, "If the Philippines fall, do you think the government should get General Douglas MacArthur out beforehand so he can fight again, or have him stay with his troops to the end?" Those favoring his evacuation and the ones who believed he should stay each constituted 42 per cent, with 16 per cent undecided. Five months later, however, the American public was much more interested in the future of the general. George H. Gallup's American Institute of Public Opinion found in a poll in early May that MacArthur had suddenly emerged as one of the top four men considered by the people as "Presidential material for 1944." [44] In a *Fortune* magazine survey conducted by Elmo B. Roper and printed in May the question was asked, "Would you like to see any of these men given an important position in Roosevelt's war administration?" MacArthur was well ahead of the group, with the combined totals for Wendell L. Willkie and Thomas E. Dewey, the most likely Republican contenders in 1944, barely surpassing the general's showing:[45]

Douglas MacArthur	57.3%	Charles Lindbergh	12.5
Wendell Willkie	35.8	Bernard Baruch	9.9
Henry Ford	30.9	Alfred Landon	8.9
Thomas Dewey	24.7	William O. Douglas	5.7
Herbert Hoover	16.8	John L. Lewis	2.0
F. H. LaGuardia	12.5	None of these	16.0
			233.0%*

(* Since some respondents gave more than one answer, the percentages totaled more than 100%.)

The popular support for an administration post for MacArthur was undoubtedly influenced by a number of public statements issued earlier by leading politicians in favor of bringing the general back to the States in a more responsible political role. At a Lincoln Day dinner in New York, Willkie, the titular head of the Republican Party, delivered a widely quoted speech in which he urged the President to "bring Douglas MacArthur home. Place him at the very top. Keep bureaucratic and political hands off him. Give him the responsibility and the power of coordinating all the armed forces of the nation to their most effective use. Put him in supreme command of our armed forces under the President." Willkie concluded that "then the people of the United States will have reason to hope that skill, not bungling and confusion, directs their efforts." Robert E. Wood, board chairman of Sears, Roebuck and Company and former head of the isolationist America First Committee, said he would be "delighted" if MacArthur "were in command of our whole force," both Army and Navy, at home and abroad. The San Francisco *Examiner,* a Hearst paper, and McCormick's Chicago *Tribune* were among the journals that joined the refrain. The New York *Daily News* wanted Stimson ousted so that MacArthur could be brought back as Secretary of War.[46]

It was probably inevitable that a MacArthur-for-President movement would result from the wave of public adulation, although expressions of political interest in MacArthur during the spring of 1942 were restricted to a few public statements and much informal speculation on the subject. House members Charles I. Faddis, Democrat of Pennsylvania, and Hamilton Fish, Republican of New York, among others, expressed their hopes publicly that MacArthur would run in 1944. Faddis proclaimed in a House speech that he was "the finest leader the United Nations has" and "would make a wonderful President." His remarks produced "a burst of applause" by many congressmen. The president of a leading New York public relations firm and former Willkie supporter wrote the general that he wanted to be his campaign manager: "No one can stop you from being President of the U.S.A. after you have licked the d—— Japs and then go up into Russia and lead the Russians and British to victory over Hitler and the d—— Nazis — a tall order for anyone but you." [47]

Senator Arthur H. Vandenberg, already an influential leader in the Republican Party and on Capitol Hill, disliked Willkie and was searching for someone he could support wholeheartedly against Roosevelt in 1944. The sentiments of many Americans who were disturbed and frustrated by the course of the war since December were epitomized in Vandenberg's letter to a member of his family in early February:

> I certainly envy the guy in uniform who can *see action.* [Millard F.] Tydings made a grand speech in the Senate today — giving everybody *hell.* It's too early for us to break loose on our [Republican] side of the aisle. But it won't be long now. Come what may, I'm going to "speak my piece" one of these days. Roosevelt . . . hasn't demobilized a single one of his old "social revolution" units . . . The country is getting ugly — and I don't blame 'em — *so am I.* Even we in the Senate can't find out what is going on. This is Roosevelt's private war! He sends out troops where he pleases — all over the map — and meanwhile MacArthur fights alone! *Ugh!* If he gets out alive, I think he will be my candidate for President in 1944.[48]

The stirrings of a presidential boom, which MacArthur refused to comment upon, began that spring with disgruntled anti-Roosevelt conservatives who hoped to capitalize on the widespread enthusiasm for the nation's first major heroic commander of the war. At first, the political canard was spread that supplies and reinforcements were withheld from the Philippines "to prevent MacArthur from reaping the political rewards of a military victory there." This should have been refuted by Roosevelt's decision to evacuate the general and by the subsequent award of both the SWPA command and the Medal of Honor. Later in the spring the Roosevelt opposition developed a new story based on the charges that MacArthur should have been made commander of all forces in the Pacific and that the SWPA and POA commands were created for "political reasons" and at Roosevelt's behest.[49] How far this MacArthur-for-President movement would progress if it were based on such negative and often erroneous reports, and without the general's active support, was a matter of conjecture by political observers in the spring of 1942. And MacArthur's virtual monopoly of the stage would be challenged in coming months as American operations expanded into the Mediterranean theater and other areas of the Pacific, producing more commanders with heroic images.

4. The Last Days of Bataan and Corregidor

When MacArthur moved to Australia, he planned to retain control of the Philippine forces through a small advance headquarters on Corregidor headed by Colonel Lewis Beebe, who had been supply officer on the USAFFE staff. Designating Beebe as his deputy chief of staff and recommending his promotion to brigadier general, MacArthur intended that he be responsible chiefly for overseeing the movement and distribution of supplies from the southern Philippines. The USAFFE commander planned to exercise control over operations through four separate commands in the archipelago: Moore's Harbor Defense Force, Wainwright's Luzon Force, Sharp's Mindanao Force, and Chynoweth's Visayan Force.

MacArthur's main hope now lay with the defenders in the southern islands, through whom he expected to channel supplies northward, develop an effective guerrilla movement, and thereby make easier his eventual return to the Philippines by way of Mindanao. The splitting of the forces into four distinct commands, with each commander reporting directly to MacArthur, was intended to prolong resistance. The Japanese would be compelled to defeat the forces *seriatim*. The surrender of all at one time would be impossible to negotiate because the overall commander was thousands of miles away in Australia. In view of the stinging response Roosevelt had made in early February to the neutralization proposal and his order to fight to the end, MacArthur would be in no mood to negotiate the capitulation of any of the four forces. Indeed, he would expect them to avoid surrender under any conditions, just as he had been told to do.[50]

But perhaps because of the disruption caused by his trip to Australia, MacArthur neglected to inform the War Department of his new arrangements in the Philippines. Marshall assumed that Wainwright, the senior officer remaining in the islands, was now in command, and he began sending him messages addressed to the "Commanding General, USAFFE." For several days Beebe was caught in an embarrassing position, until on March 20 the Army chief of staff formally designated Wainwright the commanding general of United States Forces in the Philippines (USFIP) and on that same day the President informed Wainwright of his elevation to lieutenant general. In one of his first acts as USFIP commander Wainwright appointed Beebe as his chief of staff. As yet not informed of the creation of USFIP, MacArthur testily asked Wainwright on whose authority he had made the appointment, whereupon the latter sent him a copy of Marshall's message of the 20th. When MacArthur received it, he hastened to send Marshall a detailed explanation of the command structure he had envisaged for the Philippines.

"Not impressed" by MacArthur's plan, Marshall replied politely but firmly that it would produce an unworkable situation if he were to try to command Philippine operations from far-off Melbourne and that Wainwright would remain in the USFIP post unless MacArthur had strong objections. MacArthur responded that he was "heartily in accord with Wainwright's promotion" and his USFIP assignment was "appropriate." According to at least one account, however, Sutherland and others on MacArthur's staff were "privately more outspoken" and did not consider Wainwright "qualified to take over-all command of the islands," one of their reservations undoubtedly being based upon the general's reputation as a heavy drinker. When Mac-Arthur formally took command of SWPA on April 18, it will be recalled, Wainwright's USFIP was one of the subordinate commands under his authority.[51]

MacArthur's seemingly gracious acceptance of Wainwright's new role was soon shaken by a number of provocations and misunderstandings. At the outset of his new command Wainwright reversed several of MacArthur's policies; for example, he relaxed the former strictures on promotions for officers in the field and he transferred some foodstuffs from the stores on Corregidor back to Bataan. When Wainwright began reporting directly to the War Department and issuing communiqués without clearance through the American headquarters in Melbourne, MacArthur protested strongly to Washington. Marshall tried to effect a compromise by requiring Wainwright to send his communiqués through MacArthur, but permitting the USFIP commander to continue sending routine daily reports directly to the War Department with copies to MacArthur. At the height of the Melbourne-Corregidor friction Marshall himself became entangled with MacArthur: he found it necessary to chide Mac-Arthur for allegedly loose censorship practices in his Melbourne headquarters, which allowed Australian reporters to obtain and publish stories, of possible assistance to the enemy, about recent SWPA air operations and ship routings. MacArthur heatedly replied that the information came from Australian defense officials, and, besides, he could not control the Australian press.[52]

On March 28 Wainwright informed the War Department that food stocks on Bataan would be exhausted by April 15. When MacArthur read a copy of the message, he sent word to Marshall that the supply levels had not been so alarmingly low when he departed, but "it is of course possible that with my departure the vigor of application of conservation may have been relaxed." No supplies had arrived at Corregidor since February 27, as the War Department learned after several queries to Wainwright and MacArthur. Marshall started in motion several hastily conceived plans to have supply-laden submarines, converted destroyers, and other ships once again penetrate the enemy blockade of the Philippines.

One scheme called for eight vessels to make the run to Corregidor loaded with supplies that had been stocked at Cebu. Since air cover was essential, both Marshall and Wainwright asked MacArthur to send some B-17's, which could still operate from Del Monte Field. Although MacArthur pledged that the bombers would be sent, for unknown reasons he and Brett delayed authorization of the air mission until April 7; it took several more days to ready the planes. On the 10th the Japanese invasion of Cebu began, and the waiting ships and their precious cargoes were destroyed to prevent their capture. The following day the B-17's finally arrived at Del Monte, flew several bombing missions in the next few days, and then returned to Australia when it was learned that the remaining USFIP positions on Mindanao were endangered by new Japanese thrusts. On April 13 MacArthur told Marshall, "I regard it as useless to attempt further general supply blockade running." He maintained that the only alternatives left were "a major effort involving grand strategic considerations to be executed within the next two months or the acceptance of ultimate defeat in Manila Bay." Nevertheless, Marshall persisted vainly for another two weeks in trying to get supplies to Wainwright.[53]

After several days of intensive air and artillery bombardment of the USFIP lines on Bataan, Homma launched his long-expected offensive against the Bagac-Orion line on April 3, Good Friday. Employing most of three infantry divisions and one brigade against Parker's II Corps on the east side of the peninsula, Homma saw his men achieve quick penetrations through the lines of the emaciated, exhausted Americans and Filipinos. Within three days the II Corps was in a state of utter collapse. USFIP commanders frantically tried to rally their troops and sometimes succeeded in establishing new defensive positions, only to have the rapidly advancing enemy envelop or overrun them in short order. Roads in the rear areas were jammed with overloaded vehicles, civilians fleeing on foot, and soldiers wandering about in confusion.

On the west side of the peninsula the I Corps was preparing to withdraw to protect its exposed right flank. Wainwright reported on April 7, "The present Japanese attack is the longest sustained drive of the enemy since operations began in Bataan. Waves of shock troops have attacked almost continuously, without regard to casualties." The end was obviously near for the valiant defenders, whose effectiveness was now almost completely vitiated by months of starvation and disease. Major General Edward P. King, Jr., whom Wainwright had appointed as Luzon Force commander in his stead when USFIP was created, faced the most agonizing of all command decisions: whether to fight on to certain defeat or to surrender.[54]

When MacArthur had been presented the Medal of Honor, Wainwright had sent his congratulations, and in his reply of April 4, while thanking him, MacArthur emphasized that "under no conditions should this command be surrendered. If food fails, you will prepare and execute an attack upon the enemy." In fact, MacArthur gave exact instructions on how the I and II Corps were to attack in coordination, envelop Olongapo, seize the enemy supplies in the depot there, and advance into northern Luzon, if necessary resorting to guerrilla operations. In explaining to Marshall his plan for a final attack on Bataan, MacArthur stated that he was "utterly opposed, under any circumstances or conditions to the ultimate capitulation of this command" and would be happy to return to the Philippines and lead the operation himself if the War Department so desired. Marshall replied, "We concur that any action is preferable to capitulation. Should it become necessary for you to direct a last-resort attack with the objectives you outlined, we feel sure that Wainwright and his forces will give a good account of themselves." Besides knowing MacArthur's position on the matter, Wainwright was also aware that the President's "no surrender" message of February had not been rescinded, as Marshall reminded him on March 24.[55]

Obediently but reluctantly Wainwright relayed the order to attack to his Luzon Force commander on April 7. King, as well as his corps and division leaders, responded in exasperation that an offensive operation was out of the question with the troops in such pitiful condition and with entire units disintegrating as organized combat forces. At midnight of April 8–9 King assembled his staff and announced that he had decided to capitulate. He was not going to inform Wainwright, he said, "because I do not want him to be compelled to assume any part of the responsibility." The next morning King started toward the Japanese lines to arrange terms of surrender. "A terrible silence settled over Bataan about noon on April 9," said Wainwright. Numbering between 71,000 and 80,000 troops at the time, the Luzon Force became the largest American army in history to surrender.[56]

MacArthur was shocked at the news and demanded of Wainwright a full explanation of King's conduct. The USFIP general replied that he had "expressly forbidden such action" and that King "did not personally broach the subject of capitulation to me." He went on to describe the chaotic situation that had existed on Bataan and stressed that King's force had faced certain destruction "in two or three days" had it not surrendered, Wainwright refused to criticize King because "the decision which he was forced to make required unusual courage and strength of character." If MacArthur was upset with Wainwright and King, Wainwright, in turn, became embittered when he received a message from Roosevelt on April 9 after the latter had learned of King's action: in it the President said he had decided to rescind his "no surrender" order and "to leave to your best judgment any decisions affecting the future of the Bataan garrison."

The message had been sent through MacArthur who had delayed in relaying it to Corregidor. Several days after the surrender MacArthur explained to Wainwright that the message "was not received until after the fall of Bataan and consequently was not forwarded as it referred entirely to the possibility of surrender on Bataan." According to a friend of Wainwright's, the only ill feeling the USFIP commander bore toward MacArthur after the war stemmed from this incident. Nevertheless, at the time misunderstandings were put aside temporarily as both Wainwright and MacArthur prepared messages on the disaster. The former wrote to Roosevelt, "I have done all that could have been done to hold Bataan, but starved men without air and with inadequate field artillery support cannot endure the terrific aerial and artillery bombardment that my troops were subjected to." MacArthur issued a press release that stated in part: "The Bataan force went out as it would have wished, fighting to the end its flickering hope. No army has ever done so much with so little and nothing became it more than its last hour of trial and agony." [57]

The Corregidor garrison fully realized that with the fall of Bataan the enemy would soon invade the island. On May 2 Beebe, without Wainwright's authorization, sent a special plea to Sutherland to prevail upon MacArthur to evacuate the USFIP commander. Sutherland responded that he had discussed the proposal with his chief, who was agreeable to evacuating Beebe, but that "General Wainwright was assigned to his command by the War Department and General MacArthur has no authority to relieve him therefrom." Meanwhile, Homma had been preparing cautiously for the assault on the bastion; for three weeks a bombardment of "unrelenting fury" by Japanese aircraft and artillery pulverized whatever defenses were left exposed.

Then on the night of May 5–6 Homma sent a regiment ashore on the eastern end of the island. For a while there was doubt that the attackers could secure a beachhead, but, as in the last days on Bataan, the USFIP troops were physically unfit and lacked adequate firepower to fight a sustained action. As Japanese tank, artillery, and troop reinforcements landed, early on the 6th, Wainwright concluded that the end was at hand for his garrison. In Malinta Tunnel lay hundreds of wounded and ill soldiers; there were also many civilians and nurses who would be helpless if the enemy broke through to the laterals.

In his final message to the President that morning Wainwright reported that he was preparing to ask for terms of surrender and did so "with broken heart and head bowed in sadness but not in shame." At noon on May 6 he ordered the white flag hoisted over Corregidor. MacArthur shortly issued a statement: "Corregidor needs no comment from me. It has sounded its own story at the mouth of its guns. It has scrolled its own epitaph on enemy tablets. But through the bloody haze of its last reverberating shot, I shall always seem to see a vision of grim, gaunt, ghastly men, still unafraid." [58]

In the final hours on Corregidor Wainwright had sent a message to Sharp, whom he had earlier placed in command again of all Mindanao and Visayan troops: he released Sharp from his authority and told him he could act on his own. On May 7, however, Wainwright delivered a terse radio address in Manila in which he announced that he had resumed authority over the southern forces and ordered Sharp to surrender his troops. The USFIP commander made the broadcast on Homma's demand and in fear that, unless all forces promptly surrendered, the Japanese would renew fighting on Corregidor, a course that would lead to a massacre since the American and Filipino soldiers had destroyed their heavy weapons and stacked their light arms.

Actually no direct evidence exists that Homma made such a threat. But Wainwright's action left Sharp in a quandary, particularly since he also received on the 7th a message from MacArthur stating that "orders emanating from General Wainwright have no validity. If possible, separate your force into small elements and initiate guerrilla operations. You, of course, have full authority to make any decisions that [the] immediate emergency may demand." MacArthur told Marshall, "I place absolutely no credence in the alleged broadcast by Wainwright." Later, when it appeared that the broadcast was authentic, MacArthur advised the War Department, "I believe Wainwright has temporarily become unbalanced and his condition renders him susceptible of enemy use." The SWPA chief was unaware that Wainwright's conduct had been dictated by his fear of a massacre of the 11,000 persons on Corregidor.[59]

When one of Wainwright's staff officers flew to Mindanao and explained the circumstances to Sharp, the Mindanao general was persuaded that the threat to the Corregidor personnel was real, so on May 10 he issued orders to his commanders to surrender. Chynoweth on Cebu, as well as his subordinate commanders in the Visayas, refused to believe that the surrender order was valid: Wainwright and Sharp were either acting under duress or without MacArthur's authorization, they reasoned. Chynoweth, the Visayan commander, never received any direct word from MacArthur and finally concluded, after talking to a courier from Sharp, that "maybe MacArthur would rather have us surrender"; he and most of his Cebu troops capitulated on May 16. Two days later Colonel Albert F. Christie surrendered his Panay garrison after repeated earlier refusals to accept Sharp's order, at one point boldly charging, the compliance "tends toward treason without the sanction of the War Department through MacArthur." The USFIP units on Leyte and Samar capitulated on May 26 and the Negro troops on June 3. Except for a few battalions that never capitulated, the small units on the rest of the southern islands surrendered by June 9. Homma, who had been expected by Tokyo to conquer the archipelago in less than two months, was soon recalled to Japan and placed on inactive status for the rest of the war.

MacArthur remained convinced that his plan of four separate Philippine forces after mid-March would have averted the wholesale surrender that the creation of USFIP had enabled Homma to exploit. "It was not a very creditable thing," he told one of his generals in March, 1945, referring to Wainwright's orders to Sharp to surrender. As the conversation continued, it was apparent that MacArthur still harbored strong feelings about several aspects of the fall of the Philippines.[60] Indeed, it seems that no major commander on either side emerged from this campaign with his reputation unsullied.

MacArthur had awarded the Distinguished Service Cross to Wainwright in January, but when Marshall asked him in the summer of 1942 to recommend the USFIP commander for the Medal of Honor, he adamantly refused. The fact that Marshall presented him with the proposed citation, which had been drafted without MacArthur's counsel, antagonized him. By then, too, MacArthur had learned some of the details of the so-called Bataan "Death March," the forced march of the Luzon Force prisoners from southern Bataan to Camp O'Donnell in the Central Luzon Plain, during which an estimated 5000 to 11,000 American and Filipino soldiers died or were killed.

Besides being embittered over the surrender order to Sharp, MacArthur was now persuaded, more than ever, that if Wainwright had compelled King to launch the Olongapo attack and breakout, many of those men need not have died on the Death March but could have escaped to become an effective guerrilla force in northern Luzon. When he answered Marshall about the Medal of Honor, his words about Wainwright were hostile: he did not think Wainwright deserved the award and argued that if it were given to him an injustice would be done to other USFIP soldiers who were more deserving. Marshall, who had affidavits from three USFIP colonels recommending Wainwright for the medal, discussed the matter with Stimson. The Secretary of War favored making the award in spite of MacArthur's feelings, but later he and Marshall decided to postpone it. "Neither Marshall nor Stimson," according to the former's chief biographer, "changed his mind," and, thanks to their efforts, Wainwright finally received the Medal of Honor after the war.[61]

In the spring of 1942 many Americans viewed the strategic significance of the stand in the Philippines as greater than it proved to be in the long course of the Pacific conflict. Pro-MacArthur writers have preserved this exaggerated notion of the campaign's importance. Willoughby, for instance, claims in his work on MacArthur that the Bataan-Corregidor operation "became a decisive factor in the ultimate winning of the war." First, he says, "it gave the United States a needed image of courage." Second, "the Japanese timetable, which called for quick conquests throughout a great fan-shaped territory . . . was disrupted in a way that was to prove crucial." Thus, according to Willoughby, because of the prolonged Philippine defense, "the Japanese never managed to detach enough men, planes, ships, and materiel to nail down Guadalcanal. Nor did they ever succeed in mopping up New Guinea or seizing a foothold in Australia." [62]

It is quite true, as confirmed in the Army's official chronicle, that "for an Allied world surfeited on gloom, defeat, and despair, the epic of Bataan and Corregidor was a symbol of hope and a beacon of success for the future." The Japanese war machine advancing through Southeast Asia had been halted and shorn of its aura of invincibility only in the Philippines. For five months the enemy had been denied use of one of the Pacific's finest harbors because of the stubborn, courageous resistance of American and Filipino soldiers, the real heroes of the Philippine campaign.

But since the Japanese enveloped the archipelago and continued moving southward, the Philippine operation was prolonged, in part, because of Tokyo's higher priority on conquering the East Indies; Homma, for one thing, lost a division and an air group at a critical time when they were transferred south. Moreover, the defense of the Philippines did not materially affect Japanese plans for the Solomons or New Guinea, where they had months after Corregidor's fall to build up defenses before the Allied counteroffensives would begin. As for the global context, the Philippines "did not in 1942 possess great strategic significance," according to the official Army history of the campaign.[63]

In retrospect, compared to the British operations in Southeast Asia in 1941–42, the defense of the Philippines has not appeared impressive to some authorities, including Australia's chief official historian of the war, who observes, "It cost a far stronger Japanese army as many days of actual combat to take Malaya and Singapore as it cost Homma to take Bataan and Corregidor." The American Army's principal authority on the reconquest of the Philippines in 1945 commends the Japanese for not copying MacArthur's example of withdrawing into the Bataan cul-de-sac, but rather moving into the northern Luzon mountains and valleys where holding defensive positions and gathering sustenance from the countryside were more practicable.[64] Apparently in 1941 no American planners, in Manila or Washington, considered that region a possible location for defensive operations since their minds were absorbed with the need to deny the enemy access to Manila Bay.

There is no question that MacArthur made mistakes aplenty — his poorly conceived beach defense plan and its disastrous effect on supplies, his hesitancy in the Clark Field incident, and his isolation from his field commanders and troops, to name a few. But his presence was a primary reason why the resistance, though virtually hopeless from the start, was successful for so long. Most of the defenders were Filipino troops, and the vast majority of them were dedicated to MacArthur with a zeal and loyalty that they would have felt toward no other American. If he momentarily flirted with Quezon's neutralization scheme, it was also MacArthur who inspired and prodded Quezon and his Filipinos to continue their support of the fight against the invaders.

It must be remembered, too, that MacArthur did everything within his power — and his influence in Washington was far greater than that of any other officer in the Pacific — to try to get reinforcements sent to the islands. In fact, he did so with such vehemence and persistence that it lost him personally no small amount of sympathy among certain key Army and Navy leaders in the Pentagon. In addition, it should be pointed out that he was neither the cowardly Dugout Doug, as some resentful soldiers claimed, nor the Lion of Luzon, as enthusiastic supporters in the States called him. His departure from Corregidor, since it was made under presidential orders, marked him as neither coward nor opportunist despite his detractors' comments.

Because he rarely revealed his inner turmoil, little is known of his emotional adjustment to the Philippine tragedy and of how deeply the traumatic experience scarred him. But it was obvious to everyone by the time he reached Australia that, rather than floundering in remorse and self-pity, he was eagerly and confidently planning for the day when he would go back to the islands in triumph. In his later years MacArthur considered the Philippine campaign of 1941–42 one of the most critical phases of his personal and professional life. When the general sat down to write his memoirs toward the end of his

long career, it was with careful deliberation that he decided to
devote three of the ten chapters to World War II and one of
those three solely to the fall of the Philippines. As will be seen
in the subsequent account in this volume of his career during the war against Japan, that experience of defeat cast a long
shadow over his personal conduct, his relations with his contemporaries, and the strategic planning of the Allied chiefs in the
Pacific conflict. The return to the Philippines became his obsession — and his redemption.

PART II

Papuan Campaign

CHAPTER IV

Offensive Preparations

1. Turning Point

HAVING ESTABLISHED BASES on the Northeast New Guinea coast
in early March, the Japanese next planned to launch seaborne
invasions of Tulagi in the Solomons and Port Moresby in Papua
during the first half of May. Since they had broken the Japanese
naval code, the Americans were soon alerted, and submarine
and aerial reconnaissance from April 10 on confirmed the
build-up of forces at Rabaul. It was known, too, that some
enemy naval units were coming from as far away as the Bay of
Bengal. Willoughby predicted that they would attack Queensland, Australia, but actually the high command in Tokyo had
no plans for invading that continent despite proposals advanced
by some of its venturesome naval officers. As air raids on Port
Moresby mounted in late April, MacArthur told Brett to concentrate his bombers at the Queensland and Moresby bases, and
to arrange for antiaircraft reinforcements to be rushed to the
latter.

Meanwhile, Nimitz agreed to dispatch Rear Admiral Frank
Jack Fletcher's Task Force 17 to the Solomon and Coral seas; it
included the carriers *Lexington* and *Yorktown* and supporting

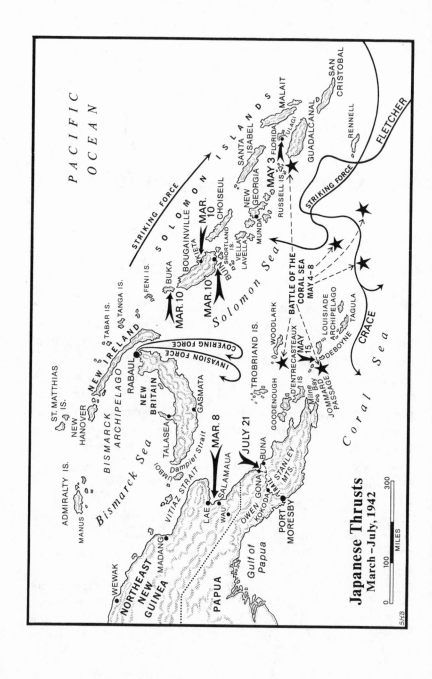

Japanese Thrusts
March – July, 1942

cruisers, destroyers, and auxiliary vessels. Leary, the SWPA naval chief, sent most of his small fleet to rendezvous with Task Force 17; the Australian-American group of cruisers and destroyers was commanded by Rear Admiral J. G. Crace of the Royal Navy. Also Rockwell, now commanding one of the SWPA submarine groups, sent his submarines to patrol the routes into the Coral Sea that were most likely to be used by the enemy.[1] Thus in the first major engagement since the establishment of the new American commands in the Pacific, Nimitz's forces would be operating in MacArthur's theater. The naval elements would be under Nimitz's strategic command, and the land-based aircraft and ground forces would be controlled by MacArthur. It was to be an interesting test of whether cooperation could prove effective in lieu of unity of command, the traditional military principle that had been warily laid aside by the Joint Chiefs in drafting the March directive for the two Pacific commanders.

When he was sailing south of the Solomon Islands on May 3, Fletcher received a message from MacArthur that SWPA planes had spotted enemy transports debarking troops off Tulagi. The *Yorktown* sped north; its planes attacked the invasion force but did little damage. In response, the main Japanese striking force, which lay northeast of the Solomons and included two large carriers, started south at full speed. MacArthur's bombers undertook reconnaissance missions over a wide region and bombed enemy bases in the Lae, Rabaul, and Bougainville areas, but neither they nor Fletcher's search planes uncovered the enemy surface units. The Moresby invasion force, consisting of eleven troop transports and several destroyers, was headed from Rabaul toward Jomard Passage, off the southern tip of Papua. Moving parallel to it on the east was a covering force made up of a carrier and several cruisers and destroyers. The Japanese striking force was speeding down the east side of the Solomons; it turned west on May 5, passing the southernmost of the Solomon Islands and entering the Solomon Sea.

B-25 medium bombers out of Townsville and Moresby sighted enemy ships north of Jomard Passage and others south of Bougainville on May 4 and 5. Their reports precipitated a number of missions by SWPA heavy and medium bombers in the next three days, and the airmen claimed that their bombs hit several ships. Postwar interrogations of Japanese officers and studies of their official files, however, showed that no serious damage was inflicted by any land-based aircraft. More significant, Brett did not relay news of the early sightings to Fletcher, whose scout planes finally spotted the Moresby invasion force on the 7th. Naval aircraft sank the covering force's carrier and another ship, whereupon the invasion force turned back to Rabaul.

While these raids were under way, the American carriers were open to attack, but the Japanese striking force did not notice them and concentrated instead on sinking a destroyer and an oil tanker nearby. When the Japanese striking force commander learned of the air attacks against the Moresby invasion fleet, he immediately sent out planes again to locate and bomb the carriers. But it was almost dusk and the search proved fruitless. So uncoordinated was the Japanese planning that the striking force, which boasted the greatest firepower of the three enemy groups, rendered no assistance to the Moresby invasion force, whose withdrawal negated the fulfillment of the primary objective of the whole operation.[2]

Early on May 7 Fletcher had ordered Crace's support group to hasten northwest to Jomard Passage and attack the Moresby invasion force. Beginning at about 2:00 P.M., three waves of Japanese bombers dropped bombs and torpedoes in the midst of Crace's fast-moving ships, which amazingly survived the raids without suffering a scratch. Within a few minutes of the departure of the enemy aircraft, however, three SWPA B-26 medium bombers attacked two cruisers and a destroyer of the support group, sinking none but causing nine casualties among the sailors. The airmen returned to Townsville and duly reported their attack on "enemy" ships. Crace later remarked, "Fortunately their bombing, in comparison with that of the Japanese formation a few moments earlier, was disgraceful!" The airmen had obligingly taken photographs of the vessels attacked; they were clearly Crace's ships. But the Allied Air Forces records at Townsville showed only that eight B-17's had attacked some enemy vessels about ninety miles from Crace's location at the time of the mistaken-identity incident; no B-26's were listed as having been in the area.

Brett firmly denied that his aircraft had bombed the ships, and he refused Leary's offer of a plan "to improve Army recognition of naval vessels." MacArthur remained in Melbourne during the entire Coral Sea battle; his office diary briefly notes conferences with Brett at noon on May 8 and with Leary an hour later. No evidence has been uncovered indicating MacArthur's opinion of or intervention in the affair, but the shameful matter undoubtedly did not improve his regard for either Brett or Leary. Fortunately for relations between MacArthur and Nimitz, the episode did not involve Fletcher's ships.[3]

The height of the battle of the Coral Sea occurred on May 8, by which time both sides had finally located each other's carriers. About 240 carrier-based aircraft, half of them Japanese, were in action that busy morning in dogfights, bombing missions, and torpedo raids. The Americans came out slightly ahead on enemy aircraft destroyed, shooting down forty-three planes while losing thirty-three of their own. One Japanese carrier was heavily damaged, but both American carriers were hit. About noon the Japanese broke off the engagement and their ships turned north toward Rabaul. Several hours after the aerial action had quieted, a motor generator inadvertently left running on the crippled *Lexington* ignited gasoline vapors; a series of explosions followed and uncontrollable fires spread across the carrier. The *Lexington* was abandoned without loss of life and an American destroyer sank the flaming ship with torpedoes. Until then the losses of the two sides were about even, but the sinking of the *Lexington* gave the tactical victory to the Japanese. Strategically, the Allies won because the Moresby invasion had been prevented.

The Coral Sea battle, which was actually fought in the Solomon Sea, was the first naval engagement in which all losses were caused by air action; the opposing surface craft did not fire a single shot at each other nor did they come within sight of each other. In the judgment of the foremost naval historian of the war, "So many mistakes were made on both sides that it might be called the Battle of Naval Errors; but more were made by the enemy, and he failed to profit by them." In lessons absorbed by the Americans, the battle was "an indispensable preliminary" to the triumph at Midway a month later. Because of pilot losses and ship damage, neither of the enemy's large carriers in the Coral Sea action would be ready in time to participate in the Midway operation.

Since the defeat of the seaborne thrust at Port Moresby immediately followed the surrender of Corregidor, the Coral Sea news had a positive impact on Allied morale, particularly in Australia, where the population had feared an invasion. MacArthur's early reaction was that a tactical as well as a strategic victory had been won; judging from reports prepared before the fog of battle had cleared, he thought that no American ships had been lost and that two enemy carriers had been sunk. According to Brigadier General Robert H. Van Volkenburgh, who headed the SWPA component antiaircraft command, MacArthur relished telling the story of how his planes discovered the Japanese ships: "He told it all in the most wonderfully theatrical fashion. I enjoyed every second of it." MacArthur was still pleased when he wrote Nimitz on May 19: "[I] consider your forces in [the] recent action were handled with marked skill and fought with admirable courage and tenacity. [I] am most anxious to perfect air-naval cooperation . . . Call upon me freely.

You can count upon my most complete and active cooperation." [4]

The Army Air Force's contribution had been limited; its
reconnaissance work had been significant, but its bombing missions against moving surface craft had done little damage. The
airmen had had little training in ship recognition, and neither
Brett nor Fletcher had any information on each other's battle
plans and movements; no identification signals between aircraft and ships had been established. Lack of coordination between Brett's units and the naval forces prevented pursuit of
the withdrawing enemy units. Brett's B-17's, for instance, might
well have finished off the large Japanese carrier crippled on the
8th after it returned to Rabaul, but for some time Fletcher did
not inform the Allied Air Forces that the important vessel had
been hit badly and probably would soon be an inviting stationary target in harbor. After studying the battle reports Nimitz
told King on May 20 that "much must be done to bring about
coordination" between fleet task forces and commanders of
land-based aircraft involved in the same operation.[5]

In a message to Marshall a week earlier MacArthur implied
that much of the confusion attending the Coral Sea battle could
have been averted if he, as commander of the theater in which
the action took place, had commanded both the land-based aircraft and the naval forces:

> There is an element of danger in the coordination of opera-
> tions of this kind in that a task force commander is responsible
> only for immediate tactical execution, but movements of this
> nature to exercise a successful influence must be oriented with
> the past and the future with regard to the campaign being car-
> ried out in the area affected. Coordination of effort between
> air and naval forces can be effected without difficulty, but in
> any case in which land forces are involved the operations must
> be handled as to planning and execution by the commander of
> the area in which the operation takes place.[6]

The Joint Chiefs in Washington immediately assigned their Joint Staff Planning Committee "to draw up a directive for effecting closer cooperation in joint operations in the Pacific Theater." [7] But the problem would continue to plague both planning and operations throughout the war against Japan, and in the fall of 1944, as he sat on Leyte while the greatest naval battle in history developed, MacArthur would recall his repeated warnings about the dangers if unity of command in the Pacific were not achieved.

After the Coral Sea battle Japanese radio propaganda, which was beamed daily to Australia, took a turn that would characterize its treatment of defeats for the next three years: each new loss produced an increase of bravado and efforts not merely to cover up the defeat but to prove it was a victory. Thus Japanese propagandists repeatedly boasted of the great triumph in the Coral Sea and quoted an Imperial General Headquarters report that the United States had lost two carriers and a battleship in the action. This new propaganda phenomenon in May, together with demands by the Australian press and public for news of the battle that they thought might result in an invasion of their shores, led MacArthur, through Diller's public relations office, to issue a number of dramatically worded communiqués about the course of the naval battle and its consequences. On the other hand, the Navy was reticent about issuing press releases on the action, in part for fear of revealing something about the fleet that might assist the enemy.

As MacArthur's communiqués poured forth and were repeated widely in the press in all Allied nations, not only the Navy in the Pacific and its leaders in Washington but also the President himself came to resent them and to assume that the SWPA commander was trying to garner for himself the glory of defeating the Moresby invasion armada. On May 18 Roosevelt wrote to Prime Minister Mackenzie King of Canada, "As you have seen by the press, Curtin and MacArthur are obtaining most of the publicity. The fact remains, however, that the naval operations were conducted solely through the Hawaii command!" [8]

Alleged news leaks by MacArthur's general headquarters (GHQ), which had earlier produced friction with the War Department, reached a new height during the Coral Sea battle. A press dispatch bearing the dateline "Allied Headquarters, Australia, April 27" revealed details of the enemy naval concentration under way at Rabaul. Marshall told MacArthur that the Japanese must be aware that reconnaissance alone had not obtained such data and they "would be justified in believing their codes had been broken." The Army chief of staff frankly stated, "This together with previous incidents indicates that censorship of news emanating from Australia including that from your headquarters is in need of complete revision."

MacArthur responded that "a careful check" showed that "such material was not given out by direct communique, inference or discussion" by his GHQ. He said that reporters used the term "Allied Headquarters, Australia" loosely and it "does not imply any control or approval by military authorities." He traced the dispatch in dispute to an Associated Press correspondent; it was "released by an Australian censor without reference to any military authorities." MacArthur continued, "As I have explained previously, it is utterly impossible for me under the authority I possess to impose total censorship in this foreign country." [9]

At MacArthur's request the Australian Advisory War Council took an unprecedented action on May 6 by investing him with broad powers over publicity and censorship relating to SWPA operations. Henceforth Australian newspapers would have to rely almost solely on his GHQ communiqués for news of the war in the Southwest Pacific. According to an official Australian chronicle, "This control was exercised with a free interpretation of 'operations,' and often in an arbitrary manner, and was the cause of considerable irritation in both American and overseas circles." Within a week the War Council may have regretted its action. A SWPA GHQ communiqué reported that ten enemy ships were sunk and five badly damaged in the Coral Sea action, and the War Council was grievously upset when it later learned the true story of the battle. On May 13 it concluded that the results of the battle of the Coral Sea were "rather disappointing, the more so as we had ample warning . . . As it was, an opportunity to inflict [heavy] losses on the enemy was lost." Curtin defended the role of SWPA aircraft, but the War Council expressed doubt "as to whether the maximum degree of attack by land-based aircraft had been brought to bear to counterbalance the enemy's superiority in aircraft carriers."

On the day after the naval engagement had ended, Marshall sent a message to MacArthur telling him of King's and Nimitz's irritation with his communiqués: "The commander-in-chief of the Pacific Fleet considers that premature release of information concerning action of forces under his command imposes definite risks upon participating forces and jeopardizes the successful continuation of fleet task force operations." On King's demand, in the future all news of operations involving Nimitz's forces "will be released through the Navy Department only." [10] MacArthur's reply was a prompt and vigorous defense of his policy:

> Absolutely no information has been released from my headquarters with reference to action taking place in the northeastern sector of this area except the official communiques. By no stretch of possible imagination do they contain anything of value to the enemy nor anything not fully known by him. The release of such information by this headquarters is specifically provided for in the general directive approved by all the nations concerned.
>
> The forces engaged in the present action involve all my naval force, which includes the major portion of the Australian Navy; a large part of my air force, involving many Australian

components; and my ground forces, which are the actual objective of the hostile movement and which are almost exclusively Australian. This is an action in Australian waters involving Australian forces and the very fate of the Australian people and continent, and it is manifestly absurd that some technicality of administrative process should attempt to force them to await the pleasure of the United States Navy Department for news of action . . .

If I do not issue communiques involving this area, such control as I have of the situation will entirely disappear. The Australians will resume their own publicity, and their views on censorship differ so materially from the standard desired that the information that will flow out will be infinitely more liberal than at present. My communiques and all information from this headquarters are given only in the broadest generalities. They emanate personally from me and so far as secrecy is concerned cannot be objectionable . . . Under these circumstances I feel that it is absolutely essential that communiques such as those put forth be issued as circumstances demand.[11]

The Army chief of staff did not respond to this radiogram, but five days later MacArthur, in a more conciliatory mood, informed Marshall that he had had "a series of conferences" with Curtin on "limiting the freedom of publicity in this country." Now MacArthur was "hopeful that real results will be obtained." For the time being the matter ended there, but it was by no means permanently resolved. Coincidentally, in its usual babbling manner Radio Tokyo on May 31 reported that "MacArthur is now a nervous wreck." [12] Had the battle over censorship continued much longer than it did, the Japanese propaganda might have come closer to the truth than Tokyo realized.

American correspondent Theodore H. White, then on assignment in Australia, wrote to a friend on May 11, "I half expect the Japanese to come down again, for they're not like ones to be smacked and not nurse a grudge. But if they don't come I think there'll be damned little action out of here for a hell of a long time." White's first sentence probably voiced the consensus of most persons in Australia at that time; his second sentence proved to be an accurate prediction of SWPA developments. The Japanese military and naval leaders in Tokyo, despite the recent setback, were still determined to take Moresby; their revised plans called for that undertaking to follow invasions of New Caledonia, Fiji, and Samoa. But Admiral Isoroku Yamamoto, the brilliant commander of the Japanese Combined Fleet, persuaded his superiors in Tokyo to approve his ambitious plan to seize Midway and the Aleutians, as well as his Central and North Pacific operations, which would precede further thrusts in the southern regions. Yamamoto confidently predicted that he would be able to lure Nimitz's Pacific Fleet into a decisive confrontation and administer an overwhelming defeat that would make the South and Southwest Pacific operations much easier.

Meanwhile, in Washington, about the time of the Coral Sea battle, a climax of sorts had been reached in Roosevelt's decision-making on Pacific-versus-Europe priorities. The many messages from MacArthur, Evatt, and Curtin urging greater reinforcements for the Southwest Pacific had been a factor in influencing the President briefly to consider siphoning to the Pacific some shipments scheduled for Operation Bolero, the massive build-up in Britain for the eventual invasion of the European continent. After taking counsel with Marshall and King, however, Roosevelt reaffirmed his commitment to the Europe-first policy and decided for the present not to add to the forces and supplies already in or en route to the Pacific theaters. In a message to MacArthur on May 6 the President said that he appreciated MacArthur's critical needs, but in grand strategy the logistical build-up for a second front in Europe took precedence. He added, "I know that you will feel the effect of this . . . I well realize your difficult problems, and that you have to be an ambassador as well as supreme commander."

MacArthur continued to maintain that the next likely Japanese thrust would be against Australia or New Guinea, but American cryptanalysts' decodings of enemy messages pointed clearly toward a major strike against Midway. With no significant increases in reinforcements expected soon in his theater, Nimitz anxiously searched for ways to strengthen his forces. Persuaded by King to do so, the Joint Chiefs temporarily assigned to the Central Pacific Area several squadrons of heavy and medium bombers that were due to go to MacArthur. Also, Fletcher's task force was recalled from the Southwest Pacific to assist in the impending engagement.

MacArthur was deeply displeased with these actions and cautioned the War Department that he would face a catastrophe unless he received both carriers and large air reinforcements. On May 23 he told Marshall, "The Atlantic and the Indian oceans should temporarily be stripped" in order to provide naval and air forces to ensure Australia's security. "If this is not done," he warned, "much more than the fate of Australia will be jeopardized. The United States itself will face a series of such disasters and a crisis of such proportions as she never faced in the long years of her existence." Marshall patiently explained that a monumental crisis was already shaping west of Midway, where the Pacific Fleet's outnumbered ships and planes were assembling to meet Yamamoto's oncoming force.[13]

As the great air-naval battle of Midway turned out, it was most fortunate, despite MacArthur's earlier dissatisfaction, that the air units scheduled for his theater had been retained in Hawaii and that Task Force 17 had departed from the Solomons area in time to participate in the Midway action. It took everything the Pacific Fleet could muster, from individual heroics to brilliant tactical decisions — together with Japanese mistakes and a lot of luck — to defeat Yamamoto's armada. Like the Coral Sea engagement, the battle was largely decided by the action of carrier aircraft, although this time submarines also played an important role. After losing four carriers, a heavy cruiser, 322 aircraft, and 3500 lives during the wide-ranging combat of June 3–6, Yamamoto decided to turn back toward Japan, but not before small Japanese forces had captured Attu and Kiska in the Aleutians — small compensation for the disaster suffered by his fleet. Nimitz's forces, ably led by Rear Admiral Raymond A. Spruance in the naval-air actions, had lost a carrier (*Yorktown*), a destroyer, 150 planes, and 307 men. Forgetting the antagonisms of previous weeks, MacArthur sent his congratulations to Nimitz: "The splendid victory at Midway has aroused the greatest enthusiasm throughout this area . . . My own pride and satisfaction is [*sic*] boundless. We will not fail."

The loss of first-line carrier pilots was a disaster from which Yamamoto's fleet would not completely recover. As Allied submarine and air attacks later cut oil shipments from the East Indies, the Japanese pilot training program would be crippled further, and the enemy would be compelled more frequently to employ pilots with far less training than their American opponents. Moreover, four days after the Midway battle ended, Imperial General Headquarters ordered a two months' postponement of the invasions of New Caledonia, Samoa, and Fiji, and later permanently canceled the operations.

The Japanese high command did not give up its intention to seize Moresby, but after Midway the plan for another seaborne invasion had to be abandoned in favor of one for a more difficult overland drive across the Owen Stanley Mountains to the Papuan port.[14] This ground operation in New Guinea would be the last major offensive by the Japanese in the Southwest Pacific, although few of the leaders in Tokyo in June, 1942, fully comprehended the far-reaching consequences of the Midway disaster. Henceforth not they but the Allied commanders would concentrate more on planning and preparations for offensive operations. The Pacific war had reached a turning point.

2. *Preparing for the Next Encounter*

During his stay in Melbourne, from March to July, 1942, two contradictory images of MacArthur emerged, the picture usually affected by the closeness of the observer to the SWPA commander. His pronouncements and public demeanor impressed the Australians as those of a dynamic, determined general who was supremely confident that he could lead his forces to victory. Nelson Johnson, American minister to Australia, reported to the State Department, "I do not think that any other person could quite have caught the imagination of this people like MacArthur . . . No Britisher could, that is certain. It is doubtful that any Australian has the confidence of the whole people."

MacArthur Day, June 13, was celebrated as widely and joyously in Australia as in his own country. That day programs and rallies in Melbourne, Canberra, Sydney, Brisbane, and other Australian cities produced innumerable speeches in his honor, and flattering messages poured into his office from persons high and low. Curtin was host at a grand party at the Menzies Hotel for the general and also played a prominent part in several MacArthur Day programs. He declared in one speech, "Were these times of peace, the United States could have no more popular ambassador than this soldier, who has won not only our hearts but our strongest regard." In an opinion survey conducted by the Sydney *Daily Telegraph* two months later, the persons polled were asked to name the three most important public figures in Australia. MacArthur was the leader with 60 per cent of the voters listing him, Prime Minister Curtin was named by only 41 per cent, and no one else was near these two in the poll's results. There is little doubt that MacArthur's presence in Australia had boosted the morale of that nation and that his SWPA leadership had strong public support.[15]

The other image of him, revealed principally in his private talks and messages, and by his remoteness, was that of a tired, bitterly disappointed commander whose desire to undertake a major offensive was being frustrated by Washington and London leaders who discounted the relative significance of his theater. According to Willoughby, the apparent procrastination of the Joint Chiefs in approving an offensive plan of action for his SWPA forces produced occasional moods of despair in MacArthur, but, as on Corregidor, few persons detected them.

May and June marked a period of particular sadness and distress for him. He was shocked by the death of General George in a freakish airplane accident on the ground. George had been the only airman to gain entry into the inner circle of MacArthur's close friends. At his funeral on May 4 MacArthur was so grief-stricken that he was barely able to talk to friends. In addition, the first escapees from Japanese prison camps in the Philippines arrived in Australia in June, and MacArthur was profoundly disturbed to learn for the first time the details of the Bataan Death March and of other atrocities and privations suffered by the American and Filipino captives. He was also upset and disappointed by the performances of Brett and Leary; his relations with them were becoming tense and he was already considering relieving his air commander. And he was sensitive about growing criticism of the SWPA's operations and training program by members of the Conservative Party in the Australian Parliament. Actually, most of their barbs were aimed at embarrassing the Labour Party ministry of Curtin, who could be counted upon to join the fray if the opposition attacked the SWPA general.

MacArthur appeared to some observers more remote and withdrawn than ever during his months in Melbourne. To be sure, because of the duties of his office he daily held numerous conferences with political, civic, and military leaders, but most of those meetings, at his insistence, took place at his headquarters, which was in an old insurance building at 401 Collins Street. His daily route back and forth from the Menzies Hotel to his office seldom varied except when he had to attend sessions of the Australian Advisory War Council at Victoria Barracks, or of the Allied Supply Council or some other high-level defense agency at the Government House in Melbourne. His public appearances in the city were chiefly limited to participation in an "Anzac Day" program on April 25 and the inauguration of a war bond drive on June 27. Mrs. MacArthur represented him at most social and civic functions, and rarely did they entertain at their hotel suite. The only journey that he made outside the city between March 28 and July 16 was a brief trip to Seymour, sixty miles to the north, where he inspected the American 41st Division at its training camp on June 29.

Huff stated that MacArthur received several anonymous notes in early July, "some of them threatening harm to the family or suggesting the possibility of an attempt to kidnap Arthur." Normally not one to pay heed to such "crank letters," this time MacArthur told Huff, who functioned as an aide to Mrs. MacArthur, "Just keep on as you've been doing, Sid, but get yourself armed." When the general moved his SWPA headquarters to Brisbane on July 20, his train coach "was protected by armed guards and machine guns." No matter how withdrawn and busy he was, however, the general took time in late June to answer a letter from a ten-year-old boy in Utica, New York, who wanted his assurance that Pearl Harbor was not in enemy hands. The general could not have been too depressed; he replied, "The Japs have not 'got' Pearl Harbor and are not going to get it." [16]

An unexpected problem that required MacArthur's attention during the Melbourne period was lend-lease. In fact, one of his most frequent office visitors was William S. Wasserman, chief of the lend-lease mission to Australia. For several months Wasserman and the Allied Supply Council in Australia had been wrestling rather unsuccessfully with determining which requisitions should be made and then getting the supplies assigned to Australia. Some Australian military leaders justifiably objected to requisitions for American ammunitions, for example, since most of their current weapon stocks required British-made ammunition. Also the lend-lease administrator was besieged by demands for materials either not essential to the war effort or already amply stockpiled in Australia. Certain Australian industrialists requested plant equipment that obviously would benefit their postwar expansion aims rather than their immediate wartime needs. At first, moreover, all requisitions were reviewed in Washington and then relayed to London for another review. "By the time they had gotten through the London review," said Wasserman, "the British had taken out of the requisitions whatever they felt they could use and what was left was spared to Australia."

MacArthur's influence and counsel were indispensable in resolving some of these problems, according to Wasserman: "I have never seen a man grasp a problem more quickly or settle it more justly and decisively." With MacArthur's assistance a system of reverse lend-lease was developed whereby Australia supplied goods and services to the American forces. "I am proud of the fact," Wasserman stated, "that Australia was the one country that actually returned to us more in Lend Lease goods than we gave them."

On July 10 Curtin, MacArthur, and Wasserman signed a formal agreement, sanctioned by the Combined Chiefs of Staff, whereby military requisitions and shipping priorities on all lend-lease materials sent to Australia would be under the jurisdiction of MacArthur. Wasserman claimed that thereafter, thanks to MacArthur's leadership, the lend-lease program in Australia worked smoothly and "there was a considerable stoppage of unnecessary demands." MacArthur was empowered to divert supplies from one SWPA national force to another in whatever manner he deemed best, but he soon found it prudent to refrain from redistributing supplies assigned to specific forces. By mutual agreement with the Australian government later in 1942, MacArthur relinquished his control over receiving and handling supplies at Australian ports; the government was developing adequate facilities to handle this aspect of the operation. MacArthur acted as a sort of lend-lease comptroller, reviewing requisitions and assigning shipping priorities.[17]

His ability to select able officers, experienced in supply administration, was important to the success achieved in that area. Colonel Lester Whitlock, the new SWPA G-4, soon became one of his most indispensable staff leaders in solving the never-ending, complex problems of supply. A tall, slender, quiet individual, Whitlock was one of the most hard-working, methodical men at the Melbourne headquarters. Brigadier General Paul W. Johnston, the firm, tactful SWPA general purchasing agent, had the responsibility of processing reverse lend-lease transactions, which ultimately totaled over a billion dollars, and of administering the procurement of Australian supplies and equipment for American forces. MacArthur later said of Johnston's work, "His success was outstanding and his service of major importance in the supply of our forces in the Southwest Pacific Area and the maintenance of our cordial relationships with the Australian Government."

In July MacArthur dissolved the USAFIA command, which had been set up originally as a rear-area organization charged with supply support of the Philippines. Barnes, who was said to be "incompatible" with Sutherland and others at GHQ, was relieved, but most of the other USAFIA personnel were brought into a new command, United States Services of Supply (USASOS). MacArthur chose his experienced deputy chief of staff, General Richard Marshall, to head USASOS, which controlled SWPA supply establishments, lines of communication, and various other agencies essential for the support of the combat forces. Marshall and his capable, energetic chief of staff, Brigadier General Dwight F. Johns, provided excellent leadership in the development and execution of supply policies. During the Melbourne phase, logistics ranked with training of combat troops in warranting more of headquarters' attention than did the headline-catching arena of combat operations.[18]

Because of the unexpectedly large contributions of supplies and services by the Australian nation in the next three years, said Willoughby, "no American force in any other theater was remotely so self-sufficient or so successful in the assignment of local exploitation as was our Army and Air Force in the Southwest Pacific Area." He estimated that 65 per cent to 70 per cent of the supplies consumed by American forces in that theater during the last half of 1942 were produced by the Australians. The American Army's official history corroborates his statement: "Within the framework of this system, the pooling of resources was achieved in such manner as to conserve shipping to the utmost degree possible. In no other theater did lend-lease and reciprocal aid serve these ends so well." The Australian contributions that were especially important included food, housing, clothing, petroleum, tires, ships, airfields, repair facilities, and hospitals. At the same time lend-lease from the United States in the form of construction, transportation, and industrial equipment did much to boost the Australian economy and to assist in the production and movement of the supplies needed by the SWPA command.

With MacArthur's encouragement, Australian industry even turned to ordnance and tank production, and the country's foremost medical researchers and public health experts undertook extensive programs of research on tropical diseases and sanitation problems which would benefit troops operating in New Guinea. A large amount of MacArthur's time, particularly during his first six months in Australia, was devoted to working with the Allied Supply Council, Allied Work Council, and numerous other agencies involved in the gigantic program of providing goods and services for the theater's armed services. If the Australian-American forces had been obliged to depend solely on American sources for their general supplies and services, they would have been in dire need; the theater was assigned relatively low priorities in these areas as well as in combat personnel and matériel.[19]

Despite an impressive output in Australia, the labor force, both civilian and military, was never adequate to meet wartime demands in the expanding factories, ports, and military installations. In no theater was the shortage of service troops more serious than in the Southwest Pacific. The War Department felt that MacArthur should utilize Australian labor as much as possible, but Australian Army service units were barely able to fill the most essential jobs needed by that force, and most SWPA supply officers were dissatisfied with Australian civilian workers, especially the longshoremen. Despite appeals by Curtin and other officials of his Labour Party ministry for the cooperation of organized labor, Australian unions were often recalcitrant and unenthusiastic in their support of the war effort. In the case of port strikes, according to the American Army's official chronicle, "the Australian Government, at least in the eyes of many U.S. Army observers, gave in to every demand of the longshoremen because of its dependence upon organized labor for political support." [20]

A G-2 estimate submitted to MacArthur in June portrayed a dismal labor situation:

> In Government-owned plants, morale and drive is [*sic*] lacking, and slowdowns are frequent. The coal miners have shown a distinctly non-cooperative spirit and strikes continue . . . Stevedores have also shown a recalcitrant spirit. Those at Darwin have used every emergency for their own benefit, are completely unreliable, and even in critical times were guilty of intentional slowdowns, stoppages and strikes . . . At Sydney they [stevedores] have been very troublesome and unreliable . . . In road, railway and airdrome building, unit accomplishment is only a little above the WPA standard.[21]

If the conditions were as appalling as reported in this estimate, the tremendous production levels achieved by Australian industry over the next three years could not have been reached. But the vexatious problem of too few American service troops and the consequent need to depend upon civilian labor and Australian Army service units continued to be a headache for MacArthur throughout the war. When his forces moved in large numbers to New Guinea in the following months, the lack of service personnel there would result in a situation even more critical than that in Australia.

Up to June, 1942, the SWPA theater had little intelligence equipment or personnel. There were aerial and submarine patrols, but the Central Bureau, a low-order intercept service run by British cryptanalysts, and the Royal Australian Navy's Coastwatcher Service, whose agents operated radio transmitters at isolated posts from Borneo to Bougainville, provided the main sources of information on enemy activities. MacArthur soon found that geographic, topographic, and hydrographic data on New Guinea and adjacent areas were obsolete, erroneous, or entirely lacking. More information was needed also on current enemy strength, dispositions, equipment, and plans. Under Willoughby's general jurisdiction, several agencies were created between June and September to augment intelligence data on the areas of likely future operations. The Allied Translator and Interpreter Section (ATIS) was the most important; it was charged with interrogating enemy prisoners and translating and printing captured documents.

Under the brilliant, resourceful leadership of Colonel Sidney F. Mashbir, a master intelligence agent of long and distinguished experience who knew well the Japanese mind and language, ATIS grew in the next three years into an almost independent staff division of great significance in SWPA planning and operations. By the end of the war, Mashbir's section would have interviewed over 14,000 prisoners and published more than twenty million pages of enemy documents; its large staff would include over 4000 Japanese-Americans as interpreters and translators.[22]

The Allied Intelligence Bureau was established to collect intelligence through clandestine operations in enemy territory. It also had the duties of conducting sabotage and espionage and encouraging guerrilla resistance movements. By the war's end this agency had sent 264 missions behind enemy lines, in the course of which its agents transported over 300,000 pounds of supplies to guerrillas and fellow agents, rescued more than 1000 trapped or captured Allied personnel, took 1100 Japanese prisoners, and killed 7000 enemy troops in commando and paramilitary operations.

A third valuable intelligence agency was the Allied Geographical Section, which was formed to collect, evaluate, and disseminate geographical information on areas of operations. Ultimately this section distributed 200,000 copies of its 110 terrain studies, sixty-two terrain handbooks, and 101 special reports on all phases of SWPA geography. Its pocket-size handbook became highly regarded as "a sort of individual 'Baedeker' for the assault echelons when they hit the landing beaches."

The work of these intelligence organizations and their many subsections was of keen interest to MacArthur, especially when the groups operated in the Philippines. The SWPA commander was so satisfied with their work that he refused a proposal of the Office of Strategic Services (OSS) in Washington to send its agents into the theater. In turning down the OSS, however, MacArthur was also motivated by his dislike of having any military personnel in his theater whom he could not control and by his knowledge of Willoughby's deep-seated resentment of anyone interfering in what he believed was his own domain. This strong feeling of Willoughby's was the Achilles' heel of the SWPA intelligence structure, and led to numerous ugly clashes between him and the leaders of his intelligence agencies when the fiery G-2 thought his subordinates were infringing upon or working counter to his own plans. Nevertheless, the SWPA intelligence system was far superior to that of the enemy and functioned effectively in the long run without the assistance of the highly touted OSS. A Japanese staff officer testified after the war, "Allied intelligence activities were responsible in great part for our losses in New Guinea," although he added that SWPA intelligence "gained its great effectiveness through the failure of our own intelligence to combat it." [23]

Through March the build-up of American Army troops and matériel in Australia represented about half of the troops sent out of the States and one-third of the cargo shipped overseas during the first quarter of 1942. After that month shipments to Europe began to increase quickly, and there was a correspondingly rapid drop in reinforcements to the Southwest Pacific. By June most of the troops MacArthur was to receive for the year had arrived and were stationed in training camps around Melbourne and Adelaide. The principal units were the 32nd and 41st infantry divisions. Meanwhile, the Australian Army had expanded to seven infantry divisions, two motorized divisions, and one armored division. The only veteran infantrymen of either national force on the Australian continent were those of the Australian 6th and 7th divisions, who had distinguished themselves in the Libyan desert war; much to MacArthur and Blamey's disappointment, the 9th Division would be retained in the Middle East until early 1943.

Besides a Dutch squadron of medium bombers and a small Royal Australian Air Force, which included about 180 obsolete aircraft, Brett had the following American air units: two heavy, two medium, and one light bombardment groups, three fighter groups, two transport squadrons, and one photographic squadron. A disappointingly large number of SWPA aircraft, however, were not in operational condition. Leary's naval force still consisted of only a handful of Australian and American cruisers and destroyers, although several American submarine divisions operated out of Australian bases. The SWPA land, air, and sea forces were perhaps adequate for the defense of Australia, barring a large-scale enemy invasion, but they were by no means satisfactory for the northern offensive that Mac-Arthur was anxious to launch.

Actual combat activities from April to July were confined for the most part to air operations, which were ineffective against enemy shipping on the seas but did considerable damage to Japanese bases from Bali to Bougainville. The most frequent targets were Rabaul, Lae, and Salamaua. The Allied Air Forces shot down eighty enemy aircraft and destroyed another twenty on the ground, but lost eighty-three planes in combat, eleven on the ground to enemy action, and a disappointing seventy-seven to accidents. The deterioration of morale was a growing problem among Brett's airmen, a consequence of primitive living conditions at isolated bases in New Guinea and northern Australia, exhausting flights of great distances to targets, almost daily encounters with tropical storms, and the lack of parts and maintenance crews to keep the aircraft in top condition.

Most depressing to the high command was the lag in replacement aircraft: in May and June, for example, 106 fighters and forty-two bombers were lost, but gains for that period were only sixty-two bombers. Nevertheless, Brett's airmen held their own against Japanese aircraft, and the enemy had not enjoyed numerical superiority in the air in the Southwest Pacific since early May. Although MacArthur and Brett insisted that the SWPA strength of about 500 combat planes should be at least doubled, General Arnold, chief of the United States Army Air Forces, contended that, except for replacements, no additional air units would be needed in that theater for some time.[24]

Surprisingly little had been done by the end of June toward strengthening defensive positions in New Guinea, despite cryptographic and other evidence pointing toward another enemy attempt to seize Port Moresby. The American 32nd and 41st divisions were moved from training camps near Adelaide and Melbourne to ones in the Rockhampton area of Queensland, but, although some antiaircraft, engineer, and service troops were sent to Moresby and Milne Bay, few Americans were transferred to Papua. The first American troop unit that MacArthur sent to New Guinea was the 96th Engineers, a Negro battalion; it arrived at Moresby in late April and proved valuable in constructing airfields, docks, and hospitals. In June a brigade of the Australian 7th Division began moving to Milne Bay to protect airfields under construction at the southern tip of Papua. The Kanga Force, made up of several Australian companies, guarded the airfield at Wau in the gold-mining country of the Owen Stanley Mountains and conducted sporadic, indecisive attacks against the Japanese around Salamaua.

In early June Willoughby reported to MacArthur that his intelligence agencies had gathered "increasing evidence that the Japanese are displaying interest in the development of a route from Buna on the north coast of southern New Guinea through Kokoda to Port Moresby." MacArthur notified Blamey on June 9 that "minor forces" might try to use that mountain route to attack Moresby or to supply a new seaborne operation against the port. "Whatever the Japanese plan may be," he stressed, "it is of vital importance that the route from Kokoda westward be controlled by Allied forces, particularly the Kokoda area."

Major General Basil M. Morris, Australian commander of the New Guinea Force, was not as alarmed as MacArthur and sent only a reinforced battalion of Australian and native constabulary troops to hold Kokoda, which lay near the Owen Stanley divide and astride the principal trail from Buna to Moresby. Chamberlin, MacArthur's G-3 and probably the most competent of his GHQ staff section chiefs, warned the SWPA commander that this force would not be adequate to insure the security of the Kokoda Trail. MacArthur discussed the problem with Blamey, who instructed Morris to strengthen the Kokoda garrison and also to "take all necessary steps to prevent a Japanese surprise landing along the coast north and south of Buna." When Morris reported that he was executing the orders, MacArthur and Blamey let the matter rest pending further intelligence or an overt move by the enemy.[25]

Some of the reasons why the transfer of troops northward to New Guinea had progressed slowly were evident in the findings of Major General Robert C. Richardson, who, as the "personal representative" of Marshall, inspected the SWPA command in early July. The American divisions, he found, were handicapped in their training by want of practice ammunition, instructors with knowledge of enemy tactics, and quartermaster, ordnance, signal, labor, bakery, shoe repair, railhead, police, maintenance, and medical units. Until these shortages were remedied, mainly by action of the War Department, the 32nd and 41st divisions could not be properly prepared for service in a combat area. Richardson also found that much of the equipment of the air units was either lacking or in poor repair. He reported, "The present organization of the American Air Forces, under which our pilots receive their combat missions from Australians, is resented throughout the entire command from top to bottom." Richardson's criticisms of the air command and its policies carried an indictment, by implication, of Brett for permitting the Australians too much authority at the policy-making level. When he visited New Guinea, Richardson discovered "great confusion in the minds of the command" as to what their duties and mission were.[26]

MacArthur took these criticisms in stride not only because they confirmed some of his own thinking, especially about air force conditions, but also because they came from one of his oldest friends. The War Department had authorized MacArthur to establish an American corps headquarters, so, after discussing the matter with Richardson, he nominated him to be his corps commander. Marshall, however, notified MacArthur on July 30 that "it is not advisable to send him back to Australia." The Army chief of staff explained, "The difficulties inherent in any allied command organization and your especially difficult problems as commander-in-chief in a country not your own, combined with Richardson's intense feelings regarding service under Australian command, made his assignment unwise."

Richardson later told MacArthur that he had looked forward to the job and had his headquarters staff ready to go, but Marshall had concluded that he was prejudiced after he had commented on the "unsoundness" of the March directive to MacArthur. Richardson said he had recommended that "the directive be changed so that all American troops could be headed up as a national force serving directly under the supreme commander." [27] Before the year ended, MacArthur would reach a similar conclusion himself. The honeymoon period with the Australian Army would not last long.

3. A Directive and a Surprise

Throughout the spring of 1942, King and his naval planners in Washington had been unwilling to trust the Pacific Fleet to MacArthur and wanted the future offensive against Japan to be in Nimitz's theater. Nevertheless, King and MacArthur lined up against the President, Marshall, Arnold, and the Army planners in insisting that the Bolero build-up in Britain should be delayed in order to improve the Allied position in the Pacific. In fact, as early as February the outspoken chief of naval operations had advocated the establishment of bases in the New Hebrides, Tonga, and Ellice islands not merely to secure the line of communications to Australia but to provide springboards for offensive thrusts. In early March the President tentatively endorsed King's basic idea of "offensive rather than passive" use of such bases, although, as previously mentioned, Roosevelt changed his mind in May and decided again to increase Bolero shipments at the sacrifice of Pacific reinforcements.

Meanwhile, in April King's planners had developed a four-stage draft plan for future Pacific operations: (1) base expansion and build-up of forces in the South and Southwest Pacific theaters, (2) seizure of Papua and the southern Solomons, with simultaneous carrier strikes in the Central Pacific, (3) capture of the Bismarck Archipelago and the Caroline and Marshall islands, and (4) invasion of the East Indies or the Philippines, depending upon which route offered "the most promising and enduring results" by that stage.

The Joint Chiefs did not act on this plan, but on May 28 Nimitz proposed to MacArthur that they cooperate in an attack on Tulagi; the admiral believed a Marine battalion, supported by SWPA naval forces, could secure the island. MacArthur responded that he did not yet have sufficient naval strength for such an undertaking. The Navy and War departments also looked askance at the proposal. Sensing MacArthur's anxiety about the Navy's intentions regarding his theater, Marshall reassured him that if such an operation were executed the SWPA chief would retain strategic control. "All decisions, including the extent to which you accede to any further proposals by CINCPAC [Nimitz] rest with you," Marshall added. But on that same day, June 1, Nimitz notified Rear Admiral Robert L. Ghormley, his South Pacific commander, that he would control the amphibious forces if an assault on Tulagi were undertaken, even though the island lay in MacArthur's theater. The problems of control and coordination of forces and operations were emerging well before the plan for an initial Pacific offensive had been settled.[28]

One of the most important decisions MacArthur made in 1942, as well as one of the least known, was to resist the temptation to invade Timor. Australian and Dutch units were still operating in the hills of Timor, and on June 3 Blamey proposed that SWPA forces invade the island. If MacArthur did not favor this, Blamey argued, the troops presently on Timor should be evacuated. King, a worthy and wily protagonist of MacArthur's, learned of the proposal and seized on the Timor invasion plan with relish, possibly because it would divert MacArthur's forces into the East Indies and make easier Nimitz's future control of all Pacific operations.

Knowing the word would get to MacArthur, King told Leary that he would work to get two carriers from the British Eastern Fleet in the Indian Ocean to support the Timor operation. The SWPA commander would have been delighted to obtain the carriers but had no intention of being sidetracked into the East Indies, so he simply told Blamey that SWPA ships and landing craft were inadequate for a seaborne invasion: "Without them such an expedition has little chance of success and cannot therefore be considered with the means now available." MacArthur realized that an invasion of Timor would drain his forces and permanently derail his objective of returning to the Philippines. He decided instead to establish a regular supply run to Timor by air and sea in order to maintain the existing forces there, with the intention of ultimately withdrawing them, which he did in 1943.[29]

That he had another northern route in mind was apparent when, on the day following the termination of the Midway battle, MacArthur sent a proposal to the War Department for an immediate offensive against Rabaul, the Japanese stronghold on New Britain. With his current SWPA strength plus two carriers and an amphibious division, he claimed, "I could retake that important area, forcing the enemy back 700 miles to his base at Truk with manifold strategic advantages both defensive and offensive [and] with further potential exploitation immediately possible. Speed is vital." Marshall said he would present the idea to the Joint Chiefs and their planning staff but cautiously warned MacArthur that agreement with King "is the most critical factor" and it would have to be "handled carefully."

The SWPA general's audacious proposal won surprisingly quick favor with a majority of both Army and Navy planners in the Pentagon, who preferred a rapid move against Rabaul to King's more gradual approach. The planners drafted an outline scheme that called for intensive air attacks to paralyze enemy air bases along the Papuan and Solomons flanks, followed by a direct assault on the Rabaul area. They were confident that the 1st Marine Division, which could be ready for the seaborne invasion by early July, would be able to seize Rabaul. Army divisions would then be employed to occupy the stronghold and later reduce Japanese positions in Papua and the Solomons at a more leisurely pace. Most of the Army and Navy planners were in agreement that MacArthur should have strategic control of the Rabaul operation, while an admiral should be in tactical command of the assault stage.

But King and his war plans chief, Rear Admiral Charles M. Cooke, objected strongly to the command arrangement, refusing to permit carriers and the necessary support ships from the Pacific Fleet to come under MacArthur's control. The two admirals also challenged the presumed effectiveness of air power in paving the way to Rabaul and preferred a slower approach to New Britain, seizing Papuan and Solomons bases and eliminating enemy air strength in step-by-step moves northward.[30]

Learning of King and Cooke's criticisms, MacArthur sent word through Marshall that his proposal "was merely of the ultimate objective of the attack and did not contain the details of the progressive steps of the plan." He, too, favored advancing up the Papuan and Solomons ladders since "it would be manifestly impracticable to attempt the capture of Rabaul by direct assault supported by the limited amount of land-based aviation which can now be employed from the presently held bases." He refused, however, to yield on the question of command, asserting that the operations would occur in his theater; unless he had strategic control, the principle of unity of command within the Southwest Pacific theater would be violated and would "result in nothing but confusion."

On June 27, three days after MacArthur sent this message, his GHQ planners completed a plan called Tulsa I, which was not transmitted to Washington; it called for the capture of Rabaul in two weeks, including the seizure of Papuan and Solomons bases on the way. Chamberlin thought the time element was unrealistic, so a revised plan, Tulsa II, was drafted and sent to Washington; it provided for the capture of Rabaul in eighteen days.[31] Neither MacArthur nor Chamberlin explained to Marshall how the New Guinea and Solomons sites could be occupied and developed into air bases in time to support the assault on Rabaul. The Tulsa plans were so grandiose and unrealistic that they appear to have been conceived without careful consideration of logistics or of enemy strength and dispositions. For a while in June it seems that euphoria was unrestrained both in Washington and Melbourne, probably because of the Midway triumph and the desire to follow up quickly before the Japanese recovered their balance.

In the meantime, King and Cooke persisted in refusing to consider MacArthur for command of the Rabaul offensive despite the fact that their concept of the operations now differed little from his. Marshall and Handy, the Army's war plans chief, tried in vain to dissuade the two admirals, repeatedly emphasizing that the offensive would take place in MacArthur's theater. Despairing of reaching any agreement with the generals, King brazenly ordered Nimitz to begin preparations for the offensive, informing him that there might be a delay in determining the Army's role and that he should plan for the contingency that only his own naval and Marine forces would be available. Marshall, showing patience and self-restraint, asked King to meet with him to work out a compromise so that the Army and Navy could get on with the fight against the Japanese.

About that time MacArthur obtained copies of the King-Nimitz exchange regarding the Navy's plan to go ahead with the Rabaul campaign alone if necessary. The messages revealed that Nimitz intended to use MacArthur's air and naval forces in support, although the admiral would hold strategic command of the operations. MacArthur was already irritated by the fact that King continued to correspond directly with Leary after the general had earlier protested that this practice made a "mockery" of his command structure in the Southwest Pacific.

On June 28 MacArthur sent an angry message to Marshall charging that the Navy "contemplates assuming general command control of all operations in the Pacific theater," with the Army to be relegated to a "subsidiary" role "consisting largely of placing its forces at the disposal and under the command of Navy or Marine officers." He also told Marshall that in the early 1930's, when he was Army chief of staff, he had "accidentally" learned of a Navy conspiracy to acquire control of the entire national defense system and reduce the Army to a training and supply organization. Marshall calmly replied that "regardless of the outcome of these negotiations, which I hope will be as you desire, every available support, both Army and Navy, must be given to operations against the enemy." By the time he received Marshall's reply, MacArthur had composed himself; he reassured his superior that however the matter was resolved, he would abide by the Joint Chiefs' decision and would employ his forces against the Japanese "at all times and under any conditions." [32]

During the last two days of June, King and Marshall finally worked out a compromise, thanks mainly to the Army chief of staff's tactfulness and amazing forbearance. Except for minor changes, this plan, largely the work of Marshall, was approved by the Joint Chiefs on July 2. The new directive, which was immediately sent to MacArthur, Ghormley, and Nimitz, stated that the Rabaul offensive would be divided into three "tasks," or phases, of which Ghormley would command the first under Nimitz's strategic direction and MacArthur would control the remaining two. Task One would be the seizure of the Santa Cruz Islands, Tulagi, "and adjacent positions." Task Two would be the capture of Lae, Salamaua, the northeast coast of New Guinea, and the rest of the Solomons. Task Three would be the taking of Rabaul "and adjacent positions in the New Guinea–New Ireland area." As of August 1, the eastern SWPA boundary would be moved westward from 165° to 159° east longitude, thereby placing the Tulagi-Guadalcanal area within Ghormley's theater. MacArthur was to provide naval and air support as called for by Ghormley during Task One, which was originally assigned a target date of August 1 and was later postponed to the 7th. The Joint Chiefs reserved to themselves the authority to decide what forces would be employed, the timing of the tasks, and when MacArthur would assume strategic command after Task One.

When Marshall notified the SWPA commander of the decision, he admitted that "this agreement was reached with great difficulty," but he felt that "a workable plan has been set up." He appealed to MacArthur "to make every conceivable effort to promote complete accord in this affair." Anticipating that MacArthur would be less than overjoyed with the compromise, Marshall added, "There will be difficulties and irritations inevitably, but the end in view demands a determination to suppress these manifestations." MacArthur's response was encouraging: he pledged his full cooperation, invited Ghormley to Melbourne to plan their coordinated efforts, and suggested that the admiral be retained later as naval commander for Tasks Two and Three. MacArthur probably realized that, though the directive was not altogether to his liking, it represented the first significant departure from the basic Anglo-American strategic policy of merely containing the Japanese until the defeat of the Germans was assured.[33]

In view of the new directive from Washington, MacArthur ordered Chamberlin and his planners at Melbourne to revise Tulsa II to provide for the immediate construction of a major airfield at Buna for the support of later operations against Lae and Salamaua. He confidently assumed that Task Two could be launched within "a matter of weeks" after Task One was begun. He ordered a six-man reconnaissance team to go to Buna on July 10 to ascertain whether a long-neglected emergency air strip near the village could be expanded into a large base. The team reported that the terrain was poorly drained and unsuitable but that there was an excellent site at nearby Dobodura. After several hasty meetings with Chamberlin, Blamey, Brett, Casey, and Marquat, MacArthur issued a plan on July 15 for Operation Providence, which provided for a SWPA task force to construct and protect a major airfield in the Buna-Dobodura area. Van Volkenburgh was to command the Buna Force's movement to the site, and an Australian brigadier would take over on location. The Buna Force was to move to the region in four echelons: the first, consisting of four Australian infantry companies and a few American engineers, would leave Port Moresby by foot on July 31 and arrive at Buna about August 10–12. The other three echelons, totaling approximately 3000 men, were to arrive before the end of August.[34]

Van Volkenburgh, who was at Moresby, learned on July 18 that a large number of enemy ships had been spotted at Rabaul the previous day, as well as some vessels loaded with troops under way off Talasea, New Britain. He notified his assistant commander, Lieutenant Colonel David Larr, then at Townsville, and both men concluded that the troop transports were bound for Buna. Larr made contact with Sutherland and Chamberlin at Melbourne, where everything was in confusion because they were preparing to move GHQ to Brisbane in two days. Larr, on behalf of Van Volkenburgh, urged them to get MacArthur to launch Providence at once, but the GHQ generals discounted the threat and said that, according to Willoughby's intelligence, there was no evidence that the enemy ships were headed for Buna. They did say that every effort would be made to speed up Providence, but logistical problems would make it impossible for the first echelon of the Buna Force to get to Buna before August 8 at the earliest. Van Volkenburgh had earlier pressed for sea transportation of the first echelon to Buna, but Chamberlin, probably influenced by Leary, believed that "coral heads in the sea off the north coast of New Guinea were so numerous and so dangerous the ships couldn't go through it."

MacArthur informed Brett of the transports off the New Britain coast, but since his airmen were exhausted and their morale was at an ebb, Brett decided to suspend all bombing missions on July 18 and 19 except for a lone sortie against a target on Bougainville. By the time he ordered strikes against the convoy from Rabaul, his aircraft could not locate the ships; bad weather had set in and visibility was poor. Finally, on the morning of July 21 the Allied Air Forces discovered the convoy off Salamaua, steaming southward without air cover. One B-17 and six B-26's attacked but scored no hits. At 6:30 the next morning an Australian patrol bomber spotted the transports unloading troops and equipment between Buna and Gona.

Brett's aircraft flew eighty-one sorties that day against the invasion force, but, because a dense haze hung over the beaches, bombing was inaccurate and the results disappointing. A transport and a barge were sunk, but the landing operations were already far advanced when the Allied planes attacked on the 22nd. The Japanese quickly moved their equipment and supplies into the dense jungle and set up antiaircraft guns. Major

General Tomitaro Horii's South Seas Detachment encountered no ground opposition in securing Buna. His 3000-man assault force would soon be reinforced by more than 13,000 troops as the Japanese busily transformed Buna into a formidable bastion.

MacArthur's Operation Providence had been precluded by the surprise move, and his hope for an early inauguration of Task Two was blasted. It would take six months and over 3000 Australian and American lives, as well as 12,000 Japanese lives, before the dismal Buna area would be secured by the Allied forces — a heavy price to pay for taking a place that MacArthur's forces could have occupied without opposition as late as July 20. Van Volkenburgh remained convinced in later years that "had we been furnished sea transportation a few days earlier, the Japs would have found us at Buna when they landed." Morris, Brett, and the Melbourne GHQ staff could be faulted, but the principal reason why the enemy got to Buna first was the prolonged debate over Pacific strategy and command by the Joint Chiefs of Staff, which delayed the issuance of a directive on South and Southwest Pacific operations.[35]

The next month MacArthur wrote to a friend in Washington that there were "tragic lessons to be learned from our experiences in this war." Defeated in one campaign and off to a disappointing start in the new one, he lamented, "The way is long and hard here, and I don't quite see the end of the road. To make something out of nothing seems to be my military fate in the twilight of my service. I have led one lost cause and am trying desperately not to have it two." [36] Only a year and a half away from the statutory retirement age for Army personnel, MacArthur was tired and was feeling his age, but he was also fiercely determined to taste victory. He was correct in predicting that the "end of the road" in the Papuan campaign would be difficult to reach, but his "twilight" period was destined to be extended far beyond what he then imagined.

CHAPTER V

Across the Owen Stanleys

1. Shifting to the Attack

AFTER HE MOVED HIS HEADQUARTERS to Brisbane in July, Mac-
Arthur's unusual combination of aloofness and showmanship
fascinated the people of that city as much as it had those of
Melbourne. He continued to work seven days a week and
made few appearances in public other than his daily trips to
and from his suite at Lennon's Hotel, the city's only air-conditioned hotel, and the nine-story AMP Insurance Building,
which was taken over for the main offices of his GHQ. Mac-
Arthur's brief excursions became one of the sights of the city
that many residents, as well as soldiers and sailors stationed in
the area, felt they had to witness at least once. Riding in his
"long, high, black limousine that would make a doorman in-
stinctively reach for the red carpet," the only four-star Allied
general in the Pacific always carried "an admirably flourishable
cane," said one observer, and was never seen in public without
"his floppy hat" with "the gold braid swarming on the brim."
Sergeant E. J. Kahn, Jr., of the 32nd Division, commented after
beholding "Brisbane's wonder" that "he is an awesome, dramatic spectacle, and Australian civilians, who after several years

of war were used to soldiers of all ranks, never tired of hanging around his car waiting for him to approach and display, as he crossed the sidewalk, his inimitable, strolling magnificence."

The hotel management added an awning from the entrance to the curb for MacArthur's benefit, which itself became an attraction since it was the only one in Brisbane. An Australian correspondent who encountered the general numerous times in the next two years observed, "Always he was grim and unsmiling [in public]. He could have been the lion of the Australian social world. Hostesses used every lure in vain. He went nowhere except between his hotel and his headquarters. The atmosphere of mystery grew rapidly. In Australia, where even policemen don't carry nightsticks, let alone guns, it was strange to see stern-faced guards swinging tommy-guns wherever MacArthur went."

Clark Lee, a correspondent who had escaped from Corregidor, found the general "was hard to get along with in those early Australia days." Brett conjectured that MacArthur seemed to be "suffering a feeling of guilt in having left his men at the most critical moment of their hopeless fight." Others on the GHQ staff closer to their chief than Brett, however, maintained that if he was irritable at times, it was because he was overworked and under great stress in his new command position. It was true that he had taken no leave and only a day or two off from his work since the war began. At any rate, Lee concluded, "if MacArthur was troublesome, his staff was worse," particularly the Bataan Gang, which "formed an exclusive group that resented and suspected 'outsiders.' "

In view of the fact that the clique's experiences of war had been limited mainly to Corregidor, one disgruntled newcomer's remarks are especially interesting: "The defense of Bataan seemed to have an extraordinary effect on them. They wore an air of superiority that was most irritating to men who had endured the hardships and perils of other fronts." Brigadier

General Elliott R. Thorpe, who headed the SWPA counter-intelligence section and was considered an outsider, said that "MacArthur's little party remained for some time an exclusive little coterie . . . Frustration and defeat produce strange emotions." Thorpe did notice, nevertheless, that "this divisive feeling" at GHQ was at its height during the Melbourne days and decreased after the move to Brisbane. The decline probably coincided with the succession of victories that came later.[1]

George H. Johnston, an Australian reporter, was one of the few newspapermen who were privileged to interview MacArthur alone in Brisbane in 1942. If MacArthur was depressed or despairing when the correspondent entered, Johnston never observed it. But he found that it was "impossible to get behind the real MacArthur" because of "the streak of showmanship that is part and parcel of the man." Johnston, who admired MacArthur as both commander and actor, described the general's performance at press conferences:

> When he was interviewed, the four-star general would always have a stage property — a long, unlighted cigar one time, a chunky bulldog pipe another. And he used the properties, for gesticulation and emphasis, with the histrionic ability of Sir Henry Irving. When he was asked a question he never hesitated in giving an answer that was not only utterly complete but was in itself, taken down verbatim, a polished essay on military lore. He could talk continuously for two hours and never grope for a word. Each talk would hold the complete interest of two score hard-bitten foreign correspondents without a second's flagging of their interest.
>
> The General would race up and down incessantly (whenever he was thinking some problem out the whole staff would know and comment on the fact that "the Old Man is rug-cutting upstairs!"), drawing for parallel and metaphor on writings of Napoleon, on a line or two from a melodrama he had seen in New York a quarter of a century before, on a speech by Lincoln, on a statement by Plato, or sometimes on a passage

from Scripture. The tone of his voice would vary from almost a whisper to a ringing shout followed by a long period of thoughtful silence.[2]

Contributing to his moodiness was his dissatisfaction with Brett, which had grown perceptibly since March, although Arnold, the Army Air Forces chief, may have exaggerated in claiming that "from the first it became evident that he and General Brett could not get along." Arnold blamed Brett, who "should have done the 'getting along,' as he was the junior." On the other hand, Major General George Kenney, who succeeded Brett as Allied Air Forces commander on August 4, maintained that Brett's relationship with MacArthur was undermined, in part, by Sutherland, who convinced his superior that the air officer was incompetent: "Nothing that he did was right . . . None of Brett's staff or senior commanders was any good, the pilots couldn't hit anything, and knew nothing about proper maintenance of their equipment or how to handle their supplies." According to Kenney, Sutherland also "thought the Australians were about as undisciplined, untrained, over-advertised and generally useless as the Air Force," but Brett held the Australian airmen in high esteem, carrying the Allied partnership so far as to require every American bomber pilot to have an Australian copilot and vice versa.

In late June MacArthur decided Brett must go; he wanted in his stead Lieutenant General Frank M. Andrews, but he was not available. Marshall suggested Brigadier General James H. Doolittle, who had led a daring raid on Tokyo in April, or Kenney, whose long flying career included forty-seven missions against the Germans in World War I and, most recently, command of the Fourth Air Force. On July 14 MacArthur curtly notified Brett by letter, "You are to be replaced here by General Kenney, for whom orders were issued yesterday to proceed by air without delay."

In his first visit with MacArthur in Brisbane, on July 30, Kenney noticed that the SWPA commander appeared "a little depressed . . . tired, drawn, and nervous." After exchanging a few pleasantries, MacArthur launched a lengthy, angry tirade against the Allied Air Forces, said Kenney, "until finally there was nothing left but an inefficient rabble of boulevard shock troops whose contribution to the war effort was practically nil . . . He had no use for anyone in the whole organization from Brett down to and including the rank of colonel." MacArthur told Kenney that he would demand his total personal allegiance because under his predecessor "the air personnel had gone beyond just being antagonistic to his headquarters" and had opposed him "to the point of disloyalty." Kenney pledged that he would do his best but added that he would have to make a quick inspection to determine for himself what changes were needed immediately.

Kenney took off for New Guinea that night and in the next few days made a rapid tour of the air bases there and in Australia, besides observing the situation at air headquarters in Brisbane. He returned to MacArthur and explained in detail what he thought was wrong and what corrective measures were needed. After he had outlined his offensive objectives, the first of which was "to take out the Jap air strength until we owned the air over New Guinea," Kenney said that "General MacArthur approved this program and said to go ahead, that I had carte blanche to do anything that I wanted to. He said he didn't care how my gang was handled . . . as long as they would fight."

Kenney immediately inaugurated a number of reforms in air administration, operations, and services, which soon showed their effect in improved performances by the Allied Air Forces. He "blew through the torpid and discontented American Army Air Force organization like a cleansing breeze," commented an Australian authority. Five general officers whom Kenney regarded as "deadwood" were relieved in the first two weeks, and other air officers of Brett's staff soon followed them back to the States as Kenney wielded his ax against inefficiency.

With the new air commander putting a premium on maintenance, the daily in-commission rate of SWPA combat aircraft soared to 90 per cent, doubling the average figure under Brett's leadership. "With 90% the Jap could have had twice as many airplanes as I had," Kenney remarked, "but I could put more in the air than he could." Only three days after taking command, Kenney sent his planes in a highly successful attack on Rabaul's airfields. The bombing mission was the largest conducted to that time in the Pacific war, and it pleased MacArthur greatly.

Dynamic, decisive, and as self-confident as MacArthur, the stockily built Kenney was one outsider who quickly won the friendship and admiration of the SWPA commander. "Of all the brilliant air commanders of the war, none surpassed him," said MacArthur, "in those three great essentials of combat leadership: aggressive vision, mastery of air tactics and strategy, and the ability to exact the maximum of fighting qualities from both men and equipment." Kenney, who came to regard MacArthur as "the best general this country has ever produced," proved to be a rejuvenator for both the Allied Air Forces and his SWPA chief: "MacArthur's restoration to full health and activity," claimed Lee, "might well be dated from the day that Kenney walked into his headquarters in Brisbane." [3]

Several days after Kenney became head of the Allied Air Forces, MacArthur requested and shortly obtained authorization for an American air force; on September 3 the Fifth Air Force, named in honor of his fighter and bomber commands in the Philippines, was officially constituted. Kenney assumed command of the new American air force while continuing to head Allied Air Forces. The latter organization also included Air Vice Marshall William D. Bostock's Royal Australian Air

Force as well as several Dutch units, which were designated the Coastal Command and were responsible mainly for the defense of Australia and missions against the East Indies west of New Guinea.

Though Australian squadrons were sometimes employed in New Guinea, especially during 1942 and early 1943, the Fifth Air Force was intended to be the principal air arm supporting MacArthur's offensives to the north. Both Kenney and Mac-Arthur were highly pleased with the leadership later displayed by the officers whom the former chose to head the Fifth Air Force's fighter and bomber commands, Brigadier Generals Paul B. Wurtsmith and Kenneth N. Walker. The Fifth's deputy commander, Brigadier General Ennis C. Whitehead, who also headed the advance echelon in New Guinea, enjoyed "the complete confidence of both MacArthur and Kenney." Mac-Arthur later praised Whitehead's "masterful generalship . . . brilliant judgment and inexhaustible energy" as factors "of the highest importance in Allied successes" in the Southwest Pacific. Kenney was proud that, in the ensuing months, he converted MacArthur from a skeptic to an ardent supporter of air power.

Both Brett and his luckless predecessor, Brereton, had lacked the forcefulness to tackle Sutherland, but Kenney, once he got his carte blanche from MacArthur, did not hesitate to enlighten the widely feared chief of staff regarding the lines of authority. On his first day in command of the Allied Air Forces, Kenney's orders for an air attack were returned by Sutherland with the numbers of aircraft, bomb tonnages, times of takeoff, and other details drastically altered. Kenney rushed to the chief of staff's office for an immediate showdown with him: he angrily took a piece of blank paper from the chief of staff's desk, put a tiny penciled dot in the corner, and informed Sutherland that the blank area represented his knowledge of air matters and the dot symbolized Sutherland's.

Kenney firmly told the astonished chief of staff to rescind the orders that he had revised and not to interfere again with his command. According to Kenney, "When Sutherland seemed to be getting a little antagonistic, I said, 'Let's go in the next room, see General MacArthur, and get this thing straight. I want to find out who is supposed to run this Air Force.'" Sutherland calmed down and agreed to handle Kenney's orders as he wished. "His alibi was that so far he had never been able to get the Air Force to write any orders," Kenney stated, "so that he, Sutherland, had been forced to do it himself . . . No wonder things hadn't been running so smoothly." Years later Kenney commented about Sutherland, "He was an arrogant, opinionated, and very ambitious guy . . . I don't think Sutherland was even loyal to MacArthur. He pretended that he was and I think MacArthur thought he was, but I wouldn't trust him." [4]

As the SWPA commander explained to Kenney in their first conversation at Brisbane, the southern Solomons operation (Task One) would be launched in a few days, and Allied Air Forces' bombing missions against the Bismarcks and Solomons were to be undertaken in support of the invasion by Ghormley's forces. At a conference in Melbourne on July 8, MacArthur and Ghormley had decided to recommend to the Joint Chiefs that the Tulagi invasion be postponed beyond August 7, the date for which it was scheduled. They felt that the ground, air, and naval units in the South and Southwest Pacific were inadequate to guarantee success and that it would be wiser to continue the build-up until they had the means to follow Task One quickly with the remaining two tasks.

But the Joint Chiefs rejected their advice on the grounds that it was imperative to remove this threat to the line of communications and, moreover, the expected Japanese concentration in Papua might improve the chances of surprise and success in the Solomons. In addition, word had just been received that the Japanese were constructing an airfield on Guadalcanal, so the Joint Chiefs added that island as an objective of Ghormley's assault.

King did not miss the opportunity to point out to his colleagues that only a few weeks earlier MacArthur had boasted that, with the addition of two carriers and an amphibious division, he could take Rabaul in quick order. "Confronted with the concrete aspects of the task," King sarcastically remarked, "he now feels that he not only cannot undertake this extended operation but not even the Tulagi operation." MacArthur resigned himself to defeat on the matter of dissuading the Joint Chiefs and sent most of his small naval force, under Rear Admiral V. A. C. Crutchley, to assist Ghormley, while Kenney prepared to mount strikes against Rabaul and the northern Solomons to hamper enemy staging activities. On August 7 Major General Alexander A. Vandegrift's reinforced 1st Marine Division landed on Guadalcanal and Tulagi, setting in motion a fiercely fought campaign that for a time seemed destined to fulfill MacArthur and Ghormley's darkest forebodings.[5]

By the time the invasion of the southern Solomons was under way, the Southwest Pacific theater had become the scene of another action that produced mounting concern at Brisbane: the Japanese were advancing rapidly along the Kokoda Trail and on July 29 entered the village of Kokoda. The march across the Owen Stanleys surprised MacArthur because Willoughby had persuaded him that the Japanese South Seas Detachment's mission was merely to establish and garrison air bases in the Buna-Gona area, from which aircraft could raid Moresby and Queensland. As the enemy advance across the mountains continued, SWPA G-2 reports so grossly underestimated the enemy's strength that MacArthur believed Morris' troops had yielded Kokoda to a numerically inferior force. In truth, Horii's soldiers on the Kokoda Trail were far superior to the defenders in numbers, quality, and firepower. MacArthur explained to Marshall on August 2 that his plans for defending Papua had been seriously handicapped by "a critical shortage of transportation, especially sea transport, and by [a] dearth of naval convoy ships," which at the time was true of his naval units, then en route to support Ghormley's operations. But the paucity of troops in Papua when the enemy offensive began, suggests one authority, "scarcely supports MacArthur's later claim that from the moment of his arrival in Australia he decided to defend that country in New Guinea."

Whereas the SWPA priority had recently been the completion of airfields in the Townsville-Cloncurry and Moresby-Milne areas, MacArthur now ordered the veteran Australian 7th Division to be rushed to Papua, with two of its brigades going to Moresby and one to Milne Bay. Lieutenant General Sydney F. Rowell, a distinguished Australian commander in the Mid-East war, was appointed to command the forces in New Guinea, which his predecessor, Morris, had led poorly in the view of MacArthur and his Brisbane staff. Meanwhile, on the Kokoda Trail the Australians fought back valiantly and on August 8 briefly recaptured the air strip at Kokoda. But with fresh reinforcements from Buna, the Japanese resumed their advance and by the third week of August had captured Isurava, which lay southwest of Kokoda and only sixty-five air miles from Port Moresby. The experienced Australian 21st Brigade had been thrown into action on the trail, yet even with those reinforcements the Australians had succeeded only in slowing down, not halting, the enemy advance. The situation was rapidly reaching a critical point.

The astounding ignorance at GHQ in Brisbane concerning conditions on the rugged, jungle-tangled trail across the Owen Stanleys became evident when Sutherland wrote to Rowell on the 13th that his men could stop the enemy advance at a spot called "the Gap," about twenty miles south of Kokoda; the chief of staff assured him that "the pass may be readily blocked by demolition." Apparently Sutherland imagined it to be a typical mountain pass — a narrow trail between high rock walls — but actually there were numerous side routes at the Gap for the Japanese infantry to use in enveloping a blocking force on the trail and no one location where demolitions could stop the advance. Rowell pointed this out and informed Sutherland that even if the explosives plan were to work, there was not enough time for hundreds of native porters, carrying explosives, to make the walk of at least five days from Moresby and that "some parts of the track have to be negotiated on hands and knees." He tartly suggested that "such explosives as can be got forward would be better employed in facilitating our advance than for preparing to deny the enemy." [6]

In late August Horii himself traversed the wild reaches of the Kokoda Trail to lead his soldiers in the final push to Port Moresby. The Australians, mainly the 21st Brigade, hotly contested every mile of the Japanese advance, and by early September the enemy's supply and reinforcement situation was becoming desperate as the numbers of defenders grew. The tortuous route over the mountains from Buna was a logistical nightmare in itself, but Kenney's planes were making it even more difficult for the Japanese to bring forward provisions and ammunition. Savage Australian resistance finally stopped the Japanese offensive southwest of Ioribaiwa on September 17.

By then Horii had already received orders to go on the defensive in Papua because the Japanese high command had shifted its priority to the Guadalcanal campaign. As soon as that island was secured, Horii was informed, large reinforcements would be sent to him so that he could complete his original mission, the seizure of Port Moresby. Thus the Japanese offensive ended with Horii's advance troops on Imita Ridge within twenty miles of Moresby — so close that they could see the port's searchlights crisscrossing the sky at night. But the last grain of rice had been issued to his troops on Sep-

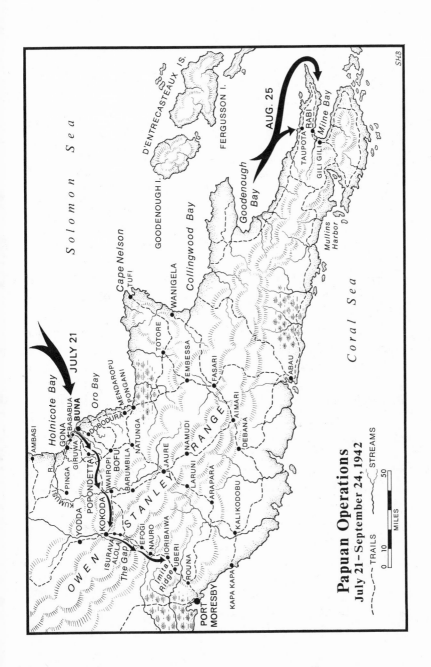

Papuan Operations
July 21 – September 24, 1942

Solomon Sea

D'ENTRECASTEAUX IS.

GOODENOUGH I.

FERGUSSON I.

AUG. 25

RABI
TAUPOTA
GILI GILI
Milne Bay

Goodenough Bay

Collingwood Bay

Mullins Harbor

ABAU

Coral Sea

Cape Nelson
TUFI

WANIGELA

TOTORE

EMBESSA

FASARI

AIMARI
DEBANA

NAMUDI
LARUNI

JAURE

ARAPARA

KALIKODOBU

KAPA KAPA

Holnicote Bay   JULY 21

GONA
BASABUA   BUNA
GIRUWA   Oro Bay
AMBASI   DOBODURA   MENDAROPU
PINGA   WAIROPI   PONGANI
KUMUSI R.   POPONDETTA   BOFU'   NATUNGA
YODDA   BARUMBILA
KOKODA
ISURAVA   EFOGI
ALOLA   NAURO
The Gap   ORIBAIWA
Imita Ridge   ROUNA
UBERI

OWEN   STANLEY   RANGE

PORT MORESBY

TRAILS
STREAMS

0   10   50
MILES

SHB

tember 17, and Horii realized that in their disease-ridden, starved condition they probably could not have captured, much less permanently held, Moresby.

In announcing on September 20 the decision to withdraw, Horii praised his men for their efforts in gaining the hard-won positions on the southern slopes of the Owen Stanleys: "No pen or words can depict adequately the magnitude of the hardships suffered. From the bottom of our hearts we appreciate these sacrifices and deeply sympathize with the great numbers killed and wounded." MacArthur had expected Horii to make a tenacious stand at Ioribaiwa, north of Imita Ridge, but the Japanese quietly and quickly pulled out of their forward positions on September 24 in a masterfully conducted withdrawal and headed back toward Kokoda and Buna. The last threat to Port Moresby had ended as suddenly and surprisingly as it had begun.[7]

Three weeks before Horii halted his attack along the Kokoda Trail, a second prong of the Japanese offensive on Moresby had come through by way of Milne Bay. An enemy convoy of nine ships was sighted by Allied aircraft north of Milne Bay on August 24, but land-based air attacks were limited by adverse weather conditions that day and the next. MacArthur sent an urgent appeal to Ghormley for carrier support, but the admiral felt their employment in the Solomons region "is a greater contribution to MacArthur's assistance than any sacrifice given at this time of carriers in the Milne Bay area." Ghormley did agree, however, to return Crutchley's support group, which proved valuable in covering the sea approaches to Milne Bay during the last days of the operation.

On the evening of the 25th, about 2000 Japanese marines landed at the east end of the twenty-mile-long peninsula on the north side of the bay and started moving toward the Allied base and three partially completed air strips at the west end. Japanese intelligence reported only two or three Australian companies in the Milne Bay area, but Major General Cyril A. Clowes's Milne Force comprised two brigades, about half of whom, including Clowes himself, had become combat-hardened in the Libyan desert campaign of the previous year. In addition, two RAAF fighter squadrons, equipped with American P-40's, and part of a RAAF reconnaissance squadron of American-built Hudson patrol bombers were stationed at Milne Bay. Clowes's total strength, including about 1300 American engineers and antiaircraft personnel, was nearly 9500 men.

For almost two weeks the Japanese, gaining a few hundred reinforcements by sea and at night, tried to maintain their beachhead on the bay, but the issue was, in fact, decided during the first three days of heavy fighting when the invaders' advance toward the air strips was hurled back with severe losses to the Japanese. RAAF planes continuously bombed and strafed their troop concentrations, barges, and supply dumps, while Clowes's troops counterattacked to the east. On the night of August 29 Japanese warships raced into the bay and successfully evacuated part of the troops, returning on September 7 to withdraw some of the remnant; a total of about 600 escaped in this manner. Meanwhile, the Australians wiped out a 200-man enemy force that had landed at Taupota, northwest of the bay; this Japanese unit had apparently intended to rendezvous with the main force near the air strips. Heavy jungle growth impeded Clowes's main push eastward along the peninsula but he eventually wiped out the beachhead. Although Clowes's soldiers and airmen suffered approximately 370 casualties, they inflicted over 2000 casualties on the enemy.

The victory at Milne Bay marked the first time that a Japanese amphibious force had been defeated and dislodged after it had established a beachhead. In a communiqué on September 10 MacArthur proudly reported that the enemy move against Milne Bay was "anticipated" and "prepared for with great care. With complete secrecy the position was occupied by our forces and converted into a strong point. The enemy fell into the trap with disastrous results to him." In the following weeks Milne Bay was developed into a major SWPA port, which by early 1944 would handle more tonnage monthly than any other port in the theater. Also, once the Milne airfields were completed, Kenney's aircraft could attack the Bismarcks and Solomons without crossing the Owen Stanleys. "Equally important," as the official American Army history points out, "the stage was set for a successful investiture of the north coast of Papua from East Cape to Buna." [8]

Unfortunately, the aftermath of the Milne Bay battle was less pleasant than could have been expected from the victory and MacArthur's communiqué. The SWPA chief had been eager, ever since the Guadalcanal invasion began, to get a counteroffensive started in Papua. He had proposed, through the Tulsa Plan, that all three tasks could be accomplished in less than three weeks, provided, of course, that he was adequately reinforced. On August 28 he became upset over the scanty reports coming from Clowes and told Blamey to instruct him "at once to clear the north shore of Milne Bay without delay" and to submit full daily operations reports thereafter. Through Blamey, MacArthur had previously put similar pressure on Rowell to "energize" his forces against the enemy on the Kokoda Trail.

Major General George A. Vasey, the deputy chief of the Australian general staff who was soon to command the 6th Division in Papua, confided to Rowell, "Sutherland stated that MacArthur was very concerned about the apparent lack of activity on Cyril's part. I replied that it was not necessarily lack of activity, but lack of information . . . You possibly do not realize that for GHQ this is their first battle, and they are, therefore, like many others, nervous and dwelling on the receipt of frequent messages." He continued, "By the tone of this morning's conversation with Sutherland, I feel that a wrong impression of our troops has already been created in the minds of the great." On another occasion Vasey informed Rowell, "GHQ is like a bloody barometer in a cyclone — up and down every two minutes . . . They're like the militia — they need to be blooded."

On August 30 MacArthur told Marshall that he was "not yet convinced of the efficiency of the Australian units." Even after the triumph at Milne Bay he remained unconvinced, as was clear in his report to the War Department: "The enemy's defeat at Milne Bay must not be accepted as a measure of relative fighting capacity of the troops involved. The decisive factor was the complete surprise obtained over him by our preliminary concentration of superior forces." He went on to deprecate Clowes's leadership, charging that he should have "acted with great speed" in destroying the entire enemy force and preventing the evacuations. Blamey meekly supported MacArthur's criticisms, but Rowell lashed back in defense of Clowes: "I'm sure that he was right. Inability to move except at a crawl, together with the constant threat of further landings, made it difficult for him to go fast or far."

Both Sutherland and Kenney visited Papua in the wake of the Milne Bay action and returned with reports of Australian ineptitude and passivity that further buttressed MacArthur's dissatisfaction with Rowell, Clowes, and their troops. Despite the fact that Blamey, who toured the Papuan front about the same time in September, came back with the optimistic report that the Australians were ready and able to drive the Japanese out of Papua, MacArthur persuaded Curtin of his negative view of their performances. With a ready acquiescence which Australian military authorities later criticized, Blamey agreed that the Papuan commanders and their soldiers could have been more aggressive both at Milne Bay and on the Kokoda Trail. MacArthur insisted, and Curtin readily agreed, that it was time for Blamey to take command personally in New Guinea.

Blamey arrived at Port Moresby on September 23, a week after Rowell's troops had stopped the Japanese drive south of Ioribaiwa. After several days of argument about the nature of the new command arrangement, tempers flared, according to one source, when Rowell accused Blamey of being too subservient to MacArthur. Blamey relieved Rowell and took command of the New Guinea Force on the 28th. "He charged me with having failed to safeguard his interest," Blamey reported to MacArthur, "and said he felt he was being made to eat dirt." He found that "Rowell is competent but of a temperament that harbours imaginary grievances . . . [It is] essential to have [a] commander of cheerful temperament and who is prepared to co-operate to the limit." Blamey appointed Lieutenant General Edmund Herring to command the Advance New Guinea Force and assigned, as his first task, a counteroffensive on the Kokoda Trail in late September. Herring would turn out to be a brilliant commander in the operations in New Guinea, but MacArthur's criticisms were not forgotten by the Australians — nor would they be his last.[9]

Of all times for MacArthur to receive his first visit by a member of the Joint Chiefs, late September, 1942, was not the most ideal, but Arnold arrived at Brisbane on the 25th to confer with him and Kenney, and flew on to Moresby the next day to talk to Blamey and Rowell. Kenney said he enjoyed "chuckling at General MacArthur practically ordering Hap to give me everything I wanted." In his diary Arnold briefly noted the main points of MacArthur's monologue, which ranged widely:

1. Japs are better fighting men than Germans.
2. Pick of Japs in South[west] Pacific.
3. MacArthur does not have the troops to hold Japs. Only two divisions — and those partially trained. Australians are not even good militia. Navy support is nil.
4. Air has passed from below average under Brett to excellent under Kenney. Walker and Whitehead outstanding. Would not exchange Air Force units for any others.

5. Japs can take New Guinea at will. Can take Fijis. Will then control Pacific for 100 years.

6. Japs' move into Aleutians is part of the general move into Siberia.

7. Need 500 more airplanes to hold Japs. Our planes are fine — excellent. Give him any kind of combat type.

8. England can only be considered as a besieged citadel.

9. No second front can possibly be established from England.

10. Any move into North Africa is waste of effort.

11. Sufficient numbers of air bases can never be established in England to provide air cover for second front.

12. Japs have much better coordinated team than Germans.

13. Our present cordon defense system across Pacific is as old and out of date as a horse and buggy.

14. Our plan should be to give more aid to Russia. Put troops in there. Work from interior lines against Germany and Japan.

15. We should stop building up an Army that we can't use — building tanks and autos that we can't send overseas.

16. Build up Australia as a reservoir of supplies, troops, and planes — use them in any direction against Japs.

Arnold added at the end of that day's entry in his diary: "Thinking it over, MacArthur's two-hour talk gives me the impression of a brilliant mind — obsessed by a plan he can't carry out — frustrated — dramatic to the extreme — much more nervous than when I formerly knew him. Hands twitch and tremble — shell shocked." [10]

Nevertheless, Arnold's opinions of personalities and problems in the Pacific war were strikingly similar to MacArthur's. "Kenney has destroyed since August 2nd, with loss of only 40 of his planes, the following Jap planes: 150 in air, 175 on ground," the Army Air Forces head jotted in his diary. "He is a real leader and has the finest bunch of pilots I have seen. All those who were worn out and nervous wrecks are now eager to fight and withdrawing their requests to go home." He was also impressed by Whitehead, Walker, and the recently arrived commander of the American I Corps, Lieutenant General Robert L. Eichelberger. Of the last-named, Arnold wrote, "I believe that he will put some pep in the Aussies. He already has plans to go from defensive to offensive." After his conferences and inspections in Papua, Arnold concluded that Blamey "seems highly pleased with the way things are going . . . General Blamey has no idea of attacking unless he is forced into it." His opinion of the Australian soldier was brutally unfair and was probably influenced by the views he picked up at GHQ in Brisbane: "Australian is not a bushman. He is not a field soldier. He is nothing but a city slum dweller. The Massachusetts soldiers knew more about the New Guinea jungle in 2 days than the Australians in 2 years."

After a conference in Noumea, New Caledonia, with Ghormley and his commanders, which Kenney and Sutherland also attended, Arnold made these observations in his diary: "(1) Navy is not going to help MacArthur to get to Rabaul before they do. (2) What was started as a big offensive now is classed as a limited offensive to stop Japs from further advance. (3) Navy and MacArthur can see no other operations than these in the Pacific — Germany does not present danger that Japs do." The air chief's opinions of the top admirals in the South and Central Pacific theaters were almost as harsh as his views of the Australians.

When he returned to Washington in early October, Arnold proposed that the entire Pacific be placed under a single commander. For that position he nominated MacArthur, Lieutenant General Joseph T. McNarney, and Lieutenant General Lesley J. McNair, each of whom he considered "perfectly capable of conducting the combined operations" in the war against Japan.[11] Unity of command was never to be achieved in the Pacific, but if MacArthur learned of Arnold's support of him — and he undoubtedly did through his high-ranking confidants in the Pentagon — it must have been of some consolation to the troubled SWPA commander during this critical period. Of course, he probably wondered why Arnold would have nominated McNarney and McNair also.

2. *Other Commitments*

A second front in Europe was under consideration by the Combined Chiefs of Staff even during the gloomy days of early spring, 1942, and the American members, especially Marshall and Arnold, already were talking in favor of an invasion of France as soon as practicable. In April they persuaded their reluctant British counterparts, who preferred an attack in North Africa, to agree tentatively to two proposals of action against the Germans: a limited assault against the Continent in the autumn of 1942 in case of a disastrous defeat of the Soviet Army (Operation Sledgehammer) and a massive invasion of Europe in the spring of 1943 (Operation Roundup). In either case, the concentration of forces in the British Isles (Operation Bolero) would be necessary. The fall of Tobruk and other disasters in the Libyan campaign in June resulted in the diversion to the Middle East of all British shipping involved in Bolero. Fearful that the German-Italian offensive would overrun the Suez region, Churchill and his chiefs proposed that a North African invasion be undertaken instead of Sledgehammer, even if it meant delaying Roundup.

Suddenly Marshall, "tearing a page from MacArthur's book," quipped one authority, took the position that if the British were going to balk on Sledgehammer the United States should concentrate its might on defeating Japan. Although dedicated to the Germany-first strategy, he reasoned that the North African operation would violate the hallowed military principle of concentration of force, involving the Allies in a large-scale offensive that would not have a decisive impact on the Germans and would cause the indefinite postponement of the cross-Channel attack. Therefore he proposed turning with full force to the war against Japan, which would avoid the wasteful dispersion of American men and matériel and would surely produce the defeat of that member of the Axis. But when Marshall and King presented the idea to Roosevelt in mid-July, he squelched it promptly on the grounds that it "amounted to the abandonment of the British." The President concluded that if Sledgehammer was not feasible, "then we must take the second best — and that is not the Pacific."

As Marshall, King, and Harry Hopkins, Roosevelt's trusted adviser, prepared to leave for England to negotiate a plan of action against the Germans for 1942, the President emphasized to Hopkins, "Under any circumstances I wish BOLERO and ROUNDUP to remain an essential objective, even though it may be interrupted." In late July a preliminary Anglo-American agreement was reached to undertake Operation Torch, as the invasion of Algeria and French Morocco was soon code-named. Eisenhower, then war plans chief under Marshall, was selected to command Torch, which would be launched on November 7. The American chiefs agreed to the abandonment of Sledgehammer only on condition that some Bolero units and supplies be detoured to the Pacific for a limited counteroffensive. But before and after its initial landings, the North African operation would consume troops and supplies at a rate that distressed both the advocates of a European second front and the supporters of an expanded effort in the Pacific. In fact, many military leaders from the Pentagon to Brisbane would wonder if the Allies had the resources to execute concurrent operations in North Africa, Guadalcanal, and Papua.[12]

MacArthur was keenly aware by August that his theater was already playing second fiddle in the Pacific to Ghormley's and that when the Allies began offensive operations against the Germans the Southwest Pacific's priority would drop even lower.

He perused radiograms from the Pentagon and even newspapers for hints of future developments and became extremely sensitive about any suggestions in print that his theater faced further subordination in global strategy and logistical planning. In early August, for example, the New York *World-Telegram* published an editorial that stated that Curtin and MacArthur should not expect top priority for their area since, with the greatly increased Allied commitments around the world, "President Roosevelt and Mr. Churchill must take a wider view . . . They cannot now give Australia a larger share of planes and shipping without jeopardizing global strategy." MacArthur notified Marshall that the editorial "has been featured in all Australian papers and has caused a tremendous upheaval of bitter resentment throughout this country . . . If possible, such an incorrect and damaging statement should not be passed by American censors. It tends to destroy the morale of the Australian public with a corresponding reaction throughout the armed forces, both Australian and American." [13]

Marshall's reply on August 10 was a lucid exposition of the place of MacArthur's theater in Allied global planning and of the impression he was creating among the Joint Chiefs on that matter:

> The publication in Australia of editorials such as the one you quote in your Number C RPW C-219 of August 8th is damaging to morale. The last statement, "Australia no longer can count on priority," is untrue and seriously detrimental in its effects. The delivery of troops and munitions to Australia is made under allocations determined by the Combined Chiefs of Staff in accordance with the over-all strategic concept. The needs of the Southwest Pacific theater are weighed against those of all other theaters, and once determined, they have equal priority with those of other theaters.
>
> You can do much to counteract the ill effects of this editorial through the medium of press releases emanating from your headquarters. General Richardson was sent to inform you of

the broad Allied strategy proposed by the Combined Chiefs of Staff and approved by the President and the British War Cabinet. You are aware of what has been done and what is being done to supply your theater to meet the needs of the strategy adopted. You are also familiar with American newspaper practice regarding freedom of the press with particular reference to the editorial pages. Editorials have no official status or approval, and as yet our government has not set up censorship control in regard to them.

Under dateline from your headquarters of August 6 the Washington *Post* and other papers have published an article by Lee Van Atta. He stated that his information was from "authoritative military and civilian circles," the spokesmen for whom made seven points which Van Atta listed categorically. Each of the seven points was designed to deprecate the part played by the United States in aiding the war effort in your theater. This press release originating from your headquarters can only serve to fan the indignation and resentment that has resulted from the editorial of which you complain.

Your problems are appreciated by the Combined Chiefs of Staff and by the Secretary of War and me personally. We know that opportunities are not taken advantage of because of our inability to provide you with additional means. You must rest assured, however, that these factors have been carefully considered.

Van Atta's article mentioned above creates the impression that you are objecting to our strategy by indirection. I assume this to be an erroneous impression. You should be aware that the pressures to meet the growing dangers of the situation in the Aleutians, to build up again the depleted air force in Hawaii, to meet the debacle in the Middle East, not to mention Russia, China, the losses in ocean tonnage, and the urgent necessity of creating new air squadrons sufficiently trained and equipped to go overseas, make our problem exceedingly difficult and complex.[14]

As MacArthur probably noticed, Marshall's last sentence was a summary of the thesis of the *World-Telegram* editorial.

The SWPA chief responded, "You are entirely correct in your

assumption that this headquarters is not by indirection attempting to influence strategic control from higher headquarters. The complete opposite is the case." He went on to explain that Van Atta's article stemmed from the *World-Telegram* editorial and to describe the Conservative Party's reaction to it in Australia: "The opposition seized upon this as a great opportunity, and criticism of the present Australian government and the general strategy of the war as dictated from Washington and London became the ruling political issue." He denied that Van Atta obtained his information from his headquarters and assured Marshall that "the Solomons attack has completely silenced all criticism." As another member of the Joint Chiefs, Arnold, was soon to learn, MacArthur was severely critical of the Combined Chiefs' strategy since he was convinced that "no second front can possibly be established from England" and a North African invasion would be a "waste of effort." Nevertheless, the Combined Chiefs, mainly because of Marshall and Arnold's support of him, chose to interpret his objections and demands as the justifiable efforts of a zealous, aggressive commander to obtain more logistical support for his theater's operations.[15]

In the meantime, Curtin took the stage to reopen with Churchill the question of retention of the Australian 9th Division in the Middle East. Curtin expressed his War Council's "willing agreement" to allow the division to remain there until Rommel's offensive had been hurled back if Churchill would do his utmost to insure the allotment of enough aircraft to equip seventy-three RAAF squadrons by June, 1943. The British prime minister responded that the United States government had assured him that sufficient measures were being taken to protect Australia, but he would present the seventy-three-squadron proposal to the Combined Chiefs.

In late August that body agreed to equip thirty RAAF squadrons by April, 1943. Curtin protested that this was not enough to "assure even the defence of Australia as a base," much less to undertake offensive operations, but Churchill said that the Combined Chiefs' plans for a combined strength of over 1100 aircraft in the Southwest Pacific theater and another 1000 in the South Pacific by spring, 1943, would be sufficient. Next Curtin began pushing for the transfer of the British Eastern Fleet from the Indian Ocean to the Southwest Pacific, this time appealing to Roosevelt also. He made no request for additional troops and expressed gratitude for the 98,000 American soldiers and airmen who were in Australia (by August 31), but he did remind Roosevelt that "Australia's capacity to help herself has been limited by the fact that 48,000 men are still serving overseas and our casualties in dead, missing and prisoners of war total 37,000 or an aggregate of 85,000."

There is little doubt that Curtin's overtures were precipitated by his talks with MacArthur. On August 30, the day before Curtin importuned the President with the above message, MacArthur warned the Joint Chiefs that "unless the strategic situation is constantly reviewed in the light of current enemy potentialities in the Pacific and unless moves are made to meet the changing conditions, a disastrous outcome is bound to result shortly." Not then knowing that Clowes had already turned the tide of battle at Milne Bay or that Horii's drive toward Moresby would soon falter, MacArthur ominously predicted, "It is no longer a question here of preparing a projected offensive. Without additional naval forces, either British or American, and unless steps are taken to match the heavy air and ground forces the enemy is assembling, I predict the development shortly of a situation similar to those that have successfully overwhelmed our forces in the Pacific since the beginning of the war."

Both Curtin and MacArthur continued their urgent pleas for help until September 16, when Roosevelt frankly told Curtin, "After considering all of the factors involved, I agree with the conclusions of the Combined Chiefs of Staff that your present armed forces, assuming that they are fully equipped and effectively trained, are sufficient to defeat the present Japanese force in New Guinea and to provide for the security of Australia against an invasion on the scale that the Japanese are capable of launching at this time or in the immediate future." With the North African invasion only seven weeks away and of paramount concern to him, Roosevelt pointed out to Curtin that the Allied leaders were bound by "the necessity of rigidly pursuing our overall strategy that envisages the early and decisive defeat of Germany in order that we can quickly undertake an all-out effort in the Pacific."

For several weeks the Brisbane pot simmered but began to boil anew when on October 6 MacArthur reminded Curtin, "The concept that the 9th Division's presence in Egypt would be offset by British or other naval reinforcements no longer exists." This and new crises in the Pacific set off another series of requests to Washington and London by the two friends in their never-ending struggle to elevate SWPA's priority. But if they remained set in their conviction that the major Allied effort should be exerted first against Japan, Roosevelt, Churchill, and the Combined Chiefs were just as determined to pursue the course of global strategy they had decided upon, which left the Southwest Pacific a secondary theater in logistical considerations.[16]

In the autumn of 1942 priorities were complicated by the Torch preparations and also by the situation on Guadalcanal, which had been critical ever since the third day after the landing. On the night of August 8–9 Japanese warships surprised Ghormley's fleet off nearby Savo Island, sinking four heavy cruisers, including the Australian *Canberra*. The remaining Allied vessels, some of them heavily damaged, retired from the area, and for a time Vandegrift's division was stranded without naval or air support. During the next several weeks the enemy miscalculated the Marine assault as merely a reconnaissance in force, while, on the other hand, the Joint Chiefs, despite the Savo disaster, misjudged the Japanese determination to hold the island and began plans to start Task Two. But the enemy, especially by early September, was reacting with unexpected ferocity and strength and for four months would unleash such devastating ground, air, and sea attacks against the invaders that the ability of the Marines to remain on Guadalcanal would be in serious doubt.

In August, however, at least Ghormley and Nimitz realized they had struck a hornet's nest and sent repeated pleas to Washington for reinforcements. Marshall diverted to Ghormley twenty-nine B-17's and sixty-one medium bombers that had been scheduled to go to Australia. He also told MacArthur to intensify his supporting air attacks and to send a fighter squadron to Ghormley. SWPA bombing missions against the Bismarcks and northern Solomons were stepped up, and Kenney sent a squadron of P-39's to the South Pacific, though Ghormley had requested the far superior P-38's; the only ones in the Pacific were in MacArthur's area. In the Joint Chiefs' sessions King crusaded for greater air support for Ghormley, but Marshall and Arnold stood by their commitments to Torch and Bolero, refusing at first to allow any more aircraft for the Pacific. Eventually, as the crisis worsened, they agreed reluctantly to the transfer of three air groups from the Bolero allocation, though King had hoped to get fifteen shifted to the war against Japan.

When MacArthur appealed for additional planes and shipping to support Task One and also to help drive the enemy out of Papua, Marshall firmly told him that he, Ghormley, and Nimitz would have to coordinate their air plans and cooperate in pooling the aircraft already available in their theaters. As for shipping, Marshall suggested that he obtain vessels from Australian sources or from Nimitz because the Torch preparations were tying up virtually all American cargo vessels outside the Pacific. For a brief period in early September it looked as if the 7th Marine Regiment might be transferred from Samoa to Australia, giving MacArthur some of the amphibious troops he had long pressed for, but at the last moment they were withheld from him and shifted to Guadalcanal instead.[17]

Beginning about the middle of September, South and Southwest Pacific intelligence sources reported the build-up of large numbers of enemy troops, aircraft, and ships in the Rabaul and Bougainville-Buka areas. Since the first of the month the Japanese high command had changed its top priority from Horii's Papuan operations to the Guadalcanal campaign. Despite attacks by Allied air and naval forces, including another large-scale sea battle, the Japanese managed to get several thousand more soldiers to Guadalcanal in the early days of October.

On the 16th Marshall alerted MacArthur to a new naval force staging off the Shortland Islands and urged him to send his planes to attack it. MacArthur apparently interpreted the message as a request that he give Ghormley better support. In reply he defensively maintained that he had been assisting the admiral as well as he could, Ghormley had expressed "his appreciation" in radiograms on three different occasions, and coordination was excellent between the two theaters. Furthermore, he said, he was already aware of the Shortlands activity and, in fact, had called it to the attention of the War Department previously. The SWPA chief continued with a summary of the needs of his area, calling again for increases in shipping, troops, and planes, and for the transfer of the British Eastern Fleet to his theater. He boldly appealed for a thorough review of global strategy by the Combined Chiefs and for the commitment of what amounted to the largest share of Anglo-American resources to counter the Japanese in Papua and the Solomons. His efforts were, of course, to no avail.

As it turned out, from September through November, 1942,

the War Department's allocations to Army forces in the four Pacific theaters indicated that rumors of a Japanese thrust at Alaska, which was never attempted, seemed to cause more concern among the Army planners than the threat to Papua and Australia: 16,000 troops and 547,000 tons of cargo were shipped to the North Pacific during that period, 25,000 troops and 333,- 000 tons to the Central Pacific, 36,000 troops and 310,000 tons of cargo to the South Pacific, and only 8300 troops and 157,000 in cargo tonnage to the Southwest Pacific. In fact, MacArthur's headquarters claimed that "in the last half of 1942 the Southwest Pacific received a smaller tonnage of supplies from the United States than the theater itself shipped out to the neighboring South Pacific." [18]

At the beginning of the final week of October, Roosevelt became extraordinarily anxious as the Japanese began their long-awaited offensive to retake Guadalcanal. The President directed the War Shipping Administration to find quickly twenty additional ships for supply runs to the South Pacific, and he told his military chiefs "to make sure that every possible weapon gets in that area to hold Guadalcanal." The War Department had earlier decided to send the 43rd Division to New Hebrides and New Caledonia, and now the 25th Division, originally slated to go to MacArthur, was reassigned to Guadalcanal, although the situation there had long passed the dangerous stage by the time it arrived. The understanding with Mac-Arthur was that, when the 25th Division relieved the 1st Marine Division, which would be in early December, the Marines would be transferred to Australia. (As it developed, the exhausted, battered, malaria-ridden Marine division would need a year before it would be ready for combat again.) Meanwhile, in October Nimitz rushed major elements of the Pacific Fleet to the southern Solomons, and on the 18th, in a move to get the best possible leader to handle the crisis, he appointed gruff, aggressive Admiral William F. Halsey to succeed Ghormley as South Pacific commander. Halsey would prove equal to the challenge and, as an unexpected benefit, would win the friendship and cooperation of MacArthur.

On Guadalcanal the Marines, now reinforced by an Army regiment, held firm as the climactic Japanese assault struck during the last week of October, while off the Santa Cruz Islands Halsey's fleet turned back a large enemy naval force with heavy losses on both sides. By the first of November the worst crisis of the campaign had passed, but two weeks later the persistent Japanese tried again to drive the Americans off the island. In several fierce battles in mid-November, the Japanese fleet and its troop-laden convoys were decisively defeated by the American Navy. In a communiqué on November 16 the Navy Department announced that "General MacArthur's aircraft were of great assistance to our naval forces, both before and during the naval actions. Army bombers made repeated successful attacks on units of the Japanese invasion fleet at Rabaul and at Buin." In addition, MacArthur finally sent eight P-38's to Henderson Field for the period November 13–22. The effort by the enemy to recapture Guadalcanal in November was the last major threat during the campaign; thereafter Halsey had no doubt that his forces could hold, but more than two months of vicious fighting lay ahead before Guadalcanal was finally secured. Task One required a six-month campaign during which the Japanese suffered 27,500 casualties and the Americans 6111.[19]

Their anxious efforts in October to find the means to alleviate the Guadalcanal crisis made more clear than ever before to the Joint Chiefs, as well as to the South and Southwest Pacific commanders, the significance of shipping and port facilities. They found that not only was there a shipping shortage in that region of the Pacific but that the lack of shipping was a worldwide problem for the Allies, affecting even the preparations for the top-priority Torch operation. Serious difficulties developed, which were not solved for over a month, in getting the twenty ships that Roosevelt had wanted immediately for the South Pacific run.

MacArthur had repeatedly stressed that cargo vessels, especially light shipping that could operate in the treacherous coastal waters off Papua, were desperately needed in his theater; their absence would seriously cripple his offensive efforts along the northern shores of Papua. In addition, at times in the South and Southwest Pacific ports, particularly at Noumea in September and October, unloading could not keep pace with ship arrivals because of administrative inefficiency, poor Army-Navy coordination, and a dearth of longshoremen. The ships became "floating warehouses" at the very time when their cargoes were in great need at the front. The chaos at some ports aggravated the already alarming shipping shortage, which did not begin to ease until after the vessels that had been committed to Torch were released later in the fall. Torch cast more than one long shadow across the Pacific.[20]

Confusion in the handling of supplies produced a singularly unfortunate episode which handicapped the Marines during the campaign. In early July, Vandegrift sent one of his intelligence officers to Melbourne to obtain topographic data on Guadalcanal because the South Pacific staff had none. Since the island lay outside the SWPA bounds, Willoughby's geographic section had compiled no information, but MacArthur ordered a photoreconnaissance mission to make aerial photographs of the island. This was done a few days later. Three sets of the prints were made at Townsville and sent to the South Pacific's rear base at Auckland, New Zealand. There the maps were misplaced; they never reached Vandegrift. It was "a matter of considerable surprise" at MacArthur's GHQ when it was learned, long after the campaign ended, that the Marines had not received the maps.

Colonel E. F. Kumpe, the SWPA map chief, stated, "An investigation after the [Guadalcanal] operation brought out the information that the maps had been lost in the tremendous pile of boxes incident to the organizing of the base establishment of South Pacific (SOPAC)." Kumpe admitted that "the story does not sound too good in its reflection on the coordination between theaters. However, in this particular case, every effort was made from the western Pacific [SWPA] to send forward all they had to meet the operational dates." Vandegrift thought that the maps were "improperly addressed," and that Willoughby's staff was at fault. Regardless of who erred, the Marines paid the penalty by having to rely during the opening phases of the campaign on captured enemy maps and the personal recollections of former residents, none of which was very accurate.[21]

During the worst period of the Guadalcanal operation — August to mid-November — most of the support given by the SWPA was in the form of bombing missions against airfields in the Bismarcks and northern Solomons. Ghormley wanted the air strikes directed primarily against shipping, but Kenney felt that it was more important to both theaters that his planes achieve air supremacy over Papua and the western portion of the Solomon Sea. Besides, in the battle of the Coral Sea SWPA's land-based bombers had established a sorry record against moving ships, and in the early naval actions off Guadalcanal Kenney's bombers had mistakenly attacked Allied submarines on the surface — and had fortunately missed them. His aircraft did win superiority in the skies over Papua that fall, and their destruction of Japanese planes in the air and on the ground in the New Britain and Bougainville regions helped significantly to relieve the air situation over Guadalcanal. Ghormley and Halsey both attested to the importance of the air support from the Southwest Pacific squadrons, even if MacArthur was rather late in sharing his P-38's.

The quarrel over those aircraft arose because, although they were the only type of American fighter superior to the vaunted

Zero, they were in short supply. MacArthur's determination to get an offensive under way in Papua before the completion of Task One, in this instance and in others, lessened the air support he gave to the South Pacific, but his increasing pressure on the Japanese in Papua did keep the high command at Rabaul off balance and deterred the sending of even more enemy air and ground units to the Guadalcanal campaign.

MacArthur had some skirmishes with admirals during the Guadalcanal campaign, but it would be an exaggeration to claim that his relations with Navy leaders in the Pacific that autumn were hostile. The SWPA naval support group under Crutchley was involved in several major naval engagements in the waters around the Solomons in August. MacArthur's request for its return in early September seemed justified by his needs for convoys and for patrols off the coast of New Guinea. "MacArthur's Navy," as it was then called, was still small; it consisted of only five cruisers, eight destroyers, twenty submarines, and seven small auxiliary vessels. According to Admiral Thomas C. Kinkaid, who would later command the SWPA fleet, Leary "had rather a rough time" in his relations with MacArthur in August. For one thing, Leary persisted in communicating directly with Nimitz and King, which was contrary to MacArthur's belief that all such communications should go through his office first. More important, Leary was wary of endangering his vessels in the uncharted waters off the Papuan coast. On September 11 MacArthur obtained a new Allied Naval Forces commander, Rear Admiral Arthur S. Carpender, with whom he soon experienced similar difficulties.

In late October MacArthur and Nimitz clashed briefly over the latter's request that all SWPA submarines be placed under his control for the duration of the Guadalcanal crisis. The general refused, probably feeling, as one official historian suggests, that by then "the co-operation between the two theaters was a one-sided affair." Nimitz appealed the matter to the Joint

Chiefs, who shortly reassigned twelve SWPA submarines to Halsey over MacArthur's protests. Marshall and King received information, perhaps from Nimitz, implying trouble between MacArthur and Ghormley, but both theater commanders denied it and no evidence has been found to contradict them. Except for a skirmish in November, to be discussed later, Mac-Arthur and Halsey seemed to have a healthy respect for each other's ability and fiery temperament.

Much has been printed about MacArthur's differences with the Navy, but the attitude in both Nimitz's and Ghormley's headquarters toward the Army did, in fact, leave much to be desired that fall. The admirals tended to treat with disdain the opinions of Army and Army Air Force officers assigned to their staffs, and the Guadalcanal operation was a "Navy show" at the decision-making levels. Probably the most serious blunder of the campaign was the South Pacific command's failure to finish Henderson Field quickly and bring in land-based airpower, a fault that could have been corrected had the admirals listened to Army Air Force counsel. With Halsey's arrival, inter-service friction in the South Pacific command diminished because he earnestly solicited the advice of the former outsiders at his headquarters.[22]

As now was becoming all too usual, there occurred some unpleasant exchanges between Washington and Brisbane over alleged press releases by MacArthur. On August 16, for instance, Marshall radioed MacArthur that the Navy was "greatly concerned over [the] character of press statements on [the] Tulagi operation emanating from Australia. As all are labelled 'General MacArthur's Headquarters,' this promotes [the] feeling that you can control [the] matter." MacArthur replied, "I am distressed by your [message] . . . because of the complete coordination and absolute cordiality that exists between myself and all naval commanders in this general theater." He maintained that "there is in Australia absolutely no source of information regarding this operation," so it must have been copied from dispatches from "outside sources," especially in the United States. "The fault, if fault exists, is due to the lack of censorship at these outside points," he stated. He promised to discuss the matter of censorship again with Curtin, but emphasized that the real solution was "censorship at the receiving offices in the United States of incoming messages, irrespective of the fact that they have been censored here."

As on similar occasions in the past, MacArthur told the Army chief of staff, "There is growing resentment against the lack of news of the Solomons operation on the part of the people of Australia" since the action "is in their immediate neighborhood, affecting directly their security, and the Australian Navy is actively engaged." Especially irksome to him and Curtin was the Navy Department's refusal until October to permit a news release on the sinking of the Australian cruiser *Canberra,* which had gone down with heavy loss of lives on August 8.[23]

The Guadalcanal operation provided another trial of the Joint Chiefs' command experiment for the Pacific, which was based on coordination and cooperation between the Army-dominated Southwest Pacific Area and the Navy-controlled Pacific Ocean Areas. To some observers the campaign pointed anew to the need for unity of command in the Pacific war, but neither the Joint Chiefs nor their planners could reach a consensus on who should be appointed. In the debates the list of candidates was usually narrowed down to MacArthur and Nimitz as the chief nominees. Arnold, it will be recalled, returned from his Pacific tour that fall convinced that it must be an Army general. Brigadier General St. Clair Street, who was in the War Department's operations division and would later become one of MacArthur's air commanders, proposed in late October that the "sane military solution" would be to remove MacArthur to a post such as the ambassadorship to Russia and then give the Pacific command to Nimitz or McNarney. Nothing came of his suggestion, and, in practice, the Joint Chiefs continued to function as a corporate supreme command for the Pacific.

There had been some misunderstanding and disagreement between MacArthur and the admirals of the neighboring theaters, and they would continue to arise, especially when theater interests overlapped. But the fact that these differences, according to the official Army study of Pacific strategy and command, "had little effect on operations and the vigor and speed with which the war against Japan was conducted is a tribute to the determination of all concerned to make common cause against the enemy." [24]

3. Approaching the Beachhead

As Blamey and Herring prepared in late September to send the New Guinea Force on the counteroffensive, the training and morale of their troops were far superior to those of the Australian militiamen and native constabularies who had first tried to stop the Japanese drive across the Owen Stanley Range. The two brigades of the veteran 6th Division, which had been detoured from the Middle East to Ceylon, arrived in Australia in August, and by late September one of them had reached Port Moresby. Already in Papua by that time were the other two brigades of that division, now commanded by Vasey; Major General Arthur S. Allen's 7th Division; and at Milne Bay two more Australian brigades.

Over half of the Australian soldiers in New Guinea now were men who had earlier seen combat against the Germans and Italians. In addition, two American regiments of Major General Edwin F. Harding's 32nd Infantry Division had arrived at Moresby, although most of these troops were National Guardsmen whose training had been hasty and incomplete. The 126th Regiment came by sea and the 128th was transported by Ken-

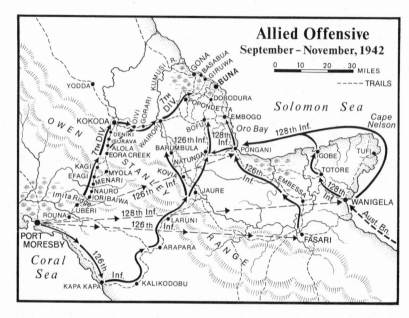

Allied Offensive
September – November, 1942

0   10   20   30 MILES

----- TRAILS

YODDA

Solomon Sea

Cape Nelson

GONA
BASABUA
GIRUWA
BUNA
DOBODURA
POPONDETTA
EMBOGO
Oro Bay
KOKODA
DENIKI
ISURAVA
ALOLA
EORA CREEK
BARUMBULA
NATUNGA
PONGANI
GOBE
TUFI
TOTORE
126th Inf.
128th Inf.
126th Inf.
128th Inf.
7TH DIV.
OIVI
GORARI
KUMUSI R.
WAIROPI
BOFU
EMBESSA
WANIGELA
KAGI
MYOLA
EFAGI
MENARI
NAURO
IORIBAIWA
Imita Ridge
UBERI
KOVIO
JAURE
128th Inf.
126th Inf.
ROUNA
128th Inf.
126th Inf.
LARUNI
ARAPARA
FASARI
Aust. Bn.

OWEN
STANLEY
RANGE

PORT MORESBY

Coral Sea

KAPA KAPA
KALIKODOBU

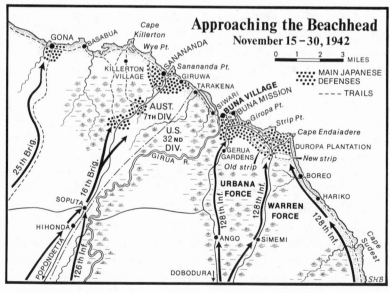

Approaching the Beachhead
November 15 – 30, 1942

0   1   2   3 MILES

• MAIN JAPANESE DEFENSES

----- TRAILS

GONA
BASABUA
Cape Killerton
Wye Pt.
SANANANDA
KILLERTON VILLAGE
Sanananda Pt.
GIRUWA
TARAKENA
SIWARI
BUNA VILLAGE
BUNA MISSION
Giropa Pt.
Strip Pt.
Cape Endaiadere
DUROPA PLANTATION
New strip
BOREO
HARIKO

AUST. 7TH DIV.

U.S. 32ND DIV.
GIRUA R.

GERUA GARDENS
Old strip
URBANA FORCE

WARREN FORCE

25th Brig.

16th Brig.

SOPUTA
HIHONDA
128th Inf.
128th Inf.
128th Inf.
POPONDETTA
126th Inf.
ANGO
SIMEMI
DOBODURA
Cape Sudest

SHB

ney's aircraft. The latter's successful movement was the largest troop-carrying operation the United States Army Air Forces had undertaken in its history up to that time. "General MacArthur was happy as a kid over the way the movement was going," said Kenney. The air commander, nevertheless, had experienced difficulty in selling the idea of the airlift because of the skepticism of Sutherland and other GHQ staff officers.

MacArthur issued his Papuan offensive plan on October 1, the immediate objective being to drive Horii's forces across the Kumusi River, which crosses the Kokoda Trail near Wairopi, about twenty miles east of Kokoda. The Australian 7th Division would advance along the Kokoda Trail, while part of the American 126th Regiment would converge on Wairopi by way of trails that crossed the mountains farther south. An Australian battalion would seize lightly defended Goodenough Island off the northern coast of Papua, where an air base was to be constructed, and the 128th Infantry would move by air, land, and sea in an advance on the Buna region from the southeast.

As the main overland drive along the Kokoda Trail got under way, the Australians soon found that their service troops and nearly 4000 native carriers could not keep the advance troops adequately supplied, so tedious was foot travel along the track. The 126th's troops moving along the poorly mapped, rugged tracks to the south came to depend on air drops also. Kenney initiated a large-scale program of air supply, but often the weather was so rough over the Owen Stanleys that his transports could not complete their missions. Frequently the drops in wild jungle reaches were off the mark and either were not located by the Allied soldiers or were seized by the enemy.

Carpender, conducting naval operations along the northern coast, refused, like Leary before him, to allow his cruisers and destroyers to venture into the coastal waters between Milne Bay and Cape Nelson for fear of the numerous reefs and the proximity of Japanese aircraft at Lae, Salamaua, and Rabaul. Finally, in late October a safe channel was charted to Cape Nelson, and small Australian and Dutch lighters and barges, manned by Australian, Dutch, Papuan, and Javanese crews and sometimes escorted by Australian corvettes, began to work their way up the coastline with men and matériel. As Kenney's airmen won supremacy in the skies, more and more small ships made the trips to and around Cape Nelson. By December the seaborne traffic to Pongani and Oro Bay, which lay between Cape Nelson and Buna, would be contributing much to Allied operations: in one eighteen-day period that month over 2000 troops, as well as supplies and some tanks, were shipped to Oro Bay by the sea route. But Carpender proved to be right on the use of larger vessels since, according to the leading naval historian on the Pacific war, "up to May 1943 every merchant ship of over 2000 tons which ventured around East Cape got bombed, and many were sunk." [25]

With the start of the advance, MacArthur decided to make his first visit to New Guinea. American newspaper articles, whose sources were not cited, had been describing him as personally leading the defense in Papua for some time. Accompanied by Kenney, Diller, and Morhouse, MacArthur flew to Moresby on October 2. Immediately upon arriving that evening MacArthur plunged into conferences with Blamey, Herring, and other ranking officers. On the 3rd, as noted in MacArthur's office diary, he "spent the entire day inspecting Port Moresby area, going beyond the advanced artillery posts by 'jeep.' Addressed the members of the Engineer Company who were working on landing strips and decorated Vernon Haugland, Associated Press newspaper man, and inspected the wharves." In a brief excursion along the beginning stretch of the Kokoda Trail, said Kenney, MacArthur "made quite a hit with the Aussies. They were glad to see him up on the trail. Good psychology." The SWPA chief remarked to Brigadier John E. Lloyd, whose 16th Brigade was about to move out to the front far up the trail, "Lloyd, by some act of God, your brigade has been chosen for this job. The eyes of the Western world are upon you and your men. Good luck and don't stop." MacArthur also inspected some American infantry at Moresby and, stated Kenney, found them to be "fresh and full of pep and ready to go, although they were far from being seasoned troops." The next morning at 7:00 MacArthur departed on a B-17 for Brisbane.[26]

His next trip to Papua was to have been on November 4. That morning he and Kenney boarded a B-17 at Brisbane and took off for Moresby. About 100 miles out at sea an engine quit, and Kenney told the pilot to turn back to Brisbane. Kenney describes MacArthur's reaction to the development:

> I went back to where MacArthur was still peacefully sleeping. I touched him on the knee. He opened his eyes, smiled, and said, "I guess I must have dozed off. Did you want something?" "Oh, nothing in particular," I answered, "I just wanted to tell you that this is a good airplane." He nodded. "In fact," I went on, "It flies almost as well on three engines as it does on four." "I like to listen to you enthusiastic aviators," said MacArthur, "even when you exaggerate a little." "All right," I said, "we've been flying on three engines for the last twenty minutes and you didn't know it. In fact, you didn't even wake up. If you look out that window you can see the propeller of number-two engine standing still."
>
> He looked out the window, listened carefully for a while, grinned, and said, "Nice comfortable feeling, isn't it?" and leaned back in his seat and relaxed. He took it a lot more coolly than I did the first time I had a bomber engine quit.
>
> We landed back at Brisbane, got the engine fixed up, and the next day flew to Port Moresby without incident, except that we flew through heavy rain most of the way. It took us six hours. MacArthur slept through three of them.

MacArthur arrived at Moresby on November 6 and remained there until January 9.[27]

During his first visit to Moresby and for several weeks afterward, MacArthur received disturbing reports from the front that the supply situation was critical despite the air drops. At least 50,000 pounds daily were required by the troops in the mountains, but about one-third of what was sent in had to be discounted as wastage because of the problems of dropping from aircraft. Gradually the air supply system improved as both airmen and troops on the ground became more experienced at making contact with each other and after some emergency air strips were constructed along the routes of advance.

During the last half of October the supply crisis, however, was not as alarming to MacArthur as were the possible consequences to his forces of a collapse on Guadalcanal. On October 16 he warned Marshall, "It is now necessary to prepare for possible disaster in the Solomons. If we are defeated in the Solomons, as we must be unless the Navy accepts successfully the challenge of the enemy surface fleet, the entire SWPA will be in the greatest danger." Foreseeing a shift of Japanese concentration back to Papua if the enemy succeeded in retaking Guadalcanal, he began to prepare a plan for withdrawing his forces from the north where the 128th Regiment, part of the 126th, and an Australian battalion had worked their way to within approximately thirty miles of Buna.[28]

But the fateful last week of October was marked by irremediable setbacks to the Japanese in Papua as well as in the Guadalcanal area. On the 28th the 7th Division soundly defeated the Japanese at Eora Creek, about ten miles south of Kokoda. Until then the advance along the Kokoda Trail had been excruciatingly slow. Now the Australians' forward momentum picked up, and on November 2 they captured Kokoda and its valuable airfield. MacArthur jubilantly sent his congratulations to the Australian units, and Kenney's aircraft soon were landing at Kokoda with troop reinforcements and much-needed supplies, including heavier equipment than could be sent in by air drops.

In the next two weeks Vasey, who had assumed command of the advance, caught a large part of Horii's troops in a well-executed envelopment east of Kokoda. The Japanese force in the mountains was virtually annihilated. Hundreds died in the fighting between Kokoda and Wairopi, and many others, including Horii, were drowned when they tried to escape by raft across or down the flooded Kumusi River. Quickly seizing Wairopi, the Australian 16th and 21st brigades crossed the swollen Kumusi on November 14–15 on flimsy wire-and-log suspension bridges constructed by their engineers. As they pressed on past the last foothills of the Owen Stanleys and began the descent in the final twenty-mile trek to the coast, it seemed that the four-month struggle to regain control of the entire Kokoda Trail was almost finished.[29]

In the meantime, another part of MacArthur's plan was executed successfully when an Australian battalion, transported by two destroyers, landed on Goodenough Island on the night of October 22–23. At first they encountered fierce opposition from the 290 Japanese who had been stranded there during the battle at Milne Bay. But an enemy submarine evacuated about 250 of the Japanese; the remaining stragglers were rapidly mopped up by the Australians. Completing another part of the offensive plan were the 126th and 128th regiments which, together with several Australian battalions, had made their way — some units by the coastal sea route, others by airlift, and some overland across the mountains — to a position about fifteen miles south of Dobodura, where they were ready to close in on the Buna area from the south and southwest. Colonel L. Jack Sverdrup, Casey's deputy, was a key figure in reconnoitering routes and leading prodigious engineering feats in airfield construction to support the advance of the 126th and 128th infantries. Thus, just as the last major enemy thrust at Guadalcanal was broken in mid-November, so on the eastern side of the Owen Stanleys the Papuan campaign was moving toward a final phase. In both theaters the last stage would take much longer than anticipated, but whereas on Guadalcanal the scale of operations would decrease, the fighting at the Papuan beachhead would reach its height during the two months ahead.

When the issue on Guadalcanal was much in doubt in October and he was pessimistic about the situation in Papua, MacArthur had prodded Blamey, Herring, and Allen to speed up the advance to Kokoda. On October 17 Allen was stung by a message from Blamey: "General MacArthur considers extremely light casualties indicate no serious effort yet made to displace enemy." Four days later MacArthur sent a message through Blamey to Allen stating that "progress on the trail is NOT satisfactory. The tactical handling of our troops in my opinion is faulty." Allen told Blamey that he was "singularly hurt" by the criticism, and he tried to justify the slow advance on the grounds of rugged terrain, supply difficulties, and stubborn Japanese rear-guard defenses.

On October 23 Blamey made it clear that he supported MacArthur's charges when he informed Allen that his response "does NOT confute any part of General MacArthur's criticism in his message sent to you on [the] 21st. Since then progress has been negligible against an enemy much fewer in number . . . [who] appears able to delay advance at will." Blamey notified Allen on the 27th that Vasey would relieve him in two days. Allen replied, "It is regrettable that it is has been found necessary to relieve me at this juncture especially since the situation is improving daily and I feel that the worst is now behind us." On the 28th, as mentioned, the 7th Division, led by Allen, won its crucial victory at Eora Creek, which resulted in the rapid advance to Kokoda a few days later. At Brisbane in November, Allen personally explained to MacArthur the conditions on the trail up to Eora Creek and stated that the SWPA commander's critical messages had "distressed" him. MacArthur looked surprised and commented, "But I've nothing but praise for you and your men. I was only urging you on." Allen responded drily, "Well, that's not the way to urge Australians."

The Australian brigadier remained bitter about the failure of MacArthur, Blamey, or Herring to visit him on the Kokoda Trail during his operations. When a lieutenant colonel from Herring's staff had visited Allen briefly on October 22, it was the first time that any of his three superiors had sent a staff officer forward to investigate conditions at first hand. The official Australian account of the campaign is sympathetic toward Allen and suggests that the problems and misunderstandings "could have been overcome in some measure through the use of competent and experienced liaison officers." It concluded that "a theatre commander must rely largely on that and similar means to develop a picture denied generally to his own eyes by the demands of the desk from which necessarily he must discharge most of his responsibilities." Since Allen was well liked and trusted by the troops, his departure produced widespread ill feelings toward the high command, even though the able Vasey was his successor. "Throughout it was at Brisbane and Canberra," maintains the Australian Army history, "that there was lack of confidence, not at the front."

MacArthur's plan of attack on the beachhead was issued on November 14 and called for the Australian 7th Division to advance against Gona and Sanananda and the American 32nd Division to attack Buna. The divisional boundary generally followed the Girua River, whose mouth was just west of Buna, but each division was to attack across the boundary if an opportunity to hit the enemy's rear or flank presented itself. In the American sector, which was east of the Girua, Harding would employ the Warren Force on the coastal flank against the enemy positions at Duropa Plantation and the two air strips, while the Urbana Force would operate on the river flank and attack the Japanese around Buna Village and nearby Buna Mission. Harding's troops were divided into the two task forces because the water-logged, almost impassable area in the middle of the American sector forced the separation. The 32nd Division was also given the task of establishing and protecting an airfield at Dobodura, about ten miles from Buna Village. Moreover, it was to protect the coastline northward from Oro Bay to prevent seaborne attacks against the right flank and rear of the Allied lines.

MacArthur had earlier rejected a bold plan by Blamey to employ one of the brigades at Milne Bay in an airborne attack on Nadzab, 200 miles to the north near Lae in the Markham Valley. The SWPA commander believed that the Japanese, who controlled the sea north of Cape Endaiadere, could easily reinforce their troops in the Lae region and thus overwhelm the isolated brigade. He also later refused Blamey's request to move one of the Milne brigades to the Buna-Gona front since he felt that another enemy attack at Milne Bay was still a possibility.

While the Allies were organizing their front and reshuffling some units on the Papuan front, at Rabaul the setbacks that the Japanese had recently suffered brought a command reorganization: the Eighth Area Army was constituted on November 16, with Lieutenant General Hitoshi Imamura as its commander, and under him were the Eighteenth Army in New Guinea, headed by Lieutenant General Hatazo Adachi who arrived at Rabaul on the 25th, and the Seventeenth Army in the Solomons.[30]

The coastal region where Vasey's and Harding's divisions were operating was mostly swamp and thick jungle. Patches of shoulder-high, razor-sharp kunai grass, groves of coconut palms, some growing 125 feet in height, and heavy underbrush were scattered through the dry areas. The rainy season had begun, and the overflowing Girua River and other streams in the vicinity sent waters into the swamps in front of the beachhead, making it impossible in many locations for large numbers of troops to concentrate in preparation for attacks and presenting difficulties in the transfer of units from one place to another. The daily temperature averaged 96° Fahrenheit and the humidity 85 per cent; the frequent torrential rains seemed to worsen the hot, muggy conditions. As the troops on both sides soon found, numbers of diseases were endemic to the region, including scrub typhus, malaria, amoebic and bacillary dysentery, dengue fever, jungle rot, ringworm, and dhobie itch. Harding and Vasey realized that unless they could capture the beachhead in a short time, these diseases were likely to decimate their ranks. But ahead of them the Japanese had cleverly utilized every parcel of dry ground in the swamps to construct well-concealed bunkers that covered every possible stream crossing, the few jungle tracks, and all usable exits from the swamps. If the Allied soldiers got past this honeycomb of jungle and swamp defenses, they would still face heavily fortified pillboxes all along the coast for about eleven miles from Gona to Cape Endaiadere, three miles south of Buna Village.

Any possibility of an amphibious operation against the beachhead was ruled out when Carpender frankly told MacArthur on November 10 that he could not comply even with a request from Blamey for a destroyer escort for some small transports moving from Milne Bay to Oro Bay. The admiral refused, as he had in October, to endanger his vessels in the shallow, reef-ridden waters south of Buna, where they would also be subject to air assaults. The Japanese Navy, on the other hand, continued to reinforce the beachhead by way of a deep-water route from New Britain to a landing area just north of Buna Village. MacArthur had repeatedly requested amphibious engineer and assault forces, as well as landing craft, but none was available in time for this operation. An amphibious officer from Washington who visited the Papuan front in December reported to the War Department that there was "every reason to believe that Buna could have been taken during November if one of our units could have put a minimum of one combat team afloat."

To make matters worse for the Allied attackers, their intelligence estimates of the enemy's numerical strength were far too optimistic: Willoughby's estimate was 1500 to 2000 Japanese in the Buna-Gona area, which was the same as that calculated by Vasey's G-2, and Harding's G-2 estimated there was "not more than a battalion" in the beachhead. Harding informed Sutherland that he expected the capture of Buna to be "easy pickings, with only a shell of sacrifice troops left to defend it." The Allied troops, according to the official American Army chronicle, were "told by their officers that the operation would be an easy one, and that only a small and pitiful remnant of the enemy force which had fought in the Owen Stanleys remained to be dealt with." Actually the Japanese forces at Gona and Sanananda, which were led by Colonel Yosuke Yokoyama, and those at Buna, under Navy Captain Yoshitatsu Yasuda, totaled approximately 8000, of which about 6000 were effective combatants. With ample stocks of ammunition, excellent defensive positions, and more reinforcements and supplies expected from Rabaul, the Japanese were well situated to make the reduction of their beachhead a long and costly operation.[31]

The Allied forces learned the truth quickly and brutally when they launched the first of many attacks against the beachhead in mid-November. The Australians were repulsed before Gona, and the Americans made little headway in their attempted advance against Buna. When Japanese planes on November 16 destroyed an important convoy of luggers and barges loaded with supplies, the impact on the offensive was "a catastrophe of the first magnitude." Harding himself and several of his officers narrowly escaped death in the attack near Cape Sudest and had to swim ashore. Despite this disruption to the coastal supply line, both divisions attacked repeatedly in the next week or so, but with little success. The unexpected enemy resistance, torrential downpours, supply shortages, and the ravages of disease sent morale, especially among the inexperienced

Americans, plunging to an alarmingly low level. Discipline was rapidly becoming a problem in the 32nd Division, and, to add to Harding's woes, on November 19 Herring ordered the 126th Infantry shifted to the Gona sector to assist the Australians. This order and Herring's requests for heavier weapons gave Harding cause to complain that Herring was uncooperative.

By late November the American division was down to one-third of the normal daily ration; it lacked tents, gun oil, entrenching tools, and other basic equipment and supplies. What was particularly frustrating was that the Americans did not have the weapons they needed to reduce the powerful bunkers that blocked their advance — tanks, flame throwers, mortars, artillery, and close air support. Both sea and air traffic to the embattled Allied forces had been sharply reduced because of Japanese air attacks east of the Owen Stanleys and unusually bad weather west of the mountains.

Nevertheless, on the evening of November 22, MacArthur told Harding to launch an all-out attack the next day "regardless of cost." When his troops were soon brought to a standstill by well-directed enemy firepower, Harding ordered them to cease the attack and pull back; to those in Moresby his cessation of the assault appeared premature. Brigadier General Hanford MacNider, the Warren Force commander who had ably led the earlier advance along the coastline from Pongani, was wounded by a grenade on the 23rd and had to be evacuated. Under new pressure from MacArthur, Harding sent the Urbana and Warren forces in a general attack on November 30, which also was viciously hurled back by the Japanese. Both the American and Australian divisions had suffered heavy casualties during the two weeks of repeated assaults against the beachhead, and the number of men succumbing to serious diseases was climbing at an appalling rate.[32]

Blamey reported to MacArthur that he had conferred with the port naval commander at Moresby and that officer had

ridiculed the idea that "navigational difficulties prevent the use
of naval forces in the Buna area. Moreover, Japanese naval
units have no hesitation in moving into these waters on that
account." So Blamey proposed an amphibious landing at the
beachhead, transporting the troops in destroyers. MacArthur
thought it "an excellent idea," but when he consulted Carpender, he learned again to his dismay that the stubborn admiral still would not risk his ships in that area; besides, no
landing craft were available anywhere in Papua. Frantically
MacArthur appealed to Halsey for the use of his naval forces,
but the admiral replied, "Until the Jap air in New Britain and
[the] northern Solomons has been reduced, [the] risk of valuable naval units in [the] middle and western reaches of [the]
Solomon Sea can only be justified by [a] major enemy seaborne
movement against [the] south coast [of] New Guinea or Australia itself."

On one of the few occasions when he became upset with
Halsey, MacArthur heatedly radioed Marshall that although
he had faithfully supported the South Pacific command during
its crises, when "I have been under acute pressure and have
appealed for naval assistance that was available in contiguous
areas, I have not only been refused but occasion has been taken
to enunciate the principles of cooperation from my standpoint
alone." Although MacArthur portrayed the crisis in blackest
terms in late November, Halsey, Carpender, Nimitz, and King
were unanimous in opposing the dispatch of fleet units to the
Buna area.[33]

On November 25 MacArthur called a conference of his high-
ranking officers at his Moresby headquarters, which was in the
large, comfortable but not luxurious Government House where
the Papuan territorial governor had resided before the war. At
the meeting MacArthur stated that the crisis at the Buna-Gona
beachhead made it necessary to bring in the American 41st Division, though it was then still in training near Rockhampton.

Blamey frankly told him that he would prefer an Australian brigade instead because "he knew they would fight." The SWPA chief agreed after Blamey and Herring elaborated on reports from the front about the poor morale and discipline of the 32nd Division, but it was, observed Kenney, "a bitter pill for MacArthur to swallow." He sent Sutherland to visit the front, and the chief of staff, like Herring on an earlier visit to Harding's sector, concluded that the American leadership was unaggressive and its soldiers lacked the will to fight. On November 27–28 Chamberlin also went to the front and returned with a similar adverse report on the 32nd's leadership.

Harding told both GHQ visitors that he was solidly behind his regimental officers, although Sutherland and Chamberlin had serious doubts about the competence of several of them. Sutherland tried to warn Harding that command changes would have to be made by him if the troops were to be revitalized, but the divisional commander insisted that no advance could be made until he got tanks, infantry replacements, and more artillery. Before leaving Harding's headquarters, Sutherland informed him that MacArthur had already ordered Eichelberger, the I Corps commander, to report to him at Port Moresby.[34]

On the afternoon of November 30, Eichelberger, along with Brigadier General Clovis E. Byers, his chief of staff, and others of his corps headquarters, arrived at Moresby. Shortly after reaching their rooms at the Government House, they were summoned to a conference with MacArthur, Kenney, and Sutherland on the long, wide veranda across the front of the house. Kenney was smiling and friendly, but Sutherland, whom Eichelberger learned had just returned from the Buna front, wore a stern look. MacArthur also looked grim as he opened the meeting with a long monologue on the condition of the 32nd Division and his humiliation over reports that the Americans would not fight. Like Sutherland, he placed the blame chiefly on Harding and was convinced that "a real leader could take these same men and capture Buna." He told Eichelberger to go to the front immediately and relieve Harding and all other unaggressive American officers "or I will relieve them myself and you too." He expected the enemy to land reinforcements "any night" and emphasized that "time is of the essence." Restlessly pacing up and down the veranda and speaking with great intensity, he told Eichelberger, "Go out there, Bob, and take Buna or don't come back alive." Pointing his finger at Byers, he added, "And that goes for your chief of staff, Clovis, too."

Before Eichelberger departed for the front the next morning, MacArthur conferred briefly with him once again. On the previous day MacArthur had impressed Eichelberger as "angry and harassed"; now he seemed affable and relaxed. He cautioned the I Corps commander to take care of himself since he was of "no use to him dead," but he also told him to seize Buna regardless of casualties. Taking him to one side, MacArthur quietly promised Eichelberger that if he captured Buna he would award him the Distinguished Service Cross, recommend him for a British decoration, and cite him prominently in his press releases. Eichelberger later stated, "I did not know . . . what would happen if I had disobeyed General MacArthur's directive" regarding Harding's relief. He learned afterward that part of the reason for MacArthur's ire had been that he "was being gloated over by the Australian High Command who had been criticized in turn by him previously." [35] Eichelberger had indeed walked into a tense situation at SWPA headquarters, where his chief was bristling because he felt that his pride and honor were at stake. But when the I Corps commander would get to the Buna front he would find that, as reported, the 32nd Division was at the breaking point and that human lives, not just reputations, were at stake there.

CHAPTER VI

Belated Victory

1. Far from the Guns of Buna

THE LIFE OF THE MACARTHURS at Lennon's Hotel was, in the words of a reporter-friend, "one of simple dignity, almost monastic in its call to duty." Mrs. MacArthur, with the help of the faithful Ah Cheu, who lived with the family, devoted herself to taking care of her young son and her busy and often exhausted husband. The MacArthurs occupied an apartment formed from three suites in a private section of the hotel that was served by a small elevator, with a guard posted at the landing to keep uninvited persons from getting off at their floor. Kitchen facilities were provided in the quarters, but for a while Jean, who was not an experienced cook, preferred to order the family's meals from the hotel kitchen. General Mac-Arthur eventually tired of certain items on the hotel menu, so Jean and Huff, with the assistance of Ah Cheu and a hotel maid, prepared many of his meals. Since the general's office hours were very irregular, he always called around noon and in the evening just before he left GHQ, so that his meals would be waiting when he arrived. Jean did everything possible to make a peaceful home life for him in Brisbane's busiest hotel, and he, according to friends, reciprocated as a considerate, adoring husband and affectionate father.

Because he rarely took off long periods of time from work, MacArthur tried to give his son as much attention as possible when he was home. He started the practice of bringing a small gift, usually a toy, to Arthur every day, but Jean had to persuade him to forgo this daily routine lest he spoil Arthur. The boy's play areas were restricted by the location of the downtown hotel, and he had few playmates because most of the American officers who resided in the hotel had not brought their families. He did find a few friends of his age, including the hotel manager's son, and they particularly enjoyed playing in the small park across the street near the Supreme Court buildings. Huff, who often took time to play games of chase with Arthur, found him to be "a child of great enthusiasms," who, though missing some of the normal activities of childhood, "seemed able to adapt himself easily to almost any circumstances." [1]

Kenney, on his arrival in Australia, introduced into the life of the SWPA chief an informal camaraderie which he had lacked and which Sutherland, still his principal professional confidant, did not have the warmth and amiability to offer. Outgoing, good-natured, and devoted to MacArthur, Kenney became a frequent visitor at the MacArthurs' apartment and was one of the few persons who felt free to call on them without notice.

Kenney relates the way a typical evening get-together developed:

I'd get some bright idea and go see them. They were two floors above me in Lennon's Hotel there in Brisbane. I would go up and knock on the door, and Jean would come to the door.

I would say, "Jean, this Australian coffee we are getting here isn't too good. Do you have any of that good-tasting San Fran stuff that they had a little left of at the commissary a few months ago?"

I'd hear the "Old Man" in there say, "Jean, let him in. He doesn't care anything about coffee. He wants to come in and give me the dope on some new idea he's got."

So they both would laugh, and I would go in. Jean would sit down and listen till she finally would get sleepy and fall sound asleep. We would talk till about 2:00 in the morning, discussing some move we should make. We came to quite a lot of decisions that way.[2]

Yet even in informal conversations with a friend like Kenney, rarely did MacArthur's discussions venture far from the topics of strategy, tactics, logistics, and leadership. The military life for him was both his profession and his principal recreation.

When MacArthur moved to Port Moresby in early November for a two-month stay, he came to a community that most Americans considered, in the words of one soldier, "a dry, dusty, dirty town consisting of a few houses, hotels, warehouses, and docks squatting on a hill that rises from a curving harbor. Most of the buildings are made of wood and many of them, today [fall, 1942] are rather splintered after months of being subjected to enemy bombing." By the time of MacArthur's arrival Allied aircraft controlled the sky overhead, though on the night of November 24 two enemy air raids hit the town. None of the bombs, however, fell near MacArthur's residence. The Government House where he lived was a large, rambling, one-story white house set apart on a small knoll overlooking the busy harbor. Around the house were palms, tropical shade trees, and a beautiful garden with scarlet poinciana and pink frangipani. A number of native servants were employed at the headquarters, and a colorful detachment of Papuan constabulary soldiers, attired in knee-length white skirts bound with red sashes, handled the daily rituals of raising and lowering the American and Australian flags in front of the Government House. The scene was an idyllic one in contrast to the unimpressive, noisy town crowded with Australian and American servicemen.

A correspondent who had known the general in Melbourne and Brisbane observed that at Moresby MacArthur "is just as remote, just as mysterious as he has been ever since he reached Australia eight months ago . . . He is rarely seen." In fact, a glimpse of him on the Government House grounds was so rare for passing soldiers that they regarded the phenomenon as worthy of retelling to their buddies. One who saw him strolling before breakfast said he wore "a pink silk dressing gown with a black dragon on the back" — considered so newsworthy an item that *Time* magazine mentioned it. Another told of seeing the general pacing the grounds in deep meditation while holding some messages in one hand and a head of green lettuce in the other.[3] As in Brisbane, the more MacArthur seemed to withdraw, the more interested the public became in tales and glimpses of his private life.

Kenney, who roomed across the hall from MacArthur, found him far from aloof and fondly remembered those days of fellowship with him. The SWPA chief's human side was revealed on one occasion at the Government House when he decided that the stifling heat at night was unbearable in his breeze-forsaken bedroom. He noticed that the wind seemed to blow steadily against the side of the house where Kenney roomed. After one of Kenney's flights to Australia, he returned to find that MacArthur had "stolen" his room. Kenney took it good-naturedly, particularly when "with the advent of the rainy season the prevailing winds shifted 180° and MacArthur then had the hottest room in all New Guinea, and it remained that way during our entire stay." Kenney commented, "However, the General never mentioned the subject again and I don't believe it was because he had gotten used to the heat." [4]

Far away in the United States the war drums of the anti-Roosevelt groups were building up excitement in the summer and fall of 1942 for the presidential candidacy of MacArthur. Some influential conservative newspapers and speakers were savage in their denunciation of what they said was the President's failure to provide adequate military support for Mac-Arthur's theater, charging that Roosevelt feared the political consequences in 1944 if the popular general, after several glorious military campaigns, decided to enter the presidential race. Romulo, formerly MacArthur's aide and now on Quezon's staff in Washington, spent much of that summer and autumn on a tour of the United States, giving speeches before large political and civic groups in which he praised MacArthur as America's greatest leader, the clear implication being that he was politically as well as militarily great. He and a number of politically minded Army officers, editors, and business executives wrote to MacArthur giving him their views on the potential support for his candidacy, described by most as overwhelming.

The general's answers to their letters usually exhibited interest but were noncommittal and emphasized his concern over combat developments in his theater. When organizations in the States solicited public statements from him, however, he issued them with the politician's gusto, whether on behalf of the Doughboy Committee or the Congress of American Industry. The magnitude of the number of public messages that he sent to such groups, extolling their war production figures, praising each organization's high principles, or commemorating the particular society's anniversary, undoubtedly led many of the general's admirers to think that he would not look unfavorably upon a political draft.[5]

Stimson and probably Marshall were annoyed by Mac-Arthur's apparent acquiescence in the growing MacArthur-for-President movement. The Secretary of War wrote in his diary in late October, "MacArthur, who is not an unselfish being and is a good deal of a prima donna, has himself lent a little aid to the story by sending people here who carry a message from him that he was not a presidential candidate, thereby playing into the hands of the people who would really like to make him a candidate." Stimson felt that he should handle the affair "as soldier-like Marshall would treat it of never saying a word on the subject and assuming that all talk of one's candidacy is nonsense." [6]

In Brisbane on October 28, the day before Stimson recorded the above, MacArthur issued the following statement to the press:

> No nation is making a more supreme war effort than Australia. It is rapidly gearing to full capacity. Its resources are relatively meagre, but it is utilising them to the utmost. Its effort is universal and embraces equally all classes and all parties. It has unanimously and completely supported me in my military command, and the harmony and co-operation between Australians and Americans in this area are inspirational.
>
> Such internal party differences as exist are largely based upon the desire of one group or the other to accelerate rather than retard the war potential. I am deeply grateful for their magnificent spirit of friendship and understanding, without which it would have been difficult to go on.
>
> I have noted the statement quoted in the morning papers from the Christian Science Monitor's Washington correspondent [Joseph C. Harsch] that "political Washington was largely responsible for the establishment of two separate commands in the Pacific, partly because of the conservative opposition which launched the MacArthur for President campaign." I have no political ambitions whatsoever. Any suggestion to the contrary must be regarded as merely amiable gestures of good will dictated by friendship.
>
> I started as a soldier, and I shall finish as one. The only hope and ambition I have in the world are for victory for our cause in the war. If I survive the campaign I shall return to that retirement from which this great struggle called me. [7]

Commenting on MacArthur's statement, Curtin pledged his government's "complete and unequivocal backing to the commander in whose capacity and person it has whole-souled confidence." In an unusual move for an Australian prime minister, he lashed out against MacArthur's detractors, who were prominently voicing their opinions of the general that fall: "What has been done and is being done is better understood by the enemy than is apparently the case with certain critics, and it is a matter for reflection that so inspiring and great a leader should have been obliged by astigmatic minds to stress the obvious." Nelson Johnson, who had returned to Washington from Australia, wrote to MacArthur that he "admired" his statement and "appreciated the peculiar difficulties under which you have had to labor in silence." Johnson hoped "the air has been cleared now," for in Washington he had become "exasperated almost beyond control by the kind of irresponsible whispering that has been the main capital of the pub-strategist."

Major General George Van Horn Moseley, a long-time friend of MacArthur, believed the "subversives" would unite to defeat him if he ran in 1944. Moseley predicted that the "mongrelization" of the nation by the Jews, Negroes, "low-bred" immigrant laborers, and leftists would so arouse the rest of the people that in a few years they would demand that MacArthur be returned to the States as a temporary dictator. He felt MacArthur's "greatest task" in life would come after the war when he could, by "brushing all opposition aside, restore our Republic by the temporary institution of the most drastic methods." Moseley assured him, "You would be damned for the moment, but in the end you would make for yourself a place in history unequalled except by our first President himself." MacArthur chose not to comment on this in his friendly but brief and carefully worded reply. Another interesting response to MacArthur's announcement was that of the San Francisco *Examiner,* a Hearst organ, which stated, "The politicians, having nothing further to fear from him politically, should now be willing to send him sufficient men and equipment for the fulfillment of his military job . . . It is not good Americanism to obstruct him. It is not even good politics." [8]

The public opinion polls indicated that, although MacArthur was held in high esteem by many Americans, most did not view him as a potential political figure in the league with Roosevelt. That fall, in a *Fortune* poll in which respondents were asked to name the greatest living Americans, MacArthur ranked a close second to Roosevelt; MacArthur's total was more than double the grand total for the ten men below him on the list. On the other hand, surveys by the American Institute of Public Opinion through March, 1943, showed him well behind Roosevelt, Willkie, Dewey, and sometimes Henry A. Wallace as the respondents' likely choice for President in 1944, with his support, as expected, suffering a sharp drop after his announcement that he had no interest in politics.[9]

Then in February, 1943, came a *Fortune* poll of a national cross section of factory workers, which gave the general's supporters new hope. The workers were asked, "If the war is over before the next election, which one of these men do you think would make the best President in 1944?"[10]

	All Factory Workers	Well-informed	Uninformed
Roosevelt	37.8%	30.2%	46.1%
Willkie	20.2	27.6	13.1
MacArthur	15.2	11.2	17.9
Dewey	9.8	13.3	6.3
Wallace	5.0	8.1	3.2
Murray	1.7	1.3	.9
Lewis	.5	.9	.5
Don't know	10.6	8.7	12.9
	100.8%*	101.3%*	100.9%*

* Since some respondents named more than one, the percentages exceed 100.

It will be noted that among uninformed workers MacArthur was the leading potential Republican candidate, although the records do not indicate the criteria used for distinguishing "well-informed" from "uninformed" workers. His supporters would have been wise to observe, however, that Roosevelt had his largest percentage and an almost three-to-one margin over the general among this grassroots element. Nevertheless, this poll, together with the Democratic setbacks in the congressional elections in November, gave the MacArthur-for-President movement a new impetus, regardless of what the general stated publicly.

If his supporters in the States had known of the problems with which MacArthur was wrestling, perhaps they might have understood his disinclination to become involved in politics at that time. His troops were finding it difficult to seize the area that the enemy had not even controlled when Task One was planned; relations with the Australian high command had deteriorated sharply; the Guadalcanal operation continued to require aircraft that Kenney would have preferred to use in support of the Papuan drive; and both headlines and supplies seemed to be very nearly monopolized by Eisenhower's offensive in North Africa.

Three weeks after MacArthur moved to Port Moresby, another problem, which had been smoldering for some time, suddenly became a conflagration, namely, the friction between Australian and American troops. In New Guinea their relationship was reasonably satisfactory since most of the men had more than enough to occupy their minds and time. But it was when multitudes of Australian and American servicemen, bearing passes and leaves, intermingled in their leisurely enjoyments of the large cities that trouble erupted. As has been almost a tradition with soldiers and sailors, various combinations of sex and liquor precipitated most of the brawls.

On the evening of November 26 Australian soldiers and American military police clashed outside the American post exchange in Brisbane, and after the police resorted to their guns, there were Australian casualties of one dead and nine wounded. The next night angry bands of Australian servicemen roamed the streets of the city, viciously attacking American troops and some officers with their dates. Twenty-one Americans were injured, some seriously. More American and Australian military police were rushed to Brisbane, and with the restoration of order in the streets the tension began to lessen.

Allied Land Forces headquarters conducted an investigation, and the report on December 4 listed six major factors contributing to Australian-American friction:

> (a) drunkenness, (b) the higher rates of pay and the smarter uniforms of the American Army, (c) discrimination in favour of Americans in shops and hotels and by taxi drivers, (d) the spectacle of American troops with Australian girls, particularly wives of absent soldiers, and the American custom of caressing girls in public, (e) boasting by some American troops, and their tendency to draw guns or knives in a quarrel, (f) the taunting of Australian militiamen by Americans.

The report pointed out also that the strong-arm methods of the American military police were antagonistic to all Australians, whose own police rarely employed weapons and physical force. The official Australian history adds, "In the United States the display of batons and firearms in the hands of police is an effective way of quelling a riot whereas in Australia it is an effective way of starting one."

After further study by his staff, Blamey proposed some measures designed to improve relations, including the transfer of selected officers and noncommissioned personnel from each national force to battalions and companies of the other, the interchange of staff officers at higher levels, lectures by "good men" from each national force to assemblies of the other force, and "a concerted but unobtrusive effort" by each side's public relations sections to promote better understanding.[11] In a message to Blamey on February 12, however, MacArthur rejected his plan:

grievance was that the majority of persons patronizing the establishments on such occasions were not American soldiers but Australians who were trying to undermine "the defence against Sabbath desecration." The ministers asked MacArthur to get his officers to withdraw their requests for the Sunday openings and, if necessary, to prevail upon government officials to take action to close these so-called dens of iniquity. Mac-Arthur assured the church leaders that he stood four-square with them in support of the principles of the faith, but he discreetly refused to become involved. Instead, he suggested that they might consider his own countrymen's way of handling similar problems: "In most places where Christianity flourishes, local communities, through the due processes of law, regulate such questions." The clergymen apparently were satisfied with the general's counsel on Caesar and Christ and did not bother him again on the matter.[14]

A more explosive issue was the employment of Negro soldiers in a nation where, as MacArthur explained to the War Department, a policy of "exclusion against everyone except the white race, known locally as the 'White Australia' plan, is universally supported here." Nevertheless, he believed "by utilizing these troops in the front zones away from great centers of population that I can minimize the difficulties involved." When the War Department cautiously began sending black troops overseas in 1942, it first solicited the views of commanders in the areas where it was planning to ship Negroes. MacArthur told Marshall that he was willing to accept Negro soldiers because "there are basic policies which while contrary to the immediate circumstances of a local area are absolutely necessary from the higher perspective and viewpoint." Racial incidents inevitably occurred when, as he accepted more and more black troops, some were assigned to posts in Australia, mainly on engineer and supply duties, yet there were no major episodes of violence.

By the end of 1942 American Negroes had not been employed

in front-line combat in the Southwest Pacific, but 8.14 per cent
of the United States Army personnel in Australia and Papua
were black. This was double the percentage Eisenhower then
had in his command in North Africa (4.09 per cent) and was
a higher proportion than existed in the American Army commands in Great Britain (6.85 per cent), Hawaii (4.63 per cent),
and New Caledonia (5.15 per cent).[15] MacArthur's long and
cordial association with Filipinos had rid him of any tendencies
toward racial prejudice, a fault widespread among American
white officers of his time but one that even his harshest critics
have not leveled against him.

The miscellaneous problems, both major and minor, with
which MacArthur dealt in late 1942, aside from those directly
related to operations, included one concerning the relocation
of the 1st Marine Division, which, it will be recalled, was to be
transferred to his theater. Vandegrift's troops, beginning with
the 5th Marine Regiment on December 9, were gradually relieved on Guadalcanal by Army units. They arrived in Australia when MacArthur was at Port Moresby, and Sutherland
assigned them to an abandoned camp forty-five miles from
Brisbane. Army engineer and service troops assisted in readying the camp's facilities for them, and an Army surgeon assured
Vandegrift that the site was free of malaria. This fact was vital
because the incidence of malaria in the division then was 75
per cent, with the time for rehabilitation estimated at three to
six months. But on December 21, shortly after the Marines
settled in at the camp, the division surgeon, according to Vandegrift, "declared us to be smack in the center of an anopheline
mosquito area — the same malaria-bearing breed we encountered on Guadalcanal." The director of the Queensland Health
Service, whom the GHQ officers had not consulted, backed the
Marine surgeon's findings. Within days hundreds of men were
reinfected, and the number of new cases of malaria mounted
rapidly.[16]

Vandegrift sent an urgent appeal to MacArthur to authorize the movement of the division to an area free of malaria. At the same time the Marine commander sent several of his officers to reconnoiter the cooler, more salubrious Melbourne region for a camp site, which they soon found. On January 1 MacArthur authorized the division's transfer to the Melbourne area, but he added that "no transportation facilities are available . . . to effect the move . . . The already overburdened railroad facilities of Australia cannot cope with such a movement without jeopardizing operations upon which our forces are now engaged." Vandegrift radioed Halsey for help, and the admiral quickly dispatched a transport to move the Marines by sea from Brisbane to Melbourne. By mid-January the division was encamped thirty-five miles outside Melbourne under satisfactory conditions, but about 7500 of the men were hospital cases. Vandegrift was soon succeeded as divisional commander by Major General William H. Rupertus, but before leaving for his new Washington assignment the former decided to pay a final courtesy call on MacArthur.[17] Vandegrift relates their first comments at the meeting on January 24:

> I was certain that I had annoyed him in the process of getting the division transferred to Melbourne, so I was agreeably surprised when he greeted me with a smile and outstretched hand.
> "Vandegrift, what are you going back to the States for? To become President?"
> I looked him in the eye. "General, I thought maybe you would know why I was going back."
> He recoiled slightly, then recovered. "No," he said, "you were dead right in taking your division to Melbourne." [18]

As in other cases of GHQ decision-making, beginning with the Clark Field affair, evidence is wanting to determine finally how much Sutherland's interpretations influenced MacArthur, whether the chief of staff was acting on his own in some situations, or to what extent MacArthur used Sutherland as a lightning rod to attract charges that might otherwise have struck him. Nevertheless, one thing is certain about the Marines' experience in Australia during the winter of 1942–43: they were not likely to forget soon the camp near Brisbane. It was fortunate that the division would have nearly a year not only to recuperate but also to lose some of its bitterness before MacArthur would order it into combat in his theater.

2. *Fall of Gona and Buna*

A discouraging stalemate had developed in the Buna sector when Eichelberger, Byers, and several other officers of I Corps headquarters flew to Dobodura on December 1. Harding met them at the air strip, where Eichelberger confided to him, "I have been ordered to relieve you but get behind me and I'll see if I can't hold you here." Harding did not reply. Later when Eichelberger inquired about what command changes should be made at regimental and lower levels, Harding defensively responded that his officers should be decorated, not relieved. That evening while still at Dobodura, about ten miles from Buna, Eichelberger wrote to Sutherland that the situation did not seem as dismal as he had expected, judging from Harding's comments and a report on progress by the Urbana Force from its commander, Colonel John W. Mott.

The next morning, traveling by jeep at first and then walking the rest of the way, Eichelberger undertook a thorough inspection of the Urbana Force's front. He was accompanied by Harding and Brigadier General Albert W. Waldron, the division artillery commander. At the same time he sent Byers, Colonel Clarence A. Martin, his G-3, and Colonel Gordon Rogers, his G-2, to inspect the Warren Force, which held the front on the right, or coastal, flank of Mott's troops. Arguing that it was too dangerous since the enemy had just launched a powerful counterattack, Harding and Mott tried to keep Eichelberger from walking forward to the front lines, but the corps commander insisted on seeing combat conditions at first hand. He was enraged when he discovered that not only did his exposure of himself draw no enemy fire but there had been no recent Japanese attack. "It was evident," he concluded, "that a very pallid siege was being waged. In any stalemate, it was obvious that the Japanese would win, for they were living among the coconut palms along the coast on sandy soil while our men lived in the swamps." He found that the supply situation at the front was bad and the troops' physical condition deplorable: "At three o'clock in the afternoon these men had had nothing to eat since the previous day and had had no hot food in ten days." [19]

Eichelberger decided that he had no recourse except to comply with MacArthur's instructions because the conditions in the 32nd Division were appalling. He later explained the circumstances that led him to relieve Harding and Mott:

> When we arrived at the front, which was a pathway around the village, in some places not over 100 yards from the Japanese bunkers, I found conditions far worse than those responsible would have been willing to admit. There was no front line discipline of any kind. Our men were walking around and the crew of the heavy Browning at the right of our line were entirely exposed . . .
>
> [A corps staff officer with him suggested to some troops that they fire at certain palm trees which allegedly contained snipers, but the soldiers objected, "Don't fire! They won't shoot at us if we don't shoot at them."]
>
> There was never any idea of men going forward down the pathway . . . As near as I could find out, nobody had gone forward five yards, ten yards, or fifty yards . . .
>
> There were many soldiers at the rear, at aid stations and on the roots of trees. Undoubtedly some of these men had been

sent back for a rest, and others had left the front without permission. The reasons given by Colonel Mott of all the trials and tribulations of his men before I arrived were, of course, true. A glance at the men would show what they had been through, but my orders were . . . to take Buna and I was not there to excuse myself or others. I found that the information given me at Port Moresby, that the front lines were weak and the rear areas strong, was true. Personally, I think half the command was back there . . .

I believe that 19 out of 20 combat officers would have agreed about conditions surrounding the village. There were many excuses to include hunger, fatigue, fever, but . . . these were the tools I had been given to accomplish a task. When I told Colonel Mott . . . how conditions looked to me, he lost his temper, as did General Harding, who took a cigarette out of his mouth and threw it on the ground at his feet in anger. For Colonel Mott to insist that the conditions I described were not correct, and to insist in an angry manner, placed him outside the pale. For General Harding to lose his temper at a criticism of these conditions put him out on thin ice, and particularly so when I could remember all that General MacArthur had described about General Harding's failings and my orders to relieve him. I ordered Colonel Mott to report next morning to our headquarters near Dobodura, and when they both lost their tempers a second time, I reluctantly directed that they report to Port Moresby.[20]

Byers, Martin, and Rogers reported that similar conditions existed on the Warren front. "There was no question in our minds," Byers later recalled, "of certain actions that should be taken." Eichelberger relieved Colonel J. Tracy Hale, Jr., the task force commander there, as well as five of six battalion commanders on the Warren and Urbana fronts. He placed Waldron in command of the 32nd Division; Martin and Colonel John E. Grose were selected to take over the Warren and Urbana task forces respectively. Eichelberger had assumed overall command of American forces in the Buna area on December 2, the day he landed at Dobodura, and now the responsibility for taking Buna rested on him and his new appointees.[21]

The day before he relieved Mott, Eichelberger told him that he was to receive the Silver Star and the Purple Heart. The latter was a mistake, as Mott pointed out, since he had not been wounded. Later he remarked, "I really should have got that too since I got my throat cut." Harding was convinced that Eichelberger had been "sent here to get heads." When Harding reported to MacArthur the next day at Moresby, according to Kenney, MacArthur told the "broken-hearted" officer that after such prolonged combat activity "anyone would be exhausted and it would be a good thing for him . . . to go to Australia, get rested, and then come back, and he would be given a job." That same day, MacArthur wrote to Curtin that, regarding the prime minister's desire to nominate several senior officers for prestigious British decorations, "in the case of General Harding I am sorry to say that I will have to withdraw my approval."

The War Department elevated Harding to command of the Department of the Canal Zone and Antilles in May, 1943; later he served as head of the Army's historical office and on a committee of the Joint Chiefs of Staff. When news came of Harding's transfer to Panama, Eichelberger said he "asked the Big Chief [MacArthur] what he thinks of Forrest's job — he didn't know whether it was aimed at him or at me but thought at both." The postwar historian of the 32nd Division wrote that Harding's relief was "highly disturbing" to the troops, and he was careful to point out Harding's later "important contributions to the winning of the war." He also observed that the Buna area was not taken until a reinforced Australian brigade and another American regiment were brought in, clearly implying that with such help Harding could have achieved victory. What the divisional historian did not write was that, whereas Harding had tried in vain to get reinforcements, Eichelberger was able to obtain them in a hurry. Harding had

lost face with Herring, Blamey, and MacArthur and could no
longer effectively make demands. MacArthur was impatient for
an end to the dragged-out campaign, and he chose well in
selecting the aggressive Eichelberger to finish the job. Eichelberger summed up his own feeling about the Harding affair
thus: "I was very sorry the way that turned out but there was
nothing else I could do." [22]

Meanwhile, in the Australian sector, west of the Girua River,
Herring's troops had also faced malaria, dysentery, supply shortages, and heavy combat losses in their attempts to advance in the
Gona area since mid-November. They had no serious problems
of morale or discipline because, in contrast to the inexperienced
Americans on their right flank, the Australian officers and enlisted men were, for the most part, hardened veterans of earlier
Mid-East campaigns. Relatively rested and fresh units gradually replaced the exhausted brigades of the 7th Division, which
had borne the brunt of the drive across the mountains and the
early fighting at the beachhead. The 25th Brigade, for example,
was down to less than a third of its authorized troop strength
when it was relieved by the 21st Brigade. (An Australian brigade's strength was roughly equivalent to an American regiment's.)

In one costly attack after another, the 21st steadily worked
its way toward Gona. On the afternoon of December 9 the
Australians finally overran the last Japanese positions at Gona,
having suffered 750 casualties in taking the stronghold. They
had to bury about 640 enemy corpses; the Japanese had fought
with such "single-minded ferocity" that they had not taken time
to bury their dead. The defenders had donned gas masks while
firing over the piles of corpses, so appalling was the stench. It
took another ten days of heavy fighting to capture the three-mile
stretch of coastline just west of Gona.

Having secured one of his two main objectives, Herring now
turned his forces against the Japanese positions in front of

Sanananda Point. These fortifications extended along the beach and also inland for about five miles along the Popondetta-Sanananda track. The Sanananda sector contained the largest concentration of Japanese strength, with very strong positions established around a track junction about four miles from the beach. The recently arrived 30th Brigade, relieving the worn-out 16th, succeeded in enveloping some of the enemy's track defenses and created several roadblocks to sever the line of communications to Sanananda Point.

But the Japanese along the track fought tenaciously even when they were cut off. The Australians' daily progress slowed down to gains measured in yards, until by late December a bitter stalemate existed in the Sanananda sector. As mentioned earlier, Herring had called upon the American 126th Regiment and later upon some Australian militia battalions in reserve, but now there were no more units available in Papua to use as reinforcements. The regular Australian Army brigades had already been used to exhaustion and relieved or were currently committed to combat, except for one brigade at Milne Bay, which MacArthur and Blamey refused to release, and one that was manning the defenses of northern Australia.

All the while, the American 41st Division, which Eichelberger earlier had tried to convince MacArthur was better prepared and led than the 32nd, had been continuing its training near Rockhampton, Australia. With the crisis developing on the Sanananda front, MacArthur approved Blamey's request to have its 163rd Regimental Combat Team dispatched to assist Herring's forces. But when the unit arrived at Moresby in late December, MacArthur suddenly changed his mind and told Blamey to send it to the Buna front. Blamey, a rotund, jovial gentleman who was known at GHQ as a heavy drinker and a "fourteen-carat politician," was a former police chief of Melbourne. He was also a talented commander who had compiled a distinguished war record in the Middle East and was generally

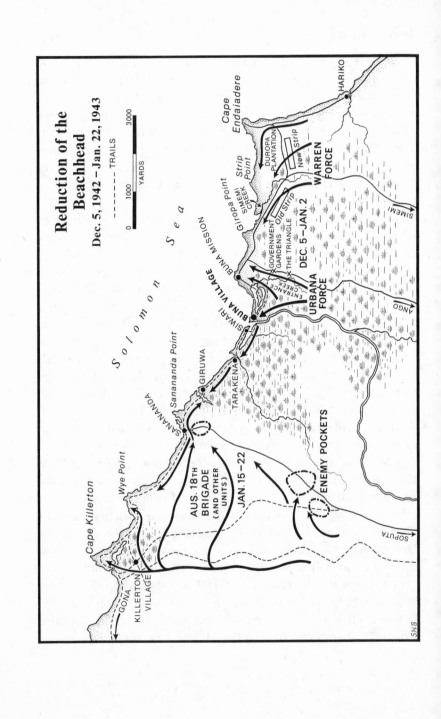

Reduction of the Beachhead

Dec. 5, 1942 – Jan. 22, 1943

TRAILS

YARDS

0   1000   3000

Solomon Sea

Cape Endaiadere

HARIKO

Strip Point

DUROPA PLANTATION

New Strip

WARREN FORCE

Giropa Point

SIMEMI CREEK

GOVERNMENT GARDENS

Old Strip

THE TRIANGLE ×

× **DEC. 5–JAN. 2**

SIMEMI

BUNA MISSION

BUNA VILLAGE

ENTRANCE CREEK

URBANA FORCE

ANGO

SIWARI

GIRUWA

Sanananda Point

SANANANDA

TARAKENA

Wye Point

Cape Killerton

GONA

KILLERTON VILLAGE

AUS. 18TH BRIGADE (AND OTHER UNITS) JAN. 15–22

ENEMY POCKETS

SOPUTA

SHB

underrated by the Americans. When he learned of MacArthur's change of orders, he told the SWPA commander that he deeply regretted his unwarranted interference in the matter. Blamey frankly stated that he did not "for one moment question the right of the Commander-in-Chief to give such orders as he may think fit," but nothing was "more contrary to sound principles of command" than that MacArthur personally should "take over the direction of a portion of the battle."

The SWPA chief "apparently saw the point," says the official American Army chronicle, and canceled his order, thus permitting the American unit to go to the Sanananda front. Otherwise, as Blamey made him realize, MacArthur would have violated the March directive of the Joint Chiefs, which expressly forbade him from commanding any national force directly or interfering with its internal administration. Although Blamey usually supported MacArthur even to the point of incurring the wrath of his Australian commanders, the jovial Allied Land Forces commander was surprisingly effective when he chose to challenge his august superior.[23]

In the meantime, on the Buna front Eichelberger had not performed miracles overnight with the 32nd Division. For several days after Harding's departure the I Corps commander found it necessary to halt all attacks in order "to effect the unscrambling of units and an orderly chain of command." During the interim, forty tons of much-needed food and ammunition arrived, along with five Bren gun carriers, which proved ill-suited for swampy terrain. On December 5 Eichelberger ordered his first general assault, but the gains were disappointing and the casualties heavy. He and several of his staff officers "took [an] active part in the assault, pushing and leading troops forward, and in general operating as troop leaders." Waldron was seriously wounded, and Byers functioned as both corps chief of staff and acting divisional commander. While the Warren Force undertook holding actions on the coastal flank in front of heavily defended Duropa Plantation, the Urbana Force hammered away at the defenses around Buna Village, launching over a dozen savage attacks during the week of December 7–13.

Suddenly, on the night of December 13–14 the Japanese evacuated the village and successfully moved up the coastline to join the garrison at Giruwa, so the next day the Urbana troops walked into Buna Village without having to fire a shot. As in the case of the fall of Gona, however, it took several more days of heavy fighting to clear the remaining Japanese forces, who were entrenched in a nearby coconut grove. Byers was wounded during this action, and Eichelberger's aide was shot while standing next to the corps commander, who always seemed to be in the thick of battle.[24]

Just as Eichelberger and his officers were preparing to break open some liquor bottles following the capture of Buna Village, the following message, dated the 13th, arrived from MacArthur for the corps commander:

> Time is fleeting and our dangers increase with its passage. However admirable individual acts of courage may be; however important administrative functions may seem; however splendid and electrical your presence has proven, remember that your mission is to take Buna. All other things are mere[ly] subsidiary to this. No alchemy is going to produce this for you; it can only be done in battle and sooner or later this battle must be engaged. Hasten your preparations and when you are ready — strike, for as I have said, time is working desperately against us.[25]

Soon after the news of the victory reached Moresby, however, Eichelberger was able to write to his wife that he had received another message from MacArthur — "a grand letter from the Big Chief" congratulating him on the triumph. Although aware that the enemy's strongest defenses still lay ahead in the stretch from Buna Mission to Duropa Plantation, Eichelberger jubilantly reported that there had been a dramatic rise in the morale of his soldiers, who were "coming to life all along the line." [26]

The prospects on the American front were further brightened, not long after the seizure of Buna Village, by the arrival of a battalion of the Australian 18th Brigade from Milne Bay and four American tanks manned by Australian crews. Eichelberger now planned a pincers movement to be launched on December 18: the Warren Force, assisted by the newly arrived infantry and tanks, would attack Duropa Plantation, Cape Endaiadere, and the two air strips, while the Urbana Force would assault the so-called "Triangle" stronghold in front of Buna Mission and then drive through to the coast between the mission and Giropa Point. These objectives were attained, but it took two weeks of the most intensive fighting the Americans had experienced to secure the areas. The rest of the 18th Brigade and additional artillery had to be summoned from Milne, and the Japanese resisted so fiercely that the attackers had to wipe out large and small defensive positions literally to the last man before proceeding farther.

Faced with damaging Japanese air attacks and bloody repulses in the ground fighting on December 25–27, Eichelberger wrote to MacArthur that this was "the low point of my life." Recalling that at their Moresby meeting the SWPA chief had bewailed, "Must I always lead a forlorn hope?" Eichelberger now wondered if Buna was to be "an American military disaster." A few days after Christmas, Sutherland visited the front and offered his unsolicited advice on how to conduct the operation; the I Corps commander wrote in a letter on the 30th that Sutherland "is a queer duck but he is plenty hard." It was well that the depressed Eichelberger did not know that Herring, equally alarmed by the Sanananda situation, visited MacArthur on Christmas Day and was greeted with this opening by the tense SWPA chief: "Well, we're not getting on very fast, are we? . . . . If we do not clean this position up quickly, I will be finished and so will your General Blamey, and what will happen to you, young man, I just don't like to think."

Gradually the Warren Force, now ably led by Australian Brigadier George F. Wootten, began to achieve minor, then major breakthroughs on the eastern end of the front. Japanese resistance crumbled as the Allied troops completed the conquest of the region from Cape Endaiadere to Simemi Creek at the end of December. After savage battles at the Triangle, Government Gardens, and the mouth of Entrance Creek, Grose's reinvigorated Urbana Force overran Buna Mission on January 2. In the ensuing mop-up a number of Japanese were killed when they tried to escape by swimming and wading through the surf. Starvation was obviously an important factor in the final collapse of enemy resistance; it was evident in the horribly emaciated condition of the Japanese bodies as well as from a number of definite cases of cannibalism. The cost of taking the Buna area had been high for both sides.[27]

Congratulatory messages from Eichelberger, Blamey, Herring, Grose, and Wootten to each other, to subordinate commanders, and to troop units were sent out in rapid fashion. Churchill, Curtin, Stimson, and Marshall, among other dignitaries, sent congratulations to MacArthur. In his reply thanking Marshall for his message, MacArthur added the almost paranoid sentiment, "However unwarranted it may be, the impression prevailed that this area's efforts were belittled and disparaged at home, and despite all my efforts to the contrary the effect was depressing. Your tributes have had a tonic effect." Strangely missing from the flurry of congratulations was one from MacArthur to Eichelberger. On January 6 the corps commander, in a bitter if not self-pitying mood, confided in a letter to his wife, "When I was sent here, I was told by the one who should know [MacArthur] that conditions were desperate and . . . things . . . would be done for me if I were successful . . . I didn't expect much, but a good many days have passed and as yet I have not received a 'thank you, dog' and I do not expect to receive any."

Nevertheless, on the 8th, six days after the fall of Buna Mission and one day before MacArthur returned to Brisbane, he wrote to Eichelberger, "I was so glad that you were not injured in the fighting. I always feared that your incessant exposure might result fatally. With a hearty slap on the back. Most cordially, MacArthur." This change of tone by the man who had given him an emphatic win-or-die ultimatum was at first slightly difficult for Eichelberger to adjust to. Two days later the corps commander commented, "The boys tell me that last night San Francisco radio carried word of what troops are here and that I have been in command . . . The Big Chief . . . returned to the mainland and he evidently released the information after his arrival." This was the first time that a GHQ communiqué had mentioned the presence of Eichelberger or the 32nd Division in the Papuan campaign.[28]

3. *Sanananda and Retrospect*

To the astonishment of American and Australian commanders at the front, MacArthur issued a communiqué on January 8, 1943, announcing the virtual termination of hostilities in Papua:

> The Papuan campaign is in its final closing phase. The Sanananda position has now been completely enveloped. A remnant of the enemy's forces is entrenched there and faces certain destruction. With its elimination, Papua will be entirely cleared of the enemy. One of the primary objects of the campaign was the annihilation of the Japanese Papuan army under Lieutenant General Horii. This can now be regarded as accomplished.[29]

Approximately 16,000 to 18,000 Japanese troops had been committed to the operations in Papua since July, of which about

7000 remained quite alive in strong defensive positions around Sanananda in early January, so MacArthur's communiqué was premature, to say the least. Eichelberger commented, "Everyone [at the front] feels that the Sanananda campaign is going to be every bit as difficult, if not more so, than the Buna campaign."

Shortly after Blamey followed MacArthur back to Brisbane on January 11, Herring took command of the New Guinea Force, with headquarters at Moresby, and Eichelberger became the head of the Advance New Guinea Force, comprising all Allied forces at the front. Australian units had been engaged in combat near Sanananda for nearly two months, and, as mentioned earlier, although their attacks had accelerated since the fall of Gona in the second week of December, little progress had been made toward reducing this last portion of the enemy beachhead. Wootten's 18th Brigade, Colonel Jens A. Doe's 163rd Regiment, several militia battalions, and an armored troop were brought in, but the all-out assaults on January 12 were disappointing, with only small yardage gained and at a frightful cost in casualties. The untried Americans and Australian militia were disappointing in their first performances, reminiscent of the inexperienced troops in the early attacks against Buna. Determined to win but by now exhausted and disillusioned with the Big Chief, Eichelberger believed he had figured out the meaning of MacArthur's early exit and communiqué: "The inference of course is that when the Sanananda campaign is concluded it was of such unimportance that the high command did not need to give it its personal attention, whereas if it fails I have been in command of an unsuccessful venture and will return under a cloud." But such misgivings did not affect his aggressiveness; he called in reinforcements, including the American 127th Regiment, and set about planning a new course of attack.

As Eichelberger conferred with his commanders on what tactics to employ next, Herring's chief of staff, Major General Frank H. Berryman, who maintained that the area was not worth the mounting cost in lives, proposed a blockade of the Sanananda region, bypassing the stronghold and forcing the defenders to perish by starvation. In later Southwest Pacific operations, neutralizing and bypassing strong points would be frequently practiced, but not at this stage. According to the Australian Army chronicle of the campaign, "With the desirability present of lifting the Allied morale as high as possible by finishing the operations in Papua decisively and completely — the decision to press the coastal fighting to the bitter end was probably inevitable." After all, several times MacArthur had reminded both Australian and American commanders that the time element was paramount in his considerations and they must press on at all costs.[30]

The attacks were therefore renewed, while, unknown to the Allied command, Eighth Area Army headquarters at Rabaul received word from Tokyo to start evacuating its troops from both Guadalcanal and Papua. Major General Tsuyuo Yamagata, in charge at Sanananda, received orders on January 13 to begin evacuating his forces northward to the mouth of the Kumusi River from where they would be taken by ship to Salamaua and Lae. An estimated 2200 Japanese troops, mainly the sick and wounded, were successfully withdrawn to the north during the next week. But frequent attacks by Allied aircraft and increasing ground action made it impossible for Yamagata to get the rest of his men out of the doomed beachhead.

On January 17 one of Wootten's battalions on the left flank of the Allied line broke through to the coast at Cape Killerton, while other units of the 18th Brigade overran Killerton Village and pushed to the western edge of the hamlet of Sanananda. Meanwhile, on the Popondetta-Sanananda track the American 163rd's troops cleaned up one of two Japanese pockets of resistance on the 16th and was steadily reducing the second and

larger one. After four days of fierce battling, a complex laby-
rinth of Japanese fortifications just outside Sanananda was seized
by the Australians, and on that same day, January 21, American
and Australian units closed a pincers movement on the beach
positions around Giruwa, east of Sanananda Point. As the 163rd
destroyed the last enemy defenses on the track inland, the 18th
Brigade overcame the final Japanese resistance west of Sanananda on January 22.

That afternoon Herring issued an order of the day announcing the real end of the Papuan campaign and proudly proclaiming that seldom in history had soldiers "been called on to endure
greater hardships or discomfort" while fighting "a dour and
determined enemy on ground of his own choosing in well prepared defenses." In a letter to "Miss Em," his wife, Eichelberger bitterly recalled the premature GHQ communiqué and
departure of the SWPA commander: "General MacArthur announced his return to Australia by saying that there was nothing
left in Papua but some 'mopping up' at Sanananda. This was
just an excuse to get home as at that time there was no indication of any crackup of the Japs at Sanananda . . . If General
MacArthur had known we could do it, he would have waited to
celebrate a great victory." But, despite the fact that Allied casualties at Sanananda were nearly 3500, about 700 more than in
the Buna operation, MacArthur's communiqué and subsequent
press releases on the fall of the Buna area were more widely
broadcast in the newspapers of Allied nations, and the Sanananda operation continued to be generally regarded as merely
a mopping-up activity.[31]

From his own viewpoint, MacArthur more than fulfilled the
promises he had made to Eichelberger. For his heroic leadership at Buna and Sanananda the I Corps leader received an Oak
Leaf Cluster to his Distinguished Service Cross (first won in Siberia in 1919), a Presidential Unit Citation for his corps headquarters, and a coveted honor from King George VI, Honorary

Knight of the Military Division of the Most Excellent Order of the British Empire, all of which were issued on recommendations by the SWPA chief. Moreover, the revelation in GHQ communiqués that Eichelberger had led the Allied forces in their victories at Buna and Sanananda brought him a good deal of publicity in newspapers and magazines as America's newest heroic general.

But Eichelberger, who seemed at times to be as sensitive about his position and reputation as MacArthur, was irked because his DSC award was announced by the SWPA commander in an order of the day that included the names of eleven other officers to receive that decoration, of whom the majority had not really served at the front. MacArthur's blanket citation praised them all for "extraordinary courage, marked efficiency and precise execution of operations during the Papuan Campaign" and made no distinction between those who had been involved in actual combat and those who had merely visited the front briefly. The former group included Eichelberger, Herring, Vasey, Wootten, and Brigadier Kenneth W. Eather, the hard-driving commander of the 18th Brigade. The members of the latter group, Blamey, Kenney, Sutherland, Willoughby, Whitehead, Walker, and RAAF Group Captain William H. Garing, may have deserved the Distinguished Service Medal but, in the opinion of the combat officers, not the Distinguished Service Cross, which ranks next to the Medal of Honor among American Army awards for heroism in battle. Eichelberger grumbled, "My citation was worded exactly like the others and the principal expression, 'for precise execution of operations,' speaks for itself." He continued to be upset also by the fact that "the great hero went home without seeing Buna before, during or after the fight while permitting press articles from his GHQ to say that he was leading his troops in battle." [32]

Eichelberger became even more disgruntled later when he found out that "Colonel Gordon Rogers, who had been my

G-2 and who is now in Washington in the Ground Forces had submitted a great number of certificates with a recommendation for the Medal of Honor for me. He told Clovis [Byers] that the War Department was all set to approve it, but that it was disapproved by radio by my Chief." Byers confirmed this story recently and added, "I started a recommendation for a Medal of Honor for Bob, got all the necessary documents, sent them to GHQ, and the paper was lost," which seemed strange to him. "So we had duplicates made," he continued, "and when our first staff officer [Rogers] returned to the United States from Buna, we sent the duplicates to the War Department." The War Department was agreeable to the award, according to Byers, but wanted MacArthur's approval. "He said he didn't think a Medal of Honor was warranted . . . This hurt Bob, but it didn't affect his loyalty" to the SWPA chief.

A popular superintendent at West Point in 1940–42 and widely esteemed in high Army circles — Eisenhower was one of his many friends — Eichelberger had an engaging personality, a bag full of first-hand combat stories, and rapport with correspondents that made it easy for them to portray him as the heroic, battle-hardened but likable general about whom the American public was eager to read. But he quickly found that the publicity that followed his feats in Papua did not improve his relations with MacArthur. After the appearance of flattering articles about him in magazines such as *Life* and *Saturday Evening Post,* Eichelberger stated, "General MacArthur sent for me . . . He said, 'Do you realize I could reduce you to the grade of colonel tomorrow and send you home?'" Eichelberger answered, "Of course you could." MacArthur responded, "Well, I won't do it."

The lesson Eichelberger took from this odd encounter was to dread publicity in a theater where only one general was supposed to be in the limelight. He later wrote to a friend who worked in the War Department's public relations bureau, "I would rather have you slip a rattlesnake in my pocket than to have you give me any publicity." Later Eichelberger told his brother, "I went through many unhappy months because of the publicity that came out about me after Buna. I paid through the nose for every line of it . . . While I realize that publicity is the thing that brings one in the eyes of the people, it also may prove more dangerous than a Japanese bullet." [33]

Eichelberger's musings and mutterings seem like those of an officer intensely hostile toward his superior, which was far from true because all the while he retained a deep admiration for MacArthur and regarded him as the outstanding commander in the Pacific war. Both men were extremely sensitive and susceptible to dark moods, yet both possessed the ability to project an air of confidence to their immediate staffs as well as to their troops and the public. While offering some penetrating insights into MacArthur's ways and wiles, Eichelberger's writings must be judged in context and in light of his moods. For example, his charge above of supposed vindictiveness by MacArthur because of the publicity he garnered was in reference to the SWPA chief's appointment of a general with much seniority and experience to command the first American army in the Southwest Pacific, which was created shortly after the Papuan campaign, a story to be told later. It is difficult to believe that MacArthur considered this selection as anything more than a matter of choosing the ablest man available for the position, and subsequent operations would prove that he again chose wisely.

MacArthur's communiqués produced a storm of controversy throughout the Papuan campaign. The Navy and War departments objected to the leaks of vital information they were said at times to contain. Many soldiers at the front expressed resentment not only at his premature announcements of victories but also at his interpretations of operations, which arbitrarily reduced costly battles to mop-up actions and transformed skir-

mishes into major engagements. MacArthur's communiqué on
Christmas Day, for example, piously stated that at the front "our
activities were limited to routine safety precautions. Divine
services were held." Actually, large-scale battling was under
way at Buna, and the troops were so occupied that they scarcely
realized it was Christmas. "The fighting was desperate," said
Eichelberger, "and the outcome of the whole miserable, tor-
tured campaign was in doubt" that day. On several occasions
during the campaign, Curtin's press censorship advisory committee voiced strong criticism of the GHQ press releases. Reviewing MacArthur's handling of censorship and news releases
during the period since July, the committee, on March 12, 1943,
reported that its principal grievances had been against "censorship of criticism of the High Command, inaccuracies and over-
optimism in communiqués and the dissatisfaction of correspondents." [34]

Australian troops at the front became sardonic about Mac-
Arthur's policy of referring to "Allied troops" when the only
units in a mentioned action were Australian, but citing "American troops" when Americans were involved, even if only in a
minor supporting capacity. The exaggerations and mendacious
statements that appeared too frequently in GHQ communiqués
inevitably produced, as on Bataan, some crude, mean doggerel
which was widely, if surreptitiously, circulated among the combat troops. The following lampoon, probably written by an
Australian, is typical of the jibes with language fit to print:

> Here, too, is told the saga bold,
>   of virile, deathless youth
> In stories seldom tarnished with
>   the plain unvarnished truth.
> It's quite a rag, it waves the flag,
>   Its motif is the fray,
> And modesty is plain to see in
>   Doug's Communiqué . . .

"My battleships bombard the Nips from
    Maine to Singapore;
My subs have sunk a million tons;
    They'll sink a billion more.
My aircraft bombed Berlin last night."
    In Italy they say
"Our turn's tonight, because it's right in
    Doug's Communiqué . . ."

And while possibly a rumour now,
    someday it will be fact
That the Lord will hear a deep voice say
    "Move over, God — it's Mac."
So bet your shoes that all the news
    that last great Judgment Day
Will go to press in nothing less than
    DOUG'S COMMUNIQUE! [35]

The deepest resentment felt by the veterans of the Papuan campaign was probably reserved for MacArthur's audacity in depicting the casualty rate as relatively light. To the astonishment of commanders who had been pressed by him to finish off their operations quickly "regardless of costs," he stated that the figures on Allied losses in Papua "reverse the usual result of a ground offensive campaign, especially against prepared positions defended to the last. There was no reason to hurry the attack because the time element was of little importance. For that reason no attempt was made to rush the positions." He concluded, "The utmost care was taken for the conservation of our forces with the result that probably no campaign in history against a thoroughly prepared and trained Army produced such complete and decisive results with so low an expenditure of life and resources."

When the losses in Papua are compared to those on Guadalcanal, MacArthur's claim appears fantastic. The fight to take and hold Guadalcanal was regarded then and since as a rough, grueling, and bloody operation. In the ground fighting the

American troops, Marine and Army, suffered 5845 casualties, including 1600 killed. But during approximately the same time span the Allied forces in Papua had 8546 combat casualties, of which 3095 were killed. Moreover, about 60,000 Americans fought on Guadalcanal, whereas about 33,000 Allied troops were committed in the Papuan operations. Thus, one in eleven Allied combat soldiers in Papua lost his life compared to one out of thirty-three on Guadalcanal. In some of his later campaigns MacArthur would have reason to boast of the economy in lives, but surely not in the Papuan fighting. The official United States Army history of the campaign states the unpleasant truth: "The conclusion is inescapable that the fighting in Papua had been even costlier than had at first been thought, and that the victory there, proportionate to the forces engaged, had been one of the costliest of the Pacific war." [36]

The question of authorship of the GHQ communiqués was raised earlier with reference to those of the Corregidor period, and it will be remembered that Diller maintained that MacArthur either wrote or carefully edited many of them. Textual evidence supports this contention because the style and grammar, especially of the more controversial ones, are strikingly similar to MacArthur's. Eichelberger, among others, was convinced that "General MacArthur was in charge of his own public relations." Several days after he arrived in Brisbane as I Corps commander in August, 1942, according to Eichelberger,

Diller, the PIO, asked me to talk to the press off the record, at the request of a number of Australian correspondents. Worried a bit about what I might say, I made up my mind to say little, if anything, except to tell them that I would like to have them brief me. Later I asked Sutherland if there was anything General MacArthur would like me to say to these correspondents and he answered, "You know, General MacArthur handles his own public relations." Sutherland made a dash for the door and didn't come back out of MacArthur's office for a long time.

Later MacArthur asked me to cancel this engagement. Sutherland repeated this statement many times, and I am convinced that MacArthur's greatest interest was in the picture the world gained of him. That alone will explain how headlines went out of Port Moresby that MacArthur was leading charges at Buna, et cetera.[37]

MacArthur faced a "dilemma" during the Papuan campaign, in the opinion of a correspondent who knew the general reasonably well: "He had to win the war every morning in his communiqué . . . Yet he had to convince the public that Roosevelt and the dastardly Chiefs of Staff were withholding from him the weapons that were rightfully his." He added that although the Southwest Pacific was a secondary theater, "yet the American public believed all along that MacArthur was the one who was licking the Japs. Does history offer a comparable public relations coup?"[38] Nevertheless, it can be argued that at least during this period MacArthur's motivation was not mainly a desire to prepare the way for political candidacy but rather an interest in channeling the principal Allied war effort to the Pacific and specifically to his theater.

Persuaded by the brilliant leadership of air commanders like Kenney and Whitehead and the prodigious feats of their airmen, MacArthur had become a zealous exponent of air power during the Papuan campaign. When Colonel Edward V. Rickenbacker, the famous ace of World War I, visited him at Port Moresby on December 1, MacArthur remarked, "You know, Eddie, I probably did the American Air Forces more harm than any man living when I was chief of staff by refusing to believe in the future of the airplane as a weapon of war. I am now doing everything I can to make amends for that great mistake." Powerful air coverage would be an important part of his later operations. Each phase of his future advances would include the seizure and development of airfield sites, the completed bases serving as steppingstones to the next objective.[39]

With the Sanananda operation terminated, MacArthur released a statement on January 24 giving his review and preview of operations in the Southwest Pacific:

> The outstanding military lesson of this campaign was the continuous calculated application of airpower . . . employed in the most intimate tactical and logistical union with ground troops. For months on end, air transport with constant fighter coverage moved complete infantry regiments and artillery battalions across the almost impenetrable mountains and jungles of Papua, and the reaches of the sea; transported field hospitals and other base installations to the front; supplied the troops and evacuated casualties. For hundreds of miles bombers provided all-around reconnaissance, protected the coast from hostile naval intervention, and blasted the way for infantry as it drove forward . . . The offensive and defensive power of the air and the adaptability, range and capacity of its transport in an effective combination with ground forces, represent tactical and strategical elements of a broadened conception of warfare that will permit the application of offensive power in swift, massive strokes, rather than the dilatory and costly island-to-island advance that some have assumed to be necessary in a theater where the enemy's far-flung strongholds are dispersed throughout a vast expanse of archipelagos.[40]

The Allied Air Forces' role in direct support of ground operations in Papua had not actually achieved the level of excellence he described. Poor ground-to-air communications especially had marred the efforts, and sundry errors demonstrated that the airmen still had much to learn about direct support of troops. But the air forces' logistical and reconnaissance achievements were as superb as MacArthur pictured them. Moreover, the inestimable importance to future operations of the air bases later built in the Dobodura area justified his insistence that the beachhead be secured rather than bypassed, as some Australian officers favored.

MacArthur and his commanders learned many valuable lessons from this campaign and proved it by avoiding any other operation proportionately so costly during the rest of the war. On the tactical level, they found through study of the mistakes made in the Papuan fighting that there were many tactical and logistical methods and techniques that needed to be discarded entirely or drastically altered. More suitable jungle equipment of various types was placed on order, and training programs were transformed as the officers worked to improve their units in areas ranging from artillery-infantry coordination and radio communications to education on jungle survival and malaria control.[41]

Allied Naval Forces had provided minimal support during the Papuan operations: two destroyers were used to transport troops in the Goodenough landing, several corvettes escorted a few convoys from Milne Bay up the northern coast, and a squadron of PT boats was active in the waters between New Guinea and New Britain. Carpender seems to have been justified in refusing to employ his cruisers and destroyers off the beachhead, but the virtual absence of his fleet contributed to the prolongation of the campaign. If, as Van Volkenburgh proposed, the Navy had transported his advance echelon to Buna in July, its presence might have deterred the enemy from trying an invasion of Papua or repulsed the assault if it had been attempted, since Horii's landing force was not formidable. Blamey's proposal for an amphibious attack against the beachhead in November, had it been adopted, would probably have broken the siege much more quickly, particularly in view of the fact that the principal Japanese defenses were positioned on the inland side of the beachhead.

MacArthur's demands for amphibious troops belatedly brought him the 1st Marine Division, though it would be of no use in combat for a long time. More important, his many requests resulted in the transfer to the Southwest Pacific in January, 1943, of Rear Admiral Daniel E. Barbey, a tough, energetic amphibious specialist who would prove indispensable in the future in planning and directing the landings during fifty-six amphibious operations in MacArthur's theater. Barbey's VII Amphibious Force was born as a direct consequence of the obvious need for amphibious craft and trained amphibious personnel during the Papuan campaign.

The most problematical aspect of MacArthur's plans for future operations was the support he could count on from the Navy's major surface units. There was little prospect of measurable increases in his Allied Naval Forces, and King and Nimitz seemed to be determined to keep any sizable part of the Pacific Fleet out of his theater. MacArthur's relations with admirals in the Pacific and in Washington other than Halsey had not improved since his skirmishes with Hart in the Philippines a year earlier. The general was to blame, in part, because, as Barbey soon discovered, he "was outspoken in his criticism of his senior naval commanders."

As late as Christmas week, King had tried in vain to persuade Marshall to support Nimitz for overall command of Pacific operations, and the chief of naval operations and his planners in Washington were raising new objections to the Joint Chiefs' earlier decision to place MacArthur in strategic command of Tasks Two and Three in the advance to Rabaul. Stimson found that the admirals in the Pentagon were venomous on the subject of the SWPA commander, who was "a constant bone of contention" between the leaders of the Navy and War departments. The Secretary of War admitted that "the extraordinary brilliance of that officer was not always matched by his tact, but the Navy's astonishing bitterness against him seemed childish." [42]

After fourteen months of war which had included the defeat in the Philippines, the worst in the American Army's history, and the Papuan campaign, so disappointing in its length and high casualties; after being on the job virtually seven days a week during the entire period, wrestling with diplomatic as well as military problems; and after finding that his strongest protests had availed little in securing a higher priority for his theater in Allied strategic and logistical planning, MacArthur was understandably tired, tense, and sometimes angry and frustrated. Many of the difficulties and mistakes that had marred his two initial campaigns had resulted from actions that enemy moves forced him to undertake with insufficient forces and before adequate preparations could be made. His often fiery, sometimes harsh behavior in dealing with individuals was rooted in his own exhaustion and disappointment.

But an Australian correspondent who visited him soon after his return to Brisbane on January 9 found MacArthur again brimming with self-confidence and more determined than ever to return victoriously to the Philippines:

> He looked younger than at any time since he had arrived in my country. His hair was black, his eyes alert, his step springy. At sixty-four [sixty-three] he was the youngest looking man for his age I had ever seen. He was no longer wearing his decorated uniform. This time he wore a pair of slacks and a simple leather flying jacket. The leather name tab on the pocket bore the word "MacArthur," and four silver stars were painted on each shoulder. There was no sign of the early bitterness. He looked happy, he joked with correspondents, he answered every question they asked with frankness and, for him, a complete absence of theatricals. His confidence that the Japs could be licked could be detected in every remark, seen in every gesture. Perhaps the crusade seemed less of an illusion. Perhaps he felt that he had dealt out at least some retribution for the men of Bataan. At any rate, his only comment was, "The dead of Bataan will rest easier tonight." [43]

MacArthur had rebounded strongly from over a year of pressures and tribulations that would have broken the spirit of a lesser mortal. More significant, as his later string of successful operations would demonstrate, he had learned from his mistakes, which unfortunately is not a common practice among commanders. He had changed his mind entirely on air power and would soon alter his views drastically on some strategic and tactical matters also, which was unusual for an officer only a year away from the statutory retirement age. In addition, his record as SWPA commander, considering the lack of support he received in carrying out the Joint Chiefs' directives, was not unimpressive. The enemy threat to Port Moresby and Australia had been permanently erased, and crippling losses had been inflicted on Japanese ground, air, naval, and shipping strength in the Southwest Pacific. By launching his counteroffensive quickly, he took advantage of the enemy's dispersion of forces between Papua and Guadalcanal and produced the first victorious Allied campaign of the Pacific war, and at the same time rendered air and naval support to the South Pacific operations. (Guadalcanal was not secured until February, 1943.) Under his leadership, in the words of a distinguished historian of the war, the SWPA forces "not only defeated experienced troops with units inexperienced in battle but we met the enemy in his deliberately chosen and fortified positions and crushed him."

In spite of no small degree of bickering and friction, he still commanded the respect and support of his superiors in Washington, the Curtin ministry, and his commanders in the theater. He had acquired a large number of critics, but, with the exception of King and some of his staff, no one in high-level positions with whom he had differed — from Roosevelt, Stimson, and Marshall to Halsey, Blamey, and Eichelberger — would have suggested in early 1943 that a better theater commander could be found for the Southwest Pacific than MacArthur. "Warts and all," he still had their trust, as well as that of the vast majority of people in America and Australia.[44] As a commander, he would more than repay their faith in him, for the Old Man's finest hours still lay ahead.

PART III

Cartwheel Operations

CHAPTER VII

Northward to Huon Gulf

1. Two Bright Victories and an Ugly Controversy

IN EARLY JANUARY, with the losses of Papua and Guadalcanal certain, the Japanese high command decreed a new first line of defense in the Southwest Pacific, to run through Northeast New Guinea, New Britain, and the northern Solomons. Special emphasis was placed on holding the region from Salamaua to Madang, loss of which would expose the right flank of the defense perimeter and give the Allies a springboard into the strategic Bismarck Archipelago. Adachi's Eighteenth Army, with headquarters at Madang, was sent a considerable number of reinforcements, and new airfields were developed on the Huon Peninsula and in the Salamaua-Lae area. The newly arrived 51st Division was ordered to seize Wau, which lay about thirty miles inland from Salamaua and was held by the small Australian Kanga Force. For the Japanese the capture of Wau meant securing the right flank of the defensive line and also gaining an excellent position from which to begin another overland drive against Port Moresby when the opportunity arose.

On January 14, while heavy fighting was still under way on

the Sanananda front, a 3000-man detachment of the 51st Division began the march across the mountainous area from Salamaua to Wau. After several brief encounters with the Kanga Force on the way, they arrived on the 27th at a ridge about six miles northeast of Wau. MacArthur, Blamey, and Kenney had kept up with the situation carefully from Kanga reports, but, except for a small portion of the Australian 17th Brigade, airborne reinforcements to Wau had been delayed by bad weather over the Owen Stanley Range. On January 28 the Japanese launched an all-out assault, but the outnumbered Kanga defenders stopped them about 400 yards short of the air strip. A spell of clear weather fortunately set in on the 29th, and promptly that day Allied transports began flying into Wau the major portion of the 17th Brigade as well as badly needed supplies and ammunition. By February 4 the Japanese detachment, now outnumbered and running short of provisions, began retreating eastward. With the Australians in close pursuit until they neared the coast, the Japanese lost heavily in the Wau operation. Only 2200 of them reached Salamaua, and an estimated 70 per cent of those were suffering from disease and malnutrition. Later that spring the Australian 3rd Division established headquarters at Wau, and its troops consolidated the Allied hold on the Bulolo Valley, kept the enemy confined at Salamaua, and pushed northward almost to the Markham River near Nadzab, threatening the Japanese position at Lae.

The official Australian history praises the Allied Air Forces' support at Wau as "the adaptation of air power in its most dramatic form to the needs of the army in the field." MacArthur commented, "This engagement proved to any remaining skeptics that tactical movement of troops by aircraft had become a strong and trusty adjunct of the armed forces." Air bases in the Wau region would give important help to the later offensives against Lae and the Huon Peninsula, and ground units from the Bulolo Valley would assist in the capture of the Nad-

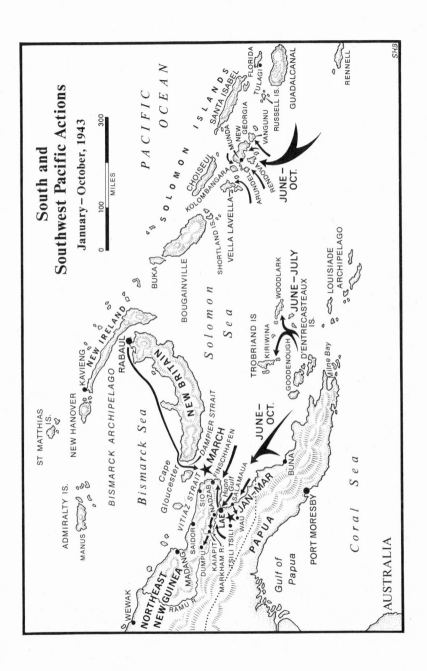

**South and
Southwest Pacific Actions**

January–October, 1943

zab-Lae region. The Wau offensive, which was the last Japanese attempt to capture new territory in New Guinea, was the only significant ground fighting in the Southwest Pacific from the end of the Papuan campaign until the middle of 1943.[1]

At Eighth Area Army headquarters in Rabaul, Imamura and his staff interpreted the Allied victory at Wau as a serious threat to Japanese positions along the shoreline of Huon Gulf. Imamura decided to reinforce the garrison at Lae as soon as a convoy could be readied and a weather front blanketed the route from Rabaul to Huon Gulf to hide the ships from Allied aircraft. Beginning on February 27 a wide, dense cloud cover gathered over the region, with stormy conditions predicted for the next few days. At midnight on the 28th, the convoy steamed out of Simpson Harbor at Rabaul — eight destroyers and eight transports carrying about 6000 soldiers, 400 marines, 2340 crewmen, and cargoes of troop equipment, provisions, munitions, and aviation gasoline.

Earlier Japanese convoy successes had been due mainly to astounding luck in having, when they needed it, the bad weather necessary to slip their vessels into New Guinea ports without serious damage by the Allied Air Forces. Willoughby's intelligence reports had indicated the build-up of enemy strength in the Salamaua-Lae region ever since the Japanese had abandoned their efforts to reinforce the garrisons at Buna and Sanananda. On February 19 Willoughby alerted MacArthur and Kenney to the strong possibility of a large troop convoy to Lae departing from Rabaul during the first week of March, an uncannily accurate estimate. Kenney and Whitehead stepped up the movement of combat aircraft to Papuan bases and the training of their airmen in various techniques of low-level strikes against shipping. Long-range reconnaissance missions over the Bismarck and Solomon seas were accelerated, and 207 bombers and 154 fighters were stationed at bases in Papua, with another ninety-five fighters and eighty-six bombers ready at Queensland bases to stage to Moresby on short notice. The

Japanese grossly underestimated both the accuracy of Willough-by's intelligence on their plans and movements and the Allied Air Forces' formidable strength of combat-ready planes in Papua.[2]

The enemy's meteorological data also proved to be faulty, for on the afternoon of March 1, as the convoy moved westward off the northern coast of New Britain, instead of the weather worsening as anticipated, large breaks began to appear in the cloud veil. Several patrolling B-24's spotted the vessels and relayed the welcome news to their Moresby and Milne bases. A force of B-17's took off to attack, but darkness and bad weather closed in before the convoy could be located again. As an early morning cover of heavy clouds began to dissipate over the convoy on March 2, twenty-eight B-17's flew through a patrol of Zeros to bomb the ships, which were heading into Dampier Strait. At least one transport was sunk and two others heavily damaged. Two destroyers picked up survivors and sped with them to Lae, returning to the slow-moving convoy the next day. Toward dusk on the 2nd, eleven more B-17's attacked, leaving one ship sinking. Through the night Allied patrol bombers kept contact with the convoy off Huon Peninsula. During the first attacks on the 2nd, Allied aircraft had accurately reported sixteen ships, but because of the departure and return of the destroyers, together with exaggerated and confused reports by excited pilots, later figures on the composition of the convoy were less dependable. Some airmen claimed that a second convoy joined the first during the night of March 2–3.

Kenney and Whitehead's main show was reserved for the 3rd when the hapless ships, now nearing Finschhafen, came within range of the rest of the Papuan-based aircraft, which were fueled, armed, and ready for the kill. After an unsuccessful dawn attack by torpedo-carrying Australian Beauforts, which encountered bad weather, the skies began to clear by midmorning, exposing the convoy in loose formation with a forty-plane cover overhead. Suddenly, out of the south appeared thirteen B-17 heavy bombers, thirty-one B-25 medium bombers, twelve A-20 light bombers, twenty-eight P-38 fighters, and thirteen Australian Beaufighters. While the P-38's kept the enemy fighters engaged in dogfights, the rest of the Allied air armada unleashed its firepower on the doomed ships. The attacks continued through much of the day as more planes roared off the Moresby and Milne runways that afternoon to join the slaughter. Before nightfall over 330 Allied aircraft had participated in the action against the convoy or in attacking air bases in the Lae area to keep the remaining Japanese fighters from getting to the scene. Except for four destroyers, which hastily rescued survivors from the water and fled northward, by dusk on the 3rd all of the enemy ships were sunk, sinking, or badly damaged. The area of devastation was covered with floating debris, lifeboats, swimmers, and burning hulks as Allied fighters returned to strafe survivors.

During the night of March 3–4 eight PT boats roamed the waters, attacking the remaining crippled ships and sending one to the bottom. On the 4th, Allied bombers returned to finish off two destroyers. For the next day or two, PT boats and low-flying planes systematically hunted down and killed hundreds of survivors who were clinging to debris, swimming toward shore, or crowded into lifeboats. Some of the airmen "confessed to experiencing nausea" as "the terrible yet essential finale" of machine-gunning survivors took place. "It was a grisly task," commented one authority, "but a military necessity since Japanese soldiers do not surrender and, within swimming distance of shore, they could not be allowed to land and join the Lae garrison."

When MacArthur received the news of the ships' destruction, Kenney observed, "I had never seen him so jubilant." The SWPA chief sent a message through Whitehead to all air units involved in the operation congratulating them on "the magnificent victory which has been achieved. It cannot fail to go down in history as one of the most complete and annihilating combats of all time. My pride and satisfaction in you all is boundless." When MacArthur began preparing a press release citing the enemy losses as given in the first reports from the battle, Diller cautioned his chief that the aviators might be in error or might have claimed too much. "I trust George Kenney," responded MacArthur emphatically, and that was the end of the matter. Diller later remarked, "It wasn't up to me to verify the communiqués." [3]

In his release of March 4, based on preliminary reports from air commanders in the battle as compiled by Kenney's office, MacArthur proclaimed:

> The battle of the Bismarck Sea is now decided. We have achieved a victory of such completeness as to assume the proportions of a major disaster to the enemy. His entire force has been practically destroyed. His naval component consisted of 22 vessels, comprising 12 transports and 10 warships — cruisers or destroyers. They represented a tonnage estimated at approximately 90,000 tons. They have all been sunk or are sinking. His air coverage for this naval force has been decimated or dispersed, 55 of his planes having been shot out of combat and many others damaged. His ground forces, estimated at probably 15,000, destined to attack in New Guinea, have been sunk or killed almost to the man.
>
> The original convoy of 14 ships was joined during the afternoon by 8 other vessels. Our Air Forces in all categories constantly attacked throughout the day, and ship after ship was hit again and again with heavy bombs from low altitude. The enemy air coverage became weaker and weaker; his forces more scattered and dispersed; and finally his remnants, isolated and bewildered, were gradually annihilated by our successive air formations as we sent them into combat.
>
> Our losses were light, one bomber and three fighters were shot down. A number of others were damaged but returned to base.
>
> Our decisive success cannot fail to have the most important results on the enemy's strategic and tactical plans. His cam-

paign, for the time being at least, is completely dislocated. A merciful Providence guarded us in this great victory.[4]

The battle bore the name of the Bismarck Sea thereafter, although, like the misnamed Coral Sea battle, the action occurred elsewhere — in Dampier Strait and the western part of the Solomon Sea. Three days later MacArthur issued another communiqué on the battle, this time raising enemy aircraft losses to 102 and restating the above figures on ship and personnel losses. His and Kenney's later official reports to Washington, with slight modifications, included the figures of March 7.

In the aftermath of the battle that spring, MacArthur's claims about losses may have raised some eyebrows in Washington, but they did not create as much stir as a statement he made to the press that the Navy considered to be provocative and insulting. Secretary of the Navy Frank Knox, responding to recent Australian expressions of anxiety over a story that the enemy was preparing to invade down under, released a statement that said, in part, "You must remember that an attack on Australia must be accompanied by a tremendous sea force, and there is no indication of a concentration pointing to that." Still jubilant over the display by Kenney's airmen in the Bismarck Sea action, MacArthur retorted in a communiqué that the Japanese, despite the efforts of the United States Navy, "have complete control of the sea lanes in the western Pacific and of the outer approaches toward Australia." But he assured the Australians that "control of such sea lanes no longer depends solely or even perhaps primarily upon naval power, but upon air power operating from land bases held by ground troops . . . The first line of Australian defense is our bomber line." As if he had not made his point clear, he continued, "A primary threat to Australia does not therefore require a great initial local concentration of naval striking power. It requires rather a sufficient concentration of land-based aviation."

If MacArthur wished to provoke a rise from the admirals in

Washington, who considered the Pacific war mainly a naval show, he succeeded. The next day Brigadier General Albert C. Wedemeyer, serving in the Operations Division, informed Marshall, "The Navy (Admiral Cooke) phoned me this morning and expressed strong disapproval of remarks which have been appearing in the press the past few days concerning the role of the Navy in the Pacific as visualized by General MacArthur." Wedemeyer suggested that the Army chief of staff could expect a visit from an irate Admiral King shortly. Marshall prudently stayed out of this latest dispute between MacArthur and the Navy, and that relationship soon returned to a simmering, rather than a boiling, level.[5]

Looking back over the campaigns in the Southwest Pacific, MacArthur in September, 1945, still regarded the battle of the Bismarck Sea as "the decisive aerial engagement" of the war in his theater. The principal history of the United States Army Air Forces in World War II describes the operation as a "brilliant achievement . . . A major effort to reinforce Lae was turned back with mass destruction upon an enemy who never thereafter dared renew the effort." The Japanese high command was shocked by the disaster, its projected second offensive against Wau proved abortive, and its troops already in New Guinea would have to live and fight with less food and equipment. The Allied Air Forces maintained "an effective if not absolutely tight air blockade" of the Huon Gulf region for months in advance of Allied ground operations against Salamaua, Lae, and Finschhafen, thereby greatly facilitating the conquest of the area. By relying heavily on Kenney's aggressive airmen, MacArthur, indeed, showed that he could manage without the help of the vaunted Pacific fleet, at least at that stage of his operations.[6]

It would be impossible to prove that some admirals in the Pentagon suggested the idea to Arnold's staff, though MacArthur and several of his officers suspected it, but Air Force headquarters in Washington somehow became wary of the SWPA reports on the Bismarck Sea battle and launched an investigation that in thoroughness and industry far exceeded the usual review of operations reports. The painstaking investigation took several months to complete and was based on all records of the operation forwarded from Kenney's and Whitehead's headquarters, including captured enemy documents and SWPA transcripts of interrogations of prisoners who had been aboard the convoy vessels. It was routine for Kenney's staff to relay such data to Washington, but the depth of the study and its secrecy were anything but routine. The investigating committee concluded from the evidence that the SWPA reports on enemy losses were nearly double the actual figures. There was only one convoy, and it consisted of eight destroyers and eight transports, of which four of the former and all of the latter had been sunk. About 2900 Japanese personnel died in the action, and only twenty to thirty enemy planes were destroyed in aerial combat. Allied losses were about as light as MacArthur and Kenney had reported: six American and Australian aircraft were lost, four of them in combat, with thirteen airmen killed and eight wounded.

The results of the Air Force study were bluntly reported to the unsuspecting Kenney on August 12, 1943. Having heard nothing about the matter from Kenney or MacArthur during the next three weeks, Marshall reminded MacArthur on September 7 that "this corrected data was forwarded on August 12th from A-2 [air intelligence] of the Army Air Forces in a letter to General Kenney with a suggested corrected communique which to date has not been issued." The Army chief of staff said that his biennial report to the Secretary of War was due on September 8, and he wanted it to "incorporate only uncontested factual material." He told MacArthur, "In view of this it is desired that if the facts are as stated in the Air Force letter, I be advised immediately and a corrected communique be issued." [7]

MacArthur replied promptly and strongly, but, instead of is-

suing a revised communiqué, he concluded with a brazen suggestion on how the matter should be handled:

> The bases for the communique [March 7] were official reports
> from air headquarters to GHQ. Information acquired later
> from captured documents, photographs, and other data, while
> making minor changes in [the] original knowledge, showed in-
> creased rather than diminished losses. The communique as
> issued is factual, and definite data available here, including that
> acquired later, supports every essential item . . .
>
> My official operations reports submitted to the War Depart-
> ment coincide with the information released in the communi-
> que, and that of the A-2 indicates a challenge of that official
> report as well as the communique. Operations reports and com-
> muniques issued in this area are meticulously based upon
> official reports of operating commanders concerned, and I am
> prepared to defend both of them either officially or pub-
> licly . . .
>
> I request that you personally intervene to correct this situa-
> tion, which I feel must be merely a matter of routine compila-
> tion of an annual report. If such not be the case, I request that
> any report emanating from the Office of the Commanding Gen-
> eral, Army Air Forces, challenging the integrity of my opera-
> tions reports, of which the Chief of Staff is taking cognizance, be
> referred to me officially in order that I may take appropriate
> steps, including action against those responsible if circumstances
> warrant.[8]

Kenney, in turn, contested the Air Force committee's findings
point by point in a lengthy letter to Arnold. The matter of a
new communiqué on the Bismarck Sea battle was dropped,
though the Air Force historical office quietly accepted the deflated figures on Japanese losses. Marshall chose to retain Mac-
Arthur's version in his biennial report, perhaps in order to
quiet the troubled waters but more probably because the report's deadline was at hand and, for want of time to check the
data further, he felt compelled to trust the former military head
of the American Army.[9]

The issue lay dormant until September 3, 1945, when, at a press interview in Japan, while reviewing the course of the Pacific war, MacArthur reiterated that twenty-two enemy ships were involved in the battle of the Bismarck Sea. "Some people have doubted the figures in that battle," he stated, "but we have the names of every ship sunk." A few days later Kenney's Far East Air Forces headquarters in Tokyo set up a committee to re-examine the details of the operation in the hope, said one of the investigators, "that Japanese sources would bear out the Kenney-MacArthur position." The committee comprised five officers and a sergeant, all of the Thirteenth Air Force, which had been under MacArthur and Kenney's command since 1944; no Fifth Air Force personnel or participants in the battle were included. The group spent several weeks studying the available Allied and Japanese documentary evidence and interviewing a number of Japanese participants, including the admiral who commanded the convoy. The documentary and oral evidence clearly showed, stated a committee member, that "the number of Japanese personnel lost was 2890, not 15,000, the number of vessels sunk twelve, not twenty-two." Thus the findings bore out the Washington study of the summer of 1943.

An officer on the committee maintained, "When the statement of the findings was submitted by the committee, the Far East Air Force officer who received it for transmittal remarked, 'It is a fine job and I have no doubt the report will be immediately burned.'" No copy of the full report was sent to Washington, and, according to one account, "on November 19, 1945, MacArthur's headquarters ordered that the report be destroyed." Only the notes made by an Air Force historical office representative who read the report reached Air Force headquarters in Washington.[10]

Late that fall Brigadier General Jarred V. Crabb, who had been one of the Fifth Air Force unit commanders in the Bismarck Sea action, headed another GHQ-instigated inquiry into the matter. The Crabb report of December, 1945, in essence left open the possibility that MacArthur and Kenney could have been correct. Crabb wrote, "It is regrettable that much of the supporting data has been lost and destroyed, leaving this report incomplete." He concluded:

> The number of ships possibly sunk could well reach the number twenty-two, or even more, if Japanese reports had been carefully made and saved. In any survey of the Bismarck Sea Battle it is advisable and necessary to consider the abundance of miscellaneous shipping and submarine activity [and sinkings in the vicinity of the main battle] during the period of February 28 to March 6th inclusive.[11]

In a recent interview Kenney maintained that the chief of the Japanese naval staff told him in Tokyo in the fall of 1945 that the figure of twenty-two ships was a gross underestimate since "we sent about forty down there about that time, but I don't remember if we got any back." Kenney also conferred that autumn with a ranking officer of the headquarters staff at Rabaul in March, 1943, who confirmed that a second convoy of "seven or eight ships that were smaller in tonnage than the main Rabaul convoy . . . joined them in the [Dampier] strait." In addition, Kenney talked to Imamura immediately after American naval officers had interrogated him at length, undoubtedly in connection with the studies of the war later prepared by the naval analysis division of the United States Strategic Bombing Survey. He found that Imamura now "disavowed everything he ever said" in support of the Kenney-MacArthur claims on sinkings and took the position that "the convoy was as the Navy had said in Washington two years before."

As for MacArthur's views at the time on the controversy, Kenney commented:

> MacArthur said he thought the Navy was trying to belittle the whole thing because they weren't in on it. He said, "You

know, it's against the rules for land-based airplanes to sink ships, especially naval vessels. It's bad enough for them to sink merchant vessels. They ought to be sunk by battleship gunfire or by submarines. But for airplanes to do it, especially if they aren't naval airplanes, it's all wrong." Then he would laugh. But that was his only remark.

I don't accuse the Navy of anything; I don't accuse anybody. All I know is that there were a lot of ships sunk, and the Japs didn't get the troops and supplies into Lae which they were trying to do. That's what the story was all about.[12]

In his memoirs, published in 1949, Kenney insisted that nineteen or twenty ships were sunk, sixty aircraft surely destroyed and another twenty-five probably destroyed, and that Japanese personnel losses "might have been as high as 15,000." MacArthur's memoirs, completed shortly before his death in 1964, state that twelve to twenty ships were sunk out of "eight to twelve transports and a similar number of destroyers" involved in the battle, and "most of the enemy's troops were lost." Strangely, in the *Reports of General MacArthur*, edited by Willoughby and his G-2 staff at GHQ in Tokyo in the late 1940's (but not published until 1966), Japanese losses in the Bismarck Sea battle approximate closely the deflated figures given in the Washington study of mid-1943.

In 1954–55, biographical studies of MacArthur were published by Willoughby, correspondent Frazier Hunt, and Major General Courtney Whitney, each of whom had MacArthur's confidence and was given access to his files. Despite the defensive tone of all three books, Willoughby's and Whitney's accounts of the Bismarck Sea action generally follow the Washington findings; Hunt's figures on losses, however, are similar to those announced in MacArthur's communiqués of March, 1943. All of the official American and Australian Army, Navy, and Air Force histories of the war against Japan that discuss the Bismarck Sea controversy, though each involves a somewhat different approach and uses new studies of the evidence, closely agree on the figures of Japanese losses determined by the Washington study of 1943 and the suppressed Tokyo report of 1945.

The MacArthur-Kenney position on the data, as one authority observed in 1950, "to be sure, was what the aviators reported at the time, and what was stated in the official communiqué; but such mistakes are common in war and inevitable in air war. It would be more creditable to acknowledge the truth, which is glorious enough for anyone, than to persist in the error." [13] Some officials in the Pentagon had long suspected hyperbole and mendacity in MacArthur's communiqués. Whether King, Cooke, and their staffs were of any influence in the decision by Arnold's office to make this a test case, as MacArthur suspected, cannot be decided for want of evidence. The mischief-making on both sides in this prolonged and eventually ridiculous controversy should have made it a primary exhibit in the argument for unification of the armed services. It is amazing that MacArthur would have accepted their challenge to make the affair a cause célèbre, particularly since he could have quietly excused his erroneous statements on the grounds of incomplete battle reports. Ironically, MacArthur was able to confess to his earlier mistaken notions about air power — a change of mind that was important and that vitally affected his conduct of later operations — but he could not admit to a relatively inconsequential and, at the time, understandable exaggeration in a communiqué.

If his prewar responses are revealing in this connection, undoubtedly the issue had become a matter of personal honor with him. Through more than four decades of military service his reaction in similar situations had become predictable: whether right or wrong according to the available evidence, he did not budge from his stated position, however flexible he might be on matters not involving his honor, pride, or public image.

2. *The Routes to Tokyo*

General Charles de Gaulle, Sicily, and unconditional surrender — these are the topics commonly associated with the ten-
day Casablanca Conference of January, 1943. There Roosevelt,
Churchill, and the Combined Chiefs of Staff wrestled with the
problem of reconciling limited logistical means with desired
strategic ends, and ultimately agreed on general courses of
global action for Anglo-American forces in 1943. Their discussions dealt principally with the Mediterranean and European theaters, but their decisions also affected Pacific strategy.
The British preferred a holding war in the Pacific until Germany was defeated, and wanted the immediate emphasis placed
on the expansion of Allied operations in the Mediterranean.
The Americans agreed on the Germany-first strategy, as in the
past, but feared that extending the Mediterranean operations
might entail further postponement of a cross-Channel invasion
of Europe. They also believed that limited offensives in the
Pacific were possible in 1943 without vitally affecting Mediterranean and European plans. Marshall warned that, unless the
initiative were retained in the Pacific and unremitting pressure
kept up against the Japanese, "a situation might arise in the
Pacific at any time that would necessitate the United States regretfully withdrawing from the commitments in the European
Theatre." He and King maintained that 30 per cent of the
Allied military resources should be allotted to the war against
Japan, instead of the 15 per cent that King estimated was then
being employed in the Pacific.

The British, catching the veiled threat, finally agreed that a
limited offensive should be continued in the Pacific. In the
final order of priorities of men and matériel drafted by the
Casablanca planners, however, the Pacific theater ranked far
down the list, behind such priorities as protection of communications lines against submarines, aid to the Soviet Union, Medi-

terranean operations, the strategic bombing offensive in Europe, and the Bolero build-up in England. When Wedemeyer visited Brisbane on February 19, MacArthur reluctantly accepted the Casablanca priorities and asked him "to explain to General Marshall that the momentum which appeared to be the Prime Minister's major point about continued operations in the Mediterranean had an even greater application in the Southwest Pacific." [14]

In establishing Pacific objectives for 1943, the Combined Chiefs optimistically decided that Rabaul was to be captured, the Aleutians secured, and a Central Pacific drive launched; the last, however, was not to be undertaken until the fall of Rabaul. The Combined Chiefs' thinking at the time was that after Task Three, the seizure of Rabaul, the top priority in the Pacific would be Nimitz's advance across the Central Pacific. Mac-Arthur cautioned Marshall in January that the capture of Rabaul "will require long preparation and great resources." Nevertheless, "everyone assumed," states the official American Army chronicle, "despite the experience of Guadalcanal and the pessimistic estimates of MacArthur and Nimitz, that Rabaul would be captured by May of 1943." No dates were set for any of these operations, and Nimitz's projected offensive to the Truk-Guam line was made contingent upon MacArthur's release of certain air and ground forces after Rabaul's fall and on logistical requirements of a planned offensive to retake Burma that year. Whether at Casablanca the Combined Chiefs envisioned bypassing the Philippines is not clear, but British Admiral Dudley Pound predicted that an invasion of that archipelago would surely not be possible before the surrender of Germany.

Once the general strategic aims for 1943 had been determined at Casablanca, the Joint Chiefs of Staff and the Joint Staff Planners in Washington set to work on tactical objectives and their logistical requirements for the war against Japan. Accordingly, Marshall requested MacArthur to submit his detailed plans for

1943. In February, the SWPA chief forwarded Elkton I, an ambitious plan that was strikingly similar to his earlier Tulsa Plan. The advance against Rabaul, as in Tulsa, would be carried out in five stages: (1) MacArthur's seizure of Lae, Salamaua, Finschhafen, and Madang; (2) Halsey's capture of New Georgia; (3) simultaneous invasions of western New Britain by SWPA forces and of Bougainville by South Pacific forces; (4) Halsey's capture of Kavieng, New Ireland; and (5) MacArthur and Halsey's combined attack on Rabaul.

MacArthur provided Washington with no dates for the operations, saying that the schedule would depend on what and when forces were available. He claimed that Halsey had adequate strength to fulfill his part of Elkton, but that SWPA would need five more divisions, 1800 more aircraft, and additional naval forces. Rear Admiral Theodore S. Wilkinson, Halsey's deputy, had met with MacArthur at Brisbane on February 11, and agreement was reached on the execution of Elkton, which covered Tasks Two and Three of the Joint Chiefs' directive of July, 1942. But they had not coordinated their plans and logistical requirements with Nimitz's; MacArthur simply sent a copy of Elkton to the admiral for his information.[15]

The lack of coordination, together with the unexpectedly large demands to carry out Elkton, did not favorably impress the Joint Chiefs. MacArthur quickly requested that Sutherland and others of his staff be allowed to come to Washington and personally explain Elkton to the Joint Chiefs. The latter concluded that such a meeting should include representatives from Nimitz and Halsey as well. So the Joint Chiefs on February 16 extended invitations to all three Pacific commanders to send representatives to Washington to discuss Pacific strategy; each agreed, and the conference was set for March 12. MacArthur selected as his delegates Sutherland, Kenney, and Chamberlin, whom he could trust to present faithfully his views and to fight for Elkton.

When the Pacific Military Conference was convened on the morning of the 12th, King opened the first session with a summary of the Casablanca deliberations and a review of the global situation. Although all of the Joint Staff Planners attended the conference, King was the only member of the Joint Chiefs present, and he left while the first session was still under way. Most of the rest of that session was devoted to Sutherland's explanation and defense of Elkton II, which was a slightly revised version of the earlier plan. The five-stage advance was not changed, but now MacArthur and Halsey would need even more troops and planes than they had anticipated earlier. The Joint Chiefs and their planners, who felt that they had already been generous to the Pacific theater, were taken aback to learn that MacArthur had "upped the ante" again. At that time American Army strength alone in the Central, South, and Southwest Pacific theaters totaled 374,000 men, which was, despite the Germany-first strategy, considerably greater than that in the Mediterranean (298,000) or in the United Kingdom (107,000). And, of course, the preponderance of American naval power was already in the Pacific.

As ground operations in the Mediterranean extended into Sicily and Italy and the strategic bombing offensive over Europe accelerated later in 1943, the Pacific's share of personnel and matériel would drop proportionately. But, even so, Sutherland's statement of the revised Elkton requirements, together with his imperious and sometimes tactless manner, astounded and antagonized some of the Washington planners. Had they known that MacArthur had already prepared a preliminary plan (Reno) for the invasion of the Philippines, they would have been even more aghast.

During the next two sessions, on the afternoon of the 12th and the following morning, the conferees argued over the alternatives, which were succinctly expressed by one authority thus: "provide MacArthur the forces he required, persuade him to lower his estimates, or cancel the decision to take Rabaul in 1943 and substitute a less ambitious program." Carefully weighing other global priorities, the Washington planners concluded that the maximum additional strength that could be allocated to MacArthur's and Halsey's theaters would still be short nearly six divisions and twenty-four air groups of the minimum requirements they had set for Elkton's execution.

The Pacific representatives were then asked what operations could be undertaken in 1943 with such forces. They promptly replied, showing the same unanimity they had displayed throughout the conference, that only Task Two could be carried out, not the conquest of Rabaul. They said that in the South and Southwest Pacific their forces could successfully seize the Salamaua-Madang region of Northeast New Guinea, Woodlark and Kiriwina in the Trobriand Islands, New Georgia and southern Bougainville in the Solomons, and Cape Gloucester in western New Britain. With no decision reached on this proposition, the Pacific Military Conference was terminated, and the determination of the course of future operations against Japan was turned over again to the Joint Chiefs. At their request, the Pacific officers remained in Washington for several more days in case they were needed for consultation. Kenney was invited to the White House, where he found Roosevelt eager "to hear the whole story of the war in our theater in detail." The air commander said that the President "seemed to admire what the General [MacArthur] was doing and said so emphatically several times during the conversation." [16]

In their deliberations following the conference, the Joint Chiefs readily accepted the Pacific representatives' judgment that their operations in 1943 be limited to Task Two. With Sutherland's further explanation that air bases in the Trobriands were essential to support operations in the Solomons, they also agreed to the inclusion of Woodlark and Kiriwina, which were not among the original Task Two objectives. But they strongly questioned the sequence of landings in Elkton. King argued that Halsey's fleet could be used in the Central Pacific if the South Pacific forces' landing on New Georgia was to be postponed until after the conquest of the Salamaua-Madang area, which might (and did) take many months.

On March 23 the Joint Chiefs radioed MacArthur and Halsey that their personal views were desired on this matter of sequence. MacArthur responded, "We are already committed to the campaign in New Guinea, the completion of which is only temporarily suspended because of a lack of resources. If at the same time we enter upon a non-convergent attack on the New Georgia group, we have committed our entire strength without assurance of accomplishment of either objective . . . The total means are not available in these two areas at present for two such non-related offensives." Halsey, who earlier had said he was willing to attack New Georgia in April, now replied that he was agreeable to postponing that landing until after the Woodlark-Kiriwina operations.

During the Joint Chiefs' discussion in late March, King and Cooke tried in vain to get the theater boundaries readjusted so that the Solomons would lie entirely within Halsey's jurisdiction. As it was, only the southern portion of those islands, mainly Guadalcanal and Tulagi, was in the South Pacific theater. Marshall steadfastly defended the current boundary and also the command structure provided in the directive of July, 1942, which gave the strategic command of Tasks Two and Three to MacArthur. Cooke then proposed that since the Pacific war "is and will continue to be a naval problem as a whole," the entire Pacific Ocean should constitute a single theater with "a unified Naval command" headed by Nimitz. Marshall, Arnold, and their planners were vehemently opposed to this, and once again unity of command in the Pacific was forsaken in the hope of getting effective cooperation and coordination by the separate theater commands.[17]

On March 26 Marshall submitted to the Joint Chiefs a draft
directive for the Pacific commanders, and after surprisingly
little resistance by King and only minor changes in wording,
the directive was approved on the 28th. One Naval officer suggested that in a final showdown with Marshall on an issue such
as unity of command in the Pacific, King was willing to continue with MacArthur's Southwest Pacific command rather than
damage his own relations with Marshall "beyond repair." In the
instance of this directive, King seems to have retreated a considerable distance, for the Joint Chiefs approved a modified
form of MacArthur's Elkton Plan.

The directive of March 28, 1943, canceled the Joint Chiefs'
instructions of July, 1942, which had specifically called for the
capture of Rabaul; now MacArthur and Halsey were merely to
prepare for the "ultimate seizure of the Bismarck Archipelago."
The objectives for 1943 would be threefold: the seizure of (1)
Woodlark and Kiriwina; (2) Salamaua, Lae, Finschhafen, Madang, and western New Britain; and (3) the "Solomon Islands
to include the southern portion of Bougainville." The means
and sequence of operations were not spelled out; rather, it was
stated that the necessary forces would be "determined by the
Joint Chiefs," and MacArthur was to submit to them his "general plans, including the composition of Task Forces, sequence
and timing of major offensive operations."

Although not as ambitious as the objectives envisioned for
1943 at Casablanca, the goals in the directive were realistic in
relation to the means at hand. Moreover, according to the
official American Army history, the directive "gave to the
planning in the Pacific a new urgency and an immediate goal
that had been absent before." The Allies still had not developed a long-range plan for the defeat of Japan, but "now,
for the first time since July of the previous year, realistic plans
with specific targets, forces, and dates could be made." [18]

Both MacArthur and Halsey believed in early April, 1943,

that they lacked the forces to launch immediately the operations to achieve the objectives set forth in the directive, although actually their accumulated forces seemed relatively strong from Washington's viewpoint. Halsey's naval units, recently designated the Third Fleet, were formidable, consisting mainly of six battleships, five carriers, and thirteen cruisers; his Thirteenth Air Force had about 500 planes; and his ground forces comprised seven divisions, though two of them needed rest after the Guadalcanal campaign.

In the Southwest Pacific theater Carpender's naval forces, redesignated the Seventh Fleet on March 15, had two Australian cruisers and one American as their principal vessels. Barbey's VII Amphibious Force had accumulated only four old destroyers converted to transports, six landing ships-tank (LST's), and about thirty other assorted landing craft. Kenney's Fifth Air Force had grown to 1400 aircraft, besides the Allied Air Forces' Australian and Dutch squadrons. Blamey's ground forces consisted of two American Army, one American Marine, and fifteen Australian Army divisions. But two of the three American divisions were combat-exhausted, as were two of the Australian divisions. Also two of the Australian divisions were armored, for which no combat role would be found in SWPA for a long time, several Australian divisions were barely under way in their training program, and the Australian government insisted on retaining a large defensive force in Australia. Halsey's fleet and MacArthur's air forces were powerful, but the adequacy of the other components in each theater was questionable, particularly in view of Willoughby's estimates of enemy strength.

Allied intelligence figures on Japanese strength in the Solomons and New Guinea that spring totaled about 79,000 to 94,000 troops, 380 land-based aircraft, and a fleet consisting of four battleships, two carriers, and fourteen cruisers among its major ships. They could be promptly reinforced, according to

Allied estimates, by another 12,000 troops, 250 land-based aircraft, and a considerable part of the Japanese Combined Fleet,
now at Truk. If allowed to concentrate most of their strength
against either MacArthur's or Halsey's operations, the Japanese could offer devastating resistance.

Besides the creation of the Seventh Fleet and VII Amphibious Force, the changes in MacArthur's organization after the
Papuan campaign also included the establishment of a new
USAFFE and the American Sixth Army. USAFFE was reestablished in February, 1943, as the administrative headquar-
ters, headed at first by MacArthur and later by Marshall, over
the major American Army commands of the theater — Sixth
Army, Fifth Air Force, and Army Services of Supply. The last,
USASOS, according to the official history, "became in theory
merely an agency for the execution of policies made by USAF-
FE." Lieutenant General Walter Krueger and the first echelon
of his Sixth Army headquarters also arrived at Brisbane in
February. For the coming Elkton operations in the Southwest
Pacific, MacArthur created an independent tactical organization known until July as the New Britain (or Escalator) Force
and thereafter as the Alamo Force. It was commanded by
Krueger and was made up of very nearly the identical staff as
Sixth Army headquarters and the same units that constituted
the Sixth Army. At first the major units of both the army and
task force were the 1st Marine Division, the Army's 32nd and
41st Divisions, two antiaircraft brigades, an engineer special
brigade, a paratroop regiment, and a field artillery battalion —
all American units. The Alamo Force's responsibility was to
conduct the Trobriand and New Britain operations. Blamey's
New Guinea Force, almost entirely an Australian command,
would handle the conquest of New Guinea to Madang.[19]

In effect, this not too subtle move by MacArthur withdrew
American Army units from Blamey's control, made his position
as Allied Land Forces commander practically meaningless, and

left him in charge of little more than a task force. Krueger commented that, although MacArthur never discussed with him his reasons for establishing the Alamo Force, "it was plain that this arrangement would obviate placing Sixth Army under the operational control of C.G., Allied Land Forces . . . Since [Blamey] . . . likewise could not exercise administrative command over Sixth Army [because of USAFFE], it never came under his command at all." [20]

The official Australian explanation is surprisingly devoid of bias:

> MacArthur did not consult the participating governments about this change as he should have done under the terms of his directive, nor did Blamey then raise the question with his own government, as he was entitled to do. Whether the procedure — or lack of it — was right or wrong, the new arrangement was probably the only one that, in the circumstances that had developed, would have been politically acceptable in Washington. The direction of the operations in the Pacific had been allotted to the U.S. Joint Chiefs of Staff. Although a majority of its troops were Australian, MacArthur's headquarters was not an Allied but an American organisation, although it received extensive specialist assistance from Australian staffs and individual officers. There were practical and psychological obstacles in the way of leaving an Australian commander in control of the Allied land forces in the field now that they included a substantial American contingent; and the Americans evidently considered that, if separate roles could be found for the Australian and the American Armies, difficulties inseparable from the coordination of forces possessing differing organisation and doctrines could be avoided. [21]

In Brisbane MacArthur's GHQ staff continued to be dominated by American Army officers, especially the Bataan Gang, Chamberlin, and Whitlock. Of the heads of the three tactical headquarters — Allied Land Forces, Allied Naval Forces, and Allied Air Forces — only Kenney, the air commander who through his Fifth Air Force set-up was already making certain that the American influence dominated air operations, could be considered to have an influence on MacArthur and access to him comparable to that of the elite Army group at GHQ. That MacArthur was well satisfied with the headquarters structure of his Allied command is apparent from the description of it that he provided to the Army chief of staff in the summer of 1943:

> Complete and thorough integration of ground, air, and naval headquarters with GHQ is the method followed with marked success in the SWPA . . . Naval, air commanders and their staffs are in the same building with GHQ. The land commander and his staff are nearby. These commanders confer frequently with the CinC and principal members of GHQ. In addition to their functions as commanders they operate, in effect, as a planning staff to the CinC. When operating in forward areas the same conditions exist.
>
> The personal relationships established and the physical location of subordinate headquarters makes possible a constant daily participation of the staffs in all details of planning and operations. Appropriate members of GHQ are in intimate daily contact with members of the three lower headquarters . . .
>
> GHQ is, in spirit, a headquarters for planning and executing operations each of which demands effective combinations of land, sea, and air power . . . It is only the determination that GHQ shall act as a GHQ rather than as the headquarters of a single service that will produce the unanimity of action and singleness of purpose that is essential for the successful conduct of combined operations.[22]

Actually MacArthur's careful exclusion of United States Navy and Australian officers from positions of key importance on his staff was no worse than Nimitz's bias in favor of naval officers at his Honolulu headquarters, where Army and Army Air Force representation was meager and often ignored. Richardson, Mac-Arthur's old friend, commanded Army forces in the Central

Pacific, but, in reality, his authority was as circumscribed as was Blamey's authority as Allied Land Forces commander.[23]

When the Joint Chiefs' directive of March 28 reached Mac-Arthur and Halsey, they immediately put their staffs to work revising their respective roles in Elkton to make the plan conform to the objectives set in Washington and the means available in their theaters. On April 15 Halsey flew to Brisbane for a three-day conference with MacArthur about coordination of their operations. He especially wanted to impress on the SWPA chief the need for seizing New Georgia, which had not been specifically mentioned in the directive but which Halsey felt was imperative so that airfields could be established on it before Bougainville was attacked. The admiral had little trouble convincing MacArthur of this proposal. Halsey was aware that his dual role in the forthcoming operations could prove difficult since he would be under MacArthur's strategic direction and, at the same time, was responsible to Nimitz, who was theater commander of the Pacific Ocean Areas and Pacific Fleet commander-in-chief. Halsey, however, regarded this command arrangement as "sensible and satisfactory."

Most important, he and MacArthur at this, their first personal meeting, immediately established cordial relations of mutual respect, which were destined to deepen into a friendship that lasted until their deaths. MacArthur discovered that the South Pacific commander was "blunt, outspoken, dynamic" and "a strong advocate of unity of command in the Pacific." The SWPA commander found that "the bugaboo of many sailors, the fear of losing ships, was completely alien to his conception of sea action. I liked him from the moment we met. He was about my age." The fact that "there seemed always to be an undercurrent opposed to him in the Navy Department" may have improved the admiral's position in MacArthur's eyes.[24]

Halsey, in turn, described the Southwest Pacific general as follows:

Five minutes after I reported, I felt as if we were lifelong friends. I have seldom seen a man who makes a quicker, stronger, more favorable impression. He was then sixty-three years old, but he could have passed as fifty. His hair was jet black; his eyes were clear; his carriage erect. If he had been wearing civilian clothes, I still would have known at once that he was a soldier . . . We had arguments, but they always ended pleasantly. Not once did he, my superior officer, ever force his decisions on me. On the few occasions when I disagreed with him, I told him so, and we discussed the issue until one of us changed his mind. My mental picture poses him against the background of these discussions; he is pacing his office, almost wearing a groove between his large, bare desk and the portrait of George Washington that faced it; his corncob pipe is in his hand (I rarely saw him smoke it); and he is making his points in a diction I have never heard surpassed.[25]

MacArthur, Halsey, and members of their staffs worked out a plan that was issued on April 26 as Elkton III. The operations as a group were code-named Cartwheel and consisted of thirteen amphibious landings to be completed in six months, with each theater providing the maximum possible support of the other's operations. In the first phase, to begin in June, Woodlark and Kiriwina would be occupied, as well as New Georgia, with one month allotted for the Trobriands and five to achieve the Solomons objective. About two months from the start of Cartwheel, SWPA forces would launch the second phase with the seizure of Salamaua, Lae, and Finschhafen, to be accomplished by the time New Georgia was secured. The second phase would end with the capture of Madang by MacArthur's forces and of Faisi in the Shortlands and Buin in southern Bougainville by Halsey's units. The third phase, starting about December, would consist of the SWPA landing at Cape Gloucester in western New Britain, while South Pacific forces attacked Kieta in eastern Bougainville and neutralized enemy air bases on Buka, a small island off the northern coast of Bougainville.

Although the forces and timing for this complicated schedule of operations were carefully figured by the planners at Brisbane, for some reason MacArthur delayed sending a copy of Elkton III to the Joint Chiefs after its completion in late April. King complained to Marshall in early May that MacArthur should be prodded, that the Pacific forces had been inactive for several months. Marshall asked MacArthur for his plans, which the SWPA chief then promptly sent along with a detailed explanation of Cartwheel. He told the Army chief of staff that the first phase would start about the first of June and thereafter would continue in rapid succession through the various amphibious operations for about a half-year. Although he did not give dates, the timing and sequence indicated that by January, 1944, his and Halsey's forces would be poised and ready for the final, combined assault on Rabaul. A few days after MacArthur had sent this explanation to Marshall, however, shipping and landing craft shortages compelled him to push back the date of the beginning of Cartwheel to mid-June, and about two weeks later he had to notify the War Department that the operational first phase would start in late June.[26]

These changes in the date of the launching of Cartwheel and the SWPA chief's refusal to give exact dates for later operations seemed to suggest to King some hesitancy and procrastination on MacArthur's part in carrying out the Joint Chiefs' directive. In early June, King grew impatient with what he called "inactivity" in the South and Southwest Pacific and tried, through Marshall, to get MacArthur to fix precise dates for each of the Cartwheel landings. MacArthur gave September 1 as the tentative date for the start of the Lae operation, but cautiously responded that the dates of operations beyond then were "so dependent on the degree of success attained and probable enemy reaction that an estimate of dates is pure guess work." Next King tried without success to persuade the Joint Chiefs to empower Nimitz to fix the specific dates of all future Pacific operations, which, of course, would have been a long stride toward granting the admiral overall command in the Pacific.

At the Trident Conference at Washington in May, involving Roosevelt, Churchill, and the Combined Chiefs, the idea of a Central Pacific offensive had been approved in principle. With King in the lead, the Joint Chiefs and their planners then began earnest work toward starting Nimitz's long-awaited thrust. After all, the Papuan and Guadalcanal campaigns had taken far longer than anticipated, Task Two had not even been started, and the seizure of Rabaul was not in the foreseeable future. Surely, as King argued, the Central Pacific route was now worth trying, for MacArthur had had his chance to prove that his proposed New Guinea–Philippines axis was quicker and more economical. On June 15 the Joint Chiefs notified MacArthur that landings in the Marshalls were tentatively set to begin in mid-November. The 1st Marine Division from his theater and Halsey's 2nd Marine Division, as well as most of the Third Fleet and two bomber groups from either the South or Southwest Pacific, probably would have to be employed in the Marshalls offensive.

The SWPA chief protested that the proposed troop transfers would seriously handicap Cartwheel. Moreover, he said, "It would seem to be wasteful of shipping to move troops from this forward area back to Hawaii. From a strategic viewpoint the withdrawal . . . would seem to indicate a complete reorientation" favoring the Central Pacific route. MacArthur responded strongly on the bomber proposition: "Air supremacy is essential to success. With my present strength, this [success] is problematical. The withdrawal of two groups of bombers would, in my opinion, collapse the offensive effort in the Southwest Pacific Area." He advised the Joint Chiefs, "In my judgment the offensive against Rabaul should be considered the main effort, and it should not be nullified or weakened by withdrawals to implement a secondary attack" in the Central

Pacific.[27] In arguing that the sole offensive should be along his axis of advance, MacArthur told Marshall:

> From a broad strategic viewpoint I am convinced that the best course of offensive action in the Pacific is a movement from Australia through New Guinea to Mindanao. This movement can be supported by land-based aircraft, which is utterly essential and will immediately cut the enemy lines from Japan to his conquered territory to the southward. By contrast a movement through the mandated islands will be a series of amphibious attacks with the units and ground troops supported by land-based aviation. Midway stands as an example of the hazards of such operations. Moreover no vital strategic objective is reached until the series of amphibious frontal attacks succeed in reaching Mindanao. The factors upon which the old Orange plan were based have been greatly altered by the hostile conquest of Malaya and the Netherlands East Indies and by the availability of Australia as a base.[28]

Marshall did not endorse the proposition that the Southwest Pacific route was the only feasible offensive axis or necessarily the best, but he supported the SWPA commander's protests against the diversion of his forces during Cartwheel, and the Joint Chiefs agreed not to demand them for Nimitz. But at least the threat of their loss and of the proposed Marshall Islands attack succeeded in getting MacArthur to produce an exact timetable for Cartwheel, which the Joint Chiefs had repeatedly requested and regarded as necessary for the coordination of logistical needs in the Pacific operations. The dates and forces needed would not be realized exactly as he anticipated, but MacArthur proposed the following: Kiriwina and Woodlark to be captured by two regimental combat teams, beginning June 30; New Georgia, commencing June 30, and southern Bougainville, beginning October 15, to be seized by the 43rd Division; the 1st Cavalry Division and three Australian divisions to conquer the Salamaua-Madang area, starting September

1; the 1st Marine and 32nd divisions to invade Cape Gloucester on December 1, with the 24th and 41st divisions in reserve. Marshall saw to it that MacArthur not only did not lose forces to the Central Pacific but also that the 1st Cavalry and 24th divisions were promptly dispatched to the Southwest Pacific.[29]

After the staggering defeats at Guadalcanal, Papua, Wau, and the Bismarck Sea, the Japanese high command had also been engaged in reviewing strategy in the early months of 1943. The Tokyo planners finally worked out a plan that favored the Army's desire to stress the defense of New Guinea rather than the Navy's preference for putting the top priority on the Solomons. The Army-Navy Central Agreement was issued on March 25 and sent to General Imamura at Rabaul and Admiral Yamamoto at Truk. The new strategic plan emphasized the strengthening of garrisons and bases in the Lae-Finschhafen-Madang area, but the only offensive mission was for the air forces to destroy enemy air power and interdict shipping so that the Allies could not mount new offensives in the Solomons–New Guinea region. The nature and wording of the agreement were such that this offensive task became largely a responsibility of the Japanese Navy's air arm. While Imamura set about reinforcing his troops in New Guinea, Yamamoto developed a bold plan of massive air attacks, designated the I-Gō Operation, to destroy Allied air power and shipping in the Solomons and in New Guinea. Hundreds of planes were transferred from Truk to Rabaul, and Yamamoto himself flew to Rabaul on April 3 to head the operation.

Beginning on April 7, Yamamoto hurled 228 planes against the American forces on and around Guadalcanal. Considerable damage was done, but the American airmen and antiaircraft crews took a heavy toll of the attacking formations, and the Japanese by no means succeeded in wiping out or seriously crippling Halsey's air strength and shipping. Deluded by overoptimistic reports of destruction by his planes, Yamamoto sent his air forces next against the Papuan bases: ninety-four Japanese aircraft attacked Oro Bay on the 11th, 174 hit Moresby the next day, and 186 planes struck Milne Bay on the 14th. Again, the enemy airmen reported that the raids were splendid successes, but, in reality, Allied air defenses inflicted severe losses on the attackers without suffering serious damage to their air strength, bases, or shipping.

On April 18 Yamamoto took off to inspect naval air bases in southern Bougainville and congratulate the I-Gō participants there. Thanks to the alert work of South Pacific cryptanalysts, Yamamoto's exact flight plan was known and P-38's from Guadalcanal intercepted the admiral's plane. The famed admiral, who had been the architect of the Pearl Harbor raid and was probably Japan's most brilliant naval officer, died in the flaming crash of his bomber in the jungle of Bougainville.[30] Cartwheel, the dread two-pronged Allied offensive that Yamamoto thought his air armada had thwarted, would begin a month later.

3. Cartwheel Actions and Quadrant Decisions

Halsey's key objective in the first phase of Cartwheel was the Japanese air base at Munda Point, on the northwest coast of New Georgia. On the night of June 29–30, 1943, his III Amphibious Force transported some 6000 troops from Guadalcanal to the Central Solomons, catching the enemy by surprise and quickly securing beachheads the next morning on Rendova, southern New Georgia, and Vangunu. Air support by Kenney's bombers was canceled the first day when a storm front moved into the area. During the next five days American soldiers went ashore at two beaches on northwest New Georgia. Although Rendova was secured rapidly, the enemy garrison there being small, the Americans encountered mounting resistance when they tried to advance toward Munda from the beachheads on northwest New Georgia.

In mid-July Major General Oscar W. Griswold, commander of the Army's XIV Corps, took charge of operations on New Georgia and called in troop and artillery reinforcements. By August 6, after fighting that was as bloody as the worst experienced at Buna and Guadalcanal, Griswold's divisions finally secured Munda. The mop-up operations on New Georgia were costly and took another two months. Intended to be a one-division operation, the conquest of New Georgia ultimately involved three Army divisions and elements of another, besides several Marine battalions. The campaign also precipitated large-scale naval and air battles that caused heavy casualties to both sides.

The Japanese garrison on Kolombangara, just north of New Georgia, was strongly reinforced after Munda's fall in the expectation that the island would be Halsey's next target. Instead, the admiral, with MacArthur's concurrence, decided to bypass Kolombangara and in mid-August sent his forces to lightly held Vella Lavella, the northernmost of the main islands in the Central Solomons, which they quickly seized. In late August the South Pacific forces attacked Arundel, west of Munda Point, but strong Japanese resistance delayed this conquest for three weeks. From August to early October, the Japanese Navy skillfully evacuated nearly 10,000 troops stranded in the cluster of islands around New Georgia, setting off several major naval battles with the Third Fleet.

Although the Central Solomons came under American control, the length and cost of the operations had been far greater than Halsey and MacArthur had anticipated when they planned Elkton back in the spring. Southwest Pacific support had been limited to air strikes against staging areas to the north, with the cancellation, because of bad weather, of several raids that were scheduled for critical times. No serious complaints were registered by Halsey, and generally the operational and logistical coordination between the Southwest and South Pacific theaters was satisfactory. The sensitive arrangement by which South Pacific forces operated in the Southwest Pacific theater, where Halsey's immediate superiors were MacArthur for strategic direction and Nimitz for all other matters, worked harmoniously, in no small part because of the amicable relations between Halsey and the SWPA commander.[31]

Coinciding with the South Pacific troops' initial assaults in the Central Solomons, MacArthur's Cartwheel operations began with landings on June 30 in the Trobriands, northeast of Milne Bay, and at Nassau Bay, near Salamaua. Krueger's troops occupied Woodlark and Kiriwina easily; there were no enemy defenders stationed in the Trobriands. The exercise provided valuable amphibious training for Barbey's landing ship commanders and crews, and work was promptly started on two air strips, which would prove helpful to later Cartwheel operations in both theaters. Also on June 30, elements of the American 41st Division landed unopposed at Nassau Bay, over 300 miles to the northwest. The soldiers moved inland and soon linked up with the Australian 3rd Division, which had been operating in the Wau-Bulolo region; together they gradually pushed the Japanese back to their last line of defense around Salamaua in July and August. MacArthur and Blamey, however, wanted the final assault on Salamaua delayed until operations against Lae began in early September. They hoped, according to MacArthur's reports, "to siphon off enemy strength from his Lae defenses and lure his troops and supplies southward to be cut to pieces on the Salamaua front."

The Allied strategy "to deceive the Japanese into believing that Salamaua was the prime objective" worked beautifully, for the majority of the enemy soldiers in the Salamaua-Lae region were concentrated in the defense perimeter around Salamaua. Why the Japanese fell for the ruse is difficult to understand since Allied Air Forces had already destroyed the air base and port facilities at Salamaua, and the town itself and its location were of little strategic value, especially in comparison to Lae.

The mountainous Huon Peninsula was separated from the rest of Northeast New Guinea by a trough formed mainly by the Markham and Ramu rivers. Lae was situated at the gateway to this trough, and the numerous flat, grassy areas of the valleys offered good sites for airfields as well as a route, free of mountains, to Madang, the next major Japanese stronghold up the coast. Lae's harbor would be valuable as a site from which to channel supplies to both air bases and ground forces operating in the Markham and Ramu valleys. The plan of attack against Lae was similar to that which Blamey had proposed prematurely in the fall of 1942 during the Buna-Gona operations: a pincers movement in which a seaborne Australian division landed east of Lae on the shores of Huon Gulf, while another Australian division and an American paratroop regiment attacked Nadzab, eighteen miles up the Markham River, the Allied units then converging on Lae. It was hoped that the pincers would trap the Lae garrison and that a prompt advance up the Markham Valley would cut off the enemy units on the Huon Peninsula from the larger concentration at Madang. The plan was a sound one, but at GHQ there was some worry about the Japanese Air Force's ability to disrupt the sea and air movements.[32]

In late July, as part of the general strengthening of defenses in Northeast New Guinea, the Japanese high command had ordered the transfer of the Fourth Air Army, about 200 planes, from Java to the complex of airfields around Wewak, where Adachi's Eighteenth Army headquarters was also located. During July and early August Allied Air Forces daily pounded the Japanese air bases farther south — at Lae, Finschhafen, Saidor, and Madang — but without fighter escort the bombers did not dare to venture near Wewak. Kenney ordered an airfield constructed at Tsili Tsili, which was in an isolated mountain valley north of Bulolo. The field was quickly completed without detection by the Japanese, and fighter squadrons were rushed to Tsili Tsili, which placed them within range of Wewak. A number of medium bombers were also sent there, again without being noticed by the enemy.

On August 17–18, sixty-four heavy and fifty-eight medium bombers, accompanied by large numbers of P-38's, suddenly struck the Wewak airfields, destroying about 175 planes, almost all of them on the ground. Thus the principal air threat to the impending Lae invasion was decisively removed; thereafter land-based Japanese aircraft in Northeast New Guinea would offer only sporadic resistance against SWPA forces. MacArthur was justifiably proud of the Wewak strikes and stated in a press release on the 18th, "It was a crippling blow at an opportune moment. Numerically the opposing forces were about equal in strength, but one was in the air and the other was not. Nothing is so helpless as an airplane on the ground. In war, surprise is decisive." Smaller raids against other Japanese airfields in Northeast New Guinea continued daily, but at Wewak Kenney's airmen had destroyed, completely and in spectacular fashion, the main cause for anxiety about the Lae operation.

Staging from Milne Bay and the newly constructed port at hard-won Buna, the Allied seaborne invasion force debarked from Barbey's landing vessels about twenty miles east of Lae on the morning of September 4. The Japanese at first offered only light resistance. The invading troops consisted of Wootten's 9th Division, whose Australian veterans had last seen action at El Alamein in the defense of Egypt, and Brigadier General William F. Heavey's 2nd Engineer Special Brigade, American Army amphibious engineers whom MacArthur had tried in vain to get the War Department to send him during the Buna fighting. In the next four days the Allied soldiers advanced westward along the coast to within four miles of Lae before

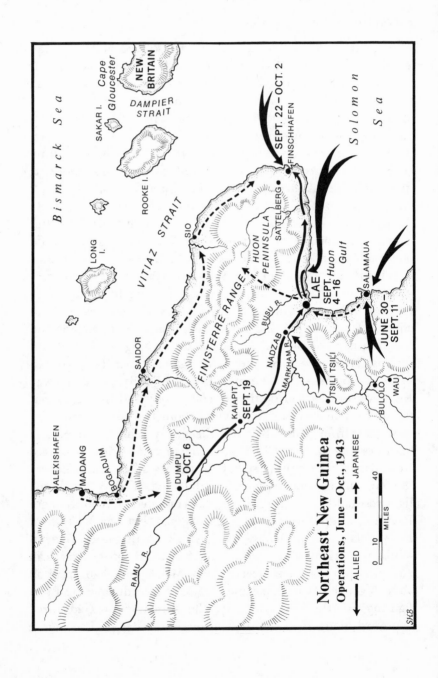

Northeast New Guinea
Operations, June–Oct., 1943

ALLISON ← → JAPANESE

Bismarck Sea

NEW BRITAIN

Cape Gloucester

SAKARI.

DAMPIER STRAIT

ROOKE I.

LONG I.

VITIAZ STRAIT

SIO

FINISTERRE RANGE

SAIDOR

ALEXISHAFEN

MADANG

BOGADJIM

RAMU R.

DUMPU
OCT. 6

KAIAPIT
SEPT. 19

MARKHAM R.

NADZAB

BUSU R.

TSILI TSILI

BULOLO

WAU

HUON PENINSULA

SATTELBERG

FINSCHHAFEN

SEPT. 22–OCT. 2

LAE
SEPT. 4–16

Huon Gulf

SALAMAUA

JUNE 30–SEPT. 11

Solomon Sea

MILES
0   10   40

ALLIED ← → JAPANESE

SHB

being halted by strong enemy resistance and the wide mouth of the Busu River.[33]

Meanwhile, MacArthur decided on the evening before the Nadzab airborne invasion to accompany the paratroops. Kenney argued that his going would be dangerous and unnecessary, but the SWPA commander replied that his presence would help the troops' morale and, besides, "I'm not worried about getting shot. Honestly, the only thing that disturbs me is the possibility that when we hit the rough air over the mountains my stomach might get upset. I'd hate to get sick and disgrace myself in front of the kids." MacArthur took Diller with him on his B-17 and, just in case, his personal physician, Morhouse. He did not get air-sick, but his bomber, called *Bataan*, made the trip on three engines because, although one quit about fifteen minutes out of Moresby, the SWPA chief insisted that they fly on to Nadzab.

That day, September 5, the American 503rd Parachute Infantry Regiment jumped over Nadzab and seized the air strip in short order against light opposition. The huge aerial show over Nadzab employed ninety-six C-47 transports escorted by 206 bombers and fighters. Again caught off guard, the Japanese Air Force did not make an appearance. MacArthur and Kenney, in separate B-17's, thoroughly enjoyed watching the spectacle from their bombers circling high above the transports. "Everything went like clockwork," commented MacArthur of this first major paratroop jump of the Pacific war. "When we got back to Port Moresby," Kenney said, "General MacArthur swore that it was the most perfect example of discipline and training he had ever seen." At Nadzab work was begun immediately on expanding the existing airfield and constructing another one. In the next two days Vasey's 7th Division began arriving, some by air transport and others overland from the Wau-Bulolo region.[34]

On September 19 the two Australian divisions, the 9th at

the Busu River and the 7th at Nadzab, began the final offensive against Lae. Six days later they captured the town, after encountering some hard fighting though less than expected. Over 9000 enemy troops, including many who had been belatedly rushed up from Salamaua, escaped the closing Allied noose by fleeing into the rugged Finisterre Mountains in an effort to reach the Japanese base at Sio on the northern coast. About 600 of them died of wounds, disease, or starvation on the way. As Halsey was learning in the Central Solomons, MacArthur and his commanders discovered that closing a trap on the wily Japanese was not easy. In the meantime, units of the Australian 5th and American 41st divisions finally received the go-ahead to launch their all-out assault against Salamaua. The last enemy positions there were overrun on September 12. Allied casualties during the long siege of Salamaua had been heavy, but that secondary front had proved its worth in diverting enemy strength from Lae, the main objective, at the critical time of the latter operations.

According to the Cartwheel schedule, SWPA forces were to attack Finschhafen, on the eastern end of the Huon Peninsula, about six weeks after the Lae operations had begun, but the unexpectedly rapid advance to Lae and intelligence reports that enemy reinforcements were headed from Madang toward the Ramu Valley and Finschhafen prompted MacArthur to hasten his operations. On September 15 he ordered an immediate offensive to capture Kaiapit and Dumpu, in the Markham and Ramu valleys respectively. Two days later he told Barbey to assault Finschhafen as soon as the amphibious operation could be mounted. As the G-2 estimates showed, Adachi was, indeed, in the process of reinforcing his garrisons at Finschhafen and in the Ramu region. The Japanese 20th Division was already well along on its 200-mile march to Finschhafen, and an additional regiment was en route to the Ramu Valley when MacArthur issued orders to seize those locations.

Elements of the Australian 7th Division moved out quickly and on September 19 captured Kaiapit. In a well-executed movement by air transport, they took Dumpu on October 6. The Markham and Ramu valleys were now securely in Allied hands, but a relatively short thrust across the Finisterres would eventually be necessary to seal off completely the Huon Peninsula. Overcoming nightmarish logistical difficulties, Barbey's VII Amphibious Force was ready to move against Finschhafen only five days after MacArthur ordered the operation speeded up. On September 22 Barbey's landing ships put ashore a brigade of the Australian 9th Division on a beach north of Finschhafen. An important factor in MacArthur's bold decision to attack Finschhafen so far ahead of schedule had been Willoughby's estimate that the defenders there numbered only about 350. In reality, nearly 5000 Japanese troops were at Finschhafen, and the Australians encountered savage fighting before they drove the enemy out of the village on October 2. An Australian battalion, marching along the coastline from Lae, arrived the next day, and Wootten soon dispatched another brigade to the area.

Nevertheless, the Australians at Finschhafen were in a vulnerable position because the Japanese garrison had not been killed but had retreated inland to nearby Sattelberg and would soon launch powerful counterattacks. Also the Japanese 20th Division's advance echelon arrived at Sio, fifty-five miles up the coast, on September 30, and the entire division could be expected to reach the lines above Finschhafen by the middle of October.[35] In a series of brilliantly planned and smoothly executed operations from July to October, MacArthur's forces had seized the Markham-Ramu trough from Lae to above Dumpu, overrun Salamaua, and captured Finschhafen, but the situation on the end of Huon Peninsula looked precarious in mid-October.

While the Cartwheel operations in Northeast New Guinea

and the Central Solomons were under way in the summer and early autumn of 1943, the planners in Washington and Brisbane were considering future operations. In early June the Joint Strategic Survey Committee, operating under the Joint Chiefs of Staff, had proposed the neutralization of Rabaul, a move strategically more feasible than its capture. By July 21 Marshall was convinced, and that day he radioed a proposal to Mac-Arthur that after Cartwheel he should seize Wewak in Northeast New Guinea, and Manus in the Admiralty Islands, and that Halsey's forces should capture Kavieng in New Ireland. By these maneuvers, Rabaul would be encircled and isolated and the need for its seizure obviated. At that time no one on the planning staffs in Washington or Brisbane expected the capture of Rabaul to come without frightful casualties.

MacArthur responded, however, by insisting that Rabaul had to be taken in order to provide him with "an adequate forward naval base" and with security on his right flank as his forces advanced up the coastline of New Guinea. The SWPA general was certain that the "capture of Wewak prior to Rabaul would involve hazards rendering success doubtful." Wewak should be heavily bombed and neutralized, but the base was too strongly fortified to be assaulted, particularly if the garrison were supported by air and naval strikes from Rabaul.[36]

In early August MacArthur sent to Washington his Reno II Plan, covering his proposed operations after the fall of Rabaul. He planned to advance along the northern coast of Netherlands New Guinea to the Vogelkop Peninsula, then jump to Halmahera and Morotai, and move from there to Mindanao. He predicted that he could capture Rabaul and the Admiralties by the middle of 1944 and the Vogelkop by the end of that year, but that he could not invade Mindanao until at least early 1945. The Washington planners were agreeable to his advance to the Vogelkop by the end of 1944, but on several important points they differed with his Reno Plan. They favored an attack on Wewak and the bypassing of Rabaul, and, what was more significant, they were persuaded that projected offensives by Nimitz's forces in the Gilberts and Marshalls should get the highest Pacific priority. From the viewpoint of the Washington planners, "two familiar threads ran through RENO II: the strong belief of MacArthur and his staff in the prime importance of their strategic goals and in the efficacy of their methods of prosecuting the war; and the familiar plea for additional allocations to step up the pace of the war" in the Southwest Pacific.

The rumors that reached the anxious SWPA commander in the first half of August said that the "Washington admirals" were about to succeed in their stratagem to halt MacArthur's northward advance at the equator and turn the Pacific war into a completely Navy-dominated performance. When he returned to Brisbane about August 9 from Washington, where he had talked to Marshall and other leaders in the War Department, Willoughby reported dejectedly that little help could be expected "until the number one job [defeat of Germany] is over . . . Something may and will be done . . . to see that the Jap is hurt and MacArthur not helped in doing it." [37]

It was with understandable anxiety, then, that MacArthur awaited news of the decisions of Roosevelt, Churchill, and their military advisers at the Quadrant Conference in Quebec, August 14–24. There, after extensive deliberations on Pacific strategy, the Combined Chiefs, on the recommendation of the American members, approved the following post-Cartwheel objectives for MacArthur's theater, to be achieved by the end of 1944:

35. Operations in the New Guinea–Bismarcks–Admiralty Islands subsequent to current operations:
   The seizure or neutralization of eastern NEW GUINEA as far west as WEWAK and including the ADMIRALTY ISLANDS and BISMARCK ARCHIPELAGO. RABAUL is to be neutralized rather than captured.

36. Operations in NEW GUINEA subsequent to the WE-
WAK-KAVIENG Operation:
    An advance along the north coast of NEW GUINEA as
far west as VOGELKOP, by step-by-step airborne-waterborne
advances.

Having canceled the assault on Rabaul, the Combined
Chiefs decided that the top priority henceforth in the Pacific
conflict would go to Nimitz's offensive, which, by the end of
1944, was expected to have secured the Gilberts, the Marshalls,
Ponape and Truk in the Carolines, and the Palaus or the Marianas, or both. The seizure of the Gilberts, on the American
chiefs' recommendation, was to be the principal Central Pacific
objective for the remainder of 1943.[38]

Since Pacific planning was primarily the responsibility of the
American Joint Chiefs, the British military leaders at Quebec
went along agreeably with most of the American proposals,
choosing to give battle over issues dearer to British interests,
such as operations in Burma and the Indian Ocean area. But
the British chiefs did raise the point that a single advance across
the Pacific would release additional forces for the future cross-
Channel invasion of Europe. It would seem, they suggested,
that since the American chiefs favored the Central Pacific offensive, MacArthur's offensive operations could be sharply reduced or canceled after Cartwheel. King countered that if military resources were withdrawn from MacArthur's area, they
should be allocated to Nimitz's drive, not to the European theater. Marshall observed that most of the forces required for
MacArthur's advance to the Vogelkop Peninsula were already
in or en route to the Southwest Pacific. The British quietly
dropped this matter, but later they proposed that the Joint
Chiefs should review the New Guinea plans and operations "to
ensure that the results likely to be obtained are commensurate
with the effort involved." The Joint Chiefs retorted that they
regularly reviewed all their operations, and, besides, the British
proposal would have "a disheartening effect" upon MacArthur

when he read it in the Combined Chiefs' final Quadrant report to Roosevelt and Churchill. The British quickly withdrew the suggestion, professing that they were not aware that the report would be made available to the SWPA commander.[39]

No decision was reached at Quebec on whether the Philippines would be invaded, much less which force, MacArthur's or Nimitz's, might undertake the operation if it were authorized. When news of the Quadrant decisions reached Australia, both MacArthur and the Curtin ministry were troubled over the further lowering of the priority of the Southwest Pacific theater. The Quebec conferees seemed to have made mockery of MacArthur's oft-quoted, if unauthorized, pledge to the Filipinos, "I shall return." In the weeks after the Quadrant Conference numerous articles appeared in Australian newspapers speculating on the future of Southwest Pacific operations. The Brisbane *Courier-Mail* of September 27, for example, carried a long article on the subject under a headline that read " 'Garrison Post' for MacArthur?" [40] Colonel William L. Ritchie, who headed the Southwest Pacific section of the War Department's Operations Division and made frequent trips to MacArthur's headquarters, reported to Marshall from Brisbane on September 28 that the SWPA chief was dismayed about the future prospects for his theater:

> In discussions with Generals MacArthur and Sutherland it is quite evident that they sincerely feel that there is an intention on the part of the Combined Chiefs of Staff to pinch off the operations of the Southwest Pacific forces at the Vogelkop. The principal basis for this belief seems to be the treatment of Far East and Pacific war strategy by the British which they assume is inspired, together with certain rather devious Navy propaganda to the effect that this would be a naval show from New Guinea on. They indicate that the Australians are beginning to feel the same way to the extent of preparing to let down in their war effort . . . I have assured General MacArthur that were this the intention of the Chiefs of Staff you would have so informed him immediately.[41]

In early October Marshall tried sympathetically to explain to MacArthur the import of the Quadrant decisions, but the Army chief of staff's honest appraisal was not especially encouraging from the SWPA chief's point of view. Marshall stated:

> Quadrant decisions as set forth in JCS 319/5 insofar as they pertain to the war against Japan were projected only so far in the future as the situation permitted when the decisions were made . . . The dispositions taken by the Japanese to meet our efforts will have considerable influence on the ultimate decisions as to the main effort for the forces from the Pacific and Southwest Pacific areas. The important thing is constant pressure from all directions until means become available for the kill.
>
> Although decision has not been made by the Chiefs of Staff covering operations in the Southwest Pacific beyond those set forth for the seizure of the Admiralty Islands, Bismarck Archipelago and the North coast of New Guinea as far west as Vogelkop, plans must be perfected for further operations beyond those phases. It appears that the next logical objective for the Southwest Pacific Forces is the seizure of Mindanao. However, it may be found practicable to make this effort from the Central Pacific or to concentrate our effort in a thrust farther north through the Bonins. Our rapid expansion and immediate availability of naval surface forces including carriers is giving us a decided advantage in naval strength. Not to make full use of this would be a serious error. We must seek the best method and the most fruitful area in which to utilize this asset.[42]

The cancellation of the Rabaul assault was not the cause but the result of the Joint Chiefs' decision to give preference to the drive across the Central Pacific. The official histories give full and proper credit to the Joint Chiefs and their planners for originating and holding to the policy of neutralizing Rabaul despite MacArthur's persistent advocacy, before the Quebec Conference, of the need to attack the stronghold. "The decision to neutralize Rabaul marked the first official pronouncement of a policy of bypassing strong centers of resistance," states the offi-

cial Army chronicle, "and foreshadowed the gradual replacement of the earlier conservative step-by-step method of operations in the Pacific."

Actually the first victims of bypassing in the Pacific war had
been MacArthur's forces in the Philippines, when the Japanese
offensive in Southeast Asia enveloped the archipelago and left
the defenders isolated and subject to inevitable reduction at the
leisure of the high command in Tokyo. The first case of bypassing by the Allies had been the reconquest of Attu in May,
1943, when Kiska was skipped, and the only other one was Halsey's bypassing of Kolombangara to invade Vella Lavella in
mid-August. No bypassing had been attempted to date by Mac-
Arthur's forces. Nevertheless, just as the SWPA chief was quick
to exploit Kenney's aggressive, imaginative use of air power to
spearhead his advances, so MacArthur was set to thinking, by
the disappointing Quebec decision on Rabaul, how he could
adapt the technique in his operations. As mentioned, the bypassing of Wewak was already on his mind, and he was soon
talking about other possible strong points, such as Madang, that
could be effectively leapfrogged. He later commented, "It was
the practical application of this system of warfare . . . to bypass Japanese strong points and neutralize them by cutting their
lines of supply . . . to . . . 'hit 'em where they ain't' — that
from this time forward guided my movements and operations." [43]

In the next two years MacArthur would become the foremost
exponent of the technique of bypassing, indeed, so much so that
in the postwar era a legend would develop that he had originated
the plan to bypass Rabaul. In truth, he strongly opposed that
decision, but once he was converted, no commander exploited
bypassing more brilliantly than MacArthur.

CHAPTER VIII

Three-Pronged Offensive

1. Increasing the Tempo

THE AUSTRALIAN BEACHHEAD on the eastern end of the Huon
Peninsula, it will be recalled, was in imminent danger by October, 1943, despite the fact that MacArthur announced on the
4th that all enemy forces between Finschhafen and Madang had
now been "outflanked and contained." For a time Wootten had
difficulty getting reinforcements sent to Finschhafen because, according to the official Australian account, "MacArthur's planners felt that Finschhafen would be a 'pushover' and that the
operation could be considered as finished" now that the base had
been captured. With the arrival of the Japanese 20th Division
in the Sattelberg-Wareo area, northwest of Finschhafen, the
enemy launched a series of savage counterattacks on October
16–25. Wootten's 9th Division, which was finally reinforced by
another of its brigades on the 20th, gave some ground but firmly
held the key positions of the perimeter around Finschhafen.
The totals on killed-in-action during the ten days of counterattacks showed that fourteen Japanese were killed for every
Australian who died in combat. The frightful casualties and the

failure to achieve a breakthrough compelled Adachi to order the Japanese forces to go on the defensive in the mountainous region from Sattelberg to Wareo. In the meantime, the 9th Division had received further reinforcements, and on November 17 Wootten's brigades began an offensive, seizing Sattelberg after eight days of heavy fighting. On December 8 the Australians took Wareo, and the Japanese retreated toward Sio, to the north. Maintaining relentless pressure on the enemy, the 9th Division captured Sio five weeks later, and the bedraggled remnants of the Japanese 20th and 51st divisions retreated west toward Saidor. Some small pockets of enemy defenders remained to be mopped up later, but the end of the Huon Peninsula was now securely in Australian hands.[1]

While the Huon operations were under way, advance fighter bases had been constructed at Nadzab, Lae, and Finschhafen so that P-38's could escort bombers on the long flight to Rabaul. Beginning on October 12, Kenney's aircraft attacked Rabaul more frequently and in larger numbers than ever before; some of the raids involved nearly 400 Allied planes. Praising the results of the attack on the 12th, Arnold told MacArthur that it was a "small Pearl Harbor in reverse." As was now almost customary, MacArthur's communiqués grossly exaggerated the damage wrought by SWPA planes, claiming for example, that a raid on Rabaul on November 2 destroyed fifty-five aircraft and sank or damaged 114,000 tons of shipping when actually the enemy lost only twenty planes and about 5000 shipping tons. Yet there was no question that the regular strikes were causing much destruction. Of a raid on the 3rd, MacArthur told Kenney, "The history of warfare shows no more valiant, no more determined, and no more effective battle than the one waged by your medium bombers and fighters yesterday at Rabaul." Except for short periods when stormy weather intervened, the massive attacks by SWPA land-based aircraft, supplemented later by hordes of planes from the Solomons air command, including New Zealand

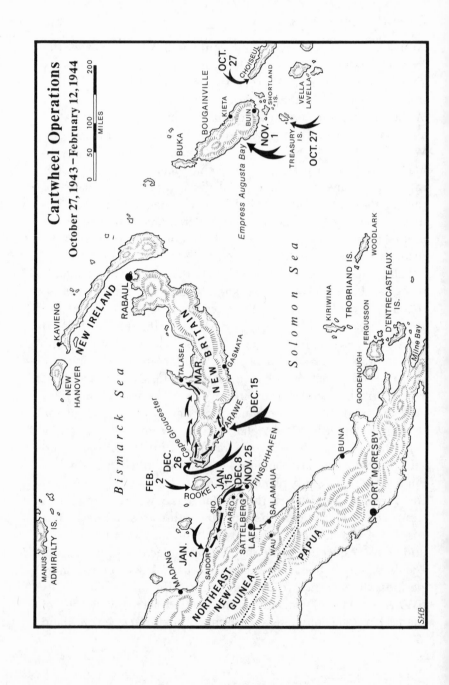

Cartwheel Operations

October 27, 1943 – February 12, 1944

MILES

0   50   100   200

squadrons, and carrier groups operating in conjunction with Halsey's offensive, would continue into early 1944 when the Japanese decided to withdraw their remaining planes from Rabaul to Truk. Also during the autumn of 1943, while Kenney's aircraft were concentrating on Rabaul, over 600 planes of Halsey's air command in the Solomons had been battering enemy air bases in the northern part of those islands and had effectively neutralized the fields on Bougainville by early November.[2]

In his planning for Elkton, MacArthur had anticipated that southern Bougainville would be secured by Halsey about a month prior to the SWPA invasion of western New Britain, at first set for early December. In July, MacArthur had agreed to Halsey's suggestion that, in view of the enemy's strength on Bougainville, the island should be bypassed altogether, while South Pacific forces seized the nearby Shortland Islands from which their artillery could neutralize the stronghold at Buin, in southern Bougainville. In September, however, Halsey suggested a new proposal: his forces would capture the Treasury Islands and the northern part of Choiseul and then invade Bougainville either at Kieta on the eastern coast or at Empress Augusta Bay on the western coast. MacArthur felt that his plan was overcautious and did not make provision for Halsey's air command to be ready to operate from bases on Bougainville in time to support the SWPA invasion of western New Britain: "I feel the intent of the J.C.S. directive would not be satisfied by seizing and operating from Treasury and Choiseul Bay . . . I believe myself the occupation of a suitable base for air operations on Bougainville proper and essential to further operations against the Bismarcks." So that Halsey might employ all his strength in the Bougainville campaign, MacArthur released the admiral from any obligation to render support to SWPA operations during November–December, 1943. When one of Halsey's planners asked MacArthur at a Brisbane conference on September 17 if he preferred an attack on either the eastern or western coast of Bougainville, MacArthur answered, "No, that is entirely as Halsey decides. To me it makes no difference." In several conferences at Brisbane in early fall, MacArthur and Halsey amicably worked out a plan in which the admiral's objectives were to seize the Treasuries and northern Choiseul in late October and Empress Augusta Bay in early November.[3]

The Bougainville campaign began on October 27 when a New Zealand brigade captured the lightly held Treasury Islands and a battalion of American Marines conducted a diversionary raid on northern Choiseul. On November 1 came the main thrust when the 3rd Marine Division successfully established a beachhead at Empress Augusta Bay against the hopeless opposition of a 270-man Japanese garrison. The area, on the west central coast of Bougainville, was geographically isolated from the major Japanese bases on the southern and eastern coasts of the islands. The Marines quickly fortified a perimeter about one mile deep and five miles long, and work was started on an airfield at Cape Torokina on the southern end of the beachhead.

Halsey's land-based aircraft from New Georgia and Guadalcanal, together with several naval surface groups on loan from Nimitz, thwarted the enemy's air and naval efforts to destroy the beachhead, and at the same time SWPA bombers stepped up their raids on Rabaul. By the end of November, the Army's 37th Division had arrived at Empress Augusta Bay, to be joined soon by the Americal Division; command of the expanded beachhead passed to Griswold's XIV Army Corps on December 15. Two days later, fighters from the Torokina airfield participated in their first strike on Rabaul from the new base; the enemy stronghold was now only 250 miles to the northwest. By that time the Japanese had expended hundreds of planes, relayed from Truk and staging out of Rabaul, in frantic efforts to frustrate Halsey's and MacArthur's offensives. With Rabaul increasingly vulnerable to air attack, the strategic significance of that huge base in enemy planning began to decline rapidly.

Indeed, Rabaul was fast becoming more of a liability than an asset to the Japanese.[4]

The next objective in Cartwheel was the invasion of the western end of New Britain. The main landing was to be at Cape Gloucester, though after the decision to bypass Rabaul was announced Kenney tried in vain to persuade MacArthur against the Gloucester assault because it would be too time-consuming to construct an air base there before the next major operation. The SWPA commander insisted, however, that control of Cape Gloucester was necessary for securing the Vitiaz and Dampier straits, which were essential passageways for his forces as they advanced along the coast of New Guinea. At first the New Britain plan, code-named Dexterity, had included a secondary landing at Gasmata, on the southern coast of New Britain, but after long conferences at Brisbane with Krueger, Carpender, and Kenney in late November, MacArthur decided to substitute Arawe, partly because it was less strongly defended and farther from the Rabaul-based aircraft.

MacArthur also found it necessary, mainly for want of ships, to postpone Dexterity for about two weeks. Barbey, whose amphibious force would play a key role in the landings, recalled the ending of one of the planning conferences: "Amid the gloom resulting from lack of ships and planes to do what we felt needed to be done, General MacArthur adjourned the meeting until the following morning. In spite of the passage of time, some words are so burned into one's memory as never to be forgotten. Among them are MacArthur's bitter words as we filed out of the room, 'There are some people in Washington who would rather see MacArthur lose a battle than America win a war.'" Carpender wanted to develop a PT boat base in the harbor at Arawe, although after the operation the commander of the PT boat command in SWPA said that he had expressed no need for such a base. Major General William Rupertus, whose 1st Marine Division was to attack Cape Gloucester, persuaded

MacArthur to abandon a proposed paratroop drop there because bad weather could prevent it and thereby disrupt the whole operation, which, as then structured, depended on the drop. After considerable and sometimes heated discussion among Army, Navy, and Marine planners at MacArthur's GHQ, the Dexterity Plan was made final.[5]

The Marine version, as written by the divisional historian, gives credit to the courageous 1st Division's staff for opposing an originally defective plan for the Gloucester landing, developed by Krueger's staff, and formulating one that was realistic and satisfactory:

> The plan for Gloucester would not jell. As summer wore into fall, and fall approached winter, there was still disagreement between Sixth Army staff and the 1st Division over some of the main points.
>
> With D-day set for 26 December, Sixth Army as late as 17 October 1943 distributed a plan that seemed to the 1st's staff as unrealistic as the early plan that had been issued in Australia. This new plan, issued as Field Order No. 4, called for only a single regiment of the Division to land in the Gloucester area on D-day. This lone regiment was to be supported by an Army parachute regiment, the 503rd, which would drop in a kunai patch southeast of the airfield. The Marines were to drive through the jungle and join the parachutists, a piece of ma-neuver that looked better on paper to the Army staff than it did to the Marines who had already learned at Guadalcanal some sad lessons about maneuver in the rain forest.
>
> This was still the plan, the fixed and set plan, when General MacArthur himself came to Goodenough in late November, primarily to make an inspection of the troops.
>
> The day he visited the CP [command post] of the 1st Division the maps were spread out and MacArthur looked at them casu-ally as the Division staff stood around. He was accompanied by Lieutenant General Walter Krueger, Sixth Army com-mander, who had heretofore been adamant with the 1st.
>
> MacArthur asked, as if in politeness only, how the 1st liked the plan for the coming operation.

"Well, General," spoke up Lieutenant Colonel E. A. Pollock, Division D-3 [operations officer], and the same Pollock who had commanded the battalion at the Battle of Tenaru [Guadalcanal], "we don't like it."

MacArthur's surprise was evident. "Well, what is it, Colonel, you don't like?" he asked.

"Sir, we don't like anything about it," was Pollock's bold reply.

MacArthur looked questioningly at Krueger, but that general was staring fixedly at Pollock. Recovering himself somewhat, MacArthur turned back to Pollock and said with a sternness still curbed by his surprise at the turn of events.

"You had better speak to General Rupertus about your questions."

"But I have," insisted Pollock. "None of us like it."

With that MacArthur turned and walked out of the tent, making no further comment, but apparently, thinks one Division staff officer, with the mental note to discuss the whole landing plan later with Krueger.

For, shortly after MacArthur's visit, word came down from Sixth Army that another joint conference was to be held between that staff and the 1st's staff. And at this conference, attended by General Rupertus and Pollock, among others, a new, and final plan was settled upon which met the Division's objections to the earlier plans.[6]

To the chagrin of some of his Army officers and to the credit of his objectivity, MacArthur approved the plan that was essentially the one proposed by the Marines.

The Dexterity operations would be the first major undertaking by Krueger's Alamo Force. The 112th Cavalry Regiment and a field artillery battalion would go ashore at Arawe, while the 1st Marine Division, reinforced by miscellaneous supporting units, including the Army's 2nd Engineer Special Brigade, would take Cape Gloucester. The 32nd Division, which, like the Marines, had had a long rest since the first campaigns, would constitute the Alamo Force reserve. In late November and early December, air attacks on New Britain targets, especially Gasmata

and Cape Gloucester, were intensified, but Arawe was left untouched in the hope of deceiving the Japanese.

MacArthur was at the wharf on Goodenough Island to bid
farewell to Brigadier General Julian W. Cunningham as his
Director Task Force started boarding its ships to depart for
Arawe. On December 15 the 112th Cavalry and its supporting
units landed at Arawe against relatively light opposition. But
Japanese reinforcements were rushed to the area, and heavy
fighting developed at intervals, especially in January when the
enemy tried to obliterate the beachhead by an all-out assault.
The American lines held, however, and by mid-February most
of the Japanese troops were withdrawn from the area. Arawe
did not prove to be worth the effort because no PT boat base
was established there nor was its air strip used much in support
of later operations. Also, this secondary operation had not succeeded in drawing Japanese troops away from Cape Gloucester,
the main objective.[7]

A few hours before the Marines embarked for Cape Gloucester on Christmas Day, MacArthur visited them on Goodenough
and wished them well. His final words to Rupertus were frank
and sincere: "I know what the Marines think of me, but I also
know that when they go into a fight they can be counted upon
to do an outstanding job. Good luck." The enemy offered only
slight resistance when the Marines landed on widely separated
beaches east and south of Cape Gloucester on December 26. But
as the main force of Marines, at the eastern beachhead, started
pushing westward toward the two Japanese air strips at Cape
Gloucester, the fighting accelerated. The air strips were overrun
on the 30th, and Rupertus received prompt congratulations
from MacArthur, but heavy battling continued for another two
weeks on the high ground west and southwest of the cape. Tactical adaptation of medium and light tanks to jungle warfare,
tried on a limited basis in the New Georgia and Bougainville
operations, proved decisive in some of the assaults around Cape

Gloucester. After that the Japanese 17th Division, which was the main defensive unit in the area, seemed to have "little heart for a resolute defense." Many of its men were in poor physical condition because Allied air strikes had virtually cut off the supply line from Rabaul for weeks before the invasion.

On February 12 Rupertus' troops seized unoccupied Rooke Island, across Dampier Strait, and later advance elements of his division moved eastward as far as Talasea, halfway between Cape Gloucester and Rabaul, without meeting any sizable groups of Japanese. The inhospitable region of jungles and mountains between Talasea and Rabaul was left as a sort of un-contested buffer zone. In May the Marines, much to their joy, were finally transferred from New Britain to Nimitz's theater. MacArthur, who was "extremely desirous" of retaining the division in his theater, protested to Washington that its mission in the Bismarcks had not yet been completed. He told the division commander he regretted losing the 1st Marines because "you know in Central Pacific the 1st Marine Division will just be another one of six Marine divisions, [but] if it stayed here it would be *my* Marine Division." [8]

MacArthur remarked to Krueger that "this war has shown no finer victory" than that at Gloucester, and most authorities agree that it was well planned and executed. But, like Arawe, Cape Gloucester was never developed into a major air or naval base and assumed little significance in the staging of future operations. "It is clear that the Arawe and Cape Gloucester invasions were of less strategic importance than the other CARTWHEEL operations," states the official Army history, "and in the light of hindsight were probably not essential to the reduction of Rabaul or the approach to the Philippines."

The chief naval historian of the Pacific war bluntly says, "Arawe was of small value. The harbor was never used by us; the occupation served only to pin down some of our forces that could have been better used elsewhere, and to divert the Japanese Air Force from attacking Cape Gloucester on D-day of that operation." About the latter invasion he comments, "The capture of Cape Gloucester was an even greater waste of time and effort than Arawe. With the Huon Peninsula in our possession a big hole had been breached in the Bismarcks Barrier and there was nothing on Cape Gloucester to prevent General MacArthur from roaring through Vitiaz Strait to the Admiralties, Hollandia and Leyte." He does admit that the operation was "well planned, well led and superbly executed" and that "in the light of the intelligence which he then had," rather than the hindsight of later critics, MacArthur "was justified in undertaking it." Some valuable lessons were learned in tactical techniques, which made the troops more effective jungle fighters in later operations. Also, some important discoveries were made about adapting new weapons and equipment to jungle warfare.[9]

On December 17, two days after the Arawe landing, MacArthur decided to launch a leapfrogging amphibious assault against Saidor to cut off the Japanese retreat from the Huon Peninsula. He assigned the mission to Krueger's Alamo Force, which marked a departure from the understanding that the New Guinea Force, comprised mainly of Australian units, would conduct all operations in Northeast New Guinea. To no avail, Krueger, cautious and conservative, opposed the mission because his forces were already committed in two other operations. MacArthur reassured him that it could be undertaken and added, "I am most anxious that if humanly possible this operation take place as scheduled. Its capture will have a vital strategic effect which will be lost if materially postponed."

The Michaelmas Task Force, led by Brigadier General Clarence Martin and consisting of about 6800 troops of the 32nd Division, made the landing at Saidor on January 2 against slight opposition. The American garrison was soon built up to nearly 15,000 men, and construction of airfields and base facilities was begun promptly. But Martin did not push his forces into the inland hill country to try to cut off the Japanese withdrawal from the Sio region. He did seek permission from Krueger, however, to advance eastward and pin the enemy forces between the Americans and the Australians. Krueger's authorization for Martin to move east was received at Saidor too late to block the enemy forces, which by then had eluded the Americans around Saidor and were moving to the west of them. Having pursued the Japanese all the way from the Finschhafen region, the Australians were delighted to hear of the Saidor landing but were astounded to learn that the Americans had bungled a grand opportunity to trap the enemy force of 11,000 to 13,000 men.

The chief reasons seem to have been Krueger's unwillingness to commit more troops to the Saidor operation, his concern lest Martin's force overextend itself and prove unable to withstand a concentrated attack, and communications difficulties, which produced some garbling of Martin's messages in transmission to the Alamo Force headquarters. On February 10, advance elements of the Australian 5th Division, which relieved the weary 9th Division after Sio's fall, made contact with American troops southeast of Saidor. The meeting was somewhat anticlimactic since the intended victims of their trap were far to the west on their way to Madang.

Actually, when Martin's task force seized Saidor, the main objectives of Cartwheel, as set forth in the Joint Chiefs' directive of March, 1943, had been achieved except for the capture of Madang. Both the Markham-Ramu trough and the Huon Peninsula had been secured in Northeast New Guinea, western New Britain had been captured, and a western portion of Bougainville had been taken (the directive stipulated the southern part). The complete neutralization of Rabaul had not yet been accomplished, but the next operations of MacArthur's and Halsey's forces, to be launched in early 1944, would be intended to achieve that goal.[10]

Nearly two years after the start of the Pacific war, Nimitz

finally began his much-debated drive across the Central Pacific with the invasion of the Gilbert Islands on November 20. That morning about 35,000 troops, supported by intense pre-assault bombardments by planes and naval guns of the Pacific Fleet, landed on the tiny coral atolls of Tarawa and Makin. Because of the heavy losses of aircraft earlier sent from Truk to Rabaul, the Japanese were unable to mount a serious air threat. The Army's 27th Division had a comparatively easy task overrunning Makin, but the 2nd Marine Division was engaged in a bloody three-day battle against 4800 Japanese in strong fortifications before it secured Tarawa. The Marines on Tarawa suffered 3300 casualties, including more than 1000 dead — about ten times the Army's losses on Makin.

Although most authorities disagree with him, Major General Holland M. Smith, the Marine commander, later concluded that Tarawa had little strategic value and should have been by-passed. Its assault, he felt, produced "a terrible waste of life and effort." MacArthur was one of the few Pacific commanders who during the war years repeatedly pointed to the Tarawa operation as a bloody blunder. The casualty toll was shocking to Nimitz, and, as in the case of the lessons MacArthur learned from the Buna campaign, it would be nearly a year and a half before the Central Pacific forces again attacked such a powerful fortress. "Of all the beaches assaulted in World War II," according to the Army chronicle, "only Iwo Jima was more strongly fortified or more stubbornly defended than Tarawa." It was not the best possible start for the Central Pacific offensive, but it should be remembered that MacArthur's troops at Buna and Halsey's on Guadalcanal had not enjoyed auspicious beginnings either.[11]

2. *Logistics, Command, and Strategy*

Although the Cartwheel operations generally had progressed well, MacArthur was convinced that "shoestring" logistics prevented him from achieving greater victories. In November, 1943, he wrote to Robert Wood, the Sears, Roebuck head who was now a major general engaged in supply work, "We are going well against the Nip just now, but working on such a shoestring as we are leaves much to be desired." MacArthur told Moseley in January, 1944, "Out here I am busy doing what I can with what I have, but resources have never been made available to me for a real stroke. Innumerable openings present themselves which because of the weakness of my forces I cannot seize. It is truly an Area of Lost Opportunity." The Southwest Pacific theater lacked resources, he contended, because "everything military seems to be so handicapped by politics that even the most basic decisions are corrupt." Two months later he sounded a similar refrain in a letter to Major General George B. Duncan, a trusted friend since their times together in World War I: "From the very beginning we have had a hard time. No resources and no supplies made the situation precarious from the start. I have done the best I could with what I had, but no commander in American history has so failed of support as here. We have come through, but it has been shoestring stuff." [12]

Nevertheless, official statistics on American overseas deployment do not indicate that the Pacific forces were fewer in number than those committed to the war against Germany or that they lacked adequate supplies. Army troops in the Pacific nearly doubled in numbers from December, 1942, to December, 1943; the total by the latter date was nearly 700,000, which was, states an Army historian, "an increase of over 100,000 more than the planners had counted upon having in the Pacific according to their estimates of early March 1943." The Southwest Pacific Area at the end of 1943 had four American Army, one United States Marine, and three veteran Australian Army divisions, with twelve more Australian divisions in reserve, on garrison duty, or in various stages of training. By that time seventeen United States Army divisions were deployed in the European and Mediterranean theaters compared to thirteen American Army and three United States Marine divisions in the Pacific.

The total number of American servicemen committed to the war against Japan, including ground, naval, and air forces in all theaters of that conflict, was just over 1,878,000 in December, 1943, while those in the theaters of the German conflict numbered approximately 1,810,000. American combat aircraft of all types and services deployed against Germany amounted to about 8800 at that time compared to nearly 7900 in the war against Japan. While 515 combat ships of the United States Navy, ranging from battleships to landing craft, were then in use in the Atlantic and Mediterranean, 713 such vessels, including a preponderance of the newer and larger types, were engaged in the Pacific. The figures located for the Pacific are not broken down by theaters, but MacArthur's area by December, 1943, had about one-third of American ground forces, the largest land-based air force, and only a small naval force, of which the most numerous ships were the landing craft of the growing VII Amphibious Force. All in all, as the official Army history concludes, "After two years of war, the balance of U.S. forces and resources between the European and Japanese areas was fairly even."

What alarmed MacArthur, however, were the recent trends of deployment, for since August, 1943, the shipments of men and matériel to the European and Mediterranean theaters had risen sharply in comparison to the Pacific's allocation, and of the deployment against Japan since August the Central Pacific had gotten the largest share. He realized that in the future both trends were likely to continue until the deployment to Europe far exceeded that to the Pacific and Nimitz's share became much greater than his. In fact, the balances would have been tipped earlier and more heavily in favor of Europe over the Pacific and of Nimitz's theater over MacArthur's if the Combined Chiefs and Joint Chiefs had been able to reach agreement sooner on plans for the cross-Channel attack and the Central Pacific thrust.[13]

Cargo and personnel shipping, which seemed to be inadequate in every theater, became an especially critical problem in the Pacific in the fall of 1943. The shortage was due to a number of developments that were enmeshed in the complexities of global logistics. Lags in output by American shipyards resulted from the retooling necessary to construct new types of vessels and also from the conversion of many cargo ships into transports and tankers to meet special theater needs. Transfers of shipping to Soviet registry under the lend-lease program were unusually heavy in the first half of the year. The start of the Central Pacific offensive and the acceleration of operations in the Southwest and South Pacific brought shipping demands that were unprecedented in the war against Japan. The increased needs in the Pacific, moreover, coincided with the tremendous speed-up of troop and supply shipments to the United Kingdom in preparation for the invasion of France, now set for May, 1944.

The shipping crisis in the Pacific that developed in the autumn of 1943 was aggravated also by MacArthur's unauthorized retention of War Shipping Administration vessels in order to carry troops and supplies in his theater. Whereas Nimitz had the combat loaders and auxiliary ships of his huge Pacific Fleet to help in relieving his shipping needs, MacArthur's local fleet of merchantmen was pitifully inadequate, consisting, in the main, of four "Liberty" ships assigned to the theater and an assortment of small Dutch and Australian vessels. The War Shipping Administration protested about the slow turn-around rate

of its ships on the Southwest Pacific run, but MacArthur steadfastly maintained that he had to use to the maximum all shipping in sight to mount the numerous Cartwheel amphibious
operations. In August he informed the War Department:

> It is coming to be evident that sustained effort may be impos-
> sible in this theater because of lack of mobility which effec-
> tively prevents taking advantage of hostile weaknesses developed
> or successes gained. Each successive operation will be delayed
> for purposes of concentration, thus allowing the Japanese to re-
> consolidate ahead of our offensive effort. This results from lack
> of shipping. If any form of limited offensive is to be contin-
> ued, heavier concentrations must be on hand closer to the com-
> bat zone and ships must be on hand to carry these concentra-
> tions to forward staging areas and maintain them there. Be-
> cause of the inadequacies of port facilities in the forward areas
> and the considerable period of time required to build them, re-
> serves of supplies, equipment and personnel must be held afloat,
> immediately available to follow our offensive efforts.[14]

There is no doubt that the lack of shipping in MacArthur's
theater was greater than in any other area involving amphibious
operations. Ritchie, who was in the Southwest Pacific early that
fall, confirmed to the War Department MacArthur's assertion
that the want of merchantmen was severely handicapping the
rate of his advance. Ritchie reported to Handy, his chief in the
Operations Division in Washington, that MacArthur could have
mounted the invasions of Saidor and Cape Gloucester shortly
after the fall of Finschhafen if adequate shipping had been ob-
tainable. Lieutenant General Brehon B. Somervell, who, as
head of the Army Service Forces, was a key figure in logistical
planning, visited MacArthur at Port Moresby on September 29–
October 4. The SWPA chief took the opportunity to "educate"
him thoroughly on the supply and shipping problems of the
Southwest Pacific. It was probably no coincidence that later in
October, after Somervell's return to Washington, the War Department and the War Shipping Administration suddenly found

seventy-one Liberty ships and five other cargo vessels which they assigned permanently to MacArthur's theater.

But the increased shipping soon produced an embarrassing congestion of loaded vessels at MacArthur's forward bases, which were not yet prepared to receive such heavy traffic. At Milne Bay in January, 1944, for example, over 140 cargo ships were waiting to be unloaded; some of them had been anchored there over a month. The rate of discharge was slowed by continuing hostile air raids, unusually bad weather which made the dirt roads quagmires, and a serious lack of port facilities, longshore-men, service troops, trucks, warehouses, and, in particular, suitable lighters. Brigadier General Harry Van Wyk, the SWPA transportation chief, later stated that the most important equipment that was lacking in the theater until late 1944 and was at the root of the shipping turn-around problem "was lighterage. It seemed like it took a year to get the stuff from the ships onto the shore. That was true in the early stages . . . because up until we got into Leyte we didn't have a single berth. Everything was lightered. We used DUKWs, barges and small LCMs but had no LSTs, which would have been ideal for that purpose."

With the War Department demanding corrective action, Mac-Arthur himself devoted considerable attention to the situation, carefully reviewing with his supply and transportation leaders the conditions at forward ports. Gradually the turn-around rate was speeded up in the spring of 1944 as problems of inefficient administration were alleviated, more and better cargo-handling equipment was obtained, and more hands were assigned to unloading details. By late March the situation had improved to the extent that Marshall commended MacArthur's efforts as an "outstanding example of vigorous and effective action in the solution of a difficult problem." But shipping shortages would recur in the Southwest Pacific, and MacArthur's arbitrary, if temporary, retention of merchant ships to serve his theater's needs would continue to antagonize shipping administrators in Washington.[15]

The scarcity of shipping made it difficult, in turn, to develop a system of regular rotation of personnel in the Southwest Pacific. The harsh climatic conditions of the region, the difficult terrain, the prevalence of jungle diseases, and the limited rehabilitation and recreational facilities, except for those in far-off southeastern Australia, made the adoption of a rotation plan imperative to avert a breakdown in morale among the Southwest Pacific soldiers, especially those who had been in New Guinea continuously for over a year.

In November, 1943, the War Department worked out a plan whereby one per cent of the personnel in "hardship areas," such as New Guinea, would be rotated to the States monthly beginning the following March, their selection to be determined by the theater commanders. But no additional shipping would be provided from outside the theater to transport them. Besides, Army Ground Forces headquarters in Washington still had not solved the problem of finding sufficient replacements for casualties of earlier operations, especially in infantry units. MacArthur protested sharply that, as much as rotation was needed, it could not be effected without handicapping operations unless Washington found solutions for the problems of shipping and replacements. Eventually some Liberty ships were converted into troop transports and assigned to rotation runs, and the vexing problem of infantry replacements was partly solved by converting and retraining men who were currently serving in other arms and services in the States. On MacArthur's suggestion, the War Department also inaugurated a policy of permitting combat divisions to refill their ranks more quickly by not charging against their actual strength many of their hospitalized personnel.[16]

In the early spring of 1944, a cautious start on rotation was attempted although the above problems were not yet solved. One day Colonel Aubrey S. Newman, chief of staff of the 24th Division, which was training in Australia after earlier duty in

Nimitz's theater, received a large parcel from GHQ. The cover letter instructed him not to open the package until a stated date and time, whereupon he was to post one copy of the enclosed papers on the bulletin board of every company. Similar parcels and instructions were sent to all American ground and air units in the theater. Each package turned out to contain copies of a letter from MacArthur to "Soldiers of the Southwest Pacific," and each of the hundreds of copies was personally signed by him.

In his message MacArthur praised the "superb fighting qualities" and "impressive victories" of the SWPA soldiers. "As military men I know you will understand," he continued, "it is imperative we exploit our successes by driving on in relentless attack before the enemy can regroup." Then he came to his main point: "Therefore, in order to have enough men to follow up our hard-won successes, and thus avoid unnecessary casualties and suffering later, I have issued orders that the Rotation Policy be discontinued until further notice." For security reasons, of course, MacArthur could not reveal that he and members of his staff were working on the plan for the invasion of the Hollandia-Aitape area, far up the coast of Dutch New Guinea. It was going to be the longest leap and the largest amphibious assault yet undertaken in the Southwest Pacific. As the time drew near, MacArthur had reluctantly concluded that continued rotation would be too costly to the operation in personnel and shipping. In his letter to the men he could only imply that a major attack was imminent.

As Newman observed, the discontinuance of the rotation plan, even if only temporary, "could be expected to cause widespread unrest." But fortunately no such reaction occurred. Newman offers his explanation of why there was no bitter response in his division:

The notice went up on every bulletin board at 11 A.M. on the date specified. As a result, when men formed up for chow at noon everybody knew it, also who made the decision and why. The basic reaction was simply disappointment because:

The order was *personally signed* by Gen. MacArthur, and its wording made it clear it was a personal message — from him, as soldier to soldier, to each one of them.

Also, they realized he knew what such a reversal of policy meant to them, and showed his confidence in them as military men that they would understand this was the proper course to follow, hard as it might be. No one had ever before seen Gen. MacArthur's personal signature, much less on an order that, in effect, bypassed every echelon of command to go from him to individual men in ranks, explaining directly to them why the decision was made, and that he had made it.

Unstated, but implicit in the wording and method of distribution — including that personal signature — was respect for his "Soldiers of the Southwest Pacific," and his understanding of the terrible disappointment this decision would be for many of them. Equally important was the fact there was no long harangue, merely his confidence that they would understand his explanation and know he had made the hard decision only after consideration of what it meant to them.

Because of MacArthur's human touch and sensitivity toward his troops, which was not often so vividly seen as in this little episode, he was able to communicate the spirit of his message to the men directly. "As a result," says Newman, "there was no loss of morale, only soldierly acceptance of a fact of war." [17] It is unfortunate that such singularly judicious acts by MacArthur were offset by the ill will that his communiqués often created.

The tie-up of shipping in the Southwest Pacific, since it involved many merchantmen that had been scheduled to make supply runs in the Central Pacific, was not appreciated by Nimitz and his commanders, who were preparing for the invasion of the Marshalls in early 1944. In fact, throughout the Cartwheel period, relations between MacArthur's headquarters and the admirals in Washington and Pearl Harbor continued to deteriorate. Since early summer MacArthur had repeatedly expressed his opposition to the Central Pacific drive and seemed to take an I-told-you-so attitude toward the costly battle Nimitz's forces had had to fight on Tarawa.

In late September the controversy over his communiqués surfaced again when the Navy Department strongly objected to a SWPA press release announcing the sinking of a Navy transport in Southwest Pacific waters. Marshall relayed to MacArthur the admirals' dissatisfaction and urged him to conform to the established policy according to which "initial announcement of loss of naval vessels will be made by the Navy Department from Washington." MacArthur heatedly replied that "it is invidious for the U.S. Navy to endeavor to exempt its personnel and ships from the terms of the directive [of March 1942]" whereby, he maintained, "I am charged with the issue of the communiques reporting American, Australian, New Zealand, British and Dutch ground, naval and air operations in the SWPA." He added, "My long established policy is to publish nothing that would assist the enemy, but within that limitation to publish the entire truth, both good and bad." Despite King's anger, Marshall dealt with MacArthur patiently and dropped the matter, hoping there would be no more such incidents.

Nevertheless, there were other issues that autumn to keep the pot boiling. Sutherland and Kenney, for instance, had a sharp disagreement with Carpender — and indirectly with Nimitz — over the contention of the former pair that naval aircraft operating within the bounds of the Southwest Pacific theater were under Kenney's control as Allied Air Forces commander. In addition, Sutherland appeared to try deliberately to antagonize ranking naval officers who visited GHQ. For example, when Rear Admiral Russell S. Berkey, who had distinguished himself as a captain in earlier Pacific actions, reported in late 1943 as the new commander of a cruiser division of the Seventh Fleet, Sutherland kept him waiting for nearly an hour before he saw MacArthur, although the SWPA chief was not in conference.

Berkey received an amiable greeting from MacArthur when he was finally ushered into his office. The SWPA commander commented, "Well, I hope you haven't been waiting long." When Berkey told him the truth, MacArthur turned to Sutherland and said sternly, "The next time that Berkey comes into the office, usher him in right away, no matter who is in here with me."

Neither Berkey nor Barbey, the amphibious force commander, experienced any difficulties with MacArthur himself. Barbey felt that the principal anti-Navy sentiment at GHQ was promoted by Sutherland, Kenney, and their subordinates. Yet MacArthur himself objected that autumn to the behavior of Carpender, because of his direct communications with Nimitz and King and his alleged failure to support fully the Cartwheel operations with his surface units. On November 26, Carpender was succeeded as commander of Allied Naval Forces and Seventh Fleet by Vice Admiral Thomas C. Kinkaid, a stern-faced veteran of the Guadalcanal and Aleutian operations. After relationships with Hart, Leary, and Carpender that had been less than satisfactory, MacArthur surprisingly took a liking to Kinkaid from the start. His able command of the Seventh Fleet during the final Cartwheel amphibious landings undoubtedly had much to do with his auspicious start at GHQ.[18]

Rear Admiral Raymond D. Tarbuck, who served as MacArthur's chief naval adviser and naval liaison officer at GHQ from mid-1943 until late 1944 when he became Barbey's chief of staff, maintained that much of the difficulty between GHQ and the Navy stemmed from the predominance of the "Army mentality" toward operational planning. He explained:

> It was surprising how little the Army officers at GHQ knew about water . . . For instance, when we went into Lae (in addition to the paratroopers in the Markham Valley), instead of landing on the beach at Lae where we could fight the Japs, we intentionally landed on the wrong side of a river [Busu] . . .

It was in full flood. Why did Chamberlin decide to land there? He did not consult me . . . Well, it would give the troops a chance to deploy, because the Japs couldn't attack across the river. But it worked in reverse. The Japs escaped over the hills . . .

Here is the mentality involved: At the Infantry School in Georgia, they teach that every stream and every body of water is a potential MLR [main line of resistance]. They treat even the smallest stream as an obstacle, but naval minds think of it as a highway. We use rivers and oceans; to us they are roads. The things we are afraid of are land, coral reefs, and rocks. The Army's maps and their topography are very accurate . . . This hill and that hill are given in exact slope and height in feet, but when their map gets to the water's edge, it just stops. They think it is just blue . . . dead, deep water, with a harmless bottom that goes on and on under the water . . . But that water is what we are interested in. The two mentalities are exactly the opposite, and some of the time Chamberlin didn't know what I was talking about. He didn't give it the proper weight.[19]

Tarbuck's theory of opposing Army and Navy mentalities can be extended to some of the basic differences between Mac-Arthur's concept of Pacific strategy and that of Nimitz and King. Whereas the admirals envisioned the vast expanses of the Central Pacific as an easily traversed pathway for the Pacific Fleet in spearheading a more direct advance to Japan, the general thought in terms of a route that could best be exploited by ground forces covered by land-based air power. No master plan for the defeat of Japan had been completed yet, but already the admirals believed that a strangling naval blockade would compel Japan's capitulation, while MacArthur and most other Army leaders assumed that an invasion would be necessary. Throughout the war the SWPA chief never fully comprehended the principles of modern naval warfare, especially the complexities and dangers inherent in operating fast carrier groups, the Navy's most potent striking force. Naval leaders, then and later, were convinced that it would have been folly to deploy carriers in the close confines of the uncharted waters of the Southwest Pacific, where they would be subject to the additional danger of attack from numerous Japanese air bases.

But as late as 1954 MacArthur still argued that carriers should have been employed extensively in support of his operations:

> The very essence of our so-called "by-passing" method of advance depended upon security [of] air control over the area covered in each forward step. In the present state of development of the art of war no movement can safely be made of forces on sea or land without adequate air protection. The limit of such protection in our case was the possible radius of operation of our fighter planes. This radius had to be measured from the actual location of our ground air bases. This required the seizing or construction of such new bases at each forward movement. The presence of carriers with their inherent movability would have immeasurably increased the scope and speed of our operations. I know of no other area and no other theater where they could have been used to such advantage. The enemy's diversion of his air forces on many different islands and fields was peculiarly adapted to his piecemeal destruction, which would have been drastically assisted if we could have utilized the mobility of carriers in surprise concentrations. For instance, with our overall inferior air strength, in order to neutralize the enemy's superior combined air strength at Rabaul and Aitape, being limited to ground air strength, I had to locate a temporary air base in New Guinea between these two enemy garrisons to operate by surprise with my entire force concentrated first on the one and then on the other. Their combined force could have beaten me, but divided I destroyed them unilaterally. The presence of carriers would have entirely altered our potential. Prime Minister Curtin did his best to persuade Prime Minister Churchill to let us have carriers, and I did the same with Washington but without success. To this day I cannot understand why the decision was in the negative.[20]

Although no carriers were permanently assigned to his Seventh Fleet, MacArthur apparently forgot that carriers of the Pacific Fleet had made brief but crucial appearances in his theater, helping to avert the Japanese seaborne invasion of Port Moresby in the spring of 1942 and to effect the neutralization of Rabaul in late 1943 and early 1944. They would also play important roles in supporting his invasions of Dutch New Guinea and the Philippines in the future.

MacArthur's relations with the Navy were not helped by the widespread talk of a higher command for the general, which was rife in some political and journalistic quarters in the fall of 1943. The re-emergence of the topic was in part a consequence of the discontent of MacArthur's admirers in the States with some of the decisions said to have been made at the Quadrant Conference, the general nature of which soon became public knowledge; of rumors that Marshall might be relieved as Army chief of staff in order to head the coming cross-Channel attack; and of the revival of interest in MacArthur's possible presidential candidacy, following the publication of national polls that showed his voter appeal increasing again. On September 9–11 five United States senators visited MacArthur at Port Moresby; he entertained them royally and frankly discussed presidential politics and global strategy. (When Mrs. Franklin Roosevelt visited Australia later that month, however, he told Eichelberger to act as host and refused to permit her to come to Moresby.) On his return from Moresby to Washington, Senator Albert B. Chandler, a Democrat from Kentucky, began crusading for legislation to make MacArthur supreme commander of all Allied forces in the war against Japan. Although Chandler's efforts to obtain such a bill got nowhere, several influential newspapers and periodicals picked up the refrain, including the *Army and Navy Journal,* which was published by John C. O'Laughlin, a long-time friend of MacArthur's. The Washington *Times-Herald* and New York *Herald Tribune,* among other papers, supported the idea and gave an unwarranted amount of attention to a statement by MacArthur to reporters on September 21 that clearly implied criticism of the Quebec decisions inaugurating Nimitz's Central Pacific offensive and appointing Lord Louis Mountbatten to head the newly formed Southeast Asia Command. MacArthur suggested that his role would be subordinated henceforth to those of Nimitz and Mountbatten despite the fact that his New Guinea–Philippines axis of advance was the quickest and most economical route to Japan.[21]

On September 30 the London *Daily Mirror* added to the excitement by publishing the following dispatch from its correspondent in New York:

> A strong group of United States senators will open a campaign in Congress next week to have General MacArthur made supreme commander of the Asiatic war theatre. This group openly expresses disapproval of the appointment of Lord Louis Mountbatten to Southeastern Asia, believing that the entire campaign should be under MacArthur. Senator [H. Styles] Bridges, who will lead the Senate campaign for MacArthur, said today: "We have recently won much new support in the Senate."
>
> The Senate battle is being preceded by a vitriolic anti-Mountbatten campaign in a section of the American press. The Ohio State Journal contrasts the "sincere attitude" of MacArthur with "the somewhat flamboyant air of Mountbatten" adding "it would be a tragic thing if MacArthur were to be shorn of his authority while a London glamour boy is elevated." Some papers are publishing letters from readers containing insulting references to Mountbatten. Here is a sample: "If it turns out that America's No. 1 hero MacArthur is to play a subordinate role to ex-playboy Mountbatten in the Far East, a wave of anger will sweep this nation that will bode certain Washington people no good." [22]

The episode reached the highest levels of state when Churchill protested to Roosevelt about the American press's slurring remarks about Mountbatten. In the presence of an American guest at Chequers, Churchill walked over to his huge globe and figured out the distance from Mountbatten's to MacArthur's headquarters; it was 6660 miles. Then he turned to the American and asked sarcastically, "Do you think that's far enough apart?" Back in Washington Roosevelt remarked at a news conference on October 5 that such stories as the one mentioned in the *Mirror* showed "an extraordinary ignorance of geography" and "carelessness on the part of some people" and were probably written "with malice aforethought." With the move to create the position for MacArthur already still-born in the Senate, Bridges, a Republican from New Hampshire and a ranking member of the Senate's military affairs committee, assured the President on October 9 that he had taken no part in the movement whatsoever: "As a matter of fact, I have never given this matter thought." [23]

As late as March, 1944, the issue was briefly and futilely revived in the House when two resolutions were introduced but failed of passage: one called for MacArthur's appointment as commander of all Allied forces in the Asian war, and the other directed the President to postpone American participation in the cross-Channel assault "until qualified American military authorities are agreed that the American forces are adequately prepared for the invasion and that the invasion is reasonably necessary to the military security of the United States." The latter resolution was partly inspired by an attempt to put greater stress on the Pacific war, especially MacArthur's theater. Surprisingly little was said in the fall of 1943 about elevating Mac-Arthur to Army chief of staff again if Marshall were relieved, but Somervell's name was prominently mentioned and sometimes Eisenhower's as the next likely military head of the Army.[24] The revival of the MacArthur-for-President campaign will be discussed in Chapter X, where the developments will be traced to their finale in the spring of 1944.

The decisions at Quebec regarding Pacific strategy disappointed MacArthur but did not deter his hope of returning to the Philippines. On October 20 he completed Reno III, which was a revision of his earlier plan for successive advances along the New Guinea coast and north to Mindanao. Listing his requirements of ground and air units for each step, he proposed the following objectives in the five-phase plan: (1) neutralization of Rabaul by seizing Hansa Bay in Northeast New Guinea, the Admiralty Islands, and Kavieng, New Ireland, beginning about February 1, 1944; (2) capture of Humboldt Bay (Hollandia) in Netherlands New Guinea and the Tanimbar, Aroe, and Tajandoe islands in the Arafura Sea, starting in June; (3) seizure of Geelvink Bay in Dutch New Guinea, beginning in August; (4) capture of Halmahera Island, Manado on the northeast coast of Celebes, and possibly the Palaus, east of Mindanao, starting in December; and (5) invasion of Mindanao, in February, 1945. Wewak and Rabaul were to be bypassed, but MacArthur still planned to capture Rabaul later and develop a naval base there. The Arafura Sea proposal was probably injected at the behest of the Australian military chiefs, who were anxious about the security of the northern coast of their country and also desired advance bases for air strikes deeper into the East Indies. Raids on bases and shipping in the Lesser Sundas, or western, area of the theater had become one of the chief missions of the RAAF and Dutch squadrons based in northern Australia.[25]

In early November Sutherland arrived in Washington to explain and defend Reno III before the Joint Staff Planners. MacArthur assured Marshall, "Sutherland is completely familiar with my tactical and strategical views and is authorized to speak with my full authority." Before the planners, MacArthur's chief of staff repeated his superior's familiar arguments for top priority to be given to the advance to the Philippines via the New Guinea route. The invasion of Mindanao, he contended, would provide excellent existing air bases from which Allied planes could interdict enemy shipping from the East Indies to Japan. And an assault on Mindanao would probably force the enemy into a decisive naval battle, which Sutherland knew the American naval leaders desired. Reno III, he argued further, would afford the most effective way of attacking the enemy "in each of his four major points of weakness: oil, naval and merchant shipping, and the air." Since only one major offensive in the Pacific seemed logistically possible until after Germany had been defeated, Sutherland reiterated the advantages of the axis proposed in Reno III and sharply disparaged the Central Pacific plan. "To attempt a major effort along each axis," he maintained, "would result in weakness everywhere in violation of cardinal principles of war, and . . . in failure to reach the vital strategic objective at the earliest possible date, thus prolonging the war."

The Washington planners, however, were not persuaded by Sutherland's reasoning or of the efficacy of the plan itself. His offensive remarks about the Navy and Nimitz's operations did not help his cause; Marshall later remarked that Sutherland was "the chief insulter of the Navy." The planners concluded that the Reno operations would demand more ground and air units than could be supplied. They rejected the Arafura Sea thrust as diversionary. Otherwise, they found the first three phases of the plan generally acceptable, but refused to commit themselves to the last two, which were rather far in the future.[26] On November 9 the Joint Staff Planners recommended to the Joint Chiefs that the following principles on Pacific strategy for 1944 be adopted, the latter part marking a disturbing setback to Sutherland and MacArthur:

> The advance along the New Guinea–N.E.I.–Philippine axis will proceed concurrently with [Nimitz's] operations for the capture of the Mandated Islands [Marshalls, Carolines, and Marianas]. These two series of operations will be mutually supporting. The fleet can be deployed to support successive operations along each axis, and to prevent interference by hostile surface units with simultaneous operations in the two areas. Transfer of our forces and resources from one area to the other is contemplated. When conflict in timing exists, due weight should

be accorded to the fact that operations in the Central Pacific promise a more rapid advance toward Japan, our ultimate objective; the earlier acquisition of strategic air bases closer to the Japanese homeland; and, of greatest importance, are more likely to precipitate a decisive engagement with the Japanese Fleet.[27]

In late November and early December there occurred the conferences at Cairo and Teheran, at which the Allied heads of state and their military chiefs deliberated strategy for the coming year in Europe, the Mediterranean, Burma, China, and the Pacific, with the chief attention given to the invasion of France and the defeat of Germany. The Sextant Conference, encompassing the Combined Chiefs' sessions at Cairo before and after the Teheran meeting, saw the relegation of the China-Burma theater permanently to the low priority which it had had in actuality all along; the Combined Chiefs agreed that the principal effort against Japan should be in the Pacific. Both MacArthur's and Nimitz's offensives were to be continued as aggressively as logistics permitted, with the two thrusts expected to converge in 1945 in an assault on the general region of Luzon, Formosa, and the southern coast of China.

At the Sextant meetings the chiefs approved a program of Pacific operations in 1944 that called for SWPA forces to seize Hansa Bay, beginning February 1; Manus, in the Admiralties, starting April 20; Humboldt Bay, to be launched June 1; and the Vogelkop Peninsula, to begin August 15. The final objective of the South Pacific forces was Kavieng, the assault on which was to start on March 20. While it seemed that MacArthur's drive northward would be stopped at the equator, with no decision at Sextant regarding Mindanao, Nimitz's theater would have an ambitious schedule in 1944, which would include invasions of the Marshalls in January, Ponape in May, Truk in July, and the Marianas in October.[28]

The Sextant decisions on Pacific strategy were based partly on the assumption that by the end of 1944 the new B-29 very-long-range bombers, operating as an independent command directly under the Joint Chiefs, would be able to start bombing targets in Japan proper from bases in the Marianas. The Combined Chiefs anticipated that, as early as May, 1944, some B-29 squadrons would be operating from bases in south China against targets in the enemy's inner zone of defenses from Singapore to the Japanese home islands. MacArthur and Kenney had tried for months to pre-empt the forthcoming B-29's for attacks on Japanese-controlled oil fields and refineries in the East Indies, but Arnold and his planners had successfully persuaded the Joint Chiefs that the powerful new bombers should be concentrated principally against targets in Japan proper. Of course, the need for B-29 bases in the Marianas gave further impetus to the Navy's arguments in favor of stressing the Central Pacific offensive. At the end of the war the summary report of the Strategic Bombing Survey supported MacArthur and Kenney's contention that the B-29's "could have been more effectively used in coordination with submarines in search, low-level attacks and mining in accelerating the destruction of Japanese shipping, or in destroying oil and metal plants in the southern area [mainly East Indies]." [29]

During the Sextant deliberations, the British chiefs introduced the idea of having their fleet in the Indian Ocean join the operations in the Pacific. Earlier and later MacArthur, who desperately wanted more naval surface units, especially carriers, expressed enthusiasm over the possibility of the British units' deployment in his theater. But the Joint Chiefs, particularly King, were not eager to have British forces operating in the Pacific yet, because, among other things, it would mean British participation in planning operations in that area. In addition, contrary to his own chiefs, who wanted to start British operations in the East Indies and the western Pacific, Churchill favored a major British offensive through Burma to Singapore, which would mean retaining the Royal Navy ships in the Bay of Bengal region.

At Cairo the American chiefs agreed in general terms to future British participation in the Pacific war but were vague and noncommittal on the specifics of what forces would be needed and when. The British chiefs cheerfully assumed that their fleet would be allowed to participate soon in the Pacific, and in early 1944 they prepared to send a task force to Australia. About the same time, the Japanese suddenly shifted some of their main fleet units from Truk and the Philippines to Singapore, which compelled the British fleet to remain in the Indian Ocean. Later Roosevelt, on the recommendation of his military chiefs, politely told Churchill that British naval units would not be needed for some time in the Pacific, perhaps well into 1945. Eventually combat ships of the Royal Navy would operate with the Pacific Fleet in the Okinawa invasion, but, as in the case of the B-29's, no British surface units would be assigned to MacArthur's operations.[30]

For months prior to Sextant, the Combined Staff Planners in London and Washington had been working on a long-range plan for the defeat of Japan. After numerous revisions of the plan, the Joint Chiefs met to consider it again when they returned from Cairo in early December. They asked Sutherland for his opinion of the plan, perhaps because he had been involved in many of the strategic discussions since his arrival in Washington a month earlier and had accompanied the planners to Cairo. But Sutherland had apparently learned little about global strategy and logistics and even less about tact, despite the opportunities to broaden his horizons in Washington and Cairo. Responding to the Joint Chiefs, he bluntly reiterated the need to adopt Reno III and to give the highest priority in the war against Japan to MacArthur's offensive. The overall plan, as finally approved later in December by both the American and British chiefs, was based on the assumption that "invasion of the principal Japanese islands may not be necessary and the defeat of Japan may be accomplished by sea and air blockade and intensive air bombardment from progressively advanced bases."

The plan was supposed to be "capable of expansion to meet

the contingency of invasion," but the Combined Chiefs and their planners, in MacArthur and Sutherland's view, obviously intended to support the efforts of the Pacific Fleet and the Marianas-based B-29's as fully as possible. Drawn almost verbatim from the November study by the Joint Staff Planners, the overall plan for Japan's defeat further stated that the aim in the Pacific "should be to advance along the New Guinea–N.E.I.–Philippine axis and to complete the capture of the Mandated Islands in time to launch a major assault in the Formosa-Luzon-China area in the spring of 1945 (i.e., before the onset of the typhoon season) from a distant base." [31] Indeed, there might be an invasion of the Philippines, but MacArthur had good reason to wonder whether it would be he or Nimitz who would command the operation. The dissonance of "I shall return" and the plans of the Anglo-American military chiefs seemed greater than ever.

When the Combined Chiefs finished their talks at Cairo in early December, Marshall, according to his chief biographer, "thought it highly important that he see the Pacific situation for himself. He also wanted to show MacArthur that he had not been forgotten." Boarding a C-54 transport at Cairo, Marshall made the long flight to New Guinea by way of India and Ceylon. He was accompanied by Handy, Cooke, Brigadier General Haywood S. Hansell, Jr., of Arnold's planning group, and Lieutenant Colonel Frank McCarthy of the Army's General Staff. In the meantime MacArthur, who had spent a total of forty-six days in New Guinea since the end of the Buna operation in January, 1943, flew from Brisbane to Port Moresby on December 12. The next day he, Chamberlin, Diller, and Morhouse journeyed by air to Krueger's headquarters on Goodenough Island, where they remained for the next four days to observe the embarkation of the Arawe invasion force. Marshall and his party landed at Moresby on the 14th; Kenney met them at the airfield and the next morning accompanied them on an aerial tour of SWPA bases from Nadzab to Buna. The flight ended at Goodenough,

where they landed on December 15 in time for lunch with Mac-
Arthur. Kenney said that Marshall "was much impressed by the
amount of work we had done by airborne means" at the forward bases in New Guinea.

At the Alamo Force headquarters that afternoon and evening,
the SWPA and Washington leaders discussed at length matters
of strategy and logistics in the Pacific. Kenney recalled that
"General Marshall briefed us on the situation in Europe and at
home and General MacArthur described the situation in the
Southwest Pacific and discussed our plans for the future operations." Cooke "spoke of the necessity for a big main effort west
across the Central Pacific," with which Kenney promptly took
issue. The SWPA air chief remarked, "General Marshall looked
as though he agreed with me." At the get-together the next
morning they talked about the upcoming invasion of Cape
Gloucester, received reports from Arawe where a beachhead had
been secured satisfactorily, and inspected some of Krueger's
troops during a tropical downpour. Shortly after 10:00 A.M.
MacArthur, Marshall, and their accompanying officers flew to
Moresby where they had lunch together, and early that afternoon Marshall and his entourage took off for Guadalcanal.[32]

Since this was the only meeting of MacArthur and his "boss"
during the entire war, it is especially regrettable that no minutes
or notes of their sessions have been located. Probably no such
notes were made. Correspondent Frazier Hunt, who arrived at
MacArthur's headquarters two months later and claimed to have
the SWPA chief's version of the affair, stated in his biography of
MacArthur that "as a result of both the present and past differences" between them, MacArthur felt beforehand that the
confrontation "might be somewhat embarrassing." So the
SWPA commander, says Hunt, "seriously considered conducting the Gloucester [Arawe] operations in person, thus relieving
Marshall of his presence." He finally decided to meet the Army
chief of staff, but predicted to one of his officers that "he'll never
see me alone. He'll always find a way to have someone else

present." Hunt, who had MacArthur's confidence, based on long years of friendship, said that, although "there was every evidence of friendly cordiality" shown by the two leaders at Goodenough, "never for a moment had Marshall sought to be alone with him. Nor did he evince any desire to confide in Mac-Arthur or to give him his own inner thoughts and ideas on the global struggle." In view of the hundreds of messages, often brutally frank, exchanged between them in the previous two years, it is doubtful that either man could have more clearly revealed his ideas in a talk tête-à-tête. Moreover, they had met on only a few brief occasions before the war, and no rapport, such as Marshall enjoyed with Eisenhower, existed between them.

MacArthur seemed to contradict Hunt when he wrote, nearly a decade after the publication of the correspondent's book in 1954, that he and Marshall had "a long and frank discussion. I called attention to the paucity of men and matériel I was receiving as compared with all other theaters of war. He said he realized the imbalance and regretted it, but could do little to alter the low priority accorded the area." According to MacArthur's memoirs, Marshall appeared to lay much of the blame for SWPA's difficulties with Washington on King, who "claimed the Pacific as the rightful domain of the Navy." Marshall, wrote MacArthur, stated that King "resented the prominent part I [MacArthur] had in the Pacific War; he was vehement in his personal criticism of me and encouraged Navy propaganda to that end." [33] They may not have been alone, but surely fiery Admiral Cooke was not present if and when Marshall said this.

Handy observed that Marshall and MacArthur treated each other with great respect and politeness during their talks:

> I didn't see any evidence of any conflict between Marshall and MacArthur . . . I figured it this way: MacArthur had been Chief of Staff of the Army, and he wasn't going to degrade that position. In other words, his talk and attitude toward General Marshall, regardless of what his personal feelings might have

been, were quite proper at the Goodenough meeting. Marshall now had the office, and I think General MacArthur respected this . . . The very fact that he had held that office himself meant he wasn't going to degrade it.[34]

Secretary of War Stimson's diary contains scattered comments throughout the war years which, though not mentioning the Goodenough meeting, indirectly support MacArthur's claim that Marshall spoke frankly about King. One of Stimson's entries in 1944 describes Marshall as speaking out at a Joint Chiefs' meeting against King's persistent hostility toward MacArthur: "It has gotten so bad that Marshall finally said to him, thumping the table, 'I will not have any meetings carried on with this hatred,' and with that he shut up King." MacArthur at least believed that Marshall left New Guinea with a more sympathetic appreciation of his theater's problems: "Upon his return to Washington he informed me that he had spoken to General Arnold, who promised greater air support. From that time on Washington became more generous to the SWPA."

On Christmas Eve morning, after having returned to Washington late the previous night, Marshall sent a radiogram to MacArthur expressing his "appreciation for the reception you gave me . . . and of the admirable organization and fighting force you have under development there. I was greatly impressed by all that I saw." He added, "Already this morning I have talked to General Arnold about some of the air matters and probably will have a little encouraging news for you in a few days." Extending his best wishes to Marshall on his upcoming birthday, MacArthur in his reply also stated, "Your trip here was an inspiration to all ranks and its effects were immediate. You have no more loyal and faithful followers than here." [35]

In a fireside chat on Christmas Eve Roosevelt commented that Marshall's talks with MacArthur "will spell plenty of bad news for the Japs in the not too far distant future," which, of course, his radio listeners were delighted to hear. The London *Times* remarked of Marshall's trip to New Guinea: "His visit and the opening of the campaign in New Britain will certainly increase the apprehension with which, as a recent Tokyo broadcast to the Japanese people has shown, the enemy's high command is beginning to regard the Pacific horizon." [36]

The Melbourne *Herald* typified Australian journalistic reaction:

> The news that General Marshall . . . has visited . . . New Guinea . . . has brought great satisfaction . . . It is fresh evidence of the importance attached by the Allied Command to operations in this area and of the attention given to them in the most recent planning . . .
>
> The absence of General MacArthur from the Quebec conference, which was mainly devoted to Pacific war planning, and from the conference in the Middle East, may have given rise to some doubts of the importance ascribed to the southern Pacific area by the Allied Command. Now that the American Chief of Staff — who has been suggested as a likely man to be given the highest command of global operations — has been to see for himself the needs and conditions of war in these parts, any such concern should be allayed.[37]

The Australian press may have been indulging in a bit of premature enthusiasm over the future role of the Southwest Pacific, but there is no question that Marshall's visit boosted the morale of the Australian civilians as well as that of MacArthur and his SWPA personnel.

Marshall would make numerous trips to the European theater during the course of the war, but he would not return to the West Pacific until MacArthur was in Tokyo. The Army chief of staff's message exchanges and personal relations with Eisenhower were often informal and amiable in contrast to the cautious formality that characterized most of the Marshall-MacArthur correspondence. Yet the minutes of the meetings of the Joint Chiefs and Combined Chiefs prove that MacArthur,

whether he fully realized it or not, had a powerful and sympathetic advocate in Marshall. When it did not mean compromising the European priority, the Army chief of staff repeatedly
defended MacArthur and his theater's interests before the American and British chiefs. There is a suggestion in MacArthur's
memoirs that at the Goodenough meeting he sensed that, if he
were permitted to lead a return to the Philippines, Marshall
would play a significant role in making it possible.

Contrary to the legend spread by some MacArthur disciples
that Marshall conspired against the military interests of the
SWPA commander, one of the most fortunate breaks of the war
for MacArthur was the emergence of Marshall by 1943 as the
dominant member of the Joint Chiefs and Combined Chiefs.
Those who disagree would do well to ponder the probable fate
of MacArthur's Southwest Pacific offensive if King had been
foremost among the Joint Chiefs or if one of the British officers
had proven to be the most influential of the Combined Chiefs.

CHAPTER IX

Climax in the Bismarcks

1. Isolation of Rabaul

IN A DIRECTIVE to his commanders on December 23, 1943, Blamey intimated that MacArthur, whose American forces would soon outnumber the Australians in forward areas, had decided to relegate the Australian Army to a role in 1944 that would be insignificant in comparison to its major burden of the fighting in New Guinea to that time. Blamey informed his officers that "the operational role of the Australian Military Forces engaged in forward operations in New Guinea will be taken over by U.S.A. Forces in accordance with plans now being prepared. Aggressive operations will be continued and reliefs necessary to maintain the initiative will be made by G.O.C. [general officer commanding] New Guinea Force until Commander, U.S.A. Forces takes over responsibility." This would probably occur after the New Guinea Force achieved its current objective —— the seizure of Madang. The veteran 6th, 7th, and 9th divisions would then return to Australia for rehabilitation, while three militia divisions would assume the main garrison duties in the rear areas of New Guinea and at the bases scattered along the northern coast of Australia.

The Madang offensive began on December 26 when Vasey's 7th Division attacked Japanese positions near Dumpu in the Ramu Valley. Intense fighting erupted about seven miles north of Dumpu on Shaggy Ridge, but the Australians secured the area in late January. Several days afterward they overran the Japanese base at Kankiryo in the middle of the Finisterre Mountains. By mid-March, two Australian brigades had broken through the last enemy defenses in the mountains and were driving toward the coast of Astrolabe Bay. Meanwhile, two battalions of the American 32nd Division had landed midway between Saidor and Bogadjim, where they encountered light opposition and were advancing westward along the coast to rendezvous with the Australians. Elements of the Japanese 41st Division fought delaying actions while Adachi moved the rest of his forces out of the Madang region and toward Wewak. On April 13, a patrol of the Australian 11th Division, which had relieved the weary 7th a week earlier, walked into Bogadjim unopposed, the last defenders having withdrawn during the previous night. With Adachi's units now in full retreat, the Australians seized Madang on April 24, and two days later they took Alexishafen against light rear-guard resistance.

On March 25, Adachi had received orders, which had not been intercepted by the Allies, to withdraw his main units all the way to Netherlands New Guinea. Imperial General Headquarters had redrawn the primary line of defense to exclude Northeast New Guinea. In the meantime, Blamey called a halt to major operations north of Alexishafen since the objective of the drive had been achieved. In their final large-scale offensive in New Guinea the Australians had performed well. In fact, they had so mastered the tactics and logistics of jungle warfare that Vasey's chief complaint during the campaign was not related to combat or supply. "These visitors are a curse! We've had 280 of them," he wrote disgustedly in late January, "16 Generals and 1 Admiral — cheap tour of the world — a lot of them being able to say they've been to the war." The situation had changed mark-edly since Vasey's dismal days in the swamps in front of Gona and Sanananda fourteen months earlier.[1]

The capture of Madang completed Cartwheel except for the revised Task Three, the isolation of Rabaul. According to the planning of late 1943, this was to be accomplished by the seizure of Hansa Bay, about midway between Madang and Wewak, beginning in February, and the invasions in March of Manus in the Admiralties by MacArthur's forces, and of Kavieng in New Ireland by Halsey's forces. Besides being ideally situated to help in severing Rabaul's line of communications, the Admiralties, consisting mainly of Manus and Los Negros islands, had one of the finest potential fleet anchorages in the Pacific, at Seeadler Harbor. MacArthur and Halsey agreed on the need for a major fleet base at Seeadler to support future operations, but in their planning sessions in December the two commanders did not see eye to eye on the necessity for taking Kavieng. MacArthur argued that its capture was essential to provide air bases to cover later advances, but Halsey contended that Kavieng, known to be strongly fortified, could be bypassed in favor of seizing lightly held Emirau, in the Saint Matthias Islands to the north. In conferences with Nimitz and King in early January, Halsey was unable to win their endorsement of his proposal to bypass Kavieng.

The Joint Chiefs ordered Nimitz to follow up his conquest of the Marshalls, to begin about February 1, with a large-scale car-rier strike in March to neutralize Truk and then to dispatch carriers and other surface units to the Bismarcks in time for the Manus and Kavieng invasions, which were postponed to April 1. At a conference of Southwest, South, and Central Pacific theater representatives at Pearl Harbor on January 27–28, 1944, Suther-land, who, together with Kenney and Kinkaid, represented SWPA, maintained that MacArthur preferred Kavieng, not Emirau, as the South Pacific forces' objective in the isolation of

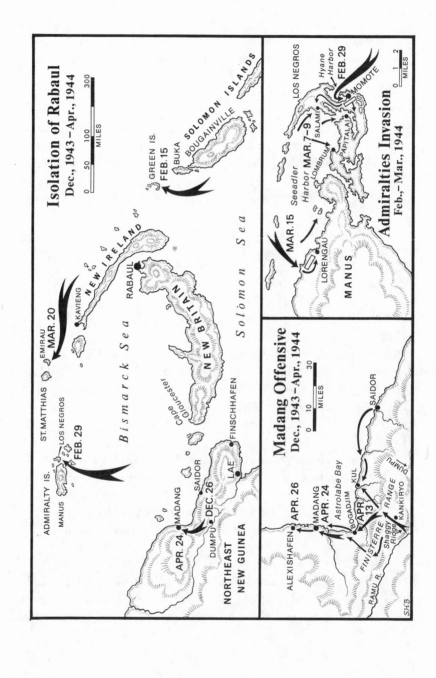

Isolation of Rabaul
Dec., 1943 – Apr., 1944

0 50 100 300
MILES

SOLOMON ISLANDS

GREEN IS.
FEB. 15

BUKA

BOUGAINVILLE

Solòmon Sea

NEW IRELAND

KAVIENG

RABAUL

EMIRAU
MAR. 20

ST. MATTHIAS

Bismarck Sea

NEW BRITAIN

Gloucester

Capе

FINSCHHAFEN

LAE

ADMIRALTY IS.

MANUS

LOS NEGROS
FEB. 29

SAIDOR
DUMPU DEC. 26

MADANG
APR. 24

NORTHEAST
NEW GUINEA

Admiralties Invasion
Feb.–Mar., 1944

0 1 2
MILES

LOS NEGROS

Seeadler
Harbor MAR. 7–9

SALAMI

LOMBRUM

PAPITALAI

Hyane
Harbor
FEB. 29
MOMOTE

LORENGAU

MAR. 15

MANUS

Madang Offensive
Dec., 1943 – Apr., 1944

0 10 30
MILES

SAIDOR

ALEXISHAFEN
APR. 26

MADANG
APR. 24

Astrolabe Bay

BOGADJIM

KUL

APR.
13

DUMPU

FINISTERRE
RANGE

Shaggy
Ridge

RAMU R.

KANKIRYO

SHB

Rabaul. Nimitz felt that his Marshalls operations could be completed in February, and he reassured Halsey's and MacArthur's delegations that his carriers would strike Truk in late March, after which at least two carrier divisions would be sent southward to operate under Halsey's command during the Manus and Kavieng landings.

Shortly after the Pearl Harbor sessions ended, action picked up again in the war against Japan. On January 31–February 1 Nimitz's invasion of the Marshalls got under way as the 4th Marine Division assaulted Roi and Namur and the Army's 7th Infantry Division attacked Kwajalein. Despite bitter fighting, especially on Namur and Kwajalein, the islands were secured in less than a week. A fast carrier task force raided Truk on February 16–17 with such devastating effectiveness that most of the aircraft stationed there were destroyed and, with about 200,-000 tons of enemy shipping sunk in the attacks, the fleet anchorage there was abandoned by the Japanese Navy. Meanwhile, Army and Marine troops landed on Eniwetok, in the northwest area of the Marshalls, and by February 23 had secured the atoll. Persuading MacArthur that he would need fighter bases within range of Kavieng before that invasion, Halsey sent elements of a New Zealand division into the Green Islands on February 15. Within five days that operation was successfully completed, and by early March a fighter strip was operational on one of the Green Islands, which lay only 220 miles southeast of Kavieng and 117 miles east of Rabaul.[2]

During January and early February the Fifth Air Force regularly and heavily bombed Japanese air bases at Kavieng and in the Admiralties. By mid-February the airmen reported no enemy planes at either of the air bases in the Admiralties, Momote on Los Negros and Lorengau on Manus. Moreover, neither antiaircraft fire nor troop activities were observed. Actually, though he had no more serviceable aircraft, the Admiralties commander, Colonel Yoshio Ezaki, possessed about 4000 troops, whom he instructed to stay carefully concealed from aerial observation. While Willoughby's intelligence sources accurately, if belatedly, determined on February 21 that virtually all enemy aircraft had been withdrawn from Rabaul, two days later Whitehead excitedly reported to Kenney that his B-25's had spent an hour and a half crisscrossing the Admiralties without spotting a sign of enemy activity. Whitehead said the airmen were convinced that the enemy base at Momote was "completely washed out," and he urged that a ground reconnaissance force be sent there to check.

Agreeing with Whitehead that "Los Negros was ripe for the plucking," Kenney rushed into MacArthur's office in Brisbane and proposed that a reconnaissance in force be dispatched to Los Negros immediately. If the opposition was nil or light, they could seize and repair the Momote airfield; if resistance was strong, they could be quickly withdrawn. According to Kenney, MacArthur "listened a while, paced back and forth as I kept talking, nodded occasionally, then suddenly stopped and said, 'That will put the cork in the bottle.'" In less than twenty-four hours, orders for the Los Negros reconnaissance were issued, and a host of frantic officers dashed about to prepare for an operation set for February 29, only four days after the decision was announced.

On February 26, the Brewer Task Force was established for the occupation of the Admiralties; it was to be under Major General Innis P. Swift, the commander of the 1st Cavalry Division. The reconnaissance in force would be led by Brigadier General William C. Chase, one of Swift's brigade commanders, and would consist of about 1000 troops of the 1st Cavalry Brigade. Another 1500 cavalrymen, as well as about 400 "Seabees" (naval construction personnel), were to be at Finschhafen on the alert to go to Los Negros forty-eight hours after D-day if MacArthur decided that the reconnaissance indicated the feasibility of an occupation. Chase's force would be transported from Oro Bay aboard three of Barbey's destroyer-transports escorted by eight destroyers. A supporting force of two cruisers and four destroyers would bombard Los Negros and the Lorengau area, the action at the latter site to be diversionary. Rear Admiral William M. Fechteler, Barbey's deputy, was picked to lead the naval attack group and Berkey to head the support group.

MacArthur's decision on the evening of the 24th to send the force to Los Negros was made quickly and boldly. Reminiscent of his hasty decision on the Finschhafen landing, his move disregarded Chamberlin's carefully laid plans for an attack on Los Negros to be undertaken over a month later, and by a division, not a mere 1000 men. "Always a man of faith, self-confidence, and buoyant optimism," states an Army historian, MacArthur "saw opportunities where other men saw problems and difficulties." Although Whitehead estimated that about 300 enemy troops were in the Admiralties, MacArthur accepted the figure of 4050 put forth by Willoughby, which turned out to be amazingly accurate. In other words, the SWPA chief bought Whitehead and Kenney's bold proposal, but was realistically aware that their estimate of Japanese strength was probably far too optimistic.

MacArthur knew that he was taking a tremendous risk that could lead to the destruction of Chase's force, the termination of offensive operations in the Southwest Pacific, and the ruin of his own career. But he was gambling on his capability to reinforce the beachhead quickly and on the Japanese commander's commitment of his soldiers in piecemeal attacks, a tendency that the enemy had frequently displayed in the Pacific fighting. In addition, by putting "the final seal on the isolation of Rabaul," he could greatly speed up operations in his theater and thus keep pace with Nimitz's forces in the advance toward the Philippines. It was feared at GHQ in Brisbane that any slowdown of SWPA operations at this stage of the competition would result in the

Joint Chiefs' determination to put all the emphasis on the Central Pacific drive. But, according to Kenney, most of the GHQ staff still opposed MacArthur's decision to invade Los Negros ahead of schedule and on such short notice because they feared the logistical difficulties were insurmountable. Kenney observed, however, that the SWPA commander "brushed aside ruthlessly any arguments that we already had outrun the capabilities of our supply system." [3]

The fact that the operation was able to be mounted on four days' notice was due in large part to the alert action of Kinkaid, Krueger, Barbey, Fechteler, Berkey, Swift, and Chase. There was better Army-Navy coordination during those hectic days than the Southwest Pacific command had experienced in its nearly two years' existence. On the 27th MacArthur flew with Kinkaid to Milne Bay, where they boarded Captain Albert G. Noble's cruiser, the *Phoenix*, which was to join the naval support group. While at sea on the afternoon of the 28th, MacArthur received news that a six-man team of scouts sent by Krueger to Los Negros the previous night had found the island "lousy with Japs." Chase's force had already departed from Oro Bay. Again confronted with a critical decision, MacArthur discounted the scouts' report as exaggerated and did not hesitate about continuing the expedition.

As to why the SWPA chief decided to go along, Barbey speculated, "We could only guess at the reason MacArthur wanted to accompany this small 'reconnaissance in force' operation. He had not taken part in any previous operations where the stakes were much larger. We guessed that he wanted to be present when the decision had to be made whether to continue the assault or to withdraw." Krueger said that, before MacArthur boarded the *Phoenix*, "I argued that it was unnecessary and unwise to expose himself in this fashion and that it would be a calamity if anything happened to him. He listened to me attentively and thanked me, but added, 'I have to go.' He had made up his mind on the subject — and that was that." [4]

The voyage on the *Phoenix* seems to have been an exhilarating and educational experience for MacArthur, who, to the best of anyone's recollection, had never traveled on a Navy combat vessel except for his PT boat journey in March, 1942. He chatted amiably with Kinkaid, Noble, and other naval officers, displayed great curiosity about the workings of the ship, and was impressed by the efficiency and discipline of the crew. Gaetano Faillace, a combat photographer whom MacArthur liked and would take along on many of his future forays into combat areas, said that the general talked casually with the sailors and consented to give autographs to them. Noble recalled that at dinner on the evening of the 28th "we gave him a good old Dixie meal" that included "some fine beef" and a pudding made of "cracked or ground corn." MacArthur liked the latter so much that he obtained from Noble not only the recipe but also a package of the cornmeal, which he took back to Brisbane. When the landing got under way the next morning at Hyane Harbor, on the southern coast of Los Negros, the first waves encountered some heavy fire from Japanese 20-mm. batteries on either side of the narrow harbor entrance. The guns of the *Phoenix* and other support ships promptly silenced them. "This performance," remarked Kinkaid, "so thoroughly converted General MacArthur into a naval gunfire enthusiast that he became more royalist than the king." On later occasions Kinkaid "frequently had to point out the limitations of naval gunfire to the general." [5]

The Brewer Task Force's landing craft began moving to the southern shore inside Hyane Harbor about 8:00 A.M. on February 29, meeting little opposition except for the early shelling by coastal batteries. Within two hours the 1st Cavalry troops captured Momote airfield. By 1:00 P.M. the entire force was ashore, and casualties on the American side so far had amounted to four dead and six wounded. Five Japanese had been killed, and no sizable enemy units had been engaged; large amounts of hastily abandoned supplies and equipment indicated, nevertheless, that a considerable force was in the Momote vicinity. Actually, Ezaki had mistaken the landing at Hyane Harbor as a diversionary effort. He held the majority of his troops on the northern side of Los Negros and around Lorengau, thinking that the main invasion would strike through Seeadler Harbor. By the middle of the afternoon, however, the enemy troops who had withdrawn into the jungle near the Momote strip were preparing for a banzai charge, to be undertaken that night. The next three days would be marked by savage attacks by Ezaki's troops, but with the beachhead secured and reinforcements soon arriving, Chase's force could not be driven into the sea.[6]

At 4:00 P.M. on the 29th, after a heavy downpour of several hours' duration began to subside, MacArthur insisted on going ashore. He was accompanied by Kinkaid and two of his aides, Colonels Lloyd A. Lehrbas and Roger O. Egeberg, the latter having recently been assigned as the general's physician. Mac-Arthur awarded a Distinguished Service Cross to a young lieutenant who had led the first wave ashore, conferred with Chase and some of his officers on the progress of the operation, and, despite sniper fire that resounded through the jungle nearby, spent an hour or so walking around the Momote area. Deciding that the beachhead could be held, he ordered the reinforcements waiting at Finschhafen to be brought to Los Negros. He commented to Chase, "You have all performed marvelously. Hold what you have taken, no matter against what odds. You have your teeth in him now. Don't let up."

In his tour of the beachhead MacArthur seemed to be determined to refurbish his image as a "fighting general" and to bury the unjust Dugout Doug legend, which still circulated among some embittered soldiers. His deliberate exposure within easy range of enemy guns and his calmness when bursts of small-arms firing erupted close by amazed both officers and enlisted men who witnessed his casual tour. At one stage an uneasy cavalry officer touched him on the sleeve and pointed toward a spot in the jungle fifty yards ahead: "Excuse me, sir, but we killed a Jap sniper in there just a few minutes ago." MacArthur responded as he continued to walk in that direction, "Fine. That's the best thing to do with them." Coming across two Japanese soldiers who had been killed less than twenty minutes before, he looked at them a long while and, as he walked away, muttered, "That's the way I like to see them." Faillace observed that "General Chase was very, very anxious to get him out of there," but, though he was in "very intimate danger" at times, the SWPA commander persisted in his tour until he was satisfied that he had "a sense of the situation."

The most dangerous moments for him came when he insisted on walking out on the air strip despite warnings that enemy troops held the area immediately beyond the other end of the runway.[7] Egeberg soon learned that it was indeed precarious to accept an invitation from the Old Man to "see what's happening" in a combat area:

> Walking along with MacArthur, I could hear gunfire a few hundred yards off the beach. I thought about my children at home. Maybe if I "accidentally" dropped something, I could stoop over, but I wondered if I ever would be able to stand again. Back at Milne there was no fighting while I was there, and though I had visited Buna after the battle there, I actually had not witnessed fighting until that day on the beach in the Admiralties. All of the officers with MacArthur were uneasy at Los Negros — uneasy about MacArthur's safety and, more vital to them, about their own safety. MacArthur always strongly advised us to wear combat helmets, which I did, but he never wore one himself when we went ashore on landings.
>
> We went inland a short distance to the air strip where an estimated 200 or 300 Japs were on the far side of the runway, all within rifle range. I was particularly uneasy on that walk because I was on the side of MacArthur toward those Japs. For some reason, however, they chose not to make us targets. The General commented that he felt they were busy preparing for a banzai charge later; it came that night after we were back

aboard ship . . . At one point MacArthur insisted on comparing the size of holes made by naval shells with those made by
aerial bombs. On this occasion we were fired at by some Japs,
but an artillery battery immediately bracketed them and silenced the firing.

General MacArthur was convinced (and I was, too), after seeing the reaction of the troops to his visit, that his presence
ashore in the first hours of combat had been an important boost
to morale for the soldiers on Los Negros. There was also the fact
that MacArthur wanted to experience the smell of gunpowder
and the sights and sounds of combat. Being in or near a battle
seemed to quicken him . . . It was almost as if battle "fed"
his system . . . It was true also that he could appreciate the
problems of his commanders and soldiers much better by getting
a taste of the fighting than by poring over maps and operations
reports back at headquarters.[8]

"Wet, cold, and dirty with mud up to the ears," MacArthur
and his entourage returned to the *Phoenix* after two hours
ashore and departed that evening for New Guinea. As he had
predicted, the Japanese troops were wasted in piecemeal attacks
during the next few days, and, with reinforcements that arrived
on March 2, Chase's men rapidly overran Los Negros. A week
later Brigadier General Verne D. Mudge's cavalry brigade entered Seeadler Harbor and invaded the northern coast of Los
Negros at Salami. On March 15–18, Mudge's troops landed
west of Lorengau and proceeded to capture that last bastion of
Japanese resistance in the Admiralties. By the end of March the
cavalrymen were engaged in scattered mopping-up activities.
The Admiralties were securely in American hands. The Momote airfield was being used by American fighters before the
end of the month, and a bomber base was already under construction. The Japanese strip at Lorengau was found to be un-
usable, but a new one was soon built nearby. Seeadler Harbor
would become an important anchorage for Allied ships in coming months.

Shortly after returning from Los Negros in early March, Mac-Arthur decided that seizure of the Admiralties had made it unnecessary to attack Hansa Bay, Wewak, and Kavieng in order to complete the isolation of Rabaul. On March 12 he received authorization from the Joint Chiefs to make the gigantic leap to Hollandia; Halsey was to assault Emirau. The latter was easily secured on March 20, and a month later SWPA forces would seize Hollandia against light opposition. Bloody encounters at Wewak, Hansa Bay, and Kavieng were averted primarily because of the gamble that had paid off on Los Negros. And the decisions to send the reconnaissance force on short notice and to keep it there were MacArthur's alone. Fechteler commented, "Actually we're damn lucky we didn't get run off the island." Barbey later remarked, "Looking backward, I have wondered if MacArthur ever questioned his own judgment in this matter." Because the general was self-confident, it is doubtful that he hesitated in making the three decisions — of February 24, 28, and 29 — which were critical to the operation's success. He was widely acclaimed as a bold, shrewd strategist in the aftermath of the Admiralties victory. Marshall and Churchill, among others, sent messages of praise, and even crusty King admitted that the Los Negros invasion was "a brilliant maneuver." The Army's chief historian of the operation states simply that MacArthur's decisions regarding Los Negros "had the very great virtue of hastening victory while reducing the number of dead and wounded." [9] Actually a commander could ask for no finer tribute.

2. *Conflict and Compromise*

It is regrettable that the triumph in the Admiralties was accompanied by a bitter dispute over control of the huge naval base planned for Manus. When the SWPA delegation returned from Pearl Harbor in late January, their reports of scuttlebutt picked up at Nimitz's headquarters made MacArthur uneasy about the future role of the Southwest Pacific forces in the advance toward Japan. On February 2 the anxious SWPA chief radioed the Army chief of staff urging him to persuade the Joint Chiefs to concentrate all Pacific forces along the New Guinea–Philippines axis after the termination of the Marshalls operations. MacArthur wanted almost all of the Pacific Fleet as well as most of the new B-29's, at least until after the reconquest of the Philippines; the former he proposed to place under Halsey as his naval commander. Since time was short and a decision was needed, he suggested sending Sutherland to explain his views to the Joint Chiefs. Marshall was agreeable to his coming, but also in early February Nimitz sent his chief of staff, Rear Admiral Forrest P. Sherman, to present his arguments before the Joint Chiefs for expanding the Central Pacific drive. The Washington planners by that time were leaning in favor of bypassing Truk and shifting even more weight to Nimitz's forces for future invasions of the Marianas and Palaus, from which they would then attack Formosa or Luzon.

While Sutherland expounded in Washington and MacArthur bombarded the War Department with radiograms defending the Southwest Pacific route, what seemed to the SWPA chief an ominous portent appeared in late February: Nimitz recommended to the Joint Chiefs, through King, that the development and control of the naval base at Manus be placed under Halsey. The Joint Chiefs, he maintained, needed only to extend the boundary of the South Pacific Area westward to encompass the Admiralties. After all, he noted, Halsey's staff had a major role in planning the layout of the base, and his Seabees then constituted the majority of the work force involved in its construction. Alarmed by the debate over Pacific strategy under way in Washington, MacArthur interpreted Nimitz's suggestion as the first step toward his assumption of supreme command in the

Pacific, which would undoubtedly result in closing out Mac-Arthur's offensive.

On February 27 MacArthur protested to Marshall that at stake in the Manus matter was not only control of the Pacific war but also the respect due the SWPA commander's honor and leadership capability. If the Joint Chiefs should remove Manus from his jurisdiction, he demanded the right to present his case personally to Roosevelt and Stimson "before finally determining my own personal action in the matter." MacArthur had reached the statutory retirement age of sixty-four in January, but neither the President nor the War Department had seriously considered the idea of forcing his retirement. Now he seemed to be implying that he would retire voluntarily if he lost on the Manus issue.

Marshall replied reassuringly that he agreed with his basic argument: "You should retain command of all base facilities in your area unless you yourself see fit to turn over control of them." But he added, "While the base should remain under your command, there should be a clear understanding that facilities for fleet operation and basing will be developed as desired by the [Pacific] Fleet and that the Fleet will have unrestricted use of them." Marshall said he would arrange for him to visit the President and the Secretary of War "at any time on this or any other matter," but, he continued, "I cannot see that a change in a boundary of your area, in itself, could be regarded as a serious reflection upon your capacity to command . . . Your professional integrity and personal honor are in no way questioned or, so far as I can see, involved." [10]

This did not soothe MacArthur, however, and in early March he radioed Halsey to come to Brisbane at once. In stormy sessions on March 3–5, they thoroughly thrashed out the Manus issue. Except for Sutherland, the top staff officers of both commanders were present, appearing at times like seconds in a duel. "Before even a word of greeting was spoken," said Halsey, "I saw that MacArthur was fighting to keep his temper." The South Pacific admiral, who had had nothing to do with Nimitz's proposal, sat through a tirade by the general in which, according to Halsey, "MacArthur lumped me, Nimitz, King, and the whole Navy in a vicious conspiracy to pare away his authority." As MacArthur continued, Halsey noticed that "unlike myself, strong emotion did not make him profane. He did not need to be; profanity would have merely discolored his eloquence."

The SWPA chief firmly stated that "he had no intention of tamely submitting to such interference; and that he had given orders that, until the jurisdiction of Manus was established, work should be restricted to facilities for ships under his direct command — the Seventh Fleet and [anticipated] British units." When he finished and asked for opinions, Admirals Kinkaid and Robert B. Carney, Halsey's deputy, as well as Captain Felix Johnson, the South Pacific liaison officer at GHQ SWPA, all joined Halsey in stating that MacArthur was wrong. Halsey bluntly told him, "If you stick to this order of yours, you'll be hampering the war effort!" MacArthur's staff "gasped," observed Halsey, adding: "I imagine they never expected to hear anyone address him in those terms this side of the Judgment Throne."

After a long argument that lasted until dinner and was continued through two tense sessions the next day, MacArthur finally yielded. "He gave me a charming smile," commented Halsey, "and said, 'You win, Bill!'" On that positive note, Halsey and his staff took off to return to Noumea. The disagreement had no effect whatsoever on the friendship of the two strong-willed commanders, and MacArthur, who intended no affront to Kinkaid, still hoped to obtain Halsey as his SWPA naval commander.[11]

Back in Washington the Joint Chiefs were deeply involved in the Manus dispute, since they viewed it as closely related to Pacific strategy for 1944 and the decision to send the main thrust north or south of Truk. Admiral William D. Leahy, the presidential chief of staff, stated that "the Joint Chiefs of Staff were receiving the sharpest criticism yet made by naval commanders in the Pacific of the actions and operations of General Douglas MacArthur. This was the most controversial single problem before the JCS during March, 1944." In the end, the Joint Chiefs rejected Nimitz's proposal and left Manus under MacArthur's control, but the fleet anchorage and facilities were to be used freely by all units of the Navy, whether they were assigned to the Seventh Fleet or to some other group. As mentioned earlier, the Manus, or Seeadler Harbor, naval base became a huge and much-used station of the Third, Fifth, and Seventh fleets in later operations.[12]

The invasion of the Admiralties caught the Joint Chiefs as well as the Japanese by surprise. The move influenced the Joint Chiefs on March 2 to return for additional study a proposal of the Joint Strategic Survey Committee to curtail MacArthur's drive after the seizure of Dutch New Guinea. That same day they directed MacArthur and Nimitz to submit their respective plans for advancing to the Luzon-Formosa-China coast triangle. The Joint Chiefs also invited Sutherland and Sherman, who were already in Washington, to present their theaters' cases on March 7–8. By that time Nimitz had arrived in the national capital and joined Sherman in his appearance before the Joint Chiefs.

The Central Pacific leaders, who spoke first, argued that the rapid capture of the Marshalls and the highly successful carrier raids recently against Truk and the Marianas made an acceleration of the Central Pacific thrust feasible. They offered alternative plans, depending upon the Joint Chiefs' decision regarding Truk. In their first plan they proposed to take Truk in June, the southern Marianas in September, and the Palaus in November. Their second plan, assuming that Truk had been isolated, called for the capture of the southern Marianas in June,

Woleai, between Truk and the Palaus, in July, the Palaus in October, and Ulithi and nearby Yap in November. Nimitz stated that, regardless of which of his plans was used to reach the Luzon-Formosa-China objective, it would be beneficial to have MacArthur's forces seize Mindanao and provide him with air support from bases there.

Sutherland's turn came on March 8, at which time he offered MacArthur's Reno IV Plan. He assured the Joint Chiefs that "the line of action presented in RENO IV will sever sea communications between Japan and the vital Borneo–N.E.I.–China Coast area at the earliest date possible under conditions that can be foreseen at this time." Unlike the previous Reno plans, the latest version omitted most of the ground operations intended to protect the flanks of the main SWPA drive, on the assumption that land-based aircraft and Nimitz's forces to the east would provide adequate flank security. Reno IV comprised four objectives: the capture of (1) Humboldt Bay and Geelvink Bay, in Dutch New Guinea, beginning April 15, (2) air bases in the Arafura Sea islands, July 15, (3) the Vogelkop and Halmahera, the latter lying between New Guinea and Mindanao, starting about mid-September, and (4) Mindanao, to be invaded on November 5.

Sutherland suggested that SWPA forces would be prepared to invade Luzon in January, 1945. Echoing MacArthur, he argued that the limited base facilities in the Marianas made the use of those islands impracticable in staging major operations against the Luzon-Formosa-China coast region. King countered that, as in the Torch invasion, ground forces could be staged from rear bases with the convoys rendezvousing at sea. He caustically pointed out that no suitable staging areas for such an immense operation existed along the coast of New Guinea. Arnold, of course, favored the seizure of the Marianas because, since the early fall of 1943, he and his planners had hoped to base the big B-29's there for raids against Japan proper.[13]

After further meetings of the Washington planners on March 9–10, the Joint Chiefs met again with the Pacific representatives on the 11th to hear their final arguments on the assets and liabilities of the Central and Southwest Pacific routes. In a closed session on March 12 the Joint Chiefs approved a directive for MacArthur and Nimitz that was to govern their operations until February, 1945:

The Joint Chiefs of Staff have . . . decided that the most feasible approach to the Formosa-Luzon-China area is by way of [the] Marianas-Carolines-Palau-Mindanao area, and that the control of the Marianas-Carolines-Palau area is essential to the projection of our forces into the former area, and their subsequent effective employment therefrom. Examination leads us to the decision that effective lodgment in the former area will be attained by the following main courses of action:

a. Cancellation of FOREARM [Kavieng invasion]. Complete the isolation of the Rabaul-Kavieng area with the minimum commitment of forces.

b. Early completion of [the] Manus operation and [its] development as an air and fleet base.

c. Occupation of Hollandia by CINCSOWESPAC [MacArthur], target date April 15, 1944. The objective is the establishment of heavy bombardment aircraft for preliminary air bombardment of the Palaus and neutralization of [the] western New Guinea–Halmahera area.

d. Establish control of [the] Marianas-Carolines-Palau area by POA [Pacific Ocean Areas] forces —

(1) By neutralization of Truk.

(2) By occupation of the southern Marianas, target date June 15.

The objective is to secure control of sea communications through the Central Pacific by isolating and neutralizing the Carolines and by the establishment of sea and air bases for operations against Japanese sea routes and long-range air attacks against the Japanese home land.

(3) Occupation of the Palaus by POA forces, target date September 15.

The objective is to extend the control of the eastern approaches to the Philippines and Formosa, and to establish a fleet and air base and forward staging area for the support of operations against Mindanao, Formosa and China.

e. Occupation of Mindanao by SOWESPAC [Southwest Pacific] forces, supported by the Pacific Fleet, target date November 15. The objective is establishment of air forces to reduce and contain Japanese forces in the Philippines preparatory to a further advance to Formosa either directly or via Luzon, and to conduct air strikes against enemy installations in the N.E.I.

f. Occupation of Formosa, target date February 15, 1945, or occupation of Luzon should such operations prove necessary prior to the move on Formosa, target date February 15, 1945. Planning responsibilities as follows: Formosa — CINCPOA [Nimitz]; Luzon — CINCSOWESPAC.[14]

The Joint Chiefs' directive of the 12th was a partial disappointment to MacArthur because his plea for concentration along the Southwest Pacific axis of advance was rejected (as was also his insistence on Kavieng's seizure, discussed earlier). Nevertheless, the SWPA commander had some reasons to be elated. Most important, his offensive would not be stalled on the Vogelkop since he was clearly slated to lead the return to the Philippines. Also, the Joint Chiefs confirmed their earlier endorsement of his proposal to bypass Hansa Bay and Wewak and to attack Hollandia instead. The directive's phrasing suggested that the Joint Chiefs were definitely in favor of an invasion of Formosa, but at least the seizure of Luzon was not ruled out. MacArthur undoubtedly realized that, when the day arrived that his forces were poised in Mindanao and Nimitz's in the Palaus, the factors of proximity and logistics would greatly strengthen his case for moving next to Luzon.

The directive, which was actually the result of numerous compromises, did not resolve the controversies over theater priorities or the primary objective within the Luzon-Formosa-China coast triangle. Again the Joint Chiefs did not try to settle the issue of unity of command in the Pacific. The dual advance would continue, though Nimitz was now directed to provide naval support during MacArthur's operations against Hollandia and Mindanao, with the specific fleet units mentioned in the details of the directive. MacArthur, in turn, was to provide facilities at Manus for the Pacific Fleet, and he was to make available air support for the Palaus invasion and other Central Pacific operations within range of Southwest Pacific bases. Willingly or not, the two Pacific commanders were now bound to coordinate their efforts better since they were under direct orders of the Joint Chiefs to do so.

The last large-scale action in Halsey's theater took place when the Japanese launched vicious counterattacks on Bougainville in March, but the beachhead remained secure. The time was now opportune to begin phasing out the South Pacific Area as a major combat zone. As soon as the Joint Chiefs completed their directive of March 12, they turned to the problem of reallocating Halsey's forces. On the 17th they issued a directive on the redeployment of South Pacific forces and resources that resulted in a distribution approximately along service lines. MacArthur was allocated the XIV Corps headquarters and corps troops as well as Halsey's six Army divisions — the 25th, 37th, 40th, 43rd, 93rd, and Americal. He also obtained the Thirteenth Air Force, but with the understanding that it was to be employed in support of Nimitz's operations at the admiral's request. The major portion of Halsey's naval resources, including all naval and Marine air squadrons, went to Nimitz. A few surface units were added to Kinkaid's fleet, bringing its total strength in American ships to three cruisers, twenty-seven destroyers, eighteen destroyer escorts, thirty submarines, eight attack transports of various types, sixty LCI's, forty LST's, and miscellaneous small auxiliary craft. A small American Army force and a New Zealand division would remain in the South Pacific. In time, the Bougainville perimeter would be reinforced by Australian units as well. Over the next four months, the transfer of American units would be accomplished gradually, and on August 1 the South Pacific Base Command, whose functions would be mostly staging and rehabilitation, was to be established. The termination of Halsey's South Pacific Area command clearly demonstrated the progress being made in the war against Japan.[15]

Although MacArthur saw his Army divisions increased from six to twelve and his air strength nearly doubled, the reallocation of South Pacific resources would not turn out to be the boon that his GHQ staff initially anticipated. The return to the Philippines, now definitely on the schedule, would require not only combat forces but also shipping and logistical support, and solutions to MacArthur's growing transport and supply needs had not been found. In fact, shortly after receiving the directive of March 12 MacArthur, because of shipping difficulties, requested and obtained from the Joint Chiefs a week's postponement of the Hollandia target date. No relief of the acute shortage of assault and landing craft in the Pacific would be possible until after Overlord, the cross-Channel attack.

Some of MacArthur's shipping problems, however, would be allayed by the Combined Chiefs' tentative decision in late March to cancel Anvil, the invasion of southern France that was to have taken place concurrently with Overlord. But offsetting this temporary relief was a mounting crisis in the Southwest Pacific over the serious shortage of service troops. As early as January, Marshall suggested that MacArthur should start "rolling up" rear bases that were no longer absolutely necessary for his operations and should employ only a basic minimum of service personnel in intermediate areas. In his reply MacArthur acknowledged that "victory is dependent upon the solution of the logistic problem," but, as yet unwilling to close down his rear bases, he maintained that the answer was to send him more service troops. If necessary, he suggested, more uncommitted combat troops in the States could be retrained and assigned to service units. Adding to MacArthur's woes in this area was the tightening manpower pinch in Australia, where Curtin's government was preparing to reduce the strength of the Australian Army, especially since its role in the combat zone was to be taken over by American units.[16]

As the Joint Chiefs' directive called for the Pacific Fleet to support the Hollandia invasion, now set for April 22, the Pentagon leaders hoped that the two Pacific commanders would confer personally on coordinating their plans. They optimistically felt that such a meeting also might dispel some of the tension between the two headquarters. Despite hints from Marshall to MacArthur and King to Nimitz, neither theater commander would take the initiative in arranging a get-together. Only slightly acquainted on a personal basis, they had not met during the war years. Each man had ample grounds for his reluctance about a meeting in view of all that had occurred during the inter-theater rivalry and maneuvering of the past two years.

But then Nimitz received word from Secretary Knox that he was planning to visit the Central, South, and Southwest Pacific commands soon and "would be pleased" to have Nimitz accompany him on the Australian leg of his journey. Major General Omar T. Pfeiffer, then serving on the Marine headquarters staff at Pearl Harbor, recalled that "this opportunity was not palatable to Admiral Nimitz because, as he expressed himself, 'it looks like Papa has come out to take the little boy by the hand and lead him over the line to meet General MacArthur,' except that the word he used was not 'General MacArthur.'" Preferring to handle the matter his own way, and to do so before Knox's trip, Nimitz got in touch with MacArthur and the two agreed to confer at GHQ in Brisbane on March 25–27.[17]

During the previous two years Nimitz had shown more patience toward MacArthur than MacArthur toward him, but the staffs of both men had been guilty of vicious remarks about the "opposing" theater commander. Sutherland's tactless, blunt comments in Washington and Pearl Harbor did much to keep relations tense. In the previous half year MacArthur had displayed increasing irritation over alleged or actual statements and actions by Nimitz. Captain Johnson, Halsey's liaison officer at Brisbane, said he could always tell when MacArthur was angry over something Nimitz had said or done because he would pronounce his name "Nee-mitz."

Sherrod, whose coverage of news took him to both commanders' headquarters, found Nimitz's attitude toward his job quite different from MacArthur's toward his. For instance, on the matter of personal publicity, said Sherrod, "the Admiral was frequently the despair of his public relations men; it simply was not in him to make sweeping statements or to give out colorful interviews." The Central Pacific commander "conceived of war as something to be accomplished as efficiently and as smoothly as possible, without too much fanfare." [18] Vice Admiral Charles A. Lockwood, who commanded the SWPA submarine force for a time and later served under Nimitz in the Central Pacific, admired both Pacific commanders and offered the following comparison:

> General MacArthur and Admiral Nimitz had much in common. Both had highly trained command minds that cut through underbrush to reach the core of projects and problems; both had that extraordinary quality of leadership that inspires loyalty; both were endowed with the champion's will to win; both respected rules and traditions but had the guts to throw them over and make the off-the-cuff decisions in emergencies; both were tall, well-knit men, lean as greyhounds and straight as ramrods.
>
> But here the similarity ceases. The admiral's eyes were serene and blue, his bushy hair was blond salted with gray, his soft speech still carried a trace of his native Texan drawl. The general's eyes were dark and fiery, his thinning hair was straight and jet black, his speech was quick and modulated. The admiral seldom rode the emotional pendulum; joy and sorrow would set the general off on lusty zooms or steep dives. During moments

of tense waiting, when great combat issues hung in the balance, the admiral would drawl appropriate Lincolnesque jokes while he calmly practiced on his pistol range or tossed ringers with horseshoes just outside his office. At such moments the general would, as a rule, sit stonily in his chair, chewing on the stem of a corncob pipe, which usually needed relighting.[19]

Nimitz sent Captain Cato D. Glover of his planning staff ahead to Brisbane "to do the initial planning for the first co-ordinate operations" between the Central and Southwest Pacific commands. When he was introduced to MacArthur on March 21, Glover said that the general gave him "a surprisingly enthusiastic greeting." But the atmosphere quickly changed as MacArthur launched into a lengthy monologue on "the differences in our strategy that might keep us fighting on separate fronts." He hinted darkly that, though he needed the Pacific Fleet's help, he was not expecting to get much support. Glover tried several times to interrupt him to deliver Nimitz's message that he was prepared "to accomplish most effectively that co-ordination and cooperation" which the general desired. "His mind seemed to have been made up," Glover lamented, "and I wasn't given the opportunity to say a word except to thank him for the meeting which had lasted a full forty-five minutes." Glover surely had cause to be anxious about the forthcoming conference.

On March 25 Nimitz and Sherman flew to Brisbane, and MacArthur met them as they got off the plane shortly after 4:30 P.M. Johnson was amazed at the SWPA chief's friendliness: MacArthur "put his arm around him" and seemed to "love Nimitz with a fervor at that time." An hour later the two Central Pacific admirals met briefly with MacArthur and Sutherland at GHQ to discuss the schedule and agenda of the sessions. That evening MacArthur hosted a lavish banquet at Lennon's Hotel in honor of Nimitz. The general's office diary states that there were "forty-eight guests, including all Allied officers of general officer rank or equivalent in the area." [20] Tarbuck, who attended the dinner, recalled that

> Admiral Nimitz made a speech, and he answered questions. Someone asked him whether he was going to continue bombing these Japanese islands in the Pacific or bypass them. Admiral Nimitz said that brought up a very difficult question as to whether it was better to bypass them and let them starve all at once by cutting off their supply, or let them live longer by reducing their number, in which case it would take him longer to get the island and use it. Jokingly he said that was the big problem: starve or bomb. It got a laugh, and it showed that he was in a happy mood. As I recall, General MacArthur didn't laugh.[21]

It could be that MacArthur interpreted the admiral's words as a mockery of the general's public statements in the fall in which he had lauded his own bypassing and criticized the costly frontal assault of Tarawa.

On the 26th, a Sunday, the conferees met in long sessions, both morning and afternoon. Besides MacArthur, Nimitz, Sherman, and Sutherland, the others present were Kinkaid, Kenney, Marshall, Glover, and Lehrbas. Why Lehrbas, an aide and PRO officer, was invited to a top-level planning conference is not known. In the talks, Nimitz stated that he planned to send the eleven fast carriers of Vice Admiral Marc A. Mitscher's Task Force 58 to conduct a series of raids in the Carolines and Palaus in early April, after which they would be dispatched to the Southwest Pacific in time to provide air support for the Hollandia invasion. But the admiral was greatly disturbed about the threat of Japanese air strength in Dutch New Guinea, which his intelligence estimated at 200 to 300 planes. Kenney said, "I promised to have them rubbed out by April 5. Everyone except MacArthur looked skeptical." Nimitz finally was persuaded that the situation would be safe for his carriers, but he insisted on withdrawing them the day after the landings.

Kinkaid talked him into delaying the departure of some of the small carriers until eight days after the assault, by which time it was expected that Kenney's aircraft could move to forward bases and provide aerial cover for the ground units.

The conferees also discussed the Joint Chiefs' directive, and the two sides repeated their familiar arguments for one axis or the other with neither yielding an inch, as expected. According to Kenney, MacArthur and Nimitz did agree, however, that "the occupation of Luzon was an essential preliminary to the movement against Formosa and that Formosa could not be attacked by any expedition springing from the Marianas-Palau line." On the evening of the 27th General and Mrs. MacArthur invited Nimitz and Kinkaid to dinner at their suite in Lennon's Hotel, which the general later described to one of his staff as "a quiet evening of congenial conversation." [22]

The next morning, March 27, MacArthur summoned an assembly of his GHQ staff; the number present was termed "huge" by Glover. The purpose of the meeting was to introduce the visiting brass from Pearl Harbor and to acquaint the staff with the general results of the planning sessions just concluded. In a letter to Nimitz many years later Glover recalled the occasion:

General MacArthur outlined the results of our conferences and stated the basic differences in our strategic thinking. There was a dead silence and as I cast about I could see only long and disappointed faces. You [Nimitz] stood to talk and your smile was encouraging, and it was apparent that your first purpose was to ease the tension with a humorous story. You began by saying that after all you and General MacArthur were not alone in having grievous troubles, "The situation reminds me of the story of the two frantically worried men who were pacing the corridor of their hotel. One finally turned to the other and said, 'What are you worried about?' The answer was immediate, 'I am a doctor and I have a patient in my room with a wooden leg and I have that leg apart and can't get it back together again.' The other responded, 'Great guns, I wish that was all that I have to worry about. I have a good looking gal in my room with both [legs apart] and I can't remember the room number.' "

Even MacArthur laughed and there was great applause.[23]

That afternoon Nimitz and Sherman flew back to Pearl Harbor. The two theater commanders were pleased with the harmonious atmosphere of the conference, but both were probably relieved that the unusual experience was past. Four days later, Sherman wrote to an admiral who was a friend of his that, despite MacArthur's "moments of forensic oratory," the conference "established a background for better cooperation in the future" between the two leaders and their staffs.[24] The Hollandia operation, only three weeks away, would be the first challenge to the Pacific commands' new era of brotherly feelings.

CHAPTER X

Political Misadventure

1. The Boom Begins

THE CONGRESSIONAL AND GUBERNATORIAL ELECTIONS in 1942, writes an eminent historian, signaled "not merely a Republican revival but also a strong conservative upsurge" across the nation. That November the Republicans gained forty-seven more seats in the House of Representatives and another ten in the Senate. The Republican–Southern Democratic coalition on Capitol Hill had grown in strength since its birth in 1938 and was now determined, war or no war, to destroy certain of Roosevelt's liberal domestic programs while cautiously supporting his leadership in matters of strategy and foreign affairs. Among some, however, there was growing anxiety about the President's seeming neglect of the Pacific war and his supposed mishandling of relations with the Allies, especially China and the Soviet Union. The gubernatorial results in 1942 produced Republican governors in twenty-six states which possessed 342 of the 531 electoral votes. New York elected its first Republican governor since 1920, Thomas Dewey, a moderate liberal whose vigor and efficiency at Albany quickly made him the likely rival of Wendell Willkie, an ardent internationalist and the party's

titular head, for the Republican presidential nomination in
1944.

As taxes, economic controls, and casualty lists mounted, war
weariness and anti-Roosevelt sentiment seemed to pervade disparate groups of the American populace, so that by late 1943
the G.O.P. leaders were very hopeful of defeating the Democratic President. Governors John W. Bricker of Ohio and
Harold E. Stassen of Minnesota, one an outspoken isolationist
and the other a favorite son with little national support,
emerged as minor Republican contenders when Willkie, accused of being too closely identified with the Roosevelt administration since 1940, lost favor with the G.O.P. hierarchy and
Dewey coyly delayed an announcement of his intentions.

The ultraconservatives and supranationalists among the leaders of the Republican national and state organizations considered Bricker the only contender of the four who was not tainted
by liberal or internationalist tendencies. A political historian
saw "an aura of old-fashioned Republicanism" emanating from
Bricker, while William Allen White, the distinguished editor,
caustically referred to him as "an honest Harding." But the
realists among the Ohio governor's supporters had to admit that
he was not well known nationally and, if nominated, would
need a tremendous organization and a prodigious campaign in
order to pose a serious threat to Roosevelt in the 1944 race.
When the so-called "Mackinac Charter," a tentative platform
for the party, was drafted at a conference of Republican leaders
in Michigan in September, 1943, the isolationist wing was upset
because it committed the party to support "responsible participation by the United States in postwar cooperative organization"
to maintain world peace. The Republican malcontents, joined
by some anti-Roosevelt Democrats, set forth in quest of a candidate who would be ideologically sound and who possessed strong
voter appeal.[1]

In early April, 1943, the War Department had inadvertently

contributed to a revival of political interest in MacArthur when Stimson restated publicly a long-standing regulation that prohibited a regular Army officer from becoming a candidate for or accepting election to any political office not held by him when he began active military duty. In a House speech, Hamilton Fish, a New York Republican and vociferous critic of Roosevelt's, charged that the Secretary's statement was aimed at MacArthur, which was probably true. Fish said, "I do not know whether General MacArthur would even consider the nomination . . . but I am quite sure that the Executive Department of the government has no power whatever to dictate to the free people of America whom they should nominate and elect as President of the United States."

Other congressmen of Fish's persuasion attacked Stimson for trying to insure a fourth term for Roosevelt. Senator Vandenberg also voiced his opinion publicly that the move "was aimed at keeping MacArthur out of the next Presidential campaign." On April 19 Vandenberg, who had not yet communicated with the SWPA commander, received a message from the general delivered by one of his staff officers who had just flown in from Brisbane. "I am most grateful to you for your complete attitude of friendship," wrote MacArthur. "I only hope that I can some day reciprocate. There is much that I would like to say to you which circumstances prevent." In a conclusion weighted with implication he said, "In the meanwhile I want you to know the absolute confidence I would feel in your experienced and wise mentorship." Vandenberg's son said this letter impressed his father and "may well have crystallized his attention on the General as a candidate."

In the next four months Vandenberg gradually and quietly assumed the unofficial leadership of a MacArthur-for-President movement. When Willoughby was in Washington in June, he and the senator had "a long talk" on the subject, and Willoughby agreed to act as liaison between MacArthur and Vandenberg. In Chicago the senator met with General Robert Wood, who, said Vandenberg, "offered to underwrite any necessary expenses." Wood, the former head of the America First isolationists, had made an unpublicized visit to MacArthur in April. Conferring and corresponding with influential friends in various sections of the nation, Vandenberg formed what he called "our cabinet" to organize the movement. The group included, among others, John Hamilton, a former chairman of the Republican National Committee, who was to serve as campaign manager; Wood, the chief financial backer; Frank Gannett, a conservative Republican publisher of several influential newspapers in the Northeast; Roy Howard, of the Scripps-Howard newspaper syndicate, who was doubtful at first but had "a total loyalty" to MacArthur; Kyle Palmer, reporter for the Los Angeles *Times* and "our key man on the Pacific coast"; Joseph N. Pew, Jr., a leading Republican of Pennsylvania; and Colonel McCormick, the Chicago *Tribune* publisher and long-time friend of MacArthur's.[2]

On August 17 Vandenberg wrote to Willoughby, "our mutual friend," briefing him on the developing organization. Elaborating on the group's approach, the senator emphasized that, in order to avoid embarrassment to MacArthur and better to insure a convention draft, they were committed to "the importance of doing absolutely nothing of a promotional nature which would involve 'our campaign' in any ordinary political atmosphere or involve us in any of the usual preconvention methods." He continued:

> The whole thing, of course, continues to be entirely a gigantic speculation in public opinion and in the evolution of events. Of course, the chances are all against us. I am sure this is fully understood out where you are. It is simply a matter of developing a situation which, in the first instance, produces a national convention in which a majority of the delegates are "uninstructed" so that they are free to make the proper decision when the

time comes; then to develop through general consciousness that "our man" is the best answer under all the circumstances . . .

Tell my friend to just "get on with the war" and to forget this whole political business back here in the States. None of us wants him to do anything else.[3]

In late August, as the Sextant Conference adjourned in Quebec, news leaks about the strategic decisions that had been made there created a flurry of journalistic speculation, as discussed previously. MacArthur's public statements in early September strongly implied criticism of what he believed to be the Allied leaders' relegation of his theater to an inconsequential role, and his many admirers became alarmed over the impending martyrdom the gallant SWPA chief would achieve because of the machinations of the Europe-first strategists. Scores of letters from persons of high and low status deluged MacArthur expressing concern and indignation over his plight, and many of them expressed a preference for him, rather than Roosevelt, as the nation's commander-in-chief. At first Vandenberg was delighted with the tremendous outpouring of sympathy: "It seems to me that the American people are rapidly coming to understand what the General is up against in the Far East. These people can easily *martyrize* him into a completely irresistible figure." The senator wrote in his diary on September 30: "I think it is desperately important that there should be no signs whatever of any centrally organized activity . . . We should give our own 'commander-in-chief' no possible excuse upon which to hang his own political reprisals." [4]

Public opinion polls indicated a moderate interest in MacArthur as a potential presidential candidate, but the race for the Republican nomination was obviously between Willkie and Dewey, with the latter far ahead by February, 1944. Below are surveys conducted by the American Institute of Public Opinion in which national cross sections of Republican supporters were asked which of a given list of possible candidates they preferred:[5]

	Dewey	Willkie	Mac-Arthur	Bricker	Stassen	Others
Apr. 27, 1943	38%	28%	17%	8%	7%	2%
June 3, 1943	37	28	15	10	7	3
Aug. 24, 1943	35	29	15	8	4	9
Sept. 28, 1943	32	28	19	8	6	7
Nov. 23, 1943	36	25	15	10	6	8
Feb. 1, 1944	45	21	19	7	5	3
Apr. 12, 1944	55	7	20	9	7	2

MacArthur's strength lay principally in the farm belt of the Middle West, a majority of whose voters were usually considered to be conservative and isolationist. A Gallup poll in September pitted MacArthur against Roosevelt, with the general receiving 42 per cent of the votes to the President's 58 per cent. But the total farm vote showed MacArthur ahead, 56 per cent to 44 per cent, and among farm voters outside the traditionally Democratic South MacArthur got 58 per cent to Roosevelt's 42 per cent. Compared to similar Gallup polls involving Willkie and Dewey against Roosevelt, MacArthur's agrarian support was larger than either of the leading Republicans. A poll by *Successful Farming* magazine in November also indicated that MacArthur was stronger than Dewey or Willkie among its subscribers. Moreover, the general's vote was nine percentage points higher than Roosevelt's among farmers nationally and an impressive twenty-five points above the President's among Midwestern farmers.

MacArthur invariably registered a high percentage on polls that were intended to indicate which leaders the people most admired. According to the various surveys, the SWPA chief stirred the greatest admiration of all current military figures. An American Institute of Public Opinion survey in March, 1945, found that 43 per cent of the respondents considered MacArthur to be the greatest American Army general of the war; Eisenhower and Patton were the choices of 31 per cent and 17 per cent respectively, with Marshall, Hodges, Stilwell, and Bradley each supported by 1 per cent. Elmo Roper, the prominent pollster, remarked of the polls that registered opinion about MacArthur, "Most people admired him as a great general, but only a small segment had faith in his abilities as a civilian leader." [6] In a *Fortune* poll conducted by Roper in March, 1944, nation-wide opinion indicated that Roosevelt was regarded as better qualified to handle domestic, diplomatic, and strategic matters than Dewey, Willkie, or MacArthur. As the results below demonstrate, the President's percentage was higher than those of the three others combined in all categories, even surpassing by far MacArthur's rating on who was the best man to run the war effort:[7]

Which of these men do you feel could	Roosevelt	MacArthur	Dewey	Willkie	No Opinion
Run the government most efficiently, as President?	42%	8%	21%	12%	17%
Do the best job, as President, of preventing unemployment after the war?	41	5	16	12	26
Do the best job, as President, of running the war?	52	22	7	5	14
Do the best job, as President, of handling our foreign affairs after the war?	43	9	10	14	24

Thus, by early 1944 the polls were accurate harbingers of the eventual convention and election outcomes: Dewey was the preferred Republican, but Roosevelt could handily defeat any of the three likely Republican contenders.

Vandenberg and Howard especially kept a careful watch on

the polls and were sufficiently realistic to recognize that the general's only chance for the nomination would occur if the convention became deadlocked between the Dewey and Willkie forces and needed a dark horse. But the polls did not deter more zealous and less prudent admirers of the general from organizing openly to promote him for the presidency in the fall of 1943. Sometimes they joined with the backers of another potential candidate in advocating a ticket with MacArthur for President and the other individual as his running mate. L. W. McCormick, for example, headed a committee promoting the general and Senator Henry Cabot Lodge of Massachusetts; this group was most active in Pennsylvania, New York, and New England. John J. O'Connor, a former representative from New York, tried to stir up interest in a "100 Per Cent Americanism" ticket that would include MacArthur and James A. Farley, the disenchanted New Dealer who had once been a key member of Roosevelt's Cabinet. Hoover and Alfred E. Landon briefly explored the possibility of a ticket made up of MacArthur and Senator Harry F. Byrd, the conservative Virginia Democrat.

Ormsby McHarg, an "Old Guard" Republican who had been assistant secretary of commerce under President Taft, and John A. Schaefer organized the National Committee to Draft Bricker and MacArthur, but the group could never decide which of the candidates it would favor for the presidency and eventually split over the issue. McHarg withdrew in January and formed the MacArthur National Associates, maintaining that his new organization was based on the "moral certainty" that the general would accept the presidential nomination if he were chosen at the Republican convention. McHarg claimed that his headquarters in New York was soon "swamped with offers of support by Southern Jeffersonian Democrats, together with support of many of the same political affiliations in the North." In addition to such organized efforts, a number of politicians, including Fish, Brewster, and Eugene Talmadge, Georgia's former governor, made individual statements in behalf of MacArthur for President.

Vandenberg, who was disconcerted by this spontaneous babel that he could not control, later stated that "the most important 'free lancers' were Joseph P. Savage of Chicago (who nationalized the 'MacArthur Clubs'), General Leach of Minneapolis and Lansing Hoyt of Milwaukee." Major General George E. Leach had served as MacArthur's artillery chief in France in 1918, as head of the National Guard during the Hoover administration, and as Republican mayor of Minneapolis in 1921–29 and 1937–41. Savage, a well-to-do Chicago attorney, organized and headed the Illinois association of MacArthur clubs from August to December. In January, 1944, he was instrumental in forming a national association of MacArthur-for-President supporters, comprised of state organizations in Illinois, Missouri, West Virginia, Wisconsin, Massachusetts, Ohio, California, Indiana, and Wyoming, as well as a number of clubs in large cities in other states. Comparatively little effort was directed toward the South by any of the MacArthur groups, although the polls indicated that the agrarian South ranked second only to the Midwestern farm belt among the areas where the general's support was strongest.[8]

Adding mightily to the clamor for MacArthur were McCormick's Chicago *Tribune,* Joseph M. Patterson's New York *Daily News,* Cissy Patterson's Washington *Times-Herald,* and the Hearst publications, such as the San Francisco *Examiner.* Despite the affection and admiration that his wife had for MacArthur and Willoughby, Henry Luce did not lend the powerful resources of his *Time-Life-Fortune* empire to assist the movement. According to one story, however, he finally dispatched a *Life* correspondent to Brisbane to start, it was said, a promotional effort on MacArthur's behalf, but the boom for the general died a week or so before the reporter arrived in Australia. Luce's reasons for remaining aloof from the MacArthur excitement are not known, but he may have been influenced by the sheer hopelessness of the quixotic crusade or perhaps by the identification of certain extremists with the movement.

When Roosevelt haters of the most venomous variety, such as Gerald L. K. Smith, Father Coughlin, and William Dudley Pelley, began beating the drums for MacArthur, John Mc-Carten, who had been an associate editor of *Fortune* and *Time,* became alarmed: "The General's more respectable backers seem to be weaving a blanket large enough to cover all the dissident elements in the country, from Yorkville Bundists disguised as patriots to grass-root legislators catering to bucolic dreams of hermetic isolation." He continued, "It may not be his fault but it surely is his misfortune that the worst elements on the political Right, including its most blatant lunatic fringe, are whooping it up for MacArthur." Although some well-known hate-mongers with totalitarian traits did espouse the idea of MacArthur for the presidency, they did so as individuals, and none was identified with the Vandenberg, McHarg, or Savage movements.[9]

As the MacArthur boom continued unabated into early 1944, the War Department and White House seemed to start catering to MacArthur as if yielding to public pressure, or so thought the general's supporters. Actually, Stimson and Roosevelt probably were trying to avoid any appearance of hostility toward the SWPA commander during this politically sensitive period in order to avoid charges by antiadministration forces that the general was being neglected or balked militarily or politically. On January 20 Stimson stole an arrow from the opposition's quiver when, upon being asked by reporters if the general would be retired next week at the statutory retirement age of sixty-four, he replied, "Definitely no. I wouldn't worry about it if I were you." Moreover, as if it were a birthday present, the War Department announced on January 25 that MacArthur had been awarded a second Oak Leaf Cluster to his Distinguished Service

Medal for "exceptionally distinguished service as Supreme Commander of Allied Forces in the Southwest Pacific since March, 1943." Two weeks later the President stated that "regular officers of the armed services can accept such nominations for political office as come to them without solicitation by themselves." This meant MacArthur could accept the nomination if he were to be drafted by the Republican convention, but he could not authorize the use of his name in any preconvention campaigning or in the upcoming primaries. (The President's ruling also affected Stassen, who was then on active duty with the Navy.)[10]

At last the War Department would find itself deeply involved after the liberal *American Mercury* in January, 1944, published an article by McCarten that was the first detailed, critical look at MacArthur's leadership in the Philippine and Southwest Pacific campaigns. All previous articles that were critical of the general and were written by correspondents in his theater had been ruthlessly suppressed by GHQ SWPA or Australian censors. McCarten's sources were not revealed, but his information on the general and his operations was far more accurate than the picture conveyed in the GHQ communiqués. Indeed, McCarten's treatment of him as a military commander, though bluntly stated, was reasonably objective when judged by the evidence later revealed in the American and Australian official histories. But he tended to exaggerate the role of extremists when he wrote about the MacArthur presidential movement. Moreover, McCarten was too harsh in suggesting that the image of MacArthur as a hero was manufactured solely by the supranationalist press for political use against the Roosevelt administration. Undoubtedly without Stimson's or Marshall's knowledge, the McCarten article was recommended by the Army War College's library service in its monthly bulletin describing printed materials being disseminated by the Army to its units' libraries all over the world.

On March 9, Vandenberg delivered a blistering attack on the Senate floor against the War Department for distributing such "smear" literature to the troops.[11] Two days later MacArthur sent the following barrage to the War Department:

> The daily press here carried the following article: "Senator Vandenberg told the Senate that prejudicial partisan magazine articles were being circulated among the troops at home and abroad through the Army War College's library service. An article in the American Mercury, he said, entitled 'General Mac-Arthur: Fact and Legend,' which was being sent to the troops, was a 'smear article written for the purpose of making a definite attack on MacArthur.' Senator Vandenberg said that an Army library bulletin described the article as 'a comprehensive objective appraisal of the General as presidential timber, with special reference to the character of his backers and an analysis of his military reputation before Pearl Harbor and his leadership afterwards.' 'What business has the War Department in presenting a comprehensive objective appraisal of any man as presidential material?' shouted Senator Vandenberg. 'The War Department had better concentrate on the war abroad, instead of a political war at home.' "
>
> The article in question has been read by me. It is full of misstatements of facts, is in places scandalous in tone and even libelous in essence. Its bias is self-evident and was written by a man who has never even seen or talked with me. It has omitted the appraisal made in official records by the government of my services and, in fact, in large part makes no mention of those services themselves. It tends unquestionably to reduce the confidence of troops and the public in my military capacity to command. It repeats much of the Japanese radio propaganda against me. Such disparagement of one of our commanders helps the enemy's sabotage efforts. I protest the action of the War Department in circulating through military channels such an article, scandalous in itself and carrying on its face the War Department caption with an implied estimate of its reliability. I request that prompt action be taken to withdraw this article from official circulation, that full investigation be made of the circumstances of its issue and that I be informed of the facts of the matter.[12]

Although the article did contribute some authentic information about the general's traits, it was published in a magazine which, like other organs of the liberal press, had shown a determination to assault MacArthur's leadership ability regardless of its impact on his effectiveness as a key commander in the war against Japan. McCarten did not reveal military information vital to security in the Southwest Pacific theater, but instead enlightened the public on the previously unknown liabilities of a military leader who seemed nearly ready to enter national politics and about whom the people knew only his favorable side. If it had been published after 1951, McCarten's article probably would have been accepted as a commendable start toward an honest interpretation of the general, but its publication in 1944 made McCarten and the *American Mercury* vulnerable to charges of irresponsible journalism.

In retrospect, unless the writer violated regulations on the use of classified data, McCarten seemed to be within the bounds of good journalism even if his findings and interpretation reflected adversely on a high-ranking officer. "Nothing should discourage our enemies more," commented the *New York Times,* "than our ability to maintain free public discussion of vital issues and important personalities in the midst of war. We are strong enough to do this and the Germans and Japanese are not strong enough; and this is one of the very reasons why we shall certainly beat them." MacArthur, however, was on solid ground in charging that the War Department erred in permitting the publication to be distributed to troops with its apparent endorsement. Stimson and Marshall quickly realized this, ordered the article banned from the list of endorsed reading materials passed out to Army libraries, and apologized to MacArthur. The McCarten affair, which received considerable attention in the press, affected the MacArthur presidential boom like a two-edged sword: it buttressed his supporters' efforts to portray him as persecuted by the Roosevelt administration, but it also provided the public with the first published criticism of the SWPA chief.[13]

In February the War Department barred from publication in *Harper's Magazine* an article critical of MacArthur that was written by Walter Lucas, a correspondent for the London *Daily Express* who had spent eighteen months in the Southwest Pacific theater. The War Department said that approval was withheld "on the grounds of security. The article as written undermines the confidence of this country, Australia, and particularly the troops in that theater in their commander and his strategic and tactical plans." The editors of *Harper's*, headed by Frederick Lewis Allen, protested in vain to the White House that "although General MacArthur is protected by censorship from adverse criticism, he has not repudiated the persistent efforts which are being made to nominate him for the Presidency." [14] In their May issue, which appeared in April, the editors of *Harper's* wrote a strongly worded editorial in which they admitted that "censorship of criticism may sometimes be justifiable if military matters alone are at stake." But, they pointed out, "the present case wears another and graver aspect. As we go to press, General MacArthur has not denied receptiveness to a nomination for the Presidency of the United States. No candidate for the Presidency, tacit or otherwise, should be hidden behind a veil of censorship."

The editorial concluded:

> One may write what one pleases about the other candidates; about General MacArthur no opinions based on recent direct observation may apparently be given publicity unless they are flattering.
>
> This situation is intolerable in a free country. It may be that General MacArthur's apparent grievances against the Administration are justified. It may be that the many unfavorable criticisms of him which we have heard — even those which we sought to publish — have been misjudged. But that a man who

stands protected by censorship should permit his name to be considered for the Presidency mocks a central principle of democracy — the right of the people to see their political candidates in the light of free discussion.

Before this page reaches print the General may have unequivocally withdrawn his name. Or the censorship may have been relaxed. Otherwise let the public stand warned. The accounts of this candidate which have been appearing are incomplete, biased by censorship, and therefore politically unreliable.[15]

The *New York Times,* among other prominent newspapers, firmly backed the position of Allen and his fellow editors. No evidence was found of a War Department statement in response.[16]

The profusion of hastily written, adulatory books and articles on MacArthur in 1942–44 was astounding. No less than twelve books on the general, several of which appeared also in serialized or condensed form in magazines and newspapers, were turned out by different American publishers. Two others were written and published abroad, in Lisbon and Buenos Aires, the capitals of two pro-fascist regimes intensely hostile toward the Roosevelt administration. Among the earliest to appear in the United States were *General Douglas MacArthur: Fighter for Freedom* and *MacArthur the Magnificent,* which were as excessive in praise as the titles suggest; the first was penned by Francis T. Miller, a former editor of *Success Magazine,* and the latter by Bob Considine, a sports writer for the New York *Mirror.* Frank C. Waldrop, on the staff of the Washington *Times-Herald,* quickly put together in book form a collection of MacArthur's prewar speeches and reports, with the selections stressing his strong beliefs in patriotism and Christianity. Besides his coast-to-coast speaking tour on behalf of the Philippines and MacArthur, Romulo, the former Manila *Herald* editor and aide to MacArthur on Corregidor, published a book on the Philippine campaign that buttressed the portrayal of the general as a grim, hard-fighting commander committed to a forsaken cause. The two books that probably had the greatest number of factual errors and surely the worst expressions of hero-worship were William A. Kelley's *MacArthur: Hero of Destiny* and Helen Nicolay's *MacArthur of Bataan*.

At the zenith of the boom in early 1944 Frazier Hunt, the correspondent and trusted friend of MacArthur, happened to appear at GHQ in Brisbane. He quickly went to work on what seemed to be intended as a well-timed campaign biography. He enjoyed many interviews with the SWPA chief and was allowed to study some of his files, which he used uncritically in view of his apparent purpose. But, alas, his book, *MacArthur and the War Against Japan*, was slowed in the process of publication and appeared on the market a few months too late to assist the presidential drive. The only ones of the spate of hasty MacArthur books of 1942–44 that merited some respect were Hunt's book, principally because he had access to material denied to the others, and *Men on Bataan*, written by John Hersey of *Time*'s staff; the latter, however, also was largely a work of veneration and probably an embarrassment to the author during his later distinguished career.

When the above array of hymns of praise is considered, it is little wonder that McCarten's lonely contribution was welcomed by some thinking citizens who, though hero-hungry in the dark days of 1941–42, were now truth-hungry as they viewed MacArthur as a possible candidate. But even if the Lucas article had been printed, its impact, like McCarten's, would have been limited, for the mass of American readers had been conditioned by propaganda to accept an uncritical, almost incredible picture of MacArthur.[17]

Affected by the optimistic contagion of the boom, nearly all of the men whose confidential advice on nonmilitary matters MacArthur had trusted for years were unrealistic in their counsel to him. Fish wrote him in mid-1943 that if he ran on a "Win-the-War ticket" he would "carry all but two states of the

Union . . . We need an Army man at the head of the government and for some time after winning the war." O'Laughlin, publisher of the *Army and Navy Journal,* told him in late December that a respected political analyst said "you could carry 35 States . . . But, as you realize, it is another thing to translate this feeling into action." That month Moseley informed him of a rumor that Roosevelt would not seek re-election: "The Jews and the un-Americans are hoping that the President may run; but they are taking no chances. I understand they are supporting Willkie with all kinds of money, so that if he should be elected they will still be in the saddle." Typical of the innuendoes in letters from such advisers was his closing comment: "I hope that the honors coming to you in 1944 will surpass anything you have yet received from our country." MacArthur answered this type of correspondence with only oblique references to the presidential movement, as, for example, when he responded to the above letter from Moseley saying that his political observations were "of great interest and give food for much thought." [18]

Most of the general's contacts with Vandenberg's group were handled through Willoughby, Sutherland, Lehrbas, and Lieutenant Colonel Philip LaFollette, then serving on the GHQ SWPA staff and in the future to follow in the footsteps of his father, Robert M. LaFollette, and become governor of Wisconsin. The principal contacts seemed to be Willoughby with Vandenberg, Sutherland and Lehrbas with Howard, and LaFollette with Wood and McCormick. According to Willoughby, Colonel Courtney Whitney, who had joined MacArthur's staff in the late spring of 1943 to head the Philippine section of G-2, was also in touch with "influential persons" in the States. In November Wood wrote to MacArthur, "You are the only man that could defeat the President in 1944," to which the general responded, without mentioning politics, "My grateful thanks to you, Bob, for your real friendship. I hope I can repay it someday." About a week later Howard informed the SWPA com-

mander, "As of today the situation is lined up in a manner to
indicate that President Roosevelt very probably will not be a
candidate and that the odds are strongly favoring Dewey as the
Republican nominee . . . I must add, however, and would like
to emphasize that the situation is still fluid and very definitely
subject to change." Howard said he wanted to visit Brisbane
"before Spring," but MacArthur was not to extend him a direct
invitation. "I believe that because of the President's knowledge
of our long-time friendship, such an invitation, which would
certainly be immediately relayed to him if it went through the
censorship, might react disadvantageously."

By late fall the uncontrollable, bewildering profusion of interest groups that were organizing MacArthur-for-President activities left Vandenberg in a quandary: how effective could his
"underground" movement be under such circumstances? Another unexpected situation bothered him, too, as he explained
in a letter to Wood on November 5: "I am disturbed about one
thing which to me is quite inexplicable. I am constantly hearing
reports that veterans returning from the South[west] Pacific are
not enthusiastic about our friend. One skeptical correspondent
has gone so far as to suggest that there is some sort of diabolical
arrangement to see to it that only anti-MacArthur veterans are
furloughed home."

When Savage announced that his organization was planning
to enter MacArthur's name in the Illinois primary, Vandenberg's
dismay grew. He called a secret meeting of his "cabinet" at
Pew's farm near Paoli, Pennsylvania, in mid-January to discuss
their future strategy. The decisions were not recorded, but, according to Vandenberg's son, "it was obvious then and later that
the group was torn between the fear that they would not do
enough to create a MacArthur organization and the fear that
they would get the General involved in a premature political
battle that might knock him out before the fighting really
started." [19]

One product of that conference may have been Vandenberg's first major statement appealing to Republicans to help in drafting MacArthur. In an article entitled "Why I Am for MacArthur" which appeared in *Collier's* on February 12, he explained at length and in campaign-style language his three principal reasons for believing "he would make the strongest President in the tough days that lie ahead":

First . . . My correspondence suggests that many of our good people think MacArthur is so good a soldier that he ought to stay where he is . . . If he is indispensable to us as a four-star general, then we simply give our country and the United Nations the maximum use of his tremendous military genius when we promote him to commander in chief and thus give him total sway over the military decisions which we think he is so incomparably qualified to make . . .

Now for Reason No. 2: . . . The next President of the United States must make hard, harsh decisions every day of his administration when the time comes to put this country back on its postwar feet . . . He must have but one unselfish devotion . . . I know that MacArthur is the embodiment of loyalty to our American destiny at any cost . . . I know that he has never shirked a tough job in his life or compromised with it. He is granite in the face of duty . . . He would be elected, in this emergency, as something vastly more than a Republican in any narrow, partisan sense. He is utterly detached from our party schisms and our party feuds and our interparty divisions. More than any other Presidential possibility, he would be elected as a great, unifying American who would win his country's unified support by deserving it. The very nature of his draft, void of any obligation, save to his country, would dramatize and implement this selfless dedication . . .

Now let's come down to Reason No. 3. Although MacArthur has been a soldier all his life, I never knew a man in whom spiritual values are more predominant. He is infinitely more than a soldier . . . I find everlasting consolation and assurance in this simple Christian's reliance upon divine grace . . .

I think I know at firsthand something about what the next Presidency will require. I believe that General MacArthur has

what it takes in full measure. He is a composite of all our necessities. He is unique in respect to many of them. He has the
maturity of vast experience, yet he is in his physical and mental
prime. If nominated, he will be elected. If elected, he will bring
a great mind, a great heart, a great capacity and a great devotion
to the proud leadership of a great nation.[20]

As the senator probably realized, the destiny of the Mac-
Arthur draft depended not upon the campaigning of his and
other pro-MacArthur groups but rather upon the outcome of
the Dewey-Willkie duel. If defeats in the approaching primaries
compelled Willkie to withdraw, there would be no dark-horse
role for MacArthur at the convention. Since the MacArthur
boom's success rested on Willkie's ability to hold his own going
into the convention, perhaps General Wood would have been
wise to make some timely investments in Willkie's campaign.

2. *Unexpected Developments*

Speculation was rife by the winter of 1943–44 on MacArthur's
political intentions. As early as October 16, radio newscaster
Arthur Hale announced on the Mutual Broadcasting System's
evening news program, "A sensational whisper making the
rounds in high political circles has it that General Douglas Mac-
Arthur has definitely agreed to be a candidate in the 1944 presidential campaign." Quoting "persistent reports of reliable persons returning from Australia," the Indianapolis *Star* on December 22 said that the SWPA chief was making "tentative plans"
to return to America after retiring in late January, with Krueger
designated to succeed him in command. An unidentified
"spokesman" at GHQ SWPA, however, promptly told reporters
that the general "had no plans to return to the United States in
the near future . . . General MacArthur's ambition is still to
fly the American flag on Bataan as soon as he can."

The day after Christmas the *New York Times* carried a long editorial on the subject, stating that it was "one of the most fascinating enigmas on the eve of the opening of the 'political season.' " Perhaps intending the pun, the editorialist said, "The primary question is whether he is or is not a candidate." That same day in Australia the Sydney *Herald* declared, "Distasteful though it might be for a soldier to make repeated personal explanations of the situation developing in the United States, a further statement would be to the interests of all concerned." But MacArthur remained silent on the matter, dodging reporters' questions on his possible candidacy with the terse remark, suggested to him by Vandenberg, "Let's get on with the war." [21]

On January 19 in Brisbane, Frank Kluckhohn, a *New York Times* correspondent, had a meeting with MacArthur, Diller, and Lehrbas. Possibly by that time the general had received some word on the strategy decided at Vandenberg's Paoli conference. Nine days later the *Times*, undoubtedly relying on a report from Kluckhohn, published the only significant revelation of MacArthur's position that had appeared:

A recent visitor to Gen. MacArthur's headquarters in the Southwest Pacific has sent a report on political sentiment there. The summary was passed through the general's own military censorship.

The general, the report suggests, believes an experienced soldier in the White House would bring an earlier victory in the war.

"It would not be surprising," it says, "if Gen. MacArthur felt — as do a good many here — that the shortest way to victory would be to place an experienced military man in the White House."

The report reflects the impression at Southwest Pacific headquarters that the general will neither declare his availability for the Republican nomination nor withdraw his name from consideration, preferring to "let events take their course." It was emphasized that he was not taking any time out from war for politics, but that no one should assume this to mean that he would not be receptive to the Presidential nomination.

"Even if he were nominated," the report continues, "sources here believe it entirely possible that MacArthur would not leave his post to campaign. Talking to MacArthur supporters, of whom there are many here, I get the impression they foresee the possibilities this way:

"Gen. MacArthur will maintain complete silence on political matters pending the Republican National Convention, but his supporters will go into the convention with a fair bloc of votes from the Midwest. One figure is 125 delegates. This presumably would place him 3rd behind Gov. Thomas E. Dewey and Wendell L. Willkie.

"They believe Dewey and Willkie are likely to deadlock, whereupon MacArthur might emerge as a compromise candidate, since he is likely to have considerable second-choice strength among both Dewey and Willkie supporters.

"If nominated, it is believed MacArthur might accept by cable, explaining that his job of beating the Japs was too important to permit him to campaign. The campaign would be the responsibility of party leaders at home, with the general tossing in an occasional radio speech or public statement."

The report continues that in "some quarters here," there is a suggestion that MacArthur might be nominated for Vice President on a ticket headed by Dewey.

"But it is felt," according to this report, "that the general probably would not be receptive to such a suggestion and would scorn any pre-convention deal with Dewey, Willkie or any other candidate.

"But whether he actually would refuse the Vice Presidency should the convention offer it is entirely unknown. Such a ticket might be as attractive as anything the Republicans could offer, especially if the Presidential nominee announced that he planned to let Gen. MacArthur handle the job of winning the war." [22]

Opinions differ sharply among those who were around Mac-Arthur in 1943–44 about his real attitude toward the presidential nomination. Kenney said that, when he was visiting the general and his wife in their apartment at Lennon's Hotel one evening in early 1944, they discussed politics for "the first time." He cautioned MacArthur against believing "a lot of conversation among members of his staff" that as a candidate he "would sweep the country." Kenney advised him, "I didn't think anyone could defeat Roosevelt while the war was going on and I hoped that MacArthur wouldn't listen to the politicians in or out of the service who might try to persuade him to throw his hat in the ring. In the first place I suspected that most of them wanted to ride his coattails for their own interest more than his." MacArthur smiled, according to Kenney, and replied, "Don't worry. I have no desire to get mixed up in politics. The first mission that I want to carry out is to liberate the Philippines and fulfill America's pledge to that people. Then I want to defeat Japan."

Willoughby stated that, despite the efforts of the general's friends to persuade him, MacArthur was interested "only in the soldier's profession" and was "absolutely not" desirous of political office. Hunt maintained that the presidential boom was "unsolicited" and "embarrassing." According to Whitney, the SWPA commander "never took the movements seriously" and also was "not interested" in an alleged bid from Dewey later to accept the vice-presidential position on the Republican ticket. Colonel Laurence E. Bunker, who was then serving as secretary of Marshall's USAFFE staff and would become MacArthur's trusted aide in 1946–52 and later serve as vice president of the John Birch Society, commented, "What he wanted for himself was purely military. I'm convinced that he did not want to be President . . . He told me so personally on a number of occasions." Major General Charles H. Bridges, one of MacArthur's few friends who felt close enough to address him in letters as "Mac," maintained that the SWPA commander "is first, last and always a soldier and would rather command armies in time of

war than be President of the world. I do not believe he wants
to be President while his country is fighting for its very life."
In his memoirs MacArthur emphasized that he "had no political
ambitions whatsoever and only hoped to see Allied victory in
the war before retiring." [23]

On the other hand, Huff observed that the "idea wasn't unpleasant to MacArthur." As on other occasions when his staff
officers journeyed to the States, MacArthur told Huff, preparatory to the aide's trip home in 1943, "Keep your ear to the
ground." Huff said the remark "obviously referred to the fact
that he was being boomed for the Republican presidential
nomination." When he returned to Brisbane, Huff told his
chief, "One of the things people asked me was this: 'Why does
MacArthur carry that cane around all the time? Is he feeble?' "
The aide concluded, "Maybe it was a better job of reporting
than I thought then, because the General never carried the
stick again."

Marshall, the SWPA deputy chief of staff, believed that Mac-
Arthur's "supporters had worked him up to the point" where
he was interested in the nomination. Frederic S. Marquardt,
who had known MacArthur for years when he was an editor in
prewar Manila and later when he represented the Office of War
Information in the SWPA theater, was convinced that "he
wanted to be President very badly, no doubt about that." After
a visit from MacArthur a few days earlier, Eichelberger, who
was then training the I Corps near Rockhampton, recorded in
his diary on June 2, 1943: "My Chief talked of the Republican
nomination for next year — I can see that he expects to get it
and I sort of think so too." In his postwar dictations Eichelberger remarked of MacArthur's intentions, "Before the 1944
election he talked to me a number of times about the Presidency, but would usually confine his desires by saying that if it
were not for his hatred, or rather the extent to which he despised FDR, he would not want it."

Several weeks after the re-election of Roosevelt, A. H. Sulz-berger and Turner Catledge of the *New York Times* visited MacArthur at his new headquarters at Tacloban, Leyte. Cat-ledge, later to become the executive editor of the *Times,* "de-tected some jealousy of Roosevelt" in the general's remarks about the election. According to Catledge, MacArthur had been "definitely" interested in running for the presidency that year: "In private he talked a great deal in political terms, far more than other generals. I believe that he was hoping for a popular avalanche of support . . . but I do not think he had the stom-ach for campaigning. When the avalanche did not come, he backed out of the political picture reluctantly."

It is exceedingly difficult to believe that Willoughby, La-Follette, and other members of his staff actively served as sources of contact with political groups promoting MacArthur for presi-dent without some encouragement from the SWPA chief. In fact, some of Wood's and McCormick's correspondence to Mac-Arthur contain suggestions that he discuss a particular point of strategy in the underground campaign with one of the active members of his staff, and the general's office diary shows appoint-ments with such officers shortly after his receipt of the recom-mendations. It might have been that, instead of deceiving some of his staff or listening only to those who were optimistic about his chances, MacArthur underwent several changes of attitude toward the prospects of his candidacy during 1943–44. After all, it would be unprecedented for a commander in the field to return home to run for president. Even Major General George B. McClellan's electoral challenge to President Lincoln in 1864, an event that was recalled by some political analysts in 1944, was undertaken after the officer had been recalled from field command.[24]

Circumstantial evidence points sharply toward MacArthur's interest in the nomination. For example, Senators Brewster, Chandler, Lodge, Russell, and Mead found him generous with his time and keenly interested in political developments when they visited Port Moresby on September 9–11, 1943. Yet, as reported above, when Mrs. Franklin Roosevelt had arrived in Australia a few days earlier after a pleasant visit with Halsey at Noumea, MacArthur refused to allow her to come to Moresby and would not return to Australia to receive her. In his memoirs the general said, "She wished to come to New Guinea, but I thought it too dangerous. We were old friends and she took my refusal in good part." But she informed her husband on September 6, "Word came last night from Gen. MacArthur that it would require too many high-ranking officers to escort me in Port Moresby & he c[ou]ld not spare them at this time when a push is on. This is the kind of thing that seems to me silly. I'd rather have a Sergeant & I'd see & hear more." Later she wrote to a friend, "General MacArthur was too busy to bother with a lady." The SWPA chief, as mentioned earlier, assigned Eichelberger to escort her during her Australian visit.

On September 13, the eve of the First Lady's departure, Mrs. MacArthur hosted a large dinner at Lennon's in her honor, but the SWPA commander adamantly refused to attend and remained at Moresby from August 25 to September 24. Certainly Cartwheel was in progress, but a theater commander's most pressing responsibilities are in the planning stages; during the actual operations he can usually just wait or observe from a distance. Unless there was some emergency not revealed in the official records, it seems that he could have spared Eleanor Roosevelt some time, especially when one regards the hospitality he bestowed upon the junketing senators. It strongly appears, in view of the political situation, that his primary consideration may have been that the news articles and photographs of him with the First Lady would have been repugnant to potential supporters among the Roosevelt haters in the States.[25]

Other aspects of MacArthur's behavior also seem, in retrospect, to have been influenced by political ambition. It is no credit to his superior mental ability, which even his critics acknowledged, to assert that his self-glorifying communiqués and careful censorship of critical news stories written by correspondents in his theater were motivated solely by his egotism.

Although his releases might merely annoy or amuse military authorities in Washington, they contributed significantly to the molding of his hero-martyr image, the widespread acceptance of which facilitated the efforts of the MacArthur-for-President groups. Moreover, to an extent far greater than any other theater commander, he was eager to cooperate with every civic, labor, industrial, church, or other organization that requested a message from him for some occasion. The voluminous files of his correspondence with civilian associations and individuals reveal an amazing network of contacts with a wide variety of interest groups in every region of the country, which, again, proved invaluable to those leaders engaged in promoting his political fortunes.

Yet one of the most telling bits of evidence that he desired the presidency was his response to a letter from Wood on December 30, 1943. The Sears executive, exhibiting some consternation, notified him that Savage's organization was entering the general's name in the Illinois presidential preference primary. Wood also relayed advice from McCormick, with which he apparently agreed, that it would be "unwise" to test the general's vote-getting strength at that time. Wood enclosed a certificate of withdrawal from the primary for MacArthur to sign and return if he so decided, and he urged the SWPA chief to discuss the matter with LaFollette. MacArthur refused to sign the certificate.[26]

In his article of January, 1944, McCarten pointed out MacArthur's failure to visit his troops on the front lines of Bataan and New Guinea. Whether this accusation had some bearing on his decision to land at Los Negros in February is debatable, but it was true that he had not been near the front after his exit from the Philippines in early 1942. Since a theater commander's duties did not require frequent trips to areas of battle, it was not incumbent upon MacArthur to defend his absence, much less to try to refurbish his reputation as a combat leader, which he had firmly established in World War I. But MacArthur apparently decided that a counterattack was necessary lest McCarten's revelation damage his image as a fighting general during the critical period of the presidential boom.

On January 26, 1944, which was his sixty-fourth birthday and which was also Australia Day, the 156th anniversary of the commonwealth's founding, MacArthur made a bizarre visit to Eichelberger and his I Corps, then engaged in a command post exercise in the hilly jungle country near Rockhampton, about 300 miles north of Brisbane. Diller and Lehrbas, his top public relations officers, accompanied him on the flight to Rockhampton, where they obtained a Packard limousine and drove to Eichelberger's field post. At the time, Eichelberger said, the troops were engaged nearby in "a very realistic scene" of mock jungle warfare.

MacArthur insisted on transferring from the Packard to a jeep, and Eichelberger personally drove him around the area of the field exercise. "There was quite a battery of photographers" taking pictures of him in the jeep and as he stood talking in front of some jungle tents, observed Eichelberger, who was somewhat puzzled by the amount of picture-taking. At the end of the tour, he said, "We were directed to send all negatives to his [MacArthur's] headquarters and he selected the ones which were not to be destroyed. A number of these were sent to all the papers in the United States under such captions as 'General MacArthur at the Front with Gen. Eichelberger in New Guinea.'" Eichelberger was "amused" later when he saw one of the photographs bearing that caption in an American newspaper. "The dead giveaway," he noticed, "was the unmistakable nose of a Packard motorcar in one corner of the picture. There weren't any Packards in the New Guinea jungle in early 1944." [27]

As voters and political hopefuls braced themselves for the approaching spring primaries, various MacArthur-for-President groups, excluding Vandenberg's, were busy circulating petitions to get the general's name on the primary ballots in states where the laws did not require the consent of the man named as a candidate. They succeeded in getting the required number of petitioners in Illinois and Wisconsin, thanks to the energetic MacArthur organizations in those states. In California several large-circulation newspapers, especially the Los Angeles *Times* and San Francisco *Examiner,* were pro-MacArthur, and early prognostications indicated that he would get a strong vote if his name were entered in that state's presidential preference primary, to be held in May. O'Laughlin reported to MacArthur on December 23 that an authoritative political observer had told him that the general "could win handily" in California. Also that month, John Hamilton released a private survey that showed MacArthur's voter appeal as "strongest on the West Coast but tapering off as you come eastward."

Nevertheless, the MacArthur boom was never effectively organized in California, and when the time expired in March for certification of slates for that state's primary, only 390 of the necessary 6377 signatures were on the petition to qualify the MacArthur delegation. Allen H. Worcester and John Mac-Loghlin, leaders of the MacArthur-for-President organization in the Los Angeles area, sought an order from the California Supreme Court to require county clerks to provide a special space on the ballot so voters could write in the MacArthur slate, but in late April the court denied their request without comment.[28]

From the standpoint of entries and consequences, the most important of the 1944 primaries was that in Wisconsin. It was the only one in which the names of Dewey, Willkie, MacArthur, and Stassen were entered; Bricker was the only serious Repub-

lican contender who did not compete. Willkie conducted a
vigorous seventeen-day campaign in Wisconsin during which he
journeyed 1500 miles and delivered forty speeches. His book,
One World, published in April, 1943, had already sold a million
copies, and Willkie told his Wisconsin listeners that its popularity indicated the nation's mood, which was moving away from
narrow partisanship and isolationism. Dewey, somewhat wary
of the Wisconsin primary, tried in vain to have his name withdrawn, but his followers campaigned actively for the slate bearing his name. Stassen was still on naval duty in the Pacific, but
his supporters hoped for strong backing in the counties bordering Minnesota, where he had been a popular two-term governor
and was widely regarded as "an earnest young man with a sense
of mission." Besides the efforts of the Leach and Hoyt forces,
John Schaefer, head of the Bricker-or-MacArthur national organization, came to Wisconsin to campaign for the MacArthur
slate. "The real choice before the State's electorate," claimed
Schaefer, "is a favorite son, General MacArthur, or an out-
lander, Wendell Willkie."

Three weeks before the primary, which was held on April 4,
Vandenberg commented dejectedly, "I have simply had to wash
my hands of the Wisconsin situation. It is entirely too complex
to be handled intelligently at arm's length. But I still hope that
we shall be spared a catastrophe at that point." It seemed to him
that "the trends have more definitely turned in Governor
Dewey's direction." The primary returns in Wisconsin proved,
indeed, to be a major victory for Dewey: of the twenty-four
delegates to the Republican convention, he won fifteen, with
two uninstructed delegates also favoring him. Stassen got four
delegates, MacArthur three, and Willkie none. The popular
vote approximated the delegate count, with Willkie delegates
finishing last in every part of the state. His last-place finish
prompted Willkie a few days later to announce his withdrawal
from the race for the Republican presidential nomination.

Schaefer thought that "General MacArthur's showing, considering the fact that he was silent during the campaign, was highly complimentary to his Wisconsin advocates." But Vandenberg correctly saw MacArthur's chances as having disappeared, now that a convention deadlock was impossible. "It is all over but the shouting," he said on April 10. "I have written Australia and frankly presented this picture." [29]

Yet MacArthur was to have a brief but hollow moment of political glory a week later in the Illinois presidential preference primary where he won easily because none of the other major Republican contenders was entered. He got over 550,000 votes compared to about 37,000 for his Republican opponent, Riley Bender, a Chicago real-estate man who was a political unknown. But Arthur Krock, a respected journalist and political observer on the *New York Times* staff, did not scoff at the general's seemingly empty triumph. Looking ahead to June, he warned that "the danger in the acceleration of the MacArthur movement" was that at the Republican convention the Midwestern isolationists would try to force the presidential nominee to defer to their supranationalism by threatening him "with the loss of areas essential to his election." [30]

Krock was severely critical of the role of McCormick's *Tribune* in influencing the voters:

Illinois Republicans seem still to be represented by the opinions of the *Tribune*, which published on its first page the day before the primary a recommended list of candidates who, or the most important of whom, were overwhelmingly chosen.

The Republican party in the nation must face this regional fact, just as the Democrats must accept strong objection to a fourth term and other dissatisfactions with the administration which exist widely in that party, particularly in the South. One condition will plague the candidates and platform to be selected by the Republicans in June. The other will plague the candidates and platform to be selected by the Democrats in July.

The half million or more Republicans in Illinois who registered a preference for Gen. MacArthur as President can know
little or nothing of his views on the issues that agitate the *Tribune,* both national and international. But on its first page
Monday they read: "The chance to express sentiment against
the New Deal by voting for Gen. MacArthur . . . will increase
tomorrow's turnout in a generally dull state-wide primary, political sages said yesterday." And in a banner headline across page
one they read: "Sanction Red Land Grabs: Polish, Baltic Seizures are O.K.'d by Hull." To all who share such interpretations,
and in Illinois they are numerous, the name of the General on
the ballot was a beckoning beacon, and substantially he had no
rival.

Also, it is generally believed, and the impression is not confined to readers of the *Tribune,* that Gen. MacArthur is dissatisfied with the military strategy of the war as approved by the
President and Prime Minister Churchill. This made an attractive psychological combination for voters, conditioned, as Illinois Republicans so long have been, to oppose the administration's record at home and abroad and to suspect its post-war
plans.[31]

Krock's prediction, of course, would be proved correct in June
when Dewey was compelled to accept as his running mate the
outspokenly isolationist Ohio governor, Bricker.

With the chances of the general's nomination waning, a
well-meaning admirer, who had hitherto played no significant
role in the drive, came to the fore with a maneuver intended to
preserve the boom. On April 14, Representative Albert L.
Miller of Nebraska, a conservative Republican and surgeon-
turned-politician, startled the nation by releasing to the press his
correspondence with MacArthur during the previous half year,
consisting of two letters to the general and two revealing ones
from him. On September 18, 1943, Miller had written the
SWPA commander denouncing the domestic and military policies of the President and urging MacArthur to accept the presidential nomination, which the congressman was "most certain"
the Republican Party would offer him. "You owe it to civiliza-

tion and to the children yet unborn" to run and defeat Roosevelt, said Miller, for "unless this New Deal can be stopped our
American way of life is forever doomed." MacArthur replied
on October 2: "I thank you so sincerely for your fine letter . . .
I do not anticipate in any way your flattering predictions, but I
do unreservedly agree with the complete wisdom and statesman-
ship of your comments."

Miller wrote a second letter to the general on January 27, in
which he continued his denunciation of the Roosevelt administration: "If this system of left-wingers and New Dealism is continued another four years, I am certain that this Monarchy
which is being established in America will destroy the rights of
the common people." He wanted MacArthur, as "Commander-
in-Chief and President of a free America," to "destroy this
monstrosity . . . which is engulfing the nation and destroying
free enterprise and every right of the individual." On February
11 MacArthur answered Miller, thanking him for his "scholarly
letter." The general said, "Your description of conditions in
the United States is a sobering one indeed and is calculated to
arouse the thoughtful consideration of every true patriot." He
continued, "Like Abraham Lincoln, I am a firm believer in the
people, and, if given the truth, they can be depended upon to
meet any national crisis." As for the Southwest Pacific situation, he added, "Out here we are doing what we can with what
we have. I will be glad, however, when more substantial forces
are placed at my disposition." Miller remarked on April 15
that he had recently written another letter "urging the General to state definitely that he was available for the Presidency,"
but he declined to make its exact contents public.[32]

Senator Gerald P. Nye, the isolationist Republican from
North Dakota, told reporters that the letters "mean that if the
people of the United States want General MacArthur for President, they can have him." Senator John Thomas, Republican
of Idaho, agreed that the letters suggested MacArthur was "in
a receptive mood," but he felt the publication of the corre-

spondence had "come too late" to help in getting him nominated. Senator Dennis Chavez, Democrat of New Mexico, thought the Democrats should "beat the Republicans to the gun and draft MacArthur for Secretary of War." The *New York Times* said that the general reaction noted by its reporters interviewing various political leaders was that MacArthur was receptive and "did not push aside the suggestion." Ernest K. Lindley, a *Newsweek* columnist, commented that the letters "supported a conclusion based on earlier evidence: MacArthur is a receptive, at heart possibly eager, candidate for the Republican Presidential nomination." John O. Donnell, of the Washington *Times-Herald,* was sharply critical of Miller's "political judgment" in giving "to the ears of the world a communication written in the honest conviction that it was a private and personal communication." Isidor F. Stone, writing in *The Nation,* stated bluntly that the letters revealed MacArthur "in a very unsoldierly posture — disloyal to his Commander-in-Chief and a rather pompous and ignorant ass." [33]

"A furor was raised by the unauthorized publication," MacArthur later said, so he "tried to clear the atmosphere" by issuing the following statement on April 17:

> My attention has been called to the publication by Congressman Miller of a personal correspondence with him. In so far as my letters are concerned they were never intended for publication. Their perusal will show any fair-minded person that they were neither politically inspired nor intended to convey blanket approval of the Congressman's views. I entirely repudiate the sinister interpretation that they were intended as criticism of any political philosophy or any personages in high office. They were written as amiable acknowledgments, to a member of our highest law-making body, of letters containing flattering and friendly remarks to me. To construe them otherwise is to misrepresent my intent. I have not received Congressman Miller's third letter in which he is reported to advise me to announce candidacy for the office of President of the U.S.

The high Constitutional processes of our representative and republican form of government, in which there resides with the people the sacred duty of choosing and electing their Chief Executive, are of so imposing a nature as to be beyond the sphere of any individual's coercion or decision. I can only say as I have said before, I am not a candidate for the office nor do I seek it. I have devoted myself exclusively to the conduct of war. My sole ambition is to assist my beloved country to win this vital struggle by the fulfillment of such duty as has been or may be assigned to me.[34]

Vandenberg called Miller's action a "tragic mistake" and a "magnificent 'boner' " which made the general's position "untenable." The senator became exasperated when "after making his first raw mistake (and getting himself limelighted on all the first pages of the country) Miller proceeded to continue his *public* bombardment of MacArthur (*after* the whole thing was practically all over)." On April 18, referring to MacArthur's statement, Miller told the press that it "indicates definitely that he is receptive, and I feel that he will wait no longer than six weeks to make it certain and definite in an announcement." Miller then proceeded to deliver a speech in the House of Representatives extolling MacArthur and defending his own action. He told his fellow congressmen that he "wanted to be just a good chore boy and assume full responsibility for the release of the correspondence."

On April 22 he wrote to MacArthur, "I have been just a bit unhappy and a bit apprehensive that the release of our correspondence may have caused you a little embarrassment . . . My purpose was to bring before the people a great American whom I considered most competent to lead us for the next four years." Enlightening the general further, he added, "I do want to be your servant and do your bidding. Perhaps my surgeon technique will help you to appreciate the fact that I have frequently, as a physician, found it necessary to make a swift, clean stroke to the root of the problem. The medicine is sometimes bitter but the result in the final end is good." [35] There is no record of an answer from MacArthur.

Miller continued his embarrassing, fumbling efforts to defend his action, and public dissatisfaction mounted over what seemed to many to be only a halfhearted denial by MacArthur — "I am not a candidate for the office nor do I seek it" — which did not exclude acceptance of a draft. Because his "formal disavowal failed to pacify the angry critics," MacArthur said, he "felt it necessary" to issue another statement on April 30:

> Since my return from the Hollandia operation I have had brought to my attention a number of newspaper articles professing in strongest terms a widespread public opinion that it is detrimental to our war effort to have an officer in high position on active service at the front, considered for nomination for the office of President. I have on several occasions announced I was not a candidate for the position. Nevertheless, in view of these circumstances, in order to make my position entirely unequivocal, I request that no action be taken that would link my name in any way with the nomination. I do not covet it nor would I accept it.[36]

Remarkably knowledgeable about the episode, the Soviet newspaper *Izvestia* informed its readers that with MacArthur's withdrawal "President Roosevelt had increased his chances for a 4th term." This apparently was not disappointing to *Izvestia,* as it pointed out that the MacArthur movement "had been strongly supported by the McCormick press," which was vehemently anti-Communist and isolationist. The London *Times* commented that the general's statement "helps to clear the political air . . . He would have been a source of trouble. His genuine admirers, like, for instance, Senator Vandenberg, of Michigan, are one thing, but those who would inevitably have tried to use him to promote their own brand of reaction are quite another." The *New York Times* praised his decision as "blunt and unequivocal" and added that his "friends and well-wishers should take this as final, as it was obviously meant to be taken . . . Gen. MacArthur can continue to serve his country best precisely in the position he holds. He is a fearless and inspiring military leader. His strategy in the Pacific area — particularly when one considers the limited forces at his disposal — has been not merely well but brilliantly executed."

Most of the general's friends in the States praised his withdrawal as a wise decision, but some intimated that he should not consider it as binding four years later, and other persons, mainly admiring citizens of little or no acquaintance, pleaded with him to reconsider. On April 30, Vandenberg recorded an entry in his diary under the heading "The MacArthur Boom Bursts," in which he disputed MacArthur's stated reason for his action, namely that "widespread public opinion" indicated "it is detrimental to our war effort to have an officer in high position on active service at the front" considered for the presidency. Vandenberg wrote, "That is not the *real* reason. If it were, he would have said it long ago." The senator's opinion was that MacArthur had two reasons: the embarrassing Miller episode and the overwhelming momentum of the Dewey drive. "I can fully understand why MacArthur found it necessary to act summarily," wrote the senator, "and (deeply as I regret that he cannot be nominated) I applaud his statement." Curtin, who was in Washington that spring, told MacArthur that Roosevelt was "obviously delighted" when the prime minister assured him "in utter honesty and sincerity" that the general would not run against him. This story, told by MacArthur, does not jibe, however, with Leahy's statement about a talk with Roosevelt shortly after they heard the news of MacArthur's announcement of April 30. According to the admiral, "The President did not show much interest in the announcement," though Leahy observed that MacArthur "would be a very dangerous antagonist for anybody." [37]

As much as MacArthur and Vandenberg must have yearned by that time for the boom to expire quickly and quietly so that they might avoid further humiliation, McHarg suddenly proclaimed on May 13 that "nothing short of General MacArthur's personal appearance in this country and his personal veto when made familiar with the facts would prevent presentation of his name as a candidate for President at the [Republican] National Convention." When the Republicans met at Chicago on June 26–29, the business of the convention moved along smoothly until the roll was called for presidential nominating speeches. Vandenberg was suddenly tipped off that Dr. John Koehler of Wisconsin "was about to ruin everything (including Mac-Arthur) by making a 30-minute nominating speech for him." The Michigan senator "felt it would be an insufferable humiliation" for MacArthur "to wind up with only one or two votes. I was also afraid the convention would yell down the Wisconsin delegate (which might be a further reflection on MacArthur)."

Vandenberg warned Chairman Joseph E. Martin, who agreed to rush along the roll call while he kept Koehler in conversation on the convention floor. According to Martin's version, Vandenberg "engaged him just long enough for me to give Wisconsin the barest time I decently could on the roll call. By the time Koehler got past Vandenberg, Wyoming had been called, and I ruled him out of order." The maneuver so infuriated farmer Grant A. Ritter, another member of the Wisconsin delegation, which included three MacArthur supporters, that he kept the convention's final presidential nominating vote from being unanimous, as is customary. Instead, the final ballot read: Dewey, 1056 votes; MacArthur, one vote.[38] Almost hopeless from the start but reflecting an important, continuing facet of the nation's political spectrum, the MacArthur boom finally was buried — at least for four more years.

PART IV

Advance to the Philippines

CHAPTER XI

Victories and Complications

1. A 580-Mile Leap

THE CARTWHEEL OPERATIONS had left at least 140,000 Japanese isolated by April, 1944, principally at Rabaul, Kavieng, and Bougainville. But, whereas in November, 1943, nine enemy divisions had been stationed east of Java, now there were seventeen defending the new primary line of defense, which ran from Timor through Dutch New Guinea and the Palaus to the Marianas. Lieutenant General Fusataro Teshima's 50,000-man Second Army, together with the 300 or more aircraft of the 6th and 7th air divisions, were dispatched to the Wakde, Sarmi, Biak, and Manokwari bases in Dutch New Guinea. Imperial General Headquarters was much more concerned about MacArthur's expected drive along the New Guinea coast than with the offensive in the Central Pacific. In Northeast New Guinea, Adachi's Eighteenth Army, battered but still 55,000 strong, was retreating to the Hansa Bay–Wewak region. Because Imamura's Eighth Area Army headquarters at Rabaul was cut off, Adachi's forces were placed under the Second Area Army of General Korechika Anami, whose headquarters was at Davao. Anami also controlled the Nineteenth Army, stationed in the Banda

Sea islands, west of New Guinea, and the Second Army, whose headquarters was set up at Manokwari on the northeast coast of the Vogelkop Peninsula.

Although two Japanese armies now defended New Guinea, they were widely separated: between Teshima's 36th Division in the Wakde-Sarmi vicinity and Adachi's 51st Division at Wewak lay a 300-mile stretch of coastline that was lightly defended. In late March and early April, the Fifth Air Force virtually wiped out the aircraft of the Japanese 6th Air Division at Hollandia and Aitape. The garrison at Hollandia numbered about 11,000 and that at Aitape roughly 1000 men, but only a fifth of them were combat troops; the rest were service personnel and pilots and crews without aircraft. The 51st Division was scheduled to move to Hollandia in conjunction with the projected development of a major air and supply base there, but Adachi told Anami that it would be July before the entire division could get to the newly assigned station. The Eighteenth Army commander fully expected MacArthur's next move to be against Hansa Bay or Wewak in May. After all, the nearest SWPA base to Hollandia in mid-April was at Saidor, nearly 600 miles down the coast. Anami was distressed by the weakness of the defenses at Hollandia and sent his chief of staff to Wewak on April 12 to expedite the 51st's westward movement. Adachi reluctantly agreed to release two regiments to march to Hollandia. Their expected date of arrival was early May.

At SWPA GHQ in February and March, evidence garnered from enemy radio messages, which Akin's cryptanalysts intercepted and decoded, as well as from captured Japanese documents, which Mashbir's translators and interpreters analyzed, clearly revealed the defensive weakness of Hollandia. Willoughby was persuaded as was Fellers, planning section chief of G-3, but Chamberlin considered an assault against Hollandia too much of a gamble and preferred to go ahead with the scheduled landing at Hansa Bay. Fellers said that when he tried to

discuss the idea with Chamberlin, "he hit the ceiling and ordered me to drop the wild scheme." Instead, Fellers went
around the G-3 and presented the plan to MacArthur, who was
very interested. This maneuver infuriated Chamberlin, and
Fellers shortly found himself relieved of his G-3 position. He
was subsequently appointed MacArthur's military secretary and
also worked with the psychological warfare section of G-2.

Meanwhile, MacArthur had studied the Hollandia proposal
and boldly decided to bypass both Hansa Bay and Wewak and
attack Aitape and Hollandia in the third week of April. Hollandia's harbor, on Humboldt Bay, would provide the only
sheltered anchorage between Wewak and Geelvink Bay. Also,
MacArthur figured, "we would have air strips from which our
ground-based aircraft could dominate the Vogelkop, and our
advance westward would be hastened by several months." For
the first time Barbey's amphibious force had enough landing
vessels to transport a sizable invasion force, and, as mentioned
earlier, Mitscher's fast carriers were soon promised by Nimitz to
provide air support. Aitape was added to the plan not only because it would provide additional air strips but also because its
seizure would prevent the Japanese Eighteenth Army from advancing westward to Hollandia. At a GHQ staff conference on
April 9, Chamberlin proposed that the 24th Division land at
Tanahmerah Bay, twenty-five miles west of Humboldt Bay,
while the 41st Division struck inland from Hollandia to catch
the Japanese in a pincers movement near Lake Sentani. Kenney
protested that his aerial photographs showed Tanahmerah Bay
had no beaches suitable for landing a division. MacArthur,
however, accepted Chamberlin's plan, assuring Kenney that he
would be present at the Tanahmerah landing himself and, if
the beaches were unsatisfactory, would send the 24th Division
to Humboldt Bay to debark.[1]

Eichelberger, in his first combat assignment since Buna,
was appointed by MacArthur to head the Reckless Task Force,

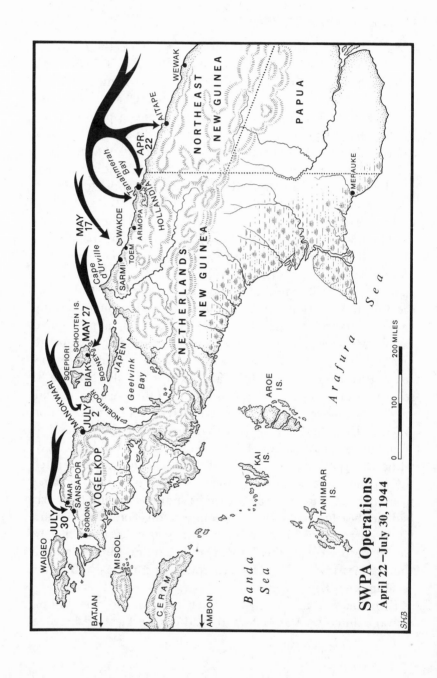

SWPA Operations
April 22–July 30, 1944

whose units would seize the region between Tanahmerah and Humboldt bays. Major General Horace H. Fuller's 41st Division, less one regiment, would land at Tanahmerah Bay and advance inland toward Lake Sentani, while Major General Frederick A. Irving's 24th Division would seize Hollandia and push on to rendezvous with Fuller's troops near the three Sentani air strips. North of fifteen-mile-long Lake Sentani and lying between the two bays were the Cyclops Mountains; both divisions were to avoid the rugged range in favor of quicker movement along the lake shoreline. Brigadier General Jens A. Doe would head the Persecution Task Force, whose mission was to seize Aitape and the nearby air strips at Tadji. Doe would have the 163rd Regimental Combat Team of Fuller's division and the 127th Regiment of the veteran 32nd Division. Altogether, 217 ships would be employed to transport, protect, and land nearly 80,000 men, of whom about 50,000 were combat troops. This was to be the largest SWPA operation to date, and the logistical problems were many, especially for Barbey, whose VII Amphibious Force had the responsibility of carrying the invaders to the beaches from three far-off staging areas, the principal one being at Goodenough Island, over 1000 miles to the south.

Fortunately, Japanese air power would be no immediate threat; true to his promise to Nimitz, Kenney had sent his planes against the air bases at Wewak, Hansa Bay, Aitape, and Hollandia so regularly and relentlessly that by D-day only twenty-five serviceable enemy aircraft were left in the entire area. Meanwhile, everything possible was done to confirm Adachi's belief that Hansa Bay or Wewak would be the next invasion target. Both bases were bombed by the Fifth Air Force more frequently than the actual objectives of the invasion, and Kinkaid's destroyers made several bombardment sweeps against Wewak and Hansa Bay in March and early April. In addition, PT boats conducted nightly patrols in that area, dummy parachutists were dropped near Wewak, and submarines dumped life rafts offshore, all to delude Adachi into believing that the Wewak–Hansa Bay area was being reconnoitered prior to an invasion.[2]

The huge invasion force's several convoys rendezvoused on April 21 west of the Admiralties and headed north, intending to keep the enemy from determining the objective should the expedition have been spotted by reconnaissance planes. Suddenly, the armada swung southwest during the night, and on the muggy morning of April 22, after heavy air and naval bombardments, the three landings began simultaneously at Tanahmerah Bay, south of Hollandia, and east of Aitape. One Japanese commander later admitted, "The morning that we found out that the Allies were going to come to Hollandia, they were already in the harbor . . . It certainly was a surprise." As Kenney had predicted, the Tanahmerah beaches were unsuitable and backed by deep swamps, so after one of Fuller's regiments had debarked, the other regiment was transported to Humboldt Bay. Fortunately, the astonished defenders offered only weak resistance during the chaotic debarkation. The regiment that went ashore, the 21st, was hampered more by heavy rain and difficult terrain than by Japanese opposition as it pushed inland. It reached the westernmost of the three air strips near Lake Sentani on April 26 and secured it that day against sporadic resistance.

The 24th Division also encountered negligible opposition when its troops landed three miles south of Hollandia. On D-day the 186th Regiment captured Pim, four miles south of Hollandia, and struck inland toward Lake Sentani, while the 162nd Regiment turned north, seizing Hollandia on the 23rd. Using amphibious tractors, some elements of the 186th crossed the lake to Nefaar, a village near the air strips, and the rest of the regiment arrived there on the 25th. The next day they seized the other two air strips and made contact with the 21st

Regiment. The only serious enemy counterattack occurred on the 27th near the westernmost air strip, but it was easily repulsed. The Tanahmerah-Hollandia area was secured at a cost of 159 American lives; 3300 Japanese were killed, most of them in the mop-up during the following weeks, and over 600 surrendered, the first sizable haul of prisoners taken in MacArthur's theater. Caught without adequate defensive positions, the other 7000 Japanese fled through the jungles toward Sarmi, 140 miles to the west, but, because of deaths from disease, starvation, and wounds, only about 1000 reached the base. Anami had wanted to send the 36th Division to attack the Hollandia invaders, but General Hisaichi Terauchi, the Southern Army commander, then at Manila, insisted that the division remain in place to defend the Wakde-Sarmi area.[3]

Meanwhile, nine miles east of Aitape on April 22 there had been little opposition to the debarkation of Doe's troops, many of whom had fought at Sanananda fifteen months earlier. They quickly turned westward and seized the Tadji air strips; Aitape was captured on the 24th, and three tiny offshore islands were secured on April 23–25. In shore-to-shore operations, April 28–May 1, the Persecution Task Force advanced as far as Babiang, thirty-five miles east of Aitape, again meeting only token resistance. Three Americans died in the Aitape operation; about 625 Japanese were killed and twenty-seven surrendered. The rest, about 300, fled toward Wewak, 100 miles east of Aitape.[4] MacArthur triumphantly reported in a communiqué on April 24:

> Complete surprise and effective support, both surface and air, secured our initial landings with slight losses . . . The operation throws a loop of envelopment around the enemy's Eighteenth Army, dispersed along the coast of New Guinea in the Madang, Alexishafen, Hansa Bay, Wewak sectors, similar to the Solomons and Bismarck loops of envelopment. To the east are the Australians and Americans; to the west the Americans; to

the north the sea controlled by our Allied naval forces; to the south untraversed jungle mountain ranges; and over all our Allied air mastery. This enemy army is now completely isolated . . . His invested garrisons can be expected to strike desperately to free themselves and time and combat will be required to accomplish their annihilation, but their ultimate fate is now certain. Their situation reverses Bataan. The present operation when completed frees British New Guinea from enemy control, and is the first recapture of Dutch territory in the war.[5]

As he had pledged to Kenney, MacArthur was on hand for the invasion of the Hollandia area. On April 18, he, Diller, Lehrbas, Egeberg, and Johnson had flown in the general's B-17, *Bataan,* to Port Moresby. There they picked up photographer Faillace and several correspondents, flew on to Finschhafen, and, with Krueger joining the caravan, departed aboard the cruiser *Nashville* on the morning of the 19th. Before joining the Hollandia invasion force, the *Nashville* detoured to Cape Gloucester where MacArthur went ashore briefly to pay his first and only visit to Rupertus' 1st Marine Division, marooned there since December but soon to be relieved by the Army's 40th Division. "The General shook hands all around," stated one of Rupertus' staff. "He was very affable and gave you the impression that he was very glad to see you again (although he had never seen you before)." The divisional band tried to play for MacArthur, but "their lips began to go flabby from lack of practice. They had to stop." In view of the Marines' bitterness after being stuck on the desolate western end of New Britain for four months, MacArthur's surprise visit there may have required more courage than his widely publicized trip to the beachheads in Dutch New Guinea.

MacArthur eagerly watched the pre-invasion bombardment of the Hollandia-Pim beaches from the *Nashville* on April 22. At 11:00 A.M., exactly four hours after the first assault wave had landed, the SWPA commander visited the Pim area, accom-

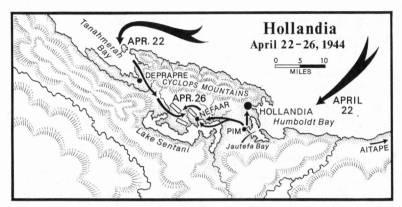

Hollandia
April 22–26, 1944

Tanahmerah Bay

APR. 22

0 5 10
MILES

DEPRAPRE
CYCLOPS MOUNTAINS

APR. 26

NEFAAR

Lake Sentani

PIM

HOLLANDIA
Humboldt Bay

Jautefa Bay

APRIL 22

AITAPE

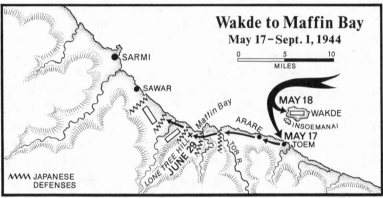

Wakde to Maffin Bay
May 17–Sept. 1, 1944

SARMI

SAWAR

0 5 10
MILES

Maffin Bay

MAY 18

WAKDE

INSOEMANAI

ARARE

MAY 17
TOEM

LONE TREE HILL
JUNE 29

TOR R.

MMMM JAPANESE
DEFENSES

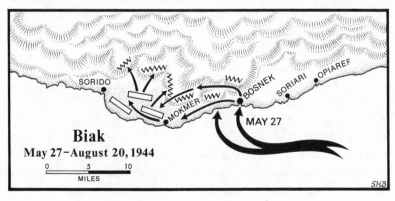

SORIDO

BOSNEK

SORIARI

OPIAREF

MOKMER

MAY 27

Biak
May 27–August 20, 1944

0 5 10
MILES

SHB

panied by Krueger, Eichelberger, Egeberg, Lehrbas, and Diller. For two hours he inspected beach positions and supply areas, chatted with Fuller and some of his staff, and thoroughly enjoyed the taste of victory. Egeberg said that the sixty-four-year-old SWPA chief was in such fine physical shape that he left the rest of his party "panting hard" and far behind as he kept a "lively" stride for three miles along the equipment-littered beach. Back on the *Nashville* after lunch, he celebrated with Eichelberger, Barbey, and Krueger by ordering for all a favorite dessert of his, chocolate ice-cream sodas. The day was unusually hot and humid, so the treat was more welcome than champagne. "When I finished mine with celerity," Eichelberger remarked, MacArthur "grinned and gave me his own untouched, frosted glass."

Next MacArthur insisted that the *Nashville* captain transport him to Tanahmerah Bay, and at 3:00 P.M. on D-day the general and his entourage boarded a landing craft and set out for the shore. About halfway to the beach the *Nashville* signaled that an enemy plane was approaching. Barbey, who was on the landing craft, ordered the coxswain to head for the protection of a nearby destroyer. "An open boat without protection," commented Barbey, "seemed hardly the place to concentrate most of the brass of the Southwest Pacific when there was a Japanese plane on the loose. MacArthur, however, thought otherwise. He asked that I direct the boat to continue to the beach, which I did. A few minutes later a lone plane came in, swooped over us, then continued in the direction of Hollandia."

After MacArthur's group landed at Tanahmerah Bay and conferred with Irving and his staff, according to Eichelberger, "we walked for an hour along a narrow stretch of mud and sand behind which rose a dense rain-forest. The sun poured down mercilessly, and my uniform was soggy and dark with wetness. I remember my astonishment that General MacArthur, despite the sweltering heat and the vigorous exercise, did not perspire at all." On the return trip to the *Nashville* they passed the anchored flagship of Fechteler, who commanded the Humboldt Bay naval task force. MacArthur turned to Johnson and asked if he could wigwag. Although the naval captain admitted that he had not used wigwag flags in two decades, the general, said Johnson, pointed to the engine box and told him, "Get up there and wigwag, 'Well done, MacArthur to Fechteler.'" Johnson did not state whether he succeeded, but he did try for the enthusiastic theater commander.

The next morning MacArthur had the *Nashville* carry him to Aitape where he went ashore at 7:00 A.M., visited with Doe and some of his men, and took a long jeep tour through the area. At 3:00 P.M. he reboarded the *Nashville* and seemed to be fully satisfied with what he had seen; the cruiser took him back to Finschhafen where the following morning he took off in the *Bataan* for Moresby. Soon the pleased SWPA chief was receiving many congratulatory messages, including one from Marshall saying, "The succession of surprises effected and the small losses suffered, the great extent of territory conquered and the casualties inflicted on the enemy, together with the large Japanese forces which have been isolated, all combine to make your operations of the past one and a half months models of strategical and tactical maneuvers." [6]

Not all of the distinguished visitors at the Hollandia beachhead had as exhilarating an experience as MacArthur. Near the Pim jetty, Lieutenant General Herbert Lumsden, the British liaison officer at GHQ who had been personally assigned by Churchill, fell into a freshly dug latrine that had not yet been covered. "Lumsden was bedraggled," Eichelberger observed, "but his dignity was undismayed . . . As he shook himself like a dog after a swim, he remarked to me without even a smile, 'At least it may be said, in England's interest, that I was the first thing through the hole.'" [7]

The Hollandia area rapidly lost its primitive appearance

as a huge complex of military, naval, and air facilities was developed there. The fighter strips at both Hollandia and Aitape were soon in use by the Fifth Air Force, and construction of bomber bases near Lake Sentani was shortly under way. MacArthur had been impressed by the beautiful setting along the shores of Lake Sentani with the majestic Cyclops Mountains in the distance and commented that it would be an excellent location for his GHQ; the decision to move from Brisbane, however, was postponed until after the destruction of Adachi's forces that summer.[8] Eichelberger, the Reckless Task Force commander who supervised the base development at Hollandia, described the immense project:

> Road construction had proceeded simultaneously [with building runways], and this was a gigantic task. Sides of mountains were carved away, bridges and culverts were thrown across rivers and creeks, gravel and stone "fill" was poured into sago swamps to make highways as tall as Mississippi levees . . . Hollandia became one of the great bases of the war. In the deep waters of Humboldt Bay a complete fleet could lie at anchor. Tremendous docks were constructed, and 135 miles of pipeline were led over the hills to feed gasoline to the airfields. Where once I had seen only a few native villages and an expanse of primeval forest, a city of 140,000 men took occupancy.[9]

2. *To the Vogelkop*

MacArthur issued a warning order to his commanders on April 10 that the seizure of the Wakde-Sarmi area might soon follow the Hollandia invasion and would require a full division. Krueger favored the use of a division then at Goodenough, but MacArthur maintained that if the opposition at Hollandia was light the 41st Division could be employed, especially since the available shipping would be already at hand. Staging a division

from rear areas 800 to 1000 miles to the south would be so difficult logistically that the assault could not be launched until
mid-June, which was unacceptable to the anxious SWPA chief.
Aboard the *Nashville* at Tanahmerah Bay on April 22, according to Barbey, "MacArthur made another one of his startling
proposals. In view of the apparently overwhelming success of
the day's operations, why not continue on to the Wakde area —
140 miles further along — and strike the Japanese there while
they were still off balance?" Barbey said his amphibious force
was ready, but Krueger was "noncommittal" and Eichelberger,
wary of a counterattack at Hollandia, "was vehemently opposed
to the idea."

It was soon learned, however, that soil conditions at Hollandia precluded the speedy development of a bomber base
there to support the advance to the Vogelkop, so in early May
MacArthur decided that the Wakde-Sarmi area must be taken
soon to provide the necessary airfields. Whitehead said his
reconnaissance pilots reported that Sarmi, headquarters of the
Japanese 36th Division, "is fuller of Nips and supplies than a
mangy dog is with fleas" and the Maffin Bay area, between Sarmi
and Wakde, was unsuitable for a bomber base. So MacArthur
revised his plan, canceling the Sarmi assault and including only
the seizure of Wakde Island, where an excellent air strip was
known to exist, and the region around Toem, a village on the
nearby mainland shore. He decreed that the invasion of Toem
would occur on May 17 and Wakde the next day. The Tornado
Task Force was created for the missions, to be headed by Doe
and to consist mainly of the 163rd Regimental Combat Team,
which was also to be used first at Aitape. Noble would command the assault force until the landings, Berkey and Crutchley's cruisers and destroyers would provide naval gunfire support, and the Fifth Air Force would pulverize further the
airfields and known defensive positions in the vicinity. Mac-
Arthur decided, too, that an assault on the island of Biak in

Geelvink Bay, the location of excellent sites for bomber bases, would be undertaken on May 27, with that attack covered by Wakde-based aircraft.

The capture of tiny Wakde, May 18–21, involved difficult fighting; the enemy was entrenched in coral caves. Forty Americans and nearly 800 Japanese died before the island was secured. While engineers quickly went to work expanding the Wakde air strip from shore to shore to accommodate bombers, Doe's mainland troops became heavily engaged west of Toem. About 10,000 Japanese troops were dug in along the mountainous eighteen-mile shoreline between Toem and Sarmi. When it was decided in late May to send another regiment to Doe so that the enemy air strips in the small coastal plain along Maffin Bay could be seized, the Japanese 36th Division fought back tenaciously, particularly at Lone Tree Hill, a heavily fortified area between the Americans and the air strips. Despite the arrival of Major General Franklin C. Sibert's 6th Division on June 12, Lone Tree Hill was not secured until the end of that month. The fanatical defenders prevented the Americans from securing the Maffin Bay shoreline until early September, although Sibert, who became Tornado commander in June, also brought in elements of the 31st and 33rd divisions. In fact, at the end of the war the Japanese were still holding Sarmi.

About 400 Americans and nearly 4000 Japanese were killed in the fighting from Toem to Maffin Bay, most of them falling in the vicinity of Lone Tree Hill. Nevertheless, the Tornado Task Force's objectives, when secured, proved valuable. Wakde was developed into a key air base, supporting two heavy bomber groups, two fighter groups, and two reconnaissance squadrons. Planes from Wakde were important in covering the forthcoming invasions of Biak, Noemfoor, and Morotai, and they later flew support missions for Nimitz's assault of the Palaus. In addition, Maffin Bay became an important staging area for five invasions — Biak, Noemfoor, Sansapor, Morotai, and Leyte.[10]

After visiting the Hollandia beachhead on April 22, Mac-Arthur had sent word to Sutherland in Brisbane that "amazing weakness" characterized the defenses at Hollandia and Aitape and "this extreme weakness exists throughout the remaining Japanese bases in northern Dutch New Guinea." The SWPA chief's optimism was buttressed when news was received in early May that a convoy carrying 20,000 troops from China to reinforce the Second Army had been attacked by American submarines, which sank four troop transports, drowning about 10,000 soldiers. The rapid captures of Wakde and Toem also fed his enthusiasm, although on the eve of the assault on Biak the protracted struggle west of Toem was not foreseen. Willoughby's intelligence, moreover, estimated the enemy garrison on Biak, the next objective, to number 2000 at most, which Fuller's 41st Division (less one regiment) was expected to overrun in short order. The landing on Biak would mean that Mac-Arthur's fast-moving offensive had advanced 800 miles in thirty-five days, but the record pace was destined to come to an abrupt, if temporary, halt on Biak.

In early May Admiral Soemu Toyoda, the aggressive new commander of the Combined Fleet, issued a plan, designated Operation A-Gō, which called for Vice Admiral Jisaburo Ozawa's First Mobile Fleet, comprising the largest and best ships left in the Japanese Navy, to lure Nimitz's Pacific Fleet into the Palaus region, where Ozawa's firepower and land-based aircraft would destroy it. If MacArthur seized air bases in the Schouten Islands of Geelvink Bay, however, his planes could disrupt A-Gō. Therefore an attack on Biak, the largest of the Schoutens, would produce a violent reaction from the Japanese, who were planning to rush troop and air reinforcements to Dutch New Guinea. If it were necessary for the launching of A-Gō, Toyoda was prepared to drain most of the naval land-based aircraft from the Central Pacific and send them to defend Biak. Moreover, unlike the garrisons at Hollandia, Aitape, and Wakde, the Biak Detachment, commanded by Colonel Naoyuki Kuzume, was expecting an invasion and for some time had been busy constructing powerful defensive positions in the cave-pocked hills and defiles overlooking the southern coastal area where the island's three air bases were located. Kuzume based his defensive plan on the sound assumption that the principal objective of the invaders would be the airfields. Rather than try to defend the entire island, he concentrated his troops and firepower on the rugged terrain overlooking the narrow coastal plain so that his forces could prevent the Americans from using the airfields there as long as possible.

Following an intensive aerial and naval bombardment on the morning of May 27, which actually hurt the defenders little since they were inland or protected by caves, Fuller's Hurricane Task Force landed on several beaches near Bosnek, nine miles east of the airfield area. They encountered little opposition during the first several days as they consolidated their beachhead and prepared to advance west toward Mokmer. Fuller planned to send the 162nd Regiment down the beaches, above which rose steep cliffs, while the 186th Regiment pushed along a parallel route in the hilly inland region. By May 29, however, both units were stopped by fierce, well-positioned enemy fire, with the 162nd forced to retreat from the vicinity of Mokmer village. The 163rd Regimental Combat Team was rushed to Biak from Wakde, and the advance picked up again slowly. On June 7 the easternmost air strip was captured by the 186th, which had descended from the high ground, but the Americans were soon pinned down by heavy fire from the hills nearby. For a while a plan to evacuate the troops at the Mokmer airfield by sea was considered, so critical was the situation. American planes could not use the captured field, and the other two fields seemed unattainable. As was now obvious to the regimental commanders, Kuzume had used the fields to lure the Americans into his trap of withering fire from the hills and caves above.[11]

In a communiqué on May 28, MacArthur stated that the impending capture of Biak "marks the practical end of the New Guinea campaign." On June 1 he reported that enemy resistance was "collapsing," and on the 3rd his communiqué announced that "mopping-up was proceeding" on Biak. As a stalemate developed, with Fuller's men covered by enemy guns and unable to advance, MacArthur, who was in Brisbane, read the daily operations reports with increasing anxiety. Bomber runways at Hollandia and Wakde would not be ready in time for Nimitz's invasion of Saipan, set for June 15, so the longer runways on Biak were needed for the SWPA planes that MacArthur had promised Nimitz would attack Japanese bases in the Carolines during the admiral's thrust into the Marianas. The SWPA chief decided on June 4 that, in view of the delay in securing Biak, the air bases on nearby Noemfoor would have to be seized, but shipping and other logistical difficulties would make it impossible to launch the Noemfoor operation for another month.

On the 5th MacArthur radioed Krueger, who was at Finschhafen, "I am becoming concerned at the failure to secure the Biak airfields . . . Is the advance being pushed with sufficient determination? Our negligible ground losses would seem to indicate a failure to do so." Krueger replied that he had been prodding Fuller and had "seriously considered" relieving him "some time ago," but was "awaiting a full report on the situation from my Chief of Staff before taking further action." On June 8 Krueger notified MacArthur that the report of his chief of staff, Brigadier General George H. Decker, indicated that Fuller "was faced with a most difficult task." Krueger added that, after studying the report, he was "glad" he had not removed Fuller earlier and that his relief "would be unwarranted now when, I'm sure, he is about to accomplish his mission successfully."

On the 13th, Fuller informed Krueger that enemy reinforcements had landed on Biak and he needed another regiment.

Krueger reluctantly agreed to send one of the 24th Division's regiments, but, according to the official history, he "placed little credence on the reports of enemy reinforcements" and concluded that "Fuller was overburdened by his dual function of task force and division commander." Postwar studies of Japanese documents, however, showed that about 1000 enemy troops were sneaked by barge at night from Manokwari to Biak during June 1–12. The decisive moment occured on June 14 when Krueger received more pressure from MacArthur: "The situation at Biak," stated the SWPA commander, "is unsatisfactory. The strategic purpose of the operation is being jeopardized by the failure to establish without delay an operating field for aircraft." Later that day Krueger informed MacArthur that he had just ordered Eichelberger to succeed Fuller as commander of the Hurricane Task Force. When he arrived at Biak on June 15, Eichelberger later wrote to his wife, Fuller "had already submitted a letter asking for relief from his division and requesting his retirement. He says he does not intend to serve under a certain man (Walter) again if he has to submit his resignation every half hour by wire." Fuller was angry and adamant, so, at Eichelberger's suggestion, Doe was appointed commander of the 41st Division. Fuller left on the 18th and later served ably as deputy chief of staff to Mountbatten in the Southeast Asia Command.[12]

Even with additional firepower, improved tactics, and aggressive leadership, Eichelberger and Doe still faced tremendous difficulties in reducing the many strong points that the Japanese fiercely defended in the caves, hills, and defiles overlooking the air strips. The easternmost field was first used by American fighters on June 22, but the other strips were not secured for several more weeks and did not become operational until early August. Krueger officially declared the end of the Biak operation on August 20. By then the Hurricane Task Force had lost about 400 men killed, 2000 wounded, and 7400 noncombatant

General MacArthur and President Quezon on Corregidor, c. February, 1942.

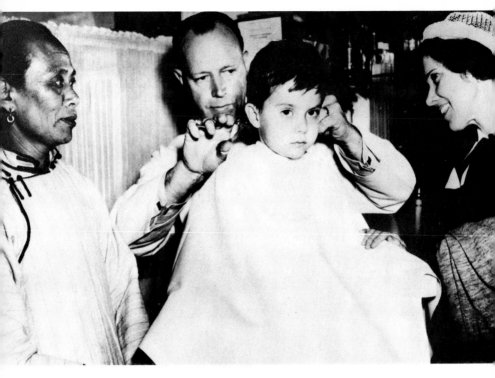

Arthur MacArthur gets his first haircut in Australia as Mrs. MacArthur and Ah Cheu watch. Melbourne, c. March 23, 1942.

Generals Blamey and MacArthur with Prime Minister Curtin at Melbourne, c. June, 1942.

Inside his B-17, "Bataan," 1943.

Left. At Port Moresby, late August, 1942.

Chief of Staff Marshall visits Southwest Pacific commanders on Good-enough, December 15, 1943. From left to right: Generals Kenney, Krueger, MacArthur, and Marshall.

Observing an enemy corpse on Los Negros, February 29, 1944. The three officers nearest to MacArthur are, from left to right: Colonel Lehrbas, Admiral Kinkaid, and General Chase.

Brisbane conference, March 25–27, 1944. Admiral Nimitz and General MacArthur plan future operations.

Generals MacArthur and Rupertus at Cape Gloucester, New Britain, April 20, 1944. General Krueger may be seen in the background to the right.

Left. Walking with General Fuller at the Tanahmerah Bay beachhead, Netherlands New Guinea, April 22, 1944.

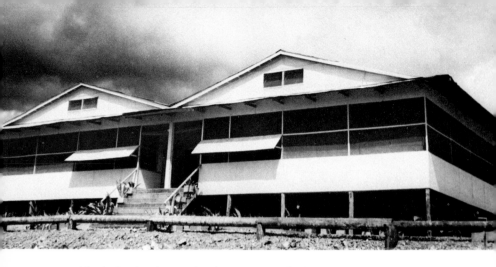

MacArthur's advance headquarters overlooking Lake Sentani near Hollandia, c. September, 1944.

Pearl Harbor conference, July 26–28, 1944. From left to right: General MacArthur, President Roosevelt, Admiral Nimitz, and Admiral Leahy.

En route to the beachhead at Morotai, September 15, 1944. Admiral Barbey can be seen to MacArthur's left.

Headed for the beachhead at Leyte, October 20, 1944. From left to right: General Kenney, General Sutherland, President Osmeña, Colonel Lehrbas, General MacArthur, Colonel Egeberg, and General Romulo.

Right. Wading ashore at Leyte, October 20, 1944. Inscription written by MacArthur.

General MacArthur and President Osmeña shortly after arriving at the Leyte beachhead, October 20, 1944.

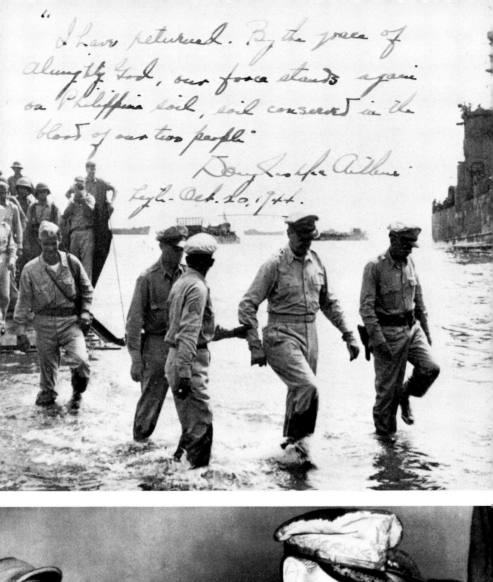

"I have returned. By the grace of Almighty God, our force stands again on Philippine soil, soil consecrated in the blood of our two people."

Douglas MacArthur
Leyte. Oct. 20, 1944.

Arrives at provincial capitol, Tacloban, for ceremony restoring Philippine civil government on Leyte, October 23, 1944. General Sutherland can be seen bending over in the rear of the jeep.

MacArthur's advance headquarters at Tacloban, Leyte, c. November, 1944.

Standing in front of his new "Bataan," a C-54, 1944.

Observing operations west of Clark Field, Luzon, February 1, 1945. From left to right: Colonel Lehrbas, Colonel Egeberg, and General MacArthur.

Left. Strolling with Secretary of the Navy Forrestal at Hacienda Luisita, near Tarlac, February 28, 1945.

Raising the American flag again over Corregidor, March 2, 1945. MacArthur can be seen in the center foreground, to the left of the mast, with his back to the camera. Inscription by MacArthur.

In front of the ruins of his former headquarters on Corregidor, MacArthur poses on March 2, 1945, with some of the officers who escaped with him from that island three years before. From left to right: General Diller, Colonel McMicking, Generals Willoughby, Akin, Sutherland, MacArthur, Marshall, and Casey, Colonel Huff, General Marquart, and an unidentified soldier.

At Caloocan, MacArthur and several officers of his staff board the "General MacArthur Special," the first train to enter Manila after the capital's recapture, March 15, 1945.

Observing the naval bombardment in Brunei Bay, Borneo, June 9, 1945.
From left to right: Generals Whitney, Kenney, and MacArthur.

Walking through swampy area on Labuan Island during Brunei invasion,
June 10, 1945.

Confers with the governor of Jolo and the sultan of Sulu on Jolo Island, June 12, 1945.

Observes Australian operations at Balikpapan, Borneo, July 1, 1945. Admiral Barbey is the second officer on MacArthur's right.

Addressing the Philippine Congress, Manila, July 9, 1945. Senator Roxas is seated to MacArthur's right and President Osmeña to his left.

With Lord Mountbatten at Manila, July 13, 1945.

The first meeting of Generals MacArthur and Derevyanko, at Manila, August 26, 1945.

Right. Arrival in Japan, August 30, 1945. MacArthur leaves the "Bataan" with Generals Sutherland and Eichelberger to his immediate left.

An emotional reunion at Yokohama, August 31, 1945. From left to right: Generals Percival, MacArthur, and Wainwright.

Right. General MacArthur and Colonel Egeberg in front of the New Grand Hotel, Yokohama, August 31, 1945.

With Generals Wainwright and Percival standing immediately to his rear, MacArthur signs the Japanese surrender document aboard the U.S.S. *Missouri*, September 2, 1945.

casualties (hospitalizations due to accidents and illness). Approximately 4700 Japanese were killed and 220 captured. None of the Biak airfields was available in time to assist Nimitz's invasion of Saipan, but they were used extensively in support of later SWPA offensives, as well as in the bombing of enemy targets in the East Indies.

The delay at Biak kept MacArthur from fulfilling his pledge to send bombing missions against the Carolines before and during the Saipan operation. But the timely assault against the Marianas by the Central Pacific forces saved the American forces in Geelvink Bay from probable disaster. When he learned of the Biak invasion, Toyoda ordered his surface units and naval aircraft into action. The land-based aircraft coming from the Central Pacific bases struck hard at Wewak; in one surprise attack, they destroyed on the ground about sixty Allied planes that had been flying missions in support of the Biak operation. Seventh Fleet vessels provided a strong umbrella of antiaircraft fire around Biak, keeping the enemy air assault from seriously crippling combat and supply activities on the island. The Japanese air attacks were part of Operation Kon, an intensive effort to defend and reinforce the strategically important island. In a stroke of good luck for the SWPA forces, Toyoda's air assault, the first stage of Kon, was curtailed prematurely when many of the naval aviators who had been rushed to Vogelkop bases from the more salubrious Central Pacific area rapidly succumbed to malaria and other jungle diseases. The other three stages of Operation Kon were to be runs to Biak from the Philippines by Ozawa's fleet bearing troop and supply reinforcements. The first run was aborted off the northern coast of the Vogelkop when the convoy was spotted by Wakde-based reconnaissance planes. The convoy commander also received an erroneous report that a huge American fleet had just arrived off Biak. A second Kon expedition, loaded with troops, approached Biak several days later, but was driven off by Allied aircraft and a cruiser-destroyer force under Crutchley on the night of June 8–9.

The third Kon reinforcement attempt prepared by Toyoda and Ozawa was to be so overwhelmingly powerful that success would be assured. On June 11 Vice Admiral Matome Ugaki assembled the huge expedition at Batjan in the Moluccas; besides a number of troop transports and cargo vessels, it included the two largest battleships in the world, *Yamato* and *Musashi*, as well as a strong force of cruisers, destroyers, destroyer escorts, and auxiliary ships. The armada could have easily destroyed Kinkaid's surface units off Biak, severed the supply line to Fuller, and smashed his combat positions and supply areas, all of which were close to the beaches. And, of course, the troop reinforcements the convoy carried would have been welcome to Kuzume, who could then have counterattacked in force. As Ugaki's ships prepared to steam out of the harbor at Batjan on the short run to Biak, news came from Saipan that the American Fifth Fleet was bombarding that island in obvious preparation for an invasion. Toyoda declared Operation A-Gō in effect, Operation Kon was canceled, and Ozawa led the First Mobile Fleet, which included Ugaki's combat vessels plus carriers and other surface units, northward to engage the Fifth Fleet in a decisive confrontation. On June 19–20 in the Philippine Sea, west of the Marianas, Spruance and Mitscher's formidable fleet, built around four carrier groups, dealt a stunning setback to Ozawa. In the so-called "Marianas Turkey Shoot" on June 19, over half of his planes were shot down. By the next evening the toll was 476 Japanese aircraft destroyed and one of Ozawa's main carriers sunk, with others badly damaged. The Japanese fleet, having lost its air cover, fled westward rather than commit its surface units to certain devastation. There was no talk among the admirals of renewing Operation Kon.[13]

The lack of unity of command in the Pacific and of a single axis of advance produced some liabilities in prosecuting the war against Japan, but coordination by the theater commands along the dual lines of advance sometimes brought about a degree of teamwork and mutual support that was effective and impressive. The movements by MacArthur's and Nimitz's forces during the period from mid-1943 to mid-1944 provide excellent examples of the assets of the existing command and strategic arrangements. The Cartwheel operations siphoned off Japan's air power in the Central Pacific in defense of Rabaul, enabling Nimitz to occupy the Gilberts and Marshalls without serious aerial opposition. The Pacific Fleet's destructive raids from Truk to the Palaus forced the Japanese Combined Fleet out of the waters north of New Guinea, thus allowing MacArthur's leapfrogging to be undertaken without the need for powerful naval protection. The invasion of Biak, in turn, drew to Dutch New Guinea much of the Japanese air strength in the Central Pacific, which otherwise would have been used against the Saipan invasion force. Most important for MacArthur's plans, the attack on Saipan lured to the north the Japanese fleet that was poised to strike and destroy the SWPA forces in Geelvink Bay. As stated in a naval history that Nimitz co-authored, "The two Allied forces advancing across the Pacific operated as a team, each relieving the other of a portion of its burden . . . Had there not been a Central Pacific drive to attract and hold Japanese forces elsewhere, the Southwest Pacific forces would have met far greater resistance in the New Guinea area." Yet MacArthur saw no benefits accruing from the Saipan invasion and viewed it as an unwise frontal assault against a strongly held island that cost more American casualties than all of his SWPA operations from Aitape to Morotai.[14]

The final operations in Dutch New Guinea were rather routine and anticlimactic. While the battle was still raging on Biak, the Cyclone Task Force, headed by Brigadier General Edwin D. Patrick and comprising about 8000 troops, mainly of the 158th Regimental Combat Team, landed on Noemfoor on July 2. At first there was no organized resistance, but on the 6th the defenders counterattacked from the island's hilly interior. The Japanese were repulsed, and thereafter opposition was sporadic, though mopping-up activities were not completed until the end of August. Seventy Americans and nearly 2000 Japanese died on Noemfoor. Construction of airfields on the island was begun in mid-July.

The final operation on the Vogelkop Peninsula took place on July 30 when approximately 7300 soldiers of the 6th Division, designated Typhoon Task Force and commanded by Sibert, made unopposed amphibious landings at Sansapor and Mar. The beachheads were established in an isolated region about 100 miles west of Manokwari, the Japanese Second Army's headquarters, and sixty miles northeast of Sorong, a smaller Japanese base. Two airfields were constructed at Mar in time for use in the forthcoming Morotai operation. The beachheads were consolidated and gradually expanded, but no offensive against Manokwari or Sorong was attempted. The total enemy strength at those two bases was one division and three brigades, but the Japanese inexplicably never mounted a serious counterattack against the Sansapor-Mar area. Except for occasional Fifth Air Force raids, they were left in their isolation to eke out a pitiful existence until the end of the war.[15]

When queried by Marshall as to the ultimate disposition of such bypassed Japanese garrisons, which were scattered from Sorong to Bougainville, MacArthur replied on August 9:

> The enemy garrisons which have been bypassed in the Solomons and New Guinea represent no menace to current or future operations. Their capacity for organized offensive effort has passed. The various processes of attrition will eventually account for their final disposition. The actual time of their destruction is of little or no importance and their influence as a contributing factor to the war is already negligible. The actual process of their immediate destruction by assault meth-

ods would unquestionably involve heavy loss of life without adequate compensating strategic advantages. The present allotment of shipping and assault craft would not permit such operations except at the expense of those which are now scheduled.[16]

MacArthur's offensive had advanced 1100 miles in the last two months. The spectacular achievement was later marred, however, when some of the Japanese garrisons that had been cut off decided not to accept the passive role allotted to them by MacArthur. The Australian Army would learn that the above policy applied only to American forces, as will be discussed later. The distasteful, unheralded lot of Blamey's troops for the rest of the war would consist largely of fighting bypassed enemy forces which the SWPA chief had dismissed as "of little or no importance."

3. Complications of the Grand Alliance

During 1942–44 there were sporadic talks among Dutch, Australian, and British authorities about invading the Netherlands East Indies west of New Guinea. The colonial interests of the Dutch and British, the defense-mindedness of the Australians, and the petroleum needs of the Allies made that archipelago a tempting objective. The Australian chiefs drew up the Madrigal Plan in late 1942 for a three-division invasion of Timor. When it was presented to Blamey, he responded, "Many years of training have produced in me a dislike for profanity in writing. This alone prevents me from giving my complete opinion of this imbecility . . . The preparation of a scheme for the capture of Timor is, at the present juncture, a pure waste of time." On January 25, 1943, MacArthur ruled out the presentation of Madrigal to the Joint Chiefs, maintaining that he "definitely did not possess the resources" for the operation, which, if undertaken, would have to be "a long-distance project." Dr. Antonio Salazar, the Portuguese prime minister, had opposed the landing of Australian troops to defend the half-Portuguese, half-Dutch island in December, 1941, but he suddenly advocated an Allied invasion of Timor, using Portuguese troops, in mid-1943. The Combined Chiefs decided, nevertheless, that an attack on Timor would have to be postponed until after the seizure of "higher priority Japanese-held objectives."

As MacArthur's advance northwestward along the coast of New Guinea provided his air forces with bases to strike deeper into the East Indies, he gave some thought to future landings in Celebes and Borneo. Although he probably could not have found the amphibious forces to mount it, he recommended in vain to the Joint Chiefs the seizure of some of the islands in the Arafura Sea. In early 1944, Kenney proposed the capture of the enemy air base on Selaru, a small island 250 miles north of Darwin. MacArthur was against it, but told him to go ahead with the planning "as he might want to carry that operation out if anything went wrong at Hollandia or the Japs decided to put too much strength on the north coast of Dutch New Guinea for us to handle" — a contingency that did not materialize. In the spring of 1944, several committees under the Joint Chiefs prepared studies on the feasibility of invading petroleum-rich Borneo, but, in view of enemy strength in the Greater Sundas, it was concluded the operation would have drained MacArthur's resources.[17]

That summer the British chiefs of staff developed a plan that called for an attack on Ambon in the Moluccas by three Australian divisions supported by a British naval task force from the Indian Ocean. They proposed also that the SWPA theater be placed under the Combined Chiefs, rather than the Joint Chiefs, and that the Ambon forces function as "a distinct Command with British Commanders under General MacArthur's supreme direction." Curtin strongly opposed the plan on the ground that it presented "a danger of the gravest misunderstandings with the U.S. if Australian Forces were taken away from General MacArthur's direct command and placed under a new Commander." The Joint Chiefs were against it because of its diversionary strategy, logistical demands, and command arrangement. Leahy commented further, "The exact British intentions were not known, but past experience indicated that if they did get control of some Dutch territory, it might be difficult to pry them loose." [18]

In a radiogram to Marshall on August 27 MacArthur argued that the Ambon scheme would be strategically unsound and would violate the international agreement by which the SWPA command was established in 1942. He continued:

> The addition of British Forces would be welcome. Every effort has been made without avail to secure their participation. This is particularly true with regard to British Forces in which this area has always been lamentably weak . . . The British [Naval] Task Force which has been contemplated would be admirably suited for this duty. British Forces, however, if assigned should come under the present setup . . .
>
> Under an agreement entered into by the five interested nations, the Southwest Pacific Area has operated under American command for more than two years. We have passed through dark days and are now on the threshold of decisive victory. It is appropriate that this command be maintained to the successful conclusion of the campaign. Entirely aside from any consideration of equity, the decision of the area and the assignment of the major portion thereof under a British Commander would be completely destructive of American prestige in the Far East and would have the most serious repercussions. It is my belief that such a line of action would not receive the approval of the American people and that if consummated, would give rise to a condition that would be prejudicial to the maintenance of cordial relations between the United States and Great Britain during the post-war period.
>
> It is my belief that any proposal to alter drastically the pres-

ent command setup at this late date should be met with complete firmness; that any form of appeasement will be followed in due course by deterioration not only of British-American relationships but of American prestige and commercial prospects throughout the Far East.[19]

The British chiefs dropped the Ambon proposal in view of the vociferous opposition from Australian and American leaders and also because their own strong-willed superior had other notions about Britain's role in the war in Southeast Asia. In September Churchill told Lieutenant General Hastings Ismay, his personal chief of staff, that British policy should be to "give naval assistance on the largest scale to the main American operations" in the Pacific, seize Rangoon as "a preliminary operation," and then launch "a major attack upon Singapore." Churchill viewed Singapore as "the supreme British objective in the whole of the Indian and Far Eastern theatres. It is the only prize that will restore British prestige in this region." [20]

With a variety of such schemes for implanting Allied forces in the East Indies and with intelligence reports that Indonesian nationalists were most receptive to the "Asia for Asians" doctrine propounded by the Japanese, the Dutch government-in-exile was anxious to obtain an agreement with Allied authorities regarding the administration of liberated territories in the East Indies. In March, 1944, as SWPA forces prepared to enter Netherlands New Guinea, Dr. H. J. van Mook, the lieutenant governor-general of the East Indies, conferred with MacArthur in Brisbane about the possible terms of such an agreement. When the SWPA chief forwarded his report of the meeting to Washington, the State Department and civil affairs sections of the War and Navy departments went to work on the matter. The agreement was delayed because Secretary of State Cordell Hull wanted it to include "(1) specific dates when independence or complete (dominion) self-government will be accorded, (2) specific steps to be taken to develop native capacity for self-rule, and (3) a pledge of economic autonomy and equality of economic treatment toward other nations."

But the van Mook–MacArthur Agreement, signed December 10, 1944, was devoid of such idealism and contained only these basic provisions: (1) MacArthur would, "to the extent necessitated by the military situation, possess *de facto* authority to take all necessary measures"; (2) the Dutch government would "resume as rapidly as possible, even in combat areas, full responsibility for the civil administration of reoccupied Netherlands territory"; (3) the Dutch authorities would cooperate with MacArthur in assuring the continued use of native labor, billets, supplies, ports, lines of communication, airfields, and other facilities needed by the military; and (4) SWPA personnel would be immune from Dutch legal jurisdiction and taxation.[21] With a war to fight, neither MacArthur nor the War Department was willing to become entangled in the dismantling of the Dutch empire. Inadvertently, of course, they were participating in planting one of the many seeds that would grow into the bloody post-1945 Indonesian revolution against Dutch rule.

If the British and Dutch were thinking already in terms of their postwar interests in the Southwest Pacific and Southeast Asia, Dr. Evatt, Australia's energetic, outspoken minister of external affairs, was just as concerned about establishing his nation's position so that it could influence developments in that region during and after the war. Like Curtin, Evatt became a close friend and ardent admirer of MacArthur's, and it is impossible to determine how much each of the three men affected the others' views on a specific topic, though all of them were strong in their insistence on a Pacific-first strategy. For example, Evatt's repeated but futile demands that Australia be represented on the Anglo-American Munitions Assignments Board were not unrelated to the SWPA commander's frequently expressed desire for a greater share of the resources distributed by that body. Moreover, neither the Australian leaders nor Mac-

Arthur were happy with the impotence of the Pacific War Council in Washington and its counterpart in London where, though Australia was represented, her interests were of little consideration in high-level Allied decision-making. New Zealand's governmental leaders also shared this sense of neglect, and the newspapers of both nations were sharply critical of Roosevelt and Churchill for not including their foreign ministers in conferences such as those at Quebec and Cairo in 1943.

The Australian–New Zealand Agreement was drafted in January, 1944, at a meeting in Canberra to establish a regional pact for the purpose, among other things, of insuring those two nations' "right to representation at the highest level in executive bodies running the war, planning armistices, or planning and establishing a future 'general international organization.' " The agreement declared that no negotiations on postwar military bases or territorial changes in the Southwest or South Pacific "should be effected except as a result of an agreement to which they are parties or in the terms of which they have both concurred." This and other clauses of the Canberra agreement antagonized some leaders in Washington and London; they seemed audacious and offensive. One United States senator accused the drafters of developing "their own brand of imperialism."

When Evatt's stance sometimes became too aggressive and threatened to hurt Australia's relations with the United States, her chief wartime benefactor, Curtin tried to placate Washington with a more moderate position or interpretation. According to the official Australian war history, MacArthur appears to have had some influence on Curtin's less grandiose views of Australia's rightful position in the family of nations: "There is scant documentary record in the Australian archives of what advice MacArthur gave to Curtin but his known views would have confirmed the idea that Australia should not seek to play a more active part in operations beyond the South-West Pacific Area."

In Evatt's case, the effort to establish Australia's position at the top levels of Allied strategy formulation merged by 1944 into a crusade on behalf of the small powers against the large powers in organizing the United Nations. At the San Francisco Conference in the spring of 1945 at which the United Nations charter was completed and signed, Evatt would become the foremost spokesman for the small nations and also would be instrumental in obtaining declarations in favor of "full employment" and other socioeconomic principles advocated by the Australian Labour regime. MacArthur endorsed the wartime pro-Pacific views of Evatt, but the general parted company with the external affairs minister when the latter's ideas conflicted with American and capitalistic interests. MacArthur also did not share the Australian leader's euphoric view of the possibilities of the embryonic United Nations organization. In Evatt's mind, remarks one authority, "the U.N. was a refuge in a flight from power politics which Australia could not hope effectively to play." [22]

In early 1944 an Australian correspondent wrote, "General MacArthur's popularity in Australia has never waned . . . It is generally said that Prime Minister Curtin would cut off his right arm and send it by air freight to MacArthur if the hero of Bataan asked for it. He hasn't needed it so far." The general's public support was strong, but there were an increasing number of Australian press comments critical of his brief involvement in American politics and his failure to give Australian forces due attention in his communiqués. Nevertheless, the reporter was correct about the closeness of the Curtin-MacArthur relationship. It was, indeed, a strange but enduring friendship that developed between the Labour leader, who was working hard to convert Australia into a socialist state while at the same time pushing the war effort, and the American general, who was committed to a Hoover-style conservative philosophy. Each was fully aware that the other was important to his own success, so when one faced a crisis the other faithfully rallied to his side.

In addresses and public messages, MacArthur made clear to the Australian people his wholehearted support of Curtin. Although MacArthur disliked civic gatherings, he joined Curtin in launching several war bond drives, and the general contributed large sums himself on at least two occasions. After the sweeping Labour victory in the parliamentary elections of August, 1943, MacArthur enthusiastically sent a telegram to Curtin: "Hearty congratulations on your magnificent victory. That was a fight worth winning. May God bless and preserve you for the great destiny that lies ahead." Curtin, in turn, regularly backed MacArthur's efforts to get reinforcements for SWPA, with pleas to both Churchill and Roosevelt. On March 17, 1944, Parliament gave a grand dinner at Canberra in honor of the second anniversary of MacArthur's arrival in Australia. As was customary when he came to the capital, MacArthur stayed overnight with the Curtins. Other high-ranking Labour officials who also were close to MacArthur included Lord Gowrie, the governor-general until August, 1944, Joseph B. Chifley, minister for postwar reconstruction and prime minister after Curtin's death in June, 1945; and Frederick G. Shedden, defense secretary.[23]

Australian industrial production hardly seems a likely field to have absorbed a large amount of MacArthur's time, but the War Council, Department of Aircraft Production, and other governmental agencies often sought his advice on the types of weapons and military equipment that should be manufactured. In general, MacArthur recommended that the highest priorities be placed on the production of items that were difficult to obtain from the United States. For example, in 1943 when his opinion was requested on whether a heavy bomber program should be started, he sensibly pointed out that, whereas long-range aircraft could be flown from the States, the transportation of fighters aboard ships took up much of the SWPA's limited shipping capacity. "It is evident therefore," he advised, "that local manufacture of fighter aircraft would not only provide us with airplanes required in this category but would at the same time release worthwhile cargo ship space which could be used for other requirements." The Mosquito fighter-bomber was built in Australian factories in considerable quantity, as well as some smaller types of military aircraft. Late in the war, a limited production of Lancaster heavy bombers (called Lincoln in Australia) was attempted, but the RAAF did not receive the first one until 1946. MacArthur spiritedly defended the Munitions Department's decision to build a tank wholly designed and made in Australia, but industrial manpower shortages curtailed the construction of the Mark tanks; only sixty were delivered to the Australian Army before the termination of hostilities.

Some of the outstanding achievements, as well as the worst labor problems, occurred in the area of maritime construction and services. The principal accomplishment of the Australian shipyards was the production of a class of fast, powerful destroyers generally regarded as equal or superior to their American and British counterparts. One of these, the *Bataan,* was launched by Mrs. MacArthur in early 1945 and was in combat later that spring. A major headache of the Labour government ironically was continual trouble with organized labor, especially with longshoremen and maritime unions. Sometimes the unions' strikes or other forms of obstruction so paralyzed SWPA shipping that MacArthur became alarmed. In early 1943, for example, he wrote to Curtin about a mutiny aboard an American cargo vessel; the Australian Seamen's Union backed the cause of the mutineers and refused to allow another crew to board the ship until the rebellious group was freed from jail. MacArthur charged that the union "was directly obstructing the war effort . . . Fifth-column activities may be behind these occurrences." Even a Labour ministry and the SWPA commander, however, could not bring some of the recalcitrant unions into line, and labor troubles continued to plague Australia's efforts on the homefront throughout the war.[24]

A valuable Australian contribution to the SWPA cause was food production. "Despite the fact," claims the official Australian history, "that a large proportion of her most active young men were in the Services, Australia supplied more food per head of population to the Allied larder than did any other country." The Foreign Economic Administration in Washington stated in September, 1944, "Australia and New Zealand have provided as reverse Lend-Lease over 95 per cent of all the food used by our forces in the Pacific Area under General MacArthur's command." This was accomplished in spite of a nearly continent-wide drought in 1943–45, the most severe in four decades. Privation and austerity affected the Australian homefront almost as seriously as the shortages that hit the British during the dark days of 1940–41. Soon after Curtin announced in June, 1943, that the imminent danger of invasion had passed, his Cabinet voted to begin successive reductions in the strength of the Australian Army. Because of the homefront manpower shortage, the men were not released but were redeployed in industry or agriculture, with 15,000 of the first 20,000 directed into farming. Most of the later redeployments of servicemen were also to agriculture, but the shortage of farm labor persisted to the end of the war. The United States eased the pressure somewhat after September, 1944, by taking over the provision of about half of the food supply of its SWPA troops, who by then were no longer based in Australia in large numbers.

In November, 1944, however, Blamey, who was rarely critical of MacArthur's command when addressing Curtin, complained to the prime minister that the American forces in Australia were storing up "vast reserves of food" in warehouses constructed under reverse lend-lease. He charged that the huge stocks were "far in excess of legitimate operational requirements." He told Curtin that the American authorities reputedly planned on "making them available in the Philippines, China or America itself for civilian or relief purposes, thus buying favorable publicity for American interests, both Government and private, at the expense of our sadly drained and depleted Australian resources." [25] MacArthur's explanation of the proposed disposition is not known, but the overstocking may have been due to a miscalculation in Washington. By early fall of 1944, it was widely believed that Germany's defeat and the start of the enormous redeployment of European forces to the Pacific might occur before Christmas.

MacArthur's dealings with the Australian military establishment in 1943–44 covered a wide range of activities. An important and little known tie was with the Combined Advisory Committee on Tropical Medicine, Hygiene and Sanitation, a group of experts drawn from the Australian and American medical services to advise him on "the medical problems of tropical service." The chief authority on its history says, "This committee, collecting information from many sources, had far reaching influences, and many important directives were made by General MacArthur on its advice." Set up in March, 1943, as a result of the alarm over the high rate of disease among the troops on the Papuan front, the committee soon found that no matter what its research uncovered about ways to combat diseases, education and discipline of troops on disease control were fundamental to success. Accordingly, MacArthur ordered his commanders to implement strictly the committee's advice and insisted that they be exacting with their subordinates about education and the enforcement of disease control regulations. Gradually losses to most jungle diseases declined, but malaria continued to take a heavy toll. Nearly 10,000 men were evacuated from forward areas as malaria victims during Cartwheel; in the Finschhafen operation 1300 Australian troops were killed or wounded, but 3400 contracted malaria.

MacArthur, who took pride in his light losses, was sensitive about the situation. He became incensed when he read a *Collier's* article of April, 1944, that reported rather sensationally the SWPA malaria situation. He told the War Department that the publication violated censorship, and, because of the article, the

malaria problem "is a burning topic here which has been discussed freely in the Parliament and in the press . . . The situation is rendered more acute by the fact that statements in the
Collier's article are completely misrepresentative of the true
situation in the Southwest Pacific Area. Such misrepresentations
can well be seized upon by opposing political factions here."

Evidence indicates that, indeed, the losses to malaria had begun to drop by the time he wrote, and they slowly, but steadily,
continued to decline. The successful battle against malaria was
due, in large measure, to improved supply positioning of food
stocks, adequate stores and use of Atabrine and nets, and efficient mosquito control. MacArthur was pleased that "by the
time we were ready to go into the Philippines it [malaria] was
reduced to secondary importance as a cause of disablement."
But Blamey's troops, operating in the inhospitable regions of
New Guinea, New Britain, and Bougainville during the last
months of the war, still suffered more casualties from malaria
than from Japanese bullets.[26]

Like the malaria menace, some problems in American-Australian military relations admitted of no wholly satisfactory solutions. A few of these with which MacArthur had to wrestle were
inequitable pay scales, differences in operational planning, and
the chaotic RAAF command structure. Australian servicemen
were paid 18 per cent to 29 per cent less than Americans of
equivalent rank and service. This was at the root of much of
the friction which seemed to reach its height when the men
were on leave, vying for female attention, attracting waiters,
bidding for liquor or hotel rooms, and enjoying similar activities
that required cash at hand. Various proposals for solving the
pay situation were voiced in the War Council, Parliament, and
the press. One that received considerable press notice called for
the United States to reduce its pay standards to the Australian
levels. MacArthur quickly retorted that he was "utterly opposed" to this: "There is not the slightest chance that the pay of

American servicemen will be lowered or withheld." He suggested, instead, that the Australians' pay be increased to the American levels, which was not realistic in view of the great difference in financial resources of the two countries. Ultimately Parliament did approve an upward adjustment of its troops' pay, but not to the American levels.[27]

Differences in operational planning resulted in some stormy exchanges between Sutherland and Chamberlin on one side and Blamey and his chief of staff, Berryman, on the other. Chamberlin claimed that the Australian plans for specific operations were "elementary and incomplete . . . The most serious defect is the total lack of appreciation of the logistic problem." Berryman said that the GHQ planners did not understand Australian methods: "Our system was to allow commands concerned to work out plans together with Air and Navy on the spot in accordance with the general outline plan . . . The difference is we work on a decentralised basis whilst G.H.Q. have a highly centralised one." Since MacArthur strongly backed Chamberlin's system, it was the Australians who inevitably had to yield.[28]

Referring to an American-Australian clash over plans for the seizure of Lae, Finschhafen, and the Markham Valley in mid-1943, the official Australian account states:

> This misunderstanding underlined the weakness whereby since April 1942 an American general headquarters on which there was quite inadequate Australian representation reigned from afar over a field army that was, for present purposes, almost entirely Australian, and whose doctrines and methods differed from those of G.H.Q. It was evidence of the detachment of G.H.Q. that, after 16 months, its senior general staff officers had little knowledge of the doctrines and methods of its principal army in the field.[29]

The clashes diminished by the fall of 1944, not through better coordination and understanding but because the Americans were moving north while the Australians were assigned to operations far south against bypassed enemy pockets.

Troubles in the high echelons of the RAAF dated from September, 1942, when MacArthur proposed to Curtin a plan for reorganizing that air force. What subsequently developed, with the SWPA chief's endorsement, was a dual set-up with the RAAF Headquarters, commanded by Air Vice Marshal George Jones, who handled administrative, supply, maintenance, and construction matters, and the RAAF Command, headed by Air Vice Marshal William Bostock, in charge of operations. There was a sharp personality clash between the two officers; in addition, Jones expressed the view that a single RAAF head would be more effective, and Bostock complained that his duties were being usurped by Jones. MacArthur and Kenney preferred to continue the dual system and personally favored Bostock, whom they knew better, while A. S. Drakeford, the air minister, and the Air Board believed Jones was right and his plan sound. A struggle for power between Jones and Bostock ensued, says the RAAF's official history, producing "an atmosphere of personal bitterness, heated exchange, and reaction to frustration . . . The acute personal tension between Jones and Bostock was certainly a serious check on Service efficiency and the cause of a distressing division of loyalties within the R.A.A.F."

MacArthur told Curtin in March, 1943, that Jones was violating the SWPA chain of command when he tried to get operational control from Bostock since in that area Kenney was really Bostock's superior: "The basic issue is a military one which does not properly admit of doubt. Reduced to its simplest terms it is that the forces placed at my disposal shall not be vitiated by outside control . . . To deny [this] would produce a situation the gravity of which I cannot overemphasize." Curtin politely reminded the SWPA commander that it was he who had initiated the set-up. When Jones later tried to explain his unitary plan to MacArthur, the SWPA chief responded that it was not "comprehensive enough to be used as a basis for further discussion."

The Jones-Bostock feud continued to divide and confuse the RAAF's high-level echelons. In June, 1944, Curtin proposed to MacArthur that a single commander should be appointed over Jones and Bostock to integrate the RAAF's administrative and operational functions, as well as to control the rivalry. The SWPA chief replied that the matter was entirely up to the Australians and he would cooperate with the new commander if they created the position. For the new headship, the Cabinet selected British Air Chief Marshal Keith Park of the Southeast Asia Command. Before negotiations were begun in September with the Royal Air Force, however, MacArthur suddenly informed Curtin that it was "too late to make such a change" now. Besides, the SWPA general felt that "any differences that had existed in the past were now quiet," so there was no need for Park. The dual system continued, but, unhappily, so did the ugly episodes between Jones and Bostock. The RAAF history concludes, "There can be no doubt that failure to overcome the conflict within the R.A.A.F. had an unsettling effect on the force. The War Cabinet did a disservice to the force by failing to take decisive action. A strong inhibiting factor was the desire to keep on friendly terms with the American commanders. This may explain the failure but does not fully justify it." [30]

The first overt step in delimiting Australia's military role in the war came on February 19, 1943, when the Citizens Military Forces Bill became law. It provided for the first time that conscripts could volunteer for service beyond the bounds of Australia, but they could not be deployed outside the "South-West Pacific Zone." That zone's eastern boundary, as set forth in the bill, would be the same as SWPA's, 159° longitude, but on the west the new zonal boundary would be 110° longitude, which excluded the SWPA territories of western Java and western Borneo. The important difference between the new zone and SWPA was that the former's northern boundary would be the equator, which excluded the SWPA territories of Morotai, the Philippines, and northern Borneo. Curtin strongly backed the measure, and MacArthur sent him a congratulatory message when the bill was passed, indicating that the general approved the restriction of Australian conscripts below the equator.

As earlier mentioned, in June, 1943, the Curtin government inaugurated a systematic reduction of its land forces. That summer the Australian Army was cut to eleven divisions and by July, 1944, to six infantry divisions and two armored brigades; only three of the divisions by the latter date were considered combat ready. The RAAF was kept at fifty-three squadrons, and the Royal Australian Navy was continued at its current strength, with a few additions later from construction then under way. As to Curtin's motive for pushing the reduction of ground forces, the official Australian chronicle says, "Whatever other thoughts may have been moving around in the privacy of Curtin's own mind, the public evidence suggests that his calculation of political chances at the coming election and his shrewd response to the political campaigning of the Opposition were the decisive influence." Far from being upset by the cuts, MacArthur informed the War Council in December, 1943, that he was in "full agreement with the general principles laid down" and it was up to the Australian government to determine the nature and extent of its own military contribution.[31]

MacArthur had fifteen American Army divisions under his command by September, 1944, but six of them were engaged in mopping-up operations or in holding the line against bypassed Japanese units, principally in Northeast New Guinea, New Britain, and Bougainville. At the fast pace his northward offensive was moving, there would be a shortage of troops for the invasion of the Philippines unless he could free some of the units to the south. By turning over the responsibility for containing the isolated enemy garrisons to the Australians, he not only would release more American forces for combat to the north but also would, in effect, "snap the link" with Blamey's headquarters. He and Blamey had tried to coordinate operational planning, an arrangement that had never been entirely satisfactory to either side. MacArthur broached the new plan to Curtin and Blamey in November, 1943. Curtin was most receptive since he felt the Australian people would highly favor the use of their troops in ejecting the enemy from the British-Australian-controlled territories and mandates. Not wishing to play a static role, Blamey hoped that at least the three veteran Australian divisions would be employed in the main SWPA offensive against Japan.

MacArthur informed Blamey on July 12, 1944, that his Australian forces were to "assume the responsibility for the continued neutralization of the enemy in Australian and British territory and mandates in the SWPA [excluding the Admiralties] by the following dates: Northern Solomons–Green Island–Emirau, 1 Oct. 1944; Australian New Guinea, 1 Nov. 1944; New Britain, 1 Nov. 1944." Blamey felt that six brigades (in addition to one already in action in Northeast New Guinea) would be sufficient, but MacArthur insisted on twelve, the equivalent of four Australian divisions. This disappointed Blamey because it would commit some of the forces he had hoped to use in the Philippines where MacArthur, for a while that summer, had talked of using two Australian divisions. Nevertheless, Blamey's loss of this argument later worked to his advantage since he was desperately anxious to keep his forces engaged in large-scale combat. "At this time," says the official account, "Blamey was fighting a rearguard action against the possible further reduction of the Army." His "grave misgivings" gave way to relief once he realized that he had gained the strength necessary to launch offensives, which would probably induce Parliament to renew its support of the Australian Army.

MacArthur expected the Australians to become involved only in "the continued neutralization" of the bypassed enemy, and,

of course, the SWPA chief took justifiable pride in his bypassing strategy, which had spared many lives. Should the Australians heavily engage the isolated Japanese garrisons, the assets
of MacArthur's strategy would be nullified to an embarrassing
extent. The reason why the SWPA chief insisted on double the
number of brigades Blamey wanted to employ is not known, but
it would afford the Australian commander his offensive opportunity. MacArthur would not have been amused by the suggestion in the official Australian Army history: "The question
arises whether considerations of *amour-propre* were involved:
whether G.H.Q. did not wish it to be recorded that six American divisions had been relieved by six Australian brigades." [32]

CHAPTER XII

Approaching the Philippines

1. Actions South and North of the Equator

TWENTY-TWO MONTHS and 1500 miles separated the operations at Milne Bay and Sansapor, as MacArthur's forces advanced from one end of New Guinea to the other. Fully anticipating more trouble from the bypassed Japanese, the SWPA commander warned on April 24, 1944, that Adachi's troops, trapped between Aitape and Alexishafen, "can be expected to strike desperately to free themselves." Surely enough, about that time Adachi announced to his soldiers at Wewak, "I am determined to destroy the enemy in Aitape by attacking him ruthlessly with the concentration of our entire force in that area." Gill's 32nd Division was concentrated in the Aitape area when the first patrol clashes with Adachi's forward units occurred in May about thirty-two miles east of the American beachhead.

At first MacArthur "considered it improbable that an 18th Army assault could seriously menace the Allied position at Aitape," but SWPA G-2 studies indicated that Adachi would attack about July 5–10 with a force of 20,000 to 30,000 men. Intelligence data, said Willoughby, "built up so unmistakable a picture of enemy intentions that Allied forces were able to take

complete countermeasures well in advance of the actual attack."
In view of the G-2 reports, MacArthur dispatched Major Gen-
eral Leonard F. Wing's 43rd Division and elements of two other
divisions to the beachhead. On June 27, he sent Major General
Charles P. Hall, the commander of the XI Corps, to lead the
Persecution Task Force at Aitape.

Hall ordered an initial defensive line prepared along the west
side of the Driniumoor River, twenty-two miles east of Aitape.
A second line was established four miles to the rear, and a third
in the Aitape-Tadji vicinity. As Adachi's main force, consisting
of the 20th and 41st divisions and parts of two other divisions,
moved slowly through heavy jungles toward the Driniumoor,
elements of the Australian 5th Division pushed forward to the
Sepik River, sixty miles east of Wewak. Although they lacked
the troops and firepower to attack the Eighteenth Army's rear,
the Australians maintained enough pressure to compel Adachi
to keep a substantial force on rear-guard duty between Wewak
and the Sepik.

Despite their defensive preparations, the Americans at the
Driniumoor were thrown off balance by the ferocity and power
of Adachi's expected attack when it suddenly began on the night
of July 10–11. Japanese units crossed the river and broke
through the lines of the American covering force. Hall ordered
a withdrawal to the second defensive line, but he received a
critical message from Krueger, who felt the retreat was unnecessary and demanded a counterattack. In spite of the confusion that reigned temporarily in the American lines, Adachi
committed his forces piecemeal and was unable to exploit the
breakthrough. Hall's units soon counterattacked and within a
few days restored their line on the Driniumoor. American
artillery and machine guns demolished the remnants of Adachi's
units west of the Driniumoor.

In late July Adachi began trying to outflank the right, or
south, end of the SWPA line in the foothills of the Torricelli

Mountains. Afua, a village on the Driniumoor, anchored the right flank of Hall's line; it was lost and retaken several times before the Japanese were finally forced to withdraw on August 9. Meanwhile, to the north Hall had launched a double envelopment that, during the first ten days of August, penetrated the center and coastal portions of Adachi's line and swung southward across his rear, trapping and killing many Japanese. The battered Eighteenth Army fell back to the Dandriwad River, fifteen miles east of the Driniumoor. His mission of protecting the Aitape beachhead fulfilled, Hall chose not to attack the Dandriwad line but turned his forces to mopping up enemy pockets in the Driniumoor region. On August 25 Krueger announced the official termination of the Aitape-Driniumoor operation.

The Driniumoor battle, with heavy fighting lasting a month, was one of the bloodiest but least known of all SWPA actions to that date: Hall's force lost 440 men killed and over 2500 wounded; according to Adachi, the Eighteenth Army's deaths amounted to about 10,000. If Adachi's offensive had overrun Aitape, MacArthur's operations to the north would have been seriously affected. The SWPA chief sent a message to Hall expressing his "admiration for the splendid conduct of the campaign east of Aitape. The operations were planned with great skill, were executed with great determination and courage, and were crowned with great success." The action at the Driniumoor was significant in destroying permanently the striking power of the Eighteenth Army and protecting the Aitape-Tadji area, which would prove valuable to future SWPA operations. Planes from airfields there would fly support missions for landings in Dutch New Guinea, and Aitape would become a key staging base for several future operations, including the invasion of the Philippines.[1]

While his forces were engaged simultaneously in July at the Driniumoor, Maffin Bay, Biak, Noemfoor, and the Sansapor-

Mar area, MacArthur was already deeply involved in planning his first offensive north of the equator. At first he thought in terms of advancing from the Vogelkop to southern Mindanao with only an intermediate operation to Halmahera. After a conference between his and Nimitz's planners at Pearl Harbor in early July, MacArthur altered his plan, for want of adequate shipping and carrier support, to include hops to Morotai and the Talauds before undertaking the invasion of Mindanao at Saragani Bay.

Intelligence reports indicated that the Japanese Second Army had almost 30,000 troops on Halmahera and there were no known landing spots on the islands that the enemy could not defend strongly. On the other hand, Morotai, the adjacent island to the north, had a garrison estimated at 1000 soldiers (actually about 500), seemingly good beaches on the southwestern tip, and an overgrown airfield at Pitoe near the best landing location. MacArthur set up a schedule that called for the invasion of Morotai on September 15, the Talauds in mid-October, and Mindanao a month later. Nimitz, whose forces had finally secured Saipan and then seized Guam and Tinian in the Marianas in late July, was to launch his invasion of the Palaus on the same day the Morotai operation began.

Hall, still at Aitape, was selected to command the Tradewind Task Force, which was to capture the Pitoe area of southwestern Morotai. He was given 61,000 troops, of which two-thirds were service and engineer personnel whose job would be to build airfields quickly for use in the hops to the Talauds and Mindanao. Tradewind's main combat unit was to be the 31st Division, led by Major General John C. Persons; most of its troops were then on duty in the Maffin Bay operation. Barbey would command the naval attack force and Berkey the Seventh Fleet's support group. The Pacific Fleet's Task Force 78, headed by Rear Admiral Thomas L. Sprague and including six carriers, would provide air support, as would Fifth Air Force planes fly-

Approaching the Philippines
June–Sept., 1944

CHINA
OKINAWA
RYUKYU IS.
IWO JIMA
FORMOSA
HONG KONG
HAINAN

South
China
Sea

LUZON
MANILA
PHILIPPINE IS.
Philippine
Sea

MARIANAS IS.
JUNE 15
SAIPAN
TINIAN
JULY 24
GUAM
JULY 21

SEPT. 23
ULITHI
YAP
TRUK

Sulu Sea
PALAU IS.
SEPT. 15
PELELIU
ANGAUR
DAVAO
CAROLINE IS.

NORTH BORNEO
BRUNEI
MINDANAO
SARAWAK
BORNEO
BALIKPAPAN

TALAUD IS.
SEPT. 15
MOROTAI
ASIA IS.
MAPIA IS.
NOV. 15
JULY 30
MANOKWARI
JULY 2
MAR-
SANSAPOR
BIAK
NOEMFOOR
SARMI
HOLLANDIA
CELEBES
HALMAHERA
CERAM
AMBON
AITAPE
DRINIUMOOR R.
ADMIRALTY IS.
WEWAK
RABAUL
MADANG
NETHERLANDS NEW GUINEA
NORTHEAST NEW GUINEA
NEW BRITAIN
LAE
PAPUA
BUNA

Java Sea
JAVA
Banda Sea
TIMOR
Arafura Sea
PORT MORESBY
Milne Bay

AUSTRALIA
DARWIN

0 200 400 600
MILES

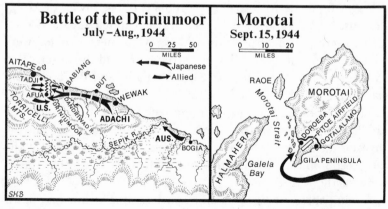

Battle of the Driniumoor
July–Aug., 1944

0 25 50
MILES

Japanese
Allied

AITAPE
TADJI
BABIANG
BUT
AFUA
DANDRIWAD R.
WEWAK
U.S.
TORRICELLI MTS.
DRINIUMOOR R.
ADACHI
SEPIK R.
AUS.
BOGIA

SHB

Morotai
Sept. 15, 1944

0 10 20
MILES

RAOE
MOROTAI
Morotai Strait
HALMAHERA
DOROEBA
PITOE AIRFIELD
GOTALALAMO
Galela Bay
GILA PENINSULA

ing from the new Vogelkop-Geelvink bases. In order to achieve tactical surprise and preclude the arrival of enemy reinforcements from nearby Halmahera, MacArthur insisted that no air strikes or naval bombardments be conducted against Morotai until the morning of the invasion.

The landings at Morotai on September 15 were made on three beaches close to the Pitoe airfield. None of the landing units faced opposition; indeed, by noon only two Japanese had been sighted, the rest having fled into the mountainous interior when the naval bombardment started. The amphibious operation, nevertheless, experienced difficulties because of previously undetected coral heads and mud flats, which forced the landing vessels to unload at a considerable distance offshore. The troops sank up to their armpits as they struggled to the beaches. After a weak banzai attack was repulsed that night, the task force's combat role soon resolved itself into minor patrol skirmishes and mopping-up in the Pitoe vicinity. By October 4, when the operation was belatedly declared completed, the Americans had lost thirty-one men killed and the Japanese about 300. Two-thirds of the enemy deaths occurred during an attempt to escape to Halmahera by barge, which was intercepted by American PT boats.

As on Bougainville, no effort was made to occupy all of Morotai; instead, the Pitoe beachhead was expanded into a twelve-mile-square perimeter, within which several new airfields were begun after it was found that the ground around the deactivated Japanese strip was too boggy. SWPA aircraft and PT boats constantly patrolled the waters off Morotai and effectively kept the Japanese from mounting a counterattack from Halmahera. The air bases built on Morotai were of much use later, during the invasion of Leyte. The Morotai operation ranks as one of the most economical and worthwhile undertakings of the Southwest Pacific war.[2]

Accompanied by Egeberg and Lehrbas, MacArthur had flown

from Brisbane to Port Moresby on September 9, then on by air to Hollandia the next day. There they boarded the *Nashville* on the 12th, and the cruiser steamed out to join Berkey's support group en route to Morotai. Early on the morning of September 15, MacArthur spent nearly an hour on the bridge watching in fascination as the *Nashville* and other ships of the Seventh Fleet pounded the Japanese base at Galela Bay, Halmahera, where it was suspected that an expedition to reinforce Morotai might be staged. At 10:15 A.M., less than two hours after the first American troops hit the Morotai beaches, MacArthur, Egeberg, Lehrbas, Hall, and Barbey went ashore near the Pitoe airfield, talked to Persons and some of his men, and observed the confusion attending the unloading of equipment and supplies. By 1:00 P.M. MacArthur was back aboard the *Nashville,* which soon got under way to Hollandia. J. E. Vine, an Australian correspondent on Morotai, reported that MacArthur commented to a group of GI's, "You have done well. You now dominate the last stronghold which barred our way to the Philippines. The enemy, as usual, was not in the right place at the right time." Lehrbas described a more dramatic encounter: While talking to a group of officers on the beach, the SWPA chief remarked, " 'We shall shortly have an air and light naval base here within 300 miles of the Philippines.' He gazed out to the northwest, almost as though he could already see through the mist the rugged lines of Bataan and Corregidor. 'They are waiting for me there,' he said. 'It has been a long time.' " [3]

Looking back over the SWPA operations from April through September, 1944, MacArthur could be pleased with the relatively low American losses and high Japanese casualties, the strategic advantages obtained preparatory to the invasion of the Philippines, the improved coordination of air and sea support of ground operations, the progress in meeting logistical needs, the experience gained by new units that would harden them for the greater battles to come, and the emergence of excellent field officers who would be essential to the reconquest of the Philippines. His forces had suffered about 1630 combat deaths and had killed over 26,400 Japanese during the following operations, which spanned 1400 miles: Madang-Alexishafen, Hollandia–Tanahmerah Bay, Aitape-Driniumoor, Wakde–Maffin Bay, Biak, Noemfoor, Sansapor-Mar, and Morotai.

During the same period Nimitz's forces had advanced 2600 miles closer to the general objective of the Luzon–Formosa–China coast triangle. His conquests of the Marianas and Palaus had contributed immensely to the attrition of Japan's air, sea, and ground strength in the Pacific and had gained base sites for the autumn inauguration of the bombing program by the B-29's against the Japanese home islands. The loss of Saipan was a major cause of the fall of General Hideki Tojo's ministry in Japan. In addition, the Pacific Fleet had rendered valuable assistance to MacArthur's operations. But the Central Pacific forces had captured the Marianas and Palaus at a frightfully high cost in American lives: the total number of Americans killed in action was nearly 7000, and about 46,000 Japanese died in those actions. Over 3400 American troops died in the seizure of Saipan alone. This battle had been particularly distressing because it caused not only appalling casualties but also a prolonged, ugly inter-service controversy after Marine Lieutenant General Holland Smith, the commander on Saipan, relieved Major General Ralph Smith, who headed an Army division in that operation.

American newspapers, especially those of Hearst, McCormick, and Patterson ownership, gave much attention to the Smith versus Smith episode. The New York *Journal-American,* a Hearst publication, charged that the high casualties and inter-service wrangle on Saipan could have been averted if Mac-Arthur had been given "the supreme command in the Pacific." Commenting on the "high and dreadful price" of Saipan, the

Journal-American stated on July 18, "The important and significant thing the American people DO know is that equally difficult and hazardous military operations conducted in the Pacific War under the competent command of General Douglas MacArthur have been successfully completed with little loss of life in most cases and with an obvious MINIMUM loss of life in all cases." Actually, not since the battle of Buna had MacArthur's troops encountered Japanese defenses as powerful as those on Saipan.[4]

When, on the same morning, Nimitz's forces invaded the Palaus and MacArthur's troops landed on Morotai, the receptions were quite different. In the Palaus the Army's 81st Division, led by Major General Paul J. Mueller, attacked Angaur, while Rupertus' 1st Marine Division assaulted Peleliu, just to the north. Mueller's troops ran into heavy opposition from the first, but it seemed to get worse as the days wore on. Mueller, who would later become MacArthur's chief of staff in Tokyo, prematurely declared the island secured on September 21, but the so-called mopping-up proved costly and lasted until late October. The division lost about 260 men killed on Angaur, and accounted for nearly 1300 Japanese dead. Rupertus' Marines faced an enemy garrison of over 11,200 troops entrenched in strong fortifications on Peleliu. Hostilities did not end there until November 26, by which time the Marines had lost 1250 killed and 5275 wounded; except for a few hundred who were taken prisoner, the Japanese defenders were wiped out. In striking contrast was the occupation of undefended Ulithi atoll, northeast of the Palaus, by one of Mueller's regiments on September 23. Ulithi was soon developed into the most important fleet anchorage and staging base in Nimitz's theater west of Hawaii.

Nimitz later admitted that the Peleliu operation "cost the attackers the highest combat casualty rate (nearly 40 per cent) of any amphibious assault in American history." The Army's official history says of the campaign in the Palaus, "It was so costly, in fact, that one wonders if the results were worth the effort." In view of last-minute changes in plans for the invasion of the Philippines, to be discussed later, the Angaur and Peleliu landings may have been needless, for, as the Army chronicle euphemistically points out, it subsequently became "impossible to fit the Palaus into the operational role originally planned for them." Airfields and an emergency anchorage were later developed in the Palaus, but heavy fighting was still under way at Angaur and Peleliu when the invasion of Leyte began in October. Although the anticipated support of American land-based aircraft in those islands would not come in time for Mac-Arthur's re-entry to the Philippines, at least the presence of Nimitz's embattled forces in the Palaus prevented the Japanese from using their bases to threaten the SWPA operation.

Some uncritical admirers of MacArthur's have cited the Palaus as an example of a strong enemy concentration that the SWPA chief would have bypassed. The truth is that of the high-ranking Pacific commanders only Halsey had advocated bypassing the Palaus. Based on the data available in late summer, 1944, not only Nimitz but also MacArthur and the Joint Chiefs of Staff had fully believed that the seizure of the Palaus would be essential to the success of the invasion of the Philippines. Thus the Palaus tragedy does not afford an illustration of the kind of blundering that MacArthur's strategic sense would have averted. In his memoirs MacArthur, in comparing the Morotai and Palaus operations, stated simply that Nimitz's forces "had been less fortunate." [5] The general's choice of adjectives was wise, for the relative easiness of his advance and the difficulty of Nimitz's in 1944 had resulted from the interplay of many causal factors other than brilliant or poor strategic planning, not the least of which was luck.

2. *Problems of Growth*

At the same time that a naval base, several airfields, and other military facilities were constructed in the Hollandia–Lake Sentani area during the summer of 1944, a sprawling headquarters complex was erected on a hillside overlooking the lake. Eichelberger and others who resided there considered the setting to be one of the most beautiful they had ever seen. With the destruction of the Japanese Eighteenth Army's offensive power in August, the move from Moresby and Brisbane to the new location was made by the advance headquarters of MacArthur, Kenney, Kinkaid, and other high-level SWPA organizations, including part of Blamey's staff. The various headquarters were situated on tiers up the side of Engineer Hill, with MacArthur's advance GHQ at the top level.[6]

Kenney, who moved to the Sentani area before MacArthur arrived, described the SWPA commander's house and its setting:

The house in which he lived, which was also occupied by several members of his staff and held his and Sutherland's office, a conference room, and the staff dining room, was located on the top of a hill about eight hundred feet high overlooking Sentani Lake and the airdrome area on its shores, about ten miles south of Hollandia village. The house was made of three Army-type prefabricated houses joined together and was quite comfortable. To make it look better, I had several striking aerial photographs enlarged, framed, and hung up on the walls. From MacArthur's office in Brisbane had come a few rugs and some furniture and, while not luxurious, it was quite good for New Guinea. Admiral Kinkaid's headquarters on the same hill about half a mile away was quite a lot better and my headquarters, farther down the slope and nearer the airdromes, although much smaller, was very livable, in spite of the fact that we were living on the edge of the jungle only two degrees from the equator. Perhaps the scenery had something to do with our feeling of comfort. The camps were all built part way up the slope of Cyclops, the six-thousand-foot mountain mass just to the north of Lake Sentani. Across the deep blue waters of the lake, which was about twenty miles long and varied in width from a half a mile to a hundred yards, the deep green hills of central New Guinea formed a backdrop of peaks, ravines, and jungle growth that was almost unreal. Little cone-shaped green islands, with native houses on stilts clinging to their shores, dotted the lake. To complete the picture, directly in back of the camp and perhaps two miles away, a five-hundred-foot waterfall seemed to spring out of the center of Cyclops Mountain, dark and forbidding, with its crest perpetually covered with black rain clouds.[7]

Thorpe, one of Willoughby's section chiefs, commented on MacArthur's structure: "Sitting on top of a beautiful hill, this white structure seemed a splendid thing from the beach far below and the war correspondents made the most of it." Long before MacArthur saw his prospective dwelling at Sentani, stories began to circulate, eventually appearing in print, that MacArthur and his family were already living in luxurious isolation in the "White House of the Southwest Pacific." According to the myth, a million dollars was spent on his mansion, its lavish furnishings, and the specially built drive leading to it. Actually, MacArthur passed his first night there on September 11 and departed on the 12th for Morotai. Returning from that operation, he was at the Sentani headquarters on the 17th and 18th, then flew on to Moresby and Brisbane. From September 20 to October 14 he was in Brisbane; on the latter day he flew to Moresby and from there to Hollandia for the night of October 15–16. The next day he left aboard the *Nashville* to join the Leyte attack force. According to his office diary, MacArthur never returned to the Hollandia area. After the Leyte landing, he set up his headquarters at Tacloban and later moved to Luzon.

Thus, in reality, he spent a total of four nights at the headquarters overlooking Lake Sentani, though the vicious stories persisted that he had spent months residing at his luxurious

Sentani mansion. The rush of events from mid-1944 on un-doubtedly was a determinant in the small amount of time he actually spent there, but he was sensitive about the cruel "White House" myth, which may have made him shy away from the area.[8] Huff recalled that on one occasion, possibly in late September, Mrs. MacArthur tried to jest with her serious-minded husband about the story:

> Not long after the establishment of the Hollandia advance headquarters, MacArthur returned to Brisbane and told Jean that he was preparing for the big push. "I won't be back," he added. Jean knew immediately what he meant.
> "You've got to send for me the minute you think it's safe for me to come to Manila," she said. They talked about the impending return to the Philippines for a few minutes and then she remarked, "When I go to Manila I want you to fix it so I can stop off at Hollandia. I want to see that mansion you built there — the one where I'm supposed to have been living in luxury!" [9]

Huff did not record the general's response.

By the time of his move to the Hollandia base, Kenney, who for two years had headed the Allied Air Forces and Fifth Air Force, now commanded the first organization as well as the Far East Air Forces (FEAF), established in June, 1944. Under the old set-up, the Fifth Air Force's rear echelon staff had also served as the Allied Air Forces headquarters, with the single exception of an RAAF officer who was the latter's intelligence director. The redeployment of the South Pacific theater's forces had brought into SWPA the Thirteenth Air Force and the 1st Marine Air Wing in the Solomons. Unless a new command were created, the Fifth's rear echelon would be controlling another Army air force and a Marine unit, which would not have been acceptable to Washington or the SWPA newcomers. So the FEAF came to be, and Kenney appointed Whitehead, his hard-driving, able deputy, as commander of the Fifth. MacArthur had wanted to call the new organization the "First Air Army," but Arnold objected to the unusual designation, and they settled on the plural version of the old FEAF which had tried to defend the Philippines in 1941–42. The most significant innovations in the organizational revision provided for the creation of an FEAF service command and an FEAF training center to take over supply and maintenance functions and training activities common to both of the Army air forces.[10]

In taking command of the Fifth Air Force, Whitehead gained a well-deserved elevation in the SWPA command structure; he had been the Fifth's field commander in fact if not in title since mid-1942. He was perhaps better known to the Japanese public than the American, for the Nipponese press often referred to him as the "Murderer of Moresby" after he had learned from New Guinea natives in early 1943 when Japanese troops would congregate at the village market in Lae to buy weekly supplies and then sent his planes to attack them at that very hour, killing hundreds gathered in the marketplace. Aggressive and eager for combat, he often flew with reconnaissance and combat missions, though Kenney eventually made him curtail that practice.

Because of its 1200-plane striking power as well as the close Kenney-Whitehead relationship, the Fifth would serve as the assault air arm for MacArthur's operations during the rest of the war, with Major General St. Clair Streett's Thirteenth Air Force cast in the supporting role. Lieutenant General Earl W. Barnes, who in 1944 headed the XIII Fighter Command and became commander of the Thirteenth Air Force in the spring of 1945, recalled that Whitehead was "caustic" toward the Thirteenth's officers and was "constantly sniping at us." In Streett's outfit there was "some chaffing on the part of the staff" about their missions, and in January, 1945, Streett disgustedly proposed that the Thirteenth be deactivated and its air units absorbed into the Fifth. MacArthur and Kenney assured him that the Thirteenth was to have a key role in the future invasion of Japan. Yet the majority of the Thirteenth's bomb tonnage in the last year of the conflict was dropped on targets in the East Indies, Rabaul, Bougainville, and Truk.

Despite his pleas for a role for his Marines in the advance to the Philippines, Major General Ralph Mitchell's Marine units, whose command was designated Aircraft Northern Solomons (AIRNORSOLS), also got only a supporting role from Kenney. Their targets were limited to the Rabaul, Kavieng, and Bougainville areas. The FEAF chief told Mitchell that his Marine flyers would be used during the assault of the Philippines, and, indeed, they were to play a crucial part in support of the Leyte operation that autumn. Whatever their differences, however, the American air commanders never approached the degree of bitterness toward each other that was attained in the RAAF's ugly Jones-Bostock feud.[11]

An unexpected blessing came to Kenney and his airmen in July, 1944, when he learned from a reporter that Colonel Charles A. Lindbergh was on a special mission in SWPA to study combat performances of fighter aircraft and get ideas on how to improve their design and capabilities. Although astounded that Washington had authorized Lindbergh's trip without informing him, MacArthur was "the soul of cordiality" when Kenney brought the famed flyer to his Brisbane office. Lindbergh explained that he knew of ways to extend greatly the combat range of the FEAF's P-38's; MacArthur and Kenney were enthusiastic and persuaded him to prolong his stay to assist the FEAF. Lindbergh remained in the Southwest Pacific until late August and succeeded in getting the radius of the P-38's up to a hitherto unimagined 750 to 850 miles. He also managed to sneak in a combat mission or two as a fighter pilot, shooting down one enemy plane and nearly getting himself killed. MacArthur and Kenney were most grateful for the "superb job" that Lindbergh did in extending fighter ranges. An outstanding example of the

FEAF's exploitation of the increased combat radius of its P-38's was the devastating raid of October 10 by 125 Noemfoor-based B-24's against the oil installations at Balikpapan, Borneo, which produced nearly 40 per cent of the Japanese requirement for lubricating oils. That day the bombers were escorted by several squadrons of P-38's based at Morotai; the fighters flew 1670 miles on that mission, a distance considered impossible by the FEAF leaders before Lindbergh's unexpected visit.[12]

Like Whitehead, Eichelberger was another experienced SWPA officer whom MacArthur elevated to a position of much greater responsibility during the summer of 1944. With the transfer of Halsey's Army units to SWPA under way, MacArthur radioed Marshall on May 11, "The nature of operations in this theatre and the size of the ground forces, which will comprise seventeen divisions and four corps, now require the establishment of an additional army headquarters." He requested that "an army headquarters and headquarters company" be sent to SWPA and added, "It is contemplated that Lieut. General Eichelberger will be assigned to the command." Marshall quickly approved his recommendation, and orders were cut assigning the headquarters personnel of the Second Army, which had been training in the States for over two years, as the staff for MacArthur's new army, to be designated the Eighth.

For some reason, MacArthur kept Eichelberger in suspense until August regarding the forthcoming command, though scuttlebutt about it was rife as early as June. When Eichelberger returned from Biak, he found Krueger in an ugly mood: "The impression I get is that the Sixth Army staff take a very poor view of General MacArthur's desire to have an Eighth Army. Walter acts as though he had been spanked." A month later Eichelberger observed that Krueger's attitude had worsened: "Walter acts as though he considers it [Eighth Army] more or less as an illegitimate child and as though he would like to strangle it or put it in a sack." Later, on Luzon, Mac-

Arthur told Eichelberger that Krueger "had steadfastly opposed the creation of another Army headquarters" in the Southwest Pacific. Willoughby maintained that in the creation of the Eighth Army "MacArthur was either influenced by Eichelberger or by the people in Washington who backed Eichelberger and with whom he had constant links . . . Eighth Army was intended to be used as relief. There was no urgent necessity for it."

By early September, the new headquarters staff, consisting of about 250 officers and 700 enlisted men, had arrived, and on the 7th MacArthur formally appointed Eichelberger as commander of the Eighth Army. Byers became its chief of staff, and several others of the old I Corps staff were added to Eichelberger's new headquarters at Hollandia. On September 25 MacArthur dissolved the Alamo Force, thus casting aside the disguise that Krueger's Sixth Army had worn for over two years. By then Blamey's position as commander of the Allied Land Forces had become almost meaningless. Actually, he had effective command of only the Australian ground forces, of which the First Army was about to relieve the American units containing the bypassed Japanese in Northeast New Guinea, the Bismarcks, and the Solomons while the Second Army was on duty in Australia. MacArthur himself gradually had assumed the unofficial command of the Allied Land Forces.

At the outset the Eighth Army was assigned two corps, including nearly 200,000 troops, or about half of the American Army strength in the Southwest Pacific in September, 1944. For the near future, the new army's principal tasks would be to relieve Krueger's units of mopping-up chores in Dutch New Guinea and assist the Sixth in its training and staging activities preparatory to that army's invasion of the Philippines. In early October, mop-up operations in the Maffin Bay, Biak, Noemfoor, and Sansapor areas were assumed by Eichelberger's command. On November 15, the Eighth Army undertook its first offensive mission, a minor one, when elements of the 31st Division seized the Asia and Mapia islands off the northern coast of the Vogelkop. The Eighth's first major combat assignment would not come until late December, when it would relieve the Sixth on Leyte.

For a time the Eighth's commanders must have felt like the Thirteenth Air Force — relegated to a supporting role. But MacArthur kept assuring Eichelberger that his day of glory would come, and it surely did in the spring. By then Eichelberger's army would include three corps, and at various times twenty-two divisions would be under his command in wide-ranging operations.[13] As will be seen, the jealousy and rivalry between the Sixth's and Eighth's commanders and staffs would produce a tense competition for MacArthur's accolades, which may have been anticipated by the wily SWPA chief when he created the second army. After all, a confirmed believer in laissez faire like MacArthur knew that the best results would come from wide-open competition.

In addition to Whitehead and Eichelberger, another prominent SWPA general to whom MacArthur assigned increased responsibilities in the summer of 1944 was Casey, his chief engineer. On July 23, MacArthur established the SWPA Army Service Command (ASCOM) as an agency to provide immediate logistical support and to start base and airfield construction in the early phase of a task force's assault. Casey was appointed to head ASCOM, and Sverdrup, his deputy, became the SWPA chief engineer. ASCOM was created primarily to cope with the emergency supply and construction problems anticipated during the coming invasion of the Philippines, an operation of far greater scope and logistical complications than any yet undertaken in MacArthur's theater. ASCOM was placed "under direct control of General Krueger, meanwhile maintaining close liaison with Services of Supply from which it drew materiel and personnel." [14]

ASCOM would prove to be a valuable asset to the assault

forces, but unfortunately most of the theater's logistical problems could not be solved so readily. The old areas of concern
in the field of supply caused new anxieties by mid-1944, particularly the shortage of service troops and a new shipping crisis.
For example, the troops of Major General Percy W. Clarkson's
33rd Division, which were eager to get into combat, found themselves detoured when they arrived at Finschhafen:

> During the month of June [1944] the 33d was launched into
> the most distasteful assignment in its World War II history.
> Base F, organized at Finschhafen to receive and break down
> Stateside supplies for forward operational units, was hopelessly
> behind in its vital work. This impairment, caused by a severe
> shortage of port personnel, resulted in Dreger Harbor being
> crowded with scores of ocean-going vessels impatiently waiting
> to be unloaded. Theater policy gave base operations a high
> priority. It also empowered the base commander to employ
> all troops in his area, combat or service, if they were needed to
> accomplish this mission. Accordingly, General Clarkson was
> asked to supply several thousand men for an indefinite period
> to augment Base F's slim port forces.[15]

A report on vessels at Hollandia on October 18 stated that of
the eighty-seven noncombatant ships anchored in the harbor
there were "12 discharging, 3 loading, 24 awaiting call to Leyte,
33 waiting to discharge, 5 waiting to load, and 10 miscellaneous"
— a scene unfortunately too common at that port on other days
and typical of other SWPA forward ports as well. The SWPA
theater, states the Army's official chronicle, "was caught in a
triple squeeze by shortage of receiving capacity, service troops,
and cargo shipping, all in a continual process of interaction."[16]

MacArthur's retention of cargo vessels to use as floating warehouses or to meet his theater's shipping needs rose from 70
in January, 1944, to 112 in May and 190 in November. As had
happened during the previous two autumns, the Allied shipping
crisis in the fall of 1944 became worldwide and was the subject

of anxious deliberations by the Joint and Combined Chiefs and their planners. In December, the Joint Chiefs decreed that henceforth ocean-going vessels must not be used for harbor storage and that theater requisitions for cargo shipping must be adjusted realistically to the discharge capacities of the ports. Moreover, the Joint Chiefs declared that MacArthur must reduce his retentions to 100 cargo vessels by mid-January, though his forces would then be involved in their largest operation, the conquest of Luzon. MacArthur protested that changes in strategic plans, swift-moving advances, inadequate port facilities, and lack of service troops necessitated the larger retentions of shipping. Among other solutions that he and Marshall considered was one to send 50,000 coolies a month from China, by way of Calcutta, to the SWPA theater to help in unloading cargo. The War Department was interested in the scheme, but no evidence has been found of its progress or failure.

Van Wyk, who headed the GHQ transportation section, said that the SWPA commander appeared quite upset about the shipping congestion at a staff meeting that fall: "MacArthur got up and walked up and down in front of us for about an hour, talking continuously . . . He was complaining that Somervell had sent a telegram to him and that he didn't want to get another one. He wanted the ships unloaded and told us to get to work and find ways to unload them." By utilizing LST's as lighters, among other techniques, Van Wyk said, "we were able to discharge ships at tremendously increased rates. That reduced the backlog markedly, but the main reasons for the huge backlog were that we had no out-loading facilities and no real restrictions placed on the Army, Navy, or Air Force to hold down their requisitions." Until the end of the war, shipping problems of various sorts would continue to plague MacArthur, as they did Eisenhower and other theater commanders. When MacArthur sent Brigadier General Harold E. Eastwood, his assistant G-4, to Washington to urge restoration of the SWPA shipping cut, the officer found out that Eisenhower's command, "the top-priority theater, had suffered far deeper proportionate cuts in shipping than had as yet been applied against SWPA." [17]

The rapid advance of MacArthur's forces in 1944, like that of Eisenhower's across northern France and the Lowlands, posed tremendous difficulties in keeping the forward units supplied. In the Southwest Pacific there was the additional problem of "rolling up" rear bases. Some of the largest ones were over 1000 miles behind MacArthur's assault spearheads by the time they hit Sansapor and Morotai. The War Department had repeatedly tried to get MacArthur to close down some of those rear bases and move their personnel and matériel closer to the combat areas. The SWPA chief had responded that such moves would take shipping that was needed in operations and also would produce time-consuming entanglements of his supply system at critical times in the northward advance. Nevertheless, the development of the huge Hollandia base seems to have been undertaken partly in response to such pressure.

The roll-up that caused most concern to the authorities in Washington and Pearl Harbor involved the movement of the Army personnel and matériel of the South Pacific theater, which had been assigned to MacArthur. In late June, Nimitz proposed to the Joint Chiefs that any Army troops or stores not physically transferred to SWPA by September 1 be assigned to the Central Pacific theater. MacArthur responded heatedly that this would violate the March directive of the Joint Chiefs regarding the redeployment of the South Pacific theater's resources. The Joint Chiefs refused to rescind the directive but urged the two commanders to work out a solution satisfactory to both.

Not unlike two hostile tribes warily trying to settle a dispute over grazing lands, representatives of MacArthur and Nimitz met at Hollandia in early November and drew up an agreement, which the two theater chiefs endorsed. In the agreement, it was pledged that Nimitz would not further press his claims regard-

ing Army resources still at South Pacific bases if the SWPA
commander provided staging and rehabilitation facilities in the
Philippines, once they were reconquered, for the parts of
Nimitz's forces that were to be employed in the future invasions
of the Ryukyus and Japan. Unfortunately, developments during the spring of 1945 would lead both commanders to renege
on the Hollandia agreement, precipitating another period of
tense inter-theater relations.[18] The era of good feelings between
the Brisbane and Pearl Harbor headquarters, inaugurated at
the MacArthur-Nimitz conference in March, 1944, had endured,
alas, no better than the proverbial summer's romance.

3. *Philippine Affairs*

In January, 1942, it will be recalled, Homma set up the Executive Commission, headed by Vargas, Quezon's former secretary,
and comprised of leading Filipino politicians, to administer
Philippine governmental affairs. Many prominent Filipinos
served in public positions during the occupation, usually excus-
ing their collaboration on the ground that it was the best way
to protect the citizenry from worse manifestations of Japanese
totalitarianism and brutality. Filipino political parties were
abolished, and in their stead the Japanese established in late
1942 a puppet political organization known as the Kalibapi, or
Association for Service to the New Philippines. Although the
Kalibapi was supported primarily by some of the prewar oligarchy, Premier Tojo, on his visit to Manila in May, 1943,
expressed satisfaction at the Filipino people's cooperation and
pledged that they would soon have their independence.

The next month a Kalibapi-chosen commission started drafting a new Philippine constitution; its chairman was José P.
Laurel, an influential member of Quezon's prewar Nacionalista

party who had served under Vargas as commissioner of justice and of the interior. Also active on the constitutional commission was Manuel Roxas, formerly a key politician in Quezon's regime and an aide to MacArthur, who until then had refused to cooperate with the Japanese. The new constitution, approved by a Kalibapi-controlled assembly in September, provided for a nominally republican form of government, but by its provisions the president was given powers that were almost dictatorial and could appoint half of the unicameral National Assembly, its other half to be chosen in elections carefully supervised by the Kalibapi.[19]

Laurel was "elected" president of the puppet republic and was inaugurated in October, 1943. For a time Roxas served as administrator of food resources in the new regime. A trusted collaborator but also a believer in the pan-Asian movement, Laurel headed a Filipino delegation later in 1943 that participated in the Assembly of Greater East Asiatic Nations in Tokyo. In the fall of 1944, the Laurel government issued a declaration of war against the United States and Great Britain. Representing mainly the pre-1941 elite who had monopolized political power and wealth, the new regime was never popular with the Filipino masses, many of whom had detested their own nation's oligarchy before the war as much as they hated the Japanese during the occupation. Disappointed by late 1944 with Laurel's failure to rally the people's support, the Japanese organized the Makapili, or Patriotic League of Filipinos, in which the most extremely pro-Japanese Filipinos tried to stir up interest in behalf of the Japanese cause. About 5000 Makapili formed a volunteer unit to assist the Japanese in defending the islands. By the time of the American invasion of the archipelago, the Laurel regime was discredited, powerless, and on the verge of being toppled by the Makapili.[20]

Karl L. Rankin, an American Foreign Service official in prewar Manila who was interned in early 1942 and freed in an exchange in late 1943, thought the main reasons for the Japanese political failure in the Philippines were as follows:

> The first was the impossibility of persuading any important number of Filipinos that the United States could lose the war . . . The second cause . . . may be found in the repetition of the worst mistakes made by Americans. At his best the invader was condescending and patronizing to the Filipino; at his worst he was grasping and brutal . . .
>
> Guerrilla activity in the provinces was a major factor in increasing the population of Manila to a point where housing, food and unemployment problems, difficult enough in any case, added fuel to Filipino hatred of the Japanese . . . Rationing and price control measures in general did not work smoothly and the cost of living rose to unprecedented heights. Business was all but stagnant.[21]

As a group of American prisoners was herded through the streets of Manila in the summer of 1943, one of the men, Major John Wright, observed that the Filipino onlookers' sympathy for the Americans clearly indicated that "the Greater East Asia Co-Prosperity Sphere had failed to make loyal members of the Filipinos . . . Their eyes showed a defiance" of the Japanese.[22]

With Wainwright's surrender of all USFIP forces in May, 1942, MacArthur's initial plan for guerrilla resistance by those units outside Bataan and Corregidor collapsed. Before surrendering themselves, however, some USFIP divisional commanders, especially Brougher of the 11th Division, had released those among their officers who wanted to escape to the hills and organize guerrilla bands. Colonel Russell W. Volckmann, one of Brougher's officers, fled to the North Luzon mountains where he gradually gathered a force that numbered 18,000 by the spring of 1945. Other active guerrilla leaders who emerged included Colonels Wendell W. Fertig on Mindanao, Macario Peralta on Panay, and Ruperto K. Kangleon on Leyte. Fertig's command, which had about 38,000 men by January, 1945, was the largest and best equipped of all the guerrilla organizations.

Some of the fiercest resistance on Luzon was supplied by the Hukbalahaps, or The People's Army Against Japan. The Huks, as they were nicknamed, were led by Luis Taruc, a zealous Marxist who sometimes had as many as 30,000 guerrillas under his command. They gained control of large areas of Luzon, including the rich agricultural regions of the Central Luzon Plain where relations between landlords and tenant farmers had long been explosive. As they drove out the Japanese, the Huks also killed or put to flight many collaborationist landlords, redistributed their lands to peasants, and created Soviet-style cooperatives. Some of the Huks were Communists, and many more would be converted to that ideology from 1945 to 1950, as they would continue to seek social justice according to their terms. The guerrilla movement in the Philippines also included many bandits who engaged in looting and other acts of lawlessness under the guise of resisting the Japanese.

Until early 1943, when radio and submarine contacts with the widespread guerrilla groups began to grow, MacArthur was uncertain how numerous and effective the members of the Filipino underground were. Actually, during 1942–44 the strength of the guerrillas was considerable, totaling perhaps 180,000 or more individuals, whose stay with a unit, however, was informal and might last two days or two years. Of the major organized guerrilla units with which GHQ SWPA was eventually in contact, there were eighteen separate forces on Luzon, fourteen on the Sibuyan-Visayan islands, and thirteen on Mindanao and the Sulus. As SWPA submarines and aircraft brought them increasing amounts of supplies, munitions, and equipment, the guerrillas began to play a valuable role not only in raiding Japanese garrisons and lines of communications but also in relaying to GHQ much important (and some unreliable) intelligence data on enemy strengths, dispositions, and activities. By late 1944, the guerrillas' resistance had become so formidable that they kept the Japanese from effectively controlling thirty-six of the forty-eight Philippine provinces, but the dozen that were strongly held by the enemy included the most heavily populated and strategically vital areas, such as Manila and Davao.[23]

For the most part, guerrilla bands were not uniformly organized or under central direction, and not infrequently they fought against other guerrilla groups. On Leyte, for example, Kangleon's force and that of a rival leader fought a bloody battle in August, 1943, for overall control of guerrilla operations on that island. To avoid further bloodshed among the Filipinos, MacArthur sent a message to the island's guerrilla bands informing them that he had appointed Kangleon as the "Leyte Area Commander." In the Sulus in mid-1943 another situation arose that also brought personal action from MacArthur. A group of tough Moro guerrillas challenged the rank and authority of a youthful USFIP lieutenant named Frank Young. The enterprising officer averted violence by announcing that he was a captain and had his appointment as leader of the unit directly from MacArthur. He then sent a desperate message to the SWPA commander: "I have stopped a rebellion single-handed. But I had to be a captain to lead them. Do not make a liar out of me. Make me a captain instead. At once, please." According to Ind, of the Allied Intelligence Bureau, MacArthur told him to send a reply at once that "Young was to be a captain, not only because Young said so, but because General MacArthur said so." [24]

During the years 1942–44, relations between the guerrillas and MacArthur's GHQ evolved in two phases: (1) the initial contacts and exploration of the guerrilla movement by Ind's Philippine subsection of the Allied Intelligence Bureau, June, 1942–May, 1943; and (2) logistical support, guerrilla training, intelligence gathering, and psychological warfare activities by Whitney's much larger Philippine Regional Section, ostensibly under G-2 but reporting directly to MacArthur, May, 1943– October, 1944. During the last half of 1942 radio contacts were rare, but some information on embryonic guerrilla organizations reached GHQ through a few USAFFE soldiers who escaped from the Philippines to Australia that fall. Although intensely interested in promoting Filipino resistance efforts, MacArthur could do little at that time to provide Ind's agency with supplies, equipment, and transportation in view of the immediate needs of his combat units in the Papuan campaign. Nevertheless, SWPA submarines carried several parties of Allied agents to and from the islands where they made contacts with guerrilla leaders and conferred with them on plans for expanding support and communications. Among these daring pioneers in penetrating the enemy-held archipelago were Captain Jesus Villamor and Major Emigidio Cruz of the Philippine Army and Commander Charles Parsons of the United States Navy. Parsons had been a long-time resident in the Philippines.

By the spring of 1943 growing numbers of submarine trips were under way to and from the islands; the underseas craft bore weapons, supplies, and highly trained agents. A widespread network of radio stations was being developed from Mindanao to Luzon, and the intelligence feedback to GHQ was beginning to mount. MacArthur insisted that all escaping prisoners and returning agents, if they were able to walk, report to him personally. His many questions and keen interest in details about conditions in the islands revealed the concern of a man whose yearning to get back to his beloved "second homeland" had become virtually an obsession.[25]

At Sutherland's suggestion, in May, 1943, MacArthur sent for Whitney, then on duty in the States, to take charge of the newly created Philippine Regional Section. An attorney for many years in Manila, with wide contacts among influential Filipinos, Whitney was charged with developing a vastly expanded and varied program of organizing and promoting resistance activities in the Philippines. American officers were dispatched to guerrilla units to assist in improving their organization and training.

With Quezon's authorization and American assistance, the guerrillas began issuing their own currency, operating postal systems, and carrying out well-planned agricultural production and distribution programs in provinces where enemy control was weak or nonexistent.

Whitney's section also became involved in the preparation and distribution in the islands of a variety of propaganda materials, including mirrors, matchboxes, needle cards, cigarette packages and a myriad of other small merchandise items all conspicuously stamped with the words "I shall return. MacArthur." How effective the slogan was in inspiring Filipino morale is conjectural, but the scheme had the endorsement of Quezon, who, of all persons, should have known the Filipino mind. The SWPA commander was highly pleased with Whitney's work, and the latter was seen going into MacArthur's office more and more frequently as the months passed. Whitney was on his way to becoming the general's chief confidant, which he would, in fact, be within another two years.[26]

Mashbir's ATIS personnel and Feller's psychological warfare group were utilized more and more in intelligence and propaganda efforts in the Philippines, sometimes under Whitney's program and at other times in activities under Willoughby's aegis. Also Frederic Marquardt, a Manila journalist who had left on the eve of war, returned to MacArthur's theater as a representative of the United States Office of War Information and helped to develop radio programs and printed news materials that were channeled into the Philippines. Robert Sherwood, who headed the OWI's Pacific section, refused a GHQ request, however, to print leaflets bearing the general's pledge to return, so Whitney had to get such work done in Australia. Meanwhile, MacArthur still refused Brigadier General William J. Donovan's repeated offers to send his OSS agents into the Philippines and other parts of the SWPA theater. Willoughby assured MacArthur that they were not needed, and the SWPA chief, in turn, was not about to have Allied personnel in his theater who were not under his control, as would have been the case with the OSS.[27]

MacArthur never forgot that the Philippines contained not only collaborators and guerrillas but also many thousands of American civilian internees and USFIP prisoners of war. For the most part the internees were kept at Baguio and Manila throughout the war, but the Japanese gradually transported many of the American soldiers from Philippine camps to work in mines and factories in Manchuria, Korea, Japan, and Formosa. This movement northward was accelerated in the last half of 1944, and possibly two-thirds of the USFIP prisoners had left the Philippines prior to MacArthur's return. Several thousand of them died on Japanese transports, which were known as "hell ships," from starvation, suffocation, disease, and Allied air and submarine attacks on these mistaken targets. At the outset of their imprisonment, Wainwright and the other senior American, Dutch, and British officers captured during the Japanese conquest of Southeast Asia were segregated from their junior officers and enlisted men. In August, 1942, Wainwright's group was transferred from Luzon to Formosa and in the fall of 1944 to a Manchurian prison camp.

Severity of prison conditions in the Philippines differed greatly, depending on the dispositions of the camp commandant and his guards, adequacy of facilities, availability of supplies, and responsible leadership among the prisoners. There were unquestionably many instances of brutality and some atrocities, but much of the prisoners' suffering stemmed from the unpreparedness of the Japanese to care for such a large number of captives, the traditional samurai disdain for soldiers who surrendered, and misunderstandings which arose from language differences. The camps were closely guarded, so the prisoners had little contact with guerrillas, but usually in each prison an enterprising individual or two had a hidden radio by which he and his companions kept reasonably well informed on the course of the war.[28]

Most of the prisoners' thoughts and conversations centered on food, clothing, family, and prison gossip, but when they talked occasionally of their defeat in 1942, some evidence of deep-seated bitterness toward MacArthur was manifest. Examples of anti-MacArthur sentiments are not uncommon in the prisoners' diaries, notes, and memoirs. On August 1, 1943, for example, Brougher began another volume of his diary in a school note-book obtained at the post exchange of the Shirakawa prison camp on Formosa: "Well, here I am beginning another book far beyond the latest date I had originally conceived as the longest possible time it would take for the help that was 'on the way' to arrive and rescue us. I suppose now that MacArthur's promised help for the Philippines is still 'on the way.' " He noted that he was "still hungry as a wolf, but still well and hope-ful" — a condition and attitude that most of the prison survi-vors shared.[29]

In the summer of 1943, three USFIP officers, William E. Dyess, Steve M. Mellnik, and Melvin H. McCoy, escaped from a Mindanao prison camp and made their way to Australia with the help of guerrillas and Whitney's personnel. MacArthur awarded the Distinguished Service Medal to each of them and later listened in shock to their stories of atrocities against the USFIP prisoners. "As we described the disease and deaths at O'Donnell, Cabanatuan, and Davao," said Mellnik, "the general tightened his lips, 'The Japanese will pay for that humiliation and suffering,' he said in a grave voice." MacArthur requested permission from the War Department to get out a press release on the officers' stories. Because of delicate negotiations then under way indirectly with Tokyo to get an internee exchange and Red Cross parcels to Allied prisoners in Asia, Washington forbade the release of their accounts of atrocities. Somehow McCormick's *Tribune* cornered the news scoop, but had to hold it until the War Department authorized its release in January, 1944. The news sent shock waves through the American public, setting off new demands for accelerating the war against Japan.[30] No available evidence ties McCormick's role in this with his political efforts at the time, but the sensational revelations did not exactly handicap the particular presidential candidacy that the *Tribune* was championing.

Back in Washington, Quezon and his small group of Filipino officials tried to maintain the semblance of a functioning administration. According to one authority, however, the Philippine government-in-exile "was primarily the vehicle for Quezon and [Vice President Sergio] Osmeña. It cloaked them with the appurtenances of office, continued the legal claim of the Commonwealth, and served as a propaganda force, publicizing the plight of the Filipinos to the American people." The Quezon group "was a symbol of the past and the hope for the future, serving as the continuing focus for loyalty of the majority of the Filipinos in the archipelago."

Seriously ill with tuberculosis, Quezon continued to complain to Roosevelt about his emphasis on the European war; he corresponded frequently with MacArthur, offering advice and soliciting information about happenings inside the Philippines; and he dispatched his staff regularly to the offices of Washington politicians to stir up interest in early Philippine independence and financial support for reconstruction. The men who were closest to the Philippine president during the exile were Romulo, who handled public relations, Colonel Manuel Nieto, Quezon's military aide, and Major General Basilio J. Valdes, the Philippine Army's chief of staff. Osmeña was carefully kept on the edge of the inner circle, which had been the case before the war when he was considered Quezon's chief political rival. Quezon made it apparent that his preference of a presidential successor was Roxas, not Osmeña.[31]

The voluminous correspondence between MacArthur and

Quezon from 1942 to 1944 reads like the letters of two devoted brothers. MacArthur treated Quezon with great respect and understanding, trying to carry out his every request, even to the point, in 1943, of sending Cruz on a harrowing mission to Manila mainly to carry a message from Quezon to Roxas. When, in the autumn of 1943, Quezon's term of office was about to expire, MacArthur anxiously wrote to the War Department that "nothing could be more harmful to our Philippine military effort than to let this situation go by default" and thereby lose Quezon's leadership, which was "symbolical of Philippine aspirations." A joint resolution was passed by Congress on November 13 providing for Quezon to continue in office for the duration of the war. The SWPA chief, busy as he was, also agreed to write the introduction for the reminiscences Quezon was laboriously writing — *The Good Fight,* published in 1944. In his introduction, MacArthur praised the ailing Filipino as "one of the greatest living statesmen," a man possessing "complete loyalty to America," courage, wisdom, and "uncanny premonition." [32]

While in exile, Quezon had the satisfaction of seeing several measures that were dear to him adopted by the American government. For nearly two years Congress and the White House wrestled with the problem of postwar relief and rehabilitation for the Philippines, finally establishing a Filipino Rehabilitation Commission in June, 1944. This would eventually result in the Philippine Rehabilitation Act of April, 1946, by which about $620 million were allocated for war damages and reconstruction funds. Also in June, 1944, a congressional joint resolution provided for a mutual defense agreement under which there would be American bases and forces in the Philippines. MacArthur heartily approved of the projected arrangement. The action in which both Quezon and MacArthur were most interested was Senator Millard F. Tydings' bill in 1943 stipulating Philippine independence as soon as practicable and authorizing the President to proclaim it even before the previously agreed date of July 4, 1946. The bill was not passed, but the basic provisions were included in a joint resolution passed by Congress in 1944.[33]

MacArthur had written to Quezon on September 27, 1943, while the bill was under consideration:

> With the passage of the bill for Philippine independence providing for mutual plans for its national defense, I desire to offer you my services at the appropriate time to command the combined military forces there under my commission in the Philippine Army but without salary. I would be glad to dedicate the remainder of my life to this great cause with which I have been associated so many years. Such a solution might be effective in bridging any gap in defense matters which might arise between the two governments. If this suggestion, however, embarrasses you in any way, please disregard it.[34]

The gesture greatly pleased Quezon.

At Saranac Lake, New York, on August 1, 1944, Quezon's long-expected death occurred. MacArthur commented, "President Quezon's death will be a great shock to the people of the Philippines, who so keenly anticipated his return to Manila. He was the very apotheosis of the aspiration of the Filipinos for the higher things of life. A great liberal, his fame and glory will increase as his policies gradually approach fruition. I mourn him." In his first message as the new Philippine president, Osmeña radioed MacArthur, "I wish to reiterate my faith in your military leadership and assure you that the close cooperation of the Philippine Government with you in the achievement of our common objective will remain unbroken." On August 11, MacArthur responded, "On your ascendancy to the Presidency I wish you to know the absolute confidence I feel towards you in that great office and to assure you of the complete support I shall give you in the critical days that lie ahead. It would be a greatest possible benefit if I could confer with you personally in Brisbane to outline our mutual plans." [35]

In spite of such agreeable messages, the new Philippine president knew that he would face difficulties with MacArthur. Osmeña had been sharply critical of MacArthur's Philippine defense program in the late 1930's, and the general had not forgiven him for his part in getting defense funds cut on the eve of war. Before and during the war years, Osmeña had enjoyed the friendship of Secretary of the Interior Harold L. Ickes, the curmudgeon who had long feuded with MacArthur. The Interior Department's Bureau of Insular Affairs was responsible for overseeing Philippine affairs until independence, and Ickes took special delight in meddling in the bureau's relations with the Quezon regime. Partly to give more support to Osmeña in offsetting MacArthur's strong influence among the Filipinos, Ickes tried in vain to get Roosevelt to appoint a new American high commissioner for the islands, to hold office until the inauguration of the postwar republic. MacArthur received a strange proposal through the War Department, possibly sent at the suggestion of Ickes, that Associate Justice Frank Murphy of the United States Supreme Court, who had been Philippine high commissioner in the 1930's and was close to Osmeña, be sent to assist the guerrillas on Mindanao. The SWPA chief refused to cooperate on the grounds that Murphy "has not been connected with the Philippine war effort in any way, and his previous views opposing Filipino preparedness for war would make his proposed visit psychologically inadvisable. His life would be in jeopardy not only by the enemy but by the guerrilla elements."

As one historian has stated, "Osmeña's great dilemma was that he could neither compete with Quezon, a dead hero mourned by the people, nor with MacArthur, a living symbol already revered as a demigod." Moreover, Osmeña knew that, like Quezon, MacArthur strongly preferred Roxas as the future head of the Philippine government, regardless of his alleged collaboration. Ickes warned Osmeña against returning to the islands while their reconquest was in progress: "The country will be entirely under military command, and you as a civilian leader will be powerless. Your people will expect many things from you that you will be unable to give them." Refusing to go to Brisbane in August as MacArthur wanted, Osmeña sent Valdes there in early September to act as his liaison with the American commander, but he was granted only two audiences with MacArthur. The Philippine president, with strong misgivings, finally decided to join MacArthur's triumphal return to the islands that fall, but he was determined to wait until the eleventh hour and met the general at Hollandia as the attack force set forth.[36]

Although Washington officials began work on a Philippine civil affairs policy in January, 1944, the Army's official history states that "strong disagreements developed between the War and Interior Departments as to who should administer civil affairs in the Islands." With no directive forthcoming from the War Department or the Joint Chiefs, MacArthur, aided by the counsel of Whitney and Fellers, devised his own plan for civil affairs during the reconquest of the islands. After the invasion was well under way he would receive a directive from Washington on the subject, but it substantially agreed with the principles and instructions he had already developed.

According to MacArthur's plan, a GHQ civil affairs section was established in September, which, in turn, was to supervise civil affairs units attached to the Sixth Army, the invading force. The units would begin restoring normal political and economic organization to communities and areas as soon as the combat situation permitted. They would temporarily select local Filipino officials, with Osmeña's government holding the power of ratification of appointments. The civil affairs units would also serve in advisory capacities on political, fiscal, and economic matters to local and provincial officials and would administer initial relief efforts. As soon as possible after the end of hostilities in a given area, Osmeña's government would take over civil administration and relief.[37]

MacArthur explained the main principles of his policy in a letter to the War Department on September 2, 1944:

> It is essential, in my opinion, in any plans for the control of civil affairs that the measure of freedom and liberty given to the Filipino people be at least comparable to that enjoyed under the Commonwealth Government before the Japanese occupation . . . The only restrictions which should be imposed are the minimum required by military necessity and these should be removed as soon as possible.
>
> During the actual military operations, it is planned to have President Osmeña and his cabinet at General Headquarters. The psychological effect of their presence would rally active national support of all elements of Philippine society behind not only the combat operations but also the essential economic measures promulgated by the military.
>
> Throughout the military period, the Commonwealth Government operates under my supreme authority . . . It would appear preferable that the High Commissioner should not be introduced into the local scene until he can assume his primary function as the personal representative of the President of the United States and thereby be the senior American official present . . .
>
> In general, the removal of collaborationists by Americans is a delicate task. Their removal is primarily a responsibility of the Commonwealth Government. A specific directive on this subject might seriously handicap me during the military phases. I do not believe any general rule could be drawn which would not tend to create embarrassment in handling such a delicate question . . .
>
> [Regarding the War Department's detailed proposals for financial and economic regulations, which he opposed,] their general effect might have been, not to restore the economy of Philippine life as it existed before the war, but to alter materially and permanently the basis of industry and commerce along restrictive and arbitrarily controlled lines . . .
>
> The utmost care should be taken that an imperialistic attitude not be introduced into the situation under guise of military operations and necessity.[38]

Besides the matter of the high commissioner's return, Osmeña differed with MacArthur's civil affairs policy on two major points, both related indirectly to Roxas. The SWPA commander intended to have Osmeña assume political control in liberated areas much sooner than the Filipino desired since Osmeña initially lacked the staff and funds to cope with reconstruction and relief. As Ickes predicted, Osmeña's efforts, made with only the semblance of a government, would exacerbate the discontent of the people in the devastated areas and would cost him dearly in future political support. Although MacArthur probably had no deliberate scheme in mind, Osmeña foresaw that if the general forsook civil responsibility for the liberated areas immediately after his forces advanced elsewhere, the Philippine president's plight could lead to his political ruin and make Roxas' ascension to power much easier.

In addition, Osmeña and MacArthur differed on the issue of collaboration. MacArthur's general position in early September, as stated earlier, was sensible as far as it went, but shortly thereafter he adopted the simplistic view held by many Washington officials that the Laurel regime and other collaborators had been disloyal to the United States and should be purged, with trials to come later. As Roosevelt put it, "Those who have collaborated with the enemy must be removed from authority and influence in the political and economic life of the country." Unlike Roosevelt, the War Department, and MacArthur, who wished the Philippine government to determine the final fate of collaborators, Ickes wanted the American Army "to shoot or hang any Filipino who had anything to do with the puppet government, no matter what reasons they may have had for cooperating." Yet MacArthur came to regard Filipino disloyalty, especially by the oligarchy, as a personal affront to him. Soon after returning to the Philippines that fall, he would issue a proclamation demanding the arrest of all citizens "who voluntarily have given aid, comfort and sustenance to the enemy." Such individuals were to be turned over to the Philippine government after the war "for its judgment upon their respective cases."

On the other hand, Osmeña's view of collaboration was more complex, based on the belief that the individual's motivation was more important in the assessment of his guilt or innocence than his overt acts. Osmeña's hostility toward the puppet government was tempered by the fact that both he and Laurel's politicians were from the same prewar oligarchic elite and, in many cases, were old friends. Osmeña did condemn those who professed and practiced zealous dedication to the Japanese cause, such as the Makapili, but he could sympathize with individuals who collaborated with the Japanese in running the government as choosing the lesser of two evils, the alternative being a wholly military administration like those set up in several areas of Southeast Asia. To Osmeña, the purge of accused collaborators before their guilt was proven would spell future disaster for law, order, and responsible government in the islands, since, as one scholar says, he "saw the oligarchy as the last bulwark preserving Philippine institutions and preventing chaos."

In essence, the American position on collaboration, expressed and implemented by MacArthur, "posited general culpability until the individual could establish his innocence; the Osmeña policy posited individual innocence until treasonable motivation could be assessed." Of course, the easier route was MacArthur's, because assessing motivation would prove difficult and, in the long run, perhaps unrealistic. Before re-entering the Philippines, however, it was obvious to Osmeña that MacArthur would insist on making Roxas an exception to any purge or charge of collaboration. Osmeña was worried lest, with MacArthur's blessing, Roxas would be set on the road to victory over him and would become the first president of the postwar republic. And that is precisely what would happen.[39] The impending reoccupation of the Philippines was shaping up to be more than a matter of defeating the Japanese.

CHAPTER XIII

Decision and Attack

1. Decided with Reluctance

IN THEIR STRATEGIC PLANNING in 1943, the Combined Chiefs of Staff had assumed that an invasion of Japan would be necessary to force that nation's surrender. Besides a tight blockade and intensive naval bombardments, the preliminaries to invasion would have to include heavy aerial attacks on the home islands. For these attacks, the Joint Chiefs felt that B-29 bases would be needed in both the Marianas and eastern China, and that a Chinese port, preferably Amoy, would be essential not only for establishing and supplying air bases in China but also for severing the Japanese lines of communication to Southeast Asia. By early 1944, the Joint Chiefs and their planners believed also that the capture of Formosa would be necessary to secure an oceanic route of supply to China. Moreover, from Formosa the Allied air and naval forces could more effectively interdict Japan's connections with the south than from either Luzon or the China coast, and B-29's could operate against Japan from Formosan bases.

Although the Joint Chiefs' directive of March, 1944, provided for the invasion of Mindanao in mid-November, many Wash-

ington planners in late spring had become so persuaded of the
strategic superiority of Formosa that discussion of bypassing the
Philippines was revived. At the Combined Chiefs' conference
in London in early June, proposals were brought up for attacking Formosa rather than the Philippines and even for bypassing
Formosa and advancing directly to Kyushu, the southernmost of
the main Nipponese islands. The possibility of an advance
against Japan from the North Pacific was not ruled out if the
Soviets could be persuaded to join the war against Japan or at
least permit the construction of American bases in Siberia. The
Anglo-American chiefs were flexible in their thinking and ready
to try the unexpected in order to defeat Japan quickly, but they
could not reach agreement on a course of action.

Upon their return from England, the Joint Chiefs notified
MacArthur and Nimitz on June 12 that they were "considering
the possibilities of expediting the Pacific campaign" and desired
"their views and recommendations" on three different means of
achieving this: "(a) By advancing the target dates for operations
now scheduled through operations against Formosa. (b) By bypassing presently selected objectives prior to operations against
Formosa. (c) By by-passing presently selected objectives and
choosing new objectives, including Japan proper." [1]

In his reply on the 18th MacArthur argued forcefully that the
seizure of the Philippines would be a much wiser course than an
assault on either Formosa or Japan in the near future:

> Due to logistic considerations it is not deemed feasible to ad-
> vance target dates for scheduled operations. Our resources will
> be strained to the utmost to meet dates now fixed.
>
> The Formosan campaign differs radically from operations
> that have been executed thus far in the Pacific. It is my most
> earnest conviction that the proposal to bypass the Philippines
> and launch an attack across the Pacific directly against Formosa
> is unsound. That operation would have to be launched with-
> out appreciable support from land-based aviation and be based

upon the Hawaiian Islands at a distance of 5,000 miles. Assuming the success of FORAGER [Marianas invasion], there still will be no bases west of Oahu along this line of advance. Under these conditions and with [the] enemy solidly established in strength on Formosa, susceptible of rapid reinforcement from Japan or the mainland and with his air bases in a flanking position at effective range in Luzon, I do not believe the campaign would succeed. The hazards of failure would be unjustifiable when a conservative and certain line of action is open. The occupation of Luzon is essential in order to establish air forces and bases prior to the move on Formosa. Assault forces could then be launched at short range with effective air support and with every assurance of success.

The proposal to bypass all other objectives and launch an attack directly on the mainland of Japan is in my opinion utterly unsound. There is available in the Pacific only enough shipping to lift about 7 divisions. That fact alone would preclude such an enterprise in the predictable future. Even with unlimited shipping I do not believe a direct assault without air support can possibly succeed.

Since the initiation of our advance the enemy has executed delaying actions within his out-post positions. Our successes in these operations must not mislead us into a suicidal direct assault without air support and with inadequate shipping and bases against heavily defended bastions of the enemy's main position.

It is my opinion that purely military considerations demand the reoccupation of the Philippines in order to cut the enemy's communications to the south and to secure a base for our further advance. Even if this were not the case and unless military factors demanded another line of action, it would in my opinion be necessary to reoccupy the Philippines. [The] Philippines is American territory where our unsupported forces were destroyed by the enemy. Practically all of the 17,000,000 Filipinos remain loyal to the United States and are undergoing the greatest privation and suffering because we have not been able to support or succor them. We have a great national obligation to discharge. Moreover, if the United States should deliberately bypass the Philippines, leaving our prisoners, nationals and loyal Filipinos, in enemy hands without an effort to retrieve them at [the] earliest moment, we would incur the gravest psychological reaction. We would admit the truth of Japanese propaganda to the effect that we had abandoned the Filipinos and would not shed American blood to redeem them; we would undoubtedly incur the open hostility of that people; we would probably suffer such loss of prestige among all the peoples of the Far East that it would adversely affect the United States for many years. I feel also that a decision to eliminate the campaign for the relief of the Philippines, even under appreciable military considerations, would cause extremely adverse reactions among the citizens of the United States. The American people, I am sure, would acknowledge this obligation.

In this dispatch I have expressed my firm convictions with a mere outline of the military factors that enter into the problem. If serious consideration is being given to the line of action indicated in paragraphs B and C of your radio, I request that I be accorded the opportunity of personally proceeding to Washington to present fully my views.[2]

When Stimson and Marshall discussed MacArthur's response, the Secretary of War stated that the lack of land-based air support in attacking Formosa was an important consideration, but he discounted the SWPA chief's other points. Marshall, who for some time had been leaning in favor of the plan to attack Formosa, countered that both the Pacific Fleet's great carrier forces and the Allied aircraft based in China would be available. He felt that MacArthur's plan to reconquer the Philippines would be "the slow way . . . We should have to fight our way through them and it would take a very much longer time than to make the cut across." King and his naval planners had long favored bypassing the Philippines, and in recent months Arnold and his air staff, foreseeing more and closer B-29 base sites, had come to support an invasion of Formosa. Somervell seems to have been one of the few Pentagon leaders who thought the entire Philippines should be secured before the Allies advanced to Formosa or the China coast. In his reply to the Joint Chiefs' query, Nimitz argued that the next step after the capture of

Morotai and the Palaus should be the seizure of the southern or central Philippines, where air bases would have to be established as a prerequisite for an offensive against the Luzon–Formosa–China coast triangle. The admiral's preference among the latter objectives was Formosa. The advice of Halsey, the next highest naval officer in the Pacific, was not sought by the Joint Chiefs at that time, but he preferred to invade Luzon, bypass Formosa, and then attack Okinawa in the Ryukyus. Most of the senior commanders and planners of the Central and Southwest Pacific commands, unlike the majority of the Washington planners, were opposed to a Formosa-first strategy.

In his reply to MacArthur on June 24, Marshall voiced the general sentiments of the Joint Chiefs and the Pentagon planners in defending their Formosa and Kyushu studies: "Neither operation in my opinion," he told MacArthur, "is unsound in the measure you indicate." Citing some of the liabilities of the SWPA commander's plan, including recent intelligence reports of a strong build-up of enemy forces in the path of his proposed advance, Marshall chided him, "We must be careful not to allow our personal feelings and Philippine political considerations to override our great objective, which is the early conclusion of the war with Japan." He reminded MacArthur that "bypassing" was not "synonymous with abandonment" and the defeat of Japan by the quickest course would best produce the Philippines' liberation. Marshall frankly admitted that he had been "pressing for the full use of the fleet to expedite matters in the Pacific and also pressing specifically for a carrier assault on Japan."

The Army chief of staff's blunt rebuttal must have been a bitter pill for MacArthur, but his response was to produce on July 10 his Musketeer I Plan for retaking the Philippines. In this plan, the SWPA commander confidently figured that his forces could assault Mindanao on November 15 and Leyte on December 20; his Musketeer II Plan in late August also included an attack on Lingayen Gulf (Luzon), to begin on February 20. At an inter-theater conference at Pearl Harbor in early July in which some of MacArthur's and Nimitz's top planners participated, the Central and Southwest Pacific representatives agreed that a move into the southern or central Philippines should precede an advance to Luzon or Formosa. By this time the Washington planners were coming to the same conclusion; the Joint Chiefs therefore reluctantly went along with Mac-Arthur's plan through the proposed invasion of Leyte but deferred a decision on whether Luzon or Formosa should follow that operation.[3]

So matters stood in the deliberations on Pacific strategy when the President, for reasons never made known, decided to journey to Pearl Harbor and confer with Nimitz and MacArthur. With the Democratic national convention nearing its end in Chicago after nominating him for a fourth term, Roosevelt departed from San Diego aboard the cruiser *Baltimore* on July 21. Those in his party included Samuel I. Rosenman, one of his key speech writers; Dr. Ross T. McIntire, the President's physician; Brigadier General Edwin "Pa" Watson, an aide; Admiral Leahy; and some lesser luminaries of the White House staff. It was Roosevelt's first trip overseas without the Joint Chiefs, who, except for the presidential chief of staff, were not invited. To avoid embarrassment, King, who had been visiting Nimitz, left Hawaii to return to Washington on the 22nd while the presidential party was at sea. King speculated that Roosevelt was particularly eager at that time to display himself in the role of the nation's commander-in-chief. A few weeks earlier the President had told King that there should be only one such title and for the admiral to cease referring to himself as Commander-in-Chief of the United States Fleet, which King promptly ignored.

Sherwood, probably voicing Harry Hopkins' opinion also, felt that the trip was politically motivated, as did many others then and since. In a speech supporting Dewey's campaign, Rep-

resentative Everett Dirksen of Illinois remarked that Mac-
Arthur "is no longer a fourth-term threat. But he is still exceedingly popular in America. And in an election year it's a good
idea to be seen as much as possible with as many popular people
as possible." MacArthur later confided to Eichelberger that he
thought the President's excursion was "purely political." [4]

Shortly before the President left for Hawaii, MacArthur received a "summons" from Marshall to be at Pearl Harbor on
July 26 for an important conference, though neither the topic
nor Roosevelt's coming was mentioned. When he boarded his
B-17 at Brisbane for the long flight to Hawaii, MacArthur carried no planning data and took along only Colonels Fellers and
Lehrbas and three minor aides. The flight took nearly twenty-
six hours with fuel stops at Tontua, New Caledonia, and Canton
Island. During the journey, the SWPA chief appeared "disgruntled and angry at the idea of being called away from his war
duties," pacing up and down the *Bataan*'s aisle and exclaiming
at one point, "The humiliation of forcing me to leave my command to fly to Honolulu for a political picture-taking junket!"
The general's plane landed at Hickam Field, Oahu, an hour or
so before the *Baltimore* docked at Pearl Harbor. MacArthur
went to Fort Shafter where he was to stay at the quarters of his
old friend, General Robert C. Richardson, who commanded the
Army forces in Nimitz's theater.[5] When the *Baltimore* docked
at 3:00 P.M. on July 26, Roosevelt immediately sent word for
Nimitz, MacArthur, Richardson, Halsey, and the other senior
officers in the area to come aboard ship for a reception.

Rosenman describes the arrival of MacArthur:

> At the dock an area of about two acres had been cleared off; a
> tremendous crowd stood in back of this space. They cheered
> as the gangplank was lowered to receive on board Admiral
> Nimitz, General Richardson and some fifty other high military
> and naval officers. The officers came aboard to greet the Presi-
> dent on the quarter-deck.
> One officer was conspicuously absent. It was General Mac-

Arthur. When Roosevelt asked Nimitz where the General was, there was an embarrassing silence. We learned later that the General had arrived about an hour earlier, but instead of joining the other officers to greet the Commander-in-Chief, he had gone by himself to Fort Shafter.

After we had waited on the *Baltimore* some time for the General, it was decided that the President and his party would disembark and go to the quarters on shore assigned to them. Just as we were getting ready to go below, a terrific automobile siren was heard, and there raced onto the dock and screeched to a stop a motorcycle escort and the longest open car I have ever seen. In the front was a chauffeur in khaki, and in the back one lone figure — MacArthur. There were no aides or attendants. The car traveled some distance around the open space and stopped at the gangplank. When the applause died down, the General strode rapidly to the gangplank all alone. He dashed up the gangplank, stopped halfway up to acknowledge another ovation, and soon was on deck greeting the President.

He certainly could be dramatic — at dramatic moments.

"Hello, Doug," said the Commander-in-Chief. "What are you doing with that leather jacket on — it's darn hot today."

I understand that the MacArthur jacket was still nonregulation.

"Well, I've just landed from Australia," he replied. "It's pretty cold up there."

Greetings all around — and we proceeded to leave the ship.[6]

Returning to Richardson's quarters, MacArthur, as one account has it, "angrily reiterated" that Roosevelt apparently "felt it would be good politics to show himself intent on winning the Pacific war and conferring in complete harmony" with him. That evening the SWPA general dined with Richardson, whom he had known since their days together at West Point. According to MacArthur, he learned that Richardson "is an unhappy man. He lives like a prince with fine cars and a fine home, but he has no authority. He is a fine, courteous gentleman, so the Navy have him licked. They have beaten him so many times there is nothing more he can do." Later that night, probably in the company of Fellers, MacArthur paced the floor of his bedroom, reminiscing about "his long years of struggle and his many defeats and frustrations." So went the story as given to Hunt. Feeling "depressed and frustrated," the SWPA leader "seemed to unburden himself in a way he had seldom if ever done before in all his life."

The President's schedule for the next day, July 27, seemed to confirm MacArthur's suspicions, for he chose to spend from 10:30 A.M. to 4:30 P.M. rushing about, said Leahy, on "a schedule so crowded with inspections of Army and Navy activities in Oahu as to leave him not a minute to spare." The open car in which the President rode was probably the same one MacArthur had used the previous afternoon for his grand arrival at the dock. Nimitz maintained that only two open cars could be found in Honolulu: one belonged to a well-known brothel madam and the other was the fire chief's bright red automobile. The latter was chosen by Richardson for the distinguished guests since the madam's vehicle, says one account, "would be readily identified." Roosevelt insisted that Nimitz and MacArthur accompany him; the admiral found himself squeezed in the middle between the other two on the rear seat, while Leahy rode in the front with the chauffeur.

The conversation was monopolized by Roosevelt and MacArthur; Nimitz and Leahy were, for the most part, ignored. MacArthur said he and the President "talked of everything but the war — of our old carefree days when life was simpler and gentler, of many things that had disappeared in the mists of time." Nimitz sensed that, despite the general's lack of staff advisers and planning data for the impending strategy sessions, MacArthur had a tremendous advantage since he knew Roosevelt better, having served as Army chief of staff under him. In recounting the experience to Eichelberger several weeks later, MacArthur said, "I talked to him [Roosevelt] for six hours and the Navy remained mute." [7]

That evening the President invited MacArthur, Nimitz, Leahy, and Halsey to dinner at the "cream stucco mansion" where he was residing. Formerly the residence of wealthy Christopher Holmes and "one of Hawaii's showplaces overlooking Waikiki," the palatial house had been turned into quarters for Navy aviators, who had been dislodged for the occasion. Admiral Lockwood, formerly MacArthur's submarine chief in the Southwest Pacific and now commander of the submarine base at Pearl Harbor, had had his repair gangs working for a week to get the place in shape for the President and his party. After dinner the five men, three of whom were admirals, moved to the large living room where, MacArthur observed, "the Navy had a tremendous paraphernalia of maps, plans, manuscripts, statistics of all sorts, and other visual adjuncts. I began to realize I was to go it alone."

Roosevelt "stated the general purpose of the conference, which was to determine the next phase of action against Japan." He picked up a long bamboo pointer, touched the Philippines on the large wall map, turned to MacArthur, and asked, "Well, Doug, where do we go from here?" MacArthur launched into an impressive, well-organized defense of his proposal to invade the Philippines; his argument was the same as that put forth in his message to the Joint Chiefs on June 18. He laid particular stress on the "moral obligation" of the United States to the Filipinos and the Americans imprisoned in the islands, as well as the adverse reaction the American people would display, presumably at the polls in November, should the archipelago be bypassed. Then Nimitz presented his argument. Although he was in agreement with MacArthur on the need for seizing the southern or central Philippines, he emphasized that Formosa should be the next objective, instead of Luzon, which MacArthur wanted.

The session lasted until midnight, and though no consensus was reached, the participants remained congenial throughout the evening. MacArthur said that Nimitz showed "a fine sense of fair play," even if the plan which the admiral presented "was King's and not his own." The general thought Roosevelt was "doubtful" of the Formosa plan, but he remained "entirely neutral" in acting as the "chairman" of the session. MacArthur added some remarks for harmony's sake, though one of his efforts probably astonished the admirals: "I spoke of my esteem for Admiral King and his wise estimate of the importance of the Pacific as a major element in the global picture, however I might disagree with some of his strategic concepts." Leahy remarked that "it was both pleasant and very informative to have these two men who had been pictured as antagonists calmly presenting their differing views to the Commander-in-Chief. For Roosevelt it was an excellent lesson in geography, one of his favorite subjects." Leahy said that when Nimitz and MacArthur described their proposed operations, "it was highly pleasing and unusual to find two commanders who were not demanding reinforcements."

At the session the next morning, July 28, the Central and Southwest Pacific commanders elaborated further on their proposals as Roosevelt, according to Leahy, "tactfully steered the discussion from one point to another and narrowed down the area of disagreement between MacArthur and Nimitz. The discussion remained on a friendly basis the entire time." MacArthur brought up the subject of the British chiefs' desire to have their forces move into the East Indies; Roosevelt agreed with him that British ground operations in the Dutch territory would not be permitted. The SWPA chief talked briefly of his own plan to use the Australian Army in a future thrust into the East Indies, but Roosevelt's response to this is not known. The second and final session ended at noon. Leahy was relieved that "these two meetings were much more peaceful than I had expected, after what I had been hearing in Washington . . . It was no secret that in the Pentagon Building in Washington there were men who disliked him [MacArthur], to state the matter mildly." But Leahy determined that "MacArthur and Nimitz were, together, the two best qualified officers in our service for this tremendous task . . . Both told the President they had what they needed, that they were not asking for anything, and that they would work together in full agreement toward the common end of defeating Japan." [8]

MacArthur had planned to depart for Australia that afternoon, but Roosevelt wanted him to go along on another round of military installations in the area. Leahy went along this time, but not Nimitz. MacArthur used the opportunity to impress on the President again the moral and political factors in favor of the reconquest of the entire Philippines. With Leahy riding in the front seat, the two were also able to talk about some "confidential" matters. When MacArthur inquired about Dewey's chances in the upcoming presidential election, Roosevelt's first response was to say that he had been too busy to consider politics. MacArthur said, "I threw back my head and laughed. He looked at me and then broke into a laugh himself." Roosevelt, according to MacArthur, went on to observe that "Dewey was a nice little man but inexperienced." MacArthur said the President "seemed completely confident. In turn, he inquired what I thought were the chances. I told him I knew nothing of the political situation in the United States, but that he, Roosevelt, was an overwhelming favorite with the troops. This seemed to please him greatly." So went the conversational game played by the master politician and his most politically minded general.

That evening there was a party on the lawn of the Holmes house for the President and his group; the "native entertainment," in Leahy's words, consisted of "an orchestra, a vocalist, and a hula dancer who performed beautifully." MacArthur did not attend; shortly after midnight he boarded the *Bataan* and took off for Tarawa, arriving in Brisbane about twenty-five hours later; the return flight had taken an hour less than the trip to Hawaii. Everyone had parted on amiable terms, and MacArthur found himself sympathetic toward Roosevelt: "I had not seen him for a number of years, and physically he was just a shell of the man I had known. It was clearly evident that his days were numbered." Lockwood had likewise observed that "the President's appearance was distressing . . . His skin had that grayish tinge one often sees in the very ill." Roosevelt's outward behavior belied his condition, however, for he spent the day of the 29th enjoying another arduous round of military inspections, finally going aboard the *Baltimore* late that afternoon and departing at 7:30 P.M. On the cruiser he sent a message to his wife: "Just off — hectic 3 days — very good results. All is well." [9]

Apparently MacArthur and Nimitz hid from the President their current dispute over control of Army resources in the South Pacific. Nimitz had recently informed King that he would need about 200,000 more troops, mainly service units, if the Formosan invasion were mounted. In telling Eichelberger later about the conference, MacArthur made the following remark, possibly in reference to a conversation with the admirals only: "The Central Pacific authorities asked that they be given 200,000 of my troops, and that is a sign of weakness." At some point in the six weeks following the Pearl Harbor Conference, Nimitz came to the conclusion that an attack on Formosa would not be feasible before Luzon was secured. Whether the get-together with MacArthur had had any influence on him is arguable; as will be seen, it was probably the insurmountable logistical difficulties alone that changed his mind. After July 28, both Roosevelt and Leahy preferred Luzon over Formosa, though the admiral had never been convinced of the soundness of the Formosa-first plan.

There is no doubt that the Pearl Harbor talks improved personal relations between MacArthur and Roosevelt, who had not seen each other since 1937. Back at his GHQ in Brisbane the

SWPA chief gave an oral report "in some detail" on the conference before his assembled staff, during which he spoke highly
of the President's support of his ideas. He told them that "the
President accepted my recommendations and approved the Philippines plan," yet he later confided to Eichelberger, "The question of whether or not the route will be by Luzon or Formosa
has not yet been settled in Washington." MacArthur's communiqués through the rest of the summer and autumn pictured
the war as going unusually well in his theater, which did not
hurt the President's standing with his constituents on the eve
of the election. In fact, on October 30, only ten days after the
Leyte landing and a week before the election, MacArthur suddenly proclaimed that two-thirds of Leyte had been secured and
enemy resistance had collapsed in many regions.

Some war correspondents on the island, who knew that the
major fighting was just starting, protested to GHQ, but a public
relations officer told them confidentially, "The elections are
coming up in a few days, and the Philippines *must* be kept on
the front pages back home." The communiqués and this statement suggest that an informal deal was made at Pearl Harbor,
probably without explicit verbalization, whereby MacArthur's
releases would portray great battlefield successes stemming from
increased Washington support, and the President's influence in
behalf of the Philippines plan would be exerted on the Joint
Chiefs. Both Roosevelt and MacArthur were clever schemers of
the first order, so such an understanding is not implausible, even
if unprovable.

In the wake of the conference Roosevelt surely made manifest
his pleasure with the meetings, MacArthur, and the reconquest
of the Philippines. At a press conference on July 29 after Mac-
Arthur's departure, Roosevelt remarked that they had enjoyed
"two very successful days" together. "We are going to get the
Philippines back," he told the reporters, "and without question
General MacArthur will take a part in it. Whether he goes

direct or not, I can't say" — an acknowledgment that the Joint Chiefs might have some say in the matter. The President wrote to the SWPA chief on August 12 referring to their "most successful" conference and "the splendid picture" he had gotten of the Pacific situation. He continued, "You have been doing a really magnificent job . . . Personally, I wished much in Honolulu that you and I could swap places and personally, I have a hunch that you would make more of a go as President than I would as General in retaking the Philippines." He added, "Some day there will be a flag-raising in Manila — and without question I want you to do it."

The general replied, "Nothing in the course of the war has given me quite as much pleasure as seeing you again." Rather than raising the flag himself, MacArthur said he had "an even higher and more soul-filling vision. It is my fervent hope that you will come to our ranks that day and as The Commander-in-Chief preside in person at that ceremony. Your presence would enhance beyond measure the benefits that will flow in perpetuity. It would mark the highest drama of the greatest of wars." In a nation-wide radio address from the navy yard at Bremerton, Washington, on August 12, Roosevelt spoke of the "complete accord" attained with "my old friend General MacArthur" during the "extremely interesting and useful conferences" at Pearl Harbor. Writing to MacArthur on September 15 from Quebec, where he was attending the Octagon Conference, the President expressed himself as if they were comrades pitted against the British and the Joint Chiefs: "I wish you were here because you know so much of what we are talking about in regard to the plans of the British in the Southwest Pacific . . . In regard to our own force, the situation is just as we left it at Hawaii though there seem to be efforts to do bypassing which you would not like. I still have the situation in hand." [10]

In his highly regarded study of Harry Hopkins' relations with Roosevelt, Sherwood made an erroneous statement about the

Pearl Harbor Conference that has been repeated with slight variations in many publications ever since: "The main decision to be made there, as I understand it, was between the Navy plan to devote the ground forces to landings on Formosa, and the MacArthur plan to liberate the Philippines; Roosevelt ultimately decided in favor of the latter." Some writers claim that MacArthur so effectively persuaded the President that he made a firm decision at Pearl Harbor in favor of seizing Luzon; other chroniclers maintain MacArthur's persuasiveness at least won a definite commitment from Roosevelt not to allow the Philippines to be bypassed. Actually, as one of the official Army volumes states, the conference "did little to clarify the strategy picture." [11] Another volume in that series says:

> Apparently, no decisions on strategy were reached at the Pearl Harbor conference. The Formosa versus Luzon debate continued without let-up at the highest planning levels for over two months, and even the question of bypassing the Philippines entirely in favor of a direct move on Formosa came up for serious discussion within Washington planning circles again. The net result of the debate through July 1944 was the reaffirmation of the decision to strike into the southern or central Philippines before advancing to either Formosa or Luzon. The Joint Chiefs still had to decide whether to seize Luzon or Formosa, or both, before executing any other major attacks against Japan.[12]

Through much of the summer of 1944, King and Cooke pressured Marshall, Arnold, and their planners to agree to the formulation of a directive providing for MacArthur to seize the southern and central Philippines and Nimitz to invade Formosa. Although Marshall and Arnold preferred Formosa over Luzon as an objective, they wanted to defer the formal decision until they were certain of the means for successfully executing the enormous operation. The situation in West Europe was changing every day, and some planners were forecasting Germany's surrender by Thanksgiving, which might produce a sufficient redeployment from that theater to carry off an invasion of Formosa, Luzon, the China coast, or Kyushu, depending on many conditions which themselves were fluid. Yet if the alternatives were Luzon or Formosa, which they were in most of the planning sessions, Formosa was strategically preferable, offering the quickest course to the defeat of Japan; tactically and logistically, however, the Luzon route seemed surer, if slower. Leahy cast his lot with the generals in preferring to schedule no operations beyond Leyte for the time being. King grudgingly yielded, and on September 8 the Joint Chiefs issued a directive calling for MacArthur to attack Leyte on December 20, with the Pacific Fleet supporting the assault. The target dates for the intermediate operations were set at October 15 for the Talauds and November 15 for Saragani Bay, Mindanao. The next objective beyond Leyte was left hanging; the directive read: "Southwest Pacific and Central Pacific forces then [will] combine to occupy either (1) Luzon to secure Manila by 20 February 1945, or (2) Formosa and Amoy on the China coast by 1 March 1945." [13]

That same day, September 8, Halsey's Third Fleet carriers mounted devastating air attacks against the Palaus and Yap, then against Mindanao on the 9th and 10th. Two days later, as the invasions of Morotai and the Palaus neared, Halsey sent his carrier aircraft by the hundreds on wide-sweeping raids in the central Philippines. On the 13th, he excitedly reported to Nimitz that his planes had destroyed all but a handful of the Japanese air forces in the Mindanao-Visayan region. His pilots found the "enemy's non-aggressive attitude unbelievable and fantastic"; the central Philippines lay "wide open" for assault. One pilot who was downed and rescued from Leyte reported that the Filipinos claimed no Japanese troops were on that island. Halsey recommended cancellation of the projected operations against the Palaus, the Talauds, Mindanao, and Yap and urged instead an immediate invasion of Leyte.

Because the Palaus attack force was already at sea, Nimitz did not recommend its recall, but he did endorse Halsey's other dramatic proposals and sent them immediately to the Joint Chiefs of Staff, who, with Roosevelt, Churchill, and the British chiefs, were then participating in the Octagon Conference at Quebec. In his message Nimitz also said that for the Leyte attack he would send MacArthur his III Amphibious Force and XXIV Army Corps, then at Pearl Harbor preparing to embark for Yap. Marshall promptly decided to send a message to Brisbane asking MacArthur's opinion of the drastic changes. Ritchie, who helped to prepare the message, said it was only three terse sentences and took "one minute and seventeen seconds to be slammed on the teletype." The SWPA chief, however, was aboard the *Nashville,* which was observing radio silence as it steamed with the Morotai invasion force, so Sutherland took counsel with Kenney, Chamberlin, and other senior GHQ officers about their course. Kenney said, "Quite naturally everyone was reluctant to make so important a decision in General MacArthur's name without his knowledge of what was going on, but it had to be done. I argued that whatever we had been ready to do on October 15 could now be switched to Leyte, as long as the Navy would take care of the air cover till we could get our land-based air in place." They concluded that any speed-up of operations would probably meet with their chief's approval. Sutherland replied in MacArthur's name that the intermediate operations could be dropped in favor of a direct assault on Leyte, though he disputed Halsey's claim that the island had no enemy forces.

Marshall received Sutherland's message while the Allied chiefs were seated at a formal dinner given by Canadian Prime Minister Mackenzie King on the evening of September 15. King, Leahy, Arnold, and Marshall excused themselves and withdrew to confer. About ninety minutes later they sent out a directive ordering MacArthur and Nimitz to cancel the Talauds, Mindanao, and Yap operations and to attack Leyte on

October 20; MacArthur would provide the assault force, and he and Nimitz were to coordinate planning for the Central Pacific forces' support role, including air strikes and the loan of the III Amphibious Force and XXIV Corps. Later that evening a message arrived from GHQ SWPA: "Subject to completion of arrangements with Nimitz, we shall execute Leyte operation on 20 October . . . MacArthur." Again Sutherland had made the final decision and sent the message, though except for the use of "we" instead of "I," there was no indication to the chiefs at Quebec that they were not communicating with MacArthur. The SWPA chief learned of the action when he disembarked from the *Nashville* at Hollandia on September 17. His staff had judged correctly; he was delighted with the news.[14]

Six days later MacArthur informed the Joint Chiefs that their decision about Leyte would make it possible for his forces to invade Luzon on December 20, two months ahead of the earliest date they then contemplated. He felt the Formosa assault could be launched in mid-February, but added that, with the prior capture of Luzon, it would be unnecessary. Still favoring an attack on Formosa first but unable to resolve the logistical problems associated with it, the Washington planners realized that, without the Luzon operation, the Japanese would have a lengthy interim between the Leyte and Formosa assaults to readjust and strengthen their defenses. And whether the Luzon attack were launched or scrapped, logistical factors made it impossible to consider invading Formosa earlier than February.

Nimitz now proposed concurrent operations against southern Formosa and the Amoy area, which greatly complicated the study of ways to provide adequate amounts of troops, matériel, and shipping. The lack of service troops at hand proved to be a serious liability to Nimitz's proposal, but MacArthur pointed out that the Filipinos constituted a huge reservoir of potential service and combat strength to assist his forces. The Washington planners also became more keenly aware that lines of communication to Luzon would be shorter and safer than to Formosa, particularly if the latter were attacked while the enemy still controlled Luzon. By mid-September, Marshall and Arnold were agreeing with Leahy that the invasion of Luzon would be much more economical in terms of lives and material resources. Also MacArthur assured them that he could conquer Luzon rapidly: at Brisbane on August 6–7 he had told Lieutenant General Barney M. Giles of Arnold's air headquarters, Major General John Hull of the Operations Division, and five other visiting officers from the War Department that he could complete the conquest of Luzon in four to six weeks after the main landing at Lingayen Gulf.

Two developments in mid-September helped to bring the Luzon-versus-Formosa debate to a climax: (1) the Leyte decision, which made it feasible to advance by two months an attack on Luzon, and (2) major Japanese offensives that erupted in eastern and southeastern China, threatening to overrun all American air bases there that might have supported a Formosa assault. The Japanese action thus nullified the need for a Chinese port, which had been intended as a supply area for the air bases. In turn, Formosa became less appealing since, in large part, its seizure was to be justified by the need to open and protect an oceanic supply route to China. As the B-29 bases in the Marianas neared completion, the interest of Arnold and his planners in Formosa declined, especially when they considered that, if Formosa were invaded in February or March, it would be May or June before B-29 bases there would be completed. Also Marshall, King, and Arnold were quite aware after Roosevelt and Leahy's return from Pearl Harbor that the President and his chief of staff favored the seizure of Luzon and gave considerable weight to MacArthur's moral and political arguments regarding the Philippines.[15]

Nevertheless, the Joint Chiefs, Leahy included, were swayed mainly by military factors in their decision about Luzon and

Formosa. "By the end of September 1944," states the Army's official chronicle, "almost all the military considerations — especially the closely interrelated logistical problems concerning troops and timing — had weighted the scales heavily in favor of seizing Luzon, bypassing Formosa, forgetting about a port on the China coast, and jumping on to Okinawa." Now standing virtually alone in his crusade for the Formosa plan, King tried a last maneuver in late September to undermine the Luzon plan by charging that MacArthur would thereby tie up all the fast carrier forces for six weeks, a period unacceptable to the Navy. General Richard Marshall, MacArthur's deputy chief of staff, who was in Washington at that time, was tipped off in advance of King's final salvo and notified MacArthur in time for him to prepare a sound rebuttal. MacArthur got off a message to the Joint Chiefs on the 28th in which he argued that his need for carriers after the assault phase would be limited to a small number of escort carriers for several days only until an airfield could be readied on Luzon for Kenney's aircraft. The SWPA leader shrewdly pointed out that the fast carrier forces would be committed for much longer and under more precarious conditions off Formosa, particularly if King's proposed invasion were attempted while Japanese air bases on Luzon were still operative. Unable to figure how King could carry off his projected Amoy–southern Formosa operations without many more troops, Nimitz threw his support behind MacArthur's plan on the 29th. King reluctantly gave in, and on October 3 the Joint Chiefs produced a new directive that called for MacArthur to invade Luzon on December 20 with Pacific Fleet carrier support, and for Nimitz to attack Iwo Jima on January 20 and Okinawa on March 1. MacArthur was to provide air support from Luzon for the latter operation.[16]

Thus the Joint Chiefs terminated their long, often acrimonious debate of 1944 on Pacific strategy, their verdict being determined primarily by military considerations, especially logistical

factors. Strategically their preference was for an invasion of Formosa, but they simply could not delay the Pacific advance until
Germany's collapse would provide the redeployed resources necessary to undertake that assault. Upon arriving in Australia two
and a half years earlier, MacArthur had confidently announced,
"I shall return." For over a year preceding the Joint Chiefs'
decision on the Luzon plan, GHQ SWPA had been deluging the
Philippines with materials proclaiming the general's forthcoming return, while in the States pro-MacArthur newspapers had
made famous his words in a tremendous promotional effort to
convince the Roosevelt administration, the Joint Chiefs, and
the American public of the value of his pronouncement. Mac-
Arthur was informed of the Joint Chiefs' major decisions but
was not privy to all of their agonizing deliberations on the
Luzon versus Formosa questions. So not until after the war did
he fully realize that his unauthorized "I shall return" narrowly
escaped becoming a humiliating mockery.

2. *The First Week on Leyte*

"Leyte roughly resembles a molar tooth," explains the official
Army history, "with its crown toward Samar and its roots pointing to Mindanao." Not to be outdone, the Navy's chronicler
compares the island's shape to "a very roughhewn Winged Victory of Samothrace." About 115 miles long and ranging from
fifteen to forty-five miles in width, the odd-shaped island had a
population in 1944 of approximately 915,000, yet the provincial
capital of Tacloban, lying on the northeast coast, was the largest
city and had only 31,000 inhabitants. Leyte is mostly mountainous, but in the north two plains interrupt the rugged terrain:
the densely cultivated Leyte Valley in the northeast, where most
of the population is concentrated, and the smaller Ormoc Valley
in the northwest. MacArthur hoped to develop a large complex

of air and logistical bases in the Leyte Valley to support future operations, and he planned that the Seventh Fleet would take advantage of the spacious anchorage in Leyte Gulf, off the east coast. He also wanted the six airfields the Japanese had built on Leyte. In addition, possession of the island would enable Mac-Arthur to support offensives against the islands to the north or south. "Leyte was to be the anvil," he remarked, "against which I hoped to hammer the Japanese into submission in the central Philippines — the springboard from which I could proceed to the conquest of Luzon, for the final assault against Japan itself." On Leyte he could count on the support of Kangleon's guerrilla force as well as on thousands of Filipinos who would volunteer to assist his service units.

Seizure of the Leyte and Ormoc valleys and the high ground bordering them was the key to military control of the island. At the southeastern end of the Leyte Valley were some beaches along Leyte Gulf that were regarded as the best for amphibious landings that SWPA reconnaissance had discovered in the entire theater. Intelligence indicated that the northeastern shoreline was not strongly defended, so MacArthur decided to strike along the eighteen-mile stretch between Dulag and San Jose. An assault there, he observed, "would permit the early capture of the important Tacloban Airfield, and make possible the occupation and use of the airfield system under development at Dulag. It would permit domination of vital San Juanico Strait, and place the invading force within striking distance of Panaon Strait to the south." The strongest enemy forces were accurately predicted to be in the vicinities of Ormoc on the west coast and Carigara on the north coast.[17]

GHQ planners had been at work on Leyte operational studies through most of the summer, though MacArthur did not approve them or issue the final plan, called King II, until September 20. The SWPA chief chose Kinkaid to command the Central Philippine Attack Force (mainly Seventh Fleet), which

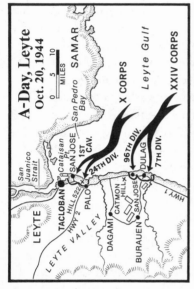

A-Day, Leyte
Oct. 20, 1944

MILES
0   5   10

SAMAR

San Juanico Strait

LEYTE

TACLOBAN

Cataisan Pt.
San Pedro Bay
SAN JOSE
1ST CAV.
HILL 522
HWY 2
PALO

X CORPS

Leyte Gulf

24TH DIV.

LEYTE VALLEY

CATMON HILL×
DAGAMI
SAN JOSE
BURAUEN

96TH DIV.
DULAG
7TH DIV.

XXIV CORPS

HWY 1

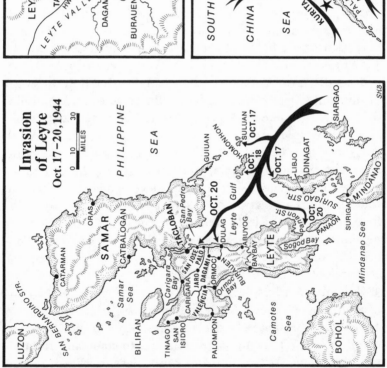

Battle for Leyte Gulf
Oct. 23-26, 1944

0   50   100

OZAWA ★

Cape Engaño

LUZON

MANILA

SOUTH CHINA SEA

Sibuyan Sea

San Bernardino Strait

SAMAR

PACIFIC OCEAN

TACLOBAN
Leyte Gulf
Surigao Strait

LEYTE

NEGROS

PANAY

MINDANAO

SHIMA

KURITA

PALAWAN

NISHIMURA

Sulu Sea

Invasion of Leyte
Oct. 17-20, 1944

MILES
0   10   30

PHILIPPINE SEA

LUZON
SAN BERNARDINO STR.

SAMAR

ORAS

CATARMAN

CATBALOGAN

Samar Sea

BILIRAN

TINAGO
SAN ISIDRO
CARIGARA
Carigara Bay
JARO
VALENCIA
DAGAMI
ORMOC
Ormoc Bay
PALOMPON

GUIUAN

SULUAN   OCT. 17
HOMONHON   OCT. 17

OCT. 18

OCT. 17

DINAGAT
LIBJO

SIARGAO

SURIGAO STR.

OCT. 20

MINDANAO

TACLOBAN
San Pedro Bay
SAN JOSE
PALO
BURAUEN
DULAG
Leyte Gulf
ABUYOG
BAYBAY
Panaon Str.
PANAON
Sogod Bay

LEYTE

SURIGAO

Mindanao Sea

Camotes Sea

BOHOL

SHB

would be responsible for the invasion from staging through the amphibious landings and until Krueger's Sixth Army headquarters arrived at the beachhead and assumed control of ground operations. Barbey's VII Amphibious Force was to land Sibert's X Corps between Palo and San Jose, just south of Tacloban; and Wilkinson's III Amphibious Force would set Major General John R. Hodge's XXIV Corps ashore near Dulag. Kinkaid would command directly Task Force 77, the Seventh Fleet's main combat vessels, which were to furnish close air and naval fire support for the landings. Altogether the Central Philippine Attack Force comprised 738 ships. Halsey's Third Fleet would provide strategic support by attacking enemy naval and air forces from Okinawa to the Sulu Sea. Nimitz, Halsey's superior, instructed him that if an opportunity arose to engage and destroy a "major portion" of the Japanese Combined Fleet, "such destruction becomes the primary task" of the Third Fleet rather than the protection of the Leyte beachhead's line of communication. Under Halsey's command were 105 combat ships, including eighteen fleet carriers. The total naval strength committed to the Leyte operation was slightly fewer in number but much stronger in firepower than that assigned to Eisenhower's enormous cross-Channel invasion in June. Indeed, the Leyte armada was, as the Navy's history states, "the most powerful naval force ever assembled," but it would be surpassed by the Luzon force in January and the Okinawa force in March.[18]

Although he had only a month's notice, Kinkaid's planning of the amphibious attack progressed smoothly:

> We had to work fast, but I think when you work fast you work better. We didn't have a lot of time to sit around and discuss things and loaf. The plan was made in my headquarters at Hollandia, and Wilkinson came down there . . . His planners were in one quonset hut opposite my planners in another, and they could talk across the little distance through open windows about any questions that came up there. If there was any dif-

ference of opinion, they could walk about seventy or eighty
feet to my office and get a settlement right then and there — a
decision. The planning went beautifully.

In addition to that, Admiral Barbey was at anchor in Hollandia Harbor, General Krueger just across the harbor in tents
camped there. General Kenney, the Air Commander, was only
about ten or fifteen minutes away by jeep, and General Mac-
Arthur's [advance] headquarters were [sic] up on the next hill
about five minutes away. So we were all within close touch, and
we could get questions asked and answered in a very short
time.[19]

MacArthur, as noted earlier, was at Hollandia only four days
during this period, but he stayed in close touch with the planners there and all final decisions were referred to him.

Whitehead's Fifth Air Force was designated the air assault
force for the Leyte operation, but Halsey's and Kinkaid's carrier
aircraft were to carry the burden of the ten days of pre-invasion
raids, mostly against Formosa, Luzon, Cebu, and Leyte, as well
as to provide the main air cover for the landings and the first
days on Leyte until airfields could be readied for SWPA land-
based planes. During that critical early phase, the Fifth and
Thirteenth air forces, plus several RAAF squadrons, were to
neutralize enemy air and naval forces within range of their bases
on Morotai, the Vogelkop, and Manus. Just before the landings,
moreover, B-29's based in China and the Marianas were to strike
Formosa, while Mountbatten's RAF bombers undertook heavy
support raids against enemy bases in the Malaya-Singapore area.
Thus three Allied theaters would be cooperating with the Southwest Pacific Area Theater's invasion of Leyte: Nimitz's Pacific
Ocean Areas Theater, Stilwell's China–Burma–India Theater,
and Mountbatten's Southeast Asia Command.

Krueger's Sixth Army would have nearly 203,000 troops involved in the Leyte operation, with all of the divisions battle-
tested except the 96th. The major ground units for the operation consisted of the following:[20]

Unit	Commander	Phase	Landing Point
Sixth Army	Gen. W. Krueger		
6th Ranger Bn.	Lt. Col. H. A. Mucci	Assault	Leyte Gulf islands
21st RCT	Lt. Col. F. R. Weber	Assault	Panaon Island
2nd ESB	Brig. Gen. W. F. Heavey	Follow-up	Leyte
32nd Div.	Maj. Gen. W. H. Gill	Follow-up	
77th Div.	Maj. Gen. A. D. Bruce	Reserve	
381st RCT	Col. M. E. Halloran	Assault	
X Corps	Maj. Gen. F. C. Sibert		
1st Cav. Div.	Maj. Gen. V. D. Mudge	Assault	Leyte
24th Div.	Maj. Gen. F. A. Irving	Assault	Leyte
XXIV Corps	Maj. Gen. J. R. Hodge		
7th Div.	Maj. Gen. A. V. Arnold	Assault	Leyte
96th Div.	Maj. Gen. J. L. Bradley	Assault	Leyte
20th Armored Gp.	Lt. Col. W. A. Jensen	Assault	
11th A/B Div.	Maj. Gen. J. M. Swing	Follow-up	
503rd Prcht. RCT	Col. G. M. Jones	Follow-up	

Casey's ASCOM would provide logistical and construction services on Leyte until Major General James L. Frink's SWPA Army Services of Supply could take over in an estimated thirty days after the landings. To supply the huge invasion force during the landing period alone, according to War Department estimates, "1,500,000 tons of general equipment, 235,000 tons of combat vehicles, 200,000 tons of ammunition, and 200,000 tons of medical supplies were required. Thereafter, 332,000 tons of equipment would be required every thirty days." The Pacific shipping situation, already strained, was made worse by the huge requirements for Leyte, the sudden change in target dates, and the substitution of Nimitz's XXIV Corps for MacArthur's XIV Corps. The immensity of the logistical difficulties was magnified by the necessity of using nine staging bases widely scattered over the Southwest and Central Pacific: Oro Bay, Finschhafen,

Manus, Hollandia, Biak, Noemfoor, Morotai, Guam, and Oahu. "The staff work," says one authority, "that solved the monumental logistical problem involved was almost unbelievable." [21]

When General Tomoyuki Yamashita, the renowned conqueror of Singapore, arrived in Manila on October 9 to assume command of the Fourteenth Area Army (about 224,000 troops) and the overall defense of the Philippines, he determined, as had his predecessor, that the top priority should be given to troop build-up and defensive construction on Luzon rather than on the islands to the south. Lieutenant General Sosaku Suzuki's four-division Thirty-fifth Army, which was under Yamashita's control, was spread out at bases on Mindanao, Cebu, and Leyte. Contrary to Halsey's wildly optimistic estimate, the Leyte garrison consisted of nearly 23,000 troops, of which Lieutenant General Shiro Makino's 16th Division was the major unit. Recalling the lessons of previous island campaigns, Imperial General Headquarters instructed Yamashita and his commanders to abandon plans for "annihilation at the beachhead" and prepare instead for "resistance in depth" at strong fortifications in the interior out of range of the fearsome American naval bombardments.

Accordingly, Makino prepared his main defensive line in the middle of the Leyte Valley and built his principal supply base at Jaro in the central mountains. But, compromising with his instructions, he planned to have a sizable mobile force prepared to rush to the beaches not merely to harass the invaders but to contest fiercely their intrusion and delay their advance inland as long as possible. The land-based air defense of the Philippines was the responsibility of the Fourth Air Army, which boasted up to 1500 planes in early September, most of them located at Luzon bases. In addition, Admiral Toyoda confidently believed that, when the Americans invaded the Philippines, his Mobile Fleet could destroy the beachhead's shipping and naval cover force. He planned to activate a complicated do-or-die plan called Shō-1, which would send the bulk of the Japanese Navy's remaining firepower in three formidable task forces to converge on the invaders while a fourth task force acted as a decoy to lure Halsey's fleet away from the area of the intended concentration and massacre.

From late September until the eve of the invasion, Halsey sent his Third Fleet aircraft in frequent, massive strikes against the Philippines, Formosa, and the Ryukyus, inflicting severe losses on Japanese air power and shipping. When they seriously damaged two American cruisers off Formosa, Japanese airmen were so gleeful that they grossly exaggerated the Third Fleet's losses: all Japan celebrated when Radio Tokyo subsequently quoted an official communiqué reporting their airmen's sinking of eleven carriers, two battleships, and three cruisers. Amazingly, Imperial General Headquarters gullibly accepted its own propaganda and concluded that the Allies would be unable to mount an invasion of the Philippines before December because of their great naval losses. Moreover, despite their naval intelligence estimates to the contrary, they continued to believe that, when the invaders came, Mindanao would be their objective. About the time the Leyte landings began, the Navy Department in Washington issued a communiqué: "Admiral Nimitz has received from Admiral Halsey the comforting assurance that he is now retiring toward the enemy following the salvage of all the Third Fleet ships recently reported sunk by Radio Tokyo." Thanks to Halsey's strikes and Tokyo's myth-making, the invasion of Leyte would achieve the strategic surprise for which MacArthur had hoped. But his forces would still be striking a hornet's nest: with Tacloban lying only 195 miles from Manila, the enemy's reaction could be swift in coming.[22]

On October 17–18, while the far-flung invasion convoys began closing in for the final approach, the 6th Ranger Battalion seized Dinagat, Suluan, and Homonhon islands at the entrance to Leyte Gulf. Only Suluan had any enemy occupants; they were few and were quickly killed. After the rangers installed navigational lights on the islands, mine sweepers and underwater demolition teams scoured the entrance to the gulf as well as the vicinity of the landing beaches, but the only enemy obstacles encountered were mines along the approach to the gulf entrance.

Accompanied by Egeberg and Lehrbas, MacArthur had flown from Eagle Farm Air Drome, Brisbane, to Port Moresby on October 14, where he had conferred with Blamey and his staff about the Australian Army's impending relief of the American units that were containing bypassed enemy forces to the north and east. The next day the SWPA chief and his two aides flew on to Hollandia where Sutherland and Kenney were waiting at the airfield to greet them. MacArthur spent the rest of the day and evening in conference with commanders about last-minute details of the invasion. Osmeña was also there yet had only a brief chance to talk with the busy SWPA chief; the Philippine president, together with Valdés and Romulo, sailed with the Leyte-bound convoy, but not on MacArthur's ship. At 11:00 A.M. on October 16, MacArthur, Sutherland, Kenney, and a number of aides, including Colonels Herbert Wheeler, Egeberg, and Lehrbas, boarded the *Nashville,* which moved out of the harbor to join the northbound armada.[23] The following days at sea must have passed excitedly but too slowly as the cruiser carried MacArthur to the climax of his arduous thirty-one-month struggle back to the Philippines.

Years later when he recalled the Leyte expedition in his memoirs, the exhilaration and high drama of the historic occasion obviously still moved him as he wrote:

> On October 16th, I left Hollandia and went aboard the *Nashville,* which was to serve as my flagship. On the waters around me lay one of the greatest armadas of history. America's rebuilt strength consisted of new battleships that replaced those lying

at the bottom of Pearl Harbor, and many of the veteran ships that had survived that initial assault itself; of aircraft carriers, cruisers, and destroyers in massive array; of transports and landing craft of a type that had not even existed three years before . . .

It is difficult even for one who was there to adequately describe the scene of the next two days. Ships to the front, to the rear, to the left, and to the right, as far as the eye could see. Their sturdy hulls plowed the water, now presenting a broadside view, now their sterns, as they methodically carried out the zigzag tactics of evasion.

We came to Leyte just before midnight of a dark and moonless night. The stygian waters below and the black sky above seemed to conspire in wrapping us in an invisible cloak, as we lay to and waited for dawn before entering Leyte Gulf. Phase one of the plan had been accomplished with little resistance. Now and then a ghostly ship would slide quietly by us, looming out of the night and disappearing into the gloom almost before its outline could be depicted. I knew that on every ship nervous men lined the rails or paced the decks, peering into the darkness and wondering what stood out there beyond the night waiting for the dawn to come. There is a universal sameness in the emotions of men, whether they be admiral or sailor, general or private, at such a time as this. On almost every ship one could count on seeing groups huddled around maps in the wardrooms, infantrymen nervously inspecting their rifles, the crews of the ships testing their gear, last-minute letters being written, men with special missions or objectives trying to visualize them again. For every man there were tons of supplies and equipment — trucks and vehicles of all kinds, and more than one ton of ammunition for every man who would storm those shores. Late that evening I went back to my cabin and read again those passages from the Bible from which I have always gained inspiration and hope. And I prayed that a merciful God would preserve each one of those men on the morrow.

The big guns on the ships opened fire at dawn. The noise, like rolling thunder, was all around us. The *Nashville*, her engines bringing to life the steel under our feet, knifed into Leyte Gulf. The ominous clouds of night still hung over the sea, fighting the sun for possession of the sky, but the blackness had given way to somber gray, and even as we saw the black outline of the shore on the horizon, the cloak of drabness began to roll back. On every side ships were riding toward the island. The battle for Leyte had already begun.

I was on the bridge with Captain C. E. Coney . . . Just as the sun rose clear of the horizon, there was Tacloban. It had changed little since I had known it forty-one years before on my first assignment after leaving West Point. It was a full moment for me.

Shortly after this, we reached our appointed position offshore. The captain carefully hove into line and dropped anchor. Our initial vantage point was 2 miles from the beaches, but I could clearly see the sandstrips with the pounding surf beating down upon the shore, and in the morning sunlight, the jungle-clad hills rising behind the town. Landings are explosive once the shooting begins, and now thousands of guns were throwing their shells with a roar that was incessant and deafening. Rocket vapor trails crisscrossed the sky and black, ugly, ominous pillars of smoke began to rise. High overhead, swarms of airplanes darted into the maelstrom. And across what would ordinarily have been a glinting, untroubled blue sea, the black dots of the landing craft churned toward the beaches.[24]

After several hours of intensive naval and air bombardments of the landing sites, the assault waves of four divisions landed simultaneously at 10:00 A.M., October 20, quickly securing beachheads near Dulag in the XXIV Corps' sector and between Palo and San Jose to the north in the X Corps' area. Major General Verne D. Mudge's 1st Cavalry Division seized the most important of the A-day (assault day) objectives, the Tacloban airfield. His troops captured San Jose and, crossing Highway 1, the main road along the east coast, advanced to within a mile of the city of Tacloban. The 1st Cavalry met only sporadic opposition, but Irving's 24th Division, immediately to the south on the X Corps front, encountered strong resistance. The Japanese permitted the first five waves to land, but opened up with murderous mortar and artillery fire against the later waves. Nevertheless, by nightfall of A-day Irving's men had intersected Highway 1 and captured strategically important Hill 522, which overlooked Palo and dominated Highway 2, the key route into the Leyte Valley.

About ten miles to the south, in the XXIV Corps' sector, the 96th Division, led by Major General James L. Bradley, captured the barrio of San Jose (not to be confused with the town of the same name in the X Corps' sector) and penetrated about a mile and a half inland. Japanese resistance in the XXIV Corps' sector had been spotty and seemingly uncoordinated. Beyond the 96th's right flank, however, lay strongly fortified Catmon Hill, the most prominent physical feature along the coastline between Dulag and the Tacloban airfield. To the south of Bradley's troops, the 7th Division, commanded by Major General Archibald V. Arnold, landed at beaches in front and on either side of Dulag. Although the town was quickly overrun, the Dulag air strip was not taken on A-day. Meanwhile, the 21st Infantry Regiment of Irving's division, landing seventy miles to the south, encountered no enemy troops as it occupied points on both sides of Panaon Strait at 9:30 A.M. on A-day. On all fronts forty-nine American troops were killed that day. Most of the Japanese 16th Division troops in the Dulag-Tacloban area had withdrawn inland during the terrific pre-invasion bombardment. Because of light ground opposition and the appearance of only a few hostile aircraft, over 107,000 tons of equipment and supplies were discharged onto the Sixth Army's beaches in the first twenty-four hours. Kinkaid said of A-day, "The execution of the plan was as nearly perfect as any commander could desire." [25]

MacArthur spent the morning of A-day intently watching the panorama on the beaches from the *Nashville*'s bridge. He notified Osmeña and his party on a nearby transport to be ready, so that he could pick them up on the ride to shore at 1:00 P.M.

Shortly before that hour the SWPA chief, observed a correspondent, "appeared on deck in fresh, smooth-pressed suntans,
bebraided hat, and sun glasses . . . looking all the time a picture of composure and dignified good humor" as he and his
American entourage descended a ladder into the *Nashville*'s
motor whaler. MacArthur remarked with a broad smile to
Sutherland, "Well, believe it or not, we're here." After stopping
at the transport *John Land* to get the Filipinos, they continued
on the two-mile trip to the beach. MacArthur took a position
atop the engine house in the stern with photographer Faillace
just behind him; seated beside the SWPA chief was Sutherland,
while to the front were Kenney, Akin, Stivers, Egeberg, Lehrbas,
Wheeler, Osmeña, Valdes, Romulo, and several other officers.

The SWPA commander chose to make his first trip ashore to
Red Beach, just north of Palo, where the 24th Division was encountering the stiffest resistance any of the landing forces met on
A-day. Over half of all American and Japanese casualties that
day occurred on Red Beach. At the time of MacArthur's landing, Irving's troops had penetrated inland less than a half mile
in that area and mortar and small-arms fire could be heard frequently in the direction of Highway 1 and Hill 522. "Four of
the big landing craft, beached where we went in," said Kenney,
"had been hit by Jap mortar fire and one was burning nicely
when we landed. One light landing craft had just been sunk.
There seemed to be a lot of Nip snipers firing all around the
place."

Having changed into a fresh uniform for the occasion and
being accompanied by the Philippine president, MacArthur had
no intention of wading through knee-deep water. When one
of the general's aides learned that the beach shelved too little
for the whaler to get to dry land, he telephoned the beachmaster
for a small landing craft to which the SWPA chief and his group
could transfer. At the moment the beachmaster was overwhelmed with the unloading of supplies and equipment. Ac-

cording to Lockwood, whose account is confirmed by several participants, "Hundreds of small landing craft were squeezed onto the beach, ramps down, and bulldozers were unloading them. Everywhere was bustle and confusion. Bullets fired by snipers hidden on the thickly wooded slope [of Hill 522] whizzed by like angry bees. It was no time to disturb an overburdened beachmaster. Angrily, he told the lieutenant to 'let 'em walk.' " Perhaps some of MacArthur's wading episodes at later landings were deliberately staged, especially after he saw the worldwide publicity received by the photographs of his A-day walk ashore, but his plans for the drama at Red Beach certainly did not include stepping off in knee-deep water. Indeed, his grim expression on that occasion may have simply reflected his discomfort and disgruntlement rather than the contrived "sense of destiny" look described by his detractors.

At the beach MacArthur was met by Sibert and Irving, who had rushed ashore by separate craft just ahead of the dignitaries. For nearly an hour MacArthur wandered about chatting with officers, enlisted men, and one old local Filipino who addressed him as "Sir Field Marshal"; he inspected the cluttered beach and strolled inland about 200 yards, as usual, to get "the feel of the fighting." [26] Although MacArthur and most other high-ranking commanders from the beginning of warfare have been convinced of the great morale-boosting value of their visits to the front, the sentiments of Jan Valtin, who served as both rifleman and combat reporter with the 24th Division, probably reflected those of the typical combat soldier on Red Beach:

> The fighting moves inland in tortuous eddies. You note by the sun that it is early afternoon. The first self-propelled guns and the first jeeps have cleared the beach to join the pioneering bulldozer men. You watch them go and you feel the sun's heat strike through your helmet in liquid hammer-blows. You feel it even in the erratic shade of the broken palms. You have become indifferent to things. You are too

numb to feel fear. All you hope is that no mortar shell will tear off your leg and leave you alive. Your canteens are empty. Green coconuts knocked down by the shells are everywhere. You chop off the end of one with your machete and drink the milk. It tastes good. While you drink your eyes fall on some dead. The Japs are twisted shapes with twisted faces. Most of your own dead lie as if they were asleep. You wonder why that is so, until you see an American whose eyes have burst out of his face. The horror does not halt the little things of life. You pee and you wipe your nose. You grab to feel if that piece of soap you pocketed that morning is still there.

A small group of men is wading up from the beach. You pay no attention to them until you see some sweating, bare-torsoed GI's tear away and wriggle hastily into their shirts. You hear a sergeant bluster, "Button up, button up," and for a moment you think he is crazy.

The small group of men is moving steadily up from the water's edge. They cross the tumultuous strip of sand, and then you notice that one of the group, the leader, wears no helmet. He wears a cap and he is smoking a corncob pipe. He walks along as if the nearest Jap snipers were on Saturn instead of in the palm tops a few hundred yards away. You stare, and you realize that you are staring at General Douglas MacArthur.

The General is trying to find the Division command post. With him is his Chief of Staff. They stop to ask a sergeant the way. The sergeant doesn't know. He is too busy to bother with gold braid. Just then Lieutenant Art Stimson — he of the Texas flag — comes running along the rim of the coconut plantation. He grins a salute and takes the general in tow.

A few yards away you hear a begrimed soldier ask: "Who's those two guys?"

"They're the generals," somebody replies.

"What the hell are they doing up here?"

"Damfino . . . they just come around, I guess."

A correspondent from the Chicago *Tribune* buttonholes you and says that he has something to show you. You figure that he wants to show you MacArthur. But his interest is in a Jap pillbox that has been knocked out twice but insists on coming back to life . . . From a distance you watch the bulldozer approach like a crack of doom. Riflemen cover its progress [as it buries the pillbox]. Then your squad leader throws a handful of dirt at you to catch your attention, and when you look, he says, "Come on." [27]

As rain began to fall on the beach, Sixth Army signal corpsmen brought up a weapons carrier with a radio transmitter mounted on it for the scheduled broadcasts by MacArthur and Osmeña to the Philippine nation. William J. Dunn, a CBS correspondent who acted as master of ceremonies, explained, "The portable transmitter was linked to a master transmitter aboard *Nashville* which broadcast on several wave lengths, supposedly known to guerrilla forces in the islands and some of the Filipino people who still had radios." For about fifteen minutes Dunn transmitted at frequent intervals the announcements that the two leaders were about to speak. Then at 2:00 MacArthur took the microphone and delivered a two-minute, emotion-packed address: "People of the Philippines, I have returned! By the grace of Almighty God, our forces stand again on Philippine soil . . . Rally to me! Let the indomitable spirit of Bataan and Corregidor lead on. As the lines of battle roll forward to bring you within the zone of operations, rise and strike! . . . For your homes and hearths, strike! In the name of your sacred dead, strike!" He concluded, "Let no heart be faint. Let every arm be steeled. The guidance of divine God points the way. Follow in His name to the Holy Grail of righteous victory!" One listener observed that the general was "genuinely moved" as he spoke: "His hands shook and his voice took on the timbre of deep emotion."

The Philippine president followed with a ten-minute speech about the restoration of civil government and plans for independence, picturing the days ahead as "a new challenge to our sense of national responsibility." Osmeña said that, before he left Washington, Roosevelt asked him "to be the bearer of a message of congratulations to the people of the Philippines on the regaining of freedom." Romulo closed the program with a brief talk announcing the restoration of his daily radio program, "The Voice of Freedom," begun on Corregidor in early 1942. Afterward, MacArthur and Osmeña sat down under a palm and talked awhile before returning to their ships for the night.[28]

MacArthur had written his address for the Leyte program about a month before the landing, or shortly after the Quebec decision. One day he called in Fellers and Mashbir to read a draft and offer their opinions. They bravely criticized three paragraphs in particular in which he seemed to be speaking too much in religious terms. Fellers recalled that after they voiced their criticism the general said nothing, but "for fifteen minutes he paced up and down. The tension was building. Then he walked up and shook his finger under our noses and said, 'Boys, I want you to know when I mention the Diety I do it with the utmost reverence in my heart. Furthermore, I have fired staff officers for "yessing" me. I'll leave off the three paragraphs.'" He also showed an early version of the speech to Egeberg, who persuaded him to delete a portion "about the tinkle of the laughter of little children returning to the streets of the Philippines." On September 29, MacArthur went to Marquardt's OWI office in Brisbane and had him make a recording of the final version just in case the transmission was faulty on A-day. Even there the SWPA chief had trouble: after he had finished a dramatic reading of the speech, Marquardt, with some trepidation, told him the recorder had not been working while he spoke. The general waited in terrifying silence while Marquardt got the recorder operating, and then MacArthur delivered his beloved speech again.

This trouble was nothing, however, compared to the sneers that greeted his speech in certain newspapers and periodicals in the States and in some books in later years. The speech was pounced on by his critics as "sacrilegious," "in poor taste," "flamboyant," and "proof of MacArthur's supreme egotism." In defense, Kenney argued that "it was not meant for the people back home. It was meant for the Filipino people and they really liked it . . . The results were apparent immediately. We got pledges for help and calls for instructions from all over the country . . . It was an emotional appeal to an emotional people." Egeberg maintained that because of the great faith the majority of Filipinos had in MacArthur, " 'I shall return' was to them a commitment. 'I have returned' was similarly a statement of promise to finish the campaign and free the Philippines, and it was accepted as such" by the Filipinos. Nevertheless, criticism of his address, as well as allegations that his wading ashore on A-day was faked or carefully staged as an act of showmanship, would follow MacArthur the rest of his life. Even Yamashita was a disbeliever at the time: when he saw photographs in Allied newspapers of MacArthur at Leyte on invasion day, he thought they were mockups staged in New Guinea. Otherwise, as he said after the war, he would have avenged Admiral Yamamoto's death by hurling all of his planes in a suicide attack on Mac-Arthur's headquarters.[29]

Some of the confused tales about MacArthur's landing on Leyte stemmed from the fact that the next day he went ashore to inspect the 1st Cavalry's White Beach positions near Tacloban airfield and on the 22nd visited the XXIV Corps' beachhead around Dulag. It was not unnatural that when soldiers of the 7th or 96th divisions, located in the Dulag vicinity, later saw published photographs of the SWPA chief with captions saying they were of him going ashore on A-day, they charged fakery, since he had visited their sector on the third day after the assault. At White Beach on the morning of October 21, MacArthur, Egeberg, and Kenney traveled in a jeep along Highway 1 to the Tacloban airfield. Kenney was sorely disappointed to discover that "the place was nothing but a sandspit," which might hold one fighter group "if we parked them wingtip to wingtip." Egeberg said they drove on toward Tacloban "until we were stopped by fire"; after three hours on White Beach they returned to the *Nashville*. About dusk the news came that Mudge's cavalrymen had already seized Tacloban, the capital of Leyte, though a bitter fight was developing in the hills west of the city. Another unexpected development for MacArthur when he returned to the cruiser that afternoon was a surprise message from Osmeña announcing the award of the Philippine Medal of Honor to him; the Philippine president noted it was "the highest award in my power to give." Also on the 21st, Krueger, Sibert, and Hodge established their headquarters ashore as command of the beachhead operations passed from Kinkaid to the Army. The *Nashville* moved down to the waters off the XXIV Corps' beaches on Sunday, the 22nd, and MacArthur, accompanied by Hodge and several other officers, made a tour by jeep of the Dulag area, including a trip to the airfield west of town, which had recently been captured. In the meantime, congratulatory messages were pouring into MacArthur's temporary headquarters on the *Nashville* from many of the leading Allied statesmen and military chiefs. Churchill praised the invasion as a "brilliant stroke," and Roosevelt wrote, "I know well what this means to you. I know what it cost you to obey my order that you leave Corregidor." [30]

The X and XXIV corps steadily enlarged their beachheads on October 21–25, but against increasing resistance west of Dulag, near Catmon Hill, and in the hills beyond Tacloban to the northwest. On the 23rd, with fighting under way only two miles outside the city, MacArthur, Osmeña, and all of the senior officers of the operation assembled at Tacloban for a ceremony marking the official re-establishment of the Commonwealth government in the Philippines. The brief program was held on the steps of the provincial capitol, a large, columned building near San Pedro Bay. Tarbuck, who was present, said the structure's exterior was intact, but the interior was "a shambles." Two 1st

Cavalry troops of "dirty and tired, but efficient-looking soldiers" formed the guard of honor. A microphone was set up in the center of the front steps, and the ceremony was broadcast throughout the archipelago. MacArthur and Osmeña made short addresses, and Sutherland read a proclamation from Roosevelt making official the restoration of civil government. A bugler sounded colors, and the flags of the United States and the Commonwealth were hoisted simultaneously at opposite ends of the building. (The Philippine flag had been sewn by a sailmaker's mate on the *Nashville*.) MacArthur then presented the Army's Distingushed Service Cross to Kangleon, the guerrilla leader who was also to serve as acting governor of Leyte. Tarbuck observed that "there were practically no Filipinos present except representatives of the local government. Apparently the inhabitants of Tacloban had not been informed of the ceremony, or perhaps did not know they were permitted to attend." The word belatedly spread through the city, and by the time MacArthur and Osmeña started to leave, crowds of Filipinos lined the streets to cheer them.[31]

While at Tacloban that day MacArthur visited the Walter Price residence, which his staff suggested for his quarters and main GHQ offices. The spacious house was located at the corner of Santo Niño and Justice Romualdez streets in the center of Tacloban; it was three blocks from the provincial capitol, which was to serve as the Philippine capitol until Osmeña could return to Manila. MacArthur approved of the Price house, and his staff went to work getting it ready for its new functions. Hostile air raids on Tacloban increased sharply after the general's broadcast on the 23rd. The city was attacked over thirty times during the last week of October, but the Price house was not seriously damaged. At the same time, the ships in Leyte Gulf also began to get more attention from Japanese planes. Aboard the *Nashville*, MacArthur enjoyed staying on the bridge during air raids, though several times bombs and crashing planes nearly hit the ship. The nearby cruisers *Honolulu* and *Australia* were badly damaged.

On October 25 the enemy introduced the American Navy to its Kamikaze Corps, the formidable group of suicidal aviators whose crashing tactics would become a terror to all Allied vessels in the western Pacific in the months ahead. Three escort carriers were hit off Samar on the 25th by kamikaze attacks, and several suicide crashes were attempted on ships in Leyte Gulf but the planes were shot down. On the 24th Kinkaid asked MacArthur to transfer his headquarters ashore so that the *Nashville* could participate in the defense of Surigao Strait, where a Japanese fleet was about to try to force its way into Leyte Gulf. "The General indicated his desire to remain on board regardless of *Nashville*'s employment," states the Navy's history of the Leyte operation, but Kinkaid, "not wishing to risk the life of her distinguished passenger, did not allow the cruiser to take part in the Battle of Surigao Strait." On the 25th, however, Kinkaid insisted that MacArthur transfer to Barbey's flagship, the *Wasatch,* "as *Nashville* was badly needed with combatant forces." MacArthur grudgingly did as his naval commander wished, and after a night on the *Wasatch* he moved ashore on the morning of the 26th and formally opened his new GHQ at the Price residence in Tacloban.[32]

By the time MacArthur transferred to Tacloban, the naval battle for Leyte Gulf was history. The greatest sea fight of all time erupted when Toyoda decided to put his Shō-1 Plan into effect. Vice Admiral Jisaburo Ozawa's Northern Force, comprised mostly of carriers without aircraft, was sent to the Philippine Sea off Cape Engaño, Luzon, to act as a decoy in luring Halsey's Third Fleet away from Leyte Gulf. Vice Admiral Takeo Kurita's Center Force, the most powerful of the Japanese fleets, was to thread its way through the Sibuyan Sea and San Bernadino Strait and come down on Leyte Gulf from the east side of Samar. Meanwhile, Vice Admiral Shoji Nishimura's Southern Force, followed by Vice Admiral Kiyohide Shima's Fifth Fleet, was to break through Surigao Strait into Leyte Gulf.

When his reconnaissance planes spotted Ozawa's carriers off Cape Engaño, Halsey abandoned his patrol off San Bernardino Strait and took the Third Fleet northward in pursuit. The only part of Toyoda's operation that succeeded was tricking Halsey so that he fell for Ozawa's decoy and did not inform Kinkaid that the vital strait above Samar was being left unguarded. Kinkaid placed virtually his entire force of battleships, cruisers, destroyers, and PT boats at the north end of Surigao Strait under the tactical command of Rear Admiral Jesse B. Oldendorf. Torpedo attacks by destroyers sank a battleship and three destroyers of Nishimura's fleet as it came through the strait on the night of October 24–25. Oldendorf then performed the classical naval maneuver of "crossing the T" as his battleships and cruisers, lined across the strait, created havoc with the enemy's Southern Force, wiping out all but one destroyer. Astonishingly, Shima had not coordinated his plans with Nishimura and blundered into the massacre in Surigao Strait later that terrible night. After a brief encounter with the devastating American firepower, Shima turned his fleet southward and fled. Carrier planes harried his ships as they retreated the next day.

Meanwhile, Kurita's strong Central Force had been doggedly continuing toward San Bernardino Strait despite the loss of two cruisers to American submarines off Palawan on October 23 and the super battleship, *Musashi,* to carrier aircraft in the Sibuyan Sea the next day. Kurita, to his surprise, was able to get through San Bernardino Strait undetected, and just after dawn on the 25th he attacked a group of escort carriers under Rear Admiral Clifton Sprague off the southeastern coast of Samar, about eighty miles from the Leyte beachhead. The small American force put up one of the most gallant, heroic defenses in naval annals. Suddenly, when Kurita was in a position to finish off Sprague's

dwindling force, the Japanese admiral broke off action and retired northward back through San Bernardino Strait. Kurita
later explained that intercepted messages led him to conclude
that Halsey's fleet was bearing down on him. Actually Halsey,
after sinking all of Ozawa's carriers in the Philippine Sea, had
sent southward part of the Third Fleet, but Kurita would probably have had time to move into Leyte Gulf and wreak untold
destruction on shipping and beachhead positions. "What was
needed on the flag bridge of the *Yamato* on the morning of the
25th," says a distinguished authority on the battle, "was not a
Hamlet but a Hotspur — a Japanese Halsey instead of a Kurita."
The Central Force commander, however, had the type of mind
that "hesitates to act regardless of the necessity for action." [33]

Sixth Army headquarters reported that if the Shō-1 Plan had
succeeded, "the effect on the Allied troops on Leyte in all likelihood would have been calamitous . . . An enemy naval victory
would have had an adverse effect of incalculable proportions not
only upon the Leyte Operation, but upon the overall plan for
the liberation of the Philippines as well." Halsey scoffed at this
grim possibility, arguing that such thinking was based on the
false premise that "our naval forces would be almost totally
destroyed." Although the American Navy lost six combat ships
in the battle for Leyte Gulf, October 23–26, these represented
less than 3 percent of the total tonnage of United States
ships involved in the action. On the other hand, the Japanese
committed the bulk of their fleet, of which nearly half of their
tonnage was sunk, including three battleships, four carriers,
ten cruisers, and nine destroyers. Admiral Mitsumasa Yonai,
the Japanese Navy Minister, said "that was the end" of the Japanese Navy's surface fleet and the defeat "was tantamount to loss
of the Philippines" from a naval viewpoint.

MacArthur never blamed his friend Halsey for his decision to
forsake the Leyte beachhead to pursue Ozawa, though some of
the general's staff and a number of naval authorities were critical

of the admiral's action. At dinner with some members of his staff at the Price house on the evening of October 26, according to Kenney, "as he sat down MacArthur heard Halsey's name mentioned, accompanied by certain expressions that might be classed as highly uncomplimentary. The General pounded the table for attention. 'That's enough,' he said. 'Leave the Bull alone. He's still a fighting admiral in my book.'" On October 29, the SWPA commander thanked Halsey for his role in the naval victory and added, "Everyone here has a feeling of complete confidence and inspiration when you go into action in our support."

MacArthur later commented, "I have never ascribed the unfortunate incidents of this naval battle to faulty judgments on the part of any of the commanders involved. The near disaster can be placed squarely at the door of Washington. In the naval action, two key American commanders were independent of each other, one under me, and the other under Admiral Nimitz 5,000 miles away, both operating in the same waters and in the same battle." [34] To the end of his days he was convinced that the failure to achieve unity of command in the Pacific was a colossal blunder on the part of the Joint Chiefs.

CHAPTER XIV

From Leyte to Mindoro

1. Advance and Stalemate

IMPERIAL GENERAL HEADQUARTERS' original version of the Shō-1
Plan called for the Combined Fleet, Fourth Air Army, and
Thirty-fifth Army to exert maximum force against an invasion
of the southern or central Philippines. But most of Yamashita's
Fourteenth Area Army was to be held on Luzon where the
decisive ground phase of Shō-1 would be fought. Implementation of the air and ground aspects of Shō-1 was "left entirely" to
Terauchi, commander of the Japanese Southern Army. Having
moved his headquarters from Singapore to Manila in May,
1944, Terauchi was in the latter city during Yamashita's first
five weeks there as Fourteenth Area Army commander. After
several tense planning sessions prompted by the invasion of
Leyte, Terauchi ordered Yamashita on October 22 to "muster
all possible strength to totally destroy the enemy on Leyte."
While Yamashita favored making the all-out ground effort on
Luzon and was apprehensive about the capability or worth of
reinforcing Leyte, he grudgingly announced to his officers that
"the Japanese will fight the decisive battle of the Philippines on
Leyte."

Terauchi and his staff, observed a Japanese general in Manila at the time, were "in extremely high spirits and very optimistic" on the evening of the 22nd. They were supremely confident that the Shō-1 naval and air attacks "would, at any moment, destroy the American forces which had entered Leyte Gulf." Optimism ran high also at Suzuki's headquarters on Cebu: "We were determined," remarked his chief of staff, to undertake "offensive after offensive and clean up American forces on Leyte Island . . . We seriously discussed demanding the surrender of the entire American Army after seizing General MacArthur." The scheme to capture the SWPA chief was not attempted because, by the time Makino could move sizable forces into the hills northwest of Tacloban, the American defenses around the city were very nearly impenetrable.

Within four days of Terauchi's decision about Leyte, the great naval battle for Leyte Gulf had spelled the doom of the Japanese Navy as an effective fighting force. Beginning on October 24, the Fourth Air Army, heavily reinforced and now possessing up to 2500 planes, undertook a massive offensive against the Leyte beachheads on a scale MacArthur had not seen since his days on Corregidor. The frequent day and night raids did considerable damage to Fifth Air Force planes and facilities at Tacloban airfield, as well as to supply dumps along the beaches and shipping anchored in Leyte Gulf. Nevertheless, by late November the combined efforts of American carrier and land-based aircraft, together with bristling antiaircraft defenses aboard ships and on shore, produced staggering Japanese losses of planes and pilots, for which adequate replacements were not available. The Fourth Air Army was badly crippled, and, as one official study says, "what had once been a formidable weapon was transformed into a sacrificial army of guided missiles."

Despite the failure by naval and air forces to defeat the invaders, Terauchi persisted in demanding that Yamashita send large ground reinforcements to Leyte. At least nine convoys were dispatched between October 23 and December 11. Although American aircraft sank nearly 80 per cent of the ships, the costly reinforcement runs succeeded in getting 45,000 to 50,000 troops and about 10,000 tons of supplies and equipment to Leyte. Besides the opposition of the 16th Division of the pre-invasion garrison, Krueger's Sixth Army in coming weeks on Leyte would be faced with all or most of the Japanese 1st, 26th, and 102nd divisions and two independent brigades, as well as elements of two other divisions. Suzuki moved his Thirty-fifth Army headquarters to Leyte on November 2, but Terauchi, having upset Yamashita's plan for defending Luzon, transferred his Southern Army headquarters from Manila to Saigon on November 17 at the height of the Leyte campaign.[1]

Monsoon rains and frequent Japanese air attacks during the week following the capture of Tacloban airfield made it difficult for the engineers to lay the 2500 feet of steel matting for a runway for the waiting Fifth Air Force fighters on Morotai. Barbey's LST crews and service personnel added to the problem by unloading cargo on the air strip until an enraged Kenney threatened to have his men forcibly evict the next sailor to intrude. When the first two squadrons of P-38's landed at the field on October 27, MacArthur and Kenney were waiting to greet the pilots as they stepped down from their fighters. Later in the day MacArthur prematurely declared that the Far East Air Forces could now assume control of Leyte air operations, so the admirals happily began withdrawing their carriers toward Ulithi. After all, the carriers had already remained in the area longer than Nimitz and Halsey desired; they were especially anxious about the rising number of kamikaze attacks.

Beginning on October 28, a typhoon raged across the island, followed by two more in the next ten days; thirty-five inches of rain fell during the American's first forty days on Leyte, making grading of runways impossible in some areas where airfield construction was attempted. Furthermore, Japanese air assaults came in unprecedented fury during the first week of Kenney's command of Leyte air defenses. By November 3, the original thirty-four P-38's were down to twenty serviceable fighters, but they and the Sixth Army antiaircraft batteries had destroyed 117 enemy planes that week. The V Fighter Command, indeed, would be so busy for another month in fighting enemy air raiders that only slight attention could be given to missions in direct support of ground troops.

With the airfields west of Dulag water-logged and construction on matted runways moving slowly, Kenney was able to get only about 150 fighters onto Leyte. Sometimes they were outnumbered fifteen to one in dogfights, but they still took a heavy toll of the enemy attackers. MacArthur had no recourse except to swallow his pride, admit to Nimitz that he was wrong about his airmen's ability to cope with the situation, and plead for the return of the carrier aircraft. On November 10, he, Kenney, and Rear Admiral Forrest Sherman, representing Nimitz, met at Tacloban to discuss the air crisis. The SWPA chief painted a gloomy but accurate picture, insisting that the air power of Task Force 38, the fast carriers, was essential to the Sixth Army's success. Halsey, then at Ulithi, had planned to employ Mitscher's formidable carrier groups in a strike against Japan proper in mid-November. Sherman, with Nimitz's concurrence, agreed, however, to resume fast carrier operations in support of the Leyte ground forces until November 25. Halsey, it was reported, "accepted this decision, a bitter disappointment to him, with good grace."

No sooner had the carriers departed for the second time than MacArthur asked Nimitz on November 27 to send him several squadrons of crack Marine night fighters from the Palaus and Solomons. Nimitz was agreeable, and the fighters began arriving at Tacloban on December 3; for the next five weeks the eighty-seven Marine aircraft proved invaluable in defending the Tacloban–Dulag–Leyte Gulf area against enemy night raiders,

which had been causing much damage. On MacArthur's recommendation, one Marine night fighter squadron, VMF (N)-
541, was awarded a Presidential Unit Citation.[2]

From A-day to Christmas, 1944, Army, Navy, and Marine
planes and Sixth Army and Seventh Fleet antiaircraft guns accounted for an estimated 1480 enemy aircraft destroyed in operations over Leyte. Celebrations of new aces became common
occurrences at the Tacloban base. After the V Fighter Command's Major Richard I. Bong downed his thirty-eighth plane,
MacArthur presented him the Medal of Honor in a ceremony
amid a half circle of P-38's at the Tacloban airfield on December 12. Within five days Bong had his fortieth "kill," after
which he was sent back to the States, only to die in a plane crash
in California eight days before the war ended.

By early December, fighter bases were operational at Dulag,
Bayug, and Tanauan, and the runway at Tacloban had been
extended to 6000 feet. All three fields, however, were badly
overcrowded; poor drainage and unsuitable soil conditions kept
the engineers constantly busy working on the runways. Airfields that were under construction at San Pablo and Buri had to
be abandoned because of unending engineering difficulties.
Not one of the captured Japanese airfields proved satisfactory,
and no bombers could be stationed on Leyte during the campaign. The Army Air Forces' history states that "the inability
of Sixth Army engineers to provide planned air facilities on
Leyte cost that army an easy victory" and "continued construc-
tional delays threatened to jeopardize the whole schedule of
future operations." Leyte's terrain and climate, especially on
the northeast coast, were so unsuitable for air bases that the
engineers faced an impossible mission.

In terms of potential air bases to support the invasion of
Luzon, Leyte was a keen disappointment to MacArthur. In addition, air support of Sixth Army operations was weak and had
to be left largely to carrier aircraft. The Sixth Army report on

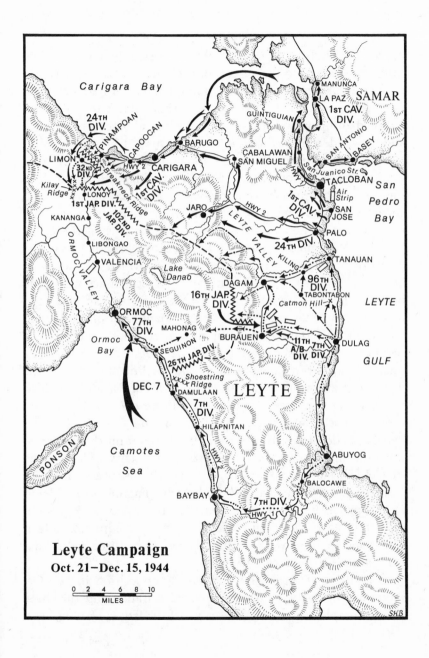

Leyte Campaign
Oct. 21–Dec. 15, 1944

0 2 4 6 8 10
MILES

the campaign concluded that the Leyte experience "brought out very strongly, although in a negative way, the vital relationship of air power to the success of the offensive as measured by the period of time required to complete the utter destruction of the hostile force." It was the first time MacArthur had attempted an operation without adequate land-based air support, and he was determined that it would be his last.[3]

In the meantime, Krueger's forces pushed ahead in their muddy operations on Leyte, advancing rapidly at first but slowing down subsequently as monsoon rains washed out roads and Japanese reinforcements joined the 16th Division in resisting the invaders. The conquest of the southern part of the Leyte Valley was assigned to Hodge's XXIV Corps. Bradley sent one of his regiments up the coast to Tanauan, which fell on October 25; north of the town that day the first contact was made between the X and XXIV corps. At the same time another regiment of the 96th Division had struck inland, capturing Tabontabon, an important enemy supply center, on the 26th. This regiment and another moving westward from Tanauan erased a small but stubborn Japanese garrison at Kiling and secured the Tanauan-Dagami road to within two miles of Dagami. A third regiment moved inland from the 96th's beachhead in a northwesterly direction between Tabontabon and Catmon Hill. A fierce fight developed on Catmon Hill, and not until October 30 were the more than sixty pillboxes and twenty caves on the rugged hill mass finally overrun. The territory secured by the 96th Division in late October yielded what engineers considered to be a promising airfield site near Tanauan, and work was immediately started on a runway. Its eventual completion alleviated some of the overcrowding at the other three fields that Whitehead's airmen were trying to use.

Arnold's 7th Division ran into strong opposition in late October, but by the 27th it had captured Burauen and the three partly completed airfields nearby — San Pablo, Bayug, and

Buri. Striking northward along the Burauen-Dagami road, the 7th encountered strong artillery fire from the hills west of Dagami but drove on to the edge of the town. There a weird fight developed in a cemetery: the enemy troops had removed Filipino bodies from their tombs and used the stone crypts and open graves as defensive positions. On October 30 Dagami was captured, Makino having earlier moved his headquarters into the hills to the northwest. While the fight for Dagami was under way, Arnold had sent a battalion down the coast to Abuyog on October 29; meeting no opposition, the troops crossed the mountains on Highway 1 and seized Baybay on the west coast on November 2. Makino had made no provision for defense of that area or of any other section of the southern half of Leyte. In addition to its small force now on the west coast, soon to be reinforced for the drive toward Ormoc, Hodge's corps was in firm control of the strategically most important portion of the southern Leyte Valley. In contrast with the corps' light casualties on A-day, 477 of its soldiers and over 6900 Japanese had been killed in the 7th and 96th divisions' sectors by November 1.

To the north in the X Corps' sector, units of the 1st Cavalry Division, led by Mudge, drove the enemy from the hills west of Tacloban on October 23–24, while other cavalrymen pushed quickly up the west side of San Juanico Strait to the end of Highway 1, fourteen miles north of Tacloban. In shore-to-shore movements, Mudge's troops on October 24–27 landed at several points on southwestern Samar and rapidly secured the entire coastline of San Juanico Strait from La Paz to Basey against surprisingly light resistance. Mudge boldly sent other elements of his division by water around the tip of Leyte into Carigara Bay. Encountering some air opposition but still no significant ground forces, they seized Babatngon on October 24 and four days later brazenly moved into Barugo, just four miles east of Carigara. Forty Americans had died in the 1st Cavalry's lightning-fast advance from Tacloban to Barugo, but about 740 Japanese had been killed. The missions along the northeastern shores had been so much easier than expected that Mudge sent the bulk of his troops to support Irving's 24th Division to the south, which was bearing the brunt of enemy opposition in the corps sector.

North of Palo the 24th Division had repulsed a fanatical charge that came on the second night it was ashore; nearly 800 enemy bodies were counted in front of the beachhead line after the wild action. Fighting their way into Palo on the 21st, Irving's soldiers met another savage enemy attack two nights later that penetrated to the town square before it was hurled back. Even when they had secured Palo, the troops of the 24th found their way into the northern Leyte Valley blocked a mile west of the town by withering fire from two hills overlooking Highway 2, the route to Carigara; it took three days of fighting to capture the hills. With the 24th Division moving along Highway 2 and the 1st Cavalry Division on its right flank, the X Corps plunged into the Leyte Valley, heading north toward Carigara. Makino had planned to make a stand between Jaro and Carigara, but the Americans pressed forward so vigorously that the Japanese general found his forces split, outmaneuvered, and forced to retreat in order to avoid envelopment. On October 31, Irving's division captured Jaro, and two days later Mudge's cavalrymen entered Carigara. A major battle had been anticipated at Carigara, but the Japanese unexpectedly abandoned the port and escaped westward into the mountains before the Americans launched their attack. In the rapid advance through the northern part of the Leyte Valley, the X Corps had killed nearly 3000 Japanese while fewer than 250 Americans had died in action. MacArthur especially relished the defeat of the Japanese 16th Division: it had been one of the two principal divisions Homma had used to capture Luzon in 1941–42.

On the day that Carigara fell, Suzuki established his headquarters on Leyte and took command of all Japanese forces on the island. He immediately set to work converting the northern entrance to the mountain barrier west of Carigara into a huge fortress. The Japanese 1st and 102nd divisions, from Manchuria and Cebu respectively, were sent to man the rugged ramparts of the mountain bastion, while the remnants of the battered 16th Division made their way south to hold the line west of Dagami. At the same time the Sixth Army's offensive momentum was beginning to feel the impact of mounting logistical difficulties and delays in the construction of air and supply bases between Dulag and Tacloban. More formidable an opponent than the Japanese so far, the almost incessant monsoon downpours continued to handicap seriously the building of runways, warehouses, hospitals, and other facilities, the transportation of supplies to the front-line troops, and the evacuation of wounded and ill combat soldiers.[4]

Despite such problems Krueger planned to launch two major drives that would converge on Ormoc: Sibert's X Corps was to push south from Carigara Bay through the Ormoc Valley, while Hodge's XXIV Corps would attack north from Baybay along the coast of the Camotes Sea. Meanwhile, the Sixth Army forces holding the western edge of the Leyte Valley were to thwart enemy efforts to break into that plain, keep pressure on the Japanese at all points, and exploit any opportunity to thrust across the mountains to the west coast.

On the northern end of the line, Irving's division started out quickly on November 3, advancing four miles along the coastal road and the next day capturing Pinampoan. But when the American troops turned south on Highway 2 and started into the mountains, they encountered the strongly fortified positions of the Japanese 1st Division on Breakneck Ridge, about halfway between Pinampoan and Limon; the latter town was often called "the gateway to Ormoc Valley." A typhoon swept across the area as Irving's soldiers launched the first of many futile assaults against the ridge fortifications. "The trickle of supplies was at a standstill" for several days because of the "angry immensity" of the storm, said Valtin of the 24th Division. The road through the swampy coastal region between Carigara and Pinampoan was temporarily washed out by the typhoon. After three days of costly attacks with gains measured in yards, Irving tried a double envelopment, sending one battalion to Kilay Ridge, two miles south of Limon, and another to establish a road block on Highway 2 near that ridge. The Japanese were unable to dislodge the valiant American battalions in their rear, and the enemy supply line was severed. Yet no immediate relief was felt on Breakneck Ridge where Irving's men, short on food and heavy weapons, continued to batter at the powerful Japanese positions.

On November 8 and 12, MacArthur conferred with Krueger at Sixth Army headquarters in Tanauan. They discussed, according to one account, "the progress of the battle, the frustrating effect of the continuous rain, and the disappointing condition of the Leyte airstrips," as well as "the lack of sufficient trained replacements to meet Sixth Army needs." It may have been on one of those occasions that MacArthur informed Krueger that the veteran 32nd Division would reach Leyte on November 14. They probably discussed also the command situation at Breakneck Ridge, where one regimental commander had already been relieved. Immediately upon the arrival of Gill's 32nd Division on the 14th, Krueger ordered the unit to relieve Irving's exhausted division. The 24th Division was assigned to defend the Jaro sector, then relatively quiet, and on November 18 Irving was relieved of his divisional command and placed in charge of garrison troops at Tanauan. Major General Roscoe B. Woodruff, his successor as the 24th's commander, said he was never told the reason for Irving's removal: "His relief was a great surprise to me." When Woodruff arrived at the 24th's headquarters, however, he noticed "some weakness in the staff, partly caused by combat fatigue." According to Valtin, about November 5 Irving had "warned higher headquarters that the road from Carigara to Pinampoan would not support a major offensive. Higher headquarters ordered that the offensive should proceed. The road dissolved and General Irving was relieved of his command." Valtin observed, "Among the rank and file who had come to admire him as a fearless, able and humane leader of men there were many who felt that their commander had been made a scapegoat for mistakes on the shoulders of higher rank." MacArthur later told Eichelberger that Irving had established "a fine record" with his division and "he is sorry that the action was taken," which suggests that the move leading to Irving's relief was instigated by Sibert or Krueger.

Meanwhile, in order to break the bloody stalemate at the northern end of the Ormoc Corridor, Gill sent two of his regiments around the enemy's left flank and a third one around the other end of the line, leaving an attached regiment of the 24th in a holding position on Breakneck Ridge's northern slopes. The maneuver worked, and on November 22 Limon was captured. With the help of the 112th Cavalry, which had pushed across the mountains from the east in an exhausting march, Gill's main forces by mid-December were astride Highway 2 about two miles south of Limon. Through the feverish efforts of engineer and service troops, plus a decline in rainfall, the supply situation had by then improved. A number of strong enemy pockets remained to be mopped up on Breakneck Ridge, Kilay Ridge, and elsewhere to the rear, but the northern gateway to Ormoc Valley had been secured at last. The death toll had been high on both sides: over 700 Americans and about 6100 Japanese.[5]

In November and early December, the front line running along the western edge of Leyte Valley, though of less strategic significance than the pincers movement closing on Ormoc, was the scene of considerable combat action. On November 2 the Japanese 16th Division, replenished with troops from assorted units arriving on convoy runs, attacked the 96th Division west of Dagami in a desperate attempt to re-enter Leyte Valley. In a week of heavy fighting the enemy was repulsed, and an American counterattack pushed the 16th Division deeper into the mountains. On the 96th's left flank, the 7th Division's scheduled movement to the Baybay region had to be postponed until the crisis subsided; then on November 22 Major General Joseph M. Swing's 11th Airborne Division began relieving the 7th's units south of Dagami. At the end of the month, the 24th and 96th divisions began a methodical drive from Jaro, pushing Japanese forces in that area to the western side of the island's mountainous backbone. Meanwhile, on orders from Yamashita to prevent the Americans from using the Burauen air strips, Suzuki planned a daring scheme whereby elements of his 16th and 26th divisions would attack Burauen while several companies of paratroopers would be dropped on the air strips by transports flying from Luzon bases. The bold attack was carried out on December 6, but because of poor coordination, garbled orders, and other mishaps, the ground and airborne troops that made it to the objective area were soon annihilated by Swing's 11th Airborne soldiers. The enemy raiders were able to destroy some fuel and supply dumps and a few parked aircraft, but ironically two of the three airfields were already in the process of being abandoned in favor of the new field under construction at Tanauan.

The 7th Division, which formerly defended the Burauen region, had moved in the meantime to the west coast where it began an advance north toward Ormoc. On November 23–27, its forward regiment was attacked by units of the newly arrived Japanese 26th Division near Damulaan, thirteen miles south of Ormoc. The American troops' situation was precarious for several days before the enemy forces were finally forced to withdraw. This so-called "Battle of Shoestring Ridge" got its nickname from the Americans' poor supply situation at the time. As the regimental commander remarked, "The old slogan 'Too little and too late' became 'Just enough and just in time' for us." From Damulaan the 7th Division launched a concerted drive on December 4 which, after eight days and numerous battles on the coastal hills and ridges, had been carried to the banks of the Panilahan River, less than six miles from Ormoc.

MacArthur had reluctantly concluded on November 30 that, because of the slowness of the Leyte conquest, the invasion of Mindoro would have to be postponed ten days, until December 15. For some time Krueger had wanted to send a division in an amphibious assault against Ormoc to close forever that avenue of enemy reinforcements and also to split Suzuki's forces. The postponement of the Mindoro operation now made available the amphibious shipping and naval support needed to mount a seaborne attack on Ormoc. MacArthur was agreeable, and the mission was assigned to Major General Andrew D. Bruce's 77th Division. Rear Admiral Arthur D. Struble's task group was given the job of transporting and supporting Bruce's division, and the Fifth Air Force would be responsible for the convoy's air cover.

The attack force arrived at the landing area, three miles south of Ormoc, on the morning of December 7, and the 77th Division went ashore against little opposition. But in less than two hours hostile aircraft began attacking Struble's vessels in Ormoc Bay; before the day was over they had made sixteen separate large-scale raids. Many of the attackers were kamikazes, and though thirty-six Japanese planes were shot down by antiaircraft fire and Whitehead's fighters, the Japanese succeeded in badly damaging five of Struble's ships. A destroyer and a transport were so crippled they had to be sunk by American gunfire. Struble was extremely upset about the inadequate protection given him by the Fifth Air Force, but at least the operation on the ground had gone smoothly and the Japanese had been caught off guard with only a few service troops in the vicinity.

As Bruce's troops advanced north toward Ipil, however, elements of the Japanese 30th Division and other reserve units, which Suzuki had intended to dispatch to the Ormoc Valley, began to offer fierce opposition. Overwhelming American firepower steadily forced the Japanese to retreat, and on December 10 the 77th Division captured Ormoc. With the 7th and 11th Airborne divisions of the XXIV Corps (besides the 32nd and 1st Cavalry divisions of the X Corps) advancing toward Ormoc at the time of the city's fall, Bruce sent a message to Hodge: "Have rolled two sevens in Ormoc. Come seven come eleven." In the drive to Ormoc the 77th Division lost 123 men killed in action; about 1500 Japanese were killed. The death toll on Struble's heavily attacked ships was over 110 sailors, and his vessels would face more punishment from enemy aircraft in the days ahead since the Navy had the task of keeping Bruce's division adequately supplied.

The seizure of Ormoc marked a turning point in the Leyte campaign. The Japanese lost the use of the key port through which reinforcements were channeled; Suzuki's army was now hopelessly divided and had suffered heavy losses; and any hope Suzuki may have had of moving his forces down Highway 2 for a final stand in southern Leyte was shattered. MacArthur joyfully announced in a communiqué the day after the Ormoc Bay landing that the operation had "split the enemy's forces in two, isolating those in the valley to the north from those along the coast to the south. Both segments are now caught between our columns which are pressing in from all fronts." The SWPA commander, as usual, was too optimistic, for at that time Suzuki was busily planning a counterattack while in Manila Yamashita was preparing to send an invasion force to Carigara Bay. In spite of MacArthur's communiqués, and to his discomfort and embarrassment, Suzuki's courageous but vastly outnumbered Thirty-fifth Army would take a long time in dying.[6]

2. *Life at Tacloban*

Although the GHQ and capitol buildings in Tacloban were only a few blocks apart, MacArthur visited Osmeña's office but four times and the Philippine president went to see him thirteen times during the ten weeks the SWPA chief resided in the city. Each leader was concerned with his own problems — MacArthur overseeing the Leyte campaign and planning the Mindoro and Luzon invasions and Osmeña coping with political, legal, economic, and social crises arising in liberated areas of the rather heavily populated island. MacArthur placed Fellers in overall charge of the Army's Philippine civil affairs units with orders to turn liberated communities over to civil authority as quickly as possible after local hostilities ceased. The units were to continue to assist Filipino officials in the distribution of relief supplies, which at first came from military stocks. Fellers said the system proved "to be simple, direct, and workable . . . Minor bungling occurs, but the entire procedure is characterized by liberality, tolerance, and sincerity."

Nevertheless, MacArthur indicated some discontent over Osmeña's reaction to bearing the burden of civil administration so soon: "I gathered that President Osmeña looked upon his trip to Leyte as a ceremonial visit, and that he fully expected to go back to the United States and continue to administer a government-in-exile until the war was over, or at least until military operations in the Philippines were concluded." [7] According to Fellers, on the other hand, the Philippine president soon saw the need for his continuing presence and vigorously tackled the problems of the freed population of Leyte:

President Osmeña's field headquarters has been bombed frequently since he took over. But this inconvenience has not prevented him from exercising energy and leadership. He has:

Appointed a provincial governor and many civil officials.

Created an organization to assist in the recruitment of civilian labor for our army.

Aided the Army in the distribution of rice and other essential supplies.

Fixed ceiling prices of commodities.

Initiated plans for the reestablishment of the hemp and copra industries.

Provided for the reestablishment of currency, of schools, and of a public health service.

And finally, President Osmeña has initiated measures for the prompt investigation of those Filipinos now confined, accused of having assisted the enemy.[8]

This last action, however, was prompted by MacArthur's intervention. At Hollandia he had told Osmeña that he would be expected to handle the matter of collaboration. But, especially since he had only a small staff at Tacloban, Osmeña placed higher priority on pressing welfare problems, while MacArthur, justifiably concerned over military security with large-scale fighting only a short distance to the west, concluded that the Philippine president was making only "feeble and ineffective" efforts to cope with collaboration. Thorpe, who headed SWPA counterintelligence, stated that by October 30 Osmeña's officials "had arrested one man and weren't quite sure what to do with him." That day MacArthur summoned Thorpe and said, "Thorpe, I'm taking the business of dealing with collaborators away from the Philippine government and giving it to you and I want action."

On November 9 a directive from the Joint Chiefs arrived at GHQ: "You will remove collaborationists from positions of political and economic influence. Their immediate disposition is a matter for your determination, bearing in mind that the ultimate disposition of all civil collaborationists is primarily the responsibility of the civil authorities." By then a massive roundup and arrest of alleged collaborators was already under way on Leyte. Osmeña wanted to give each accused person a hearing as rapidly as possible and stated that "not the mere act of occupying an office under the Japanese but the motive in doing so and the record in office would be the measure of one's loyalty." But the government was slow to act because of the lack of officials and investigative machinery, as well as the pressure of more urgent problems. "Soon the whole question" of collaboration, states one authority, "was tangled up in proceedings too heavy and complicated for the returning government to handle." Except in regard to the arrest of alleged collaborators, MacArthur seems to have stayed out of civil affairs at Tacloban, but Osmeña sensed that, when they returned to Manila, the strong-willed theater commander would exert an influence on Philippine politics that would be felt for a long time to come.[9]

The spacious, elegant two-story stucco house that served as quarters and offices for MacArthur, Sutherland, Kenney, and several other key staff members had been used by the Japanese as an officers' club after they had killed its owner, Walter Price. In the front yard the Japanese had built an air-raid shelter twenty feet deep, equipped with electric lights, ventilating fans, and furniture. According to Kenney, MacArthur looked it over and commented, "Level it off and fill it in. It spoils the looks of the lawn." Kenney later wrote, "I didn't think it made much sense, but I didn't say anything. It wouldn't have done any good, anyhow. I had tried to get him into dugouts before without any success." As more and more GHQ personnel arrived at Tacloban, it became necessary to occupy a number of buildings all over the city to house the many sections and offices. Some of the latter had to be in warehouses. The main GHQ complex was just opposite the Price house and consisted of four prefabricated buildings, each forty feet wide and 140 feet long, set in two rows. An elevated catwalk ran between them and the Price house.[10]

Sergeant Vincent L. Powers, who worked in the chief regulating officer's section at GHQ, said that he and his office mates often observed MacArthur on the long, wide veranda of the "Big House" at the end of the row:

As was his habit, the General could be seen at all hours walking up and down the veranda, smoking his elongated corncob pipe, strolling alone, or with an aide, or conferring with high-ranking military leaders. Since we had landed at Tacloban, he had spent most of his time coming in and out of his office, which opened on the patio, and pacing the porch.

We grew to know his mood from the way he walked, how he smoked and whom his pacing companions were. Watching him, some claimed they could surmise the turn of history. The speed of his pace was the indicator; the manner, the barometer.

When he walked alone, he would puff his ever-burning pipe at a slow, even pace matching his stride. Every few steps, he would look out into the clear air, his sun glasses hiding his deep thoughts. A plan appeared hatching in his fertile mind.

Then there would be times we would see him racing back and forth, an aide at his side, talking rapidly, gesticulating with quick nods, sucking his pipe with deep, long draughts. Suddenly he would take the pipe in hand, ask a rapid, short question, jam the stem back between his teeth as he listened to the answer. It was a time of crisis, quick decision.

And there would be those rare occasions he could be seen sitting quietly in a wicker chair near a small oval table at the left end of the porch, resting contentedly alone or chatting amicably with a visitor. We didn't have to reach the office to find that official communique contained good news, that a phase of a plan had been successfully completed.

Day and night, under all weather conditions, he could be seen on his porch; at night the fluorescent lights of his inner office threw his easily recognizable figure into sharp relief. Should the air alert sound, he would knock the glowing ashes from his pipe, stand by the rail in the center of the porch, peer into the sky, watching the red tracers and 90-mm's blast at the enemy. The raid over, he would resume his pacing.[11]

Even without the frequent Japanese air raids, life would have been miserable at Tacloban in the autumn of 1944 because the monsoon torrents turned the streets and walks into seas of mud through which the huge influx of American troops and vehicles floundered. Marquardt, who arrived a week after A-day, said, "It did nothing but rain. We would step out of the houses and up to our knees in mud." After a visit there in late November, Eichelberger remarked that the city's combination of heavy traffic and deep mud "defies description." The several typhoons that hit the area packed winds of 100 or more miles per hour and destroyed many temporary military structures. The soldiers in one makeshift barracks at Tacloban found that the typhoon that struck on the night of October 30–31 was able to "accomplish in five minutes what utilities hadn't been able to do in a week, i.e., install running showers, right over your cot . . . and make you realize at long last that Australia was a home on the range, Hollandia the land of sunshine and honey." Another "inconvenience" during the first weeks at Tacloban was Japanese snipers, who occasionally sneaked into the edge of the city from the nearby hills.

The first movie shown at the Mercedes Theater after Tacloban's liberation ended with a scene in which actor Fred Mac-Murray shot his double-crossing sweetheart, Barbara Stanwyck. When the "bang, bang" continued, the sound track seemed stuck and a GI grumbled, "She looked dead the first time." Then an officer announced to the audience that a sniper was firing outside the theater. He assured them, "Don't worry. The first one he shoots, we'll get him." Military police killed the sniper before he hit anyone. Reports differ as to whether MacArthur, an inveterate movie-goer, attended the Mercedes' gala reopening that night.

Because it was the largest residential structure in Tacloban, the Price house became a conspicuous, inviting target for hostile aircraft. A bomb destroyed the adjoining house of a large Filipino family, killing a dozen persons, and two war correspondents died when a bomb hit their quarters nearby, yet MacArthur's residence, though attacked many times, escaped destruction. A shell crashed through the ceiling and wall of the bedroom adjoining MacArthur's, but the missile was a dud. On another occasion the SWPA chief narrowly missed death when he stubbornly refused to quit shaving while an enemy plane strafed the house. Marquat's antiaircraft gunners hit the house once while shooting at low-flying planes. Fitch, the SWPA adjutant general, said, "One of these shells went through General MacArthur's bedroom and landed on a couch across from his bed." Fortunately it was a dud, and after having it defused, MacArthur took it with him to the general's mess the next morning. Fitch recalled that he "laid it down on the table in front of Marquat's place. He said, 'Bill, ask your gunners to raise their sights just a little bit higher.'" When Turner Catledge of the *New York Times* visited the Price house in late November, he concluded that "the Japanese must have known MacArthur was living in it, for it was a principal target for air raids. It had been strafed repeatedly and was pockmarked inside and out with machine-gun bullet holes. My room had a gaping hole through the wall made the week before by a 20-mm. shell." MacArthur's behavior did not surprise those who had seen him on Corregidor, but his calmness and courage astonished other GHQ personnel who had not been with him under fire.[12]

On November 26 Eichelberger attended a conference at GHQ during which an enemy air attack occurred. He returned to Hollandia truly awed by the SWPA commander's display of coolness in the presence of danger. Byers, the Eighth Army's chief of staff, said that Eichelberger told him of the episode:

General MacArthur was briefing a group of senior Army and Navy people . . . The Japanese bombed the house, and Mac-

Arthur was standing with a pointer in his hand, as though he were a cadet pointing out places on a map. The bomb exploded, but he went on. No one in the room noticed any hesitation or any change in his hand at all. When he finished his sentence and his thought, he turned to one of his subordinates and said, "Better look in the kitchen and outside. That bomb was close, and someone may have been hurt." At least three people in the kitchen of the house in which he was speaking were injured. One, I believe, was killed.[13]

MacArthur's principal visitors at Tacloban were SWPA generals and admirals involved in the Leyte campaign or the upcoming Mindoro operation, Filipino officials and guerrilla leaders, and correspondents. Aside from Pacific operations and strategy, MacArthur's chief topics of interest in conversations on his veranda appeared to be the presidential election, the outcome of which he stoically accepted, though Catledge noticed "some jealousy of Roosevelt"; the operations in Europe, the handling of which he criticized from the North African landing to the Battle of the Bulge, particularly Eisenhower's leadership; and the West Point football team, which under Colonel Earl H. "Red" Blaik's coaching was enjoying great success. Catledge said that he and A. H. Sulzberger "joined MacArthur on his porch for one of the most fascinating talks with a public figure that either of us had ever experienced . . . As he spoke, he was variously the military expert, the political figure, the man of destiny. Sulzberger and I later agreed we had never met a more egotistical man, nor one more aware of his egotism and more able and determined to back it up with his deeds." Correspondent Bert Andrews told Secretary of the Navy James V. Forrestal (Knox had died in May, 1944) that in his conversation with MacArthur at Tacloban the general talked much about the future of world affairs and predicted that "the lands touching the Pacific will determine the course of history for the next ten thousand years . . . and, in his strongest blast against

Washington, said 'they' were guilty of 'treason and sabotage' in not adequately supporting the Pacific while hammering Germany."

Among those who called on the SWPA commander at Tacloban were Blamey on December 6–7 to discuss the tough, unheralded operations of his Australian troops against the bypassed enemy far to the south; Dr. van Mook, acting governor-general of the East Indies, who on December 10 presented MacArthur with one of the Netherland's highest honors, the Knights Grand Cross with Swords of the Order of Orange-Nassau; and Nimitz and Sherman, who enjoyed a pleasant stay at GHQ on December 26–28 while planning with the SWPA chief and his staff the naval role in the impending Luzon operation.[14]

As would be expected of a theater commander's appointments, MacArthur's military callers were predominantly generals and admirals. Thus it is surprising to find an entry in his office diary for December 18 indicating an appointment with Privates R. J. Merisieki and Charles Feuereisen. The story of the duo's adventure is revealed in the divisional history of Swing's 11th Airborne:

> Two men of H Company, 511th [Regiment], PFC Feuereisen and PFC Merisieki, were interested in finding out why the 11th Airborne had not received more publicity for the amount of fighting it had been doing.
>
> It was around the middle of December 1944 and we were still in the thick of combat. Feuereisen and Merisieki had been in the hills with the 511th, had been wounded, and were sent back to the rear. Recovered, they were put on a detail at Tacloban Strip packaging and loading supplies for C-47 drops to our troops in the mountains. They went into Tacloban, where GHQ was located, and found themselves, by chance, in front of General MacArthur's office. A general was standing in front of the building and, since the men believed in going through channels, they asked him if there was any way they

could see General MacArthur, that they wanted to know why the 11th Airborne had been slighted in his communiques. The general replied that General MacArthur was extremely busy and could not see them. But the Commander of the Allied Forces on Leyte had heard the conversation through his open window and told the men to come into his office. Feuereisen and Merisieki again stated their mission. General MacArthur then showed them the entire situation on his own operations map, pointed out the part the 11th Airborne was playing, and indicated that he wanted to conceal from the enemy the presence and disposition of the 11th Airborne till the time was propitious for disclosing to the nation and the enemy that the 11th Airborne was carrying a large part of the fighting on Leyte. He had the men point out for him the disposition of their regiment's companies. Then he gave them a message to deliver to General Swing and the men of his Division. General MacArthur wanted them to know that he was aware of their great fight against the enemy, terrain, and the elements and that as soon as he could he would give to the division the full credit it deserved. With a mixed feeling of eminence and satisfaction, and with the feeling that their mission had been most successfully accomplished, the men departed. They had proved to themselves that their outfit was not forgotten; they had shown, at least to themselves, that the only way to find out things was to ask the man who knows. General Mac-Arthur was beyond reproach. This estimate, along with the details of the story, they hastened to make known to General Swing, and everyone else they met.[15]

During his period at Tacloban, MacArthur participated in three small celebrations, the occasions being Thanksgiving, Christmas, and his promotion to five-star rank. Normally he ate simply and avoided festivities of all kinds, but on Thanksgiving Day, November 23, 1944, with depressing news arriving hourly of the bloody stalemate on Breakneck Ridge and mounting casualties elsewhere on Leyte, he told the GHQ cooks to prepare a special menu for the generals' evening mess: princess salad, roast turkey, creamed white potatoes, candied sweet potatoes, English peas, baked tomatoes, and mince and pumpkin pies, preceded by 1929 vintage champagne and followed by demitasse. For various reasons, about half of his regular mess companions had to be absent that evening, so MacArthur enjoyed several hours of quiet relaxation with those who could come — Marshall, Stivers, Fellers, Sverdrup, Fitch, Lehrbas, and Egeberg. Each officer then returned to his desk, for the hours at GHQ were set by the Old Man's work schedule, which at Tacloban usually ended late at night.

After dark on Christmas Eve, MacArthur's lonely pacing on the veranda was interrupted by an unexpected incident which Powers describes: "That night a self-organized group of GI's gathered outside the hedge lining the porch and carolled their Commander-in-Chief . . . As he watched and listened, touched by the unrehearsed demonstration, nuisance raiders came over. The singing stopped as searchlights caught one of the intruders and antiaircraft in its very first burst shot down the Christmas Eve marauder. The General, pleased, thanked the singers and resumed his pacing."

On Christmas Day he visited Osmeña at his capitol office in the morning and went to the president's quarters for dinner that evening. Otherwise, he seems to have spent much of the day to himself, undoubtedly thinking of his wife and son in far-off Brisbane. Their last Christmas together had been their first day on Corregidor in 1941, which was spent busily unpacking and adjusting to the crowded, hectic situation on the island. On Christmas Day in 1942 and 1943, MacArthur had been in Port Moresby. Christmas at Tacloban must have been particularly lonely for him since he had not seen Jean and Arthur for nearly three months, their longest time apart. According to Huff, it was equally lonely for his little family, who were eagerly looking forward to their reunion in Manila, now destined to be postponed until March.[16]

On December 16 news was received that Congress had passed,

and the President had signed, legislation advancing to five-star rank the following officers in order of seniority: Leahy, Marshall, King, MacArthur, Nimitz, Eisenhower, and Arnold. The new title for the four Army officers was to be "General of the Army" and that for the three naval officers "Fleet Admiral." MacArthur immediately sent a radiogram to Roosevelt: "My grateful thanks for the promotion you have just given me. My pleasure in receiving it is greatly enhanced because it was made by you." The insignia of five stars in a circle was unique and had to be crafted by a Filipino silversmith at Tacloban. MacArthur had him shape the stars from a collection of American, Australian, Dutch, and Filipino silver coins, symbolizing the national forces serving under him. On the day after Christmas the handmade insignias for both lapels were ready, and in a short ceremony at GHQ Lehrbas and Egeberg stepped forward and pinned the five-star clusters on the general's uniform. The SWPA commander seemed to be especially pleased that the seniority arrangement provided for by the act placed him ahead of Eisenhower.[17]

With the prestigious theater commander on the island where the Sixth Army was engaged in combat, the situation could have been awkward for Krueger. The official Army history, which usually provides abundant source citations, offers these undocumented generalizations about MacArthur's relations with Krueger on Leyte:

> General MacArthur had full confidence in the ability of General Krueger to carry out this plan and thus bring the Leyte Campaign to a successful conclusion. Once having given the Sixth Army commander the assignment for the operation, General MacArthur did not interfere with General Krueger's prosecution of the battle. But from his headquarters on Leyte, he closely followed the progress of the campaign, frequently visited the command posts of the Sixth Army units, and made available to General Krueger additional troops upon request.[18]

It is true that MacArthur and Krueger did not confer often: the SWPA chief visited Sixth Army headquarters on Leyte only three times — October 27 and November 8 and 12 — and, other than attending three large SWPA planning conferences, Krueger called on MacArthur but seven times. Nine of their ten meetings occurred between October 27 and November 22, with none from the latter date until New Year's Day. Sibert and Hodge did not visit MacArthur nor did he go to their headquarters during the entire campaign except for the SWPA commander's visits to the beachheads on and just after A-day. During his ten weeks at Tacloban MacArthur ventured outside the city exactly four times: the three visits to Krueger and the brief trip to nearby Tacloban airfield to bestow the Medal of Honor on Bong. The many photographs of MacArthur talking to divisional and regimental officers on Leyte were made on A-day or the two days immediately after. If only meetings are considered, it is surely true that MacArthur did not interfere with the conduct of operations. But, in view of MacArthur's personality, aggressive ways, special interest in the Philippines reconquest, and past record of applying pressure on field commanders, it is difficult to believe that the theater commander established residence on the edge of the field of battle and meekly refrained from interfering with the command and tactical situation of the Sixth Army. Indeed, in a radio address in November to the Filipinos explaining the civil affairs policy of MacArthur, Fellers stated, "He is in personal command of the military campaign and proposes to take a hand in civil administration only in case of military necessity." [19]

How satisfied the SWPA commander was with Krueger's leadership by early December is obvious from an entry in Eichelberger's diary after a visit to GHQ by the Eighth Army leader:

> I talked with Big Chief [MacArthur] who explained dissatisfaction with Walter [Krueger] and stated he might have to

relieve him. Said he had held him on over-age and expected him to be a driver. He said he wasn't worried about Leyte [by that stage] but was worried about conduct [of] troops on future operations if actions here were indicative. I told him the fundamental error was made last summer when so many things were given to the 6th Army that they could not do anything well. He said he wanted me to become a Stonewall Jackson or a Patton and lead many small landing forces in from South just as the Japs had. Very cordial and when I left he yelled at me to come back often. I stayed to have luncheon with him and talked football. Walter was there . . . and tried to act real jolly without much success . . . Saw Steve Chamberlin who hoped I would come there often as he feels Kenney gives Chief wrong picture. Big Chief stated 32d never had been any good and that he was very disappointed over slow progress of 77th and 7th. He said Walter states these units have had fine records and are doing well. He says Walter makes many excuses.[20]

Almost all of the senior officers who participated in GHQ planning sessions with MacArthur were high in praise of his brilliance and tact in decision-making and administration. Major General Frank H. Britton, who joined the SWPA G-3 section in October, 1944, after earlier serving at the headquarters of the Fifth Army in Italy and also of the Army Ground Forces in Washington, recalled being quite favorably impressed with the staff set-up at GHQ SWPA. He also found that MacArthur "kept pretty darn close in touch with what was going on" and in Chamberlin had a "strong" operations chief. Fitch, in turn, was pleased that the SWPA commander "left you to do your own job and he expected you to do it," though MacArthur believed in working his staff "almost to the point of destruction." Kenney commented, "In a big staff conference, or in conversation with a single individual, MacArthur has a wonderful knack of leading a discussion up to the point of a decision that each member present believes he himself originated. I have heard officers say many times, 'The Old Man bought my idea,' when it was something that weeks before I had heard MacArthur decide to do." Kenney concluded that "as a salesman, Mac-Arthur has no superior and few equals." The SWPA chief came to staff sessions well prepared and never failed to impress the group with his detailed knowledge of their specific areas of planning, but he also expected and obtained a high level of excellence in the studies of intelligence, operations, and logistics for which they were responsible.[21]

Egeberg described MacArthur's relations with his staff in strategic and logistical planning in this way:

> When they and MacArthur had agreed on a near-term objective, they would gather to discuss the ways in which it might be attained. MacArthur would hear these planners out, ask questions, usually broad, and at the end of the conference, which might last hours or all day or lop over into the next day, he would say "Thank you very much, gentlemen," and then for a day or two he would ponder the problem himself. While we were in the jeep together he might in a way ask me questions and then answer them. From some of these interchanges I got a clear picture of the connection between chess and war. He might say, "Now if we do this which Steve [Chamberlin] suggested they might do this or if they were clever they might do that. Now if they do this we should answer in one of three ways" and he would outline what they might be, and the same for the other alternatives and then he would go to the Japanese answer to the 6 or 7 possibilities. By the time he had done this for a day or a week, he would call his staff in, establish the strategy which was amazingly frequently the opposite from the feeling of the majority and which would seem always to have been right.[22]

Friction was perhaps inevitable among the senior GHQ officers due to the irritations of wartime pressures, the personal ambitions of some among them, and their jealous jostling for MacArthur's favor. At times it seemed that their only cohesion as a staff was their common devotion to the Old Man. Kinkaid and his admirals were often at odds with Kenney, while Krueger and Eichelberger were ever aware of the attention the other got from MacArthur. Sutherland's arrogance was resented by all except MacArthur and Marshall; Whitney's overbearing disposition was obnoxious to everyone but MacArthur and Sutherland. Brigadier General Frederick P. Munson, then in G-2, said that some of the staff poked fun at "Sir Charles" (or "Prince") Willoughby so much that he "asked them to please lay off Willoughby because he would come back to our office and scream at us." The Bataan Gang continued to regard themselves as specially privileged at GHQ. "If MacArthur had a blind spot," Britton remarked, "it was his extreme loyalty to these people who had been with him in Manila before the war."

Like Roosevelt's shrewd manipulation of the contrasting personalities and divergent views of his staff and cabinet members, MacArthur appeared to relish and exploit his position as the center of his staff's attention and loyalty, the focus through which their differing opinions of people and plans were channeled. Again like the President, MacArthur cunningly used his skill at role-playing to deal separately with them, convincing each man that he had a preferred place in his esteem and inspiring him to try to outperform his staff rivals.[23] Byers saw the situation in the GHQ high echelons in another light:

> General MacArthur was positive that he knew the important things that had to be faced each day. He knew that this and that had to be considered, and he saw to these important items scrupulously. He didn't care about the rest. He'd let those things take care of themselves, but he also wanted to know the worst. So he kept his staff split in half, in two teams. He played one team against the other team, relying on the cruel things one team said about the other to keep them irritated . . . In this fashion he would be informed about the dangerous things. Aware then of the important and dangerous things, he permitted items in between to be the concern of others.[24]

The Tacloban period marked the beginning of the end for Sutherland as MacArthur's chief adviser. The SWPA com-

mander had been getting informal reports for some time that
individual members of the Joint Chiefs of Staff and of the War
Department were irritated by Sutherland's tactlessness and un-
bending hostility toward the Navy when he represented Mac-
Arthur in Washington. Marshall, Sutherland's deputy, later
recalled that some friction also arose when MacArthur "thought
Sutherland was paying too much attention to promotions . . .
He was trying to keep Sutherland on the question of what oper-
ations should be undertaken and what plans should be made.
Instead, Sutherland was looking out for the kinds of promotions
[of various SWPA officers] he saw as justified or unjustified."
The opinion of other GHQ staff officers, however, indicates
that a "considerable explosion" occurred at Tacloban when
MacArthur discovered that Sutherland had brought there an
Australian secretary with whom, it was said, he had been enjoy-
ing an affair since they met in Brisbane in 1942.

In early 1944, while Sutherland and Kenney were in Washington to discuss MacArthur's plans with the Joint Chiefs and
their planners, the two SWPA generals requested the War Department to commission three Australian secretaries at GHQ
Brisbane — theirs and Marshall's — as officers in the Women's
Army Corps. The congressional act establishing that corps restricted WAC enlistments to American citizens, but did not
clarify officer status. WAC Director Oveta C. Hobby had long
insisted that all WAC officers come from the ranks, which would
block noncitizens. She therefore objected strenuously to the
SWPA visitors' request, and she gained the backing of the War
Department G-1. But Sutherland personally went to the Army
chief of staff's office with the matter. There, states the official
WAC history, the protests of the G-1 and the WAC director
"were finally overridden when General McNarney, Deputy
Chief of Staff, was informed that the commissions were
personally desired by General MacArthur as essential to headquarters operation." Two of the Australian women were com-

missioned as first lieutenants and the other, presumably Sutherland's secretary, as a captain in the Women's Army Corps. Mrs. Hobby warned that this action would be "a great blow to the morale of the entire Corps." [25]

As the first contingent of what would become a group of 5500 American "Wacs" arrived in Australia that summer, MacArthur's theater being the last to employ them, Mrs. Hobby's prediction rang true, according to the WAC chronicle:

> This apparently minor event [of commissioning the three Australians] received widespread and generally unfavorable publicity in Australia, which had its own women's services for qualified women, as well as British women's services. An even worse reaction came from Army men, particularly young combat officers who had not yet been promoted to equal ranks. Soldier mail, in the first month before the first American Wacs arrived, showed that 90 percent of the comments about all Wacs were unfavorable, many obscene, alleging that all Wacs would be used only for "morale purposes" for officers. This situation was to cause a serious morale problem among arriving Wacs.[26]

MacArthur himself became enthusiastic about the valuable services the Wacs performed at GHQ, as well as at FEAF and USASOS headquarters, in relieving men for combat and service duties. Mrs. Hobby and high-ranking WAC officers thought it unwise when Wacs were moved to advance headquarters in New Guinea and then Leyte. But MacArthur defended the policy: "I moved my Wacs forward early after occupation of recaptured territory because they were needed and they were soldiers in the same manner that my men were soldiers. Furthermore, if I had not moved my Wacs when I did, I would have had mutiny . . . as they were so eager to carry on where needed." [27]

Sutherland's secretary's presence at Tacloban, however, was a different matter to the SWPA chief. For one thing, he and

Curtin had an agreement whereby no Australian conscripts or civilian employees would go forward with the SWPA forces as they crossed the equator. Although he and Blamey had talked about the use of two Australian divisions in the Luzon operation, the Australian government had not yet agreed to that, much less to the movement of Australian secretaries north of the equator, whether in American uniforms or not. Moreover, according to one source, MacArthur learned that the woman was supposedly being sued for divorce, which could cause unwanted sensational headlines about life at GHQ Tacloban. In early December, Fellers told Eichelberger that "the Big Chief and your old friend [Sutherland] had a row and he [Fellers] did not believe that the latter would last long." One GHQ officer said that the rapidity with which MacArthur had her shipped out of Tacloban reminded him of "the stunt in the Barnum and Bailey circus of the man shot from the mouth of a cannon. I felt that the lady was sent back to Australia with all the suddenness of the shot from the cannon. She was sent back with an official escort, a senior officer who'd been very active in politics in the United States."

Sutherland would continue as chief of staff through the first several months of the Japanese occupation, but, said a general at GHQ, "things were never the same" again between Sutherland and MacArthur after the Tacloban confrontation. MacArthur would turn more frequently to Whitney as his most trusted confidant from Tacloban on.[28] Thus Whitney, the pompous, opportunistic officer who was probably the most despised by other members of the GHQ staff, was on his way toward becoming MacArthur's alter ego during the last two decades of the SWPA commander's life. It would develop into the strangest relationship of MacArthur's entire career — and undoubtedly the most damaging to his reputation.

3. Mopping Up and Moving On

The Japanese situation on Leyte was strategically hopeless after the fall of Ormoc, yet Suzuki persisted in making preparations for counteroffensives. Among other schemes, he planned for his 16th and 26th divisions to withdraw from the area west of Burauen and Dagami, assault the Americans in the Ormoc area, and ultimately join the Japanese forces to the north in the Ormoc Valley. A reserve detachment did attack the American positions on Red Roof Hill, southeast of Ormoc, but was repulsed with heavy losses. The Japanese 16th and 26th divisions found their route northward blocked in the area between Jaro and Lake Danao by units of the American 24th, 38th, and 96th divisions, which were steadily pushing toward Ormoc, and in the Talisan Valley–Mahonag region by elements of the American 7th and 11th Airborne divisions, which had driven across the mountains from the west coast and Burauen respectively. Yamashita's plan to mount a seaborne invasion of the Carigara Bay region on December 16 had to be canceled when the Americans suddenly landed on Mindoro on the 15th. Yamashita notified Suzuki on December 19, "It is contemplated that the mission of Thirty-fifth Army will be changed to one of strategic delay . . . The Army should promptly plan for self-sufficient, sustained resistance." Although at least two Japanese convoys already at sea before the fall of Ormoc made it to western Leyte, Yamashita regretfully announced that no further reinforcements would be sent to the Leyte defenders.

Meanwhile, at the northern end of the Ormoc Valley the Japanese 1st and 102nd divisions continued to offer fierce opposition to the American 32nd and 1st Cavalry divisions. For nearly a month after the capture of Limon, the X Corps forces were stalemated three miles south of the town, unable to break

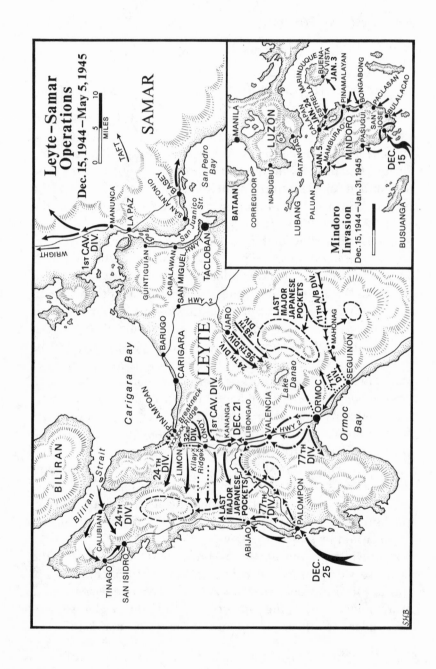

Leyte–Samar Operations
Dec. 15, 1944 – May 5, 1945

SAMAR

MILES
0 5 10

TAFT

1ST CAV. DIV.

WRIGHT

MANUNCA

LA PAZ

SAN ANTONIO

BASEY

San Juanico Str.

San Pedro Bay

TACLOBAN

SAN MIGUEL HWY.

CABALAWAN

QUINTIGUIAN

HWY 2

BARUGO

CARIGARA

Carigara Bay

LEYTE

PINAMPOAN

BILIRAN

Biliran Strait

24TH DIV.

CALUBIAN

TINAGO

SAN ISIDRO

24TH DIV.

24TH DIV.

LIMON

Breakneck Ridge

32ND DIV.

Kilay Ridge

LONOY

1ST CAV. DIV.

KANANGA

DEC. 21

LIBONGAO

VALENCIA

JARO

24TH DIV.

96TH DIV.

38TH DIV.

11TH A/B DIV

LAST MAJOR JAPANESE POCKETS

Lake Danao

MAHONAG

7TH DIV.

SEGUINON

ORMOC

HWY 2

Ormoc Bay

77TH DIV.

LAST MAJOR JAPANESE POCKETS

77TH DIV.

PALOMPON

ABIJAO

DEC. 25

Mindoro Invasion
Dec. 15, 1944 – Jan. 31, 1945

LUZON

MANILA

BATAAN

CORREGIDOR

NASUGBU

BATANGAS

LUBANG

PALUAN

BUSUANGA

MAMBURAO

MINDORO

MARINDUQUE

CALAPAN

JAN. 24

ESTRELLA

BUENA-VISTA

JAN. 3

PINAMALAYAN

BONGABONG

JAN. 5

PACLASAN

SAN JOSE

BULALACAO

DEC. 15

NASUGBU

S.H.B.

through along Highway 2 into the heart of the Ormoc Valley. Then on December 19, with the 32nd Division in a holding position astride the highway just below Limon, the 1st Cavalry enveloped the enemy's right flank and seized Lonoy, two miles to the south of the 32nd's line. While this action was under way at the northern entrance to the valley, the American 77th Division rapidly thrust northward from Ormoc in a series of enveloping maneuvers that kept the Japanese off balance. On December 18 the 77th seized Valencia and its airfield, and three days later elements of the X and XXIV corps made contact at a point between Kananga and the junction of Highway 2 with the road west to Palompon. Suzuki, who had narrowly escaped capture or death when a fast-moving unit of the 77th overran Libongao, north of Valencia, led his battered remnants toward the Palompon area on the northwestern coast, where he planned to continue resistance until his forces were destroyed.

The four divisions of the two American corps in the Ormoc Valley turned west to advance into the hills where the Japanese would offer their final organized defensive stand. While most of the troops of the 77th Division pushed along the road toward Palompon, to the north as far as the Limon area units of the 1st Cavalry, 32nd and 24th divisions started into the hills of the northwest corner of Leyte. On Christmas morning, as Suzuki's beleaguered forces were making their way toward the west, a battalion of Bruce's 77th suddenly landed at Palompon and seized the port against no opposition. About the same time a regiment of the 24th Division made amphibious landings on the northwest peninsula of Leyte along Biliran Strait and on December 28 captured the port of San Isidro against light resistance. Suzuki's remaining forces were now trapped in two large pockets, far apart, in mountainous areas: the 1st and 102nd divisions, plus a recently arrived independent brigade, between Palompon and San Isidro; and the 16th and 26th divisions, as well as several small reserve units, in the rugged wilderness east

of Ormoc. In the same month, a regiment of the 1st Cavalry
Division on Samar had advanced northward from San Juanico
Strait to capture the provincial capital of Wright and then
crossed the island to Taft, thereby completing the Sixth Army's
tactical mission on that island where enemy forces had been
small but had offered stubborn resistance.[29]

On December 25, Yamashita informed Suzuki that the Japanese high command had written off the Leyte campaign as lost,
so he was now concentrating on strengthening the defenses of
Luzon. He added that he was shedding "tears of remorse" for
the many thousands of Japanese who faced their deaths on
Leyte. The next day MacArthur's communiqué proclaimed
that "the Leyte-Samar campaign can now be regarded as closed
except for minor mopping-up . . . General Yamashita has sustained perhaps the greatest defeat in the military annals of the
Japanese Army." Eichelberger's Eighth Army headquarters assumed control of operations on December 26, relieving Krueger's headquarters and most of the X Corps so they could prepare for the invasion of Luzon. Congratulating Krueger and
his Sixth Army, MacArthur said, "This closes a campaign that
has had few counterparts in the utter destruction of the enemy's
forces with a maximum conservation of our own." The Sixth
Army phase of the campaign had cost about 2900 American and
56,000 Japanese lives. Krueger's headquarters estimated that
at the time of its relief only about 5000 Japanese remained on
Leyte and Samar.

But the mopping-up phase, delegated to the Eighth Army,
lasted until May, 1945, and, according to the divisional history
of the 11th Airborne, "it was bitter, exhausting, rugged fighting
— physically, the most terrible we were ever to know." [30] Later
Eichelberger, whose units lost nearly 700 soliders killed in the
"minor mopping-up," which took over four months, had some
choice remarks about Krueger's discounting of Suzuki's remnants and MacArthur's prematurely optimistic communiqués:

Actually the Japanese Army was still intact . . . Soon Japanese began streaming across the Ormoc Valley from east to west Leyte, well equipped and apparently well fed. It took several months of the roughest kind of combat to defeat this army. Between Christmas Day and the end of the campaign we killed more than 27,000 Japs . . .

I am a great admirer of General MacArthur as a military strategist; his plans were always fundamentally sound. But I must admit that, after serving under him for six years, I never understood the public relations policy that either he or his immediate assistants established. It seemed to me, as it did to many of the commanders and correspondents, ill advised to announce victories when a first phase had been accomplished without too many casualties.

Too often, as at Buna and Sanananda, as on Leyte, Mindanao, and Luzon, the struggle was to go on for a long time. Often these announcements produced bitterness among combat troops and with considerable cause. The phrase "mopping up" had no particular appeal for a haggard, muddy sergeant of the Americal Division whose platoon had just been wiped out in west Leyte.[31]

The triumph on Leyte marked the fulfillment of MacArthur's promise to return to the Philippines, but some of the assets and liabilities of the campaign had not been anticipated. Even with the entry of four reserve divisions of the Sixth Army, the conquest took far longer than expected, forcing delays in launching the invasions of Mindoro and Luzon and interfering with the Central Pacific theater's plans also. It had been hoped to develop airfields on Leyte from which aircraft would support the invasion of Luzon and other islands in the Philippines and would also strike at Japanese shipping and bases in the South China Sea and in the East Indies. But airfield construction proved unsatisfactory, and Leyte never became an important base for air operations.

The Japanese reinforcement of Leyte had been possible in part because of the lack of adequate land-based American aircraft there, yet, in turn, Yamashita's commitment of significant portions of his ground and air forces to the defense of the island seriously handicapped his defenses on Luzon. The introduction of the kamikaze, though a terrifying and sometimes very effective weapon, actually was the death knell of the regular Japanese air forces. Also, in choosing to fight the decisive battle of the Philippines at Leyte, the Japanese committed their main naval striking power to destruction. By the time Suzuki was killed on April 16, when American aircraft sank the ship on which he was trying to escape, Yamashita and his troops on Luzon were feeling the full impact of the consequences of having lost the ground, air, and naval forces consumed by the defense of Leyte.

The first edition of MacArthur's Mike I Plan, detailing the Lingayen Gulf invasion, had been completed in September and a revised edition in early October, but he was required to spend much of his time at Tacloban further altering his Luzon plan because of complications caused by the delays in conquest and construction on Leyte. At first he intended to send the Lingayen attack force around the eastern coast and the northern tip of Luzon. For a while, too, he considered several subsidiary operations to seize air strips on Luzon in order to cover the expedition as it moved up the eastern coast. Plans to capture the Legaspi and Aparri airfields at the extreme southern and northern ends of Luzon were eventually abandoned because the logistical difficulties would further postpone the Lingayen assault. One of the decisions reached when Sherman visited Tacloban on November 6–8 was that the Lingayen attack force should be routed through the Sulu Sea instead; Nimitz endorsed the idea and pledged the support of his fast carriers. MacArthur now dropped all plans for subsidiary operations to precede the Lingayen invasion except one, Mindoro.

It will be recalled that the Joint Chiefs had earlier set the assault on Mindoro for December 5 and the Lingayen landing for December 20, on MacArthur's recommendation. When, because of the problems on Leyte as well as recurring shipping difficulties, the SWPA commander reluctantly decided at the end of November to postpone the attack on Mindoro to December 15, he told the Joint Chiefs that he planned to launch the Lingayen invasion on the 30th of that month. Kenney, however, found that his airfields on Leyte would not be ready to handle the large number of planes essential to support the Lingayen attack, and Kinkaid pointed out that his naval forces would need more time between the Mindoro and Lingayen operations and that the full moon at the end of December would expose the convoy's night movement. So MacArthur had to inform the Joint Chiefs of another postponement of the Lingayen invasion; this time he set it for January 9. Since many of the ships to be used in that attack would be on loan from the Pacific Fleet, Nimitz had to change his target date for the invasion of Iwo Jima from the 3rd to the 19th of February, which, in turn, forced a two-week postponement, to April 1, of his assault on Okinawa.[32]

During the deliberations at Hollandia in September, which produced the Love III Plan for the invasion of Mindoro, Kinkaid "in strong language" had opposed the sending of an escort carrier group into the Sulu Sea with the attack force. When the matter was revived by MacArthur at Tacloban, Kinkaid still objected on the grounds that, in those confined waters and so near a score of enemy air bases, his carriers would be highly vulnerable to attack. The growing menace of kamikazes especially disturbed him despite the fact that Halsey's carriers were scheduled to be off the east coast of Luzon conducting strikes against Japanese fields to keep air attacks against the invasion force to a minimum.

On November 30 at Tacloban the issue was finally decided, as Kinkaid relates:

Krueger, Kenney, and myself each were [*sic*] asked by MacArthur if we were ready to go. Krueger said of course he was. Kenney said, well, he was, but he did explain that it was a little bit far out to the Sulu Sea to get the air cover there early in the morning. They couldn't take off till daylight, and they had to return early in order to land before dark. Then MacArthur turned to me, and I said, "Well, it's perfectly obvious to me what I'm expected to say. But I do not want to send CVE's [escort carriers] into the Sulu Sea to give the necessary air cover, and before giving a definite answer I'd like to talk to my people." So we went out on the porch and talked for about a half hour, and then I went back and said, "All right, we'll send the CVE's." [33]

In the admirals' huddle on the veranda, according to Noble, "All of Kinkaid's staff were against sending the big ships and CVE's into the Sulu Sea . . . I said that I would be happy to lead the way to Mindoro. My attitude seemed to help, and Kinkaid's staff began to change . . . Kinkaid was a good man, but not strict enough with his staff." [34]

That day Catledge and Sulzberger happened to be visiting GHQ at Tacloban. "After lunch," said Catledge, "MacArthur had General Sutherland brief us on the plans to recapture the Philippines. Sutherland told us everything about the still-secret plans. When we left we knew a strike was coming at Ormoc and preparations were under way for it at Tacloban and Hollandia. We knew the date set for the invasion of Mindoro and the forces to be employed." Catledge added, "We knew, in short, a great deal more than we wanted to know, since we were traveling in battle zones and it was not impossible that we might be captured by the Japanese. Both Sulzberger and I felt very uncomfortable about that briefing." [35] Before dinner that evening, Kinkaid apparently was still arguing about the employment of carriers on the run to Mindoro. Catledge relates that

while in my quarters I heard some loud talking across the hall. Looking through the door, I could see into a room where MacArthur was walking back and forth, waving his arms and giving the Navy hell about its fear of kamikazes, which had upset him greatly. Admiral Kinkaid, his naval commander, was leaning against a bedstead, silently absorbing the reprimand. At the end of his lecture to Kinkaid he suddenly placed his hands on the admiral's shoulders, smiled, and said, "But, Tommy, I love you still. Let's go to dinner!" At the dinner table with us correspondents Kinkaid appeared subdued, but MacArthur frankly related exactly what had happened in the other room.[36]

The Love III Plan stated that the task of the attack force was to "occupy Southwest Mindoro, establish control of sea routes through the Visayas, and establish air forces for direct support of operations in the Manila–Central Plain area of Luzon." Brigadier General William C. Dunckel was placed in charge of the ground units, designated the Western Visayan Task Force and comprising the 19th Regimental Combat Team of the 24th Division and the 503rd Parachute Regimental Combat Team. The latter was supposed to make an airborne assault, but, because of inadequate space on the Leyte airfields for the troop transports, the parachutists were reassigned to go ashore on the left flank of the infantry in the amphibious landing. The naval attack force was to be under the command of Struble, with air cover and support to be provided by an accompanying escort carrier group, Fifth Air Force planes flying from Leyte, and naval aircraft operating from the Third Fleet carriers in the Philippine Sea. The Japanese garrison was accurately estimated by G-2 to number about 1000 troops, most of whom were in the northeastern corner of the island. Since the goal of the mission was primarily to seize only a perimeter in the southwestern corner, around San Jose, and get airfield construction under way quickly, the ground units of the expedition included, besides the two assault teams, about 6000 service troops and 9500 air personnel.

The invasion force staged on the eastern coast of Leyte and departed on December 12, first heading south and west through the Mindanao Sea. On the following afternoon, as the convoy rounded the southern tip of Negros to enter the Sulu Sea, kamikazes, flying low and undetected by radar, suddenly attacked. One crashed into the *Nashville,* killing 133 persons and injuring 190 more. The dead included Struble's and Dunckel's chiefs of staff and a bombardment wing commander; Dunckel was painfully burned but continued in command of the ground forces. Struble, Dunckel, and their staffs transferred to a destroyer, and the *Nashville* turned back to Leyte Gulf. Two hours later a kamikaze crashed into a destroyer near Struble's, causing forty casualties; it, too, returned to Leyte. On the 14th the Japanese sent down an attack formation of 186 planes, but, believing the convoy to be headed to Panay or Negros, they missed it entirely. MacArthur had planned to accompany the invasion force aboard the *Nashville,* but had been dissuaded by his staff at the last minute.[37]

The amphibious landings near San Jose on December 15 were made without ground opposition, and by nightfall a beachhead sixteen miles long and seven miles deep had been established. Despite the efforts of P-38's and carrier aircraft, a number of kamikazes broke through the air cover that day and crashed into three landing ships, two destroyers, and an escort carrier. For the next several weeks Struble's resupply convoys were attacked repeatedly by kamikazes. "Not since the Anzio operation," states one authority, "had the Navy experienced so much difficulty supporting an amphibious operation after the initial landing." By Christmas, Fifth Air Force planes were operating from two airfields near San Jose and a third strip was nearing completion. The rapid base construction on Mindoro was fortunate because the Third Fleet had to withdraw to Ulithi on December 19 after being struck by a typhoon in the Philippine Sea that capsized three destroyers, heavily damaged seven other ships, destroyed 186 carrier planes, and took the lives of nearly 800 men. On December 26–27 a Japanese force of cruisers and destroyers attacked the Mindoro landing area, but was driven off by PT boats and Fifth Air Force planes, which sank a destroyer and damaged several other ships. Since no major American combat ships were in the vicinity at the time, it was fortunate that Whitehead had already sent forward to the Mindoro bases thirteen medium bombers and nearly 100 fighters.

On January 1, control of operations on Mindoro passed from the Sixth to the Eighth Army. That month numerous landings were made by small American forces at other points on the coast of Mindoro, mainly along the northeastern shores, as well as on the nearby island of Marinduque. By the end of January, when the mopping-up was virtually over, the Western Visayan Task Force had lost sixteen men. About 170 Japanese had died in action, and the rest fled into the mountainous interior. The Japanese had lost over 100 planes when they attacked the San Jose beachhead and Struble's ships, but they had sunk or damaged a number of vessels and killed 500 sailors.

By the time of the Lingayen invasion, the Fifth Air Force had stationed on Mindoro a powerful support force of three fighter groups, two medium bomber groups, and seven other miscellaneous squadrons. The occupation of Mindoro would prove its worth again and again in future months by providing air cover for Luzon operations and serving as an air and troop staging base for invasions of the central and southern Philippine Islands. Later, too, heavy bomber fields were established there, from which flew many valuable strategic support missions as well as strikes against enemy shipping in the South China Sea. The value of Mindoro to the upcoming Luzon invasion is made clear in the official Army history: "It seems safe to assume that without the Mindoro airfields, MacArthur would not have been able to move to Luzon when he did. Certainly, without those fields his forces would have found the invasion of Luzon, and postassault operations as well, considerably more hazardous and difficult." As previously mentioned, the Mindoro invasion also forced Yamashita to cancel a major seaborne attack on the Carigara region of Leyte. One of his Fourteenth Area Army staff officers later observed, "After the American landing on Mindoro, our supply line between Luzon and the Visayas was completely cut off. As for our communications, we had to depend entirely on wireless to contact our forces in Leyte, Cebu, Ormoc, etc., from Manila." With the landing on Mindoro, however, there was no doubt in Yamashita's mind that MacArthur intended to strike Luzon next.[38] The climactic campaign of the war in the Southwest Pacific was soon to begin.

PART V

The Last Campaigns

CHAPTER XV

Familiar Grounds

1. The Roads to Manila

MacArthur would have preferred to attack Luzon at a point where Yamashita might least expect it, but after wrestling with various proposals by Chamberlin and his planners the SWPA chief inevitably returned to Lingayen Gulf as the best route of invasion. Homma had made his main assault there in 1941 and Yamashita anticipated an attack there in early 1945, but Mac-Arthur and the GHQ planners could find no other landing site that offered the advantages of Lingayen Gulf. The beaches were the finest and most extensive on Luzon and offered direct access to the principal highway and railroad network connecting with Manila, which lay 120 miles to the southeast. In addition, the Central Luzon Plain afforded a broad area for the maneuvering of the large mechanized forces MacArthur would employ. Of the seven Mike plans for possible assaults on Luzon that the GHQ planners developed, he finally decided to use three: the main effort at Lingayen Gulf (Mike I), followed about three weeks later by secondary landings near San Antonio, Zambales Province, northwest of Bataan (Mike VII), and landings near

Nasugbu, Batangas Province, twenty miles south of Corregidor (Mike IV).

The command structure for the Lingayen assault was similar to that of the Leyte invasion. Kinkaid would be in overall charge of the attack force, made up of a large armada of Seventh and Third fleet ships ranging from battleships and carriers to small types of landing craft. Barbey's VII Amphibious Force would transport Swift's I Corps, and Wilkinson's III Amphibious Force would carry the XIV Corps of Griswold to the southern beaches of Lingayen Gulf. Whitehead's Fifth Air Force would serve as the main air assault force, supported by the Thirteenth Air Force and the carrier planes of the Third Fleet's Task Force 38, with coordinated strategic bombing attacks against targets in the Ryukyus and Japan by the B-29's of the Fourteenth and Twentieth air forces.

MacArthur chose Krueger to head the ground forces in the Lingayen invasion, with Kinkaid, as was usual in SWPA amphibious operation, retaining control of the operation as naval attack commander until the ground force commander established his headquarters ashore. All through the autumn Willoughby had steadily raised his estimates of Japanese ground strength on Luzon, and MacArthur had added more SWPA forces to his invasion plans. The final G-2 estimate before the attack placed the number of troops of all types that Yamashita had on Luzon at about 152,000. Krueger's troops would total 203,000, including 131,000 combat troops. With the addition of later reinforcements and the considerable number of organized guerrillas, the forces engaged against the Japanese on Luzon would exceed 280,000. "While it did not equal the strength of U.S. Army ground forces committed in central Europe," states the Army's chronicle, "the Luzon Campaign was by far the largest of the Pacific war. It entailed the use of more U.S. Army ground combat and service forces than did operations in North Africa, Italy, or southern France and was larger than the entire Allied commitment to Sicily." [1]

In the complicated staging of the huge operation, convoys would rendezvous in Leyte Gulf carrying troops from nine bases besides those along Leyte's east coast: Sansapor, Hollandia, Aitape, Finschhafen, Toem, Gloucester, Oro Bay, Bougainville, and Noumea. The principal ground units that were to participate in the Lingayen invasion were the following:[2]

Unit	Commander	Phase	Landing Point
I Corps	Maj. Gen. I. P. Swift		
6th Div.	Maj. Gen. E. D. Patrick	Assault	San Fabian
43rd Div.	Maj. Gen. L. F. Wing	Assault	San Fabian
32nd Div.	Maj. Gen. W. H. Gill	Follow-up	
33rd Div.	Maj. Gen. P. W. Clarkson	Follow-up	
XIV Corps	Maj. Gen. O. W. Griswold		
40th Div.	Maj. Gen. R. Brush	Assault	Lingayen
37th Div.	Maj. Gen. R. S. Beightler	Assault	Dagupan
1st Cav. Div.	Maj. Gen. V. D. Mudge	Follow-up	
112th Cav. RCT	Brig. Gen. J. W. Cunningham	Follow-up	
6th Ranger Bn.	Lt. Col. H. A. Mucci	Reserve	
25th Div.	Maj. Gen. C. L. Mullins, Jr.	Reserve	
13th Armored Gp.	Col. M. E. Jones	Reserve	
158th RCT	Brig. Gen. H. MacNider	Reserve	
4th ESB	Brig. Gen. H. Hutchins, Jr.	Assault	Dagupan
533rd EB & SR*	Col. W. S. Moore	Assault	Lingayen
543rd EB & SR*	Col. G. E. Galloway	Assault	San Fabian, Dagupan

(*Engineer boat and shore regiment)

In the later secondary assaults Hall's XI Corps, consisting of Major General Henry L. C. Jones's 38th Division and Colonel William W. Jenna's 34th Regimental Combat Team of the 24th Division, would land on the Zambales coast. Then part of the Eighth Army, they would later come under the control of the Sixth Army. Swing's 11th Airborne Division of Eichelberger's Eighth Army would make the landing at Nasugbu. Hall's mission would be to seal off Bataan as a withdrawal route for the enemy in the Central Luzon Plain and to protect Krueger's right flank; Swing's mission was to advance on Manila from the south, thus forming a pincers movement with the Sixth Army's approach from the northwest.

During the first eight days of January, hundreds of carrier and land-based aircraft struck Japanese airfields and shipping in the

Luzon-Formosa area. Despite the airmen's reports of success in destroying large numbers of enemy planes on the ground and in the air, MacArthur and his commanders sensed that the full fury of the kamikazes would be unleashed against the Lingayen attack force. Suicide tactics had wrought serious damage on naval vessels off Leyte and Samar and worse still against the ships on the Mindoro run, and it was feared that, as the Lingayen armada approached, they might break through despite the umbrella of American aircraft that was to be over the Luzon airfields to try to prevent their takeoff. Knowing also that the wily Yamashita was undoubtedly expecting the attack to come at Lingayen Gulf, MacArthur and Krueger were concerned about the reception that awaited the Sixth Army. A host of deceptive measures was used in an attempt to lure the Japanese forces into south Luzon, including minesweeping activities in southern bays, intensified guerrilla and reconnaissance missions in the Batangas region, and air strikes against targets south of Manila.[3]

MacArthur was determined to accompany the attack force and would board the cruiser *Boise* on January 4. Many of the advance GHQ personnel at Tacloban would go also since the SWPA chief planned to set up his headquarters on Luzon as soon as the beachhead was secured. Sergeant Powers, who was one of the GHQ staff assigned to go with the armada, described his emotional state the night before the attack force departed and what a brief experience with MacArthur meant to him and an office mate:

> We went to the office the night of January 3–4 to gather final odds and ends. As we passed the Big House, we noted the porch was deserted. In our own office there was much activity surrounded by somberness. The thoughts of the men who worked that night were heavy thoughts. The plan of the attack was daring in scope, risky in execution. The assault convoy which was to hoist anchor that night was to sail through narrow

straits, bypass enemy-held islands, sail up the China Sea, pass Manila, looping around fortified Bataan and Corregidor, boldly and defiantly through Jap strongholds. At no time would the convoy be moving more than 20 minutes flying time from enemy air fields, which, for the past week, the air force, in unrelenting crescendo was attempting to neutralize. Realizing that our ever-increasing wave of men and supplies was soon to engulf him, the enemy had taken to concentrating on our shipping.

His strength on Luzon was known to be heavy; his suicidal fanaticism, the last ditch of the defeated, was fully comprehended. It was not out of fear or pessimism but in the light of cold reality that many of us who were going the next day checked on the night of January 3–4 our last Will and Testament.

None of us were novices at this invasion business, but close calls of recent memories, painful scenes of hurt traveling companions, dug indelibly in our mind, betrayed in our face our emotion.

A little after 10 o'clock, the message center delivered a late wire: "Assault troop convoy for Luzon departed . . . hours Z time."

The battle was on its way. It was time for our echelon to begin moving.

We started home, walking in the silent night down the long wooden catwalk leading from the office to the street. Through the open windows of one building we could see "Plans and Operations" posting fresh, unmarked maps of Luzon. Another building revealed groups of officers holding final briefings. Armed guards stood quietly at their posts at the entrance to the buildings.

As we neared the end of the walk, we looked up. There on the porch was the same familiar figure pacing silently. For some 80 [70] days and nights since we had landed at Tacloban we had seen him, but tonight his demeanor, his pace were different from all other times. He wasn't smoking. His famous Bataan hat was missing. With head bared, he walked, hands clasped behind. The pace was measured, reverently slow. He was alone on the porch.

Never before had we stopped on the catwalk to watch him,

but something tonight impelled us to halt. The majestic figure, in silent thought, moved slowly in deep deliberation.

Quickly we realized we were staring onto something personal, intimate; we hurried away. As we turned down the street and passed the left side of the house, a friendly voice from the shadows called. It was the General's guard, who was coming off duty, and recognizing us, offered to walk with us to the barracks.

We walked without speaking for a while and then he said, "You are leaving in the morning too?"

"Yes."

Another half block through the darkened area, and our friend said, "You know what he was doing as we left? He was conferring with God. On the eve of all major operations, the moment he is notified that the assault troops have sailed, he . . ."

Early the next morning as we came up to headquarters area to join the departing convoy, the General's jeep stood at the driveway with its new, brightly painted five-star shingle. He came down the steps, walking briskly, wearing his famous fighting hat. His eyes were clear, his head held high. There was about his person a business-like expression of confidence and determination.

As the General's party left, our friend the guard with whom we had spoken last night was returning to duty.

"Didn't expect to see you again. You look much better this morning. Even in the dark, I could feel you were worried. A good night's sleep must have given you strength."

He was right — the night of January 3–4 had given us strength; but he was wrong in surmising that the strength came from sound sleep. After watching our Commander-in-Chief, we had gone to bed but we had not slept. Imbued with the inspiring sight of our leader on his porch, we had spent the night with eyes fixed to the sky, communing with Almighty God. He was the source of our strength on the morn we left on our return to Manila.[4]

Somewhere along the long path — maybe at Los Negros, Hollandia, Aitape, Morotai, or Leyte — "Dugout Doug" had disappeared from most soldiers' jargon in the Southwest Pacific.

The trip to Lingayen Gulf was a nightmare for the sailors aboard Oldendorf's support group of over 160 battleships, escort carriers, destroyer transports, and minesweepers, which went ahead of the armada. His force had the tasks of clearing mines, deploying underwater demolition teams, and bombarding the Lingayen shore defenses for three days before the assault. As his ships steamed through the Sulu Sea on January 4, kamikazes attacked, sinking the escort carrier *Ommaney Bay*. Off Bataan the next day enemy suicide planes crashed into two cruisers, an escort carrier, a destroyer escort, and a landing craft. As shore bombardment and minesweeping began at Lingayen Gulf on January 6, sixteen of Oldendorf's ships were hit by kamikazes, including the battleship *New Mexico* on which Lumsden, Churchill's liaison officer and MacArthur's good friend, was killed. The British general, like hundreds of American sailors on that terrible voyage, was buried at sea. MacArthur wrote to Churchill of "the complete courage which this officer so frequently displayed in my immediate presence during the operations in this theater in the last year. His general service and usefulness to the Allied cause was beyond praise . . . My own personal sorrow is inexpressible. "

Fortunately for the troop-laden attack force that Kinkaid was leading, Army and Navy planes and the antiaircraft batteries of Oldendorf's ships destroyed much of the enemy air strength on Luzon before the invasion force approached the Lingayen area. Yet MacArthur's trip was far from uneventful. Barbey's amphibious force, of which the cruiser *Boise* was a part, came under attack by both conventional and suicidal formations west of Mindoro on January 7. One ship was struck by a kamikaze, and the *Boise* narrowly missed being hit by a bomb; seven vessels were damaged in all. Japanese midget submarines, operating from Apo Island in Mindoro Strait, made several ineffectual torpedo runs against the convoy. One fired two torpedoes at the *Boise*, but they missed. MacArthur "calmly watched the action," says one report, when the submarine surfaced off the port side of the *Boise* and was promptly rammed by a destroyer.

The next day, as the invasion force steamed west of Manila Bay, more kamikazes attacked, seriously damaging two escort carriers, a transport, and a landing ship. Despite continuing aerial assaults, MacArthur stayed "at a battery near the quarter-deck" of the *Boise* not only to watch the action but also to catch a glimpse of Corregidor and Bataan. Suddenly, he said of the shoreline, "there they were, gleaming in the sun far off on the horizon . . . I could not leave the rail. One by one, the staff drifted away, and I was alone with my memories. At the sight of those never-to-be-forgotten scenes of my family's past, I felt an indescribable sense of loss, of sorrow, of loneliness, and of solemn consecration." That night a lone Japanese destroyer, apparently trying to escape from Manila Bay before the exit was closed, ran into Barbey's force and was immediately pounced upon by four American destroyers. "One of the enemy ship's magazines was hit," said Barbey, "and she sank amidst a tre-mendous explosion that firelighted the sky." The scene was easily visible from the *Boise*.[5]

As the sun rose over Lingayen Gulf on the 9th of January, nearly a thousand American ships lay off the southern shores. During the pre-assault naval bombardment the dreaded kami-kazes arrived, but not in the large numbers of previous days. They crashed into a battleship, two cruisers, and a destroyer escort; the cruiser *Australia* was hit for the fifth time since leav-ing Leyte Gulf. As at Mindoro, the Army had an easier time than the Navy during the early phase of the invasion, for the landings were made against no initial resistance. Griswold's XIV Corps, with the 37th Division on the left and the 40th on the right, went ashore between the towns of Lingayen and Dagu-pan, and by nightfall both towns and the enemy airfield outside Lingayen were in American hands. On the XIV Corps' left flank, the 6th and 43rd divisions of Swift's I Corps landed on either side of San Fabian. The 6th ran into little opposition on the corps' right and pushed inland over three miles, but the 43rd, though seizing San Fabian and driving beyond, encountered mounting fire from Japanese mortars and artillery in the hills to the north. There was some concern among Krueger's commanders that Yamashita had strong forces on that high ground and might be preparing a counterattack against the I Corps' left flank.

At 2:00, about four hours after the first assault waves went ashore, MacArthur landed south of San Fabian in the company of Sutherland, Akin, Marshall, Fellers, Egeberg, Lehrbas, and several others of his immediate staff. "The Seabees ashore had taken a bulldozer," said Kinkaid, "and pushed out a little sort of pier, where the boat could land . . . But when . . . MacArthur saw what they were going to do, he said, no, he wouldn't land there. So they bypassed the pier . . . and he jumped out in the water and waded ashore. He didn't want to step out on dry land. That is how MacArthur happened to wet his pants in Lingayen Gulf." His Leyte wading scene was unintentional, but this one seems to have been a deliberate act of showmanship. With the worldwide attention that his Leyte walk through the water received, apparently the Barrymore side of MacArthur's personality could not resist another big splash of publicity and surf. Surely enough, his act got both. A large crowd of Filipinos was gathered on the shore and cheered as he splashed up to the beach. Now, as was his custom on such occasions, he wandered up and down the beach, casually chatting with officers and enlisted men who were feverishly busy getting supplies unloaded.

At 3:00 he visited Patrick at 6th Division headquarters and then got in a jeep and started south toward Dagupan. At the Pantal River on the east side of the town, however, he found that the bridge had been bombed out, so he and his GHQ party returned to the *Boise*. That evening seventy Japanese motor boats, loaded with explosive charges, sneaked out of the port at Sual, west of the town of Lingayen, and set forth toward the American armada anchored in the gulf to ram as many ships as possible. In the wild night action two landing craft were sunk and four LST's damaged by the suicide boats, but most of the Japanese attackers were destroyed.

On January 10 MacArthur went ashore again, making an inspection trip through all four divisional sectors. Later that day a GHQ SWPA communiqué announced, "The decisive battle for the liberation of the Philippines and the control of the Southwest Pacific is at hand. General MacArthur is in personal command at the front and landed with his assault troops." He stayed aboard the *Boise* on the 11th and 12th, and on the afternoon of the 13th he moved his advance GHQ to the provincial building and adjoining home economics school structure at Dagupan. Before dark he, Egeberg, and Lehrbas made a tour on foot of the environs of Dagupan. Meanwhile, the beachhead had been expanded to nearly thirty miles in length and an average of about fifteen miles in depth; XIV Corps was striking rapidly toward the Agno River, but I Corps was meeting increasing resistance on its left flank. Krueger, always wary, was concerned that the uneven advance with exposed flanks would invite a counterattack.

By then the kamikazes had spent themselves; in fact, from the 9th on, their attacks had been tapering off. Since the Lingayen invasion force had left Leyte Gulf, Japanese air assaults, mostly kamikazes, had sunk four of its ships and damaged forty-three others; aboard those vessels the casualties had totaled over 2100 men, including 738 killed. By the 13th, however, the air situation had changed: the Lingayen airfield, though small, was now operational for Fifth Air Force fighters, but fewer than a dozen Japanese aircraft were estimated to be left in service on Luzon. For MacArthur's forces the terrifying kamikaze threat was over, but Nimitz's Okinawa attack force in April would meet even worse horrors from kamikazes.[6]

By January 17 Griswold's XIV Corps had driven across the Agno River to Camiling, which was twenty-seven miles from the Lingayen beaches and thirty-five miles north of Clark Field. Krueger had recently committed the 25th Division and the 158th Regimental Combat Team to the I Corps' front. But, as heavy fighting developed on the Sixth Army's left, or northern, flank, the I Corps' progress by the 17th had been virtually halted in the 43rd Division's sector, and was so slow in the 25th and 6th divisions' areas that the left flank of the XIV Corps was dangerously exposed. Part of the problem on the I Corps' front, Swift reported, was the destruction of bridges and roads caused in part by enemy demolitions but mainly by American air attacks.

On Krueger's recommendation, MacArthur ordered the Fifth Air Force to refrain from bombing bridges in the Central Luzon Plain except when specifically requested. Meanwhile, due to a host of problems arising at the beachhead, including LST's discharging cargoes in the wrong areas and shortages of men and equipment for unloading, supply operations at the Lingayen beaches had become extremely confused and many essential items needed by combat units were delayed in transit to the front. Poor soil conditions and engineering difficulties, in addition, made it sadly clear that the beachhead area was not suitable for major construction projects, especially airfields.

Anxious to secure Clark Field and Manila's port facilities before the climactic confrontation with Yamashita's army, MacArthur told Krueger on the 17th that the drive must be speeded up. Since landing at Lingayen Gulf, the Sixth Army had lost 250 men killed, all but thirty from I Corps, which indicated to GHQ that, despite exposed flanks, XIV Corps could drive toward Clark Field more rapidly. On January 25, MacArthur moved his headquarters inland to Hacienda Luisita, far ahead of Sixth Army headquarters at Calasiao, in a blatant effort to prod Krueger into more aggressive action. According to Eichelberger, Sutherland recommended that Krueger "be sent home,"

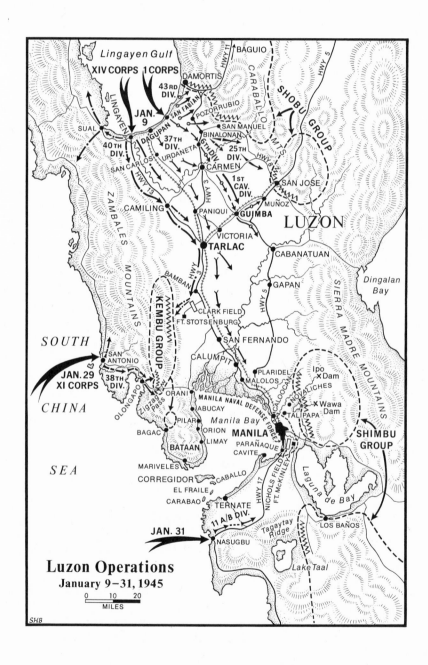

Luzon Gulf

XIV CORPS 1 CORPS

LUZON

SHOBU GROUP

BAGUIO
DAMORTIS
43RD DIV.
JAN. 9
POZORRUBIO
SAN FABIAN
SUAL
DAGUPAN
40TH DIV.
37TH DIV.
SAN MANUEL
BINALONAN
6TH DIV.
SAN CARLOS
URDANETA
25TH DIV.
CARMEN
SAN JOSE
CAMILING
PANIQUI
1ST CAV. DIV.
MUÑOZ
GUIMBA

VICTORIA
TARLAC
CABANATUAN

GAPAN

Dingalan Bay

SOUTH

KEMBU GROUP
BAMBAN
CLARK FIELD
FT. STOTSENBURG
SAN FERNANDO

SAN ANTONIO
JAN. 29
XI CORPS
38TH DIV.
CALUMPIT
PLARIDEL
MALOLOS
Ipo
×Dam

CHINA

OLONGAPO
Zigzag Pass
ORANI
ABUCAY
MANILA NAVAL DEFENSE FORCE
NOVALICHES
CALOOCAN
×Wawa Dam
TALIPAPA

SEA

PILAR
BAGAC
ORION
LIMAY
BATAAN
Manila Bay
MANILA
PARAÑAQUE
CAVITE
SHIMBU GROUP

MARIVELES
CORREGIDOR
EL FRAILE
CARABAO
CABALLO
TERNATE
11 A/B DIV.
NICHOLS FIELD
FT. McKINLEY
Laguna de Bay
LOS BAÑOS

JAN. 31
NASUGBU
Tagaytay Ridge
Lake Taal

Luzon Operations
January 9–31, 1945

0   10   20
MILES

SHB

but MacArthur, though "very impatient" and "disgusted" with his cautiousness, decided to retain him while keeping pressure on him to accelerate the pace of his advance.[7]

Even before the Lingayen invasion Yamashita had concluded that the best his troops could do was to offer a static defense and delay the Allied advance to the Japanese homeland as long as possible by tying up large amounts of Allied shipping, troops, and aircraft in the Luzon campaign. With Halsey's Third Fleet now freely roaming the waters off Luzon to the north and west, Yamashita knew that hopes for reinforcements were nonexistent. Although it had about 275,000 troops, not 152,000 as Willoughby estimated, the Japanese Fourteenth Area Army was seriously short of munitions, supplies, and transportation. Yamashita planned to concentrate his main force in the mountains of northern Luzon and to fight only delaying actions in the Central Luzon Plain and around Manila. A key factor in his defense plan was the movement of about 70,000 metric tons of supplies from Manila stockpiles to his defensive positions in the mountains, still in progress when the Americans landed at Lingayen Gulf.

Yamashita divided his forces into three regional defense zones, each centered in easily defended mountainous areas, which would cost MacArthur's units heavily in lives and time to overrun. Major General Rikichi Tsukada's Kembu Group, numbering about 30,000 troops, was charged with defense of the Clark Field area. If they were forced to yield there, the Kembu units were to withdraw into the Zambales Mountains to the west and fight delaying actions, keeping occupied as many American troops as possible. The Kembu zone included Bataan, but Yamashita did not want Tsukada's force to be trapped on that malaria-infested peninsula, where living off the countryside was well-nigh impossible. Lieutenant General Shizuo Yokoyama's Shimbu Group, consisting of about 80,000 men, was to complete the evacuation of supplies from Manila, then abandon the city and move into the mountains to the east where the Japanese could control the dams that supplied the capital's water. Rear Admiral Sanji Iwabuchi's 20,000-man defense force at Manila was included in Yokoyama's group and had orders not to attempt an all-out defense of the city but to withdraw into the mountains and join the other Shimbu units.

Yamashita himself headed the Shobu Group, which included 152,000 troops and the principal Japanese armored forces on Luzon. The Shobu units were to guard the west coast in the area above San Fabian along Lingayen Gulf. If the Americans landed to the south, as they did, the Shobu Group was to harass the invaders' left flank, but, more important, deny them access to the Cagayan Valley and the Baguio region. If forced to withdraw, Yamashita's forces were to fight to the end in the mountainous triangle between Baguio, Bambang, and Bontoc. Yamashita's Fourteenth Area Army headquarters, combined with the headquarters of the Shobu Group, was situated at Baguio.[8]

Responding to intense pressure from MacArthur, Krueger issued orders on January 18 for Griswold's corps to seize Clark Field without delay, while Swift's embattled I Corps was to push into the foothills of the mountains from Damortis on the coast to the area east of Tayug on the northern edge of the Central Luzon Plain. Swift's corps also was to extend its right flank in the plain as far south as Guimba in order to secure the left flank of Griswold's corps. In the I Corps' northern sector, the reinforced 43rd Division faced a Japanese division and a brigade in fierce fighting for two weeks before finally forcing the enemy out of the Damortis-Pozorrubio region and securing the important junction of Routes 3 and 11, the latter being the highway to Baguio. On the 30th, the 32nd Division, which had landed at Lingayen Gulf three days earlier, moved into the line on the right flank of the 43rd Division.

The 25th Division encountered savage resistance by Japanese infantry, artillery, and tanks in battles at Binalonan and San Manuel. MacArthur was visiting in that sector on January 28 when an enemy counterattack, led by tanks, hit the 25th's regiment at San Manuel. "Our lines reeled," said MacArthur, "and I became so concerned over a possible penetration that I personally hastened to the scene of action of the 161st Infantry. Its colonel, James Dalton II, was one of my finest commanders. I joined him in steadying the ranks." The Japanese detachment was repulsed and subsequently destroyed. Dalton was later killed in action; MacArthur received a second Oak Leaf Cluster for his Distinguished Service Cross.

On the I Corps' right its 6th Division, meanwhile, secured the Cabaruan Hills after a tough fight, then drove past Guimba and nearly to Cabanatuan. A ranger unit, with help from guerrillas, conducted a daring raid on a prison camp beyond Cabanatuan, rescuing about 400 grateful Bataan veterans. In hard fighting between Muñoz and Cabanatuan in the first week of February the 6th Division destroyed most of the Japanese 2nd Tank Division, Yamashita's principal armored force. The 6th then overran San Jose, but too late to interdict the final movement of troops and supplies through there for the Shobu defenses in the northern mountains.

Griswold's corps at the same time was striking southward toward Clark Field; it did not encounter sizable elements of the Kembu Group until it advanced below Tarlac. Just south of Bamban and about two miles north of Clark Field, the Japanese began offering fierce opposition on January 23. The 37th Division continued the advance down Highway 13 toward Calumpit, while the 40th Division engaged the Kembu Group in a ferocious battle for Clark Field. By January 28 the 40th Division had secured the complex of airfields known collectively as Clark Field and had also captured nearby Fort Stotsenburg. It would take three more weeks, however, to break the Kembu Group's main line in the hills two miles to the west. On the 30th, MacArthur made a jeep trip to Clark Field, where sporadic fighting was still under way and enemy shells hit frequently. After exposing himself to danger when he inspected the area, he got back in the jeep and continued down Highway 13 past San Fernando, which the 37th Division had just overrun. Impatient to accelerate even more the drive to Manila, he sent a stinging message to Krueger that day: "There was a noticeable lack of drive and aggressive initiative today in the movement toward Calumpit." Undoubtedly Krueger immediately put equal pressure on Griswold, the corps commander, and he, in turn, on Major General Robert S. Beightler, the divisional commander. The next day the 37th seized Calumpit, which lay only twenty-five miles northwest of Manila.

On January 20, Hall's XI Corps, consisting of the 38th Division and 34th Regimental Combat Team, landed unopposed north of San Antonio on the Zambales coast, northwest of Bataan. The major units of the Kembu Group were then fighting in the hills west of Clark Field, so progress for Hall's troops was at first unimpeded as they started to seal off Bataan. They moved rapidly to Olongapo on Subic Bay and started eastward, but were abruptly stopped by strong Japanese defenses at Zigzag Pass about six miles from Olongapo. On January 31, Swing's 11th Airborne Division, less one of its regiments, landed at Nasugbu on the Batangas coast, south of Corregidor. The assault troops moved inland quickly on Highway 17, the road to Manila, while on February 3 the division's 511th Parachute Infantry Regiment, aboard C-47 transports from Mindoro airfields, dropped on Tagaytay Ridge, twenty miles east of Nasugbu. The air drop was unopposed, and soon the main part of the division, pushing along Highway 17 against light resistance, joined the parachutists on the ridge. There the 11th Airborne was poised for the thrust to Manila, only thirty miles to the north. The pincers movement was now closing fast on the city, but not rapidly enough to suit MacArthur. He had dearly hoped to be able to celebrate his sixty-fifth birthday in the Philippine capital.[9]

MacArthur's role in the tactical situation on Luzon in January had been an amazing reversal of his conduct on Leyte where, though he may have exerted pressure on Krueger and perhaps intervened unilaterally in deciding Sixth Army plans, he remained at GHQ Tacloban. But ever since moving his headquarters ashore on Luzon, he had dashed from one sector to another, obviously in personal command of operations, impatiently and sometimes antagonistically prodding Krueger and his commanders, and even participating in a regimental engagement. By his nature Krueger was, like McClellan in the Civil War, painstaking in his preparations and extremely cautious in his moves. He was convinced that the Japanese intended to defend Manila, and he believed that Yamashita's strength was greater, by at least 100,000 troops, than Willoughby's estimate. Bold and confident, MacArthur discounted the Sixth Army commander's concern about a counterattack on his left flank as his forces moved southward. The SWPA commander did not believe Yamashita had any intention of defending Manila, so the Sixth Army could dash on to the capital without much difficulty. On the matter of Japanese strength Krueger was closer to the mark, but on Yamashita's plans about Manila MacArthur was correct. There was his personal desire to capture Manila as quickly as possible, but the SWPA chief had additional reasons for pushing Krueger to move faster. As stated earlier, the Lingayen beachhead, Sixth Army engineers found, was inadequate for construction of the huge air and logistical base needed to support the conquest of Luzon. The paved runways at Clark Field and the port of Manila would be essential to the expansion of operations in the weeks ahead.

In mid-January the SWPA and Central Pacific commanders became involved in a wrangle over MacArthur's refusal to release the naval units he had borrowed from the Pacific Fleet. Nimitz was busy planning the Iwo Jima attack, set for February 19, and sent a radiogram to MacArthur reminding him that, according to their agreement at Tacloban, those vessels would be returned to Ulithi by January 19 for maintenance and replenishment in preparation for the Iwo Jima assault. MacArthur, however, was still concerned about the security of the Lingayen beachhead and also was preparing to launch two more amphibious operations on Luzon, the Zambales and Nasugbu assaults. He replied that he could not rely solely on the Seventh Fleet if it were stripped of its borrowed ships; Kinkaid concurred with the general on this. Nimitz responded that Halsey's Third Fleet would continue to seek out and destroy surviving units of the enemy fleet, which would be the best protection for the Lingayen beachhead, and he agreed to let Kinkaid retain some of the borrowed ships, including four old battleships, for three more weeks. But MacArthur and Kinkaid insisted on retaining six battleships and twenty-six destroyers of the Pacific Fleet.

On January 18 Nimitz told them they could retain temporarily four battleships, two cruisers, and twenty-two destroyers. Kinkaid was agreeable to this, which annoyed MacArthur. After one particular talk with the SWPA general on the subject, Kinkaid said, "MacArthur walked out to the gate with me and put his arm around me, 'You get in the middle of everything, don't you?' I said, 'I certainly do.' He was mad at me. Nimitz was mad at me." The two battleships that Nimitz recalled were in bad shape after batterings by kamikazes, and were long overdue for repairs; they left for Ulithi on the 22nd. In his reply to Nimitz the SWPA general reassured him that he desired to keep a strong surface force in Philippine waters only during the brief but crucial period between the withdrawal of the Third Fleet's air cover and the movement of Kenney's aircraft to Clark Field. MacArthur added somewhat sarcastically that "his retention of these two veterans [battleships] of the Pacific Fleet could hardly affect the success of the massive offensive being planned by CINCPAC."

Nevertheless, MacArthur did not release the other ships in time for service in the Iwo Jima assault. Spruance, who was commander of the naval attack forces for both the Iwo Jima and Okinawa operations, later stated that "the planning for and the actual execution of the Iwo Jima operation were affected to a considerable extent by the operations in the Philippines which immediately preceded it, and by the necessity of preparing for the Okinawa operation which was to follow." He added, "The Philippines operations necessitated last-minute changes and reduced the total number of ships which had been previously allocated to the Iwo Jima operations. This applied primarily to battleships, cruisers and destroyers for the Joint Expeditionary Force, although other forces were also affected to a lesser extent." Smith, the Marine commander on Iwo Jima, felt that MacArthur's belated release of the ships significantly weakened the naval gunfire support for the Marines' landing, which, in turn, caused more American casualties than Smith had anticipated. Forrestal, who visited MacArthur at his headquarters near Tarlac on February 28, wrote in his diary, "The units General MacArthur needs to accomplish his objectives are obviously a thing of vital interest to him, but the determination of when ships need overhaul or may be necessary for other operations is obviously the interest of Admiral Nimitz." To the SWPA commander in January, 1945, however, the occupation of Manila, whether for strategic, tactical, logistical, or personal reasons, had become an obsession, blocking consideration of the Central Pacific theater's needs.[10]

2. *Conquest and Devastation*

The race to Manila began on February 1 with three divisions competing for the honor of being the first American unit to enter the most important city in the Southwest Pacific combat area: Beightler's 37th Infantry, Mudge's 1st Cavalry, and Swing's 11th Airborne. The 37th, which had driven south from

Lingayen Gulf, was at Malolos and Plaridel, preparing to move on Highway 3 along the northeast shoreline of Manila Bay to the Philippine capital, only eighteen miles away. The 1st Cavalry had been summoned from the Sixth Army reserve; it arrived at Lingayen on January 27, and by February 1 was north of Cabanatuan on Highway 5, about seventy miles north of Manila in the Central Luzon Plain. The 11th Airborne's main units were then advancing along Highway 17, approximately forty-five miles southwest of Manila in Batangas Province. Several fierce rivalries were involved in the race: Krueger's Sixth Army versus Eichelberger's Eighth Army, cavalry versus infantry in the race from the north, and airborne troops in the south versus the two older arms of the military in the north.

When MacArthur visited the 1st Cavalry's assembly area near Guimba on January 30, he gave Mudge an order to pass on to his men: "Go to Manila. Go around the Nips, bounce off the Nips, but go to Manila. Free the internees at Santo Tomas. Take Malacanan Palace and the Legislative Building." Mudge created two "flying columns" from units of Brigadier General William Chase's 1st Cavalry Brigade and sent them dashing down Highway 5 far ahead of the rest of his division. On February 1, the columns quickly forded the Pampanga River near Cabanatuan, swept through the town, and sped south on Highway 5. At Gapan the Japanese had set demolition charges under the bridge across the Peñaranda River, but the fast-moving columns captured it before the enemy troops could set off the explosives. Near Baliuag, thirty-seven miles south of Cabanatuan, the two columns took separate back roads, east of Highway 3. No serious opposition had been encountered en route, and even where the bridges were destroyed, fording places were quickly found. Near Novaliches, northeast of Manila, one of the columns arrived at a bridge just as the Japanese lit the dynamite fuzes and fled. Some cavalrymen unhesitatingly grabbed the burning fuzes and extinguished them, and the column dashed onward along Route 52. At Talipapa, farther down the road, a Japanese convoy loaded with troops and supplies started to turn onto Route 52 from a side road. Troops aboard the column's lead vehicles waved for the Japanese to halt, which the startled enemy drivers did. As the column raced by, the Americans opened fire and destroyed four of the Japanese trucks, killing about two dozen soldiers. By the time the surprised survivors at the road crossing realized what had happened, the American column, which had never slowed down, was out of sight.

Arriving in the Grace Park suburb of north Manila, the 1st Cavalry vehicles crossed the city limits about 6:00 P.M. on February 3, becoming the first American troops to re-enter the Philippine capital. They boldly sped down Rizal Avenue, encountering only scattered resistance from the astonished Japanese. Directed by guerrillas, they headed for Santo Tomas University where, after a stiff fight at the front gates, they forced their way onto the grounds and liberated about 3700 American and other Allied civilians who had been interned since 1942. Another 220 were held hostage by the Japanese survivors there until their safety was guaranteed; the hostages were released the next morning. Against increasing enemy fire from positions in south Manila, the troops also seized Malacañan Palace on the north bank of the Pasig River, which runs through the middle of Manila. By February 5, the rest of the 1st Cavalry Division arrived at Grace Park.

Meanwhile, the 37th Division had been delayed by numerous tidal streams and destroyed bridges along the Manila Bay shoreline. It also encountered heavy mortar and small arms fire from small but stubborn bodies of Japanese defenders along the way. Nevertheless, the 37th entered north Manila on the morning of February 4 and quickly moved to Old Bilibid Prison to free about 500 civilian internees and 800 USAFFE prisoners of war. The Japanese guards fled as the 37th's troops arrived. Far to the south Swing's 11th Airborne units traveled north on Highway 17 at high speed toward Manila. Dunckel, who had commanded the Mindoro assault, later told Eichelberger, who accompanied the 11th Airborne, "When you were pushing on Manila so rapidly, I visited 6th Army Headquarters and found them greatly agitated over the fact that you would be in Manila before they were." Four miles south of the city limits on February 4, however, the 11th Airborne was stopped by intense artillery, mortar, and machine-gun fire as the Americans tried to cross the Parañaque River on a partly destroyed bridge. Swing's units deployed for action and, though they did not win the race, they had the dubious distinction of becoming the first division to engage part of the main Japanese defenses of Manila, the formidable Genko Line south of Nichols Field.[11]

Founded by Spanish colonists in 1571, Manila had evolved in its modern era into a city of contrasts — secluded mansions and crowded slums, air-conditioned apartment buildings and nipa-thatched huts, medieval Spanish churches and modern American port facilities. In 1945 the city proper covered about 14.5 square miles and had a population in excess of 800,000. Greater Manila, which included the sprawling suburban area as well as the region within the city limits, extended from Grace Park southward along the bay for ten miles to Parañaque and included over one million inhabitants. The extensive port area, with its piers, warehouses, and other facilities, covered the bay front for over a mile on either side of the mouth of the Pasig River. The main business district and principal industrial plants lay north of the river, and, as already noted, Malacañan Palace, Santo Tomas University, and Old Bilibid Prison were in north Manila. South of the Pasig were Intramuros, the centuries-old Spanish "Walled City," and its stone citadel, Fort Santiago, near the bay; a number of large government buildings nearby; much of the commercial and residential construction of recent vintage; Fort McKinley and Neilson Field, just below the Pasig on the eastern edge of the city; and Nichols Field, three miles down the bay from the city's southern limits.

Many of the major commercial buildings were of sturdy concrete construction, built to withstand earthquakes and typhoons. The government structures were not unlike the massive concrete and stone edifices found in American state capitals and in Washington. Most important from a military point of view, as it turned out, was the construction of the old Walled City: "The outer walls of Intramuros," states the Army history, "up to forty feet thick at the bottom and in places reaching a height of twenty-five feet, were constructed of great stone blocks, and the buildings within the walls were constructed all or partially of stone."

MacArthur's residence from 1935 to 1941 had been a penthouse atop the Manila Hotel, on the bay shore just off the southwest corner of Intramuros; his office as Philippine military adviser and field marshal had been at No. 1 Victoria Street in Intramuros. All of the MacArthurs' furniture and his personal library of up to 8000 volumes (some of them inherited from his father) were presumed to be in place unless they had been looted, for American aircraft, on the SWPA chief's orders, had carefully avoided bombing Manila except the north port area and rail yards. To the extreme annoyance of both ground and air commanders, when it became obvious that the enemy would defend the city MacArthur persisted in banning air attacks on Manila, maintaining that indiscriminate bombing would cause great civilian casualties and alienate the friendly populace. He told Kenney, "You would probably kill off the Japs all right, but there are several thousand Filipino civilians in there who would be killed, too. The world would hold up its hands in horror if we did anything like that."

As the three American divisions approached Manila, it became apparent that the Japanese had strong forces in the city, though their dispositions were not known for some time. Because of confusion over orders and disagreements between Japanese Army and Navy commanders in the Manila area, Yamashita's plan to abandon the city after removing supplies and destroying military facilities was not implemented. Admiral Iwabuchi, who commanded the Manila Naval Defense Force of about 16,700 naval troops, ignored orders to join the Shimbu Group in the mountains east of the city and instead prepared to defend Manila. On January 27, Yokoyama grudgingly yielded to reality and formally changed the mission of Iwabuchi's troops: "The Naval Defense Force will defend its already established positions and crush the enemy's fighting strength." As the Americans closed about the city in early February, nearly 4000 of Yokoyama's Shimbu troops were caught in the encirclement. A few managed to escape to the mountains later, but the total Japanese defense force trapped in Manila was close to 20,000 men.

Iwabuchi, like most naval officers at Manila, believed the main American attack would come from the south and therefore had prepared his strongest defenses south of the Pasig. Only about 3000 troops were dispatched to the northern defenses, and many of them were cut off and later mopped up by the 37th Division on the outskirts above Grace Park. The rest of Iwabuchi's defenders were entrenched in Intramuros, at Fort McKinley, and along the Genko Line to the south. Effectively utilizing the city's strongly reinforced concrete buildings of prewar construction, the Japanese brought in heavy-caliber guns from damaged and sunken ships in the harbor. They also had a tremendous stock of automatic weapons, mortars, field artillery pieces, and grenades, and for the first time in the Pacific war the Japanese would employ rockets, including some gigantic ones of a 400-mm. naval type. But few of Iwabuchi's naval troops had been trained for ground combat, and their defensive lines seldom included mutually supporting strong points. Nevertheless, with their concrete fortifications, ample supply of weapons and ammunition, and fanatical determination to fight to the last, Iwabuchi's defenders were prepared to make the capture of Manila a bloody, time-consuming ordeal for MacArthur's forces.[12]

As the 37th and 1st Cavalry divisions arrived in force in north Manila, Griswold assigned the infantry to the west and the cavalry to the east to clear the city north of the Pasig. The remnants of Iwaguchi's northern force undertook extensive destruction of military supplies and facilities in the north port area and the neighboring San Nicolas and Binondo districts, then withdrew across the Pasig and destroyed the bridges across the river. Unfortunately, a strong wind fanned the flames of the burning port facilities in a northerly direction, and the conflagration spread into the flimsy dwellings of the heavily populated lower-class Tondo District. The fires were clearly visible to Eichelberger eight miles down the bay shoreline. Troops of the 37th Division spent much of February 5–7 halting the expansion of the holocaust. Although this incident was later cited as one of the alleged atrocities ordered by Yamashita, the Japanese do not appear to have intended to destroy anything except the military property in the southwest corner of north Manila, and Yamashita, far to the north at Baguio, knew nothing of the episode. While the 37th mopped up the remaining pockets of enemy resistance on the bay side north of the Pasig, Mudge assigned his troops to clear the eastern section of north Manila and secure the close-in water supply system of the city. By February 7 the 37th had secured the western half and by the 10th the 1st Cavalry had cleared the eastern half of north Manila. Fifty American soldiers had died in action north of the Pasig, February 3–7, and about 1500 Japanese troops had been killed. To the south, the 11th Airborne had progressed a mile beyond the mouth of the Parañaque River but was heavily engaged around Nichols Field.[13]

From his headquarters near Tarlac on February 6, MacArthur announced in a communiqué: "Our forces are rapidly clearing the enemy from Manila. Our converging columns . . . entered the city and surrounded the Jap defenders. Their complete destruction is imminent." Soon the expected congratulatory messages came pouring in from Roosevelt, Stimson, Curtin,

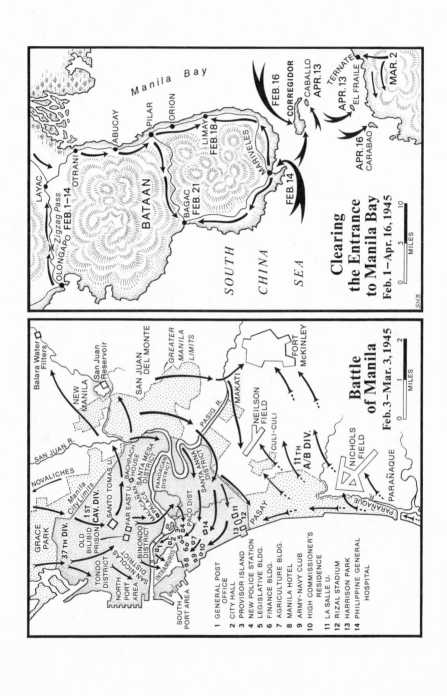

Clearing the Entrance to Manila Bay
Feb. 1–Apr. 16, 1945

Manila Bay

SOUTH CHINA SEA

LAYAC
OLONGAPO FEB. 1–14
Zigzag Pass
OTRANI FEB. 1–14
ABUCAY
PILAR
ORION
BATAAN
BAGAC FEB. 21
LIMAY FEB. 18
MARIVELES
FEB. 14
FEB. 16
CORREGIDOR
CABALLO APR. 13
TERNATE APR. 13
EL FRAILE
MAR. 2
CARABAO APR. 16

0   5   10
MILES

SHB

Battle of Manila
Feb. 3–Mar. 3, 1945

Balara Water Filters
San Juan Reservoir
NEW MANILA
SAN JUAN DEL MONTE
GREATER MANILA LIMITS
SAN JUAN R.
NOVALICHES
Manila City Limits
1ST CAV. DIV.
37TH DIV
GRACE PARK
Old Bilibid Prison
SANTO TOMAS U.
FAR EAST U.
BACHRACH HOUSE
SANTA MESA DISTRICT
PANDACAN DISTRICT
PACO DIST.
SANTA ANA DISTRICT
PASIG R.
MAKATI
NEILSON FIELD
CULI-CULI
11TH A/B DIV.
NICHOLS FIELD
PARAÑAQUE
PASAY
PASAY
FORT McKINLEY
TONDO DISTRICT
NORTH PORT AREA
SAN NICOLAS DISTRICT
BINONDO DISTRICT
INTRAMUROS
SOUTH PORT AREA

1 GENERAL POST OFFICE
2 CITY HALL
3 PROVISOR ISLAND
4 NEW POLICE STATION
5 LEGISLATIVE BLDG.
6 FINANCE BLDG.
7 AGRICULTURE BLDG.
8 MANILA HOTEL
9 ARMY-NAVY CLUB
10 HIGH COMMISSIONER'S RESIDENCE
11 LA SALLE U.
12 RIZAL STADIUM
13 HARRISON PARK
14 PHILIPPINE GENERAL HOSPITAL

0   1   2
MILES

Chiang Kai-shek, Churchill, and other Allied leaders, who justifiably assumed that the capture of Manila was at hand.[14] On the 7th, MacArthur traveled by jeep with some of his staff from the Tarlac area to north Manila. His office diary entry for that day states:

> To Manila with General Fellers and Colonels Lehrbas, Egeberg, and [Andres] Soriano, where met Generals Griswold, Beightler, Mudge, and Chase. Visited freed prisoners of war at Bilibid; visited 3,700 liberated civilian internees at Santo Tomas, receiving tremendous and dramatic ovation from all. To inspect Malacanan Palace and visit forward lines on Pasig River. Informed General Chase he had recommended him for Major General to command 38th Division. Retrieved own Cadillac automobile left on Corregidor and since driven by Jap commanding officer in Manila.[15]

About his visit to Santo Tomas, MacArthur later wrote, "I cannot recall, even in a life filled with emotional scenes, a more moving spectacle than my first visit to the Santo Tomas camp . . . When I arrived, the pitiful, half-starved inmates broke out in excited yells . . . It was a wonderful and never-to-be-forgotten moment — to be a life-saver, not a life-taker." In contrast to the noisy welcome of the civilian internees at Santo Tomas, the veterans of Bataan and Corregidor at Old Bilibid Prison, mostly men too ill to make the earlier voyages to work camps in Japan, Korea, and Manchuria, dragged themselves to "some semblance of attention" in front of their cots. As MacArthur started down the long line greeting them individually, he noticed that "they remained silent, as though at inspection." The conversational exchanges were brief:

> As I passed slowly down the scrawny, suffering column, a murmur accompanied me as each man, barely speaking above a whisper, said, "You're back," or "You made it," or "God bless you." I could only reply, "I'm a little late, but we finally came."

I passed on out of the barracks compound and looked around at the debris that was no longer important to those inside: the tin cans they had eaten from; the dirty old bottles they had drunk from. It made me ill just to look at them.

All across north Manila the SWPA commander found the Filipino residents in joyful frenzy: "Men, women, and children literally danced in the streets. I had intended to drive around the city to survey the damage, but I found myself the center of [a] triumphal procession." [16]

On the 10th the Sixth and Eighth Army commanders received word from their enthusiastic SWPA chief that he was planning a grand "victory parade" of his units through the main streets of Manila. Four days later, however, Chamberlin notified the commanders that the triumphal parade "had been put off indefinitely." During the interim, MacArthur had finally confronted the sobering reality that the battle for Manila had barely begun. The grand procession was never rescheduled. Disappointed, the SWPA commander returned to his advance GHQ at Hacienda Luisita near Tarlac and informed his staff that it might be some time before the move to Manila. Indeed, it would be nearly a month.

MacArthur had watched while the 148th Infantry of Beightler's division boarded assault boats and crossed the Pasig River near Malacañan Palace on February 7. The attack cost the regiment 115 casualties, but a foothold was established on the south bank, and soon other units of the 37th Division were across the river, taking positions in the streets and buildings of the riverside industrial section of the Pandacan District. The advance westward toward the Paco District and Intramuros faltered, however, as Japanese strong points on Provisor Island in the Pasig River and nearby buildings pinned down the 37th's soldiers with withering mortar, machine-gun, and rifle fire. Still refusing to permit air strikes, MacArthur reluctantly lifted his ban on the use of artillery within the city, and the 37th's field artillery and mortars pulverized the structures of the Provisor area. In vicious building-to-building fighting, Beightler's troops gradually pushed west through the Paco District. In the meantime, the 1st Cavalry had struck across the Pasig at several points farther east and drove steadily southwest toward the suburb of Pasay on Manila Bay.

Swing's airborne troops, which had made only small gains since February 4, continued to batter away at the powerful Genko Line defenses in the Parañaque–Nichols Field area. One company commander told Swing, "Tell Halsey to stop looking for the Jap Fleet. It's dug in on Nichols Field." On February 10 control of the 11th Airborne passed from the Eighth to the Sixth Army, and that same day Griswold promptly deployed his corps artillery in support of Swing's troops. In the next three days Nichols Field was taken, and on February 14 elements of the 11th Airborne and 1st Cavalry made contact, thereby completing the encirclement of Iwabuchi's remaining defense force.

A few days earlier, units of the 1st Cavalry had begun the arduous job of reducing the Japanese defenses at Fort McKinley, finally completed on the 19th. Iwabuchi himself, who had been at McKinley, barely escaped to Intramuros on the 11th. Yokoyama, the Shimbu commander off to the east in the mountains, sent word to Iwabuchi that Shimbu forces would counterattack in the Novaliches area; during the attack the admiral and his troops were to break out of Manila. Elements of the 1st Cavalry, however, repulsed the Shimbu attack, and Iwabuchi, hopelessly trapped along the bay in south Manila, made no attempt to break out but, instead, desperately worked on his defenses in Intramuros.

While units of the 11th Airborne turned south and secured Cavite Naval Station, and other airborne troops overran the remaining enemy positions in the Neilson Field–Fort McKinley area, the 37th and 1st Cavalry began the final push to Intramuros. Between February 14 and 16 the cavalrymen cleared the Japanese from Pasay, fighting fierce battles around Harrison Park and Rizal Stadium. In the following week, the 1st Cavalry encountered bitter opposition as it fought its way up Dewey Boulevard along the bay, overcoming die-hard Japanese defenders in battles for such landmarks as the Army-Navy Club, the Manila Hotel, the Philippine General Hospital, and the University of the Philippines. At the same time, the infantry of the 37th Division, on the cavalrymen's right flank, gradually cleared out Japanese strong points at the New Police Station, City Hall, and the General Post Office to the east of Intramuros. By February 22 Iwabuchi's surviving defenders had been driven into the northwest corner of south Manila — Intramuros, the south port area, and the Commonwealth government buildings near the Walled City.[17]

The reduction of the many strong points on the route to the edge of Intramuros during the previous ten days had produced heavy casualties among the American units, staggering enemy losses, and devastation of the city from Pasay to the Pasig River. The Japanese command structure began to disintegrate rapidly, and the doomed soldiers went on a rampage of murder, rape, and pillage against the hapless Filipinos caught within the defense perimeter. Exactly how many civilians were beaten, raped, burned, shot, bayoneted, or assaulted in other ways will never be known, but they numbered many thousands. As the American troops neared Intramuros, they came upon grisly scenes of piles of Filipino bodies burned, shot, or bayoneted, often with their hands tied behind their backs. The sickening evidence of mass murders would be worse still when they finally broke into Intramuros. An estimated 100,000 or more Filipino civilians would die in Manila before the battle ended, and though the vast majority probably were killed in the exchange of fire between the two armies, especially the artillery barrages, Japanese atrocities accounted for a shockingly high toll.

It was about mid-February that MacArthur learned the details of the massacre that had occurred on Palawan on December 14. The guards at a prison camp there panicked when they heard that an American invasion force, actually bound for Mindoro, was approaching. They herded the USAFFE prisoners into un-derground shelters, poured gasoline on them, and ignited them, then machine-gunned those who tried to break out. Over 140 died, but nine miraculously escaped. About the same time that MacArthur heard of this, he learned from guerrillas of a large internment camp behind the enemy lines at Los Baños, which was thirty miles southeast of Manila on Laguna de Bay. In a daring, well-timed raid on February 24, a task force of 11th Air-borne troops and guerrillas attacked Los Baños, killed the 250-man enemy garrison, and rescued over 2100 internees, while losing two American troops.[18]

On February 14–16, Griswold repeatedly broadcast messages to the trapped Japanese in the Intramuros area to surrender or at least release the Filipino civilians inside their defense peri-meter, but no response was forthcoming. On the 16th he asked Krueger for dive-bombing and napalm strikes against the strong-hold before he sent his troops in the final assault. The Sixth Army commander relayed the request to MacArthur, stating that it would be approved unless the SWPA chief still refused to lift his ban on air strikes. MacArthur responded immediately and firmly:

> The use of air [attacks] on a part of a city occupied by a friendly and allied population is unthinkable. The inaccuracy of this type of bombardment would result beyond question in the death of thousands of innocent civilians. It is not believed moreover that this would appreciably lower our own casualty rate although it would unquestionably hasten the conclusion of the operations. For these reasons I do not approve the use of air bombardment on the Intramuros District.[19]

Still, the SWPA commander did not object to a massive artil-lery bombardment of the Japanese positions, so from February 17 through 23 Griswold employed every available artillery piece from huge howitzers and field artillery guns to tank weapons and infantry mortars against the enemy and the Intramuros walls. The shelling finally breached the thick walls in several places in the northeast corner of Intramuros. On February 23 the first American assault troops entered the Walled City, crossing the Pasig and dashing in near the Government Mint at the north end. Soon others of the 37th Division were rushing in through Quezon Gate to the east. At Fort Santiago and other heavily fortified structures, savage fights took place before the defenders were defeated. Meanwhile, other 37th and 1st Cavalry soldiers battled their way through the port area to the west and reached the large Legislative, Agriculture, and Finance buildings just beyond the southeast corner of Intramuros. Both within and outside the Walled City, the vicious fighting involved costly room-to-room and hand-to-hand combat. On March 3 Griswold reported to Krueger that the last organized resistance in the area had ceased, and the month-long battle of Manila was finally over.

Other sources differ slightly, but the 37th Division's history states that in the fight for Manila "Japs counted dead numbered 16,665, of whom 13,006 were credited to the 37th Division." Beightler's infantry lost 461 men killed in action, while the total for the 1st Cavalry, 11th Airborne, and supporting XIV Corps units (mainly artillery) was about 710 troops. The greatest tragedy, however, was that for each American or Japanese soldier killed in the fighting for the city, at least six Filipino residents of Manila — men, women, and children — died as hapless victims of fires, shellings, stray bullets, grenades, or atrocities. The great city, once known as "the Pearl of the Orient," lay devastated, with much of the downtown area in shambles and the transportation, sewage, water, and electrical systems paralyzed.

One battle of Manila was over, but for months MacArthur and Osmeña would have to cope with the new battle of Manila just beginning — prevention of epidemics, relief of homeless and suffering civilians, restoration of law and order, repair or rebuilding of port and utilities facilities essential to both the military and civilian populace, revival of commerce, and a myriad of other problems, which for some time would make the occupation of the city more a liability than an asset to the furtherance of the conquest of Luzon. Manila had joined the ranks of Warsaw, Stalingrad, Dresden, Nanking, and other great cities of Europe and Asia that became victims of the horrors of World War II.[20]

MacArthur, accompanied by aides Egeberg, Lehrbas, and Soriano, spent the day of February 19 inspecting various areas of battle-torn Manila. After first touring north Manila, they crossed the Pasig and, according to MacArthur's office diary, visited "the front lines along the bayshore" where they got a "bird's-eye view from the 5th Cavalry OP [outpost] on top [of the] Helena Apartments." The cavalry regiment was then engaged in a bitter fight for the Philippine General Hospital. Brigadier General John A. Elmore, who was with MacArthur at the time, said that "as we came up a very narrow street, we heard firing going on no more than fifty yards from us." He persuaded the SWPA chief to turn back, though MacArthur muttered that it was not the first time he had been under fire. Later they moved over to the 37th Division's sector and observed the battle for the New Police Station. Their last stop before returning to advance GHQ near Tarlac was a visit to Swing's headquarters at Nichols Field.

On the 23rd the SWPA chief and the same three officers returned to the city and walked along the once beautiful shoreline southwest of Intramuros, which the 12th Cavalry Regiment had secured only the previous day. They went through the ruins of the former high commissioner's mansion, the Army-Navy Club, and MacArthur's home for six years, the Manila Hotel. The fight for the hotel had begun on the 21st with an assault on the east wing by a cavalry squadron supported by field artillery, 105-mm. self-propelled mounts, and a platoon of medium tanks. The east wing was seized after a brief but savage fight, but the Japanese strong points in the west wing, atop which was Mac-Arthur's former penthouse, held out until late the next day. By the time the cavalrymen and the supporting guns had overwhelmed the enemy defenders, the west wing and its penthouse were demolished. Mop-up fighting was still going on nearby when the SWPA chief arrived.

Under heavy guard MacArthur made his way up the damaged stairs to the penthouse and found his prized library and other personal possessions missing or destroyed. A Japanese colonel lay dead beside two smashed vases that the Japanese Emperor had presented to MacArthur's father when he was military attaché in Tokyo in 1905. MacArthur later commented, "It was not a pleasant moment . . . I was tasting to the last acid dregs the bitterness of a devastated and beloved home." From there he moved close to the edge of Intramuros where he observed the fighting in the Commonwealth buildings and the 37th Division's breakthrough into the Walled City. Satisfied that the horrible battle was finally nearing its end, he journeyed back to Hacienda Luisita.

On February 27 at 11:00 A.M., a ceremony was held at Malacañan Palace marking the re-establishment of the Commonwealth government in Manila. MacArthur and many of his senior staff and field officers attended. Osmeña and several members of his cabinet made brief addresses before the solemn assembly of soldiers and Filipino civilians. When it was MacArthur's turn to speak, according to Whitney, he "was deeply moved. The mask that he was able to wear at times of danger and the eve of great battles did not serve him now." [21] The SWPA chief spoke slowly, sometimes pausing as if unable to control his emotions:

> More than three years have elapsed — years of bitterness, struggle and sacrifice — since I withdrew our forces and installations from this beautiful city that, open and undefended, its churches, monuments and cultural centers might, in accordance

with the rules of warfare, be spared the violence of military ravage. The enemy would not have it so and much that I sought to preserve has been unnecessarily destroyed by his desperate action at bay, but by these ashes he has wantonly fixed the future pattern of his own doom.

Then we were but a small force struggling to stem the advance of overwhelming hordes treacherously hurled against us behind the mask of professed friendship and international good will. That struggle was not in vain! God has indeed blessed our arms! The girded and unleashed power of America, supported by our Allies, turned the tide of battle in the Pacific and resulted in an unbroken series of crushing defeats upon the enemy, culminating in the redemption of your soil and the liberation of your people. My country has kept the faith!

Its soldiers come here as an army of free men dedicated, with your people, to the cause of human liberty and committed to the task of destroying those evil forces that have sought to suppress it by brutality of the sword. An army of free men that has brought your people once again under democracy's banner to rededicate their churches, long desecrated, to the glory of God and public worship; to reopen their schools to liberal education; to till the soil and reap its harvest without fear of confiscation; to reestablish their industries that they may again enjoy the profit from the sweat of their own toil; and to restore the sanctity and happiness of their homes unafraid of violent intrusion.

Thus to millions of your now liberated people comes the opportunity to pledge themselves — their hearts, their minds and their hands — to the task of building a new and stronger nation — a nation consecrated in the blood nobly shed that this day might be — a nation dedicated to making imperishable those sacred liberties for which we have fought and many have died.

On behalf of my Government I now solemnly declare, Mr. President, the full powers and responsibilities under the Constitution restored to the Commonwealth whose seat is here reestablished as provided by law.

Your country thus is again at liberty to pursue its destiny to an honored position in the family of free nations. Your capital city, cruelly punished though it be, has regained its rightful place — Citadel of Democracy in the East. Your indomitable . . .

MacArthur's voice trembled and broke. He paused for a long moment and concluded, "In humble and devout manifestation of gratitude to Almighty God for bringing this decisive victory to our arms, I ask that all present rise and join me in reciting the Lord's Prayer." [22] He later commented on his emotional inability to complete his prepared address: "To others it might have seemed only the culmination of a panorama of physical and spiritual disaster. It had killed something inside me to see my men die." That afternoon he toured the ruins of Fort McKinley and then went back to his quarters near Tarlac. On March 5 he finally moved his headquarters to Manila. [23]

While the long battle for the capital had been taking place, the seizure of the entrance to Manila Bay had also been under way. It will be remembered that Hall's XI Corps landed on the Zambales coast on January 29, took Olongapo easily, and then was stopped by Japanese strong points in Zigzag Pass to the east. The enemy detachment was well entrenched in easily defensible terrain and kept the Americans pinned down for days. Exasperated with what he called "lack of aggressiveness," Hall relieved Major General Henry Jones, the 38th Division commander, on February 6. Chase, who had led the 1st Cavalry's flying columns to Manila, was appointed as his successor. Nevertheless, the reduction of the Japanese positions at Zigzag Pass continued to be slow and costly and was not completed until February 14. From then on, however, the conquest of Bataan moved rapidly. Staging at Olongapo, a regimental combat team of the 38th made a seaborne assault on Mariveles at the tip of the peninsula on February 14. The team then divided, its two elements reaching Bagac on the west coast by the 21st and Limay on the east coast by the 18th. Meanwhile, units of the 6th and 38th divisions drove south along the east coast, splitting at Pilar with one force moving across the peninsula to Bagac and the other continuing south to Limay where they made contact with the forces moving up from Mariveles. The Bataan operation was officially terminated on February 21, though some mopping-up of a few Japanese stragglers was necessary in the next week.[24]

MacArthur's diary entry for February 16 reads: "At 0600 to Bataan accompanied by Colonels Lehrbas, Egeberg, and Soriano, meeting Generals Hall and Eddleman. Jeeped down east coast of Bataan viewing newly recaptured areas, including Abucay, bastion of first defense line in 1941, and Balanga, bastion of last defense line in 1941. Then on a personal reconnaissance far ahead of our lines to within six miles of Cabcaben where stopped by blasted bridge." Patrolling P-38 pilots spotted the small convoy of vehicles and requested permission to attack, assuming they were Japanese. Chase would not approve it, how-ever, until further investigation, knowing that MacArthur was driving in that vicinity. The check showed that the target the P-38's were about to pounce upon was the SWPA commander's party. Not aware then of the narrowly averted attack and hop-ing to get a glimpse of Corregidor, MacArthur journeyed nearly five miles beyond the 6th Division's front lines.[25]

Egeberg described the "personal reconnaissance" mentioned in the diary entry:

> We arrived at one point of the front where a small company of soldiers had just finished repulsing a rather violent Banzai charge. There were many deaths, most of them Japanese but some were ours. We got out and MacArthur talked with the officers and enlisted men and then insisted on going on. We soon passed our forward point, a man on either side of the road stealthily proceeding down the ditch. What had earlier been a rather large cavalcade of jeeps had dwindled down to two. The jungle road with overhanging cliffs, country still in enemy hands, with sudden clearings and machine guns [possibly] point-ing towards us, certainly took the edge off my enthusiasm . . . We found a Japanese camp, the fire still going and the rice hot

in the pots . . . Finally, thank God, we reached a bridge that had been blown up and there was no way to go any farther. Through all of this General MacArthur was deeply moved . . . When he reluctantly turned back, he said, "This day has done me good." [26]

Corregidor had been under intense naval and air bombardment since January 22. Recalling that the Japanese had lost about half of their initial amphibious assault force in landing on Corregidor in May, 1942, MacArthur decided to seize the island fortress with a combined attack of paratroops and amphibious forces. The 503rd Parachute Regimental Combat Team, which had jumped at Nadzab in 1943, and a 24th Division infantry battalion were given the assignment of capturing Corregidor. The plan was risky because the drop areas on Topside were small, and the paratroops, jumping in several waves, would require about five hours to get their entire 2000-man force on the island. Moreover, the slightest miscalculations in the approach timing and wind speed would result in the paratroops' deaths on the precipitous cliffs of Topside or the rocks far below. The G-2 estimate, however, stated that there were fewer than 900 Japanese on the island, so the paratroops and about 1000 infantrymen were expected to be able to handle the situation. Actually, the enemy garrison numbered over 5200 troops.

When the assault was launched on February 16, the infantry landed with few casualties at Bottomside, but the paratroops suffered about 280 jump casualties, though few to enemy fire. The Japanese garrison, poorly led, lost over 1500 men in the next three days in wild, uncoordinated banzai charges, the type of piecemeal attacks that had cost the Japanese Army so heavily in previous Southwest Pacific campaigns. By the 20th the Americans were engaged in large-scale mopping-up activities, dislodging the enemy from caves and tunnels. The Americans controlled the surface of the island and the Japanese the subterranean area.

Suddenly, on the night of February 21–22, with American infantry in position atop Malinta Hill, an estimated 2000 Japanese below in the tunnel committed mass suicide by setting off an enormous amount of ammunition and explosives. The huge explosion blew rocks and debris in every direction and produced landslides; at least six American troops were killed in the chaotic scene. Two nights later additional explosions rocked the hill as more Japanese died underground. On the 26th, the surviving Japanese at Monkey Point on the eastern end of the island blew up an underground arsenal, killing about 200 of their own and fifty Americans who were unfortunately on top of the knoll. Colonel George M. Jones, the 503rd's commander, reported to Hall on March 1 that organized resistance was over on Corregidor. The island's conquest had cost 210 American lives and, except for twenty prisoners, all of the enemy garrison.

The clearing of the rest of the Manila Bay entrance was relegated to small forces of the 11th Airborne and 38th divisions. The former found few Japanese between Cavite and Ternate on the southern shore of the bay, though the capture of Ternate itself on March 2 involved a stiff fight in which about 350 Japanese were killed. On April 13, elements of the 38th Division used similar techniques to wipe out the small enemy garrisons in tunnels on the islands of Caballo and El Fraile, south of Corregidor: thousands of gallons of diesel fuel were pumped into the tunnel ventilators and ignited. Carabao, the last of the tiny islands to be seized at the bay entrance, was given an intensive two-day naval and air bombardment. Then on April 16 a battalion of the 38th Division landed, only to find that the sole living creature on the island was a badly frightened pig. The Japanese garrison had departed seven weeks earlier; in fact, its troops were the ones killed at Ternate in early March. Allied ships began using Manila harbor on a limited basis on March 16, but with over 300 ships sunk in the harbor and the port facilities in worse shape than that in which the Americans found Cherbourg during the Normandy operation, it would be many weeks before the harbor and port of Manila could be utilized to full capacity.[27]

At 6:00 A.M., March 2, less than twelve hours after the last fighting ended on Corregidor, MacArthur left Hacienda Luisita with Marquat, Lehrbas, Egeberg, and Soriano and went to Manila where they, along with the members of the Bataan Gang who were available, boarded four PT boats (the same number as used in the exit of March, 1942) and journeyed to Corregidor. MacArthur chatted with Hall, Jones, and officers and men of the Corregidor assault force; inspected parts of the island, including Malinta Tunnel, Wheeler Battery, and his office during the siege of 1942 on Topside, all now in ruins; and participated in a brief flag-raising ceremony on the grounds in front of the battered Topside barracks. "Bulldozers had hastily leveled off an area for the flag-raising ceremonies," said one witness. "In the center of the area stood the flag pole, a slightly bent, shell and bomb scarred ship's mast with twisted rigging and ladders still hanging from its yardarm. In the background white and camouflage parachutes dangled from the trees and wrecked buildings." With the conquering paratroops and infantry assembled in formation, Jones marched up to MacArthur, saluted, and in a firm, loud voice reported, "Sir, I present to you Fortress Corregidor." [28] MacArthur responded:

> Colonel Jones, the capture of Corregidor is one of the most brilliant operations in military history. Outnumbered two to one, your command by its unfaltering courage, its invincible determination, and its professional skill overcame all obstacles and annihilated the enemy. I have cited to the order of the day all units involved and I take great pride in awarding you as their commander the Distinguished Service Cross as a symbol of the fortitude, the devotion, and the bravery with which you have fought. I see the old flagpole still stands. Have your troops hoist the colors to its peak, and let no enemy ever haul them down.[29]

Although many moments of triumph lay behind and ahead of him, none was as personally satisfying to MacArthur as the reconquest of Manila, Bataan, and Corregidor.

3. Home Again in Manila

Making his first tour of liberated Manila on March 3, Eichelberger found the devastation shockingly worse than he imagined: "There was practically nothing that hadn't been entirely knocked down and in ruins . . . Manila in effect has ceased to exist except for some places that the Japanese thought were not worth defending or where our American troops got in by surprise." For days the horrible stench of thousands of unburied corpses pervaded the downtown area of south Manila, and a strange quietness hung over the rubble-strewn streets long after the sounds of battle faded away. Then, like the miraculous appearance of green shoots on the charred earth of a forest recently ravaged by fire, signs of life and activity began to reappear in Manila. Filipino residents came out of hiding in blasted buildings and houses, and others by the thousands began to stream back into the city from the countryside where they had sought refuge during the terrible battle.

Although large-scale fighting was under way against Yamashita's forces south of Baguio and east of Manila, MacArthur assigned a generous number of troops to assist in relief and rehabilitation activities in the stricken capital. Side by side, American soldiers and Filipinos began to clear the debris and restore the essentials of urban life. Thanks to the energetic, enlightened leadership of health, education, and welfare officers at GHQ, epidemics were averted, many thousands of tons of relief supplies from the States were distributed, and schools were reopened as soon as teachers and makeshift classrooms could be found. The State Department sent an able team to work on the problems of the thousands of American and Allied civilian internees, many of whom were in ill health and destitute. Army engineers repaired the portion of the city's water supply system in American hands, though the Ipo and Wawa dams to the northeast, which provided nearly half of the city's water, were still controlled by the Japanese. The engineers also went to work getting the harbor and port areas in workable condition, and ships were using the facilities on a limited basis in a remarkably short time. Quartermaster and other service troops in early April activated Base X, as the supply depot at Manila was designated, and by June it was in full operation. "It handled more supplies than any other SWPA base ever had," states the official Army quartermaster history, "receiving and discharging a monthly average of 380,000 long tons" from April on.[30]

By banning air strikes inside the city, MacArthur had made an earnest effort to spare the residents some of the suffering that attends battle, but his condoning of massive artillery shelling, even if a tactical necessity for conquest of the strong points, was somewhat inconsistent with the aircraft prohibition. Once the capital was secured, he continued to evince genuine concern for the Filipinos and their plight by trying to restore normal living conditions. For a time all roads into the city were clogged with Filipinos either returning to their homes in Manila or going out of the city in search of food in the countryside. Some irate officers, whose units were slowed down by the thousands of civilians jamming the roads, complained to MacArthur. He refused, however, to enact any regulation to restrict civilian traffic, maintaining that humanitarianism took a higher priority in this situation than the needs of the military, except, of course, in case of counterattack.

Although there were no epidemics, for a while the venereal disease rate among soldiers in Manila seemed to be getting serious. Egeberg discussed the growing problem with MacArthur and told him that it had been recommended by people from the United States that we should put Manila out of bounds to our own troops. He thought a moment, and then he said, "Doc, you've seen Manila. You've seen the ruins. You realize how poor the people are. You've seen the little shops they've set up to sell things, and you've seen our soldiers. Sure, some of them want to go whoring, but I'll bet most of them just want to get into a Filipino home to feel what it's like to be in a home again." He was right on that score. He said, "These men have fought their way through the jungles to get to Manila, and now you're asking me to tell them they can't go into Manila. Besides, do you realize the money they bring into town to buy things with, whether it be a bottle of liquor, or a meal, or a souvenir they send home, that is becoming the new economic life blood of Manila? Manila needs it, and these people who have been through this war need that kind of help, particularly when it comes willingly. No, I'm not going to put Manila out of bounds to our troops. Besides, they've got some pretty good treatment for that disease now, haven't they?" [31]

By the middle of March, the hard work of soldiers and civilians to restore essential services to Manila was producing encouraging results. "The lights are going on all over the city," Powers observed on March 13. Two days later MacArthur and several of his staff officers went by jeep to Caloocan, a few miles north of the city, where they boarded a flag-bedecked train and rode it back into Manila. Large crowds cheered the arrival of the first train into liberated Manila, and MacArthur made a short speech at the railway station praising the work of the Army engineers and Filipino workers in getting the line between the capital and Lingayen Gulf into operation so rapidly.[32] Another small incident symbolic of Manila's early stirrings to life took place on March 21. Powers describes it:

At dusk, on the cobbled road alongside the banks of the Pasig, in the shadows of the ruined Intramuros, the Paranaque Municipal Band, thirty strong, came on the night of the first day of Spring, to entertain their friends, the Americans . . .

Voluntarily, they had traveled ten kilometers to perform the "First Concert for the American Forces in the Philippines" . . .

At the opening clash of the cymbals, heads popped out of the shell-pocked National City Bank, in which resting combat troops were quartered . . . As the audience increased, late-comers made themselves comfortable on detonated Japanese land-mines stacked off the road . . . The soldiers sat and listened undistracted . . .

The Philippine band [at the end of the concert] cut short a native number, paused — then, with unbridled gusto and enthusiasm, burst, in full glory, into the "Washington Post March." The audience stirred in its seats. Without pause, came the finale. With every musician playing with his heart as well as his throat and hands, the band rose, playing "God Bless America." Simultaneously, the soldier audience rose too.

As the final triumphant note of the anthem sounded, you could see in the faces of the combat troops what the Paranaque Municipal Band and its music had accomplished. An amphitheatre of ruins had been magically transformed into a cathedral in which fighting men stood, their kindled spirits turning into a mockery the ravages of war around them.[33]

Slowly, all across the city, pieces of MacArthur's prewar belongings began to emerge as soldiers poked through ruins and explored the remaining buildings. His black Cadillac sedan had been found on the grounds of Santo Tomas University where it had been used by the camp commandant, who had required the internees to build a special garage for it. The city officials of Little Rock, his birthplace, sent MacArthur an Arkansas automobile license to place on his newly found vehicle. The city collector added in his letter, "Your slogan, 'On to Tokyo,' sounds rather convincing and we hope you get to use this on the streets of Tokyo before long." Some engineers recovered his set of the Cambridge Modern History series in the debris at the Manila Hotel, but few other volumes of his fine prewar library were found. On February 16, before the artillery opened fire on the hotel, MacArthur wrote to his wife that the structure was "still unharmed but not yet in our hands. Have recovered all of our silver, which had been removed from the hotel to the Watson Building near Malacanan, apparently prepared for shipment to Japan. Took Bataan today and expect to have Corregidor tomorrow or the following day. Be patient. Love, MacArthur."

When he moved with part of his advance GHQ to the Wilson Building in north Manila on March 5, MacArthur had already located a house for his wife and son, who were due to arrive the next day. The dwelling that he chose was "Casa Blanca," the Bachrach mansion in an exclusive neighborhood of the Santa Mesa District, which was less than a mile east of Malacañan Palace and a few blocks from the north bank of the Pasig. The district had been cleared by the 1st Cavalry on February 7 with relatively little fighting or damage.[34] All the way from Australia MacArthur and Kenney had been engaging in friendly competition for the better room or house, whether at Port Moresby, Hollandia, or Tacloban. How MacArthur acquired the Bachrach house is told by Kenney:

General MacArthur had stolen rooms from me before . . . I had been living in grass shacks, tents, and hastily constructed temporary quarters and had been bitten by mosquitoes and flies and had shucked scorpions out of my socks. I was getting fed up with it by the time we got to Manila, where they have real houses. MacArthur had moved to a sugar central [Hacienda Luisita] about thirty or forty miles from Manila, and I had moved down there with him.

I had a little L-5 plane on a mud strip outside there, so I hopped into Manila with some of my headquarters staff and told them to find me a good house to live in . . . They could probably find one that some Jap ambassador or admiral had. Pretty soon they got for me this house belonging to a woman called Mrs. Bachrach. The Bachrach family had the deal for all the automobiles sold in the Philippines, and it was an immensely rich family. The senior Bachrach man had been killed by the Japs, and Mrs. Bachrach was up in the hills with the guerrilla crowd. The Japs still occupied part of the city at this time [c. February 18], but we could get in through the rear . . . So I went over to look at the house. It was a good-looking house, all full of furniture and everything; some high-ranking Jap had been living there. They had a swimming pool, a massage and steam bath down in the cellar, and a nice garden. So I said, "O.K., put my name down for it."

I came back to the sugar central that evening in time for dinner. I was sitting there with the "Old Man" when he said, "Where have you been today?"

I said, "Oh, I've been in Manila getting a house. I want to get a good house to live in while we are in the Philippines."

He asked, "Did you find one?"

I replied, "Yes."

He asked, "Any good?"

I described the house and told him where it was and everything. I didn't think anything else of it till at 7:00 the next morning when I went down to breakfast. That was the one time in twenty-four hours of a day when you could find MacArthur. At 7:00 he was always sitting down at the breakfast table, no matter where he was. But he wasn't there. I waited around for about five minutes, and then I said, "Where's the General?"

Somebody said, "Oh, he took off for Manila this morning."

I asked, "About when?"

"About a quarter till six."

So I finished breakfast and put in a call to my man who was at Manila. I said, "I'll be down there in about a half hour . . . because we've got to find a house."

He said, "Well, I got you a house."

"I don't think we own it anymore," I told him. "You'd better go look around for another house."

So I got down there, and he said, "I've got you another house lined up . . . I got hold of Mrs. Bachrach, and she said her sister had a house and that her sister's instructions to the architect were simply, 'Build me a house that's better than my sister's.'"

We went over there, and it was a beautiful house. So I took it . . .

I got back to the sugar central, and MacArthur said, "George, I did a kind of dirty trick on you today. I stole your house."

I said, "I know you stole my house. I knew that was going to happen when you didn't show up for breakfast at 7:00 . . ."

He said, "I looked at that old German embassy place they had for me on the Pasig River. I wouldn't be found dead in that. It's a terrible dump. Furthermore, the Pasig River is a sewer and it smells all around that place. So I stole your house."

I said, "Alright, so you stole my house."

He asked, "What are you going to do now?"

I said, "I've got a house. I was in there today getting me another one . . ."

He asked, "Is it any good?"

I answered, "It's a better one than yours."

He asked, "Where is it?"

"I'm not going to tell you. I made one mistake, and I'm not going to repeat it," I said.

"Oh," he said, "come on and tell me where it is. Kind of describe it to me."

"No," I said, "I'm not telling one thing. Someday when you have Jean and the boy up here . . . I'll invite you over to dinner and have you served by Ramon, who is ex-chef of the Saint Francis Hotel of San Francisco and is now my cook . . . Until then I'm not telling you a thing about that house, but it's a better house than yours."

He said, "Well, I'm a son of a gun! Why didn't I wait a little longer and get that one!" [35]

MacArthur had not seen his wife and son since October 14. Mrs. MacArthur, responding on December 23 to a letter from Byers telling her about a recent meeting with the SWPA chief, revealed her longing to be with her husband:

Things go about the same with us here, except that Brisbane, as far as the American Army is concerned, is almost a ghost city, & Lennon's really seems most strange with none of the old faces around, the lobby full of civilians now . . . My days are busy with Arthur & his schedule, & now with Christmas coming there are things to be done for him, & too I have been going over the many newspapers & clippings I have packed away, trying to get them in some kind of order for packing. So you see that my days are full but I do feel lost in a way as this is the first time I have ever really been separated from the General.[36]

On January 26, MacArthur's sixty-fifth birthday, she wrote him:

Dearest Sir Boss —
    For your birthday, I send all my love to you & may it help to form a mantle of protection for you. I love you more than you will ever know. May we be able to share in peace many more of your birthdays together.
    God bless you.
                                    Jeannie[37]

Just before her departure for Manila aboard a refrigerator ship, the *Columbia Express,* she received a message from MacArthur describing the destruction of the Manila Hotel and the nearby high commissioner's house. The latter had been under consideration as their family residence. He told her, "Do not be too distressed over their loss. It was a fitting end for our soldier home." As usual, he signed it "Love, MacArthur." [38] (In none of his known correspondence to anyone did he ever sign simply "Douglas.")

Fellers flew to Brisbane to accompany Jean, Arthur, and Ah Cheu on the voyage; Huff, who had been with the family in Brisbane since 1942, had joined the GHQ staff at Hacienda Luisita in late January. The ship departed from Brisbane on February 21, stopped briefly at Hollandia en route, and steamed into wreckage-strewn Manila harbor on March 6. Since no pier was in shape yet to receive ocean-going vessels, MacArthur, along with Egeberg, Lehrbas, and Soriano, went by small boat to the *Columbia Express* to meet them. Before going to the house, they took a tour of the battle-torn areas of the city, including stops at the Manila Hotel and Santo Tomas. That evening they were dinner guests of the Osmeñas at Malacañan Palace. According to one account, "a fresh storm of criticism arose" in some circles in Washington over MacArthur's unique privilege of having his wife with him. One general at the Pentagon, possibly echoing Marshall's sentiments, remarked, "If feminine companionship serves in any way to help MacArthur, let her stay there. MacArthur is not a young man. Maybe he needs his wife." Those officers on the SWPA chief's staff who knew him best would have endorsed that statement except that they would have excluded the word "maybe." A GHQ spokesman, however, did feel it necessary to counter the criticism by stating publicly that she had come primarily "to aid and assist in such way as she can in the care of internees and rehabilitation of the city and its inhabitants." [39]

As soon as she had set up housekeeping in the Bachrach house, Mrs. MacArthur plunged into a busy schedule of volunteer relief work, more than fulfilling the assertion of the GHQ statement. In fact, her sensitivity to the suffering around her was evident that first time she visited the internees at Santo Tomas. "When we drove through the gates," she later said, "and I saw the condition of the people and the rags they were still wearing, I had a horrible feeling about my own clothes . . . So I had the driver stop, and I quickly took off my hat and gloves, but there wasn't much else I could do about it." In the following weeks, however, she did plenty, visiting former prisoners and internees, arranging through her husband for all sorts of favors for them as well as for many destitute Filipino families, regularly paying calls at the civilian and military hospitals of the city, and writing many letters to concerned families in the States regarding their loved ones imprisoned in 1942 and whom she had met after their liberation or about whom she had some news. For example, Lieutenant Colonel E. T. Thompson, commander of the 49th General Hospital, wrote to her after one of her visits to his wards, "On going thru the hospital the next morning I was frequently stopped by officers and men who told me that the patients were still talking about your graciousness, kindliness, and interest in them." As had been true in Brisbane, everyone with whom she was associated found her to be a very likable lady. Among the descriptions by some who knew her then are "modest, undemanding, unassuming, and loyal," "vivacious, charming — a delightful conversationalist, a very devoted wife, and a really superb diplomat," "a good influence not only on him [MacArthur] but on everybody that was around," and "a tremendous help to the General." [40]

The MacArthurs often entertained visiting military and political dignitaries and senior GHQ officers at lunch, but, as at Brisbane, attended no social activities and, save for rare occasions such as a dinner honoring Lord Louis Mountbatten that summer, did not act as hosts for parties or dinners in the evenings. Contrary to his behavior before his family's arrival when he almost daily toured the Sixth Army's front on Luzon, MacArthur did not leave Manila from March 5 until his departure for Tokyo in late August except on three occasions: a trip on April 27 to the Marikina Valley front, about twenty miles northeast of Manila, and two voyages to the southern Philippines and Borneo in June and July. He continued to keep his unusual work hours, arriving late and working into the evening, which was trying both for his staff's private lives and for his wife's meal schedule. According to some observers, in Manila he did make an adjustment of sorts by leaving his work earlier at night in order to devote some time for fellowship with Jean and Arthur.

When MacArthur was with Arthur, said friends of the family, he seemed to be as relaxed and playful as a young father doting over his first and only child. Now seven, Arthur was handsome and alert, though frail and reserved; he found few playmates in the Santa Mesa neighborhood. The general gave him a dog, to which the boy became greatly attached. One day an automobile, moving along the circular drive in the front yard, hit the pet and killed it. "Arthur was saddened," remarked Huff, "but the General was even more distressed. He immediately ordered the iron gates leading to the driveway closed and locked." He told the sentry there to admit no cars until he had called the house first. Kenney soon drove up, but even he had to wait until authorization came from the house for the gates to be opened. As in Brisbane earlier and in Tokyo later, MacArthur displayed a tendency to overreact when the slightest misfortune befell Arthur. Mrs. MacArthur and Ah Cheu continued to try to curb his protectiveness and extreme generosity toward Arthur for fear that the boy would become more spoiled, but he still got the almost worshipful attention of his father.

A new influence came into Arthur's life in Manila when Jean engaged Mrs. Phyllis Gibbons, an English lady, as his tutor. A divorcée, she had taught at a school in Baguio before the war and had been interned there and in Manila until her liberation in early February. It was said that Arthur picked up a slight British accent from her during the next six years, when "Gibby," as the family called her, served as his tutor. He also showed a beginning interest and talent in music, especially piano, which she encouraged.[41] How satisfied MacArthur was with the upbringing of his son at the hands of Jean, Ah Cheu, and Mrs. Gibbons is not known, but the fact that he had great expectations of his son is evident from the now famous prayer he penned:

Build me a son, O Lord, who will be strong enough to know when he is weak, and brave enough to face himself when he is afraid; one who will be proud and unbending in honest defeat, and humble and gentle in victory.

Build me a son whose wishes will not take the place of deeds; a son who will know Thee — and that to know himself is the foundation stone of knowledge.

Lead him, I pray, not in the path of ease and comfort, but under the stress and spur of difficulties and challenge. Here let him learn to stand up in the storm; here let him learn compassion for those who fail.

Build me a son whose heart will be clear, whose goal will be high; a son who will master himself before he seeks to master other men; one who will reach into the future, yet never forget the past.

And after all these things are his, add, I pray, enough of a sense of humor, so that he may always be serious, yet never take himself too seriously. Give him humility, so that he may always remember the simplicity of true greatness, the open mind of true wisdom, and the meekness of true strength.[42]

Throughout the war years MacArthur enjoyed excellent health. In his office diary there is only one day's entry mentioning his absence from duty because of illness, and that was due to a cold that he contracted shortly after arriving in Australia in 1942. The only regular exercise he got, however, was the constant pacing back and forth in his office. "I once figured that in this manner he walked at least five miles a day at about three miles per hour," observed Egeberg, adding, "He was such a restless person that even when he was at attention he was constantly shifting his feet." Although Egeberg became very close to the general, it was as his aide and not as his physician, for MacArthur would not submit to physical examinations. Egeberg commented:

> The only time I ever got a stethoscope on his chest was by a ruse. It was while we were flying at 20,000 feet with no oxygen or pressurized cabin. Larry Lehrbas, one of his aides who later died of emphysema, couldn't take it. I moved over beside Larry and felt his pulse, which was very high. MacArthur was seated beside him, so I then felt the General's pulse, which was perfectly normal. Then I put a stethoscope on Lehrbas and quickly moved over to MacArthur and put it on his chest. That was the only time that General MacArthur allowed me to even partially examine him.[43]

As in decades past, MacArthur's personality traits continued to baffle those who tried to discern a consistent pattern. To some people, particularly those who never worked closely with him or who opposed his will, he appeared egotistical, arrogant, haughty, vain, remote, and humorless. But rarely did officers who were long associated with his staff observe or admit to seeing these characteristics. An exception, Barbey, said frankly, "Mac-Arthur was never able to develop a feeling of warmth and comradeship with those about him. He had their respect but not their sympathetic understanding or their affection. He could not inspire the electrifying leadership Halsey had. He was too aloof and too correct in manner, speech, and dress. He had no small talk, but when discussing military matters he was superb." [44] LaFollette, who served on MacArthur's staff from October, 1942, to June, 1945, found him to be "endowed with a first-class mind, which he enriched with prodigious reading and study. And all was dominated by a will of iron . . . His mind was a beautiful piece of almost perfect machinery . . . Rarely was he put to his mettle by other mortals. And when he was — if in his own military field — he was superb, dazzling." LaFollette continued:

> But there was a serious flaw in this otherwise almost perfect combination of human qualities. He had no humility and hence no saving grace of a sense of humor. He could never laugh at himself — never admit mistakes or defeats. When these occurred they were never admitted, and he resorted to tricks — sometimes sly, childlike attempts — to cover up.
>
> This petty but understandable trait of wanting to be perfect, to ignore his obvious warts — warts that were insignificant against his towering intellect, superb courage, and inflexible will — became important only because they were denied. That denial convinced his detractors that they could prove the whole structure itself to be only a facade. How mistaken they were! [45]

On the other hand, the officers who knew him best found Mac-Arthur to be humble, gentle, modest, unostentatious, warmhearted, and possessing a keen sense of humor as well as a brilliant intellect, the last trait one that virtually all of his colleagues granted regardless of their opinions of him in other

respects. The GHQ inner circle's viewpoint of their commander's personality is exemplified by Kenney's description:

> He has tremendous personal charm that captivates anyone he
> likes or wishes to impress. His conversation is vivid and color-
> ful as well as interesting, and the way that he puts emphasis and
> feeling into what he says makes you remember the man, but you
> also retain the message that he is trying to put across to you.
> He is sentimental, emotional, and deeply religious. He is in-
> nately shy and retiring. While at ease with close friends, he
> does not enjoy the mob scenes which so many of our modern
> cocktail and dinner parties seem to have turned into. He is not
> a thick-skinned individual who laughs off criticism, regardless
> of whether it is just or not. If he feels that he does not deserve
> it, he is extremely sensitive to criticism, although he can take it
> and ignore it when he has a job to do.
> MacArthur is a positive individual. There is nothing vacil-
> lating about him. He believes in himself, his destiny, and in his
> place in history. While he will freely admit his mistakes after
> they have happened, he is sure that his decisions are correct at
> the time he makes them.[46]

The contradictory, enigmatic nature of MacArthur's personality, as discussed in the first volume of this work, becomes especially complicated for the observer because of his supreme
skill at role-playing. As Kenney noted in his first sentence above,
the SWPA chief could be charming to friends and to persons
whom he wanted to sway. An accomplished actor, he could play
many parts, and no one has yet finally determined which reflected the real MacArthur. He probably preferred the role of
the gentleman-warrior, the aristocrat at arms. Nevertheless, just
as the Hudson Valley aristocrat in the White House could skillfully play other parts as the occasion required, so the SWPA
leader could project a different image to suit each scheme or
maneuver in which he was engaged. He seemed no more able
to refrain from role-playing than Roosevelt, and either man, it
was said, would have rivaled John Barrymore as an actor. The

general was deeply conscious of his position on the stage of one of the greatest dramas in history. Like the foremost actors of the theater, he thoroughly enjoyed being dramatic, and he could identify himself readily and completely with the rest of the cast and even the setting. At times he would startle listeners by nonchalantly referring to himself in the third person. He once said, "Marshall proposed this, but MacArthur suggested . . ." On other occasions, as in his controversial communiqués, he would consider a decision or action as a projection of his own ego, for example, "I drove the enemy out . . . My bombers and my ships . . ." Some dismissed such language as that of an arrogant egotist, but others saw in his personal performances the supreme actor.

As to what factors impelled him to become absorbed in roleplaying, that will be left to the scholars of psychohistory to determine. There is little doubt that his role-playing was effective in his relations with his immediate staff. That his dramatic efforts had a positive impact on the soldiers of his theater is moot. Nevertheless, whereas veterans of the European operations normally responded, "First Army," "Ninth Army," or whatever was appropriate, when asked what army they served with, the Southwest Pacific veterans, even those who enjoyed the Dugout Doug doggerel, would not uncommonly reply that they were with "MacArthur's Army."

At GHQ, which moved to the Manila City Hall on May 13, Sutherland was more subdued than before the unpleasant episode at Tacloban. When Eichelberger visited GHQ, he learned that Sutherland had hoped to get command of an army but "he had lost a bit of caste now." Although MacArthur had often taken Sutherland with him on field trips, now the SWPA chief usually took along only his principal aides, Egeberg, Lehrbas, and Soriano. Since September, Soriano, like Whitney, had been enjoying more informal moments of fellowship with the Old Man, which prompted some concern and envy among certain other GHQ officers. Osmeña looked upon Soriano's rising influence with uneasiness, too, since the latter, one of the wealthiest men in prewar Manila, had been close to Quezon and Roxas. Willoughby had known Soriano well before the war and shared with him an admiration for General Francisco Franco, the Spanish dictator. Marshall, though still deputy chief of staff, was also commanding the current USAFFE, an administrative organization soon to be phased out.

The major generals at GHQ Manila included Akin, chief signal officer; Casey, chief engineer again after serving as head of ASCOM; Chamberlin, G-3; Frink, USASOS commander; Marquat, chief antiaircraft officer; Whitlock, G-4; and Willoughby, G-2. The brigadier generals included William E. Chambers, Chamberlin's operations officer; Diller, public relations officer; Eastwood, Whitlock's plans and operations chief; Fellers, MacArthur's military secretary; Fitch, adjutant general; Matthew J. Gunner, G-1; Carl A. Russell, Chamberlin's planning officer; and Whitney, chief of the Philippine affairs section. Among the American commanders of SWPA forces, Kenney, Krueger, and Kinkaid had been promoted to four stars in early 1945, while those with three-star rank now were Whitehead, Barbey, and Wurtsmith, who had recently become commander of the Thirteenth Air Force.

The vying for position at the Old Man's right or left hand continued throughout the war among a number of the staff officers who were especially devoted to him. While often critical of each other, they were intensely loyal to him. He, in turn, steadfastly supported each of them against fault-finding outsiders. Even through the period of tension with Sutherland, MacArthur did not discuss the matter except with a few confidants and refused to consider relieving the chief of staff. Sutherland, who never asked for a transfer, lasted out the storm, and gradually the relationship began to improve. The Bataan Gang may have had claim to the oldest and most sentimental relationship with MacArthur, but the ties that grew between the SWPA chief and a number of other men who joined him later seem to have been just as strong by 1945; for instance, with Kenney, Fellers, Egeberg, Lehrbas, Whitney, Whitlock, Sverdrup, Eichelberger, Krueger, Kinkaid, and Whitehead. (Appendix A gives some data on which men had the most contact with the SWPA commander.) Eichelberger, who had his differences with MacArthur from 1942 on, wrote to Miss Em, his wife, in January, "Personally I would like to see the BC [Big Chief] get a speedy victory . . . and then I would like to see him be given command of all the army troops in the Pacific. He is lucky in addition to having a very fine strategic mind. It takes a lot of courage to do what he did" in fighting for the return to the Philippines and more support for the Southwest Pacific.

Of the above-named officers, Krueger probably ranked next to Sutherland among those who felt the wrath of the Old Man. Yet, on February 18, at the height of MacArthur's intense pressure on his Sixth Army commander to be more aggressive in the drive to Manila, the SWPA chief, without telling him, recommended to the War Department that Krueger be promoted to a four-star general. MacArthur's behavior was contradictory and he surely had his faults, but to most of his high-ranking staff and field officers he possessed a charismatic appeal that made serving under him the most inspiring experience of their lives.[47]

CHAPTER XVI

Expanding Operations
and Responsibilities

1. Shobu and Shimbu Refuse to Collapse

LIKE THE TOUGH ITALIAN CAMPAIGN, the post-Manila operations on Luzon were conducted with forces that were being steadily reduced so that other commitments could be met, and were often fought in rugged terrain against a well-entrenched enemy. Krueger anticipated reconquering Luzon with the eleven divisions and four regimental combat teams under the Sixth Army's control in early February. To him the top priority for the use of those forces was the defeat of Yamashita's Fourteenth Area Army, but MacArthur had other plans. "It is possible that the destruction of enemy forces in the mountains of north and east Luzon," the SWPA chief informed Krueger on February 5, "will be time consuming because the nature of the terrain will probably channelize operations and limit development of full power." Until other objectives more vital were achieved, MacArthur concluded that "initially, hostile forces should be driven into the mountains, contained and weakened, and our principal effort devoted to areas where greater power may be applied." Instead of being able to launch decisive drives against the Shimbu and Shobu groups, Krueger soon found that, with his Sixth Army steadily drained of important combat forces, the most he could hope to accomplish in the spring and summer of 1945 would be to push Yamashita's units farther back into the mountains east and north of Manila, and, at the same time, attempt to inflict such heavy losses on them as to curtail their offensive striking power.

MacArthur shortly transferred the equivalent of three of Krueger's divisions to the Eighth Army, which inaugurated operations to retake the rest of the central and southern Philippines with an assault on Palawan on February 28. The 37th, which had suffered severely in the battle for Manila, was left on garrison and police duty in the capital temporarily, thus depriving the Sixth Army of another division. With his reduced forces, Krueger was expected to maintain pressure against the strong enemy forces south of Baguio and east of Manila and at the same time secure the extensive area from south of Laguna de Bay to the tip of the Bicol Peninsula. MacArthur was anxious to clear south Luzon for two basic reasons: (1) to secure the shoreline from San Bernardino Strait through the Sibuyan Sea, thereby enabling supply and troop ships from Leyte to use that route to Luzon, which was nearly 500 nautical miles less than the passage through the Sulu and South China seas; and (2) to establish a port and supply base on Batangas Bay to relieve the overburdened facilities at Lingayen Gulf and the supply situation at Manila, also setting up there a hospital center and a landing craft assembly plant, mostly for use in the invasion of Japan.

The wisdom of sending the Eighth Army southward rather than using it to expedite the reconquest of Luzon was highly questionable and, as will be discussed later, counter to the Joint Chiefs' intentions. The following description of the Luzon campaign is deliberately more detailed than has been usual of battle descriptions in this volume so that the reader may become aware of the crippling impact on the Sixth Army's operations that resulted from MacArthur's decision to send the Eighth Army to the south and reinforce it with units Krueger desperately needed.

Griswold's XIV Corps, reshuffled to include the 11th Airborne and 1st Cavalry divisions and MacNider's 158th Regimental Combat Team, was assigned the job of clearing south Luzon. The drive began the first week of March, and despite the little rest given the cavalrymen and airborne troops after the Manila battle, they advanced rapidly. The shorelines of Balayan and Batangas bays were seized against surprisingly light opposition. Stationed east of Lake Taal was a second-class Japanese force of about 13,000 men, most of them service and naval troops, whose primary mission was to keep the Americans from rounding Laguna de Bay on the east and hitting the Shimbu Group's main defenses east of Manila from the rear. In accordance with MacArthur's directive, however, the American thrust turned south toward Legaspi upon reaching Lamon Bay on April 10, rather than toward the north where the bulk of Yokoyama's Shimbu Group was positioned. The toughest fighting from Lake Taal to Lamon Bay occurred near Lipa, which fell on March 29, and during the mopping-up at Mounts Macolod and Malepunyo, which had been bypassed.

The Bicol Peninsula was occupied by a 1st Cavalry regiment advancing south and MacNider's troops moving north, the latter having made an unopposed amphibious landing at Legaspi on April 1. About ten miles inland, the 158th ran into fierce resistance at Daraga and was halted for a week. The enemy positions were finally overrun, and near Naga to the north MacNider's soldiers made contact with the 1st Cavalry on May 2, thus completing the seizure of the peninsula. Meanwhile, the islands of the Visayan Passages from San Bernardino Strait to Lubang, north of Mindoro, were being methodically secured by Eighth Army troops in a rapid succession of amphibious as-

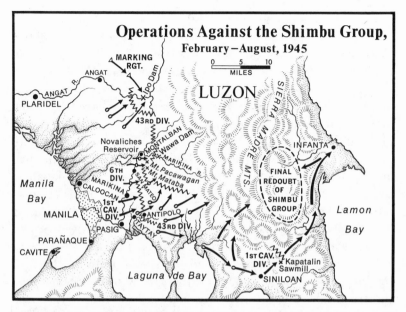

Operations Against the Shimbu Group,
February—August, 1945

0   5   10
MILES

LUZON

MARKING RGT.
ANGAT
ANGAT R.
PLARIDEL
Ipo Dam
43RD DIV.
Novaliches Reservoir
MONTALBAN
Wawa Dam
MARIKINA R.
6TH DIV.
Mt. Pacawagan
MARIKINA
Mt. Mataba
SAN MATEO
CALOOCAN
1ST CAV. DIV.
MANILA
ANTIPOLO
PASIG
TAYTAY
43RD DIV.
PARAÑAQUE
CAVITE

Manila Bay

SIERRA MADRE MTS.

INFANTA

FINAL REDOUBT OF SHIMBU GROUP

Lamon Bay

1ST CAV. DIV.
Kapatalin Sawmill
SINILOAN
Laguna de Bay

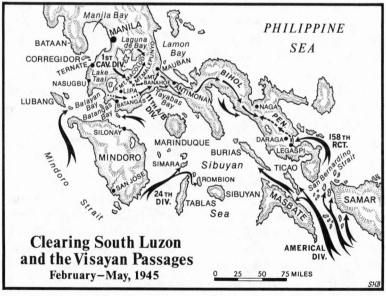

Clearing South Luzon
and the Visayan Passages
February—May, 1945

PHILIPPINE SEA

Manila Bay
MANILA
Laguna de Bay
Lamon Bay
BATAAN
CORREGIDOR
1ST CAV. DIV.
TERNATE
MT. MAQUILO
MT. LEPUNYO
MAUBAN
NASUGBU
Lake Taal
MT. MACOLOD
MT. BANAHOE
ANTIMONAN
BICOL
LUBANG
Balayan Bay
LIPA
Tayabas Bay
NAGA
BICOL PEN.
Batangas Bay
BATANGAS
11TH A/B DIV.
SILONAY
MARINDUQUE
DARAGA
LEGASPI
158TH RCT.
MINDORO
SIMARA
BURIAS
TICAO
San Bernardino Strait
SAN JOSE
ROMBION
24TH DIV.
TABLAS
SIBUYAN
Sibuyan Sea
MASBATE
SAMAR
Mindoro Strait
AMERICAL DIV.

SHB

saults. Elements of the 24th Division occupied Lubang at the end of February and some tiny islands east of Mindoro two weeks later. Units of the Americal Division made a half-dozen landings in March and April on northern Samar, Masbate, and several small islands in and near San Bernardino Strait. None of the Eighth Army amphibious operations engaged large enemy garrisons, but, as in south Luzon, the mopping-up was often time-consuming and costly. The campaign to secure south Luzon and the Visayan passages, bloodier than MacArthur had anticipated, cost about 300 American and over 8000 Japanese lives. A major supply base was already under construction at Batangas before the operations closed, and Allied shipping would rely heavily on the route through the Sibuyan Sea to resupply and reinforce the Sixth Army on Luzon.[1]

Griswold's XIV Corps also had the responsibility of holding the line against the Shimbu Group east of Manila. Elements of the 1st Cavalry and 6th divisions had held the line well during the battle of Manila, preventing Yokoyama's counterattacks from relieving the pressure on Iwabuchi's garrison within the city. (In fact, after taking the vital communications center of San Jose in early February, elements of the 6th Division had pushed through Bongabon to Dingalan and Baler bays on the east coast by the middle of the month.) Over 50,000 strong, the Shimbu forces held a line extending from Antipolo, east of Manila, northward to Ipo Dam — about twenty miles of heavily fortified positions on the western edge of the Sierra Madres. The Shimbu Group posed a triple threat to the Manila region because it was capable of launching a counterattack against the XIV Corps' thinly manned left flank or shelling the densely populated urban area with long-range artillery, and it already controlled some of the most vital installations of the city's water supply system. Ipo Dam provided about a third of the water for Manila's million or so inhabitants. The enemy also dominated the aqueducts to Novaliches Reservoir, and without that water supply only about half of the city's needs could be met from sources within the American lines. Erroneous G-2 data led MacArthur to conclude, however, that the key to the water system northeast of the city was Wawa Dam, which had actually been abandoned in 1938 after the completion of the Ipo and Novaliches installations. Apparently without consulting Filipino authorities, MacArthur told Krueger that it was imperative that both dams be taken as quickly as possible. Wawa was closer to Manila and seemed more crucial, so Krueger ordered Griswold to seize it, then advance on Ipo.

Since Patrick's 6th Division was thinly stretched along more than thirty miles of positions northeast of Manila and part of Mudge's 1st Cavalry was committed to the operations in south Luzon, the two commanders had available only about half of their divisions to employ in the drive to Wawa Dam. Against them in the Antipolo-Montalban area were approximately 30,000 of Yokoyama's troops, well armed and entrenched in terrain highly favorable to the defense. On February 20 the Americans launched their attack, crossing the Marikina River and quickly seizing the easterly side of the Marikina Valley from Pasig to Montalban. Since Wawa Dam lay less than four miles east of Montalban, it seemed at first as if the mission would be accomplished in short order. But as they drove into the foothills, the XIV Corps soldiers were stopped by intense fire. The 6th was pinned down about a mile east of Montalban by strong enemy positions on the slopes of Mounts Pacawagan and Mataba. The cavalrymen were halted in savage fighting west of Antipolo. Mudge was seriously wounded in the action, and Brigadier General Hugh T. Hoffman took over the 1st Cavalry. The Shimbu defenses incorporated numerous caves with interlocking fire on the sides of mountains and hills; in a two-day period the 1st Cavalry seized or sealed off 137 enemy-held caves, yet without showing appreciable progress in mileage. Renewing the assault on March 8–14, the Americans made some gains eastward in the middle of the line, but not toward Wawa. An enemy machine gun killed Patrick east of San Mateo on March 14; Brigadier General Charles E. Hurdis became the 6th Division's commander.

That night Hall, the XI Corps leader, arrived to take overall charge of the sector. This allowed Griswold to devote his attention to the campaign in south Luzon. Wing's 43rd Division, long embattled in the Damortis region near Lingayen Gulf, relieved the 1st Cavalry units on the right flank of the 6th Division. Hall ordered the attack renewed on March 15, but the fighting continued to be slow and costly. Gradually the Shimbu left flank began to withdraw northward, and by March 26 the 43rd Division was making considerable progress toward Wawa Dam from the south, though the 6th was still unable to make much headway from the west. As the Shimbu line was turned, a regiment of the 43rd Division swept eastward along the shores of Laguna de Bay and on April 6 made contact with the 1st Cavalry Division near San Juan at the eastern end of the large lake. In the Antipolo-Montalban sector from February 20 to March 26, 435 Americans died in action and about 7000 Japanese were killed. "Throughout the attack," states the official history, "XIV and XI Corps had been operating on shoestrings holding out scant reserves and expecting normal results from generally understrength units." In view of the Sixth Army units that MacArthur had transferred to the Eighth, it is doubtful that the American soldiers east of the Marikina River especially enjoyed hearing news of the quick, spectacular conquests of Eichelberger's forces south of Luzon.

While the 43rd Division turned south to mop up the area north of Laguna de Bay, the 6th Division resumed the attack against the Shimbu forces now backed up along the Marikina River south and west of Wawa Dam. Throughout April, the 6th fought from cave to cave and hill to hill in the rugged region, steadily pushing Yokoyama's defenders toward the dam. On April 30 the 38th Division, which had been mopping up the remnants of the Kembu Group in the Zambales Mountains, was brought over to relieve the exhausted 6th. From March 27 to April 30, the Americans had lost 175 dead and had killed about 3000 Japanese in the Wawa Dam area. Chase had his division resume the attack, but soon found his troops being counterattacked. American artillery and air strikes broke up the Shimbu counterattack, but through May 18 the 38th's gains were small and painfully achieved. Opening new attacks all along the sector front on May 19, Chase's units finally began to produce significant breakthroughs, and by the 22nd the Shimbu lines in front of Wawa Dam were disintegrating. On May 27 the 38th Division seized the dam and by the end of the month had pushed about two miles north of the Marikina. The cost to Chase's units in May had been 160 killed; they had wiped out approximately 3000 enemy troops, and many other Japanese defenders had been killed by artillery and air bombardments. The left, or southern, portion of the Shimbu Group had fewer than 5000 soldiers remaining and was finished as an effective fighting force.[2]

Before the Wawa operation had been completed, Hall had transferred the major part of the 43rd Division northward to start the drive on Ipo Dam because of the alarmingly critical water shortage in Manila. On April 19 MacArthur informed Krueger of the situation in the city and the need to press the attack:

> The low level of water in [the San Juan] reservoir now held by our forces has necessitated cutting daily consumption in Manila to one half and depriving [the] south side of [the Pasig] river of any city water except what is carried in tanks. Reduction in [the] water supply of Manila for an undeterminate [*sic*] period constitutes [a] very serious hazard to [the] health of the population and of American troops within [the] city. Many of

[the] inhabitants are driven again to drinking sewage-contaminated water from shallow wells because of [the] distance at which they live from water points. There is insufficient water for adequate cleanliness in restaurants and [a] resultant return to their filthy state of a month ago may be expected. Already many flush toilets are clogged with feces and an increase in [the] use of gutters, estuaries and vacant lots for defecation is inevitable. In summary, [the] water shortage is bringing back [the] danger of epidemic of enteric disease from which [the] city was apparently escaping. [An] outbreak of real magnitude might well prove a great military disaster. This situation will be remedied as soon as the reservoir in the Montalban area is secured. What is your estimate as to the time when this will be accomplished? [3]

Krueger responded, "Your [radiogram] . . . refers to reservoir in Montalban area. Do you mean Ipo Dam?" The Sixth Army commander now knew that Wawa Dam was not connected to the city's water system and was probably astounded that GHQ still had not learned it. Apparently for the first time, GHQ checked with the city's engineers and learned that Ipo should have been the objective from the start. On April 22 MacArthur told Krueger that Ipo was "the preferred objective." It was five days later that MacArthur, accompanied by Fellers, made a brief afternoon journey to the Marikina Valley to observe the operations in front of Wawa Dam.[4]

Ipo Dam was located on the Angat River about ten miles north of Wawa Dam. Most of the 7000 Shimbu troops guarding Ipo were in positions across Route 52, the principal approach to the dam from Manila. Wing stationed troops along a nine-mile front southwest of the dam, but planned to send his main strike force of two regiments to the right, or south, of Route 52. On May 3–5 a force of 238 Fifth Air Force fighter-bombers hit the Japanese positions southwest of Ipo with napalm and demolition bombs. Achieving surprise by starting with a night attack on May 5–6 and driving his units forward aggressively,

Wing was able to overrun or envelop some well-prepared enemy positions, and by the 15th his main force was approaching Ipo from the south. The Marking Regiment, a guerrilla unit, had been assigned to the operation, but Wing intended to employ it only in a feint from the north. The Marking guerrillas, however, proved to be excellent fighters and overran a number of Japanese positions north of Ipo Dam, setting up a race between them and the Americans moving up from the south. But the troops of the 43rd ran into the heavier opposition and had to hold up their advance until air strikes hit the enemy positions again.

On May 16–17 nearly 680 American fighter-bombers saturated the Japanese defenses with over 113,000 gallons of napalm, which according to the Army Air Forces' history, was "the largest mass employment of napalm in the Pacific war." A guerrilla patrol sneaked to the dam area briefly on the 14th, and both the Marking Regiment and the American 103rd Regiment reached Ipo in force on May 17. The guerrillas captured the dam. The Japanese defenders, after waiting too late to set off the demolitions they had placed at the dam, retreated northward into the Sierra Madres. Including the mop-up activities, Wing's units lost 120 men in the Ipo operation, May 6–31, and killed approximately 2700 Japanese. Had Ipo been given priority over Wawa, the water crisis in Manila might have been alleviated in March.

By the end of the Ipo operation, four of the five principal combat forces of the Shimbu Group had been badly mauled. The fifth, located between Laguna de Bay and Lamon Bay, had been steadily depleted by transfers to units engaged to the northwest and was down to about 2000 effective combat troops when the main American thrust came in that area. Elements of the 43rd and 1st Cavalry divisions cleared the region northeast of Laguna de Bay in small-scale operations from March 31 to June 18, losing seventy-five men and killing nearly 1500

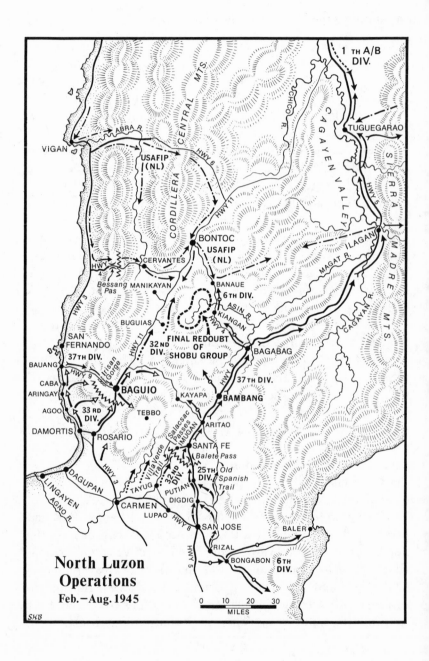

North Luzon Operations
Feb.–Aug. 1945

1 TH A/B DIV.

TUGUEGARAO

VIGAN

ABRA R.

USAFIP (NL)

HWY 6

CORDILLERA

CENTRAL MTS.

CHICO R.

CAGAYAN VALLEY

SIERRA MADRE MTS.

HWY 11

BONTOC
USAFIP (NL)

MAGAT R.

ILAGAN

HWY 5

CERVANTES

HWY 4

Bessang Pas

MANIKAYAN

BANAUE
6TH DIV.

ASIN R.

KIANGAN

MAGAT R.

CAGAYAN R.

BUGUIAS

SAN FERNANDO
37TH DIV.

HWY 11

32ND DIV.

FINAL REDOUBT OF SHOBU GROUP

BAGABAG

HWY 5

HWY 4

BAUANG

HWY 9

Ilisan Gorge

BAGUIO

KAYAPA

BAMBANG

37TH DIV.

CABA
ARINGAY

33RD DIV.

TEBBO

AGOO

Salacsac Passes

IMUGAN

ARITAO

DAMORTIS

ROSARIO

Villa Verde Trail

32ND DIV.

SANTA FE
Balete Pass

25TH DIV.

Old Spanish Trail

DAGUPAN

LINGAYEN

AGNO R.

HWY 3

TAYUG

PUTIAN

DIGDIG

BALER

CARMEN

LUPAO

HWY 8

SAN JOSE

RIZAL

HWY 5

BONGABON
6TH DIV.

0 10 20 30
MILES

SHB

Japanese. The principal action came at Kapatalin Sawmill north of Siniloan where 1st Cavalry troops were engaged for three days until the 650-man strong point was covered by napalm and artillery bombardments; it was then easily overrun on May 9. After a unit of the 1st Cavalry seized Infanta on Lamon Bay on May 25, the operation became largely a matter of mopping-up. Withdrawing deep into the Sierra Madres west of Infanta, the remnants of Yokoyama's once formidable Shimbu Group numbered about 15,000 in late June. Starving and disease-ridden, most of them were more concerned with hunting for food than engaging Americans or guerrillas in battle.[5] If Krueger had had the Sixth Army forces that MacArthur had given to the Eighth, his troops east of Manila undoubtedly could have brought the Shimbu Group to that shattered status much earlier.

In defending his triangular redoubt in north Luzon, Yamashita apportioned his principal strength in front of the two southern apexes, Baguio and Bambang, where he expected the main American assault to come. He stationed other forces in the region of the northern apex, Bontoc, and at Aparri and Balete Pass, the northern and southern gateways to the Cagayan Valley, whose rich agricultural resources he hoped to control until large food stocks had been transported to the Cordillera Centrals of northwest Luzon. Krueger's first plan of attack against the Shobu Group, by far the most powerful of the three major Japanese defense forces, was to employ four divisions of Swift's I Corps against the southern apexes: the 43rd, already in position between Damortis and Pozorrubio, and the 33rd, which arrived at Lingayen on February 10, in the drive against Baguio, now the Philippine puppet regime's capital and Yamashita's headquarters; and the 25th and 32nd divisions on the Bambang–Balete Pass front. Later he intended to land forces west of Bontoc and at Aparri to begin drives on the mountain defenses from those directions. The primary attack was to be on the Baguio front. The forces south of Bambang were to conduct a holding action until Baguio was secured. When in early February MacArthur ordered the redeployment of the 43rd Division to the area east of Manila, Krueger decided to make the major thrust against Bambang, relegating the 33rd Division to a holding position on the Baguio front. He hoped to move the 37th Division to the 33rd's front when the former was released from its garrison duty in Manila.

Fortunately he also had Volckmann's 18,000-man guerrilla force operating west, east, and north of Yamashita's defensive triangle. At first expected to be capable only of gathering intelligence and conducting minor raids, Volckmann's guerrillas, designated United States Army Forces in the Philippines, Northern Luzon, proved surprisingly effective in larger-scale operations. By late February the USAFIP(NL) guerrillas had secured much of the long shoreline from San Fernando, La Union, northwest of Baguio, on up the western coast and around the northern end of Luzon nearly to Aparri. Perhaps more significant, they had made impassable, by excellent demolitions work, several key Japanese communication routes into the triangular redoubt and controlled important portions of those routes.

Major General Percy Clarkson was not happy with his 33rd's holding role and, from mid-February, he vainly badgered Swift to give him support for an offensive, which was impossible at the time because of the Sixth Army's inadequate reserves. Nevertheless, for a month Clarkson's units conducted probing operations south and west of Baguio trying to find weak spots and the most traversable routes to the city. By the third week of March one column was gradually moving forward along Route 11, the main highway to Baguio, where resistance was expectedly heavy, and another was slowly pushing up a rugged mountain valley to the east. Astonishingly little opposition had been found along the coastal highway, Route 3, so Clarkson sent forces as far north as Bauang, which was seized on March 19.

There a unit of the 33rd started eastward along Route 9 toward Baguio, and two other units to the south began pushing inland along primitive roads and trails from Caba and Agoo. On March 23 Volckmann's guerrillas captured San Fernando, farther up the coast, and began driving toward Baguio from the northwest. Meanwhile, the supply situation of the Japanese troops on the Baguio front had seriously deteriorated because of the interdiction of supply lines by guerrillas.

A major turning point occurred during the second week of April when the largest portion of the 37th Division was dispatched from Manila to the Baguio front. The 37th took over the most promising breakthrough area, Route 9, and the 33rd pinned down the majority of the enemy units south and west of Baguio. Moving fast against light opposition along the highway northwest of Baguio, the 37th advanced to within four miles of Baguio before being stopped on April 17 by enemy defenses on the ridges above the Irisan River gorge. While the 37th was clearing the ridges overlooking the Irisan bridge, Yamashita, realizing the situation on the Baguio front was hopeless, quietly departed on the 19th for the Bambang front. (Laurel and some of the other Filipino puppet officials had long since left for Japan.) Having secured the Irisan gorge, the 37th pushed into Baguio against light resistance and captured the city on April 26. Advance troops of the 33rd arrived there the next day. During the previous week, however, over 10,000 Japanese troops south and west of the city had skillfully withdrawn from their positions unnoticed and escaped into the mountains to the northeast to avoid being trapped by the American pincers.

The American commanders were disappointed that so large an enemy force escaped, but they were still delighted that what was supposed to have been a holding action until the conquest of Bambang had resulted in the seizure of the important Baguio apex of Yamashita's defense triangle. Moreover, about 5000 troops of the Japanese division and independent brigade on that front had been killed; the Americans lost about 320 men. In early May, the 37th Division was transferred to the Bambang sector, and Clarkson's 33rd troops impatiently mopped up the area between Bauang, San Fernando, and Baguio. An excellent opportunity was missed when Krueger, always cautious, refused to allow the 33rd to push north on Route 11, for few Japanese were guarding the important Aritao supply road which intersected Route 11 above Baguio. In addition, Japanese sources confirm that, if Clarkson had been allowed to continue the drive, the retreating Japanese defenders could have been caught off guard and wiped out as they rested in hastily prepared positions to the north. All in all, though, there were no serious complaints at GHQ Manila about the situation in the Baguio sector since G-2 was not aware of the Aritao route or of the hapless enemy troops above Baguio.[6]

On the Bambang front, Swift planned to send Gill's 32nd Division northeast from Tayug along the mountainous Villa Verde Trail to Santa Fe, while the 25th Division, commanded by Major General Charles L. Mullins, Jr., was to launch a secondary attack north from San Jose along Route 5. Swift figured that the 32nd would reach Santa Fe first since the Japanese would expect an advance along the highway to the south and also would heavily fortify Balete Pass, two miles below Santa Fe on Route 5. Gill recalled elements of his division from the right flank of the 33rd Division, where they had been pushing up a mountain valley toward Baguio, and on February 21 the 32nd began its advance along the Villa Verde Trail. By March 5 it had driven northeast to the vicinity of Salacsac Pass No. 2, where it was stopped by fanatical enemy resistance. The Japanese were firing from well-prepared positions in extremely rugged terrain and were so situated that they could cover any movement along the trail. A fierce battle raged at the pass until the enemy resistance was finally broken in mid-April at a cost of 215 American and about 2500 Japanese lives. Supply and evacuation of the wounded became critical problems at the height of the fighting. By the time the pass was secured, one of Gill's regiments was shattered by combat casualties and a serious decline in morale and had to be relieved.

Next came Salacsac Pass No. 1 to the east, where again the Japanese opposition was savage. The pass was enveloped and isolated and was finally secured on May 24; even the effort to isolate the strong point took a heavy toll of the 32nd's ranks. On May 28 the exhausted, casualty-ridden division captured Imugan, only three miles from Santa Fe, but by that time the 25th Division had already reached the objective. Pitted against Gill's soldiers on the Villa Verde Trail had been a first-class force of nearly 9000, built around the reconstructed 2nd Tank Division, which, it will be recalled, had lost its tanks in the fighting on the Central Luzon Plain in January. The agonizing drive to Imugan had cost Gill's division 825 lives and the Japanese over 5700. The objective, Santa Fe, had not been reached, but the reinforced enemy division was finished as an organized fighting unit.

Unusually rough terrain, heavy rains, morale problems, logistical difficulties, and powerful enemy positions had slowed the 32nd's advance. Having fought from Buna on, including two months in the Ormoc Corridor of Leyte, the 32nd had had only two weeks' rest before being thrown into the offensive against Sante Fe. "By mid-April the only way Sixth Army could have markedly improved the situation on the Villa Verde Trail," states the official Army history, "would have been to insert a fresh division there." But, thanks to MacArthur's redeployment of units to the operations south of Luzon, Krueger was unable to provide even a reserve regiment to help the 32nd. After Buna, Breakneck Ridge, Villa Verde Trail, and several other tough operations in between, Gill's veterans were finally pulled out of the line for a well-deserved rest.

MacArthur had never been much impressed by the 32nd's efforts; he told Eichelberger in December that Gill's division "never had been any good." On the other hand, when interviewed by the Sixth Army G-2 shortly after his surrender in September, Yamashita "was asked what U.S. troops he considered the best during the Leyte operation. He replied: 'The 32nd Division.' Questioned as to the best U.S. troops encountered during the Luzon Campaign, he replied: 'The troops encountered in the vicinity of Salacsac.' " If the 32nd did not have MacArthur's esteem, at least it earned the highest tribute paid by Japan's ablest ground commander.[7]

Before the Santa Fe offensive began, Swift had expected the 25th Division to be able to advance only as far as Digdig, eleven miles north of San Jose on Routh 5, while the 32nd Division was to drive along the Villa Verde Trail to Santa Fe and turn south to Digdig. But, moving out from San Jose and Rizal on February 21, the 25th Division met only light resistance and captured Digdig on March 3. Another week or so of rapid advances brought Mullins' units to the steep, heavily wooded ridges just south of Balete Pass. They had reached the watershed from where streams flow south into the Central Luzon Plain and north into the Cagayan Valley. Two miles above Balete Pass lay Santa Fe, the gateway to the Cagayan Valley and the approach to Bambang. Guarding Balete Pass was the reinforced Japanese 10th Division, numbering about 10,000 troops and entrenched in well-concealed positions covering Route 5.

The battle for Balete Pass began on March 12 as two of the 25th's regiments attacked the ridges on either side of Route 5 and the third regiment undertook a wide flanking movement on the east along a primitive route called the Old Spanish Trail. For a month Mullins' forces were engaged in savage fights for ravines and ridge crests south of Balete Pass as hundreds of American soldiers died at places like Norton's Knob, Lone Tree Hill, and Kapintalan Ridge. A bitter stalemate developed, and Swift sent two regiments of the 37th Division from the Baguio area to help the 25th in early May. By then only about 3000 enemy defenders were left, but they continued the fight with fanatical desperation. Beginning on May 4, Mullins launched his final attack, sending enveloping columns around both flanks of the Japanese positions while another advanced up Route 5. By May 13 the pass was secured, and the Americans captured Santa Fe on the 26th. Three days later troops of the 25th Division made contact with Gill's 32nd soldiers near Imugan, west of Santa Fe, and completed the hard-fought operation.

Over 680 men of Mullins' division died in the drive to Santa Fe, including Brigadier General James L. Dalton, the assistant commander of the 25th Division, who was killed by sniper fire north of Balete Pass on May 16. The Japanese 10th Division was decimated, losing almost 8000 troops. Like Gill's division, the 25th had to be withdrawn from the lines after the Santa Fe offensive, having suffered greatly during the long, hard drive. Midway through the battle for Balete Pass, Mullins had felt compelled to withdraw his regiment moving along the Old Spanish Trail not just because it was needed elsewhere in the action but because the engineering problems along that route were too formidable for the few engineer troops available. Later studies indicate that if another division could have been sent along that trail, supported by sufficient engineer personnel and equipment, the conquest of Santa Fe might have been achieved more quickly and at less cost than by the Villa Verde Trail or Route 5. The Army's official chronicle concludes, however, that "in the end, as in the beginning, the only real solution to the problem facing I Corps would have been at least one more infantry division. As a result of General MacArthur's directive of early February, Sixth Army could make no more strength available to I Corps." [8]

Meanwhile, MacArthur and Krueger had been so pleased with the combat performances of the USAFIP(NL) guerrillas in northwest Luzon that in late March Volckmann received orders from Sixth Army headquarters to launch a drive toward Bontoc, the northern apex of Yamashita's mountain redoubt. On April 19 the guerrillas captured Vigan and started up the Abra Valley toward Cervantes, which lay seventeen miles southwest of Bontoc. The guerrillas engaged the Japanese 19th Division near Bessang Pass, just west of Cervantes, setting off a battle that lasted from early April until May 22, when the defeated enemy unit withdrew. About 120 guerrillas died in the action, but Volckmann's forces killed over 2200 of the enemy. After seizing Cervantes in late May, some of the guerrillas moved south and east in support of the I Corps' operations, and others continued to probe the defenses around Bontoc, then too strong to be overrun. Through mid-June a total of about 900 guerrillas had died in various engagements west of Bontoc, and an estimated 10,000 Japanese were killed. MacArthur commented later, "I estimated Colonel Russell W. Volckmann's northern Luzon guerrillas accomplished the purpose of practically a front-line division." [9]

As Yamashita began withdrawing and consolidating his forces deep in the Cordillera Centrals between Baguio and Bontoc, the 37th Division relieved the battered 25th at Santa Fe and began advancing north on Route 5. On June 6, only ten days after the fall of Santa Fe, the 37th occupied Bambang without a struggle. Except for a lone enemy division, which fought ineffectual delaying actions and finally fled in disorganized fashion into the Sierra Madres to the east, there was no obstacle along the 37th's path through the Cagayan Valley. The Americans seized Bagabag on June 10 and Ilagan in the middle of the valley on the 19th. Meanwhile, a ranger-guerrilla force captured Aparri on June 21, and two days later an 11th Airborne battalion parachuted onto the airfield nearby and secured it. The 37th Division reached Tuguegarao on June 25, by which time a guerrilla unit had already gained control of the town. The next day troops of the 11th Airborne and 37th divisions made contact about twelve miles to the north. The 37th then turned east and spent the rest of the war hunting down the Japanese who had sought refuge in the Sierra Madres.

At the southern end of Yamashita's mountain defenses in early June the 33rd and 6th divisions, the latter moving up from the Shimbu front, began clearing the area between Baguio, Santa Fe, and Bambang, finally meeting at Kayapa on June 27. Other elements of the 33rd, in the meantime, moved up Route 11 toward Bontoc. About twenty miles north of Baguio the 32nd Division relieved the 33rd at the end of June and resumed the drive up the western side of Yamashita's defensive perimeter. After they captured Bontoc on July 10, Volckmann's guerrillas launched a two-pronged drive. One prong was headed southwest and made contact with the 32nd on Route 11 on July 29; the other was directed southeast and met the 6th Division north of Banaue on July 23. The 6th Division had advanced against heavy resistance from Bagabag, capturing Kiangan, recently Yamashita's headquarters, on July 12. Heading northeast from Banaue, Volckmann's forces made contact with another guerrilla outfit moving west from the Cagayan Valley. By late July, the remnants of the Shobu Group were split into three pockets, two small ones east and southeast of Bontoc and a larger one containing many of Yamashita's remaining forces south of Bontoc in the Asin Valley. Gradually the lesser pockets were eliminated, but the Shobu defenses in the Asin region were strong and the guerrillas' and American troops' progress was slow. When hostilities ceased on August 15, elements of the 6th and 32nd divisions and USAFIP(NL) forces had Yamashita and his still savagely resisting troops surrounded in a rugged area of about forty-two square miles in the Asin Valley, eighteen miles directly south of Bontoc.

The Luzon campaign was the largest and bloodiest fought by MacArthur's forces in the war against Japan. Among ground combat forces only, from January 9 to August 15, 1945, about

8300 Americans, 1100 Filipino guerrillas, and 205,000 Japanese were killed in combat. That the Shobu Group was still full of fight in its final mountain stronghold was evident from the fact that during the last six weeks of the war 440 American and guerrilla soldiers were killed in north Luzon, the Japanese losing approximately 13,000. With slightly over 50,000 troops left in his Shobu units, Yamashita was prepared to continue hostilities until his supplies were exhausted; he expected them to run out in mid-September. He then planned to launch a counter-attack against the guerrilla lines on the northern edge of the perimeter and break out to a mountainous area farther north, where he hoped his men could replenish their food supply. If his forces were unable to penetrate the cordon in the September thrust, Yamashita intended to commit hara-kiri.

Whatever their fate would have been had the war continued until then, Yamashita and his soldiers, as the American Army history concludes, "had indeed executed a most effective delaying action." [10] Krueger, his commanders, and their troops, in turn, had engaged and defeated the largest Japanese army encountered during the war in the Pacific. Nevertheless, as the foregoing description of the Sixth Army's complicated, costly operations is intended to show, Krueger's forces were, time after time, severely handicapped in the execution of their missions for want of the units that MacArthur had peremptorily decided to assign to the Eighth Army for its reconquest of the rest of the central and southern Philippines. The SWPA chief may have paid only one brief visit to a Sixth Army front after the battle of Manila, but his shadow was cast over many Luzon battlefields, particularly Wawa Dam, Villa Verde Trail, and Balete Pass, where the lack of sufficient troops and firepower were sorely felt.

2. *Stirring the Cauldron of Philippine Politics*

As the Americans closed in on Baguio, the Japanese flew Laurel and some of his colleagues to Japan and allowed others of his puppet regime to depart from the city without restraint. In mid-April Roxas and three other ministers of the Laurel cabinet, as well as the chief justice of the supreme court, made their way from Baguio to the lines of the 33rd Division west of the city. On the 18th MacArthur had a special plane sent to fly Roxas to Manila, where the two friends enjoyed a reunion. The other four puppet officials were imprisoned to await trial as collaborators. The Manila *Free Philippines,* published by the OWI under the strict auspices of GHQ, announced that Roxas had been "liberated" and the 33rd had "captured four members of the collaborationist cabinet." A prewar political ally of Quezon, former speaker of the Philippine House of Representatives, and lieutenant colonel on MacArthur's Corregidor staff, Roxas found himself promoted to brigadier general and assigned to Willoughby's section. Soon after, on Roxas' request, MacArthur issued an order placing him on inactive status. Thus in rapid order the SWPA chief had arbitrarily placed his stamp of approval on Roxas as a Filipino patriot and United States Army officer and freed him to launch his campaign for the presidency of the Philippine republic. (It will be recalled that in 1944 Congress and the President had pledged independence to the Philippines on or before July 4, 1946. In the spring of 1945 it was anticipated that the presidential election would be held in Noember.)[11]

When Osmeña, having long feared that MacArthur would support Roxas' expected bid to unseat him, asked the SWPA chief why he had released Roxas but jailed the others, MacArthur replied, "We are detaining these men, without trial, because the war is still going on and their record proves they are potential threats to the military security of our armed forces in the Philippines. I have known General Roxas for twenty years, and I know personally that he is no threat to our military security. Therefore we are not detaining him." He later remarked that Roxas not only provided GHQ "with vital intelligence of the enemy but was one of the prime factors in the guerrilla movement." In his memoirs MacArthur stated, "There was never any question in the mind of President Quezon, or the guerrilla leaders, or myself, as to the exact role that Manuel Roxas played during the war. I was doubly certain because it was under my own personal orders that he stayed in the Philippines."

Citing the mission of Cruz, whom Quezon persuaded MacArthur to sneak into the Philippines in 1943 to confer with Roxas, the SWPA commander argued that Roxas' loyalty was "clearly proved" by his refusal to reveal to the Japanese the presence of Cruz in Manila, for which information "the Japanese government undoubtedly would have rewarded him highly, because Cruz was the man they most wanted." Although serving in several high positions in the puppet regimes of Vargas and Laurel, Roxas, according to his supporters, had headed the "Manila Intelligence Group," which fed to GHQ valuable information on the activities of the puppet officials and the Japanese. From the SWPA commander's viewpoint, Roxas' intelligence activities more than offset his work with the puppet regime. But, according to Roxas' critics, MacArthur initiated no investigation of the controversial Filipino's record during the occupation and no guerrillas could be found later to attest to Roxas' anti-Japanese work. A SWPA counterintelligence officer said he "tried to find Roxas' connection with the underground, but no one knew anything about it." The nature of Roxas' assistance to the guerrillas or to GHQ and his motivation in cooperating with the puppet government have never been finally determined.[12]

The Manila *Daily News,* owned by the Roxas family, repeatedly mentioned MacArthur's exoneration of Roxas. On August 26 it ran an editorial that stated that "the case of General Roxas, if there has been any touching on collaboration, has long been disposed of and that the General has already been cleared by no less an Army authority than General of the Army Douglas MacArthur." The editorial continued, "General Roxas was recognized as the leader of the underground, or guerrillas, in the Philippines during the Japanese occupation." The newspaper and Roxas' wealthy friends were engaged in promoting his presidential candidacy long before an election date had been set. Joaquin M. Elizalde, the rich landholder who had been dismissed as Philippine resident commissioner in Washington by Osmeña and would later become the republic's first ambassador to the United States, spent up to $200,000 in the following months in behalf of Roxas' candidacy. Soriano was said to have expended even more to support his campaign against Osmeña. Felixberto G. Bustos, a Manila journalist, turned out a flattering biography, *And Now Comes Roxas,* for which he was said to have been "paid handsomely" by his subject. It appeared several months before the election, which was postponed until April, 1946. MacArthur made no statements in direct support of Roxas' candidacy when he was in Manila or later in Tokyo, but his actions in April, 1945, effectively defused the collaborationist issue, which would have been an important weapon in Osmeña's campaign arsenal. MacArthur's esteem among the masses in the Philippines by 1945 was higher than that of any Filipino except perhaps the deceased Quezon, and it was obvious to all that Roxas had the general's blessing.[13]

During the spring and summer of 1945, despite a show of amenities, the estrangement between Osmeña and MacArthur grew as they found themselves differing over matters other than the Roxas situation. MacArthur tightly controlled the requisition and distribution of civilian relief supplies, mainly food, clothing, and medicine. Not only did no political credit accrue to the Philippine president from the relief program, but Osmeña, genuinely concerned about the plight of his suffering people, often learned, to his dismay, of ships with civilian supplies tied up in Manila harbor for long periods while the Army gave priority to the unloading of military cargoes. Of course, with a major campaign under way on Luzon, this situation was predictable, yet it grieved the Philippine president. He cabled the War Department on February 28: "Problems of relief and rehabilitation which are of staggering proportions face us . . . There are thousands and thousands of families without shelter and in rags, hunger and starvation are faced by millions."

MacArthur and his GHQ staff, nevertheless, performed a prodigious task in administering a relief effort in the Philippines that involved about $100 million worth of supplies obtained from Army stocks and Australia. Under the auspices of GHQ, a Foreign Economic Administration team promoted the sale of basic civilian supplies from the States at discount rates, the American Red Cross provided emergency funds and services, and volunteer organizations, including church groups and the Philippine War Relief of the United States, Inc., undertook substantial relief work. The United Nations Relief and Rehabilitation Administration sent supplies valued at one million dollars in early 1945, to be administered by MacArthur, and later added another $10 million. In August, upon the termination of hostilities, MacArthur relinquished his control over relief operations to the Foreign Economic Administration. By then Osmeña was complaining that his people immediately needed from the United States an additional $103 million in food, clothing, medical supplies, farm equipment, fertilizers, and construction materials. MacArthur was undoubtedly happy to be relieved of the burden.[14]

Osmeña's reputation was bruised when MacArthur authorized him to tell the veterans of the Philippine Army that they would get back pay of fifty pesos per month, but Washington set the amount at only eight pesos. And soldiers, ignorant of Washington's role, blamed the Philippine president. Another of Osmeña's grievances was the conditional release policy of SWPA counterintelligence, which by summer had over 5000 suspected collaborators in detention camps. On MacArthur's personal approval, a trickle of individuals was released pending trial by Commonwealth authorities. But the widespread impression among the populace was that they had been exonerated, and Osmeña appointed many of them to positions in his government; this did not please MacArthur or officials in Washington. Moreover, the Philippine president, it was said, believed that there was undue haste in the Army's hanging of seven Japanese and Filipinos who allegedly were caught in a plot to assassinate the SWPA commander.

Osmeña journeyed to Washington in the spring to plead his case for quicker independence, more relief assistance, and beneficial trade legislation. He returned to Manila in late May frustrated by the interminable delays in the working of the American Congress and federal bureaucracy, by the death of Roosevelt in April shortly after he had seemed to endorse the Filipino leader's proposals, and by President Harry S. Truman's apparent preoccupation with the multitude of other problems of worldwide importance which loomed as the European war ended and the United Nations Organization was born.

Osmeña was accompanied on his return by Senator Tydings, several economic advisers, and some members of the Filipino Rehabilitation Commission, who came to survey the Philippines' reconstruction needs. With the flurry of excitement sweeping through many influential quarters in Manila over Roxas' still informal presidential campaign, Osmeña felt that he was handicapped in his discussions with the Tydings group because they knew that he might well be out of office soon, what with MacArthur's unofficial endorsement and the wealthy backing of which Roxas boasted. Indeed, at a luncheon with two advisers among the visiting group and later with Tydings himself, MacArthur frankly expressed his displeasure with the Philippine president's leadership, stating "I can't work with Osmeña," yet praising Roxas as a worthy successor to Quezon. In early July, after the Tydings mission had returned to the States, reputedly sooner than expected, some American newspapers printed a rumor that MacArthur had advised Tydings to leave since the impasse between Osmeña and Roxas made it impossible to settle on a long-range reconstruction program until the presidential election was over. In a statement on July 5, MacArthur angrily denied the rumor as "unfounded and made without the slightest appreciation of the true facts which exist here." Tydings delivered a speech on the United States Senate floor also repudiating the story. But by then Osmeña undoubtedly believed the worst. When, later that month, Paul V. McNutt, head of the War Manpower Commission in Washington, former Philippine high commissioner, and a friend of Roxas', arrived for a visit in Manila, Osmeña suspected that he would be Truman's choice as high commissioner. Two months later McNutt was appointed to the position, thus giving Roxas another influential supporter.[15]

One of the few topics on which MacArthur, Osmeña, Roxas, and other Filipino leaders were agreed was that Generals Homma and Yamashita would be tried as war criminals, preferably in Manila. Representative Enrique B. Magalona, for example, told MacArthur that "it would be great" if they could be tried in the Philippine capital, adding, "The Filipino people would feel further indebted to you if this were done, for then it would serve as a vindication of the outrages and brutalities they suffered from the savage enemy." As early as July a war crimes section was established in the GHQ judge advocate's office, and dozens of Army lawyers were at work studying texts on international law and collecting oral and documentary evidence on atrocities. When it came to the fates of Homma and Yamashita, MacArthur would not disappoint the Filipinos, as will be related in the third volume of this work.

MacArthur and Roxas insisted that Osmeña complete the restoration of the Commonwealth government by convening the Philippine Congress. Elected in the fall of 1941, the legislature had never met. In the intervening years two members of the Senate had died, fourteen were said to have worked with the puppet regime, including seven now under arrest by SWPA counterintelligence, and the other eight had assumed neutral positions, none actively aiding the guerrilla cause. A Senate quorum would be impossible without the collaborators who were not under detention. Of the ninety-eight House members, thirty-one surviving representatives had held positions with the puppet government and seven of these were now under Army detention; about eight had died since 1941; with a few exceptions the rest, like the senators, had not engaged in anti-Japanese activities.

Although he realized that the collaborators would undoubtedly assume control of the national legislature, Osmeña, an unassuming, unassertive gentleman, as much as sealed his political fate by finally agreeing to summon the Congress. MacArthur provided Army vehicles and aircraft to transport the members from distant areas, including a number from the central and southern islands recently liberated by the Eighth Army. In fact, without Eichelberger's rapid reconquest of the Philippines south of Luzon, neither the Senate nor the House would have had quorums. As the Congress convened in Manila in early June, Osmeña's fears came true: Roxas was promptly elected president of the Senate, and hostile majorities in both houses set about obstructing legislative proposals from Malacañan Palace.

In Joint Resolution Number 2 on June 9, the first day of the special session, the Philippine Congress conveyed "the pro-

found gratitude of the Filipino people to General Douglas Mac-
Arthur and his gallant forces for the liberation of the Philippines" and resolved that, because he was "true to his plighted
word" in returning to free the islands and "in recognition of
this signal achievement and in deep appreciation of his unselfish
service as defender and liberator of the Filipino people, General
Douglas MacArthur be made, as he hereby is declared to be,
honorary citizen of the Philippines." [16] In Joint Resolution
Number 3, passed that same day, the Congress declared

> That in reverent appreciation of General Douglas Mac-
> Arthur, his name be carried in perpetuity on the company roles
> of the units of the Philippine Army and, at parade roll calls,
> when his name is called, the senior noncommissioned officer
> shall answer "Present in Spirit," and during the lifetime of the
> General, he shall be accredited with a Squad of Honor com-
> posed of twelve men of the Philippine Army.
> That coins and postage stamps to be determined by the Presi-
> dent having the likeness of General Douglas MacArthur shall
> bear the inscription "Defender-Liberator." [17]

Since MacArthur that day was observing the Australian amphibious assault at Brunei Bay, Borneo, and was quite busy the
rest of the month, it was not until July 9 that he could appear
before the Congress to express his gratitude for the honors.
Roxas introduced him as "one of the greatest soldiers of all
time." [18] The theme of the SWPA chief's fifteen-minute address
was the need for national unity. He stated, in part:

> You convene at a time when not only must your people re-
> dedicate themselves and all that is within them to the task of
> waging total war against our yet unconquered enemy, but at a
> time when many of your cities and towns lie ravished in the
> wake of that brutal enemy's retreat, with many thousands of
> your countrymen prostrate and in want. Thus the burdens
> upon you are heavy. It is absolutely essential that you operate
> without undue friction. Petty jealousy, selfish ambition and un-

necessary misunderstanding must not be permitted to impede progress and rend your country.[19]

Whatever unity in the Commonwealth government was achieved in the following months, however, came as a result of Osmeña's yielding under intense pressure from the Roxas-dominated Congress. On August 23 MacArthur released the 5000 or more Filipinos detained for security reasons, and the Philippine Congress passed legislation stipulating that upon payment of bail they could go free pending their possible trial later. Those who had been elected as congressmen in 1941 then took their seats in the national legislature, further strengthening the Roxas faction, and scores of detainees resumed their formal municipal and provincial offices. Paul P. Steintorf, the American consul general in Manila, offered his opinion in August to Secretary of State James F. Byrnes "that little or no action will be taken by [the] Commonwealth against collaborators and that [the] eventual result of MacArthur's action will be to strengthen Roxas in coming elections if they are held . . . Liberals, guerrillas and anti-collaborationists are very bitter over this matter" of generous treatment of "rich and powerful collaborators." Thorpe, the SWPA counterintelligence chief, remarked of Roxas and his colleagues, "Soon this group developed a well-organized propaganda campaign to persuade the world that all those who collaborated with the Japanese had done so only from the finest motives of patriotism and that the nation should really be grateful to them." They possessed "the money and positions of influence," he maintained, and "it didn't take long" before the Filipinos who had not collaborated "found themselves in a sadly unhappy situation."

Learning of the return of collaborators to positions of power, Ickes irately warned Osmeña in September of "the probable reluctance with which funds may be appropriated for relief, rehabilitation and support of the Commonwealth Government if it becomes generally believed that the Government has failed diligently and firmly to convict and punish those guilty of collaboration." But it was too late, for the power over Philippine national affairs had already passed from the mild-mannered Osmeña to the aggressive, collaborationist-controlled Congress. In August Osmeña sent to the Congress proposed legislation for a special judiciary body to try collaborationist cases, but it was autumn before a much-weakened version of the bill was finally passed. Lacking adequate funds even to transport witnesses, and possessing ill-defined guidelines on its duties and no definition of collaboration, the People's Court would eventually try only some cases, but few influential collaborators were ever convicted.

When Roxas defeated Osmeña in the election of April, 1946, to become the first president of the Republic of the Philippines, further prosecution of collaborators quickly ceased. The prewar reactionary elite was in control of the reins of government again, but in the following years, beset by corruption, economic difficulties, and peasant uprisings, they would sometimes find it difficult to enjoy their return to power. At first touted as an Oriental experiment in democracy, the Philippine republic actually seemed destined to failure before its formal creation in July, 1946.[20]

David Bernstein, an American political adviser to Quezon and Osmeña, later charged that, in arbitrarily exonerating Roxas, MacArthur "had determined the future course of Philippine politics." Elaborating in detail on each, Bernstein cited five charges against the SWPA commander:

1. He had hopelessly confused the collaboration question in the Philippines . . .

2. He had given the other collaborators, the puppet politicos and the buy-and-sell parasites, a powerful champion who dared to defend them publicly and effectively . . .

3. General MacArthur had added the great weight of his popularity to the Roxas cause . . .

4. General MacArthur had made inevitable the election of Manuel Roxas to the Presidency of the Philippines . . .

5. General MacArthur had made America's position seem stupid, irrational, and cynical . . .[21]

MacArthur was guilty of interfering in an explosive political situation in Manila, the full ramifications of which he probably in no way recognized. He was convinced, however, from prewar dealings with him that Osmeña was not the popular, forceful, enlightened leader that the Philippines needed during the critical reconstruction era. On that score MacArthur was probably correct, and Osmeña's defenders distort the picture in portraying him as a spokesman of the people against the elitist faction of Roxas. Actually, both Filipino leaders represented the same aristocratic interests that had long suppressed the peasantry. Widespread unrest might well have been the outcome if Osmeña had become the republic's first president, for it is unlikely that social justice would have been deemed very important in his regime.

If the Filipinos became cynical toward the United States, it was for causes more complicated and deeply rooted than MacArthur's sincere, if misguided, act of protecting an old friend. As part of the price of independence, for example, the American government required the Philippines to give ninety-nine-year leases on a number of military bases in the islands, and demanded an amendment to the Philippine Constitution providing the same commercial privileges for American businessmen as were enjoyed by Filipinos, while negotiating a trade agreement which, though of some benefit to the islands, protected certain American industries from Philippine competition. MacArthur may have blundered, but the postwar plight of the Philippines was really rooted in the unequal distribution of political and economic power within the nation and the lingering traces of imperialism in America's dealings with the new republic.

3. Rumblings from Down Under

The relief of the six American divisions that were containing bypassed enemy forces in Northeast New Guinea, New Britain, and the northern Solomons was gradually completed in the autumn of 1944 by various brigades of Lieutenant General Vernon Sturdee's Australian First Army, which amounted to the equivalent of three divisions. At Aitape in Northeast New Guinea, Cape Gloucester and Arawe in New Britain, and Torokina in Bougainville the Americans had established airfields, supply depots, and port facilities within rather closely defined perimeters. Except for limited patrolling, they had made no effort to seek out and destroy the large Japanese forces beyond the perimeters. MacArthur was proud of his strategy of bypassing large enemy forces, leaving them to "wither on the vine," instead of trying to clean them out at the cost of high Allied casualties and few strategic benefits. From November, 1944, through February, 1945, the Australians generally confined themselves to the passive role of guarding the perimeters, though they did engage in extensive patrolling, reconnaissances in force, and small-scale missions to gain more data about enemy strength and dispositions and to drive the Japanese out of certain garden areas where they had been obtaining food.

In March, 1945, however, the Australians in New Guinea and Bougainville launched offensives obviously aimed at destroying totally the opposing Japanese forces. In a report to the Australian War Cabinet on May 18, Blamey gave his reasons for accelerating operations against the bypassed Japanese: (1) Not having engaged in extensive probing, the Americans misjudged the lack of strength and passivity of the enemy forces, which actually were still powerful, self-sufficient, and, in the cases of those near Aitape and Torokina, actively hostile and dangerous. (2) Relegation of the Australian troops to passive guarding of the perimeters was "a negation of all military teaching and common sense." Blamey insisted that "it reduces the morale of the troops and leads to disciplinary troubles . . . It is a colossal waste of manpower, material and money . . . It reduces rapidly the resistance to tropical diseases and wastage of men increases rapidly. It encourages the enemy and gives him increasing influence and control over the natives." (3) At conferences with MacArthur in Manila on March 13–14, Blamey learned of the extensive plans for the Eighth Army's reconquest of the Philippines south of Luzon, and the Australian commander reached the following conclusions:

> On reaching the PHILIPPINES the "by-passing" policy of GHQ changed, and it was decided to free all the many of these [Philippine] islands completely from the enemy, although only a few of the bigger islands will be developed as bases for future operations against JAPAN. However, the reason given for the complete destruction of the enemy in these islands is to ensure the security of the bases in the PHILIPPINES. It would thus appear that the difference in GHQ policy between the PHILIPPINES and the rest of the SOUTH-WEST PACIFIC AREA is based on political rather than military grounds.
>
> Just as it is necessary to destroy the JAPANESE in the PHILIPPINES, so it is necessary that we should destroy the enemy in Australian territories where the conditions are favourable for such action, and so liberate the natives from JAPANESE domination. Were we to wait until JAPAN was finally crushed, it could be said that the Americans, who had previously liberated the PHILIPPINES, were responsible for the final liberation of the natives in Australian territories, with the inevitable result that our prestige both abroad and in the eyes of the natives would suffer much harm.[22]

On Bougainville Lieutenant General Stanley Savige's II Corps, consisting of the 3rd Division plus two brigades, launched drives to the north, east, and south from the Torokina–Empress Augusta Bay perimeter. The Japanese Seventeenth Army, earlier estimated by the Americans to have only 16,000 to 19,000 troops left, actually had about 42,000, including some naval troops. Although they outnumbered the Australians, the Japanese were seriously handicapped by starvation, disease, and shortages of supplies and munitions. Nevertheless, they fought back fanatically, suffering one defeat after another. Both sides committed their largest forces north of Buin in the southwest corner of Bougainville. At Slater's Knoll in that area the Australians defeated the Japanese in the principal battle of the campaign, an eight-day engagement in late March and early April during which over 600 enemy troops were slain. When the war ended, most of the remaining 24,000 Japanese were hemmed into the coastal areas around Buin, Kieta, and Bonis. The Australians lost 516 men killed in action on Bougainville, and about 8500 Japanese died in combat and nearly 10,000 of illness or starvation.

In Northeast New Guinea Major General Jack Stevens' 6th Division undertook a two-pronged drive, one along the coast toward Wewak and the other along the southern edge of the Torricelli Mountains toward Maprik. The Japanese Eighteenth Army, still 35,000 strong, yielded ground only after putting up stiff resistance, and sometimes tried limited counterattacks. By the end of April the Australian coastal force had seized Dagua, only twenty-one miles west of Wewak. In the interior the Australians had captured the Balif-Maprik area, where the enemy troops had been obtaining their chief food supply. Wewak fell on May 11, and the remaining Japanese fled inland. About 13,000 of them surrendered in August. In the New Guinea operations since the fall of 1944, the Australians had lost 422 soldiers killed, but over 16,000 others had been hospitalized with malaria and other tropical diseases. Approximately 9000 Japanese had been killed in combat, and over 13,000 died from malnutrition or disease.

Meanwhile, Major General Alan Ramsay's 5th Division secured the central and eastern portions of New Britain up to the Gazelle Peninsula where Rabaul is located. In several small amphibious operations, the Australians captured the shores of Open Bay and Wide Bay, then crossed the narrow neck of the Gazelle Peninsula, sealing off the Japanese Eighth Area Army by the end of March. Thereafter the Australians did not try to penetrate farther toward Rabaul since Blamey did not want to precipitate a major battle with the estimated 90,000 Japanese in the Rabaul vicinity. In contrasting this holding action with the offensives he ordered on Bougainville and New Guinea, Blamey later remarked that the New Britain operations were conducted "in accordance with the military principle: 'A detachment from the main forces is justified if it contains a force superior to itself.'" Fifty-three Australians and about 1000 Japanese were killed in the sporadic fighting on New Britain, but the Australian 5th Division would have been caught in an isolated, vulnerable position if the much larger Eighth Area Army had attacked. "Why General Imamura at Rabaul showed so little aggressive spirit," comments the official Australian history, "compared with General Hyakutake of the XVII Army on Bougainville or General Hatazo Adachi of the XVIII Army at Wewak remains a puzzle." [23]

Blamey was correct in his assessment that the Australians' assignment to the ignominious chore of containing the bypassed Japanese garrisons was destructive of his troops' morale. Judging from the following excerpt from the history of the Australian 42nd Battalion, however, they were not enthusiastic about offensive operations either:

> In the first place the [Bougainville] campaign was futile and unnecessary.
> At Salamaua men went after the Jap because every inch of ground won meant so much less distance to Tokyo. But what did an inch of ground — or a mile — mean on Bougainville? Nothing!

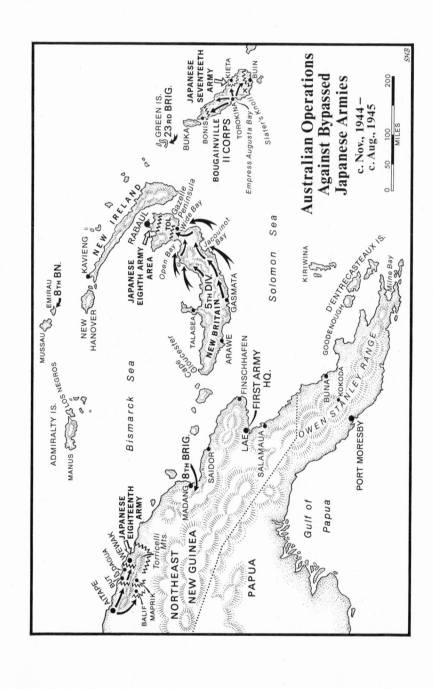

Australian Operations Against Bypassed Japanese Armies

c. Nov., 1944 – c. Aug., 1945

0   50   100   200
MILES

SHB

JAPANESE SEVENTEETH ARMY

KIETA

BUIN

GREEN IS.
23RD BRIG.

BUKA

BONIS

BOUGAINVILLE
II CORPS

TOROKINA

Slater's Knoll

Empress Augusta Bay

EMIRAU
8TH BN.

MUSSAU

NEW IRELAND

KAVIENG

NEW HANOVER

RABAUL

Gazelle Peninsula

TOL

Wide Bay

JAPANESE EIGHTH ARMY AREA

Open Bay

Jacquinot Bay

5TH DIV.

GASMATA

NEW BRITAIN

TALASEA

Cape Gloucester

ARAWE

Bismarck Sea

ADMIRALTY IS.

LOS NEGROS

MANUS

Solomon Sea

KIRIWINA

D'ENTRECASTEAUX IS.

GOODENOUGH

Milne Bay

FINSCHHAFEN

FIRST ARMY HQ.

LAE

SALAMAUA

SAIDOR

8TH BRIG.

MADANG

JAPANESE EIGHTEENTH ARMY

WEWAK

BUT

DAGUA

AITAPE

MAPRIK

BALIF

Torricelli Mts.

NORTHEAST NEW GUINEA

OWEN STANLEY RANGE

BUNA

KOKODA

PORT MORESBY

PAPUA

Gulf of Papua

Whether Bougainville could be taken in a week or a year would make no difference to the war in general. Every man knew this.

The Bougainville campaign was a politicians' war and served no other purpose than to keep men in the fight. They would have been much better employed on the farms, the mines and in building industries in Australia. Why they were not can only be answered by the few who decided that Australians must be kept in the war at all costs.

Every risk taken at Bougainville was one that could not be avoided; every life lost was begrudged. Men fought because there was no alternative. None wanted to lose his life on Bougainville . . . But despite all this men did fight and fought well.[24]

As Australian casualties increased, criticism in Australia mounted against the use of that nation's forces merely in mopping up bypassed enemy garrisons. Sir Robert Menzies, leader of the opposition in Parliament, raised the question of the usefulness of operations in areas that "cannot be regarded any longer as of primary military moment," emphasizing that it was "a matter which was gravely concerning his own mind and, he was quite sure, the minds of hundreds of thousands of other people." Menzies and his Conservative colleagues would have preferred that the Australian Army, or a portion of it, be dispatched to fight with other British forces in the probable reconquest of Malaya and Singapore. Curtin pointed out that under the SWPA international agreement MacArthur was given the authority to decide the deployment of the Australian forces assigned to his command. He added that it was to Australia's future political interests that her forces be used in occupying the territories for which she had been responsible before the war.

Turning its attack on Blamey, the parliamentary opposition charged that he was violating MacArthur's policy of simply containing the bypassed garrisons and was wasting Australian lives in strategically useless offensives. One senator claimed that there was "a widespread feeling of dissatisfaction and a lack of faith" in Blamey. Another senator sparked a new line of debate when he charged that their First Army was operating without adequate equipment and supplies although American supply depots nearby were brimming with items badly needed by the Australian combat forces. Others criticized the fact that the veteran 7th and 9th divisions of the Australian I Corps had been sidelined in Australia since the fall of 1943 and that, if they were not to be used, there should be a sharp reduction in Australia's military commitment to the Allies in order to meet pressing manpower needs at home.

Curtin, his ministers, and Labour leaders in Parliament steadfastly defended the policies of MacArthur and Blamey and blamed the logistical shortages on lack of shipping. The opposition was not satisfied, however, and the storm of controversy continued through the first half of 1945, centering primarily on the unfortunate Blamey. In a radio broadcast appealing for support of a war loan drive in April, Blamey used the opportunity for a counterattack against his critics in the newspapers and Parliament. Menzies said he was shocked by the general's "intemperate, unjust and misleading language." Another member of Parliament declared that Blamey's selection as leader of the Australian Army had been "the worst appointment made by the Menzies Government," which had preceded Curtin's Labour ministry.

MacArthur caught the brunt of Australian criticism of the nation's armed services. From the summer of 1944 through early January, 1945, there had been no mention of the Australian Army in the GHQ SWPA communiqués. According to a MacArthur-Curtin agreement, the GHQ announcements were to govern the limits of correspondents' news stories about SWPA operations, that is, they were prohibited from revealing any facts about operations that had not first appeared in the communiqués. Sometimes Australian newspapers had to quote

American or British papers which happened to get the information on an operation from news leaks, but all Allied news sources in the Southwest Pacific theater were supposedly under tight GHQ censorship. In early January, Blamey suggested to MacArthur that he should mention the Australian Army in his communiqués. MacArthur responded that he would be glad to cooperate and Blamey should watch for the release of January 9.

Amid a plethora of details about American ground and air operations in the communiqué of that date, there appeared the following meager recognition of Blamey's army: "Australian forces have relieved United States Army elements along the Solomons axis, in New Britain and British New Guinea. Continuous actions of attrition at all points of contact have been in progress. So far 372 Japanese have been killed, 20 captured and 10 friendly nationals recovered." As late as March 17 the Melbourne *Herald,* in publishing a résumé with maps of Australian operations in New Guinea and eastward, stated that it was "the first complete picture of where Australian troops are in action today." To the end of the war the GHQ communiqués never did justice to the Australian forces. The official Australian Army history states, "For Australia the results of the policies followed by G.H.Q. in the composing of its communiqués had, for three years, been most unhappy." [25]

As usual, part of the trouble arose from MacArthur's loose usage of the term "mopping-up." On April 21, 1945, for instance, Joseph Chifley, acting prime minister during Curtin's serious illness, forwarded to the SWPA chief a request from Archibald G. Cameron, a Conservative leader, who desired information relative to a debate in Parliament on the use of the Australian Army. Cameron asked Chifley to obtain a statement from MacArthur explaining

in what sense the Commander-in-Chief, Southwest Pacific Area (General Douglas MacArthur), uses the term "mopping up," and, in particular, in what sense he used it in his communique of 7th June last, in which he referred to "scattered mopping up" operations in New Guinea, and in what sense he used the term on 13th August when he referred to "final mopping up" in the Aitape area, in which we are still fighting, and what was meant in his communique of 16th February last in regard to the Solomons, and when he said "for all strategic purposes this concluded the campaign in the Aitape area."

MacArthur promptly but haughtily replied to Chifley:

> For your personal information, the military significance of the term "mopping up" implies the completion of the destruction or dispersion of all organised resistance in the immediate area of combat. The communiques to which reference is made are perfectly clear and completely accurate. Apparently the Aitape area has been confused with a sector below it where the Australian Forces are now engaged in what might be termed Wewak area. I do not believe it wise or advisable to permit myself to be drawn into what is fundamentally a political debate in Parliament. I am entirely out of touch with what is going on along these lines in Australia, and I suggest that the Government, which is completely informed and aware of the military situation and has available to it military advisers, take adequate steps to see that truth and justice are presented, in so far as the past campaigns are concerned.[26]

In early February MacArthur forwarded to Marshall a proposal to employ the 6th, 7th, and 9th divisions, comprising the Australian I Corps, in an invasion of North Borneo in April to obtain new sources of oil for the final operations against Japan. He proposed that the RAAF be the air component for the assault, thereby limiting the American commitment to the naval attack force and shipping. He requested permission to retain fifty-seven Liberty ships and ten troop transports for the invasion. In his opinion, "90 days after the beginning of such an expedition it would be possible to begin operations for the production of crude oil," though the Army-Navy Petroleum

Board in Washington estimated it would take at least a year to resume drilling and production. Yet at the Anglo-American conference at Yalta in the Crimea in February the Combined Chiefs agreed that, among other operations that might be undertaken in 1945 if the invasion of Japan had to be postponed until 1946, MacArthur's forces could go into "British Borneo," that is, Sarawak, Brunei, and North Borneo. However, because of a serious deficit of shipping in the Pacific engendered in part by the Iwo Jima and Okinawa operations, the Joint Chiefs were unable to approve MacArthur's shipping request.

Nevertheless, MacArthur continued to make plans and informed Blamey that, when adequate shipping was obtained and the Borneo operation finally approved, he wanted to use the Australian I Corps, but under the command of the American Eighth Army headquarters.[27] Blamey, who had tolerated the creation of the Alamo Force in 1943 and MacArthur's gradual assumption of the *de facto* position of Allied Land Forces commander since then, now reacted strongly. He protested to Shedden, the Australian secretary of defense, on February 19:

> You will recall that, on the establishment of the South-West Pacific Area, General MacArthur was appointed Commander-in-Chief and I was appointed Commander, Allied Land Forces . . . I have never operated as such.
> My requests for American officers to establish a joint staff were met with a face-saving acceptance that was completely ineffective . . . In fact, General MacArthur took upon himself the functions of Commander, Allied Land Forces and my own functions were limited to command of the Australian Military Forces.
> I have never raised this question definitely before, as I was always of the opinion that the Prime Minister and General MacArthur worked in close consultation and the former was fully informed of and acquiesced in the position . . .
> In the position which has now arisen, the Australian Army has been sharply divided into two components:

(a) The First Australian Army, which is dealing with the enemy elements left behind in the New Guinea and adjacent islands area.

(b) The First Australian Corps, which has been made available for offensive operations.

G.H.Q. S.W.P.A. asserts its authority to exercise direct control over the First Australian Army and . . . intends to assume direct control of First Australian Corps for operations now under consideration . . .

It is obvious to me that the intention of G.H.Q. S.W.P.A. is to treat my headquarters as a purely liaison element . . .

The insinuation of American control and the elimination of Australian control has been gradual, but I think the time has come when the matter should be faced quite squarely, if the Australian Government and the Australian Higher Command are not to become ciphers in the control of the Australian Military Forces.[28]

On February 27 Curtin wrote a tactful letter to MacArthur reminding him that the Australian 6th Division was fully committed against the Japanese Eighteenth Army near Wewak and could not be withdrawn for the Borneo assault without endangering the whole front in Northeast New Guinea. He also gently proposed that the Australian I Corps be placed directly under GHQ SWPA rather than be incorporated into Eichelberger's Eighth Army for the Borneo operations.[29] In a lengthy reply on March 5, MacArthur agreed to use only the 7th and 9th divisions, though he added, "I hope you will not eliminate entirely the possibility of using the 6th Division in the operation outlined above if it becomes a reality." He stated that he preferred Lieutenant General Leslie Morshead, the I Corps commander, to head the Australian task force, but insisted that he would have to relinquish his corps responsibilities: "It is essential that the Task Force Commander remain in the field with his troops and that he have no other duties of any kind." He agreed also to have the Australian force operate directly under him. At the same time he gave Curtin a glimpse of his purpose and plans in the East Indies:

> Current plans contemplate the elimination of the Japanese through a series of comparatively small operations in the central and southern parts of the Philippine archipelago, employing the United States Army troops that are now deployed in forward areas. Concurrently with the later phase of these operations it is proposed to attack Borneo and seize Java by overwater movement . . . For this operation I have planned to use the Australian Corps . . . operating according to the practice that has consistently been followed in the South-West Pacific Area under its own task force commander reporting direct to the Commander-in-Chief. It is estimated that the last phase of this operation, the assault upon Java, can be launched by the end of June . . .
>
> My purpose in projecting this campaign is to restore the Netherlands East Indies authorities to their seat of government as has been done within Australian and United States territory . . . It is contemplated thereafter that there will be a complete reorientation and that the British Empire and Dutch authorities will collaborate in the complete restoration of their respective territories.[30]

At their conference in Manila on March 13–14, Blamey and MacArthur worked out a compromise by which the I Corps would be directly under the SWPA chief but "the necessary administrative functions" would be handled by Blamey's advance headquarters on Morotai — a bit of face-saving for the ruffled Australian commander. Later Curtin asked Blamey's opinion of MacArthur's letter to him of March 5. The Australian general responded, "I regret that I cannot accept this as a sincere and complete statement of the matter" regarding the use of the I Corps. Blamey was also critical of MacArthur's plan, discussed in Manila, to invade the eastern coast of Borneo: "It would be the logical and strategically correct sequence in the following operations to move down the western coast of Borneo.

This would isolate all Japanese forces in Borneo, give a complete control of the South China Sea and facilitate the approach to Malaya."

Nevertheless, on March 18 MacArthur approved the first of six phases of the Oboe (East Indies) Plan, calling for the invasion of Tarakan Island off the eastern coast of Dutch Borneo on April 20. The rest of the Oboe operations which he endorsed shortly provided for landings at Balikpapan on May 18 (Oboe II), Bandjermasin on May 28 (Oboe III), Surabaya or Batavia on June 27 (Oboe IV), to be followed by the seizure of the rest of the Dutch East Indies (Oboe V) and British Borneo (Oboe VI), the target dates to be set later. Oboe III, the Bandjermasin assault, was to be undertaken only if carrier support could not be obtained for Oboe IV. Still hoping to draw the British Fleet into his theater's operations, MacArthur included the provision that if British fleet carriers were available, Batavia, rather than Surabaya, would be the Oboe IV target. Interestingly, although he had proposed only an invasion of North Borneo to the Joint Chiefs, the sole phase of the original Oboe Plan to include British territory was the last he intended to stage.

Despite a "lack of enthusiasm" for Oboe, Marshall finally agreed, and the Joint Chiefs in early April approved MacArthur's plan, which by then had been much amended and called for the invasions of Tarakan on April 29, Brunei Bay on May 23, and Balikpapan on June 15. Because of shipping difficulties and other factors, the target dates were later changed to May 1, June 10, and July 1, respectively. The Joint Chiefs, especially King, were still not enthusiastic about using the British Fleet in the forthcoming Okinawa operation. They sent the Oboe Plan to the British chiefs for their comments, pointing out that Brunei Bay would be an excellent base for the British Fleet in future operations against Japan and apparently hoping that the British would be lured into committing their fleet south of

Nimitz's area. The British chiefs, however, would not bite and responded that development of a naval base there would be a waste because their fleet had already been promised the use of Leyte Gulf and, besides, Singapore might well be captured before the Brunei base could be ready. Up until the actual invasion of Brunei Bay the British still thought the operation was useless. Blamey and Chifley found objections to the Balikpapan attack and tried in vain to persuade MacArthur against it, even threatening to withdraw the 7th Division from the Oboe operations.[31]

The factors that influenced MacArthur in developing the Oboe Plan in its various forms are still not fully known. Van Mook and other Free Dutch leaders had been promoting for some time a vague plan for reconquering parts of the Netherlands East Indies, especially Borneo and Java. King had long hoped that if the British insisted on deploying their navy in the war against Japan it could be used perhaps in the East Indies rather than in support of the American Pacific Fleet, but Churchill demanded that the British have a naval role in the main Pacific operations. Although Chifley and Blamey later had misgivings about the Oboe Plan, Curtin and Shedden appear to have favored the use of the Australian forces in seizing at least Borneo. In the eyes of the world and especially of Australian voters and members of Parliament, it would seem that Australia was again playing a significant role in the war against Japan. Indeed, there was a marked decline in Australian parliamentary and press criticism of the use of the Australian Army after the Oboe operations began.

MacArthur, who had toyed with the idea of using the Australian I Corps in the reconquest of the Philippines but later decided it was not needed, found that the Borneo scheme took some pressure off him to provide more active employment for Australian forces. Were MacArthur's stated reasons for seizing the bypassed areas of the central and southern Philippines taken to logical extremes, as Blamey was quick to do in justifying his March offensives in New Guinea and Bougainville, it would have been difficult for the SWPA chief to deny the arguments of van Mook or Curtin for the occupation of the East Indies for political reasons.

Of course, it is hard to imagine the Joint Chiefs, while possessed of some degree of sanity, approving an invasion of strongly held Java by two Australian divisions. Yet those same military sages yielded and approved MacArthur's plan to go into Borneo, fully knowing that the island's petroleum resources were not needed for the invasion of Japan and that the oil fields and refineries could not be rehabilitated before the war in the Pacific ended. On the other hand, if, during the height of the Luzon versus Formosa debate in 1944, the Joint Chiefs had foreseen that MacArthur would send his forces to reconquer all of the Philippines south of Luzon and then on to Borneo, they would have undoubtedly endorsed the King-Nimitz plan to attack Formosa instead.

From the fall of 1941, when he persuaded the Washington leaders to drop the long-accepted Orange Plan for the Philippines' defense in favor of his later aborted scheme, MacArthur had exhibited throughout the war an uncanny ability to persuade and influence both Roosevelt and the Joint Chiefs to his way of thinking, no matter what their common sense and detailed planning studies indicated. Without the support, sometimes emotional, politically motivated, or strategically unsound, offered by Roosevelt and Curtin, who died in April and July, 1945, respectively, it is unlikely that MacArthur's persuasiveness would have enjoyed such success. The future American and Australian chiefs, Truman and Chifley, did not have so high a regard for him as did their predecessors. It was most fortunate for the lives of the soldiers of the Australian I Corps, the prestige of the Joint Chiefs, and the reputation of MacArthur that the war was terminated before the SWPA chief got his way on the Java plan, for that two-division invasion could have produced the most tragic blood bath of the Pacific war.

4. Looking Ahead

OWI's Robert Sherwood, who visited MacArthur on March 10, 1945, reported back to Roosevelt that he "was shocked by the inaccuracy of the information held by General MacArthur and his immediate entourage about the formulation of high policy in Washington. There are unmistakable evidences of an acute persecution complex at work. To hear some of the staff officers talk, one would think that the War Department, the State Department, the Joint Chiefs of Staff — and, possibly even the White House itself — are under the domination of 'Communists and British Imperialists.' " Sherwood continued, "This strange misapprehension produces an obviously unhealthy state of mind, and also the most unfortunate public relations policy that I have seen in any theatre of war."

Although he did not place Marshall or Eisenhower in the above categories, MacArthur had become convinced since 1941 that those two generals headed a faction in the War Department that had conspired to deprive him of adequate logistical support and a greater strategic role. Encouraged in such thinking by some of his senior staff officers, he grew to be particularly resentful of the larger command, support, and publicity that Eisenhower, only a lieutenant colonel when he left Manila in 1939, was receiving. He attributed Eisenhower's opportunities and advancements more to Marshall's favoritism than to merit. On the other hand, Handy and Hull, the successive heads of the Operations Division, and Ritchie, chief liaison officer between the "Washington command post" and GHQ SWPA, all maintain that no anti-MacArthur faction existed in the War Department. According to them, Marshall, the other

Joint Chiefs, and their planners considered strategy and logistics as objectively as possible in terms of the tremendous global commitments of the United States and its allies. King and several of his admirals sometimes felt antagonistic toward Mac-Arthur, a feeling not infrequently prompted by Sutherland's arrogant, tactless behavior when he was in Washington, but none of the Army's high-ranking staff in Washington conspired against MacArthur's personal interests or his theater. Hull could recall only one occasion, in early 1945, when Marshall "said anything negative about General MacArthur in my presence." Marshall "felt that MacArthur had kept on constantly harassing him even when he knew what he wanted was not available." In this instance, says Hull, the Army chief of staff "drafted a bitterly frank reply to him. He then asked me what I thought of the reply. I said that it would aggravate the situation, so Marshall tore it up."

MacArthur could foresee that, just as Pershing and his lieutenants dominated the high echelons of the Army for years after World War I, Eisenhower and his European commanders, thanks to Marshall's help, would become the chiefs of staff and principal decision-makers of the Army high command for a long time after World War II. The SWPA chief thought such a development would be likely to result in few desirable appointments for his staff and in a neglect of America's defenses in the Pacific, which did become true later.[32] His attitude toward Marshall and Eisenhower, especially the latter, is evident in the following comments that Eichelberger recorded in his diary or in letters to his wife after conversations with Mac-Arthur:

> November 26, 1943: [MacArthur] thinks Geo. Patton will be remembered for 100 years as the man who struck a soldier; said he was washed up and that it would prevent Ike Eisenhower from being Chief of Staff. Said there was a crooked streak in

Ike and George Catlett Marshall which would show up in a long war . . .

January 2, 1945: The Big Chief thinks that Ike's reputation as well as Bradley's will be dimmed quite a bit because of this German penetration [during the Battle of the Bulge] . . .

March 3, 1945: [MacArthur] said he felt that Eisenhower's curve had gone down since last summer and he is not now considered the great leader he formerly was. He also agreed with me that the American public would not give the American Army on the Rhine credit for these victories but would give it to the pressure of the Russian troops from now on . . .

July 13, 1945: The Big Chief was very friendly but seemed to be depressed . . . He talked of Ike Eisenhower . . . and said there was no question in his mind now that he could have Chief of Staff if he wanted it. He remarked that he couldn't understand why we have received such an unfriendly press.[33]

In the last year of the war, MacArthur's personal feelings sometimes showed in his messages to the War Department. For example, on January 27, 1945, he radioed the Army's adjutant general that he was agreeable to the proposed use of his name in promoting a war bond drive by the Treasury Department "provided it is accorded proper relative position among Army signers. In your message you have reversed the signature of Eisenhower and myself based upon our relative rank. I presume this is merely a clerical mistake, but if it is intentional I do not care to have my name included."

Marshall and Eisenhower seem to have largely restrained their reactions to the former chief of staff's extreme sensitivity and fears of a conspiracy. However, when Hunt's adulatory *MacArthur and the War Against Japan* appeared in 1944, revealing for the first time in print some of the SWPA chief's views, Eisenhower could not resist recommending it to Marshall for "bedtime reading." Eisenhower commented, "You will be quite astonished to learn that back in the Winter of '41/42, you and your assistants in the War Dept. had no real

concern for the Philippines and for the forces fighting there —
indeed, you will be astonished to learn lots of things that this
book publishes as fact. I admit that the book practically gave
me indigestion, something you should know before considering
this suggestion further." [34] For the most part, at least, Mac-
Arthur confined his negative opinions to a few confidants, but
several of them, including Hunt, would harm his reputation
almost irreparably by echoing and sometimes exaggerating his
views in their published writings, all in the name of defending
the Old Man's honor.

On one subject of growing interest — unification of the
American armed services — MacArthur, Marshall, Eisenhower,
and most other Army leaders were in agreement: they favored a
postwar department of defense. MacArthur's position had
changed entirely since 1932 when, as Army chief of staff, he led
the fight against a congressional movement to force unification
as an economy measure. He was enthusiastic about the idea by
1945, especially after experiencing the need for unity of command in the war against Japan; yet thirteen years earlier he had
warned, "No other measure proposed in recent years seems to me
to be fraught with such potential possibilities of disaster for the
United States as this one." When MacArthur changed his
mind on a subject, the difference was not unlike the conversion
of Saul of Tarsus.

Mashbir, the able, energetic head of ATIS who became Mac-
Arthur's aide during the latter part of 1945, said that the topic
came up one evening after dinner with the SWPA chief. Someone asked the general what he would do with the armed services if he "were in complete and sole charge." According to
Mashbir, MacArthur replied, "First, I would call in every
officer over fifty, load him with honors, and retire him. There
would be no officer in the Army over fifty. Second, I would
maintain twenty-five full combat divisions, each division
equipped with the air power to transport it anywhere in the
world in fighting condition. Third, I would abolish any dif-

ference in the uniforms between the services. They would all be one service."

Extensive hearings on the subject of unification were conducted in 1943 by the Woodrum Committee of the United States House of Representatives, which decided to forgo further action pending the termination of hostilities. Little more was heard publicly on the issue for a time, though a four-man committee appointed by the Joint Chiefs continued to study the matter and gather opinions of the theater commanders and other senior officers. The committee reported to the Joint Chiefs in April, 1945, that almost all Army and Army Air Forces officers and about half the naval officers interviewed, including Nimitz and Halsey, supported consolidation of the services after the war. Except for its chairman, Admiral J. O. Richardson, who had commanded the Pacific Fleet on the eve of the war, the committee itself favored "a single department system of organization of the armed forces."

Before the spring was over, however, many formerly pro-unification naval officers turned against the idea largely because of three developments in April that made them suspect that the Navy would be the chief loser in the consolidation. With Roosevelt's death the admirals lost a President who had always been known to be partial to their service. Truman, a field artillery officer in World War I, had been outspoken in favor of the War Department's plan of unification long before he moved to the White House. Shortly after Truman succeeded to the presidency, his military aide, Major General Harry Vaughan, told a group of prominent Washingtonians, "During the Roosevelt administration, the White House was a Navy wardroom; we're going to fix that!" Another event disturbing to the admirals was the creation of the Twentieth Air Force, whose principal elements were the B-29 squadrons in the Marianas. The Twentieth was controlled directly by Arnold on behalf of the Joint Chiefs, although its major bases and targets lay within Nimitz's theater. But most upsetting to some naval leaders was a Joint Chiefs' directive reorganizing the Pacific command structure and turning over to MacArthur control of all Army ground and service forces in the Pacific as well as all Army Air Forces units there except the Twentieth. "It thus appeared to the Navy leaders," says one authority, "that as soon as the Navy's cooperation in Europe was no longer necessary, the Army was rejecting the principle of unity of command if it could not appoint and control the unified commander." [35]

The Pacific command alterations in April, 1945, resulted from the Joint Chiefs' growing realization, as plans for the invasion of Japan were formulated, that the structure created in 1942 was now obsolete. The northern SWPA boundary ran just above the Philippines, so under the directive of March, 1942, Nimitz would have complete charge of operations against the Japanese home islands. The War Department was unwilling to have MacArthur shunted aside during what promised to be the greatest ground campaign of the Pacific war, or to entrust its armies and air forces to the leadership of an admiral through the invasion of Japan. Marshall and his planners maintained that military resources under the previous command arrangement in the Pacific were so rigidly compartmentalized that they had not been utilized with maximum efficiency. Instead, the system had produced waste and overlapping, and at times the struggles between MacArthur's and Nimitz's headquarters for control of forces and bases had been detrimental to coordination of the two theaters' prosecution of the war, as in the controversies over the South Pacific service troops and base developments in the Admiralties and Philippines.

If such tugs of war and misunderstandings should occur during the climactic assault on Japan, the results could be disastrous. In addition, both Richardson, the Army commander in Nimitz's theater, and the War Department officials had been deeply displeased with the way the Army had been subordinated to the Navy in the Central Pacific theater in matters

ranging from planning decisions at the Pearl Harbor headquarters to supply distribution and conduct of combat operations. Most Pentagon leaders of both services agreed that the
best solution would be a single commander for the Pacific war,
but, as in 1942, service rivalries and differences over personalities continued to make unity of command an impossibility.[36]

From the late fall of 1944 on, some of the same influential
individuals and newspapers that were earlier involved in the
MacArthur-for-President movement had been promoting anew
the creation of a single command in the Pacific with, of course,
the SWPA chief as its head. MacArthur was without doubt
eager to lead the invasion of Japan and had long criticized the
lack of a unified command in the Pacific war.[37] Apparently
realizing that King and his admirals were not going to budge
and allow his appointment to such a position, MacArthur made
his move on December 17, 1944, for control of all Army forces
in the Pacific while still retaining his SWPA command. He
wrote to Marshall:

> I do not recommend a single unified command for the Pacific.
> I am of the firm opinion that the Naval forces should serve un-
> der Naval Command and that the Army should serve under
> Army Command. Neither service willingly fights on a major
> scale under the command of the other . . . The Navy, with al-
> most complete Naval Command in the Pacific, has attained a
> degree of flexibility in the employment of resources with con-
> sequent efficiency that has far surpassed the Army. It is essen-
> tial that the Navy be given complete command of all its units
> and that the Army be accorded similar treatment. Only in this
> way will there be attained that complete flexibility and efficient
> employment of forces that is essential to victory.[38]

(In talks with the Joint Chiefs' committee on unification of the
services and in later statements, however, he employed what
was almost the reverse of the above argument to support unity
of command.)

For a time King and his naval planners stubbornly defended

the existing arrangement, which gave Nimitz control over the assault against Japan. The War Department, on the other hand, took a firm position similar to MacArthur's, and gradually the admirals began to yield. Whether Roosevelt influenced the Joint Chiefs on this is not known, but Kenney, who was in Washington in March, said that when he met with the President on the 20th, Roosevelt remarked as he departed, "You might tell Douglas that I expect he will have a lot of work to do well north of the Philippines before very long." King's final effort to stave off capitulation to the Army was a proposal to create a third Pacific theater, designated Japan Area, so that at least the operations against Japan would be under a single commander. The generals countered that this would merely lead to more organizational complications and further inefficient compartmentalization of resources.

Finally, a compromise of sorts, though generally considered an Army triumph, was worked out, and on April 3, 1945, the Joint Chiefs issued a new Pacific directive. MacArthur was designated commander-in-chief of United States Army Forces, Pacific (AFPAC), and he was given control over all American Army and Army Air Forces units and resources in the Pacific, except those in the inactive North and Southeast Pacific subareas and the Twentieth Air Force units in the Marianas. Both MacArthur and Nimitz were to retain their current theater command positions. All naval resources in the Pacific, except those in the southeastern region, were to be under Nimitz, and the Marianas-based B-29's, as well as those in the CBI theater, would continue to be controlled by the Joint Chiefs through Arnold. By determining future strategic objectives, assigning missions, and deciding command responsibilities for major operations, the Joint Chiefs would act as the supreme command for the Pacific war, as had been true in the past.

The directive further provided that Nimitz would be responsible for naval operations and MacArthur for ground operations. In a supplementary directive that same day, the Joint Chiefs instructed Nimitz and MacArthur to complete their respective operations in the Ryukyus and the Philippines under the terms of the previous directives. The transition to the new command system was to be gradual and "by mutual agreement," thus opening the way for new disagreements over MacArthur's assumption of control over Army forces on Okinawa and the Pacific Fleet's use of Philippine bases. Nimitz was directed to make plans for a possible assault on the Chusan-Ningpo area of the Chinese coast and for the naval and amphibious phases of the assault on Japan; MacArthur was to occupy North Borneo and prepare plans for the ground attack against Japan; the two commanders were to coordinate their planning and preparations. Like the Formosa plan earlier, the Chusan-Ningpo proposal was quietly dropped in the following months.

Since he was already Pacific Fleet commander, Nimitz actually gained little or no new authority. He was to get the Seventh Fleet eventually, but MacArthur kept it busy in the southern Philippines and off Borneo until August. The main forces that would go to MacArthur were Lieutenant General Simon B. Buckner, Jr.'s Tenth Army, which was then locked in heavy combat on Okinawa and would not be formally transferred to AFPAC until August, and Major General Willis H. Hale's Seventh Air Force, which was transferred under Kenney's Far East Air Forces in July. AFPAC was officially established on April 6, with MacArthur's Army staff at GHQ SWPA constituting the new headquarters personnel. Henceforth official business designated SWPA dealt almost solely with MacArthur's jurisdiction over the Australian and Dutch forces.

Although he retained operational control of all AFPAC forces, MacArthur established two new commands, mainly to handle Army administrative and supply matters: Army Forces,

Western Pacific (AFWESPAC), commanded by Lieutenant General Wilhelm D. Styer, formerly Somervell's deputy chief in the Army Service Forces, and set up with headquarters at Manila on June 1; and Army Forces, Middle Pacific (AFMID-PAC), created July 1 and headed by Richardson with headquarters at Honolulu. Styers' command was, for the most part, a consolidation of the functions of Frink's USASOS and Marshall's USAFFE, which were dissolved. In July the Combined Chiefs decided to enlarge Mountbatten's Southeast Asia Command to include all of the Netherlands East Indies, but the arrangements had not been made final when hostilities ceased.[39]

The Joint Chiefs' April directives did not include a new logistical plan for the Pacific, perhaps because logistics was one of the thorniest, most complicated aspects of the war against Japan. "Agreement on broad principles had been hard enough to reach," states the Army's official chronicle, "and any effort to spell out the details would have delayed agreement indefinitely." In mid-April, representatives of MacArthur and Nimitz met at Guam to try to reach a consensus on the redeployment of military resources in the Pacific. Sutherland, Chamberlin, Kenney, and several other GHQ staff officers represented SWPA. Sutherland, head of the SWPA delegation, wanted to get an immediate settlement of the time for the Army resources under Nimitz's control, including those on Okinawa, to be turned over to MacArthur. The Okinawa battle was only two weeks old and was developing into the bloodiest of Nimitz's operations, with no end in sight. The admiral's representatives were understandably not in the mood to talk about releasing any resources at that stage. Moreover, the Central Pacific leaders claimed the separation of Army and Navy resources at their bases would be extremely complicated and Army service units at bases on Guam, Saipan, and the Palaus would have to be held indefinitely.

Kenney said that the "jurisdictional problems" were "so

complicated that the dates and methods of transferring" forces and installations "could not be settled at that conference." Nimitz reported to King that "very little useful discussion has taken place concerning invasion plans and preparations, and the SWPA party was apparently not prepared for such discussion." [40] Nevertheless, the talks at Guam did produce the following general principles to govern the redeployment of resources, subsequently endorsed by MacArthur and Nimitz:

1. General MacArthur and Admiral Nimitz would immediately assume administrative command of their respective services.

2. Each would release operational control of all forces of the other service, except those considered essential to the functioning, development, or defense of their respective geographical areas or to the success of previously scheduled operations. Resources to be released by each commander would include depots and supply systems of the other service.

3. Each commander would assume as rapidly as possible full supply responsibility for the forces of his own service.

4. The existing army and navy responsibilities within the Pacific Ocean Areas for the joint support of positions in the Marshalls, the Carolines, the Marianas, and the Ryukyus would continue in effect until modified by mutual agreement.

5. Both commanders would establish as quickly as possible their respective command organizations necessary for the planning and conduct of the phases pertaining to the invasion of Japan.[41]

MacArthur and Nimitz found a disproportionate amount of their time absorbed in working out the many details involved in the transfer from one command's control to the other of forces, equipment, supplies, military installations, port facilities, and, especially troublesome, shipping. Nimitz journeyed to Manila in mid-May and again in early August to confer with MacArthur on these problems as well as on preliminary planning for the invasion of Kyushu, though the latter was com-

plicated by the failure to solve the issues involved in the redeployment dispute. From April on, sharp disagreements arose
between the Manila and Pearl Harbor headquarters over the
transfer of resources, the Joint Logistics Committee wrestled
with the matter in Washington, and still the final redeployment of many units and much matériel had not been settled
when the war ended.

MacArthur also faced insurmountable difficulties in trying
to roll up his rear bases, which were no longer essential. The
War Department expected him to bring forward from his
southern bases to the Philippines by early fall over 800,000
men, mostly service troops, and about four million tons of
cargo. He complained that he lacked the necessary shipping in
view of the continuing operations in the Philippines and East
Indies. King and Nimitz were opposed to the idea of using assault ships, such as LST's, for the roll-up movement, which was
one proposal for expediting the procedure. In addition, Mac-
Arthur found that, again because of continuing operations,
base development in the Philippines was lagging, and he did
not feel that he would be able to stage from the Philippines the
thirty or more divisions that the War Department planned to
send there for the invasion of Japan. General Courtney H.
Hodges and some of his First Army staff landed in Manila during the first week of August; the famed outfit that had played
a key role in the defeat of Germany was expected to be arriving
in force soon to start preparations for the invasion of Japan.
In June, before the movement of troops from Europe was
under way, MacArthur's AFPAC command already comprised
over 1,400,000 troops, but by December the War Department
expected it to be increased by another million.[42]

In early June, the Joint Chiefs reshuffled the Army Air
Forces' organization in the Pacific, designating General Carl
Spaatz, veteran leader of the bomber offensive in Europe, to
head the Strategic Air Force, which would include the re-

grouped Twentieth Air Force and the Eighth Air Force, soon scheduled for deployment in the Ryukyus. The headquarters was to be in Guam. On a tour of Pacific air bases that month Arnold made his second visit to MacArthur, which was only the third call on him by a member of the Joint Chiefs since the war began. (The other was by Marshall in late 1943). Arnold was in Manila on June 16–19 and recorded in his diary some random notes of a "long spirited talk with General Mac-Arthur" on the 17th, which, though mainly about air force matters, are revealing of the AFPAC commander's views and problems at that stage:

(a) MacArthur is for a separate Air Force, including all air except that operated from strips, even including that supporting ground troops.

(b) He is willing to organize Army Air in Pacific along these lines now.

(c) He will be satisfied with either Kenney or Arnold as C.G., but not Spaatz.

(d) His logic is not quite clear unless I am in another league for he says that there cannot be two dominant characters in the Pacific like Kenney and Spaatz.

(e) He does not want a Supreme Commander.

(f) He says he is satisfied with J.C.S. directive as to command.

(g) He resents Navy holding back on turning over Islands and supply system.

(h) He feels that Navy is building up a post-war organization and laying plans — completing facilities for such an organization now.

(i) He thinks that Navy gives a special course of instruction to all officers that insures loyalty to Navy first and anything else second.

(j) He knows that my Strategic Air Command organization is wrong — O.K. if I keep command — O.K. if Barney [Giles] is my Deputy — but 100% mistake if command goes to Guam.

(k) Believes that bombing can do lot to end war but in final analysis doughboys will have to march into Tokyo.

(l) As far as moving his Headquarters to Guam for coordination and cooperation are concerned, the lid blew off — there was every reason why it should not be done, not one good reason for doing it.

(m) He did not understand our plan for employing B-29s in Japanese operations, destruction of 30 Jap cities and their industries, 200,000 tons for a month to destroy targets in invasion area and 80,000 tons on invasion day. He liked it.

(n) Can see no reason why we should not use gas right now against Japan proper. Any kind of gas. Sees no reason for gassing Japs in by-passed areas.

(o) Was somewhat surprised at our B-29 build up to maximum strength.

(p) Did not understand relationship of 20th Air Force to J.C.S. Neither did Sutherland.

(q) He gets excited and walks the floor, raises his voice — I thought that I was one of the few who did it.

(r) He recognizes the necessity for Army having its own supply system all the way through from U.S.

(s) He will not fight for control of Island bases.

(t) Sees Navy trying to take over Strategic Air Force and by so doing dividing Army and Air Force, and thus stopping a Department of National Defense with 3 equal sub-divisions.[43]

MacArthur, indeed, had a lot on his mind that day — and every day by the busy summer of 1945, when everything he dealt with from logistics to strategic planning seemed to be in a state of expansion or acceleration. Surely and rapidly, all activities in the Pacific war from Pearl Harbor to Manila to Tokyo were racing toward an unexpectedly quick climax.

CHAPTER XVII

South to Borneo,
North to Tokyo

1. Detours from the Road to Japan

NIMITZ'S FORCES had been called upon to "crack some hard nuts" from Tarawa and Kwajalein to Saipan and Peleliu, but even those battles were surpassed in ferocity by the Central Pacific campaigns during the first half of 1945. The capture of Iwo Jima, only 775 miles from Tokyo, took Lieutenant General Holland Smith's V Amphibious Corps of three Marine divisions from February 19 to March 16 (excluding some costly mopping-up). Nearly 7000 Marines and about 21,000 Japanese troops died on Iwo Jima. The airfields that were quickly constructed on the island proved their worth in the ensuing months as bases for long-range fighters escorting bombers to Japan and as emergency stops for over 2200 crippled B-29's, carrying about 25,000 crewmen, which made forced landings there returning from Japan. The only SWPA connection with the Iwo Jima operation was a negative one, mentioned earlier: MacArthur withheld a number of Pacific Fleet ships until it was too late for them to participate in the pre-assault bombardment, and thereby added to the ill will the Marines generally felt toward him.

The invasion of the Ryukyus — Okinawa, Ie Shima, and the Kejama Islands — was by far the bloodiest campaign of the Pacific war. Against the 120,000 Japanese on Okinawa Nimitz sent Buckner's Tenth Army, which was composed of Hodge's XXIV Corps, including the Leyte veterans of the 7th and 96th divisions, and Major General Roy S. Geiger's III Amphibious Corps of two Marine divisions. Later two reserve divisions also had to be committed to the fray. From the amphibious assault on April 1 until the island was declared secure on June 21 (followed by another ten days of mopping-up), the Okinawa campaign took the lives of about 13,000 American and 110,000 Japanese servicemen and approximately 42,000 Okinawa civilians. After Buckner lost his life in action on June 18, Geiger took over command of ground operations. Kamikazes enjoyed disheartening success off Okinawa, sinking twenty-six Allied ships and damaging another 368.

Although most of his squadrons were occupied in attacking targets in the Philippines, Kenney sent a number of strikes against Formosan ports and airfields before and during the Okinawa invasion, which took some pressure off Nimitz's forces. The SWPA contribution also included assistance in the training and staging of the XXIV Corps on Leyte. Hodge's troops departed for Okinawa on a sour note, however, when it was found that SWPA stocks in the Philippines were unable to provide the thirty-day allotment of rations and other troop supplies that MacArthur had pledged to Nimitz and Hodge. LST's loaded with reserve stocks from the Marianas had to be sent in haste to meet the corps as it landed on Okinawa.

In the aftermath of the blood bath on Okinawa, MacArthur dropped remarks to a number of officers and journalists indicating his displeasure with what seemed to him the expensive, wasteful manner in which the operations had been conducted. On one occasion he pointed out that the casualties on Okinawa "exceed the entire American losses in the SWPA from Melbourne to Tokyo." [1] He remarked to Major General James G. Christiansen, who later became AFWESPAC commander:

> The way they handled the fighting on Okinawa was awful. The Central Pacific command just sacrificed thousands of American soldiers because they insisted on driving the Japanese off the island. In three or four days after the landing the American forces had all the area that they needed, which was the area they wanted for airplane bases. They should have had the troops go into a defensive position and just let the Japs come to them and kill them from a defensive position, which would have been much easier to do and would have cost less men. [2]

MacArthur made similar comments to many visitors, but such criticism, however valid, eventually got back to Nimitz and contributed toward making the final weeks of the war the most tense period in their relations.

Confusion abounded in Washington, Manila, and Guam, Nimitz's new headquarters, about the time and the extent of MacArthur's assumption of control over the Ryukyus. At first it was planned that Lieutenant General James Doolittle's Eighth Air Force, coming from Europe, would be stationed on Okinawa, but in mid-July the Seventh Air Force, now led by Major General Thomas D. White, one of Kenney's former commanders, also began moving to that island, followed shortly by the FEAF advance headquarters, commanded by Whitehead. When Doolittle stated in a speech before a Tenth Army assembly that "one supreme headquarters" was needed in the Pacific war, the Tokyo *Nippon Times* on August 7 quoted a United Press report that said, "It is believed that Doolittle's address was approved by the censor of the MacArthur Headquarters" and that "War Department officials accepted Doolittle's statement with silent surprise."

In a communiqué two days earlier, GHQ AFPAC announced that the Ryukyus and Philippines now constituted "a great semi-

circular base which is being forged under the primary responsibility of General MacArthur for the final conquest of Japan."
The next day Nimitz countered with a tart statement of "clari-
fications" pointing out that the naval facilities on Okinawa as
well as the huge fleet in the waters off that island were still definitely under his command, not MacArthur's. The *Nippon
Times*, pouncing upon the news release, proclaimed on August
10, "The situation surrounding the command of the American
forces in the Pacific area has further been confounded by publication by the Nimitz Headquarters on Guam of a statement
denying that the bases in the Okinawa Islands have been turned
over to General MacArthur." [3]

Appointed head of Army Ground Forces headquarters in
Washington in January, 1945, Stilwell had been restless and
anxious to return to the war against Japan. In early May he
proposed to Marshall that he make a trip to the Pacific to survey
the commanders' needs. Stilwell wrote in his diary of his final
discussion with the Army chief of staff on May 10: "[Marshall]
had nothing to offer except that I could go & make my own arrangements . . . Doug obviously out of control; W. D. [War
Department] afraid of him." Stilwell toured some of the Central Pacific bases on his way to Manila, where he conferred with
MacArthur on May 26. The two had known each other since
their days together at West Point, and MacArthur had earlier
voiced his opinion that Stilwell's relief as CBI commander in
late 1944 had been an injustice to an able leader. According to
Stilwell's biographer, "MacArthur greeted him cordially and in
character: he made a speech. 'Says he wants a friend to speak
up for him.' He urged Stilwell to go everywhere, see everyone,
talk to Krueger and Eichelberger . . . make suggestions and
give him ideas."

After three weeks in the Philippines and a trip to Okinawa,
Stilwell paid his farewell call on MacArthur as he prepared to
return to Washington on June 18. The AFPAC commander

asked him if he would be willing to serve as his chief of staff, but Stilwell replied, "No, I fancied myself as a field commander." (Sutherland was ill and MacArthur had asked Eichelberger to be his chief of staff earlier that month, but the Eighth Army commander had refused on the same grounds as Stilwell.) When MacArthur inquired if Stilwell, now a four-star general, would be agreeable to commanding an army under him, the Army Ground Forces head responded that he would take a division just to be in charge of troops again. MacArthur responded, "If you would take an Army I would rather have you than anyone else I know." He added that when he could get control of the Tenth Army he wanted Stilwell to command it since Buckner was too strongly influenced by Nimitz. Stilwell departed later that day by air for Guam, where upon landing he learned the news of Buckner's death on Okinawa. He sent a radiogram to MacArthur informing him of where he could be reached and continued on to Hawaii.[4]

On June 19 Marshall radioed MacArthur:

> Reference CINCPOA [Nimitz] message 18th of June requesting you [to] designate [a] suitable general officer for 10th Army. These experienced commanders are available as indicated:
> Stilwell, now in Western Pacific, could be made available immediately. Now here in United States and could leave practically as quickly as air transportation could be made available: Patch of 7th Army, Truscott of 5th Army, Patton of 3rd Army. These that would be available in the United States in not to exceed 10 days: Simpson of 9th Army, Devers, 6th Army Group commander.[5]

MacArthur replied immediately:

> I plan, if you approve, to assign Lieut. General Oscar W. Griswold to command Tenth Army and to dispatch him immediately to Okinawa. He is eminently qualified in every respect for this assignment, having served with great distinction in extensive operations against the enemy in this theater and being completely familiar with the problems involved in amphibi-

ous warfare. He is, moreover, intimately acquainted with the personnel in the theater, including many of the officers of the Tenth Army. The vacancy in the Fourteenth Corps will be filled by Major General Roscoe B. Woodruff, who will be succeeded in the Twenty-fourth Division by Major General Frederick A. Irving.

If this command arrangement is not satisfactory, my preference for officers from outside the theater listed in your radio would be first Stilwell, second Patch, and third Truscott.[6]

Marshall curtly notified the AFPAC commander on June 20, "I have directed Stilwell to assume command of Tenth Army, reporting without delay to Admiral Nimitz at Guam." The next day the Army chief of staff radioed MacArthur, "[The] War Department will make no announcement of Stilwell's assignment. Since Geiger's assumption of command has already appeared in the press and 10th Army is now operating under Nimitz, would it not be appropriate for Nimitz to make the announcement on Stilwell? This is a suggestion only and you are free to handle the matter as you think best." MacArthur promptly issued a communiqué proclaiming the appointment and radioed Stilwell, "My heartiest welcome to the ranks of AFPAC," though acknowledging to him that the Tenth Army "is now under the operational control of CINCPOA."

The Baltimore *Sun* on the 23rd reported that "the surprise announcement from Manila that MacArthur had selected 'Vinegar Joe' Stilwell to command the 10th Army was interpreted here today as further indication of MacArthur's tightening grasp on the top Pacific command and the emergence of a 'MacArthur team' for the final assault on the Nipponese." [7] Whether MacArthur and Stilwell, two of the most strong-willed commanders in the American Army, would have been able to work together harmoniously through the invasion of Japan will have to remain a matter of interesting conjecture.

Some American newspapers claimed subsequently that MacArthur had "banned General Patton from his theater." Mac-

Arthur issued a statement denying it, and the Hearst papers rallied to the AFPAC chief's defense stating that "General Mac-Arthur has been subjected to the necessity of refuting another of the mysterious and slanderous attacks upon him, to which he has been a particular prey throughout the present war." Mac-Arthur had commented to Eichelberger in March that he would not take Patton because he "could do brilliant things but was erratic to say the least." On August 3 Marshall offered Mac-Arthur four distinguished commanders of the European theater "where it appears desirable to you to change command" of any AFPAC divisions: Major Generals Maxwell D. Taylor of the 101st Airborne, Anthony C. McAuliffe of the 103rd Airborne, James M. Gavin of the 82nd Airborne, and Robert T. Frederick of the 45th Infantry Division. MacArthur replied: "The divisions at present in AFPAC are magnificently officered not only as regards commanders but going down through all general and field ranks. I believe, moreover, that in view of the splendid record of the four general officers you named that careful consideration should be given to their appropriate assignment to redeployed divisions." [8]

As early as September, 1944, MacArthur had determined that if it were at all possible he would send the Eighth Army into the central and southern Philippines after a firm hold was established by the Sixth Army on Luzon. At the Yalta Conference in February, 1945, the American Joint Chiefs informed their British counterparts that they had no intention of dispatching major American forces to conquer the rest of the Philippines and the East Indies. Marshall, according to one authority, told the British chiefs "he assumed that the Filipino guerrillas and the newly activated Army of the Philippine Commonwealth could take care of the rest of their country, and that Anglo-Australian forces would recover the N.E.I."

Yet at the same time MacArthur was busy working on the Oboe Plan for the invasion of the East Indies and the Victor

Plan for the reconquest of the remainder of the Philippines. The Joint Chiefs finally approved three of his six proposed Oboe assaults on Borneo, but the seizure of the central and southern Philippines was well under way before their April directive retroactively authorized his liberation of the rest of the archipelago. By the time of that directive MacArthur had presented the Joint Chiefs with a fait accompli on Palawan, Zamboanga, Tawi Tawi, Basilan, Panay, Guimaras, Negros, and Cebu; the only new invasions in the Philippines after the receipt of the directive of early April were those on Jolo, Bohol, and eastern Mindanao.[9] The definitive history of American naval operations in the war states:

> It is still somewhat of a mystery how and whence . . . MacArthur derived his authority to use United States Forces to liberate one Philippine island after another. He had no specific directive for anything subsequent to Luzon. He seems to have felt that, as Allied theater commander in the Southwest Pacific, he had a right to employ the forces at his command as he thought best for the common cause; certainly he went ahead with his plans. And as Seventh Fleet and Eighth Army were not urgently required at Iwo Jima . . . or Okinawa . . . the J.C.S. simply permitted MacArthur to do as he pleased, up to a point.[10]

Astoundingly, neither the Joint Chiefs nor the War Department raised any question or objection to the eight amphibious operations executed prior to the April directive. The unauthorized initiation of his Victor Plan was surely MacArthur's most audacious challenge to the Joint Chiefs during the war, but neither he nor they seem to have regarded his action as an affront to them. It is little wonder that the same commander less than six years later would act with insolence toward his superiors in Washington.

MacArthur's reasons for launching operations in the bypassed Philippine islands appear to have been based on a mixture of political, humanitarian, personal, and strategic factors. Especially in view of the Palawan massacre in December, he and the Commonwealth officials were concerned lest the bypassed enemy garrisons turn with vengeance upon the hapless Filipino civilians of the central and southern islands. Abandonment of those Filipinos to such dangers for the lengthy period required to complete the conquest of Luzon could further tarnish America's image in the islands and in Asia generally. Roxas and other Commonwealth leaders may well have pointed out, too, that discrimination against the citizens of those islands in favor of the citizens of Luzon, particularly in Manila, who had been liberated, would undoubtedly produce a hostile political reaction later from the south, where there had long been a sense of inadequate voice in the affairs of the Commonwealth. In addition, as previously mentioned, Roxas' faction was exceedingly anxious to have the congressional representatives from the south liberated, so that quorums would not be lacking in the Philippine Senate and House at the June session. MacArthur himself had said on several occasions that he was returning to liberate the Philippine Islands — not just Leyte, Mindoro, and Luzon — and he seems to have felt a strong obligation to free all of the archipelago, especially since some American prisoners of war were believed to be in camps to the south.

As Blamey had argued for the active employment of his troops, it seemed from the GHQ viewpoint that the morale of the men not involved in the Luzon campaign could best be sustained by engaging them in operations. In general, the officers of Eichelberger's units welcomed participation in the southern operations; they provided good experience and training for their troops, who were expected eventually to invade Japan. The employment of the Eighth Army, Seventh Fleet, and Thirteenth Air Force south of Luzon, moreover, removed the possibility of their transfer by the Joint Chiefs to Nimitz's theater, a likelihood had those large forces remained idle for long. MacArthur felt that the tremendous influx of divisions from Europe, due in the Philippines for training and staging in the invasion of Japan, could not be accommodated only on Luzon, Leyte, and Mindoro, and he wanted more bases for the redeployed units, especially at good ports such as Iloilo, Cebu City, and Davao. Once he decided to attack Borneo, MacArthur had sound strategic reasons for seizing Palawan, the Sulus, and Zamboanga: he could establish air bases on them that would cover the Borneo operations. The closest other fields were on far-off Morotai. Speed in construction was essential because he wanted to have the airfields completed before the rainy summer season arrived.

As for the remaining central and southern islands of the Philippines, where, as it turned out, the principal fighting would occur, the official Army history maintains that they "had no strategic importance in the campaign for the recapture of the Philippines and the East Indies, but pressing political considerations demanded their immediate recapture as well. These subsequent offensives would be directed toward the seizure of Philippine real estate as such. They were designed for the purpose of liberating Filipinos, re-establishing lawful government, and destroying Japanese forces." [11]

In the rapid-fire series of amphibious operations from February 28 to June 25, fifty-two landings were made on various islands of the central and southern Philippines, fourteen of which could be considered medium to large operations. In contrast with Krueger's plight on Luzon, where his attacking units were sometimes outnumbered by Yamashita's strongly entrenched defenders, the 68,000 enemy troops to the south, remnants of the Thirty-fifth Army, were usually scattered in small garrisons, and only about 30,000 of them could be considered combat-effective. The best of the enemy units was the 30th Division on Mindanao, but it had lost half its troops in the Leyte campaign. The only well-prepared defenses were at Zamboanga and Cebu City; the rest of the garrisons expected to be left in their bypassed state until the war's end.

Since SWPA and guerrilla intelligence accurately estimated the enemy's weakness, it is hard to understand why MacArthur, except that he wished the operations to be concluded speedily, committed five divisions — the Americal, 24th, 31st, 40th, and 41st — and the separate 503rd Parachute Regimental Combat Team to the Eighth Army's operations south of Luzon. He knew that the Sixth Army was in urgent need of reinforcements. Some heavy fighting erupted on Cebu, Negros, and Mindanao, but most of the operations quickly developed into mopping-up activities. The principal problems were in the complicated planning of the many landings because the amphibious commanders had available only a limited number of assault craft and combat support ships.

For the reconquest of the Philippines south of Luzon, MacArthur vested command in Eichelberger of the Eighth Army and Sibert of the X Corps for ground operations, Kinkaid of the Seventh Fleet and Barbey of the VII Amphibious Force for the naval and amphibious phases, and Wurtsmith of the Thirteenth Air Force, Brigadier General Earl Barnes of the XIII Fighter Command, and Colonel Carl A. Brandt of the XIII Bomber Command for air support, with some assistance from Whitehead's Fifth Air Force. Rear Admirals Noble, Struble, Fechteler, or Forrest B. Royal usually headed the amphibious group for a particular landing, and Rear Admirals Berkey or Ralph S. Riggs led the covering group of cruisers and destroyers. The divisional commanders were Major Generals Rapp Brush of the 40th, William H. Arnold of the Americal, Woodruff of the 24th, Doe of the 41st, and Martin of the 31st.

The operations, particularly the many minor ones, usually followed the regular pattern: Staging from Leyte or Mindoro, the amphibious assault was made with little or no opposition at the beaches; the Japanese garrison would have withdrawn into the mountainous interior. The Americans would pursue the enemy for a while in hope of precipitating an all-out en-

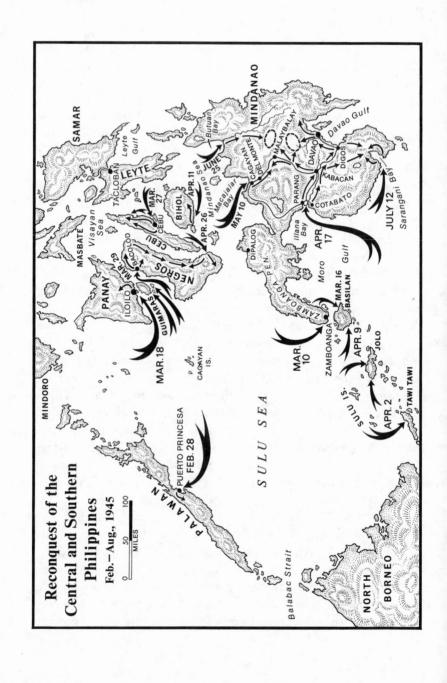

Reconquest of the
Central and Southern
Philippines
Feb. – Aug., 1945

gagement in which the Japanese force could be destroyed. Usually the enemy was too elusive, however, and only small fire fights developed. Eventually most of the American troops were withdrawn, leaving the mopping-up to guerrillas. There were several organized guerrilla units in the central and southern islands, and especially large ones on Mindanao, Panay, Cebu, and Negros. Some of the mopping-up was still under way when hostilities terminated in mid-August, but, meanwhile, in the liberated areas civil affairs had been taken over by Commonwealth officials, a semblance of law and order had been restored, and normal economic and social activities had been resumed as much as possible.

In the first of the whirlwind operations a regimental combat team of the 41st Division landed at Puerto Princesa, Palawan, on February 28. Enemy opposition was light, but about a week later a short, savage fight erupted in the hills about ten miles north of the harbor. Mopping-up activities lasted until late April, by which time ten Americans had been killed, and about 900 Japanese, half of the defending garrison, were dead. Because of poor soil conditions, airfield construction proceeded more slowly than expected; fighters were using the Puerto Princesa strip by late March, but it took much longer to construct an all-weather runway for bombers.

On March 10 two regiments of the 41st Division went ashore against light resistance and quickly captured the city of Zamboanga. Opposition by the 8900-man Japanese garrison stiffened, however, as the Americans advanced into the hills overlooking the Zamboanga airfield, and it required three weeks of arduous fighting by American and guerrilla troops to drive the Japanese farther north so that the airfield could be rehabilitated for American planes. Then the operation entered the mopping-up stage. About 220 Americans and 6400 Japanese died in the Zamboanga campaign.

Elements of the 41st Division invaded the Sulu Archipelago,

which stretches between Zamboanga Peninsula and North Borneo, long before organized fighting had ended in the Zamboanga operation. The Sulu landings, involving nine small amphibious assaults usually of company size, began on March 16 when American troops went ashore unopposed on Basilan, the northernmost of the Sulu chain. Seizing other small islands one by one, the 41st's troops attacked Sanga Sanga and Tawi Tawi, the southernmost islands, on April 2, and a week later they landed on Jolo, where a 2400-man enemy garrison offered the only significant opposition during the Sulu campaign. Approximately forty American and 2000 Japanese troops were killed in the Sulu operations. The airfields developed at Zamboanga and in the Sulus proved of great value in providing air support for subsequent landings on Borneo.[12]

The main part of the 40th Division was employed in the assault on Panay, although fewer than 2400 Japanese combat troops were there and Peralta's 23,000 guerrillas had already secured most of the island except the region around Iloilo, the principal city. The Americans landed west of Iloilo on March 18, drove the Japanese from the city two days later, and a week after turned over the mopping-up chores to the guerrillas and a battalion of the 40th. The Americans lost about twenty men and the enemy approximately 800 in the fighting on Panay, and the remaining Japanese fled into inaccessible mountain reaches. Meanwhile, on the day that Iloilo was seized, elements of the 40th Division crossed the narrow strait to Guimaras and then moved on to take nearby Inampulugan, encountering no opposition on either island. The Iloilo air strip was little used later, but MacArthur planned to stage two divisions from Iloilo in the subsequent invasion of Japan, so extensive construction was begun there.[13] In retrospect, it seems that the assignment of American advisers, arms, and equipment to the guerrillas would have enabled them to secure the remaining Japanese-held portion of Panay without the involvement of the 40th Division.

On March 29, eleven days after the invasion of Panay, two regiments of the 40th Division landed on the northwest coast of Negros. The 503rd Parachute Regimental Combat Team had planned an airborne attack inland, but because the enemy opposition was light, the paratroopers moved to Negros on assault ships. By April 2 Bacolod and almost the whole coastal plain of northwestern Negros had been secured. But when the Americans moved into the mountainous interior, they met stiff opposition from the nearly 14,000 Japanese who were in strong defensive positions. Despite the assistance of Lieutenant Colonel Salvador Abcede's 14,000 guerrillas, who had earlier gained control of nearly two-thirds of the island, the 40th Division found dislodging the enemy to be extremely rough going, and the last organized resistance in northern Negros did not end until early June.

Meanwhile, on April 26 a regiment of the Americal Division made an unopposed landing on the southeast coast of Negros and drove the 1300-man enemy garrison into the hills, where guerrillas took over the mopping-up. The Americans lost about 400 men killed in action on Negros, and nearly 8000 Japanese died in the campaign. The vast majority of all casualties occurred in the mountain warfare in northern Negros.[14] In view of the losses incurred in the strategically valueless campaign, it is difficult to understand why MacArthur and Eichelberger insisted on pushing the attack relentlessly against the trapped enemy in the mountains.

In addition to clearing the lightly held southern part of Negros, the Americal Division was given the mission of occupying Cebu and Bohol. Two Americal regiments began landing south of Cebu City on March 26, but the area just beyond the surf line had been heavily mined and ten of the first fifteen landing vehicles were blown up. As men continued to come ashore, the beaches quickly became jammed, and mine explosions took a heavy toll. Nearly 13,000 Japanese troops were in the hills overlooking Cebu City, which, along with the beaches, they had abandoned. Because of the chaos at the landing area the Japanese could have attacked and very likely driven back the American invasion, at least for the day, but instead they quietly waited in prepared positions in the hills. On the second day the Americans seized Cebu City without firing a shot, but, as on other islands, when they attempted to secure the surrounding hills and nearby airfield, the enemy began to resist. Lieutenant Colonel James M. Cushing's guerrillas, about 8500 strong, effectively contained the 2000 or more Japanese in northern Cebu and also closed in on the main defenses outside Cebu City from the north. But it took the American and guerrilla forces three weeks to break the organized resistance in the hills overlooking the city.

From then on it was largely a matter of mopping-up, which was sometimes still costly. Over 400 Americans and 5500 Japanese died in the Cebu campaign, but besides battle wounds the Americal Division suffered over 8000 noncombatant casualties in a hepatitis epidemic that swept through the troops. MacArthur ordered major construction at Cebu City, the second largest municipality in the Philippines, where he intended to stage three divisions in the invasion of Japan. Meanwhile, on April 11 an Americal battalion landed on nearby Bohol where, at a cost of seven men killed, it dispersed and drove into the hills a garrison of about 300 Japanese.[15]

Eichelberger expected the main Japanese resistance south of Luzon to come on eastern Mindanao, and he assigned Sibert's X Corps, including the 24th and 31st divisions, to capture that portion of the island. Over 43,000 Japanese troops, mainly of the 30th and 100th divisions, were in eastern Mindanao, but they were desperately lacking in leadership, artillery, ammunition, transportation, and supplies. Fertig's 24,000-man guerrilla force already controlled about 90 per cent of the island when the X Corps landed against no opposition near Parang on Illana

Bay, April 17. Rapidly advancing eastward along Highway 1 and coming ashore from landing craft far up the Mindanao River, the Americans reached Kabacan, about halfway to Davao, a week later. The 31st Division started up the Sayre Highway toward Macajalar Bay, and the 24th Division continued the advance along Highway 1 toward Davao. In permitting the Americans to take the key road junction of Kabacan without a major battle, the Japanese had foolishly allowed their two main divisions to be hopelessly separated from each other, the 30th in the north and the 100th near Davao. On April 27 the 24th Division, reinforced by elements of the 41st Division, seized Digos on Davao Gulf and turned north toward its main objective, Davao. The city was taken on May 3 against less resistance than had been expected, but the 24th had a major fight on its hands when it turned northwest and attacked the strong Japanese positions about ten miles up the Davao Valley.

Not until June 10 were the final Japanese lines overrun. The remnants of the 100th Division withdrew into the mountains to the northwest. Immediately upon the capture of Davao, MacArthur had announced that strategic victory had been achieved on Mindanao, but Eichelberger later grumbled, "There were many hard weeks ahead for the GIs who had no newspapers to tell them that everything was well in hand." Valtin, of the 24th Division, said that the soldiers of his outfit regarded the post-Davao operation as "the hardest, bitterest, most exhausting battle of their ten island campaigns" of the war.

Meanwhile, a regiment of the 40th Division had landed at Macajalar Bay and advanced southward on the Sayre Highway to Impalutao where it made contact with elements of the 31st Division moving north. The Japanese 30th Division, after fighting ineffective, desultory actions along the highway, had withdrawn into the mountains to the east. On June 24 elements of the 31st Division went ashore at Butuan Bay, driving south in the Agusan Valley to attack the trapped Japanese 30th Division from the east. The other 31st and 40th division units, in the meantime, were pushing into the enemy's mountain refuge from the west. The separate pockets containing the surviving troops of the enemy 30th and 100th divisions held out in impenetrable jungle terrain until Japan surrendered. The final operation of the Mindanao campaign was a minor one in which guerrillas and units of the 24th Division cleared the Sarangani Bay area in July, where about 2000 Japanese troops resisted briefly, then took to the hills. On June 30, however, Eichelberger had already reported to MacArthur that organized resistance on Mindanao had ceased and the mopping-up stage had begun.

From April 17 through August 15 about 820 American troops died in the eastern Mindanao operations and nearly 13,000 Japanese soldiers were killed. About 22,000 enemy troops surrendered at the end of the war, so apparently 8000 or more Japanese died from starvation or disease during the campaign. Ironically, the last operation in the reconquest of the Philippines, the seizure of Sarangani Bay, had been, from 1942 until September, 1944, the first objective MacArthur had intended to pursue on his return to the Philippines. Excluding Leyte and Mindoro, the recapture of the Philippines south of Luzon had cost the Eighth Army about 2100 lives, roughly one-fourth as many deaths as suffered by the Sixth Army in conquering Luzon.[16]

In a communiqué on July 5 MacArthur proudly, if again prematurely, announced the termination of operations in the Philippines:

> The entire Philippine Islands are now liberated and the Philippine Campaign can be regarded as virtually closed. Some minor isolated action of a guerrilla nature in the practically uninhabited mountain ranges may occasionally persist, but this great land mass of 115,600 square miles with a population of 17,000,000 is now freed of the invader.

The enemy during the operations employed twenty-three divisions, all of which were practically annihilated. Our forces comprised seventeen divisions. This was one of the rare instances when in a long campaign a ground force superior in numbers was entirely destroyed by a numerically inferior opponent . . .

Naval and air forces shared equally with the ground troops in accomplishing the success of the campaign. Naval battles reduced the Japanese Navy to practical impotence and the air losses, running into many thousands, have seriously crippled his air potential. Working in complete unison the three services inflicted the greatest disaster ever sustained by Japanese arms.

The objects of the campaign were as follows:

1. To penetrate and pierce the enemy's center so as to divide him into north and south, his homeland to the north, his captured Pacific possessions to the south. Each half could then be enveloped and attacked in turn.

2. The acquisition of a great land, sea and air base for future operations both to the north and to the south comparable to the British Islands in its use as a base for allied operations from the west against Germany.

3. The establishment of a great strangulating air and sea blockade between Japan and the conquered possessions in the Pacific to the south so as to prevent raw materials from being sent to the north and supply or reinforcement to the south.

4. The liberation of the Philippines with the consequent collapse of the enemy's imperial concept of a Greater East Co-Prosperity Sphere and the reintroduction of democracy in the Far East.

5. The liberation of our captured officers and men and of internees held in the Philippines.

6. A crippling blow to the Japanese Army, Navy, and Air Force.

All of these purposes were accomplished.[17]

Yamashita and Krueger might have disagreed with MacArthur about some of his claims in the above communiqué, American admirals might have questioned the degree of harmony attained, the invaluable guerrillas might have taken offense at the omission of any mention of their contributions, and the Joint Chiefs might have been concerned by MacArthur's almost equal stress on advancing south and north afterward. But, with the nine-month campaign in the Philippines "virtually" at an end, Mac-Arthur could rightfully claim that his forces had achieved their finest triumph and had made clear the hopelessness of Japan's efforts to stop the American advance in the Pacific.

Throughout the Philippine operations of the spring and summer of 1945, there was a marked difference in MacArthur's attitude toward the way Eichelberger was leading his army and the way in which Krueger was leading his. Krueger received no congratulatory messages comparable to those MacArthur sent to the Eighth Army commander. For example, he radioed Eichelberger that his Visayan campaign "is a model of what a light but aggressive command can accomplish in rapid exploitation." [18] Eichelberger described a conference with MacArthur in April:

> When I went in to talk to the Big Chief I never received so many bouquets in my life. He said that my operations in the Visayas, Zamboanga and the Sulu Archipelago had been handled just the way he would have wanted to have it done had he been an Army commander — speed, dash, brilliance, etc. He said that . . . [Krueger] is the old-fashioned Army general who wants to do everything by the rules. If he is given a certain number of troops to do a job he wants twice that number. The Big Chief said that if he had been trying to take the Visayas he would just now be preparing to attack Palawan (where we landed late in February) with an army corps (we used one regiment). He said he would not have dared to take in less than a division on any of these landings. He said he was the type like Meade, the Union general in the Civil War who used to make Grant so angry.[19]

In his glow of enthusiasm after talking to MacArthur, however, Eichelberger might well have recalled that it was Krueger whom MacArthur had recommended for four stars. Moreover, it would be Krueger's Sixth Army rather than Eichelberger's Eighth which MacArthur would entrust to lead the assault on Kyushu that fall. The Big Chief was capable of adopting quite contrasting views on a subject when talking to different persons, as Eichelberger would learn to his dismay during the Japanese occupation.

2. *The Big Chief Sees for Himself*

The final Australian amphibious assaults of the war, against Borneo, were conducted in spite of the reluctance of Blamey and his commanders, who seriously doubted the value of the operations. For the Seventh Fleet the invasion of Tarakan was merely an extension of its duties in support of Eichelberger's Philippine operations. Royal was assigned to command the amphibious group and Berkey the naval covering group. The RAAF and Thirteenth Air Force were to provide strikes before and during the invasion. Morshead, the Australian I Corps commander, selected Brigadier David A. Whitehead's 26th Brigade of the 9th Division to seize Tarakan. A Dutch battalion was attached, mainly to give the Netherlands Army token representation in the capture of the oil-rich island off the northeastern coast of Dutch Borneo. The assault force landed at Lingkas on the southern coast of Tarakan on May 1 against light opposition; Australian artillery units had been set up on the nearby unoccupied island of Sadau the previous day to provide fire support in addition to the naval and air bombardments. Most of the 2300 enemy defenders, however, had withdrawn inland as the preliminary shellings began. A savage fight developed for the city of Tarakan, two miles inland, and Whitehead's troops encountered strong opposition as they seized the oil fields to the northwest and drove the Japanese into the hills in the center of the island.

Organized resistance did not collapse until June 21, and mopping-up was still under way when Japan surrendered. Whitehead's force lost 225 men killed, and about 1500 Japanese died in the fighting. MacArthur's stated purposes in the operation had been to secure the oil fields and to establish an air base to support later Borneo assaults. But the oil fields had been so severely damaged by Allied air attacks and Japanese demolitions that they could not be rehabilitated for a year or more. In addition, engineers found it impossible to repair the wrecked enemy air base at Tarakan or to build a new one in time to provide support for the Brunei and Balikpapan invasions, so the air cover for those attacks had to come from the Sulu bases and escort carriers. Whitehead, Morshead, and Blamey were none too happy about the Australian losses in view of what little was gained.[20]

Barbey, who was present at the Tarakan landing, set off a furor in Australia when he charged that in making amphibious landings the Australian troops "were behind the times . . . unskilled, and knew little about their equipment." He added that the Japanese would not have had time to consolidate their defenses inland if the Australians had been faster in landing their supplies and equipment and getting them off the beaches. Australian naval observers, in turn, claimed that the Americans had not made available to Whitehead's force their modern landing equipment: "Too much manual labor was used, and the provision of more mechanical equipment would have made the operation easier."

Chifley, the acting prime minister, wrote to MacArthur on May 10 that the controversy over the "lack of adequate mechanical and engineering equipment for the Australian forces at the landing at Tarakan" has spread to the War Cabinet and Parliament, and he would appreciate a statement from him on the matter. MacArthur replied, "I am entirely at a loss to account for any criticism of the Tarakan operation. It has been completely successful and has been accomplished without the slightest hitch. The equipment and methods were essentially the same as those used in nearly 40 amphibious landings in all." He went on to praise the "splendid efficiency" of Whitehead's men and noted that there had been "light" casualties on Tarakan "in view of the great objectives attained." MacArthur's response soothed Chifley, who subsequently told Parliament, "I cannot but deplore these irresponsible criticisms which are unfair to the Supreme Commander, in whom the Government has entire confidence." [21]

But Australian criticisms and doubts about the worth of the Borneo operations did not subside. On Blamey's advice, Chifley suggested to MacArthur on May 18 that the Australian 7th Division not be used in Borneo, which would mean dropping the Balikpapan assault unless an American unit were substituted. Chifley reassured him that "it is the desire of the Government that Australian Forces should continue to be associated with your command in the forward movement against Japan." MacArthur replied firmly on the 20th:

The Borneo campaign . . . has been ordered by the Joint Chiefs of Staff who are charged by the Combined Chiefs of Staff with the responsibility for strategy in the Pacific. I am responsible for execution of their directives employing such troops as have been made available to me by the Governments participating in the Allied Agreement. Pursuant to the directive of the Joint Chiefs of Staff and under authority vested in me . . . I have ordered the 7th Division to proceed to a forward concentration area and, on a specific date, to execute one phase of the Borneo campaign. Australian authorities have been kept fully advised of my operational plans. The concentration is in progress and it is not now possible to substitute another division . . . The attack will be made as projected unless the Australian Government withdraws the 7th Division from assignment to the South-West Pacific Area . . . Withdrawal would disorganize completely not only the immediate plan but also the strategic

> plan of the Joint Chiefs of Staff . . . There are no specific plans
> so far as I know for employment of Australian troops after the
> Borneo campaign . . . I do not know whether Australian
> troops are contemplated for use to the north.

Chifley responded that his government "absolutely intends to
abide" by the SWPA agreement and therefore the 7th Division
could be used at Balikpapan.[22]

The 20th and 24th brigades of Wootten's 9th Division were
employed in the assault on Brunei Bay, June 10, with Royal
and Berkey again leading the amphibious and covering naval
groups while RAAF and Thirteenth Air Force planes provided
air support. The landings that day on Labuan and Muara islands in the bay and at Brunei Bluff ashore were unopposed.
The city of Brunei on the southern end of the bay was captured
against moderate resistance on June 15; however, a stiff battle
later developed in the hilly interior of Labuan. While the 24th
Brigade advanced about twenty miles up the coast and seized
Beaufort on June 28, the 20th Brigade in a shore-to-shore movement from Brunei attacked Lutong, seventy miles south of
Brunei Bay, and on June 20–25 captured the town and the large
Miri-Seria oil fields in the vicinity. The Australians had control
of about 160 miles of the northwestern coast of North Borneo
by July 1; they had lost 114 troops and killed about 1300 Japanese. The Labuan airfield was quickly repaired and soon in
use by Allied fighters, and a potentially excellent fleet anchorage
was secured at Brunei Bay, though, as earlier mentioned, the
British Pacific Fleet spurned it in favor of Leyte. Kinkaid lost
an able flag officer when Royal, on the way back to Leyte on
June 18, suddenly died of a heart attack.

So far the Australians had not encountered large concentrations of Lieutenant General Masao Baba's Thirty-seventh Army,
which, though depleted by transfers of units to other combat
areas in the past year, still had about 31,000 troops. Allied lead-

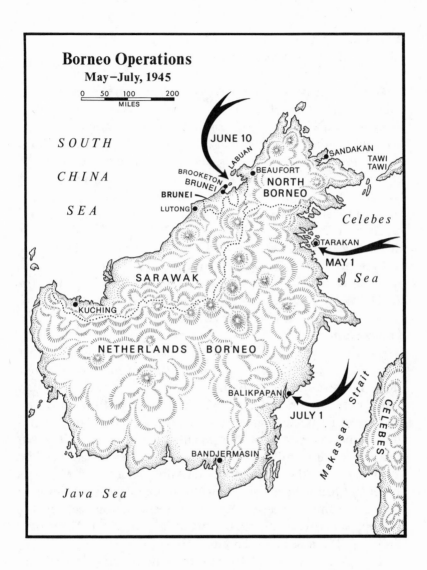

Borneo Operations
May–July, 1945

0 50 100 200
MILES

SOUTH

CHINA

SEA

JUNE 10

LABUAN

BROOKETON
BRUNEI

BRUNEI

LUTONG

SANDAKAN

TAWI
TAWI

BEAUFORT

NORTH
BORNEO

Celebes

TARAKAN

MAY 1

of Sea

SARAWAK

KUCHING

NETHERLANDS BORNEO

BALIKPAPAN

JULY 1

Makassar Strait

CELEBES

BANDJERMASIN

Java Sea

ers expected him to have a strong force in the Balikpapan area,
but actually Baba's troops were ineffectively scattered at points
on the eastern and western coasts of Borneo with only about
4000 in the vicinity of Balikpapan. The garrison there, however,
had prepared some of the most formidable coastal defenses in
the Southwest Pacific — artillery and mortars massed in the hills
overlooking the city and bay of Balikpapan, thousands of mines
in the offshore and beach areas, and an intricate system of beach
obstacles. The Japanese at Balikpapan, who had long expected
an invasion since they guarded the second largest oil center in
Southeast Asia (next in size to Palembang, Sumatra), were prepared to make an Allied assault costly. With G-2 data indicating
the strong defenses that awaited the SWPA forces, MacArthur
ordered sixteen days of naval and air attacks to precede the
Balikpapan attack, the longest pre-assault bombardment of
World War II. Extensive minesweeping operations also were
undertaken, during which six Allied ships were sunk by enemy
fire and mines.

But the preparations were so thorough and devastating that
when Major General E. J. Milford's 7th Division landed about
three miles southeast of Balikpapan on July 1 the Australian
losses were extremely light. Within two days Milford's troops
had seized Balikpapan and one of its two airfields. Heavy fighting was necessary to drive the Japanese out of their positions in
the surrounding hills, but the Australians advanced steadily.
By July 9 the other airfield was in Allied hands, and Milford's
units had firm control of a beachhead about twelve miles long
and seven miles deep. Organized resistance ceased in the
Balikpapan area on July 22, by which time about 230 Australians
and 2000 Japanese had been killed.[23]

The Brunei and Balikpapan operations were carried out
with such smooth efficiency and strong American naval, air, and
logistical support that Australian critics of the Borneo operations had little to say. The Australian Army's official history,
however, points out the ironical situation in which that nation's

combat forces found themselves during the final months of the war:

> One result of a complex of decisions, some contradictory and some illogical, was that, in 1945, while I Australian Corps, well equipped and with powerful air and naval support, was preparing for or was fighting battles of doubtful value in Borneo, an Australian corps in Bougainville and an Australian division in New Guinea were fighting long and bitter campaigns (whose value also was doubted) in which they were short of air and naval support, and suffered such a poverty of ships and landing craft that, as a rule, the best they could do was to put ashore a company or two at a time on a hostile shore.[24]

The solid support that MacArthur gave to the Borneo operations was intimately related to his plan to develop bases there rapidly for the invasion of Java, an idea that he had never dismissed despite its failure so far to win the approval of the Joint Chiefs. Eichelberger said that MacArthur confided to him in late spring that "if the Navy idea of piddling around for a long time before doing anything against the Japanese homeland carries through, he still wants me to go into Java rather than have my troops sit around and stagnate." With his previous record of success in persuading or bypassing the Joint Chiefs, Mac-Arthur probably would have sent Eichelberger's forces into Java about September. Putting it quite mildly, the Australian chronicle concludes, "In retrospect the wisdom of embarking upon this third thrust — westward against Japanese forces isolated in the Indies — seems doubtful." Yet nearly a decade later, in the wake of the triumphant emergence of Indonesian nationalism, MacArthur told Willoughby the invasion of Java in 1945 would have been a "complete success with little loss. This was one of the grave mistakes of the war and ultimately resulted in the chaotic conditions which followed in that part of Indonesia." [25]

On June 3 MacArthur left Manila aboard the cruiser *Boise* on a two-week "grand tour," as Eichelberger called it, to see the central and southern Philippines and to observe the Australian assault at Brunei Bay. Egeberg, Whitney, Fellers, Soriano, and, for part of the trip, Eichelberger and Kenney accompanied the AFPAC commander. After spending six hours of June 4 touring the military installations on Mindoro, MacArthur and his entourage traveled to Macajalar Bay, Mindanao. On MacArthur's request, the *Boise*'s captain directed his ship along roughly the same route that the general's party had taken when it escaped from Corregidor in March, 1942. The AFPAC chief insisted on making a jeep trip to Malaybalay in the interior of Mindanao near the front lines of the 31st Division on June 5. The eight-hour, 120-mile journey, mostly in the rain, seemed to be an exhausting experience for everyone except MacArthur. He also made a side excursion to the bombed-out ruins of the Del Monte clubhouse where he and his Corregidor band stayed briefly in 1942. At lunch Brigadier General Joseph C. Hutchison, the 31st Division's assistant commander, overheard MacArthur tell Eichelberger, "Bob, I think you're doing the right thing down here. Continue patrolling and keep contact with the enemy, but do everything possible to avoid a major engagement. We don't want to lose any more men than we have to, especially at this stage of the war." [26]

That night the *Boise* crossed the Mindanao Sea to Cebu City, and the next morning MacArthur made a thirty-mile jeep trip into the hills to observe artillery action against some enemy troops still holding a ridge. During the night of June 6–7 the *Boise* moved on to the port of Bacolod on northwest Negros. On the morning of the 7th MacArthur and his party, riding in captured Japanese automobiles, went to a mile-high post in the mountains east of Silay to watch the rough warfare still under way in that region. Returning to Bacolod in the early afternoon, MacArthur rode in a PT boat across the Guimaras Strait to Iloilo, Panay, where he had served as a second lieutenant of engineers fresh from West Point in 1903–04. At sea again during the night, the *Boise* took him next to Puerto Princesa,

Palawan, where he spent the day of June 8 visiting with the 41st Division's officers and men and making a trip to the nearby penal colony to talk to some Filipino political friends of high rank in the prewar era, now imprisoned as alleged collaborators. Departing about sunset with MacArthur's party aboard, the *Boise* steamed south through the night and the next afternoon rendezvoused with the attack force headed for Brunei Bay. It was perfect weather on the 9th as the convoy approached the target; MacArthur, according to Kenney, consumed four chocolate sodas that day. On the *Boise,* anchored off Brunei Bay, he eagerly watched the pre-invasion naval and aerial bombardment and seemed hardly able to wait for the landing the next morning

At 11:00 A.M. on June 10, less than two hours after the first assault troops went ashore, MacArthur and his group, now accompanied by Royal, Morshead, and Bostock, landed on the beach at Labuan Island in Brunei Bay. So far resistance had been light, and the Australians quickly secured the Japanese air base on the island. In the following days, however, it would take some stiff fighting to wipe out the 1000 or more Japanese entrenched in the hilly interior of Labuan. MacArthur strolled a mile inland, then hitched a ride back to the beach in a jeep loaded with thirteen other officers. Whitney commented, "I have never doubted since that the American jeep was the most versatile piece of equipment of World War II." On the following day MacArthur went ashore at the beach below Brunei Bluff and waded through a half mile of swampy terrain to a road where jeeps were waiting to drive his group to the port of Brooketon. From there he insisted on traveling south toward the town of Brunei, which the Australian troops were then trying to capture against mounting resistance. MacArthur was "enjoying himself hugely," remarked Kenney. About five miles below Brooketon the AFPAC chief's party halted when a brief fire fight broke out along the road ahead. A few minutes later, while MacArthur was gazing at the bodies of two snipers killed in the skirmish, a photographer standing next to him was hit in the shoulder by a sniper's bullet.

Kenney, Fellers, and Egeberg tried to persuade MacArthur to go back to the *Boise,* but he insisted on continuing until he was stopped by a stubborn Australian colonel, who was not intimidated by his five-star insignia and told him bluntly that he and the other brass of his party were forbidden to go farther since they were interrupting the operations of his combat unit. MacArthur took the order with surprising meekness and turned back toward Brooketon. Hoping to get him to halt earlier, Kenney said that he had been talking about the chocolate ice cream that was waiting for them on the cruiser and that thought may have influenced the Old Man. Aboard the *Boise* again, MacArthur issued a communiqué praising the Brunei operation and adding, "Rarely is such great strategic surprise obtained at such a low cost of life."

The next day, June 12, the *Boise* arrived at Jolo in the Sulus where the Moro sultan and the island's governor called on MacArthur and presented him with a 100-year-old *krise.* The curved sword was a gift of honor the often hostile Moros rarely bestowed upon whites. Eichelberger observed that MacArthur, for some unknown reason, appeared "indifferent and preoccupied and cut their visit short." That night the *Boise* moved on to Davao, and MacArthur spent about seven hours on June 13 inspecting the area and made a trip near the still hotly contested region of Mintal, north of Davao. Woodruff describes part of the reception provided in his 24th Division's combat sector:

> We showed them some of the units, put on a good Artillery Shoot against a village occupied far up the Trail. (The Japs must have thought we were insane wasting ammunition against such an insignificant target!) General MacArthur said I had come across the Island "in skillful and efficient manner." As he left he said, "I have heard that your Division was a superior one.

It has been confirmed by what I saw here today." I realized that somewhat the same compliment was given by him to many other Commanders and units. Nevertheless, it was good to know that our effort had been recognized.

I had been carefully warned that the General wanted the top *up* on the jeep in which he rode. It was lucky that I had been notified as my orders were that all jeeps in the Division would be wide open on the road; that is, tops and windshields flat. Caught under fire in a closed jeep can be a bit confusing.[27]

Before leaving the Davao area, MacArthur casually told Eichelberger that he "did not believe there were four thousand Japanese left alive on Mindanao." (It will be recalled that nearly six times that number surrendered later in eastern Mindanao.) After stopping at Zamboanga on June 14, Mac-Arthur and his undoubtedly tired staff group returned by sea the next day to Manila. But even before the *Boise* reached Manila Bay, MacArthur was talking about going on another such expedition soon.

Since he had taken such an adamant stand on using the Australian 7th Division in the Balikpapan assault, MacArthur decided to accompany it in what turned out to be the last amphibious operation of the Second World War. After all, it was the veteran 7th, combat-proven in the African desert war against Rommel before the division moved to the Southwest Pacific, and it had also repulsed the Japanese attack along the Kokoda Trail and had spearheaded the counteroffensive in Papua. Together with Kenney, Fellers, Egeberg, Soriano, and several other staff officers, MacArthur departed from Manila aboard the *Boise* on June 27. After a stop at Tawi Tawi on the 29th, the cruiser rendezvoused with the attack force off Dutch Borneo for the final run to Balikpapan.[28] Barbey, the war's most experienced amphibious commander, with fifty-six assault landings to his credit, describes MacArthur's visit to the Balikpapan beachhead on July 1:

About an hour after the first wave of troops hit the beach, I received a signal from General MacArthur that I join him for an inspection of the fighting ashore. I suggested a slight delay as the troops were still fanning out from the beaches and the front lines were not far away, but he wanted to go right away. I picked him up in a landing boat with a few of his staff, some war correspondents and a camera crew.

As usual, MacArthur was immaculately dressed with well-pressed khaki trousers and carrying light tan gloves. The rest of us looked shopworn and "perspiry." It was hot. MacArthur led the group along the swampland and parallel to the beach. He stopped at a little creek to speak to a group of Australian troops struggling to get a small artillery piece across the stream. They were a tough-looking lot, bare from the waist up, sweat and dirt clinging to their faces. The men paused in their work, and MacArthur, wishing to be friendly, asked, "How goes it, gentlemen?" There was a sudden silence and an immediate sense of hostility. If he had used a few epithets, the "Diggers" would have understood, but to be addressed as "gentlemen" smacked of something they didn't like. After a few more seconds of embarrassing silence, MacArthur moved on.

With his party he climbed a small shale hill, dotted with Australian foxholes, which was less than 200 yards from the enemy front lines. There he started looking over some field maps while the camera crew ground away. An Aussie major came running up and warned everybody to take cover as there was a machine-gun nest in a nearby hilltop. Before he had finished, there was the rat-tat-tat of machine-gun bullets. In a few seconds the firing had stopped, apparently smothered by the Australians, but not before all of us had dropped. But not MacArthur. He was still standing there looking over his map, quite unperturbed as I and the others took a more upright position.

I shamefacedly said something about fighting ashore being no place for the Navy, and supposed I was the first one to hit the dirt. "No," said Lee Van Atta, INS war correspondent, "I was looking up as you came down." As he turned toward me, MacArthur in a very matter-of-fact manner said, "You did exactly right," but he added no comment regarding his own actions. He gave the impression that no Japanese bullet had been made that could bring him down.[29]

That night the *Boise* weighed anchor and steamed toward Tawi Tawi, where MacArthur insisted on stopping again briefly. On the afternoon of July 3 the AFPAC chief and his party returned to Manila. Possessed of uncanny luck, MacArthur had conducted his last death-defying act during a front-line visit — at least during the current war.

3. Shifting from Olympic to Blacklist

Among other agreements reached at the Yalta Conference, February 4–11, 1945, Roosevelt and Churchill pledged generous territorial concessions in the Far East to the Soviet Union in return for Stalin's promise to unleash the Red Army against Japan within two or three months after Germany's surrender. Ritchie, who informed MacArthur in Manila on August 2 of the full details of the concessions, said the AFPAC chief was "shocked" at the deal. In a public statement a decade later MacArthur charged the concessions were "fantastic" and unnecessary since Japan at the time was near defeat. In his memoirs he stated, "I was never invited to any of these meetings [at Yalta], and my views and comments were never solicited . . . Although in 1941 I had urged Russian participation to draw the Japanese away from the South Pacific and Southeast Asia, by 1945 such intervention had become superfluous." [30]

No evidence was uncovered that Roosevelt or the Joint Chiefs solicited MacArthur's opinion in advance of the Yalta Conference regarding the concessions. Indeed, it would have been surprising if they had consulted him on such high-level Allied negotiations of diplomacy and grand strategy. Besides, as the Joints Chiefs were probably aware, MacArthur, Nimitz, and other senior commanders in the Pacific, as well as most of the Pentagon planners, favored the Soviet Union's entry into the war against Japan because it would undoubtedly terminate that conflict much more quickly and would spare many thousands of American lives, especially if it meant averting an invasion of the home islands. Colonel Paul Freeman of the War Department General Staff reported to Marshall on February 13, 1945, that he had conferred with MacArthur and was told by him that he "understands Russia's aims, that they would want all of Manchuria, Korea and possibly part of North China. This seizure of territory was inevitable; but the United States must insist that Russia pay her way by invading Manchuria at the earliest possible date after the defeat of Germany."

Brigadier General George A. Lincoln of Marshall's staff met with MacArthur on February 25 and reported back to the Army chief of staff that the Southwest Pacific commander believed "we should make every effort to get Russia into the Japanese war before we go into Japan . . . General MacArthur pointed out that politically they [the Russians] want a warm-water port, which would be Port Arthur. He considered that it would be impracticable to deny them such a port because of their great military power. Therefore, it was only right they should share the cost in blood in defeating Japan."

Secretary of the Navy Forrestal wrote in his diary of a talk with MacArthur on February 28: "He said he felt that our strength should be reserved for use in the Japanese mainland, on the plain of Tokyo, and that this could not be done without the assurance that the Japanese would be heavily engaged by the Russians in Manchuria. He expressed doubt that the use of anything less than sixty divisions by the Russians would be sufficient." MacArthur sent a message to the Joint Chiefs, read at their meeting on June 18, in which he stated that in the proposed ground assault on Japan by his armies "the hazard and loss will be greatly lessened if an attack is launched from Siberia sufficiently ahead of our target date to commit the enemy to major combat."

Although later decried by Roosevelt detractors as a treasonable sellout of America's interests and an appeasement worse than that of the Munich Conference of 1938, the Far Eastern agreement at Yalta appeared in the first half of 1945 to be reasonable and realistic to American political, diplomatic, and military leaders, including MacArthur. His close ties with leading conservative, isolationist Republicans of the postwar era apparently made it impossible for him to admit his earlier position. As Eisenhower, LaFollette, and others close to him sadly learned, MacArthur's traits included a desperate need to save face, even if it involved lying.[31]

As early as November, 1944, the Joint Staff Planners had been working on Downfall, the plan for the invasion of Japan. Late that month the Joint Chiefs of Staff tentatively approved their planning draft for Operation Olympic, the assault on Kyushu, to begin September 1, 1945, and Operation Coronet, the invasion of Honshu, to be launched December 1, 1945. The campaigns on Leyte, Luzon, Iwo Jima, and Okinawa each lasted far longer than anticipated, so that by spring, 1945, the Joint Chiefs realized that Olympic and Coronet would have to be postponed, if they were conducted at all.

Problems of redeployment of units from the European theater and base development in the Pacific for staging the attacks on Japan were also proving to be more complicated than expected, with shipping, as usual, looming as a major trouble-maker. In March the Joint Staff Planners anticipated that Olympic would entail the use of eight assault and five follow-up divisions, Coronet would require twelve assault and two follow-up divisions, and six more divisions would be needed in the forward reserve. Twenty-one Army and six Marine divisions were already in the Pacific, so fifteen more would have to be redeployed from Europe and the United States. MacArthur was told to be prepared to stage twenty-two divisions at Philippine bases by November, 1945, and eleven more there by February, 1946, the rest to go to staging bases in the Ryukyus, Saipan, and Hawaii.

In March, 1945, there were seventy-one air groups in the Pacific; the Joint Staff Planners expected to increase the number there to 142 by early 1946.

In their April directives to MacArthur and Nimitz, the Joint Chiefs, it will be recalled, told them to "make plans and preparations for the campaign in Japan." Both MacArthur and the Army planners in Washington contemplated ground assaults on the Japanese home islands as soon as practicable to force Japan's capitulation. But Nimitz, King, and the naval planners in the Pentagon favored delaying the invasion of the main islands as long as possible in favor of subsidiary operations along the Chinese coast from which more intensive air attacks and a tight naval blockade could be staged in the hope of bringing about Japan's surrender without direct ground attacks.

An actual directive for Olympic was delayed through much of the spring because of the Joint Chiefs' indecision about the best method of inducing Japan's capitulation; their uncertainty about redeployment, shipping, and base development; and their concentration on the fast-moving situation in Europe, which culminated in Germany's collapse and surrender in early May. The Joint Chiefs were aware, as MacArthur and Nimitz were not until late July, of the highly secret Manhattan Project's progress in developing an atomic bomb, which was nearing the testing stage. Like many of the Manhattan scientists, however, the Joint Chiefs were doubtful that the bomb would be as potent as some thought — indeed, that it would even detonate. Thus War Department planning for an invasion of Japan went forward based on the pessimistic contingencies that the atomic bomb would not be available, the Soviet Union would not enter the war until after the ground assault on Kyushu, and Japan could not be forced to surrender solely by air bombardment and naval blockade.

In April Marshall queried MacArthur about three of the principal alternatives the Joint Chiefs were considering: (1) encirclement of Japan by further expansion westward while simultaneously carrying out air attacks on the enemy defenses of Kyushu or Honshu preparatory to the Olympic or Coronet assaults, (2) reliance upon accelerated strategic air bombing and a strangling naval blockade to force Japan's submission, and (3) implementation of Downfall, the assault on Kyushu in November and Honshu in March.[32] MacArthur replied on April 20 that the first course had the disadvantage of "deploying the bulk of available resources off the main axis of advance" and that American forces would become enmeshed in the war in China. He believed, in addition, that reliance only on air and naval power would prolong the conflict indefinitely without necessarily prevailing upon Japan to surrender. On the other hand, MacArthur reasoned, direct assaults on Kyushu and Honshu

> would attain neutralization by establishing air power at the closest practicable distance [Kyushu] from the final objective [Honshu] in the Japanese islands; would permit application of full power of our combined resources, ground, naval, and air, on the decisive objective; would deliver an attack against an area which probably will be more lightly defended this year than next; would continue the offensive methods which have proven so successful in Pacific campaigns; would place maximum pressure of our combined forces upon the enemy, which might well force his surrender earlier than anticipated; and would place us in the best favorable position for delivery of the decisive assault early in 1946. Our attack would have to be launched with a lesser degree of neutralization and with a shorter period of time for preparation . . .
>
> I am of the opinion that the ground, naval, air, and logistic resources in the Pacific are adequate to carry out Course III . . . Logistic considerations present the most difficult problem.[33]

At Manila in mid-May MacArthur and Nimitz reached agreement on the broad principles for Olympic and submitted their proposals to the Joint Chiefs. The directive for Olympic was issued by the Joint Chiefs on May 25, setting the target date for November 1 and giving MacArthur the chief responsibility for the entire operation, including control, under certain exigencies, of the amphibious assault through the appropriate naval commander. He was also directed to make plans and preparations for Coronet in cooperation with Nimitz. The naval and amphibious phases of Olympic were assigned to Nimitz. MacArthur and his planners in Manila immediately set to work on the operational details of Olympic.

According to MacArthur's plan, the Kyushu invasion would be preceded by attacks of unprecedented magnitude by aircraft of the Far East Air Forces, the Twentieth Air Force, and Pacific Fleet carriers. The Kyushu assault was assigned to Krueger's Sixth Army, which would employ three corps in simultaneous assaults on three objective areas of southern Kyushu. A few days before X-day, November 1, the 40th Division would seize the small Koshiki and Osumi islands off the southern coast of Kyushu to establish emergency naval and seaplane bases and clear the sea routes for the main invasion forces. On X-day the V Amphibious Corps would land near Kushikino, advance to the western shore of Kagoshima Bay, and then turn north to block enemy movements from upper Kyushu. The XI Corps would go ashore at Ariake Bay, seize Kanoya, drive to the eastern shore of Kagoshima Bay, and then turn northeast to Miyakonojo. The I Corps would land at Miyazaki on the east coast of Kyushu, attack southeastward, and secure the northern shore of Kagoshima Bay. The IX Corps, actually the floating reserve, would be transported off the coast of Shikoku two days before X-day and would remain there as a tactical diversion, feinting an attack, and then after X-day would proceed to the Ryukyus to remain on reinforcement call as needed.

The principal objective of Olympic was to acquire areas for air, naval, and logistical bases to support the main assault on Honshu three months after the Kyushu landings. Bases in the

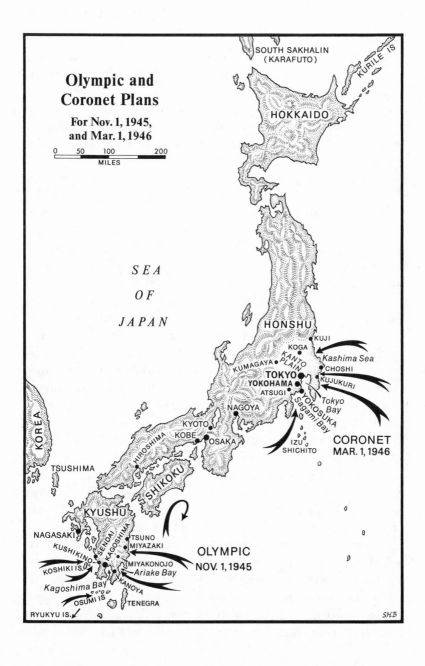

Olympic and
Coronet Plans

For Nov. 1, 1945,
and Mar. 1, 1946

0   50   100   200
        MILES

SOUTH SAKHALIN
(KARAFUTO)

KURILE IS

HOKKAIDO

SEA

OF

JAPAN

HONSHU

KUJI

KOGA

Kashima Sea

KANTO
PLAIN

KUMAGAYA

CHOSHI

TOKYO

KUJUKURI

YOKOHAMA

ATSUGI

NAGOYA

Tokyo
Bay

YOKOSUKA

KYOTO

Sagami Bay

KOBE

OSAKA

IZU
SHICHITO

CORONET
MAR. 1, 1946

HIROSHIMA

KOREA

TSUSHIMA

SHIKOKU

KYUSHU

NAGASAKI

OLYMPIC
NOV. 1, 1945

SENDAI

TSUNO

KUSHIKINO

KAGOSHIMA

MIYAZAKI

KOSHIKI IS.

MIYAKONOJO

Ariake Bay

Kagoshima Bay

KANOYA

OSUMI IS

TENEGRA

RYUKYU IS.

SHB

Philippines, Ryukyus, Marianas, and Hawaii were selected for the staging, equipping, and mounting of the Olympic forces, with Manila to serve as the principal logistical base. The unexpected end of the war in mid-August found the preparations for Olympic still very much in the planning stage. Few shipments from Europe had arrived, and the redistribution of Army and Navy resources in the Pacific between MacArthur and Nimitz was still far from completion.[34]

If Olympic preparations were barely under way, the plans for Coronet were only at the preliminary level of G-3 staff studies when the war ended. MacArthur planned to "exercise personal command of the landing forces and direct the ground operations on the mainland. With him would be the advance echelon of his General Headquarters to act as the Army Group Headquarters in the field." Hodges' First Army and Eichelberger's Eighth Army were assigned to Coronet; their principal tactical missions were to seize the Kanto Plain and the Tokyo-Yokohama area. The initial assaults would be made by fifteen divisions, followed in thirty days by three more divisions and five days later by another four divisions, thus involving a total of twenty-two divisions in Coronet. Pre-assault air and naval bombardments would be even more vast than those for Olympic. Eichelberger's forces would go ashore along Sagami Bay, seize Yokohama, and then bypass Tokyo to secure the Koga-Kumagaya area, cutting off enemy reinforcements from the north. Hodges' units would land on the Kujukuri beaches and between Kuji and Choshi on the shores of the Kashima Sea, east and northeast of Tokyo. They would proceed to clear the eastern side of Tokyo Bay, and one spearhead would strike directly toward Tokyo.

If Japanese resistance continued after the Americans had seized east central Honshu, MacArthur planned to employ Australian, New Zealand, British, French, and Canadian divisions in later stages of the Honshu campaign. In the first edition of Coronet in July, Stilwell's Tenth Army was also to be employed in the initial invasion of the Kanto Plain, but in the final edition of August 15 the Tenth's role had inexplicably been deleted.[35] Stilwell's reaction to this is not known, but it was undoubtedly vociferous.

In the early days of July, intelligence data based on reconnaissance reports of the widespread damage inflicted by air attacks, intercepted enemy messages, and Japanese efforts to get the Soviet Union to act as a peace mediator pointed more sharply to the possibility that Japan might surrender suddenly and soon, before the Russian declaration of war or the launching of Olympic. On instructions from the Joint Chiefs, MacArthur and Nimitz prepared contingency plans "for a possible peaceful occupation." Nimitz's Campus Plan called for the Navy and Marines to occupy the Tokyo Bay area and seize "key positions ashore, including, if practicable, an operational air field in the vicinity of each principal anchorage." MacArthur's ground forces were to arrive later.

MacArthur's counterproposal, the Blacklist Plan, provided for a coordinated massive movement of ground, naval, and air forces to Japan, including twenty-two infantry divisions. He objected to Campus on the grounds that "naval forces are not designed to effect the preliminary occupation of a hostile country whose ground divisions are still intact. The occupation of large land areas involve[s] operations which are fundamentally and basically a mission of the Army." Besides, he added, "It would be psychologically offensive to ground and air forces of the Pacific Theater to be relegated from their proper missions at the hour of victory."

Wedemeyer, commanding the American forces in China, urged that priority be given to occupying Manchuria and the seaports of China to prevent their seizure by the Chinese Communists. Nimitz, however, felt the occupation of Japan and Korea should take priority, and MacArthur emphasized "the prompt occupation of Japan proper" was of "paramount" importance. The Joint Chiefs gave priority to a slightly modified form of MacArthur's Blacklist: the XXIV Corps was to go to south Korea and the VII Amphibious Force was to transport two Marine divisions later to certain Chinese ports. But, at a meeting in Manila on August 18–19 of representatives of Nimitz, MacArthur, and Wedemeyer, it was determined that the shortage of shipping would make it impossible to lift the Marines to China until late September.[36]

In the meantime, events had been rushing toward a dramatic climax. On July 16 the first atomic bomb was successfully detonated near Alamogordo, New Mexico. The next day the American, British, and Soviet heads of state and their diplomatic and military chiefs opened the two-week Potsdam Conference on the outskirts of Berlin, where they deliberated problems of postwar Europe and strategy against Japan. On July 25 Truman approved a directive to Spaatz ordering the dropping of an atomic bomb on Japan "as soon as weather will permit visual bombing after about 3 August 1945." Two of the bombs had already arrived at a B-29 base on Tinian. The following day Truman, Prime Minister Clement Attlee, and Chiang Kai-shek (*in absentia*) issued the Potsdam Declaration calling upon Japan to surrender unconditionally or face "prompt and utter destruction."

The terms of surrender included military occupation until the following objectives had been achieved: elimination of militarism, limitation of Japanese sovereignty to the four main islands, prosecution of war criminals, disarmament and demobilization of military forces, removal of "all obstacles to the revival and strengthening of democratic tendencies among the Japanese people" and establishment of "freedom of speech, of religion and of thought, as well as respect for the fundamental human rights," and abolition of war-related industries, but maintenance of "such industries as will sustain her economy and permit the exaction of just reparations in kind," with access to, but not control of, raw materials and "eventual Japanese participation in world trade relations." The declaration did not mention the atomic bomb, nor did it say anything about the future status of the Emperor, a matter that was crucial in the Japanese leaders' deliberations on surrender.

When no satisfactory response was received from Tokyo, atomic bombs were unleashed over Hiroshima on August 6 and over Nagasaki three days later with horrifying results soon well known to the world. Meanwhile, on the 8th, the Soviet Union declared war on Japan, and the Red Army began a rapid advance into Manchuria. On August 10 the Japanese Cabinet agreed to the Potsdam terms on the condition that the sovereignty of the Emperor be preserved, and the next day the United States government replied, implicitly agreeing to the retention of the Emperor, though "subject to the Supreme Commander of the Allied Powers who will take such steps as he deems proper to effectuate the surrender terms." In a Radio Tokyo broadcast on August 14, the welcome news was flashed to a war-weary world that the Japanese government had decided to accept the Allied terms of surrender. When official notification reached Truman, he immediately ordered all offensive operations suspended and declared a two-day national holiday. The Japanese war machine, which had started on the road of conquest in China eight years earlier, had been wrecked at last.[37]

Late on the afternoon of August 6, before the news of the Hiroshima bombing had reached Manila, MacArthur called a conference of about two dozen correspondents at his headquarters in the City Hall. He labeled his remarks as "off the record," meaning they could not be quoted. James J. Halsema, a former internee and then a reporter for the Manila *Daily Bulletin,* made the following notes on the general's address:

> He said that the war may end sooner than some think. Things are in such a state of flux that anything can happen. The Japanese already are beaten, but their leaders hang on in the hopes of some break which will save them. The aerial sat-

uration phase of the Allied offensive is already underway. Their navy is impotent and their shipping destroyed for all practical purposes. Their army is still large and their soldiers tenacious but are spread out all over eastern Asia with no communications. It is impossible to arm the Japanese civilian population effectively. If they did succeed, it would only mean the deaths of thousands. Besides, the Japanese always have been short of arms. The conversion of the factories to war has been only 30% of the U.S. record. They have no secret weapons. The Japanese are not supermen. Let's not build up any more legends to that effect. Their emperor is a figurehead but not quite a stooge.

MacArthur said he himself would go north shortly. General Hodges (First Army) already is here and has established headquarters at Calamba (the sugar estate at Canlubang, Laguna, 30 miles SE of Manila).

Russian participation in the war was welcome. It had been planned since the days when we were much less sure of the outcome than we are now, and they would get the same deal at a peace conference even if they did not enter the war physically. Every Russian killed was one less American who had to be. If he were running their war, he would pull a double envelopment Cannae-style and commit all the Japanese in Manchuria by running one force straight down the railway to Port Arthur while another came through Chahar and Mongolia.

He hopes the Balikpapan landing would be the last show he had to pull on a shoe-string.

(Most of the people in the room had been told of the general plans for the Japan landing and although they had not been given an actual date, it was generally understood that it was safe to plan home leaves for the summer. They were actually aware of the high casualty rate expected, having seen the 30,000 beds being established in the Manila area, including a psychiatric establishment. They asked a number of questions about the modalities of reducing the high cost in American lives.) MacArthur said the use of poison gas was simply impractical: it would take months to set up an effective operation . . .

He talked for over an hour on an amazing range of subjects . . . He not only thinks of the war, but of the peace, and the possibilities of a next war with its horrors magnified 10,000 times.[38]

When the news was broadcast in Manila on August 11 that Japan had conditionally accepted the Allied terms of surrender, a crowd of several hundred GI's gathered below MacArthur's second-story office and began to yell for the AFPAC chief to make an appearance. After several minutes he came to a window and in a moving voice told the hushed group, "I hope from the bottom of my heart that this is the end of the war. If it is, it is largely due to your own efforts. Very soon, I hope, we will all be going home." He then abruptly turned around and went back to his desk.

Actually, the general felt that the use of atomic bombs at that stage "was completely unnecessary from a military point of view" to compel Japan's capitulation and said so on several occasions in later years. He was also offended that the Allied leaders had not consulted him prior to issuing the Potsdam Declaration and that the Joint Chiefs had not informed him (or Nimitz) of the existence and planned use of the atomic bombs until shortly before the Hiroshima attack. If his opinion had been requested before the Potsdam ultimatum, he would have strongly urged an assurance to the Japanese that the Emperor would be retained. As it was, he learned of the declaration through commercial radio reports, and the War Department did not send him a copy of the full text of the Potsdam statement until August 12.

Brigadier General Thomas Farrell was sent by the War Department at the end of July to inform him of the atomic bomb and to direct him to keep the skies clear of FEAF aircraft over specified cities, which were likely targets for imminent atomic attacks. On August 7, the day after the Hiroshima raid, MacArthur was more fully informed of the Manhattan Project and the future plans for using atomic bombs when he was visited by Dr. Karl T. Compton, who was a key member of the presidential advisory committee on the development of the bomb. According to one source, MacArthur reacted with "quiet indignation" when he learned that Eisenhower had known of the atomic bomb long before he was told.[39]

Some inter-service rivalry was displayed by leaders of the War and Navy departments in trying to influence Truman's selection of an officer to preside at the Japanese surrender ceremony. But the President's decision in favor of MacArthur to head the Japanese occupation, apparently made about August 8 and determined on the basis of the most experienced, best qualified officer available, also settled the question of who would accept the surrender of the Japanese. When the matter of MacArthur as the President's choice was discussed in Moscow on August 10 by Ambassador W. Averell Harriman and Soviet Foreign Minister Vyacheslav M. Molotov, the latter argued that a Red Army marshal should serve jointly with MacArthur at least over the surrender ceremony. Harriman pointed out that the United States, which had been at war with Japan for nearly four years, had no intention of sharing that authority equally with the Soviet Union, which had just entered the conflict. On August 12 Truman requested and promptly received approval from Attlee, Stalin, and Chiang to appoint MacArthur as Supreme Commander for the Allied Powers in Japan (SCAP).[40]

The next day the President approved the final wording of the SCAP directive, and on August 15, V-J Day, it was sent to the AFPAC commander as follows:

1. In accordance with the agreement among the Governments of the United States, Chinese Republic, United Kingdom, and Union of Soviet Socialist Republics to designate a Supreme Commander for the Allied Powers for the purpose of enforcing the surrender of Japan, you are hereby designated as the Supreme Commander for the Allied Powers.

2. You will require the issuance of a proclamation signed by the Emperor authorizing his representatives to sign the instrument of surrender. The proclamation to be signed should be substantially in the form appended hereto. You will take the

necessary steps to require and receive from the duly authorized representatives of the Japanese Emperor, the Japanese Government, and the Japanese Imperial General Headquarters the signed instrument of surrender. The text of the instrument is appended hereto. You will accept the surrender for the four Governments concerned and in the interests of the other United Nations at war with Japan.

3. I have asked the heads of state of China, Great Britain, and the Union of Soviet Socialist Republics each to designate a representative who may be present with you at the time and place of surrender. I have designated Fleet Admiral Chester W. Nimitz to be present as the United States representative for this purpose. As soon as I have received the other designations you will be advised. You will make the appropriate arrangements.

4. Having accepted the general surrender of the Japanese armed forces, you will require the Japanese Imperial General Headquarters to issue general orders which will instruct Japanese commanders wherever situated as to the mechanics of surrender and other details effectuating the surrender. You will effect any necessary coordination of arrangements with the Japanese Imperial General Headquarters with regard to the surrender to the Allied Commanders concerned of Japanese armed forces abroad.

5. From the moment of surrender, the authority of the Emperor and Japanese Government to rule the state will be subject to you and you will take such steps as you deem proper to effectuate the surrender terms.

6. You will exercise supreme command over all land, sea and air forces which may be allocated for enforcement in Japan of the surrender terms by the Allied Powers concerned.

7. Your appointment as Supreme Commander for the Allied Powers is effective upon receipt of this directive.[41]

MacArthur promptly responded to Truman, "I am deeply grateful for the confidence you have so generously bestowed upon me in my appointment as Supreme Commander. The entire eastern world is inexpressibly thrilled and stirred by the termination of the war. I shall do everything possible to capitalize [upon] this situation along the magnificently constructive lines you have conceived for the peace of the world." [42]

4. *"The Guns Are Silent"*

Radio messages between Manila and Tokyo became frequent in the next two weeks as MacArthur and the Japanese government worked out the multitude of details regarding surrender arrangements. On MacArthur's instructions, a sixteen-man delegation of Japanese officials, headed by Lieutenant General Toroshiro Kawabe, vice chief of the Imperial General Staff, flew to Manila on August 19 to receive directions from GHQ and provide certain data needed for the initial occupation phase. MacArthur silently watched them enter the City Hall from a nearby balcony of the building, but at no time during the conference did he meet with the Japanese. Sutherland headed the American delegation, which also included Marshall, Willoughby, Whitlock, Chamberlin, Admiral Sherman, and Brigadier General Donald R. Hutchinson, Kenney's chief of staff. Mashbir played an indispensable role as chief interpreter and sometimes conciliator.

By prior directions the Japanese brought with them a collection of reports, charts, and maps relating to the location of prison camps, airfields, military and naval installations, fortifications, minefields, and storage and billeting facilities. Lasting through the night of August 19–20 and until late the next morning, the talks went smoothly in spite of the formality displayed by both sides. When Kawabe described the unrest and violence already fomented by some military units in the Tokyo-Yokohama area opposed to the surrender, Sutherland agreed to postpone the landing of the advance American unit at Atsugi air base, fifteen miles west of Yokohama, where a large detachment of rebellious kamikaze pilots was stationed. The advance force would arrive at Atsugi on August 26th instead of the 23rd. The main part of the 11th Airborne Division would start landing there two days later.

The latter part of the conference dealt with the translation and explanation of a group of documents, most of which had been drafted in Washington, that were given to the Japanese for signing and implementation. Among others, they included the instrument of surrender to be signed at the formal surrender ceremony, a rescript that the Emperor was required to proclaim accepting the Potsdam terms and commanding his subjects to cease hostilities, a general order directing the Imperial General Headquarters to arrange the surrender of its units to various Allied commanders, and certain requirements of MacArthur's regarding the surrender ceremony and the reception of the incoming occupation forces.

The Japanese delegates were alarmed to find that the Washington-drafted imperial rescript, which began "I, Hirohito, Emperor of Japan," had as the pronoun for "I" the term *watakushi,* employed in Japan in informal conversation and as a mark of deference but never used for or by the Emperor. Pointing out that the proper, respectful pronoun for imperial use was *chin,* the Japanese delegates emphasized that the wording was "of extreme importance" in attaining their countrymen's cooperation from the start. At first Sutherland and Willoughby thought the matter was trivial and the Japanese were stalling. Fortunately Mashbir, the most knowledgeable of the GHQ group about the Japanese language and mind, was able to take the issue to MacArthur, who agreed to the change and remarked of the Emperor, "I have no desire whatever to debase him in the eyes of his own people, as through him it will be possible to maintain a completely orderly government."

At the conclusion of the Manila talks the Japanese delegation returned to Tokyo, though one of the two transports that they boarded at Okinawa had to make a forced landing on a beach near Hamamatsu toward the end of the flight, delaying those delegates' return by seven hours. Meanwhile, Emperor Hirohito had already ordered his armed forces to halt hostilities, members of the imperial family had been dispatched to the far-flung theaters to expedite compliance with the surrender edict, and Japanese units in the Tokyo-Yokohama region had begun preparations for the coming of the conquerors. Everyone in Japan was fearful and uncertain of the kind of treatment he would receive in the dark days ahead.[43]

Because of a severe typhoon that swept through the Ryukyus and southern Japan during the last week of August, the arrival of the advance American unit at Atsugi was postponed until August 28 and the Japanese surrender ceremony was rescheduled for September 2, to be held in Tokyo Bay aboard the battleship *Missouri*. On August 19 MacArthur had issued an order forbidding the acceptance of any surrenders by Allied commanders until after the main ceremony was concluded. Mountbatten, Blamey, and Chinese commanders were critical of this prohibition and later argued that the critical lapse of time in some areas, especially Java, Korea, and China, permitted disorders and seizures of power by Communists or rebellious nationalists, as well as the advance of the Red Army deep into central Korea.

The surrender and repatriation of Japanese military and naval forces, totaling over three million men scattered from the Gilberts and Solomons to Burma and Korea, involved many diplomatic and logistical complications; even the persuasion of some isolated troops to lay down their arms required several weeks. Gill, the 32nd Division's commander, opened negotiations on August 24 with Yamashita about the capitulation of his Shobu force in north Luzon. The Japanese commander delivered himself to Gill's custody on September 2 and the formal surrender of Yamashita's forces occurred the next day at Baguio, presided over by Styer, with Wainwright and British Lieutenant

General Arthur E. Percival at his side. The capitulation of each of the many other Japanese units in the Pacific and on the Asian mainland was handled by the Allied commander in the particular areas; almost none was left to complete by mid-September. The explosive international episodes that arose in connection with some of the surrenders that took place after Tokyo Bay and MacArthur's role in these will be dealt with in the third volume of this work.[44]

The last two weeks of August were one of the busiest, most disconcerting periods of MacArthur's life as he tried to cope with unprecedented, fast-developing crises of every sort. Large-scale fighting continued in many areas of northern China not only between Chinese and Japanese troops but also between Chinese Communist and Nationalist forces vying for control of strategic ports and transportation arteries. Russian troops continued to advance through northern Korea, annihilating Japanese garrisons in their path as they pushed south to the 38th parallel, the demarcation line for Soviet and American forces hastily and ignorantly agreed upon by the United States government. Appeals by Japanese officials and commanders to MacArthur to bring a stop to the continuing massacre of their soldiers in China and Korea elicited protests from SCAP to Chinese and Soviet authorities but caused little improvement in the chaotic field situations.

A false report that Soviet troops were landing on Hokkaido evoked a strong protest from MacArthur. In turn, Russian authorities, picking up wild rumors, charged that MacArthur's forces were going ashore on the Kurile Islands, promised to the Soviets at Yalta, and that the American general was trying to block their delegation from getting to Tokyo in time to participate in the surrender ceremony. There were accusations and misunderstandings by both sides. The Joint Chiefs urged Mac-Arthur and Nimitz to accept Soviet liaison missions to their headquarters shortly after V-J Day, but both commanders staunchly refused. On August 26 at their Manila residence, the MacArthurs gave a luncheon for Lieutenant General Kuzma N. Derevyanko and two other senior officers of the Soviet delegation to the surrender ceremony. This seemed to ease the tension temporarily.

Much of MacArthur's time was absorbed in wrestling with the never-ending headaches of the logistics involved in the staging of the initial occupation forces to Japan and complicated by a new shortage of shipping. In addition, a matter of foremost personal interest to him was the location, liberation, and relief of thousands of American and Allied prisoners of war and civilian internees scattered in isolated camps from Southeast Asia to Manchuria and Japan. B-29's from bases in China and the Marianas, as well as FEAF aircraft, were sent over the camps as quickly as they were pinpointed, dropping medicine, food, and other supplies and often medical teams. Even the matter of representation at the Tokyo Bay ceremony proved to be complicated and sensitive, and a disproportionate amount of MacArthur's attention had to be devoted to working out the exact number and position of the representatives of the various Allied nations on the *Missouri,* with each government, especially the British and the Soviet, anxious to have as large and conspicuous a delegation of its senior commanders as possible.[45]

For nearly two years committees in the State, War, and Navy departments had been developing a set of policies to be enacted in Japan during the occupation. Yet for two weeks after V-J Day MacArthur, now charged with the awesome responsibility of directing that occupation, had only the general principles set forth in the Potsdam Declaration to guide him in his planning. Finally, on August 29, while stopping overnight on Okinawa en route to Japan, he received by radio from Washington a document entitled "United States Initial Post-Surrender Policy for Japan," which had been prepared by a coordinating committee of the State, War, and Navy departments but was not formally approved by the President until September 6. The policy called for the implementation of the Potsdam terms, beginning with demilitarization and disarmament. It emphasized that the Japanese government "should conform as closely as may be to principles of democratic self-government but it is not the responsibility of the Allied Powers to impose upon Japan any form of government not supported by the freely expressed will of the people." Although MacArthur had "the right and duty" to demand "changes in governmental machinery or personnel or to act directly" if the Japanese government did not meet his requirements, he was normally to "exercise his authority through Japanese governmental machinery and agencies, including the Emperor, to the extent that this satisfactorily furthers United States objectives." Advisory bodies including Allied representatives would be established later, but "in the event of any differences of opinion among them, the policies of the United States will govern."

The policy statement laid the foundation for sweeping political, economic, and social reforms — encouragement of political parties and labor unions, emancipation of religion, press, and women, and dissolution of the agrarian landlord system and industrial monopolies. On the nearly unilateral control of the occupation by the United States, the continuation of the national government after its militaristic agencies and personnel had been purged, and the economic and social reforms, the philosophy of the document lay in contrast to that of the Allied occupation of Germany as it was then developing. MacArthur's own thoughts were in line with most of the Washington position, for he had told Sherwood earlier that enlightened leadership by the United States in the occupation of Japan "will make us the greatest influence on the future development of Asia. If we exert that influence in an imperialistic manner, or for the sole purpose of commercial advantage, then we shall lose our golden opportunity; but if our influence and our strength are expressed in terms of essential liberalism we shall have the friendship and cooperation of the Asiatic people far into the future." Although the directive of August 29 gave him rather wide latitude in the execution of occupation policy, he was still uneasy that Washington, and more probably the Allies, would try to hamper him in making decisions in the unpredictable circumstances that lay ahead.[46]

On the morning of August 27 the Third Fleet began moving into Sagami Bay, just southwest of Yokohama, and two days later entered Tokyo Bay, with the *Missouri,* Halsey's flagship, anchoring off the large Yokosuka Naval Base. Not only was the movement made without untoward incident, but the Japanese Navy provided navigational charts, harbor pilots, and interpreters for the American fleet, which, with the arrival of other Allied ships, seemed to be spread all across Tokyo Bay. At 9:00 A.M., August 28, about 150 AFPAC engineers and communications experts landed at the Atsugi airfield. The American force was commanded by Colonel Charles T. Tench, with Major Faubion Bowers as chief interpreter. Tench soon reported to an anxious MacArthur: "Landing of advance party proceeding according to plan . . . Reception by Japanese entirely correct." He did not mention that the Japanese had pitchers of fresh orange juice awaiting them or that they were treated by the Atsugi commander to a delicious lunch meticulously prepared and served on white tablecloths, followed by wine. As American and Japanese officers overcame their jitters and started swapping cigarettes, it was obvious to all on both sides that their fears of trouble had been exaggerated.

Early that afternoon thirty-six C-54's landed at Atsugi bearing advance troops of the 11th Airborne Division, petroleum supplies, and equipment. Beginning at dawn on the 30th and coming in at a rate of one transport every three minutes all day, the main portion of the 11th Airborne arrived at Atsugi. About the same time the 4th Marines, named for the regiment that had surrendered on Corregidor, went ashore to secure Yokosuka and its vicinity. One Marine officer admitted to Eichelberger, who also arrived that day, "Our first wave was made up entirely of admirals trying to get ashore before MacArthur."

After the war Churchill remarked, "Of all the amazing deeds of bravery of the war, I regard MacArthur's personal landing at Atsugi as the greatest of the lot." [47] Some Americans who had been there two days ahead might question the assertion, but the appearance of the Supreme Commander in Japan on the afternoon of August 30, at a time when he could easily have become the target of Japanese fanatics, was, indeed, a bold gamble. Eichelberger describes MacArthur's arrival and trip to Yokohama:

> About two in the afternoon a beautiful plane, *The Bataan*, circled the area and came in for a rubbery landing. The 11th Airborne's military band, determined that a historic event should have its proper musical background, was on hand to give the Allied commander a spirited greeting. General MacArthur ignored the panoply when he appeared at the door of his plane. His shirt was open at the throat and his corncob pipe was in his mouth. As I reported to him he grinned and said, "Bob, this is the payoff."
>
> I thought it was too. But I wasn't quite sure what the payoff would be . . . American soldiers were outnumbered thousands to one . . . The Japanese Army trusted the kamikaze pilots [at Atsugi] so little that a military expedition had forcibly removed the propellers from all planes. The air group resisted with arms, and there was fighting, with casualties, before the job could be completed [on August 23] . . .
>
> The Japanese somewhere had found for General MacArthur an American automobile of doubtful vintage; as I stepped into the car with him I was as grim-faced as the troops around me. I had heard about the discipline of the Nipponese people, but I also knew that one undisciplined fanatic could turn a peaceful occupation into a punitive expedition. With a roar and a stuttering of motors we started off. [Whitney, also present, said "a fire engine that resembled the Toonerville Trolley . . . led the way as the procession headed for Yokohama."]
>
> Some indication of the condition of transport in Japan may

be discovered from the fact that it took us two hours to go twenty miles. But it was not the snail's-pace tempo or the repeated breakdowns which made the trip memorable. In the hot bright sunlight it seemed like a sequence in a dream fantasy. On both sides of the road there were hundreds of armed Japanese soldiers, and almost all of them stood with their backs toward us. It finally dawned on me that this solid wall of men was there to assist in guarding the Supreme Commander and that the turning away of faces was an obeisance which previously had been accorded only to the Emperor himself.

Nevertheless, I did not draw an easy breath until the journey ended and General MacArthur entered his suite in the New Grand Hotel. At once I established a perimeter defense around the building with five hundred veterans of the 11th Airborne. Before nightfall of the first day the New Grand Hotel was full of newspaper correspondents, GHQ officers, Army, Air Force, and Navy satraps. In fact, it was so full that I found it necessary to scout up other living quarters for myself.[48]

Yokohama, which had been about eighty per cent destroyed by earlier B-29 raids, was soon crowded with Americans of the first incoming divisions — the Army's 11th Airborne, 27th Infantry, and 1st Cavalry and the Marines' 6th. Both Americans and Japanese conducted themselves well, although Allied correspondents made a nuisance of themselves trying to interview Japanese leaders; one expedition to Tokyo, declared off limits for the time being by MacArthur, tried without success to get an audience with the Emperor. In the days before the surrender ceremony the only charge of rape that was reported to MacArthur turned out to be an episode in which a group of airborne troops entered a brothel, made the prostitutes parade past them dumping their kimonos in a pile, and departed with the kimonos as souvenirs without touching the astounded girls. When no eggs could be located in the city for MacArthur's breakfast on the 31st, Swing donated two laid by turkeys that some of his troops had stowed away on their plane. Moved by the plight of the city's residents, who had great difficulty in obtaining food, MacArthur promptly issued an order forbidding the commandeering of local food supplies by the occupation forces. He also revoked the curfew and martial law regulations that Eichelberger, still fearful of trouble, had imposed on Yokohama.

The Japanese residents of the stricken metropolis were overwhelmingly impressed by the orderly conduct and generous attitude exhibited by the occupation commanders and their troops. Rear Admiral Yoshio Kodama, who had witnessed the Japanese rape and sack of Chinese communities and expected "unbearably dark events" and "national death" for Japan in the hands of the Americans, was pleasantly surprised at the "civilized" and "friendly" manners of the conquerors. He said that he and his colleagues stationed at Yokosuka had not felt a sense of defeat even during the worst of the B-29 fire raids, but a singular episode he witnessed in the first days of the occupation finally made him fully aware of Japan's status: "I, who had always seen the pitiful figure of war sufferers in China and had secretly sympathized with the sorrows of a defeated people, saw with my own eyes small children gathering around the soldiers of the Occupation Forces seeking for scraps of food and realized that it was we Japanese who were now tasting the sorrows of defeat." [49]

For a while after V-J Day the exact location of Wainwright, Percival, and the other senior Allied commanders in Japanese prison camps was not known. Wedemeyer learned they were near Mukden, Manchuria, and proposed to the War Department that they be flown to Chungking and that Wainwright and Percival be invited to attend the Tokyo Bay ceremony. Stimson asked for MacArthur's opinion, and the Supreme Commander promptly replied on August 21, "I would be delighted to have General Wainwright and General Percival at [the] signing of capitulation. I have asked General Wedemeyer if either or both of these officers are secured in time to send them forward to join me."

On August 28 Wainwright, Percival, and several other American, British, and Dutch generals who had been captives arrived at Chungking aboard a C-47 transport from Mukden. After a brief recuperation Wainwright and Percival, well fed and in fresh uniforms but looking haggard from their tribulations in prison, flew on to Yokohama where they arrived late on the afternoon of the 31st. MacArthur and some of his staff were having dinner at the New Grand Hotel when an officer came in and told the Supreme Commander that Wainwright had just entered the lobby. MacArthur rushed from the table to greet him. Whitney, who witnessed the emotional scene, observed that Wainwright "leaned on a cane as he walked. His gaunt close-cropped head seemed too large for his body. His cheeks were sunken and his neck scrawny and leathery. He managed a weak smile as MacArthur put both arms about him, but he choked up and was unable to say anything. MacArthur could only say 'Jim . . . Jim . . .' in a hoarse whisper."

At the dinner table Mashbir, who was present, said MacArthur assured Wainwright that he could have another command under him after the former prisoner admitted he had long thought that his surrender on Corregidor would bar him from active duty ever again. When asked what position he would like, Wainwright responded, "I want command of a corps — any one of your corps." MacArthur told him, "You can have any one that you want." As it turned out, however, the emaciated, worn USFIP general would require a lengthy recuperation, and he never again served under MacArthur.[50]

In the early daylight of Sunday, September 2, 1945, nearly 260 Allied warships lay at anchor amid the cool mists rising from Tokyo Bay. Low-hanging gray clouds drifted above the fleet as officers of the nations that had been at war with Japan began gathering aboard the *Missouri,* anchored six miles off Yokohama. The five-starred flags of the Pacific Fleet and AFPAC commanders, as well as the American flag that had flown above the United States Capitol on December 7, 1941, were raised over the huge battleship, and shortly after 8:00 destroyers arrived on its starboard side to deliver MacArthur and Nimitz. The throng of Allied admirals and generals abruptly stopped their excited conversations and snapped to attention as the two commanders came aboard. Just before 9:00 an American destroyer bearing the eleven-man Japanese delegation closed to the starboard of the *Missouri*. With Mashbir, their escort, in the lead, they slowly, grimly mounted the gangway. The four civilians of the Foreign Office, led by Foreign Minister Mamoru Shigemitsu, were dressed in formal attire, complete with top hats. His left leg had been blown off by an assassin's bomb years ago and Shigemitsu, who wore an artificial limb, appeared to be in physical agony as the completely silent Allied assembly watched his laborious journey up the ladder and across the quarter-deck to his assigned position near the railing below the No. 2 gun turret. The seven Japanese Army and Navy representatives were headed by General Yoshijiro Umezu, chief of the Imperial General Staff, who had vehemently opposed capitulation and was still angry at being forced to attend the surrender ceremony.

The documents to be signed by Shigemitsu, Umezu, and the Allied representatives lay on an old mess table that was covered with a green felt cloth. Nearby stood a throng of Allied generals and admirals, some in smart uniforms with ties, and others, including the Americans, attired informally in open-neck shirts. Cameramen and sailors were crowded on every available deck, turret, and bridge space within sight and hearing of the historic proceedings. About four minutes after the Japanese were in position, MacArthur, Nimitz, and Halsey came out of a cabin and walked briskly toward the table.[51] As MacArthur stepped up to the microphones placed beside the table, Wainwright and Percival took their positions just behind him.

The Supreme Commander began his short address with these words:

We are gathered here, representatives of the major warring powers, to conclude a solemn agreement whereby peace may be restored. The issues, involving divergent ideals and ideologies, have been determined on the battlefields of the world and hence are not for our discussion or debate. Nor is it for us here to meet, representing as we do a majority of the people of the earth, in a spirit of distrust, malice or hatred. But rather it is for us, both victors and vanquished, to rise to that higher dignity which alone befits the sacred purposes we are about to serve, committing all our people unreservedly to faithful compliance with the understanding they are here formally to assume.

It is my earnest hope, and indeed the hope of all mankind, that from this solemn occasion a better world shall emerge out of the blood and carnage of the past — a world dedicated to the dignity of man and the fulfilment of his most cherished wish for freedom, tolerance and justice.[52]

Gazing at MacArthur as he read, Toshikazu Kase of the Japanese Foreign Office noticed the Supreme Commander's hands trembling, but his attention quickly shifted to the "stirring eloquence" and "noble vision" of the general's speech. "For me, who expected the worst humiliation," remarked Kase, "this was a complete surprise . . . For the living heroes and dead martyrs of the war this speech was a wreath of undying flowers . . . This narrow quarter-deck was now transformed into an altar of peace."

MacArthur then summoned Shigemitsu and Umezu to sign the instrument of surrender. The Supreme Commander signed next, followed by Nimitz representing the United States, General Hsu Yung-chang of China, Admiral Bruce Fraser of the United Kingdom, Derevyanko of the Soviet Union, Blamey of Australia, and representatives of Canada, France, the Netherlands, and New Zealand in that order. After the last officer had signed, MacArthur solemnly declared, "Let us pray that peace be now restored to the world and that God will preserve it always. These proceedings are now closed." The time was exactly 9:25 A.M.

"At that moment," said Kase, "the skies parted and the sun shone brightly through the layers of clouds. A steady drone above now became a deafening roar and an armada of airplanes paraded into sight sweeping over the warships. Four hundred B-29's and 1,500 carrier planes joined in the aerial pageant in a final salute. The ceremony was over." [53] As the Japanese bowed stiffly and walked to the gangway, MacArthur left the ceremony area and went to another microphone; it had been arranged for him to broadcast a radio message to the world. The Supreme Commander spoke slowly and movingly:

Today the guns are silent. A great tragedy has ended. A great victory has been won . . .

As I look back upon the long, tortuous trail from those grim days of Bataan and Corregidor, when an entire world lived in fear, when democracy was on the defensive everywhere, when modern civilization trembled in the balance, I thank a merciful God that he has given us the faith, the courage and the power from which to mold victory. We have known the bitterness of defeat and the exultation of triumph, and from both we have learned there can be no turning back. We must go forward to preserve in peace what we won in war.

A new era is upon us. Even the lesson of victory itself brings with it profound concern, both for our future security and the survival of civilization. The destructiveness of the war potential, through progressive advances in scientific discovery, has in fact now reached a point which revises the traditional concepts of war.

Men since the beginning of time have sought peace . . . Military alliances, balances of power, leagues of nations, all in turn failed, leaving the only path to be by way of the crucible of war. We have had our last chance. If we do not now devise some greater and more equitable system, Armageddon will be at our door. The problem basically is theological and involves a spiritual recrudescence and improvement of human character that will synchronize with our almost matchless advances in

science, art, literature and all material and cultural developments of the past two thousand years. It must be of the spirit
if we are to save the flesh.[54]

Such were MacArthur's thoughts as mankind moved unsurely
into the morning of the atomic age and as the sixty-five-year-
old general set forth on a mission of peace that would result in
his most important contributions to history.

APPENDIXES

Appendix A

Men Who Had the Most Contact
with MacArthur, 1942–45

The following individuals mentioned in General Douglas MacArthur's Office Diary met with him individually or in a group fourteen or more times, March 17, 1942–August 28, 1945 (no diary entries for August 29–September 2, 1945):

Person	Service	Meetings with DM
*Maj. Gen. Richard J. Marshall	U.S. Army	238
Vice Adm. Arthur S. Carpender	U.S. Navy	172
Gen. George C. Kenney	U.S. Army	155
Adm. Thomas C. Kinkaid	U.S. Navy	115
*Lt. Gen. Richard K. Sutherland	U.S. Army	99
Gen. Thomas Blamey	Aus. Army	76
Col. Lloyd A. Lehrbas	U.S. Army	72
Maj. Gen. Stephen J. Chamberlin	U.S. Army	64
Gen. Walter Krueger	U.S. Army	62
*Brig. Gen. LeGrande A. Diller	U.S. Army	61
Brig. Gen. Courtney Whitney	U.S. Army	61
Lt. Gen. Robert L. Eichelberger	U.S. Army	48
Col. Roger O. Egeberg	U.S. Army	48
Pres. Sergio Osmeña	Phil. Govt.	47
Vice Adm. Herbert F. Leary	U.S. Navy	45
*Maj. Gen. Charles A. Willoughby	U.S. Army	41

*Brig. Gen. Charles P. Stivers	U.S. Army	39
Prime Min. John Curtin	Aus. Govt.	38
Brig. Gen. Bonner F. Fellers	U.S. Army	37
*Lt. Col. Charles H. Morhouse	U.S. Army	36
Maj. Gen. Arthur G. Wilson	Aus. Army	34
Defense Min. Frederick K. Shedden	Aus. Govt.	32
Lt. Gen. Herbert Lumsden	Brit. Army	31
Rear Adm. Carey Jones	U.S. Navy	25
Col. Philip LaFollette	U.S. Army	24
Vice Adm. Daniel E. Barbey	U.S. Navy	24
Lt. Gen. Ennis P. Whitehead	U.S. Army	23
Maj. Gen. James L. Frink	U.S. Army	22
Adm. William F. Halsey	U.S. Navy	20
Col. Andres Soriano	U.S. Army	19
*Maj. Gen. Hugh J. Casey	U.S. Army	18
*Maj. Gen. William F. Marquat	U.S. Army	17
Lt. Gen. Frank H. Berryman	Aus. Army	16
Adm. Chester W. Nimitz	U.S. Navy	16
Pres. Manuel L. Quezon	Phil. Govt.	16
Brig. Gen. L. Jack Sverdrup	U.S. Army	15
*Maj. Gen. Spencer B. Akin	U.S. Army	14

(* "Bataan Gang." The other members of the original Corregidor group who continued on the GHQ staff during part or all of the war years were Cols. Sidney L. Huff, Francis H. Wilson, and Joe R. Sherr.)

Appendix B

Itinerary of MacArthur
December 8, 1941–September 2, 1945*

1941

Dec. 8–24:
  Manila
Dec. 25–Jan. 9:
  Corregidor

1942

Jan. 10:
  Bataan
  Corregidor
Jan. 11–Mar. 11:
  Corregidor
Mar. 12:
  Tagauayan
Mar. 13:
  Cagayan
  Del Monte Plantation
Mar. 14–16:
  Del Monte Plantation

Mar. 17:
  Del Monte Field
  Batchelor Field
  Alice Springs
Mar. 18–21:
  Alice Springs
  Adelaide
  Melbourne
Mar. 22–25:
  Melbourne
Mar. 26:
  Melbourne
  Canberra
Mar. 27:
  Canberra
  Melbourne
Mar. 28–June 28:
  Melbourne
June 29:
  Seymour
  Melbourne

* Based mainly on MacArthur's Office Diary, RG 5, MMBA.

June 30–July 16:
    Melbourne
July 17:
    Canberra
    Melbourne
July 18–20:
    Melbourne
July 21–23:
    Melbourne
    Sydney
    Brisbane
July 24–Oct. 1:
    Brisbane
Oct. 2:
    Brisbane
    Townsville
    Port Moresby
Oct. 3:
    Port Moresby
Oct. 4:
    Port Moresby
    Brisbane
Oct. 5–Nov. 5:
    Brisbane
Nov. 6:
    Brisbane
    Townsville
    Port Moresby
Nov. 7–Jan. 8:
    Port Moresby

1943

Jan. 9:
    Port Moresby
    Townsville
    Brisbane
Jan. 10–May 26:
    Brisbane
May 27:
    Rockhampton
    Brisbane
May 28–June 6:
    Brisbane

June 7:
    Brisbane
    Sydney
June 8:
    Sydney
    Brisbane
June 9–24:
    Brisbane
June 25:
    Brisbane
    Townsville
    Cairns
June 26:
    Cairns
    Mareeba
    Port Moresby
June 27:
    Port Moresby
June 28:
    Port Moresby
    Milne Bay
    Goodenough
June 29:
    Gili Gili
June 30:
    Milne Bay
July 1:
    Dowa Dowa
    Wagga Wagga
    Samarai
    Kana Kopa
July 2:
    Milne Bay
    Dobodura
    Oro Bay
    Cape Endaiadere
    Sanananda
    Buna
    Cape Killerton
July 3:
    Dobodura
    Port Moresby
July 4:
    Port Moresby

July 5:
Port Moresby
Mareeba
July 6:
Mareeba
Brisbane
July 7–Aug. 24:
Brisbane
Aug. 25:
Brisbane
Port Moresby
Aug. 26–Sept. 4:
Port Moresby
Sept. 5:
Nadzab
Port Moresby
Sept. 6–23:
Port Moresby
Sept. 24:
Port Moresby
Townsville
Brisbane
Sept. 25–Oct. 10:
Brisbane
Oct. 11:
Brisbane
Port Moresby
Oct. 12–13:
Port Moresby
Oct. 14:
Port Morseby
Brisbane
Oct. 15–Nov. 25:
Brisbane
Nov. 26:
Rockhampton
Brisbane
Nov. 27–Dec. 11:
Brisbane
Dec. 12:
Brisbane
Port Moresby
Dec. 13:
Port Moresby

Goodenough
Dec. 14–15:
Goodenough
Dec. 16:
Goodenough
Port Moresby
Dec. 17–30:
Port Moresby
Dec. 31:
Finschhafen
Port Moresby

1944
Jan. 1–3:
Port Moresby
Jan. 4:
Port Moresby
Brisbane
Jan. 5–25:
Brisbane
Jan. 26:
Rockhampton
Brisbane
Jan. 27–Feb. 26:
Brisbane
Feb. 27:
Milne Bay
Feb. 28:
At sea
Feb. 29:
Los Negros
Mar. 1:
Finschhafen
Port Moresby
Mar. 2:
Port Moresby
Brisbane
Mar. 3–16:
Brisbane
Mar. 17:
Brisbane
Canberra

Mar. 18:
  Canberra
  Brisbane
Mar. 19–Apr. 17:
  Brisbane
Apr. 18:
  Brisbane
  Port Moresby
Apr. 19:
  Port Moresby
  Finschhafen
Apr. 20:
  Cape Gloucester
Apr. 21:
  At sea
Apr. 22:
  Hollandia
  Tanahmerah Bay
Apr. 23:
  Aitape
Apr. 24:
  Finschhafen
  Port Moresby
Apr. 25–26:
  Port Moresby
Apr. 27:
  Milne Bay
  Port Moresby
Apr. 28:
  Port Moresby
Apr. 29:
  Dobodura
  Port Moresby
Apr. 30:
  Port Moresby
May 1:
  Port Moresby
  Townsville
  Brisbane
May 2–July 25:
  Brisbane
July 26:
  Brisbane
  New Caledonia

Canton
July 27:
  Canton
  Honolulu
July 28:
  Honolulu
July 29–30:
  Honolulu
  Tarawa
  Brisbane
July 31–Sept. 8:
  Brisbane
Sept. 9:
  Brisbane
  Townsville
  Port Moresby
Sept. 10:
  Port Moresby
  Hollandia
Sept. 11–12:
  Hollandia
Sept. 13–14:
  At sea
Sept. 15:
  Morotai
Sept. 16:
  At sea
Sept. 17–18:
  Hollandia
Sept. 19:
  Hollandia
  Port Moresby
Sept. 20:
  Port Moresby
  Townsville
  Brisbane
Sept. 21–29:
  Brisbane
Sept. 30:
  Canberra
  Brisbane
Oct. 1–13:
  Brisbane

Oct. 14:
  Brisbane
  Townsville
  Port Moresby
Oct. 15:
  Port Moresby
  Hollandia
Oct. 16:
  Hollandia
Oct. 17–19:
  At sea
Oct. 20:
  Red Beach, Leyte
Oct. 21:
  White Beach, Leyte
  Tacloban
Oct. 22:
  Dulag
Oct. 23:
  Tacloban
Oct. 24–25:
  Leyte Gulf
Oct. 26–Nov. 7:
  Tacloban
Nov. 8:
  Tanauan
  Tacloban
Nov. 9–11:
  Tacloban
Nov. 12:
  Tanauan
  Tacloban
Nov. 13–Jan. 3:
  Tacloban

1945

Jan. 4–8:
  At sea
Jan. 9:
  Lingayen Gulf
  Dagupan
Jan. 10:
  Dagupan
  Lingayen

Jan. 11–12:
  Lingayen Gulf
Jan. 13:
  Lingayen Gulf
  Dagupan
Jan. 14:
  Dagupan
Jan. 15:
  Lingayen
  San Carlos
  Dagupan
Jan. 16:
  Dagupan
Jan. 17:
  San Fabian
  Damortis
  Dagupan
Jan. 18:
  Dagupan
Jan. 19:
  Camiling
  Dagupan
Jan. 20–24:
  Dagupan
Jan. 25:
  Dagupan
  Calasiao
  Santa Barbara
  Urdaneta
  Villasis
  Moncada
  Paniqui
  Hacienda Luisita
  Tarlac
  Gerona
  Camp Ord
Jan. 26:
  Capas
  Bamban
  Mabalocat
  Hacienda Luisita
Jan. 27:
  Tarlac
  Urdaneta

Binalonan
San Manuel
Pozorrubio
Manaoag
Hacienda Luisita
Jan. 28:
Hacienda Luisita
Jan. 29:
Camp O'Donnell
Hacienda Luisita
Jan. 30:
Guimba
Hacienda Luisita
Jan. 31:
Guimba
Hacienda Luisita
Feb. 1:
Clark Field
Fort Stotsenburg
Hacienda Luisita
Feb. 2:
Calumpit
Malolos
Bigaa
Hacienda Luisita
Feb. 3:
Calumpit
Bocaue
Marilao
Hacienda Luisita
Feb. 4:
Cabu
Hacienda Luisita
Feb. 5:
Calumpit
Malolos
Bigaa
Bocaue
Gaya Gaya
Hacienda Luisita
Feb. 6:
Hacienda Luisita
Feb. 7:
Manila

Hacienda Luisita
Feb. 8–15:
Hacienda Luisita
Feb. 16:
Abucay
Balanga
Hacienda Luisita
Feb. 17–18:
Hacienda Luisita
Feb. 19:
Manila
Nichols Field
Hacienda Luisita
Feb. 20–22:
Hacienda Luisita
Feb. 23:
Manila
Hacienda Luisita
Feb. 24–26:
Hacienda Luisita
Feb. 27:
Manila
Fort McKinley
Hacienda Luisita
Feb. 28–Mar. 1:
Hacienda Luisita
Mar. 2:
Manila
Corregidor
Hacienda Luisita
Mar. 3–4:
Hacienda Luisita
Mar. 5:
Clark Field
Fort Stotsenburg
Manila
Mar. 6–14:
Manila
Mar. 15:
Caloocan
Manila
Mar. 16–Apr. 26:
Manila

Apr. 27:
  Camp Murphy
  Marikina Valley
  Manila
Apr. 28–May 14:
  Manila
May 15:
  Nichols Field
  Manila
May 16–22:
  Manila
May 23:
  Nichols Field
  Manila
May 24–June 3:
  Manila
June 4:
  Mindoro
June 5:
  Cagayan
June 6:
  Cebu
June 7:
  Iloilo
June 8:
  Puerto Princesa
June 9–10:
  Brunei Bay
June 11:
  At sea

June 12:
  Jolo
June 13:
  Davao
June 14:
  Zamboanga
June 15–26:
  Manila
June 27–28:
  At sea
June 29:
  Tawi Tawi
June 30–July 1:
  Balikpapan
July 2:
  Tawi Tawi
July 3–Aug. 28:
  Manila
Aug. 29:
  Okinawa
Aug. 30:
  Atsugi
  Yokohama
Aug. 31–Sept. 1:
  Yokohama
Sept. 2:
  Tokyo Bay
  Yokohama

ABBREVIATIONS

BIBLIOGRAPHICAL NOTE

NOTES

Abbreviations

AAFWWII *The Army Air Forces in World War II*
ACS/AS Assistant chief of staff, Air Staff
AFHRD United States Air Force Historical Research Division, Maxwell Air Force Base, Ala.
AG 381 File 381, records of the United States Army Adjutant General's Office (since 1971), record group 407, National Archives, Washington, D.C.
AGS Allied Geographical Section, Southwest Pacific Area
AIB Allied Intelligence Bureau, Southwest Pacific Area
AMF Australian Military Forces
ATIS Allied Translator and Interpreter Section, Southwest Pacific Area
AW39–45 *Australia in the War of 1939–45*
CBI China-Burma-India Theater
CCS Combined Chiefs of Staff
CG Commanding general
CIC Counterintelligence Corps
CMH Center of Military History, Department of the Army, Washington, D.C.
CM-OUT (IN) Classified outgoing (incoming) message
CO Commanding officer
CofS Chief of staff
CUOHRO Oral History Research Office, Columbia University, New York
DM General Douglas MacArthur
DMBP Douglas MacArthur Biographical Papers, Mississippi State University

DM Misc. 201 Miscellaneous 201 file of General Douglas MacArthur, Center of Military History

DSC Distinguished Service Cross

DSM Distinguished Service Medal

FEAF Far East Air Force(s)

FEC Far East Command

FDR President Franklin D. Roosevelt

FDRL Franklin D. Roosevelt Library, Hyde Park, N.Y.

FRUSDP *Foreign Relations of the United States: Diplomatic Papers*

G-1 Personnel and administration section (or chief)

G-2 Intelligence section (or chief)

G-3 Operations and training section (or chief)

G-4 Supply section (or chief)

GCM General George C. Marshall

GHQ General headquarters

Hist. Com. Historical committee

Hq. Headquarters

HSTL Harry S. Truman Library

HSWWUKMS *History of the Second World War: United Kingdom Military Series*

HUSMCOWWII *History of U.S. Marine Corps Operations in World War II*

HUSNOWWII *History of United States Naval Operations in World War II*

Int. *Interview(s)*

JCS Joint Chiefs of Staff

JPS Joint Staff Planners

LC Manuscript Division, Library of Congress, Washington, D.C.

MCHD Historical Division, United States Marine Corps Headquarters, Arlington, Va.

MHRC United States Army Military History Research Collection, Carlisle Barracks, Pa.

MMBA MacArthur Memorial Bureau of Archives, Norfolk, Va.

MSU Special Collections Department, Mitchell Memorial Library, Mississippi State University

NA National Archives, Washington, D.C.

NHD Naval History Division, Department of the Navy, Washington, D.C.

OF Official file, Franklin D. Roosevelt Papers, Franklin D. Roosevelt Library

OHNZSWW *Official History of New Zealand in the Second World War, 1939–45*

OPD-EF Records of War Department Operations Division, executive file, record group 165, National Archives
POA Pacific Ocean Areas
PPF President's personal file, Franklin D. Roosevelt Papers
PRO (PIO) Public relations (or information) office (or chief)
PSF President's secretary's file, Franklin D. Roosevelt Papers
RAAF Royal Australian Air Force
RAN Royal Australian Navy
RG Record group
SCAP Supreme Commander for the Allied Powers, Japan
SecNavy Secretary of the Navy
SecState Secretary of State
SecWar Secretary of War
SWPA Southwest Pacific Area
TAG (AGWAR) Adjutant General of the United States Army (or office of)
UNRRA United Nations Relief and Rehabilitation Administration
USAAF United States Army Air Forces
USAF United States Air Force
USAFFE United States Army Forces in the Far East
USAFIA United States Army Forces in Australia
USAF (NL) United States Army Forces (North Luzon) [guerrilla forces]
USAFPAC (AFPAC) United States Army Forces, Pacific
USAFWESPAC United States Army Forces in the Western Pacific
USASOS United States Army Services of Supply, Southwest Pacific Area
USAWWII *U.S. Army in World War II*
USFIP United States Forces in the Philippines
USMC United States Marine Corps
USN United States Navy
USSBS United States Strategic Bombing Survey
WAC Women's Army Corps
WNRC Washington National Records Center, Suitland, Md.
WPD War Plans Division, War Department, Washington, D.C.

Bibliographical Note

Manuscripts

The holdings of the MacArthur Memorial Bureau of Archives, Norfolk, Virginia, provide a convenient, extensive coverage of much of MacArthur's professional activities, 1941–45. Most useful were RG 2, GHQ USAFFE records (nine archival boxes); RG 3, GHQ SWPA records (160 boxes); RG 4, GHQ AFPAC records (thirty-one boxes); RG 5, GHQ SCAP records (116 boxes), including many items predating the Japanese occupation; RG 9, MacArthur's official messages, mainly radiograms (seventy-four boxes), most of which, however, cover 1945–51; RG 10, MacArthur's private correspondence (ninety-three boxes), which contains disappointingly few letters by him and little data revealing his personal life and thoughts; and RG 16, General Courtney Whitney's papers (twenty-one boxes), principally on Philippine guerrilla affairs. Also helpful were the periodical file, newspaper collection, scrapbooks, collection of photographs, and MacArthur's personal library to which have been added since 1964 most significant publications relating to all aspects of his career. The MacArthur Memorial's oral history collection was unfortunately terminated after a brief, promising start. The MacArthur scholar must use this depository as the starting point in his research, but little will be found there that reflects adversely on the general's career.

Among federal depositories the Washington National Records Center, Suitland, Maryland, and the National Archives, Washington, D.C., contain enormous numbers of documents relating to the war in the Southwest Pacific. But the sheer mass of the materials, together with the fact that the guides and indexes are organized by geographical, topical, and unit decimal systems with virtually no biographical locators, presented difficulties in the ferreting out of information specifically on MacArthur. At Suitland the most useful collection was the G-3 journals of GHQ SWPA, comprising 271 boxes of documents of a wide assortment, ranging from operations reports and intelligence summaries to strategic and tactical planning data and messages to and from MacArthur. Other Suitland files containing information on MacArthur were found in the records of the headquarters of USAFFE, USFIP, AFPAC, Alamo Force, Sixth Army, Eighth Army, and various theater task forces. In the National Archives' Modern Military Records division are thousands of messages and documents to, from, or concerning MacArthur in RG 165, especially the Operations Division 201 MacArthur file, executive office file, message center file, strategy and policy group file, and chief of staff file; RG 218, including the records of the geographical and general decimal files of the Joint Chiefs of Staff and the Combined Chiefs of Staff and their committees; and the vast RG 407, which contains the Adjutant General central files since 1917. In the National Archives' Diplomatic Division there is a Pacific War file in RG 59 that has some items pertaining to MacArthur, but most of the important documents have been printed in the State Department's *Foreign Relations* series. The Manuscript Division of the Library of Congress in Washington has a small MacArthur collection as well as some pertinent items in the papers of Generals Henry H. Arnold and George Van Horn Moseley.

Among collections found at military installations, the Center of Military History (formerly the Office of the Chief of Military History) at Fort McNair in Washington has a variety of materials brought together largely in the process of preparing the official Army volumes on the Pacific War. They include historical studies of operations and units, official and unofficial reports, researchers' interviews with MacArthur and some of his commanders, miscellaneous 201 files of MacArthur and his senior officers, and useful newspaper and periodical files. In the Army's Military History Research Collection at Carlisle Barracks, Pennsylvania, information on MacArthur was located in the papers of Generals Charles A. Willoughby and Bradford G. Chynoweth and Colonel William C. Braly. The Archives Department of the U.S. Military Academy, West Point, New York, contains a small MacArthur correspondence file and some scrapbooks on his career. In the records of the Naval History Division at the Washington Navy Yard significant data were found in the papers of Admirals Thomas C. Hart, Francis W. Rockwell, William F. Halsey, Daniel E. Barbey, and Robert H. Ghormley; narratives of operations and transcripts of interviews with various admirals active in Southwest Pacific operations; a file of some of MacArthur's radiograms; and logs of naval ships on which MacArthur traveled. Oral transcripts of Generals Oliver P. Smith, Omar T. Pfeiffer, and Thomas E. Bourke were used in the Marine Corps Historical Division, Arlington, Virginia. The Air University's Albert F. Simpson Historical Research Center, Maxwell Air Force Base, Alabama, has information on MacArthur and his relations with his air commanders in the papers of Generals Henry H. Arnold and Ennis C. Whitehead, as well as in the Walter D. Edmonds collection; various Air Room interviews with Southwest Pacific officers; a collection of MacArthur's messages to the War Department on air matters; files of the FEAF, Fifth Air Force, and other Southwest Pacific air headquarters; and a number of valuable historical studies prepared by Air Force researchers on sundry aspects of the air war in MacArthur's theater.

Of the presidential libraries the Franklin D. Roosevelt Library, Hyde Park, New York, has material relevant to MacArthur's wartime activities in the Harry Hopkins papers and, of course, in President Roosevelt's papers. In the latter helpful data were obtained from the press conferences and the map room, President's secretary's, White House official, President's personal, and confidential War Department files. At the Harry S. Truman Library, Independence, Missouri, the official file in the Truman papers contains a number of items pertinent to MacArthur in 1945. In the Eisenhower principal file, 1916–52, at the Dwight D. Eisenhower Library, Abilene, Kansas, the MacArthur and Quezon folders have some messages of interest.

Among university collections the most significant is that of General Robert L. Eichelberger at Duke University, Durham, North Carolina. The most noteworthy excerpts from his diary and letters of 1942–45 have been largely included in Luvaas, ed., *Dear Miss Em.* Although numerous notes were made from this collection, the author relied heavily on Luvaas' more thorough search for the war years. Extensive research in both the Eichelberger and Truman papers will be necessary, however, for the post-1945 period of MacArthur's career. The Oral History Collection of Columbia University, New York, has a number of transcripts that contain comments relating to MacArthur, particularly in the reminiscences of Admirals Thomas C. Kinkaid, William M. Fechteler, Thomas C. Hart, and J. H. Hoover. The papers of Admiral Aaron S. Merrill in the Southern Historical Collection, University of North Carolina, Chapel Hill, include minor information on MacArthur and the naval war in the Southwest Pacific. Helpful data were obtained from the papers of Generals Robert C. Richardson, Clovis E. Byers, and Joseph W. Stilwell and Admiral Charles A. Lockwood in the Hoover Institution on War, Revolution, and Peace, Stanford University, Palo Alto, California. Also of value were the Henry L. Stimson papers and diary at Yale University, New Haven, Connecticut.

Over the years since this biographical study was begun, a growing body of assorted documentary material relating to MacArthur's career has been collected in the Mitchell Memorial Library, Mississippi State University. Most of it has been in the form of photocopies of thousands of individual documents which the author has obtained from various depositories across the nation. A number of items available on microfilm have been obtained, such as the trials of Generals Homma and Yamashita, the proceedings and exhibits of the International Military Tribunal of the Far East USAFFE-USFIP and SWPA operations reports and historical studies, GHQ SWPA communiqués, and files of various newspapers. Some manuscripts have been contributed by various colleagues and contemporaries of MacArthur, which have been generally grouped under the designation of the Douglas MacArthur Biographical Papers. In addition, the Mitchell Library's Special Collections Department contains some significant related papers, such as those of General William E. Brougher.

Interviews and Correspondence

The following is a list of persons who graciously consented to interviews with the author. The locations and dates of the interviews are also given. A *T* denotes that the interview was tape-recorded. Each tape and transcript has been deposited in the Mitchell Memorial Library, Mississippi State University. An *X* indicates that the person provided additional data in the form of documents, letters, clippings, photographs, or other materials. The author owes a great debt of gratitude to these interviewees: Capt. Robert H. Alexander, Norfolk, Va., May 28, 1971 (X); Lt. Gen. Edward M. Almond, Anniston, Ala., Aug. 4, 1971 (TX); Col. A. D. Amoroso, Atlanta, Ga., Dec. 17, 1966; Earl L. Ballenger, Norfolk, Va., May 27, 1971; Lt. Gen. Earl W. Barnes, Washington, D.C., July 1, 1971; Maj. Gen. William A. Beiderlinden, McLean, Va., June 25, 1971 (X); Adm. Russell S. Berkey, Old Lyme, Conn., July 9, 1971 (TX); Brig. Gen. Clifford Bluemel, Yardley, Pa., July 8, 1971 (T); Maj. Faubion Bowers, New York, N.Y., July 18, 1971 (TX); Lt. Gen. Alpha L. Bowser, San Diego, Calif., Sept. 3, 1971 (TX); Maj. Gen. Frank H. Britton, Largo, Fla., July 28, 1971 (TX); Mrs. William E. Brougher, Atlanta, Ga., December 16–18, 1966 (X); Rear Adm. John D. Bulkeley, Arlington, Va., July 2, 1971 (X); Col. Laurence E. Bunker, Wellesley Hills, Mass., July 12, 1971 (T); Lt. Gen. Joseph C. Burger, Virginia Beach, Va., June 5, 1971; Adm. Arleigh A. Burke, Washington, D.C., July 2, 1971 (TX); Lt. Gen. Clovis E. Byers, Washington, D.C., June 24, 1971 (T); Col. Frank C. Caldwell, Arlington, Va., June 18, 1971; Dr. Verna A. Carley, Walnut Creek, Calif., Aug. 23, 1971 (T); Col. James D. Carter, Kentfield, Calif., Aug. 23, 1971 (T); Turner Catledge, Starkville, Miss., Mar. 25, 1971 (T); Col. Joseph L. Chabot, Washington, D.C., Dec. 18, 1966, and July 2, 1971; Vice Adm. Alvin D. Chandler, Virginia Beach, Va., June 5, 1971; Bernard P. Chitty, Norfolk, Va., May 26–27, 1971; Maj. Gen. James G. Christiansen, Columbus, Ga., Aug. 4, 1971 (T); Brig. Gen. Bradford G. Chynoweth, Berkeley, Calif., Aug. 22, 1971 (TX); Col. James V. Collier, Santa Barbara, Calif., Aug. 20, 1971 (T); Gen. J. Lawton Collins, Washington, D.C., Aug. 30, 1967, and June 15, 1971; Brig. Gen. John F.

Conklin, Chevy Chase, Md., June 22, 1971; Lt. Gen. Edward A. Craig, El Cajon, Calif., Sept. 3, 1971 (TX); Maj. Gen. Chester A. Dahlen, San Antonio, Tex., Sept. 8, 1971 (TX); Vice Adm. Ralph E. Davison, Pensacola, Fla., Aug. 2, 1971 (T); Gen. Jacob L. Devers, Washington, D.C., June 30, 1971; Joseph H. Downs, Jr., Starkville, Miss., Nov. 17, 1970; Gen. Clyde D. Eddleman, Washington, D.C., June 29, 1971; Dr. Roger O. Egeberg, Washington, D.C., June 29–30, 1971 (TX); Gen. of the Army Dwight D. Eisenhower, Gettysburg, Pa., Aug. 29, 1967 (X); Brig. Gen. John A. Elmore, McLean, Va., June 25, 1971 (T); Maj. Gaetano Faillace, North Hollywood, Calif., Aug. 31, 1971 (TX); Brig. Gen. Bonner F. Fellers, Washington, D.C., June 26, 1971 (TX); Brig. Gen. Burdette M. Fitch, San Francisco, Calif., Aug. 26, 1971 (TX); Brig. Gen. Louis J. Fortier, Washington, D.C., June 23, 1971 (T); Lt. Gen. Alonzo P. Fox, Washington, D.C., June 26, 1971 (TX); Col. René E. Frailé, Santa Barbara, Calif., Aug. 30, 1971 (TX); Benis M. Frank, Arlington, Va., June 18, 1971 (X); Col. A. Dean Gough, Kentfield, Aug. 23, 1971, Calif. (T); Benson Guyton, Decatur, Ala., Aug. 5, 1971 (TX); Lt. Col. J. Addison Hagan, Norfolk, Va., June 3, 1971; Gen. Thomas T. Handy, San Antonio, Tex., Sept. 8, 1971 (TX); Maj. Gen. and Mrs. George W. Hickman, Jr., Solana Beach, Calif., Sept. 4, 1971 (TX); Brig. Gen. Milton A. Hill, Santa Barbara, Calif., Aug. 30, 1971 (TX); Maj. Gen. John E. Hull, Washington, D.C., June 23, 1971; Lt. Gen. Joseph C. Hutchison, Sanford, Fla., July 27, 1971; Brig. Gen. Dwight F. Johns, Piedmont, Calif., Aug. 22, 1971 (TX); Vice Adm. Felix Johnson, Leonardtown, Md., July 7, 1971 (TX); Gen. Harold K. Johnson, Washington, D.C., Dec. 18, 1966, and Valley Forge, Pa., July 7, 1971 (TX); Under Secretary of State U. Alexis Johnson, Washington, D.C., June 24, 1971 (X); Col. John M. Kemper, Andover, Mass., July 13, 1971 (T); Gen. George C. Kenney, New York, N.Y., July 16, 1971 (TX); Maj. Gen. Thomas A. Lane, McLean, Va., June 25, 1971 (T); Frederic S. Marquardt, Phoenix, Ariz., Sept. 5, 1971 (TX); Maj. Gen. Richard J. Marshall, Leesburg, Fla., July 27, 1971 (TX); Col. and Mrs. Sidney F. Mashbir, Laguna Beach, Calif., Sept. 1–2, 1971 (TX); Col. Aurelio Mendoza, Starkville, Miss., Aug. 21, 1972 (X); Chaplain Luther D. Miller, Washington, D.C., June 28, 1971; Brig. Gen. Frederick P. Munson, Washington, D.C., July 2, 1971 (T); Col. Virgil Ney, Silver Spring, Md., July 6, 1971 (TX); Col. William Niederpruem, Los Gatos, Calif., Aug. 25, 1971 (TX); Adm. Albert G. Noble, Washington, D.C., June 24, 1971 (T); Col. L. Robert Rice, Virginia Beach, Va., June 3, 1971; Brig. Gen. William L. Ritchie, Washington, D.C., June 24, 1971 (T); Brig. Gen. Paul I. Robinson, Montgomery, Ala., Aug. 3, 1971 (T); Brig. Gen. Crawford F. Sams, Atherton, Calif., Aug. 25, 1971 (TX); Gen. Frank C. Schilt, Norfolk, Va., June 5, 1971; Amb. William J. Sebald, Naples, Fla., July 30, 1971 (TX); Col. Clyde A. Selleck, Chevy Chase, Md., June 22, 1971; Adm. H. Page Smith, Virginia Beach, Va., June 5, 1971; Gen. Oliver P. Smith, Los Altos,

Calif., Aug. 25, 1971 (T); Mrs. William A. Smith, Hilton Head Island, S.C. (T); Gen. Carl Spaatz, Chevy Chase, Md., June 22, 1971; Col. Anthony F. Story, New York, N.Y., July 16, 1971; Mrs. George E. Stratemeyer, Winter Park, Fla., July 27, 1971 (X); Dr. W. Dupont Strong, Leesburg, Fla., July 27, 1971 (T); Adm. Arthur D. Struble, Chevy Chase, Md., June 22, 1971 (T); Lt. Gen. Joseph M. Swing, San Francisco, Calif., Aug. 26, 1971 (TX); Rear Adm. Raymond D. Tarbuck, Coronado, Calif., Sept. 4, 1971 (TX); Vice Adm. Edmund B. Taylor, Virginia Beach, Va., June 5, 1971; Brig. Gen. Edward W. Timberlake, Naples, Fla., July 29, 1971; Brig. Gen. Robert H. Van Volkenburgh, San Francisco, Calif., Aug. 26, 1971 (T); Brig. Gen. Harry Van Wyk, Pebble Beach, Calif., Aug. 28, 1971 (T); Gen. Albert C. Wedemeyer, Boyds, Md., July 6, 1971 (TX); Capt. Rexford V. Wheeler, Norfolk, Va., June 3, 1971; Cdr. Justus P. White, Virginia Beach, Va., June 5, 1971; Maj. Gen. Courtney Whitney, Washington, D.C., Aug. 28, 1967 (X); Maj. Gen. Charles A. Willoughby, Washington, D.C., Aug. 28, 1967, and Naples, Fla., July 30, 1971 (TX); Maj. Gen. Roscoe B. Woodruff, San Antonio, Tex., Sept. 8, 1971 (TX); Maj. Gen. Edwin K. Wright, Monterey, Calif., Aug. 28, 1971 (TX); Lt. Gen. John M. Wright, Jr., Arlington, Va., June 28, 1971 (X); and Amb. Thomas K. Wright, Naples, Fla., July 30, 1971 (T).

The following persons provided advice or information in various ways, largely through correspondence and in the form of personal reminiscences, letters, documents, clippings, and other items relating to MacArthur: Dr. Terry Alford, Philip P. Brower, Henry A. Burgess, Maj. Gen. Stephen J. Chamberlin, Maj. Gen. William G. Chase, Howard I. J. Collier, Adm. V. A. C. Crutchley, Dr. D. N. Diedrich, George Dingledy, Harold Flakser, Col. Dennis S. Forbes, Maj. Gen. William H. Gill, Dr. Grant K. Goodman, Philip C. Gowdy, James J. Halsema, Laurence Halstead, the Rev. Benson H. Harvey, Lt. Gen. Edmund F. Herring, Brig. Gen. Paul W. Johnston, Maurice Kanareck, Maj. Edward L. Kuykendall, W. R. Lancaster, Dr. Jay Luvaas, Brig. Gen. Frank McCarthy, James J. McGlynn, Maj. Gen. George O. Pearson, Dr. Forrest C. Pogue, Morgan A. Powell, George F. Qua, Capt. George L. Robson, Jr., Irving R. Saum, Gen. Lemuel C. Shepherd, Robert Sherrod, Edward J. Smith, Dr. William N. Still, Jr., William M. Taylor, Jr., Gen. A. A. Vandegrift, I. M. Wards, and Lady Muriel Wooten.

Published Sources

Especially valuable to this study was Charles A. Willoughby, ed., *Reports of General MacArthur* (2 vols. in 4 pts., Washington, 1966), although frequent reliance on GHQ communiqués and omission of episodes reflecting unfavorably on MacArthur mar the volumes. Also helpful were the following series produced under the auspices of MacArthur's headquarters in

Tokyo: Hugh J. Casey, ed., *Engineers of the Southwest Pacific, 1941–1945: Reports of Operations* — *United States Army Forces in the Far East, Southwest Pacific Area,* [*and*] *Army Forces, Pacific* (7 vols., Washington, 1947–53); and Charles A. Willoughby, ed., *The Intelligence Series: G-2 USAFFE, SWPA, AFPAC, FEC, SCAP* (18 vols., Tokyo, 1948). Other useful printed documentary materials by defense agencies included U.S. Department of the Army, *Order of Battle of the United States Army Ground Forces in World War II: Pacific Theater of Operations* (Washington, 1959); U.S. Navy Department, *Annual Report of the Secretary of the Navy for the Fiscal Year 1942* (Washington, 1942); *Navy Department Communiques 1–300 and Pertinent Press Releases, December 10, 1941, to March 5, 1943* (Washington, 1943); and *Navy Department Communiques 301 to 600 and Pacific Fleet Communiques, March 6, 1943, to May 24, 1945, with Other Official Statements and Pertinent Press Releases* (Washington, 1945). Brief but useful summaries of strategy and operations were found in the three reports each by Marshall and Arnold to the Secretary of War and of King to the Secretary of the Navy, which were published separately but later collected in Walter Millis, ed., *The War Reports of General of the Army George C. Marshall, General of the Army H. H. Arnold, and Fleet Admiral Ernest J. King* (Philadelphia, 1947).

A considerable amount of information pertaining to MacArthur's activities was obtained in the following volumes of the U.S. State Department's *Foreign Relations of the United States: Diplomatic Papers:* 1941, Vols. IV–V; 1942, Vol. I; 1943, Vol. III; 1944, Vol. V; and 1945, Vols. VI–VII. Also important were these State Department volumes: *The Conferences at Washington, 1941–1942, and Casablanca, 1943* (Washington, 1968); *The Conferences at Cairo and Tehran, 1943* (Washington, 1961); *The Conferences at Malta and Yalta, 1945* (Washington, 1955); *The Conference of Berlin (The Potsdam Conference), 1945* (Washington, 1960); and *The Axis in Defeat: A Collection of Documents on American Policy Toward Germany and Japan* (Washington, 1945).

Other federal publications of documentary materials that proved useful included U.S. Bureau of the Census, *Vote Cast in Presidential and Congressional Elections, 1928–1944* (Washington, 1946); U.S. High Commissioner to the Philippine Islands, *Sixth Annual Report of the United States High Commissioner to the Philippine Islands Covering the Fiscal Year July 1, 1941, to June 30, 1942* (Washington, 1943); U.S. Senate, Committee on Military Affairs, *Sack of Manila* (Washington, 1945); and U.S. National Archives, *Public Papers of the Presidents of the United States: Harry S. Truman; Containing the Public Messages, Speeches, and Statements of the President, April 12 to December 31, 1945* (Washington, 1961).

The Pacific studies prepared by the U.S. Strategic Bombing Survey, which contain both primary and secondary materials, were helpful, particularly the following: *Air Campaigns of the Pacific War* (Washington, 1947); *The*

Allied Campaign Against Rabaul (Washington, 1946); *The Campaigns of the Pacific War* (Washington, 1946); *Employment of Forces Under the Southwest Pacific Command* (Washington, 1947); *The Fifth Air Force in the War Against Japan* (Washington, 1947); *Interrogations of Japanese Officials* (2 vols., Washington, 1946); *Summary Report (Pacific War)* (Washington, 1946); *The Thirteenth Air Force in the War Against Japan* (Washington, 1946); *The Effects of Strategic Bombing on Japanese Morale* (Washington, 1947); *The Reduction of Truk* (Washington, 1947); and *Japan's Struggle to End the War* (Washington, 1946). Also useful was U.S. Army Air Forces, *Mission Accomplished: Interrogations of Japanese Industrial, Military, and Civil Leaders of World War II* (Washington, 1946).

The most significant published source is MacArthur's *Reminiscences* (New York, 1964), but his account of the war years must be used with great caution since it is replete with errors and important omissions. A detailed analysis of his controversial memoirs will be deferred until the concluding volume of this study. Some of his wartime messages are reprinted in U.S. Library of Congress, Legislative Reference Service, comp., *Representative Speeches of General of the Army Douglas MacArthur* (Washington, 1964); and Vorin E. Whan, ed., *A Soldier Speaks: Public Papers and Speeches of General of the Army Douglas MacArthur* (New York, 1965). The principal memoirs by his staff officers which focus on MacArthur and are all adulatory include Sidney L. Huff, with Joe A. Morris, *My Fifteen Years with General MacArthur* (New York, 1964); George C. Kenney, *General Kenney Reports: A Personal History of the Pacific War* (New York, 1949); *idem, The MacArthur I Know* (New York, 1951); Courtney Whitney, *MacArthur: His Rendezvous with History* (New York, 1955); and Charles A. Willoughby and John Chamberlain, *MacArthur, 1941–1951* (New York, 1954). By far the most important, revealing source on MacArthur and his headquarters by one of his commanders is Jay Luvaas, ed., *Dear Miss Em: General Eichelberger's War in the Pacific, 1942–1945* (Westport, 1972), upon which the author relied heavily.

Other primary works used in the preparation of this volume were Henry H. Arnold, *Global Mission* (New York, 1949); Daniel E. Barbey, *MacArthur's Amphibious Navy: Seventh Amphibious Force Operations, 1943–1945* (Annapolis, 1969); Lewis H. Brereton, *The Brereton Diaries: The War in the Air in the Pacific, Middle East, and Europe, 3 October 1941–8 May 1945* (New York, 1946); James F. Byrnes, *Speaking Frankly* (New York, 1947); Hadley Cantril, ed., *Public Opinion, 1935–1946* (Princeton, 1951); Turner Catledge, *My Life and the Times* (New York, 1971); Alfred D. Chandler, Jr., ed., *The Papers of Dwight David Eisenhower: The War Years* (5 vols., Baltimore, 1970); Claire L. Chennault, *Way of a Fighter: The Memoirs of Claire Lee Chennault*, ed. Robert Hotz (New York, 1949); Calvin E. Chunn, ed., *Of Rice and Men: The Story of Americans Under the Rising Sun* (Los Angeles, 1946); Winston S. Churchill, *The Second World War* (6 vols., Boston, 1948–53); J. J. Clark, *Carrier Admiral*

(New York, 1967); Don Congdon, ed., *Combat: Pacific Theater, World War II* (New York, 1959); *idem*, ed., *Combat: The War with Japan* (New York, 1962); Robert Considine, *It's All News to Me: A Reporter's Deposition* (New York, 1967); John R. Deane, *The Strange Alliance: The Story of Our Efforts at Wartime Co-operation with Russia* (New York, 1947); William E. Dyess, *The Dyess Story: The Eye-witness Account of the Death March from Bataan and the Narrative of Experiences in Japanese Prison Camps and of Eventual Escape*, ed. Charles Leavelle (New York, 1944); Robert L. Eichelberger, with Milton McKaye, *Our Jungle Road to Tokyo* (New York, 1950); Dwight D. Eisenhower, *Crusade in Europe* (7th ed., Garden City, 1948); H. V. Evatt, *Australia in World Affairs* (Sydney, 1947); *idem, Foreign Policy of Australia: Speeches* (Sydney, 1945); Eric A. Feldt, *The Coastwatchers* (New York, 1947); Cato D. Glover, *Command Performance with Guts* (New York, 1969); Leslie R. Groves, *Now It Can Be Told: The Story of the Manhattan Project* (New York, 1962); William F. Halsey and Joseph Bryan, III, *Admiral Halsey's Story* (New York, 1947); William F. Heavey, *Down Ramp! The Story of the Army Amphibian Engineers* (Washington, 1947); Joseph P. Hobbs, ed., *Dear General: Eisenhower's Wartime Letters to Marshall* (Baltimore, 1971); Cordell Hull, *The Memoirs of Cordell Hull* (2 vols., New York, 1948); Allison Ind, *Allied Intelligence Bureau: Our Secret Weapon in the War Against Japan* (New York, 1958); *idem, Bataan, The Judgment Seat: The Saga of the Philippine Command of the United States Army Air Force, May 1941 to May 1942* (New York, 1944); D. Clayton James, ed., *South to Bataan, North to Mukden: The Prison Diary of Brigadier General W. E. Brougher* (Athens, Ga., 1971); George H. Johnston, *Pacific Partner* (New York, 1944); *idem, The Toughest Fighting in the World* (New York, 1943); E. J. Kahn, Jr., *G.I. Jungle: An American Soldier in Australia and New Guinea* (New York, 1943); Toshikazu Kase, *Journey to the Missouri,* ed. David N. Rowe (New Haven, 1950); Ernest J. King, with Walter M. Whitehill, *Fleet Admiral King: A Naval Record* (New York, 1952); Yoshio Kodama, *I Was Defeated,* trans. Taro Fukuda (Tokyo, 1959); Walter Krueger, *From Down Under to Nippon: The Story of Sixth Army in World War II* (Washington, 1953); Philip LaFollette, *Adventure in Politics: The Memoirs of Philip LaFollette,* ed. Donald Young (New York, 1970); William D. Leahy, *I Was There: The Personal Story of the Chief of Staff to Presidents Roosevelt and Truman Based on His Notes and Diaries Made at the Time* (New York, 1950); Clark Lee, *They Call It Pacific: An Eye-Witness Story of Our War Against Japan from Bataan to the Solomons* (New York, 1943); Henry G. Lee, *Nothing But Praise* (Culver City, Calif., 1948); Robert W. Levering, *Horror Trek: A True Story of Bataan, the Death March and Three and One-half Years in Japanese Prison Camps* (Dayton, 1948); Charles A. Lindbergh, *The Wartime Journals of Charles A. Lindbergh* (New York, 1970); Charles A. Lockwood, *Sink 'Em All: Submarine Warfare in the Pacific* (New York, 1951); Ross T. McIntire, *White*

House Physician (New York, 1946); Frederic S. Marquardt, *Before Bataan and After: A Personalized History of Our Philippine Experiment* (Indianapolis, 1943); Adalia Márquez, *Blood on the Rising Sun: A Factual Story of the Japanese Invasion of the Philippines* (New York, 1957); Sidney F. Mashbir, *I Was an American Spy* (New York, 1953); Steve M. Mellnik, *Philippine Diary, 1939–1945* (Princeton, 1969); Ernest B. Miller, *Bataan Uncensored* (Long Prairie, Minn., 1949); Walter Millis, ed., *The Forrestal Diaries* (New York, 1951); Manuel L. Quezon, *The Good Fight* (New York, 1946); Juanita Redmond, *I Served on Bataan* (Philadelphia, 1943); Edward V. Rickenbacker, *Rickenbacker: An Autobiography* (Englewood Cliffs, 1967); Harold Riegelman, *Caves of Biak: An American Officer's Experiences in the Southwest Pacific* (New York, 1955); Carlos P. Romulo, *I Saw the Fall of the Philippines* (Garden City, 1942); *idem, I See the Philippines Rise* (Garden City, 1946); *idem, I Walked with Heroes* (New York, 1961); Elliott Roosevelt, ed., *F.D.R.: His Personal Letters, 1928–1945* (4 vols., New York, 1950); Elmo B. Roper, *You and Your Leaders: Their Actions and Your Reactions, 1936–1956* (New York, 1957); Samuel I. Rosenman, *Working with Roosevelt* (New York, 1942); *idem,* comp., *The Public Papers and Addresses of Franklin D. Roosevelt* (13 vols., New York, 1938–50); Francis B. Sayre, *Glad Adventure* (New York, 1957); Frederick C. Sherman, *Combat Command: The American Aircraft Carriers in the Pacific War* (New York, 1950); Holland M. Smith and Percy Finch, *Coral and Brass* (New York, 1949); S. E. Smith, ed., *The United States Marine Corps in World War II* (New York, 1969); *idem,* ed., *The United States Navy in World War II* (New York, 1966); William H. Standley, with Arthur A. Ageton, *Admiral Ambassador to Russia* (Chicago, 1955); Henry L. Stimson and McGeorge Bundy, *On Active Service in Peace and War* (New York, 1948); C. L. Sulzberger, *A Long Row of Candles: Memoirs and Diaries (1934–1954)* (New York, 1969); W. N. Swan, *Spearheads of Invasion: An Account of the Seven Major Invasions Carried Out by the Allies in the South-west Pacific Area During the Second World War, as Seen from a Royal Australian Naval Landing Ship Infantry* (Sydney, 1953); Harold Templeman, *The Return to Corregidor* (New York, 1945); Elliott R. Thorpe, *East Wind Rain: The Intimate Account of an Intelligence Officer in the Pacific, 1939–49* (Boston, 1969); Harry S. Truman, *Memoirs* (2 vols., Garden City, 1955–56); Jan Valtin, *Children of Yesterday* (New York, 1946); Alexander A. Vandegrift, with Robert B. Asprey, *Once A Marine: The Memoirs of General A. A. Vandegrift* (New York, 1964); Arthur H. Vandenberg, Jr., ed., *The Private Papers of Senator Vandenberg* (Boston, 1952); Russell W. Volckmann, *We Remained: Three Years Behind the Enemy Lines in the Philippines* (New York, 1954); Jonathan M. Wainwright, *General Wainwright's Story: The Account of Four Years of Humiliating Defeat, Surrender, and Captivity,* ed. Robert Considine (Garden City, 1946); Albert C. Wedemeyer, *Wedemeyer Reports!* (New York, 1958); Alfred A. Weinstein, *Barbed-Wire Surgeon* (New York,

1948); Edgar D. Whitcomb, *Escape from Corregidor* (Chicago, 1958); Osmar White, *Green Armor* (New York, 1945); William L. White, *They Were Expendable* (New York, 1942); Yank editors, *The Best from Yank, the Army Weekly* (Cleveland, 1945); and Ellis M. Zacharias, *Secret Missions: The Story of an Intelligence Officer* (New York, 1946).

Newspapers and Periodicals

The 1941–45 issues of the following newspapers were thoroughly searched for articles relating to MacArthur: *New York Times,* Chicago *Tribune,* London *Times,* Brisbane *Courier-Mail,* Manila *Free Philippines,* and Tokyo *Nippon Times* (sometimes *Japan Times and Advertiser*). Files of clippings on MacArthur were obtained at various depositories or through individual contributors of these newspapers: *Herald Tribune* and *Daily News* of New York; *Post, Evening Star, Times-Herald,* and *Daily News* of Washington; *Examiner* and *Chronicle* of San Francisco; Chicago *Sun-Times;* Memphis *Commercial Appeal;* Raleigh *News and Observer;* Little Rock *Arkansas Gazette;* Minneapolis *Star Journal;* Indianapolis *Star;* Phoenix *Arizona Republic;* Honolulu *Star-Bulletin and Advertiser; Daily Mirror* and *Illustrated News* of London; *Star Reporter* and *Philippines Free Press* of Manila; *Argus, Daily Telegraph, Daily Mirror, Daily Sun,* and *Morning Herald* of Sydney; and *Argus, Daily Sun, Age,* and *Herald* of Melbourne.

Numerous articles about MacArthur appeared in the wartime issues of such periodicals as *Time, Life, Newsweek, New Republic, Harper's Magazine, Fortune, Coronet, Saturday Evening Post, The Nation, Collier's,* and *American Mercury.* Among the most useful were Ernest K. Lindley, "MacArthur's Excursion into Politics," *Newsweek,* XXIII (Apr. 24, 1944), 39; Irving Brant, "The Truth About MacArthur," *New Republic,* CVII (Dec. 28, 1942), 851–53; "MacArthur and the Censorship," *Harper's Magazine,* CLXXXVIII (May, 1944), 537; and particularly John McCarten, "General MacArthur: Fact and Legend," *American Mercury,* LVIII (Jan., 1944), 7–18. Also helpful were articles and reviews referring to MacArthur's wartime career in postwar issues of the above and other periodicals, including *Military Affairs, Military Review, Infantry Journal, Army, American Legion, V.F.W. Magazine, American Historical Review, Foreign Affairs,* and *U.S. Naval Institute Proceedings.*

Official Histories

A perusal of the chapter notes herein will indicate the heavy reliance upon official histories of the war, especially the United States Army and Australian Army chronicles. A tremendous amount of information about

MacArthur's professional activities is in the numerous volumes of the official Allied histories, but locating and synthesizing that data proved to be an arduous task. Thousands of documents used in the preparation of the American series were studied (and often photocopied) not only to check the authenticity and objectivity of the official researchers' use of them but also to locate related files which might contain more information. Almost invariably the official histories were proven to be thorough, accurate, and fair in their references to and judgments concerning MacArthur.

In the Office of the Chief of Military History's *United States Army in World War II* series, the most valuable volumes were Maurice Matloff and Edwin M. Snell, *Strategic Planning for Coalition Warfare, 1941–1942* (Washington, 1953); Maurice Matloff, *Strategic Planning for Coalition Warfare, 1943–1944* (Washington, 1959); Richard M. Leighton and Robert W. Coakley, *Global Logistics and Strategy, 1940–1943* (Washington, 1955); Robert W. Coakley and Richard M. Leighton, *Global Logistics and Strategy, 1943–1945* (Washington, 1968); Louis Morton, *Strategy and Command: The First Two Years* (Washington, 1962); *idem, The Fall of the Philippines* (Washington, 1953); Samuel Milner, *Victory in Papua* (Washington, 1957); John Miller, Jr., *Cartwheel: The Reduction of Rabaul* (Washington, 1959); Robert R. Smith, *The Approach to the Philippines* (Washington, 1953); M. Hamlin Cannon, *Leyte: The Return to the Philippines* (Washington, 1954); Robert R. Smith, *Triumph in the Philippines* (Washington, 1963); Alvin P. Stauffer, *The Quartermaster Corps: Operations in the War Against Japan* (Washington, 1956); and Karl C. Dod, *The Corps of Engineers: The War Against Japan* (Washington, 1966). Numerous other volumes in the Army series were also used, as attested in the chapter notes. Two books in the War Department's *American Forces in Action* series proved valuable: *Papuan Campaign: The Buna-Sanananda Operation (16 November 1942–3 January 1943)* (Washington, 1944); and *The Admiralties: Operations of the 1st Cavalry Division (29 February –18 May 1944)* (Washington, 1945). A helpful volume in the *Army Historical Series* was James A. Huston, *The Sinews of War: Army Logistics, 1775–1953* (Washington, 1966).

In Wesley F. Craven and James L. Cate, eds., *The Army Air Forces in World War II* (7 vols., Chicago, 1948–58), valuable information on MacArthur's relations to his air commanders and air planning was found in *Plans and Early Operations, January 1939 to August 1942* (1948); *The Pacific: Guadalcanal to Saipan, August 1942 to July 1944* (1950); and *The Pacific: Matterhorn to Nagasaki, June 1944 to August 1945* (1953). Pertinent volumes in Samuel E. Morison, *History of United States Naval Operations in World War II* (15 vols., Boston, 1947–62) included *The Rising Sun in the Pacific, 1931–April 1942* (1948); *Coral Sea, Midway, Submarine Actions, May 1942–August 1942* (1949); *Breaking the Bismarcks Barrier, 22 July 1942–1 May 1944* (1950); *New Guinea and the Marianas, March 1944–*

August 1944 (1953); *Leyte, June 1944–January 1945* (1958); *The Libera-tion of the Philippines: Luzon, Mindanao, the Visayas, 1944–1945* (1959); and *Victory in the Pacific, 1945* (1960). Complementing Morison's volumes and of some benefit was Walter Karig, *et al., Battle Report* (5 vols., New York, 1944–52), a semiofficial naval account commissioned by Knox shortly before his death. The U.S. Marine Corps Historical Division's *History of U.S. Marine Corps Operations in World War II* (4 vols. to date, Washing-ton, 1958–68) was useful, as well as some of the Marine Corps monographs, especially Frank O. Hough and John A. Crown, *The Campaign on New Britain* (Washington, 1952); John N. Rentz, *Marines in the Central Solo-mons* (Washington, 1952); and *idem, Bougainville and the Northern Solomons* (Washington, 1948).

Several volumes of the Australian War Memorial's *Australia in the War of 1939–1945* (21 vols. to date, Canberra, 1952–68) were indispensable: Dudley McCarthy, *South-west Pacific Area — First Year: Kokoda to Wau* (1959); David Dexter, *The New Guinea Offensives* (1961); Gavin M. Long, *The Final Campaigns* (1963); George H. Gill, *Royal Australian Navy, 1939–1942* (1957); *idem, Royal Australian Navy, 1942–1945* (1968); Douglas Gil-lison, *Royal Australian Air Force, 1939–1942* (1962); George Odgers, *Air War Against Japan, 1943–1945* (1957); Paul Hasluck, *The Government and the People, 1942–1945* (1952); and Allan S. Walker, *The Island Campaigns* (1957). Other volumes in this excellent series were also used to a lesser extent and are cited in the chapter notes. Other Australian War Memorial publications that proved helpful were Norman Bartlett, *Australia at Arms* (1962) and Australian Imperial Forces, *Jungle Warfare with the Australian Army in the South-west Pacific* (1944). Also valuable was a volume issued under the auspices of the Australian Ministry for Information: Hugh Buggy, *Pacific Victory: A Short History of Australia's Part in the War Against Japan* (Melbourne, 1945). Some of the above Australian works contain extremely frank appraisals of MacArthur's role in the Southwest Pacific war and are essential supplements to the American official volumes in obtaining a balanced picture of Allied plans and operations.

In the *History of the Second World War: United Kingdom Military Series* there are a number of volumes containing information on Mac-Arthur, especially James R. M. Butler, *Grand Strategy, June 1941–August 1942*, Part II (London, 1964); John Ehrman, *Grand Strategy, August 1943–September 1944* (London, 1956); *idem, Grand Strategy, October 1944–August 1945* (London, 1956); S. Woodburn Kirby, *et al., The Surrender of Japan* (London, 1969); and S. W. Roskill, *The War at Sea* (3 vols. in 4 pts., London, 1954–61). Also of value in the official British history of the war was Ernest L. Woodward, *British Foreign Policy in the Second World War* (London, 1962). Several volumes were used from the *Official History of New Zealand in the Second World War, 1939–45,* commissioned by the New Zealand Department of Internal Affairs, War History Branch: *Docu-*

*ments Relating to New Zealand's Participation in the Second World War,
1939-45* (3 vols., Wellington, 1949-63); Oliver A. Gillespie, *The Pacific*
(Wellington, 1952); and J. M. S. Ross, *The Assault on Rabaul: Operations
by the Royal New Zealand Air Force, December 1943-May 1944* (Wellington, 1949).

Other Secondary Works

Regarding MacArthur biographies, see the note in *The Years of Mac-
Arthur*, I, 634-35. Three brief recent works have appeared: Gavin Long,
MacArthur as Military Commander (London, 1969); Sidney L. Mayer,
MacArthur (New York, 1971); and Lawrence S. Wittner, ed., *MacArthur*
(Englewood Cliffs, 1971). Long's work is the best of the many short biographies of the general, although sometimes a strongly pro-Australian bias
is evident. Of the several biographies published during the war years, only
Frazier Hunt, *MacArthur and the War Against Japan* (New York, 1944)
was by an author who had access to the general's papers and extensive interviews with him, but it is of little value to the serious scholar since it is
totally devoid of criticism.

Other biographical studies that proved helpful were Robert G. Albion
and Rober H. Connery, *Forrestal and the Navy* (New York, 1962); Stephen
E. Ambrose, *The Supreme Commander: The War Years of General Dwight
D. Eisenhower* (Garden City, 1970); Arthur Bryant, *The Turn of the Tide:
A History of the War Years Based on the Diaries of Field-Marshal Lord
Alanbrooke, Chief of the Imperial General Staff* (Garden City, 1957);
James M. Burns, *Roosevelt: The Soldier of Freedom, 1940-45* (New York,
1970); Burke Davis, *Marine! The Life of Lt. Gen. Lewis B. (Chesty) Puller,
USMC (Ret.)* (Boston, 1962); Corey Ford, *Donovan of OSS* (Boston, 1970);
William Frye, *Marshall: Citizen Soldier* (Indianapolis, 1947); J. Woodford
Howard, Jr., *Mr. Justice Murphy: A Political Biography* (Princeton, 1968);
Joseph P. Lash, *Eleanor and Franklin: The Story of Their Relationship
Based on Eleanor Roosevelt's Private Papers* (New York, 1971); Don Loh-
beck, *Patrick J. Hurley* (Chicago, 1956); Armando J. Malay, *Occupied
Philippines: The Role of Jorge B. Vargas During the Japanese Occupation*
(Manila, 1967); Elting E. Morison, *Turmoil and Tradition: A Study of the
Life and Times of Henry L. Stimson* (Boston, 1960); Robert Payne, *The
Marshall Story: A Biography of General George C. Marshall* (New York,
1951); Forrest C. Pogue, *George C. Marshall* (3 vols. to date, New York,
1963-73), especially Vols. II–III; Clarence Shadegg, *Clare Boothe Luce*
(New York, 1970); Robert E. Sherwood, *Roosevelt and Hopkins: An Inti-
mate History* (rev. ed., 2 vols., New York, 1950); W. A. Swanberg, *Luce and
His Empire* (New York, 1972); Theodore Taylor, *The Magnificent Mitscher*
(New York, 1954); C. David Tompkins, *Senator Arthur H. Vandenberg:*

The Evolution of a Modern Republican, 1884–1945 (East Lansing, 1970); and Barbara W. Tuckman, *Stilwell and the American Experience in China, 1911–1945* (New York, 1971).
The following military unit histories were relied on heavily: Robert Amory, Jr., and Reuben M. Waterman, eds., *Surf and Sand: The Saga of the 533d Engineer Boat and Shore Regiment and 1461st Engineer Maintenance Company, 1942–1945* (Andover, 1947); William J. Barnard, ed., *The 6th Infantry Division in World War II, 1939–1945* (Washington, 1947); H. W. Blakeley, *The 32d Infantry Division in World War II* (Madison, 1957); Kenneth W. Condit and Edwin T. Turnbladh, *Hold High the Torch: A History of the 4th Marines* (Washington, 1960); Francis D. Cronin, *Under the Southern Cross: The Saga of the Americal Division* (Washington, 1951); Orlando R. Davidson, J. Carl Willems, and Joseph A. Kahl, *The Deadeyes: The Story of the 96th Infantry Division* (Washington, 1947); Edward M. Flanagan, Jr., *The Angels: A History of the 11th Airborne Division, 1943–1946* (Washington, 1948); 40th Infantry Division Historical Committee, *40th Infantry Division: The Years of World War II, 7 December 1941–7 April 1946* (Baton Rouge, 1947); Stanley A. Frankel, *The 37th Infantry Division in World War II* (Washington, 1948); Robert F. Karolevitz, ed., *The 25th Division and World War II* (Baton Rouge, 1946); Benjamin E. Lippincott, *From Fiji Through the Philippines with the Thirteenth Air Force* (San Angelo, Tex., 1948); William F. McCartney, *The Jungleers: A History of the 41st Infantry Division* (Washington, 1948); George McMillan, *The Old Breed: A History of the First Marine Division in World War II* (Washington, 1949); Max Myers, *Ours to Hold It High: The History of the 77th Infantry Division in World War II* (Washington, 1947); James S. Santelli, *A Brief History of the 4th Marines* (Washington, 1970); 31st Infantry Division Historical Committee, *History of the 31st Infantry Division in Training and Combat, 1940–1945* (Baton Rouge, 1946); 33rd Infantry Division Historical Committee, *The Golden Cross: A History of the 33d Infantry Division in World War II* (Washington, 1948); Bertram C. Wright, comp., *The 1st Cavalry Division in World War II* (Tokyo, 1947); and Joseph E. Zimmer, *The History of the 43d Infantry Division, 1941–1945* (Baton Rouge, n.d. [c. 1946]).
Miscellaneous secondary works used in the preparation of this volume included Hernando J. Abaya, *Betrayal in the Philippines* (New York, 1946); Henry H. Adams, *1942: The Year That Doomed the Axis* (New York, 1967); Gar Alperovitz, *Atomic Diplomacy: Hiroshima and Potsdam; the Use of the Atomic Bomb and the American Confrontation with Soviet Power* (New York, 1967); *Army Times* editors, *Modern American Secret Agents* (New York, 1966); Hanson W. Baldwin, *Battles Lost and Won: Great Campaigns of World War II* (New York, 1966); idem, *Great Mistakes of the War* (New York, 1949); Charles Bateson, *The War with Japan: A Concise History* (East Lansing, 1968); James H. Belote and William M.

Belote, *Corregidor: The Saga of a Fortress* (New York, 1967); David Bergamini, *Japan's Imperial Conspiracy: How Emperor Hirohito Led Japan
into War Against the West* (New York, 1971); David Bernstein, *The Philippine Story* (New York, 1947); Hugh Borton, *American Presurrender Planning for Postwar Japan* (New York, 1967); A. Russell Buchanan, *The
United States and World War II* (2 vols., New York, 1964); Robert J.
Bulkley, Jr., *At Close Quarters: PT Boats in the United States Navy* (Washington, 1962); Robert J. C. Butow, *Japan's Decision to Surrender* (Stanford,
1954); Gilbert Cant, *America's Navy in World War II* (New York, 1943);
Demetrios Caraley, *The Politics of Military Unification: A Study of Conflict and the Policy Process* (New York, 1966); Basil Collier, *The War in the
Far East, 1941–1945: A Military History* (New York, 1969); William Craig,
The Fall of Japan (New York, 1967); John Creswell, *Sea Warfare, 1939–
1945* (rev. ed., Berkeley, 1967); Andrieu d'Albas, *Death of a Navy: Japa-
nese Naval Action in World War II* (New York, 1957); Kenneth S. Davis,
Experience of War: The United States in World War II (Garden City,
1965); Vincent Davis, *Postwar Defense Policy and the U.S. Navy, 1943–
1946* (Chapel Hill, 1966); R. Ernest Dupuy and Trevor N. Dupuy, *The
Encyclopedia of Military History: From 3500 B.C. to the Present* (New
York, 1970); Herbert Eaton, *Presidential Timber: A History of Nominating
Conventions, 1868–1960* (New York, 1964); Walter D. Edmonds, *They
Fought with What They Had: The Story of the Army Air Forces in the
Southwest Pacific, 1941–1942* (Boston, 1951); Vincent J. Esposito, ed., *The
West Point Atlas of American Wars* (2 vols., New York, 1959); James K.
Eyre, Jr., *The Roosevelt-MacArthur Conflict* (Chambersburg, Pa., 1950);
Stanley L. Falk, *Bataan: The March of Death* (New York, 1962); *idem,
Decision at Leyte* (New York, 1966); *idem, Liberation of the Philippines*
(New York, 1971); Herbert Feis, *The Atomic Bomb and the End of World
War II* (rev. ed., Princeton, 1966); *idem, Churchill, Roosevelt, Stalin: The
War They Waged and the Peace They Sought* (Princeton, 1957); James A.
Field, Jr., *The Japanese at Leyte Gulf: The Shō Operation* (Princeton,
1947); Theodore Friend, *Between Two Empires: The Ordeal of the Phi-
lippines, 1929–1946* (New Haven, 1965); C. Hartley Grattan, *The South-
west Pacific Since 1900: A Modern History: Australia; New Zealand; the
Islands; Antarctica* (Ann Arbor, 1963); *idem, The United States and the
Southwest Pacific* (Cambridge, Mass., 1961); Kent R. Greenfield, *American
Strategy in World War II: A Reconsideration* (Baltimore, 1963); *idem,* ed.,
Command Decisions (2nd ed., Washington, 1960); Samuel B. Griffith, II,
The Battle for Guadalcanal (Philadelphia, 1963); Garel A. Grunder and
William E. Livezey, *The Philippines and the United States* (Norman,
1951); D. G. E. Hall, *A History of South-east Asia* (3rd ed., New York,
1968); Paul Y. Hammond, *Organizing for Defense: The American Military
Establishment in the Twentieth Century* (Princeton, 1961); Vern Haug-
land, *The AAF Against Japan* (New York, 1948); Saburo Hayashi, *Kōgun:*

The Japanese Army in the Pacific War, trans. Alvin D. Coox (Quantico, 1959); Frank O. Hough, *The Island War: The United States Marine Corps in the Pacific* (Philadelphia, 1947); Edwin P. Hoyt, *How They Won the War in the Pacific: Nimitz and His Admirals* (New York, 1970); Rikihei Inoguchi and Tadashi Nakajima, with Roger Pineau, *The Divine Wind: Japan's Kamikaze Force in World War II* (Annapolis, 1958); Jeter A. Isely and Philip A. Crowl, *The U.S. Marines and Amphibious War: Its Theory and Its Practice in the Pacific* (Princeton, 1951); Morris Janowitz, *The Professional Soldier: A Social and Political Portrait* (Glencoe, 1960); Dudley W. Knox, *A History of the United States Navy* (rev. ed., New York, 1948); Robert Leckie, *Strong Men Armed: The United States Marines Against Japan* (New York, 1962); Werner Levi, *American-Australian Relations* (Minneapolis, 1947); Basil H. Liddell Hart, *History of the Second World War* (New York, 1970); Charles A. Lockwood and Hans C. Adamson, *Battles of the Philippine Sea* (New York, 1967); William H. McNeill, *America, Britain, and Russia: Their Cooperation and Conflict, 1941–1946* (New York, 1953); Nicholas Mansergh, *Survey of British Commonwealth Affairs,* Vol. IV, *Problems of Wartime Co-operation and Post-war Change, 1939–1952* (New York, 1958); Ralph G. Martin, *The GI War, 1941–1945* (Boston, 1967); Joseph J. Mathews, *Reporting the Wars* (Minneapolis, 1957); George H. Mayer, *The Republican Party, 1854–1964* (2nd ed., New York, 1967); L. D. Meo, *Japan's Radio War on Australia, 1941–1945* (Melbourne, 1968); Milton W. Meyer, *A Diplomatic History of the Philippine Republic* (Honolulu, 1965); Walter Millis, *Arms and the State: Civil-Military Elements in National Policy* (New York, 1958); Lennox A. Mills, *et al.*, *The New World of Southeast Asia* (Minneapolis, 1949); Samuel E. Morison, *Strategy and Compromise* (Boston, 1958); *idem, The Two-Ocean War: A Short History of the United States Navy in the Second World War* (Boston, 1963); Louis Morton, *Pacific Command: A Study in Interservice Relations* (Colorado Springs, 1961); Virgil Ney, *Evolution of a Theater of Operations Headquarters, 1941–1967* (Washington, 1967); Raymond O'Conner, ed., *The Japanese Navy in World War II* (Annapolis, 1969); Masatake Okumiya and Jiro Horikoshi, with Martin Caidin, *Zero!* (New York, 1957); E. B. Potter and Chester W. Nimitz, eds., *Triumph in the Pacific: The Navy's Struggle Against Japan* (Englewood Cliffs, 1963); Edgar F. Puryear, Jr., *Nineteen Stars* (Washington, 1971); A. Frank Reel, *The Case of General Yamashita* (Chicago, 1949); Trevor R. Reese, *Australia, New Zealand, and the United States: A Survey of International Relations, 1941–1968* (New York, 1969); Clark G. Reynolds, *The Fast Carriers: The Forging of an Air Navy* (New York, 1968); Theodore Ropp, *War in the Modern World* (Durham, 1959); Eugene H. Roseboom, *A History of Presidential Elections: From George Washington to Richard M. Nixon* (3rd ed., New York, 1970); Joseph Rosner, *The Hater's Handbook* (New York, 1965); Ward Rutherford, *Fall of the Philippines* (New York, 1971; Robert Sherrod, *History of Marine Corps Aviation in World War II* (Washington, 1952); *idem, On to Westward: War in the Central Pacific* (New York, 1945); P. C. Smith, *Task Force 57: The British Pacific Fleet, 1944–1945* (London, 1969); John L. Snell, ed., *The Meaning of Yalta: Big Three Diplomacy and the New Balance of Power* (Baton Rouge, 1956); T. Dodson Stamps and Vincent J. Esposito, eds., *A Military History of World War II* (2 vols., West Point, 1953); David J. Steinberg, *Philippine Collaboration in World War II* (Ann Arbor, 1967); George E. Taylor, *The Philippines and the United States: Problems of Partnership* (New York, 1964); Athan G. Theoharis, *The Yalta Myths: An Issue in U.S. Politics, 1945–1955* (Columbia, Mo., 1970); John Toland, *But Not in Shame: The Six Months After Pearl Harbor* (New York, 1961); *idem, The Rising Sun: The Decline and Fall of the Japanese Empire, 1930–1945* (2 vols., New York, 1970); Robert L. Underbrink, *Destination Corregidor* (Annapolis, 1971); John Vader, *New Guinea: The Tide Is Stemmed* (New York, 1971); E. Ronald Walker, *The Australian Economy in War and Reconstruction* (New York, 1947); Alan Watt, *The Evolution of Australian Foreign Policy, 1938–1965* (New York, 1967); H. Bradford Westerfield, *Foreign Policy and Party Politics: Pearl Harbor to Korea* (New Haven, 1955); John Winton, *The Forgotten Fleet: The British Navy in the Pacific, 1944–1945* (New York, 1970); Ira Wolfert, *American Guerrilla in the Philippines* (New York, 1945); George Woodbridge, comp., *UNRRA: The History of the United Nations Relief and Rehabilitation Administration* (3 vols., New York, 1950); and C. Vann Woodward, *The Battle for Leyte Gulf* (New York, 1947). Published too recently for use in the preparation of this book was John J. Beck, *MacArthur and Wainwright: Sacrifice of the Philippines* (Albuquerque, 1974).

Several graduate theses were helpful, especially Donald M. Goldstein, "Ennis C. Whitehead, Aerospace Commander and Pioneer" (unpublished Ph.D. dissertation, University of Denver, 1970). Others included Herman E. Bateman, "The Election of 1944 and Foreign Policy" (unpublished Ph.D. dissertation, Stanford University, 1952); Albert Harkness, Jr., "Retreat in the Southwest Pacific, December 8, 1941–March 4, 1942 (unpublished Ph.D. dissertation, Brown University, 1949); John J. Reed, "American Diplomatic Relations with Australia During the Second World War" (unpublished Ph.D. dissertation, University of Southern California, 1969); and William M. Taylor, Jr., "Hell Ships: Voyages of Japanese Prison Ships, 1942–1945" (unpublished M.A. thesis, Mississippi State University, 1972).

Notes

PART I. *"Defeat in the Philippines"*

Basic works in Part I that will not be cited in the chapter notes except when quoted are James H. Belote and William M. Belote, *Corregidor: The Saga of a Fortress* (New York, 1967), 1–177; Wesley F. Craven and James L. Cate, eds., *Plans and Early Operations, January 1939 to August 1942* (AAFWWII; Chicago, 1948), 201–33; Karl C. Dod, *The Corps of Engineers: The War Against Japan* (USAWWII; Washington, 1966), 55–106; Walter D. Edmonds, *They Fought with What They Had: The Story of the Army Air Forces in the Southwest Pacific, 1941–1942* (Boston, 1942); Frank O. Hough, *et al., Pearl Harbor to Guadalcanal* (HUSMCOWWII; Washington, 1958), 155–202; Frazier Hunt, *MacArthur and the War Against Japan* (New York, 1944), 1–78; *idem, The Untold Story of Douglas MacArthur* (New York, 1954), 223–72; Douglas MacArthur, *Reminiscences* (New York, 1964), 117–47; Samuel E. Morison, *The Rising Sun in the Pacific, 1931–April 1942* (HUSNOWWII; Boston, 1948), 164–83, 193–206; Louis Morton, *The Fall of the Philippines* (USAWWII; Washington, 1953); *idem, Strategy and Command: The First Two Years* (USAWWII; Washington, 1962), 131–269; Alvin P. Stauffer, *The Quartermaster Corps: Operations in the War Against Japan* (USAWWII; Washington, 1956), 1–35; Robert L. Underbrink, *Destination Corregidor* (Annapolis, 1971); Jonathan M. Wainwright, *General Wainwright's Story: The Account of Four Years of Humiliating Defeat, Surrender, and Captivity*, ed. Robert Considine (Garden City, 1946), 1–156; Courtney Whitney, *MacArthur: His Rendezvous with History* (New York, 1955), 3–59; Charles A. Willoughby and John Chamberlain, *MacArthur, 1941–1951* (New York, 1954), 16–68; Charles A. Willoughby, ed., *Reports of General MacArthur* (2 vols. in 4 pts., Washington, 1966), I, 6–30, II, Pt. I, 79–123.

CHAPTER I. *"Desperate Withdrawal"*

pages 3–45

1. Int., Dr. W. Dupont Strong, July 27, 1971; Allison Ind, *Bataan, The Judgment Seat: The Saga of the Philippine Command of the United States Army Air Force, May 1941 to May 1942* (New York, 1944), 100–01; William E. Dyess, *The Dyess Story: The Eye-witness Account of the Death March from Bataan and the Narrative of Experiences in Japanese Prison Camps and of Eventual Escape,* ed. Charles Leavelle (New York, 1944), 30. Unless cited otherwise, all interviews herein were conducted by the author.

2. FEAF Strength, Dec. 7, 1941, Charles A. Willoughby Papers, MHRC; Summary of Raids on Clark Field, Dec., 1941, File 730.01/v. 1, AFHRD; Richard L. Watson, Jr., "Army Air Action in the Philippines and Netherlands East Indies, 1941–1942" [MS study, USAAF Hist. Div., 1945], 52–58, AFHRD.

3. Richard H. Rovere and Arthur M. Schlesinger, Jr., *The General and the President, and the Future of American Foreign Policy* (New York, 1951), 51; Francis B. Sayre, *Glad Adventure* (New York, 1957), 223; Claire L. Chennault, *Way of a Fighter: The Memoirs of Claire Lee Chennault* ed. Robert Hotz (New York, 1949), 124; Edgar D. Whitcomb, *Escape from Corregidor* (Chicago, 1958), 23; U.S. Senate, *Investigation of the Pearl Harbor Attack: Report of the Joint Committee . . .* 79th Cong., 2nd Sess. (1946), Senate Doc. 244, pp. 246, 534.

4. Int., Benson Guyton, Aug. 5, 1971; Henry H. Arnold, *Global Mission* (New York, 1949), 272; Forrest C. Pogue, *George C. Marshall* (3 vols. to date, New York, 1963–73), II, 234; Samuel I. Rosenman, comp., *The Public Papers and Addresses of Franklin D. Roosevelt* (13 vols., New York, 1938–50), X, 516–17.

5. Kathleen Williams, "Army Air Forces in the War Against Japan, 1941–1942" [MS study, USAAF Hist. Div., 1945], 17–23; Juliette Abington, "Summary of Air Action in the Philippines and Netherlands East Indies, 7 December 1941 to 26 March 1942" [MS study, USAAF Hist. Div., 1945], 3–8; Lewis H. Brereton, *The Brereton Diaries: The War in the Air in the Pacific, Middle East, and Europe, 3 October 1941–8 May 1945* (New York, 1946), 34–35, 38–44, 50–51, 64–67; Arnold, *Global Mission,* 271–73; George R. Thompson, *et al., The Signal Corps: The Test (December 1941 to July 1943)* (USAWWII; Washington, 1957), 13–15; int., Gen. George C. Kenney, July 16, 1971; Brig. Gen. Bradford G. Chynoweth, Aug. 22, 1971; Col. James V. Collier, Aug. 23, 1971.

6. Brereton, *Diaries,* 38–39; Hanson W. Baldwin, *Great Mistakes of the War* (New York, 1950), 69–72. Mrs. Henry R. Luce (Clare Boothe) interviewed Brereton in Apr., 1942, at which time he stated that he and MacArthur conferred in the latter's office before daylight on Dec. 8.

MacArthur said that "there were to be no 'overt acts' on the part of the U.S. forces in the P.I. until the Japs struck the first blow at the Filipino people," according to Mrs. Luce's interview notes. When told to "stand by and wait," Brereton left, "closer to weeping from sheer rage than he had ever been in his life before." Both men later denied that they met that morning, and Mrs. Luce's interview is the only record that makes such a claim. Int., Mrs. Henry R. Luce with Maj. Gen. Lewis H. Brereton, Apr., 1942, Willoughby Papers, MHRC.

7. General MacArthur's Answers to Questionnaire Submitted by Dr. Louis Morton, Feb. 8, 1954, DM Misc. 201, CMH.'

8. George C. Kenney, *General Kenney Reports: A Personal History of the Pacific War* (New York, 1949), 27; Sidney L. Huff, with Joe A. Morris, *My Fifteen Years with General MacArthur* (New York, 1964), 30–34.

9. SCAP GHQ press release, June 25, 1943, and Sept. 27, 1946, RG 5, MMBA; *New York Times*, Sept. 28, 1946.

10. Henry L. Stimson and McGeorge Bundy, *On Active Service in Peace and War* (New York, 1948), 388; int., Kenney; George C. Kenney, *The MacArthur I Know* (New York, 1951), 82–87; D. Clayton James, *The Years of MacArthur*, I, *1880–1941* (Boston, 1970), 577–614.

11. GCM to DM, Nov. 27, 1941; DM to GCM, Dec. 8, 1941, OPD-EF, RG 165, NA; int., Rear Adm. John D. Bulkeley, July 2, 1971; Frederick C. Sherman, *Combat Command: The American Aircraft Carriers in the Pacific War* (New York, 1950), 45–46; C. L. Sulzberger, *A Long Row of Candles: Memoirs and Diaries (1934–1954)* (New York, 1969), 672.

12. Interrogation of Capt. Chihaya Takahashi, Oct. 20, 1945, in USSBS, *Interrogations of Japanese Officials* (2 vols., Washington, 1946), I, 75.

13. DM to GCM, Dec. 15, 1941; Capt. J. R. Mamerow to DM, Dec. 17, 21, 1941, RG 2, MMBA; Ind, *Bataan*, 140; Vern Haugland, *The AAF Against Japan* (New York, 1948), 31–48; Brereton, *Diaries*, 62–63.

14. Brereton, *Diaries*, 61–62. MacArthur was promoted to the temporary rank of general on Dec. 22 (date of rank from Dec. 18). Special Orders 297, War Dept., Dec. 22, 1941, DM Misc. 201, CMH. He had held this brevet rank while serving as Army chief of staff, 1930–35, but reverted to his permanent rank of major general upon leaving that position. When he was recalled to active duty in July, 1941, to head USAFFE, he was a major general but was promoted two days later to lieutenant general (temporary).

15. Air Room int., Col. Eugene L. Eubank, July 2, 1942, and Lt. Col. Richard H. Carmichael, Dec. 14, 1942, File 142.052, AFHRD; int., Walter D. Edmonds with Lt. Col. Frank P. Bostrom, File 168.7022, AFHRD; Brereton, *Diaries*, 63–72.

16. DM to GCM, Dec. 12, 15, 1941, RG 2, MMBA; U.S. State Dept., *The Conferences at Washington, 1941–42, and Casablanca, 1943* (FRUSDP; Washington, 1968), 65.

17. Rear Adm. Thomas C. Hart, Memorandum on Conversation with Gen.

MacArthur, Sept. 22, 1941; Hart, Memorandum on Conversation with Gen. Sutherland, Sept. 26, 1941; DM to Adm. Harold R. Stark, Oct. 19, 1941, Thomas C. Hart Papers, NHD; Adm. Thomas C. Hart, Narrative of Events, Asiatic Fleet, Leading Up to War and from 8 December 1941 to 15 February 1942, 16–35; Hart, Supplementary to Narrative, 15, NHD; James, *Years of MacArthur,* I, 614–16, 618; Clarence Shadegg, *Clare Boothe Luce* (New York, 1970), 126; S. W. Roskill, *The War at Sea, 1939–1945* (HSWWUKMS; 3 vols. in 4 pts., London, 1954–61), I, 561; int., Collier.

18. Walter Millis, ed., *The War Reports of General of the Army George C. Marshall, General of the Army H. H. Arnold, and Fleet Admiral Ernest J. King* (Philadelphia, 1947), 515–17; DM to GCM, Dec. 13, 1941, OPD-EF; Hart to Rear Adm. William A. Glassford, Dec. 15, 1941; DM to Hart, Dec. 19, 1941, Hart Papers; Capt. William R. Purnell to Adm. Ernest J. King, Dec. 10, 1941, RG 4, MMBA; Rear Adm. Francis W. Rockwell, Narrative of Naval Activities in Luzon Area, 1 December 1941 to 19 March 1942, 3–8, NHD; S. E. Smith, ed., *The United States Navy in World War II* (New York, 1966), 49–54; Albert Harkness, Jr., "Retreat in the Southwest Pacific, December 8, 1941–March 4, 1942" (unpublished Ph.D. dissertation, Brown University, 1949), 6–7; Hart, Narrative, 36–45; U.S. State Dept., *Conferences at Washington and Casablanca,* 56.

19. Hart, Memorandum on Last Two Interviews with Gen. MacArthur, Dec. 23, 1941, Hart Papers.

20. Hart, Narrative, 45–46; Hart, Supplementary, 15; Rockwell, Narrative, 6, 8; Hart to DM, Dec. 25, 1941, RG 2, MMBA; Walter Karig, *et al., Battle Report* (5 vols., 1944–52), I, 156–57; int., Adm. Arthur D. Struble, June 22, 1971.

21. DM to GCM, Dec. 28, 1941, Harry Hopkins Papers, FDRL; DM to GCM, Feb. 4, 1942, RG 4, MMBA; DM, *Reminiscences,* 121, 128; int., Vice Adm. Felix Johnson, July 7, 1941; Stimson and Bundy, *On Active Service,* 507.

22. Int., Bulkeley; Rockwell, Narrative, 8–22; Navy Dept. communiqué 38, Feb. 7, 1942, in U.S. Navy Dept., *Navy Department Communiques 1–300 and Pertinent Press Releases, December 10, 1941, to March 5, 1943* (Washington, 1943), 26; Karig, *et al., Battle Report,* I, 303–04; U.S. Navy Dept., *Annual Report of the Secretary of the Navy for the Fiscal Year 1942* (Washington, 1942), 49; Kenneth W. Condit and Edwin T. Turnbladh, *Hold High the Torch: A History of the 4th Marines* (Washington, 1960), 192–244; James S. Santelli, *A Brief History of the 4th Marines* (Washington, 1970), 24–25; S. E. Smith, ed., *The United States Marine Corps in World War II* (New York, 1969), 97–111.

23. Col. Glen R. Townsend, "Defense of the Philippines" [MS on 11th

Inf.], 9–12, CMH; Operations Report of U.S. Army Forces in the Far East and U.S. Forces in the Philippines [Wainwright's main rpt.], 27–29, CMH (microfilm, MSU); Clark Lee, *They Call It Pacific: An Eye-Witness Story of Our War Against Japan from Bataan to the Solomons* (New York, 1943), 71–90; D. Clayton James, ed., *South to Bataan, North to Mukden: The Prison Diary of Brigadier General W. E. Brougher* (Athens, Ga., 1971), 10–12.

24. Int., Collier; Brig. Gen. Milton A. Hill, Aug. 30, 1971; Brig. Gen. Clifford Bluemel, July 8, 1971; Col. James D. Carter, Aug. 23, 1971; Col. Clyde A. Selleck to author, June 18, 1971; John Toland, *But Not in Shame: The Six Months After Pearl Harbor* (New York, 1961), 110–13; Col. Clyde A. Selleck, 71st Division (Philippine Army) Notes, 57–58, CMH; USAFFE-USFIP Op. Rpt., 94.

25. USAFFE-USFIP Op. Rpt., 33; Baldwin, *Great Mistakes*, 66–68; DM to GCM, Oct. 28, 1941, RG 2, MMBA; James, *Years of MacArthur,* I, 594–96, 603, 607–08; int., Bluemel, Collier.

26. Edmonds, *They Fought with What They Had*, 18n; Manuel L. Quezon, *The Good Fight* (New York, 1946), 194–98; Louis Morton, "Japan's Decision for War," in Kent R. Greenfield, ed., *Command Decisions* (Washington, 1960), 158–60; int., Collier; Lt. Gen. John M. Wright, Jr., June 28, 1971; Maj. Gen. Charles A. Willoughby, Aug. 28, 1967.

27. DM, *Reminiscences*, 125; Morton, "Japan's Decision for War," 164–67; int., Bluemel, Collier.

28. Francis B. Sayre, *Sixth Annual Report of the United States High Commissioner to the Philippine Islands Covering the Fiscal Year July 1, 1941, to June 30, 1942* (Washington, 1943), 7–8, 20–22, 148–49; U.S. State Dept., *Foreign Relations,* 1941, IV, 767–68, V, 395; Manila Open-City Proclamation by DM, Dec. 24, 1941 [issued Dec. 26], RG 2, MMBA; USAFFE-USFIP Op. Rpt., 34; Adalia Márquez, *Blood on the Rising Sun: A Factual Story of the Japanese Invasion of the Philippines* (New York, 1957), 4–9.

29. Robert W. Levering, *Horror Trek: A True Story of Bataan, the Death March and Three and One-half Years in Japanese Prison Camps* (Dayton, 1948), 40.

30. USAFFE-USFIP Op. Rpt., Annex XIII, 22, and Appendix A; Col. James V. Collier, Notebooks [4 MS vols. on Philippine op., 1941–42], II, 83–84; int., Bluemel, Hill, Collier, Carter; Gen. Harold K. Johnson, Dec. 18, 1966.

31. USAFFE-USFIP Op. Rpt., Annex XIII, 19–20; Stauffer, *Quartermaster Corps,* 9; Ernest B. Miller, *Bataan Uncensored* (Long Prairie, Minn., 1949), 75.

32. Int., Chynoweth; Stauffer, *Quartermaster Corps,* 10; DM to Brig. Gen. William F. Sharp, Dec. 15, 1941, in USAFFE-USFIP Op. Rpt., Annex XI, 26; Brig. Gen. Bradford G. Chynoweth, "Visayan Castaways" [MS

on his experiences, 1941–45], 18–56, in his possession (photocopy, MSU).
33. Alfred A. Weinstein, *Barbed-Wire Surgeon* (New York, 1948), 25–47;
USAFFE-USFIP Op. Rpt., Annex XIV, 41–99; Dod, *Corps of Engineers*,
92–93; Townsend, "Defense of the Philippines," 11.
34. DM's Answers to Morton Questionnaire.
35. Int., H. Johnson; Morton, "Japan's Decision for War," 169; James A.
Huston, *The Sinews of War: Army Logistics, 1775–1953* (Washington,
1966), 538.
36. Int., Willoughby, Bluemel, Collier; Col. William C. Braly, Diary, Dec.
24–31, 1941, William C. Braly Papers, MHRC; Operations Report of
11th Infantry Regiment (Philippine Army), 1 Sept. 1941–9 Apr. 1942,
13–19, CMH; USAFFE-USFIP Op. Rpt., 28–40, Annex IV, *passim;*
James, ed., *South to Bataan, North to Mukden,* 12–19.
37. Townsend, "Defense of the Philippines," 11; int., H. Johnson, Hill;
Brig. Gen. William E. Brougher, Notes on Withdrawal of 11th Infantry
by Rail from Agno River Position, 1–2, CMH; 11th Inf. Op. Rpt., 19–
20; Lt. Gen. John M. Wright, Jr., "To Hell — and Back" [MS on
Wright's experiences, 1941–45], 10, in his possession (photocopy, MSU);
Miller, *Bataan Uncensored,* 88–97, 109–10.
38. Maj. W. H. Lage, Operations Report of 3rd Battalion, 11th Infantry
Regiment (Philippine Army), 28–29 December 1941, 16–24, CMH; 11th
Inf. Op. Rpt., 21; Operations Report of the 11th Engineers (Philippine
Army), 1941–1942, 28, William E. Brougher Papers, MSU; Col. Russell
W. Volckmann, "Combat and Guerrilla Activities in the Philippines"
[MS on his experiences, 1941–45], 13–14, CMH; Miller, *Bataan Uncensored,* 94–95.
39. USAFFE-USFIP Op. Rpt., 37; Lt. Col. H. C. Fowler to DM, Feb. 15,
1945, RG 3, MMBA; int., Hill, Carter.
40. 11th Inf. Op. Rpt., 22–24; Townsend, "Defense of the Philippines,"
12–13; int., Col. Clyde A. Selleck, June 22, 1971.
41. Morton, *Fall of the Philippines,* 230.

CHAPTER II. *"Nowhere to Retreat"*

pages 46–99
1. USAFFE-USFIP Op. Rpt., Annex IV, 16–18, Annex V, 20–23. The
Mauban-Mabatang line was also referred to as the Mauban-Abucay
line or simply the Abucay line.
2. Gavin Long, *MacArthur as Military Commander* (London, 1969), 75;
Ward Rutherford, *Fall of the Philippines* (New York, 1971), 93–102.
3. Robert E. Sherwood, *Roosevelt and Hopkins: An Intimate History*
(rev. ed., 2 vols., New York, 1950), II, 19; John Hersey, *Men on Bataan*
(New York, 1943), 255–56; FDR to SecWar Henry L. Stimson and
SecNavy Frank Knox, Dec. 30, 1941, Hopkins Papers; DM to GCM,
Jan. 1, 1942, OPD-EF.

4. GCM to DM, Jan. 2, 1942, OPD-EF.
5. Dwight D. Eisenhower, *Crusade in Europe* (7th ed., Garden City, 1952), 37; U.S. State Dept., *Conferences at Washington and Casablanca*, 109–11, 125–29; Brig. Gen. Leonard T. Gerow to GCM, Jan. 3, 1942, WPD 4639-3, RG 165, NA. Regarding the strategic decision-making at Arcadia, Prime Minister Churchill said, "On 'Grand Strategy' the Staffs agreed that 'only the minimum of forces necessary for the safeguarding of vital interests in other theatres should be diverted from operations against Germany.' No one had more to do with obtaining this cardinal decision than General Marshall." Winston S. Churchill, *The Second World War* (6 vols., Boston, 1948–53), III, 705.
6. Quezon, *Good Fight*, 244–45; USAFFE-USFIP Op. Rpt., 45; Volckmann, "Combat and Guerrilla Activities," 15; Wainwright, *Wainwright's Story*, 49–50; Robert Considine, *It's All News to Me: A Reporter's Deposition* (New York, 1967), 275–76; Carlos P. Romulo, *I Saw the Fall of the Philippines* (Garden City, 1942), 148–49; int., Bluemel, Collier; Gen. Harold K. Johnson, July 7, 1971. (Subsequent H. Johnson interview citations refer to this one.)
7. Quezon, *Good Fight*, 245; *New York Times*, Jan. 31, 1942.
8. Int., Hill; Ind, *Bataan*, 299–300; Lt. Gen. John R. Pugh to William M. Taylor, Jr., Mar. 30, 1972, William M. Taylor, Jr., Papers, MSU; Francis T. Miller, *General Douglas MacArthur: Fighter for Freedom* (Philadelphia, 1942), 271; London *Times*, Jan. 9, 1942.
9. Ind, *Bataan*, 300.
10. Int., Bluemel, Chynoweth; DM, *Reminiscences*, 131.
11. Townsend, "Defense of the Philippines," 13–14; int., Bluemel, H. Johnson, Carter; USAFFE-USFIP Op. Rpt., Annex V, 23–32; Table of Philippine Army Troop Strength and Distribution, Jan. 7, 1942, RG 2, MMBA; Steve M. Mellnik, *Philippine Diary, 1939–1945* (Princeton, 1969), 75–76; Volckmann, "Combat and Guerrilla Activities," 16–17.
12. DM to All Unit Commanders, Jan. 15, 1942, DM Misc. 201; DM to All Unit Commanders, Jan. 16, 1942, Braly Papers.
13. Maj. Gen. Jonathan M. Wainwright to Col. Jesse T. Traywick, Jr., Jan. 27, 1942, RG 4, MMBA; DM to GCM, Jan. 23, 1942, AG 381 (11-27-41 Sec. 1) Far East, RG 407, NA. The Bagac-Orion line was sometimes called the Bagac-Pilar line.
14. USAFFE-USFIP Op. Rpt., 47–48, Annex V, 36–37; Ind, *Bataan*, 237–40; Miller, *Bataan Uncensored*, 156–57; int., Bluemel.
15. USAFFE-USFIP Op. Rpt., Annex IV, 26–29; James, ed., *South to Bataan, North to Mukden*, 22–26; Townsend, "Defense of the Philippines," 17–18.
16. USAFFE-USFIP Op. Rpt., 43–52, Annex IV, 24–25; Dyess, *Dyess Story*, 38–44; Ind, *Bataan*, 277–79; Lee, *They Call It Pacific*, 217–28.
17. DM quoted in GCM to Harry Hopkins, Feb. 22, 1942, Hopkins Papers; *New York Times*, Feb. 23, 1942; Gen. Orders 16, I Philippine Corps

Hq., Feb. 28, 1942, 11th Division (Philippine Army) File, CMH; Maj. Gen. Richard K. Sutherland to Brig. Gen. Bradford G. Chynoweth, Feb. 1, 1942, RG 4, MMBA; USAFWESPAC, U.S. vs. Masaharu Homma: Transcript of Public Trial, 1945–46, XXVI, 3063, War Crimes Office Files, RG 153, NA.

18. Townsend, "Defense of the Philippines," 18; DM to GCM, Feb. 26, 1942, AG 381 (11-27-41 Sec. 2c) Far East; Brig. Gen. William E. Brougher, "Commanding a Combat Division in Action" [MS on 11th Div. op., 1941–42], 1–6, Brougher Papers; Col. Hugh J. Casey to DM, Mar. 8, 1942, AG 319.1 (1-5-42) Philippines.

19. Int., Bluemel, Carter; *New York Times*, Feb. 16, 1942; 11th Engineers Op. Rpt., 35.

20. Col. Richard C. Mallonée, "Bataan Diary" [2 MS vols. on 21st Inf. op., 1941–42], II, 76, CMH; Hough, *et al.*, *Pearl Harbor to Guadalcanal*, 182; Calvin E. Chunn, ed., *Of Rice and Men: The Story of Americans Under the Rising Sun* (Los Angeles, 1946), 1; Gen. Mateo Capinpin, History of the 21st Division (Philippine Army), 1941–1942, 41, CMH; Henry G. Lee, *Nothing But Praise* (Culver City, Calif., 1948), 81; Wainwright to DM, Feb. 26, 1942, AG 430.2 (9-11-41) Philippines; Stanley L. Falk, *Bataan: The March of Death* (New York, 1962), 33. On Jan. 17 it was reported to MacArthur that "the number of rations being issued is approximately 50% in excess of the number of troops on Bataan." The practice was reduced but never entirely eliminated. DM to All Corps and Division Commanders, Jan. 17, 1942, RG 2, MMBA.

21. USAFFE-USFIP Op. Rpt., Annex IV, 28–29, Annex XIV, 41–99; Louis Morton, ed., "Bataan Diary of Maj. Achille C. Tisdelle," *Military Affairs*, XI (Fall, 1947), 137–38; Juanita Redmond, *I Served on Bataan* (Philadelphia, 1943), 44–132; Weinstein, *Barbed-Wire Surgeon*, 25–47; int., H. Johnson.

22. Int., H. Johnson, Collier; USAFFE-USFIP Op. Rpt., Annex XIII, 33–42, and Appendix F.

23. 11th Engineers Op. Rpt., 35; Operations Report of the 21st Infantry Regiment (Philippine Army), 1941–1942, 7, CMH; Romulo, *Fall of the Philippines*, 102–58; Rosenman, comp., *Public Papers and Addresses of Roosevelt*, XIII, 105–16; Mallonée, "Bataan Diary," II, 69.

24. Int., Chynoweth, Bluemel, Carter; Col. A. D. Amoroso, Dec. 17, 1966; Col. Joseph L. Chabot, July 2, 1971; William E. Brougher, "The Battle of Bataan" [MS on 11th Div. op., 1942], 5, Brougher Papers.

25. Miller, *Bataan Uncensored*, 193–94. See also Ralph G. Martin, *The GI War, 1941–1945* (Boston, 1967), 21; Rovere and Schlesinger, *General and President*, 57; Joseph Rosner, *The Hater's Handbook* (New York, 1965), 128–29.

26. Lee, *Nothing But Praise*, 192, 195.

27. Morton, *Fall of the Philippines*, 388; Mallonée, "Bataan Diary," II, 67. On Bataan veterans' opinions of MacArthur and Wainwright, see various issues of their societies' periodicals, such as *Chit Chat, The Quan,* and *The XPW Bulletin,* in the Brougher Papers and Benson Guyton Papers, MSU.
28. USAFFE-USFIP Op. Rpt., Annex VIII, 1–79; Rockwell, Narrative, 2; Belote and Belote, *Corregidor,* 14.
29. Belote and Belote, *Corregidor,* 76.
30. USAFFE-USFIP Op. Rpt., Annex VIII, 36–38; Braly Diary, Dec. 29–31, 1941; Benson Guyton, Diary, Dec. 25, 1941–May 3, 1942, Guyton Papers; int., Wright, Hill, Guyton.
31. Int., Wright, Collier, Guyton; Col. William C. Braly, "Corregidor: A Name, a Symbol, a Tradition" [MS based on his diary, 1941–42], 10, 24, Braly Papers; Wright, "To Hell — and Back," 21; Levering, *Horror Trek,* 222–23.
32. Huff, *My Fifteen Years,* 43–44. See also Manila *Star Reporter,* June 8, 1945; Romulo, *Fall of the Philippines,* 100–01; Ind, *Bataan,* 208.
33. Int., Willoughby, Hill, Wright, Amoroso, Guyton; Sayre, *Glad Adventure,* 239; Romulo, *Fall of the Philippines,* 120–21; Belote and Belote, *Corregidor,* 54; Hersey, *Men on Bataan,* 123–25; Lee, *They Call It Pacific,* 233–34; Huff, *My Fifteen Years,* 41–46.
34. Int., Willoughby, Hill, Collier; Romulo, *Fall of the Philippines,* 171–73; USAFFE-USFIP Op. Rpt., 37; Sayre, *Report,* 150; Mellnik, *Philippine Diary,* 22.
35. Int., Kenney, Willoughby, Hill, Bulkeley, Collier; Brig. Gen. Bonner F. Fellers, June 26, 1971; Maj. Gen. Richard J. Marshall, July 27, 1971; Brig. Gen. Burdette M. Fitch, Aug. 26, 1971; DM to GCM, Feb. 3, 1944, RG 4, MMBA; Long, *MacArthur,* 52.
36. Int., officers cited in note 35 and Lt. Gen. Clovis E. Byers, June 24, 1971; Maj. William A. Beiderlinden, June 25, 1971; Brig. Gen. Dwight F. Johns, Aug. 22, 1971; Col. William Niederpruem, Aug. 25, 1971; Mellnik, *Philippine Diary,* 22; DM to Gen. Omar N. Bradley, Apr. 26, 1948, RG 5, MMBA; Belote and Belote, *Corregidor,* 73–74; Considine, *It's All News to Me,* 274.
37. Churchill, *Second World War,* IV, 105, 107.
38. Brig. Gen. Lester J. Whitlock to Brig. Gen. Richard J. Marshall, July 14, 1942, RG 4, MMBA; Don Lohbeck, *Patrick J. Hurley* (Chicago, 1956), 159–64; *New York Times,* Feb. 18, 1942; Pogue, *Marshall,* II, 232–46; Chynoweth, "Visayan Castaways," 44.
39. DM to GCM, Feb. 22, 1942, Hopkins Papers; Brig. Gen. Patrick F. Hurley and Lt. Gen. George H. Brett to GCM, Mar. 4, 1942, AG 381 (11-27-41 Sec. 3) Far East; Whitlock to Marshall, July 14, 1942, RG 4, MMBA.
40. Stephen E. Ambrose, *The Supreme Commander: The War Years of*

General Dwight D. Eisenhower (Garden City, 1970), 16; Morton, *Fall of the Philippines*, 401; Underbrink, *Destination Corregidor*, 224. The bulk of the Philippine government's bullion was dumped in the bay off Corregidor, on MacArthur's advice, but the Japanese later hauled it up after learning its location from a USAFFE prisoner.

41. Ind, *Bataan*, 280; int., Hill; Willoughby and Chamberlain, *MacArthur*, 27.

42. Int., Gen. of the Army Dwight D. Eisenhower, Aug. 29, 1967; Gen. Thomas T. Handy, Sept. 8, 1971; Maj. Gen. John E. Hull, June 23, 1971; Brig. Gen. Louis J. Fortier, June 23, 1971; James M. Burns, *Roosevelt: The Soldier of Freedom* (New York, 1970), 205–08; GCM to DM, Dec. 30, 1941, RG 2, MMBA; Ray S. Cline, *Washington Command Post: The Operations Division* (USAWWII; Washington, 1951), 84; FDR press conference, Feb. 24, 1942, Presidential Press Conferences, 1933–45, FDRL (microfilm, MSU). MacArthur sent the following "purple prose" to Roosevelt on his birthday: "For President Roosevelt, today January 30, your birth anniversary. Smoke-begrimed men, covered with the muck of battle, rise from the foxholes of Bataan and the batteries of Corregidor to pray reverently that God may bless immeasurably the President of the United States." DM to FDR, Jan. 30, 1942, PPF 4914, FDRL. MacArthur sent a similar greeting to Marshall on his birthday, Dec. 31, 1941.

43. Int., Eisenhower, Handy, Hull, Fortier; Theodore Ropp, *War in the Modern World* (Durham, 1959), 325–26; Pogue, *Marshall*, II, 374–75; Ambrose, *Supreme Commander*, 12–14; Richard W. Leighton and Robert W. Coakley, *Global Logistics and Strategy, 1940–1943* (USAWWII; Washington, 1955), 172. The earnestness of the War Department's efforts to relieve the Philippine garrison is evident in the communications reprinted in Alfred D. Chandler, Jr., ed., *The Papers of Dwight David Eisenhower: The War Years* (5 vols., Baltimore, 1970), I, 11, 13, 17, 18, 21–23, 35–37, 40–41, 51, 54–55, 63, 70, 86, 89–90, 109, 213–15, 237–38.

44. DM to Brig. Gen. Bonner F. Fellers, June 18, 1943, RG 5, MMBA.

45. Henry L. Stimson, Diary, Dec. 10, 1941, Henry L. Stimson Papers, Yale University; Sherwood, *Roosevelt and Hopkins*, II, 69–70; Burns, *Roosevelt*, 163; *New York Times*, Feb. 23, 1942; *Washington Post*, Oct. 20, 1955; Clark Lee and Richard Henschel, *Douglas MacArthur* (New York, 1952), 163.

46. Int., Robert Sherrod with Brig. Gen. LeGrande A. Diller, Feb. 15, 1967, Robert Sherrod Papers, MSU; int., Eisenhower, H. Johnson, Chynoweth; DM to TAG, Mar. 9, 1942, RG 4, MMBA; Holland M. Smith and Percy Finch, *Coral and Brass* (New York, 1949), 11–12; Lee, *They Call It Pacific*, 161, 174–75, 178, 180; Baldwin, *Great Mistakes*, 73; Miller, *MacArthur*, 276–77; Chynoweth to author, Aug. 7, 1972.

A number of the USAFFE communiqués are reprinted in Frank C. Waldrop, ed., *MacArthur on War* (New York, 1942), 351–90.

47. Int., H. Johnson, Bluemel, Chynoweth, Bulkeley; Willoughby, Aug. 28, 1967, and July 30, 1971 [hereafter, Willoughby interview citations will refer only to the latter int.]; Col. Aurelio M. Mendoza, Aug. 21, 1972; Capt. Jesus Villamor to Col. Van S. Merle-Smith, Oct. 17, 1942, RG 16, MMBA; Quezon, Proclamation to Filipino Soldiers at the Front, Jan. 3, 1941, Braly Papers.

48. Manila *Philippines Free Press*, Dec. 15, 1962; Frederic S. Marquardt, *Before Bataan and After: A Personalized History of Our Philippine Experiment* (Indianapolis, 1943), 276–77; Jorge B. Vargas, Proclamation to Our Sons and Brothers in Bataan, Feb. 6, 1942, DMBP; Theodore Friend, *Between Two Empires: The Ordeal of the Philippines, 1929–1946* (New Haven, 1965), 211–28; Sayre, *Report*, 79–84; DM, *Reminiscences*, 134–35; David J. Steinberg, *Philippine Collaboration in World War II* (Ann Arbor, 1967), 32–48; U.S. State Dept., *Foreign Relations, 1942*, I, 900–02; Armando J. Malay, *Occupied Philippines: The Role of Jorge B. Vargas During the Japanese Occupation* (Manila, 1967), 15–34, 88–101; Claude A. Buss, "The Philippines," in Lennox A. Mills, et al., *The New World of Southeast Asia* (Minneapolis, 1949), 45–53.

49. Int., Willoughby, Marshall; U.S. State Dept., *Foreign Relations, 1942*, I, 882–84, 888–90; Quezon to FDR, Jan. 13, 1942; FDR to Quezon, Jan. 30, 1942, RG 4, MMBA; Romulo, *Fall of the Philippines*, 164–65, 178; Quezon, *Good Fight*, 227–74; Huff, *My Fifteen Years*, 47–48; James K. Eyre, Jr., *The Roosevelt-MacArthur Conflict* (Chambersburg, Pa., 1950), 34–56; DM, *Reminiscences*, 137.

50. Quezon to DM, Feb. 7, 1942, RG 4, MMBA; Quezon to FDR, Feb. 8, 1942, OPD-EF; Stimson and Bundy, *On Active Service*, 397–405; Eyre, *Roosevelt-MacArthur Conflict*, 57–74; Carlos P. Romulo, *I Walked with Heroes* (New York, 1961), 218–24; U.S. State Dept., *Foreign Relations, 1942*, I 890–91, 894–99; David Bernstein, *The Philippine Story* (New York, 1947), 176–81; Friend, *Between Two Empires*, 217–23; Steinberg, *Philippine Collaboration*, 38–43.

51. DM to GCM, Feb. 8, 1942, OPD-EF. Quezon's message to Roosevelt was sent through Army channels in the same radiogram with Mac-Arthur's message to Marshall.

52. Stimson Diary, Feb. 8, 1942; FDR to DM and Quezon, Feb. 10, 1942; FDR to Quezon, Feb. 11, 1942; Quezon to FDR, Feb. 10, 1942; DM to GCM, Feb. 10, 12, 1942, RG 4, MMBA; GCM to DM, Feb. 1, 2, 10, 1942, OPD-EF; U.S. State Dept., *Foreign Relations, 1942*, I, 900; JCS Minutes, Feb. 9, 1942, CCS 371 Philippines (2-9-42); RG 218, NA.

53. DM to FDR, Feb. 11, 1942, RG 4, MMBA.

54. GCM to DM, Feb. 14, 21, 25, 1942; DM to GCM, Feb. 15, 24, 1942; FDR to DM, Feb. 22, 1942, RG 4, MMBA; DM, *Reminiscences*, 140–41.

See also messages to and from Corregidor and Washington regarding the evacuation of Quezon and Sayre, Jan. 1–Feb. 26, 1942, RG 4, MMBA. When Sayre departed by submarine on Feb. 24, MacArthur sent with him for safe-keeping "one trunk containing valuable records and documents from my personal files." Riggs National Bank in Washington held the trunk for the duration of the war. DM to Riggs National Bank, Feb. 23, 1942; Francis B. Sayre to DM, Apr. 17, 1942, RG 2, MMBA; Robert V. Fleming to DM, Apr. 17, 1942, RG 10, MMBA.

55. Wainwright, *Wainwright's Story*, 4–5; Chandler, ed., *Eisenhower Papers*, I, 127–28, 136–37, 143–44, 174–76; DM, *Reminiscences*, 142. According to Wainwright, MacArthur said, "I'm leaving for Australia pursuant to repeated orders of the President. Things have gotten to such a point that I must comply with these orders or get out of the Army. I want you to make it known throughout all elements of your command that I'm leaving over my repeated protests." Wainwright, *Wainwright's Story*, 3–4. This version is contradicted by the official records on several counts.

CHAPTER III. *"A Beginning and an End"*

pages 100–154

1. USAFFE-USFIP Op. Rpt., Annex VIII, 42–43; Rockwell, Narrative, 21–22; int., Bulkeley; DM, *Reminiscences*, 144; Romulo, *Fall of the Philippines*, 228–29; Mellnik, *Philippine Diary*, 95; Toland, *But Not in Shame*, 271–72; William L. White, *They Were Expendable* (New York, 1942), 112–28.

The passenger list by boats (with captains) was as follows:
PT 41 (Lt. John D. Bulkeley): Gen. Douglas MacArthur, CG, USAFFE; Mrs. Douglas MacArthur; Arthur MacArthur; Ah Cheu, amah; Maj. Gen. Richard K. Sutherland, CofS; Capt. Harold G. Ray, USN, Rockwell's CofS; Lt. Col. Sidney L. Huff, aide (to MacArthur); Maj. Charles H. Morhouse, medical officer.
PT 35 (Ens. A. B. Akers): Col. Charles A. Willoughby, G-2; Lt. Col. LeGrande A. Diller, aide (to MacArthur) and PRO; Lt. Col. Francis H. Wilson, aide (to Sutherland); Master Sgt. Paul P. Rogers, MacArthur's secy.
PT 34 (Lt. R. G. Kelly): Rear Adm. Francis W. Rockwell, CO, 16th Naval District; Brig. Gen. Richard J. Marshall, deputy CofS; Col. Charles P. Stivers, G-1; Capt. Joseph McMicking, asst. G-2.
PT 32 (Lt., j.g., V. S. Schumacher): Brig. Gen. Spencer B. Akin, signal officer; Brig. Gen. Hugh J. Casey, engineer officer; Brig. Gen. William F. Marquat, antiaircraft officer; Brig. Gen. Harold

H. George, air officer and CG, V Fighter Command; Lt. Col. Joe
R. Sherr, asst. signal officer.

2. Huff, *My Fifteen Years,* 62; White, *They Were Expendable,* 128–37;
int., Maj. Gaetano Faillace, Aug. 31, 1971; Lt. John D. Bulkeley,
Summary of Operations of Motor Torpedo Boat Squadron Three from
7 December 1941 to 10 April 1942, 1–3, NHD (microfilm, MSU).

3. Int., Bulkeley; Huff, *My Fifteen Years,* 63–65; White, *They Were
Expendable,* 137–43; DM, *Reminiscences,* 145; DM to Brett, Mar. 14,
1942; DM to GCM, Mar. 14, 1942, RG 4, MMBA; GCM to DM, Feb.
27, Mar. 14, 1942, OPD-EF.

4. Willoughby and Chamberlain, *MacArthur,* 54; Benson H. Harvey to
author, Oct. 12, 1970; Ind, *Bataan,* 348–51; FDR to DM, Feb. 22, RG 4,
MMBA; Chynoweth, "Visayan Castaways," 9, 28, 42, 88, 102.

5. Int., Walter D. Edmonds with Lt. Col. Frank P. Bostrom, Sept. 9,
1944, and Master Sgt. George R. Graf, Oct. 13, 1944, Edmonds Papers;
Kenney, *MacArthur,* 87–89; Maj. Gen. William E. Bergin to Mrs. C. H.
Black, Mar. 27, 1952, DM Misc. 201. The B-17 pilots and crews later
received the Distinguished Flying Cross for the mission. Gen. Orders
37, USAFIA Hq., Apr. 5, 1942, File 704.193, AFHRD.

6. Office Diary of Gen. Douglas MacArthur, Mar. 17, 1942, RG 5, MMBA;
Huff, *My Fifteen Years,* 67–71.

7. DM, *Reminiscences,* 145; DM Diary, Mar. 18–20, 1942; London *Times,*
Mar. 21, 1942; Huff, *My Fifteen Years,* 72; Toland, *But Not in Shame,*
277.

8. DM Diary, Mar. 21, 1942; Hersey, *Men on Bataan,* 306–08; Robert
Sherrod to author, Nov. 8, 1971; press release by DM, Mar. 24, 1942,
Sherrod Papers.

9. Vorin E. Whan, ed., *A Soldier Speaks: Public Papers and Speeches
of General of the Army Douglas MacArthur* (New York, 1965), 115–16.
See also *New York Times,* Mar. 21, 22, 1942.

10. *New York Times,* Mar. 21, 1942; Hersey, *Men on Bataan,* 308.

11. *New York Times,* Mar. 25, 26, 29, Apr. 3, 7, 1942; DM Diary, Mar.
22–27, 1942; Whan, ed., *A Soldier Speaks,* 117–18; Robert Sherrod,
Excerpts from Notebook, Mar. 26, 1942, Sherrod Papers; London
Times, Mar. 29, 1942; Hugh Buggy, *Pacific Victory: A Short History
of Australia's Part in the War Against Japan* (Melbourne, 1945), 32–33;
DM to Prime Minister John Curtin, Mar. 28, 1942, RG 5, MMBA. The
actual medal arrived later, and on June 30 a ceremony was held at
MacArthur's headquarters with Johnson presenting the award to the
general. DM Diary, June 30, 1942.

12. Quezon, *Good Fight,* 298–301, 316–25; U.S. State Dept., *Foreign
Relations, 1942,* I, 902–06; DM to GCM, Mar. 27, Apr. 19, 24, 1942;
FDR to Quezon, Mar. 27, 1942; GCM to DM, Apr. 29, 1942, OPD-EF;

DM to Quezon, May 19, 1942, RG 4, MMBA; Lionel Wigmore, *The Japanese Thrust* (AW39-45; Canberra, 1957), 183-84; E. Ronald Walker, *The Australian Economy in War and Reconstruction* (New York, 1947), 56-58; Churchill, *Second World War*, IV, 8; Alan Watt, *The Evolution of Australian Foreign Policy, 1938-1945* (New York, 1967), 49-59.

13. Werni Levi, *American-Australian Relations* (Minneapolis, 1947), 150-55; James R. M. Butler, *Grand Strategy*, Vol. III, *June 1941-August 1942*, Pt. II (HSWWUKMS; London, 1964), 492-97; C. Hartley Grattan, *The Southwest Pacific Since 1900* (Ann Arbor, 1963), 160-66; William H. McNeill, *America, Britain, and Russia: Their Cooperation and Conflict, 1941-1946* (New York, 1953), 154-56; Nicholas Mansergh, *Survey of British Commonwealth Affairs*, Vol. IV, *Problems of Wartime Co-operation and Post-war Change, 1939-1952* (New York, 1958), 141; F. L. Wood, *The New Zealand People at War: Political and External Affairs* (OHNZSWW; Wellington, 1958), 218-22.

14. Brig. Gen. F. S. Clark to Brett, Mar. 15, 1942, SWPA G-2 Journals, File 98-GHQ-1-32, RG 407, WNRC.

15. Hurley to GCM, OPD 381 (2-21-42 Sec. 1) SWPA, RG 165, NA; Long, *MacArthur*, 85-86; Sherwood, *Roosevelt and Hopkins*, II, 83-86; Dudley McCarthy, *South-west Pacific Area — First Year: Kokoda to Wau* (AW39-45; Canberra, 1959), 111-13; Lt. Gen. Iven Mackay to Army Minister Francis M. Forde, Apr. 2, 1942, SWPA G-3 Jnls.; Lt. Gen. Edmund F. Herring to author, May 22, 1972.

16. Watt, *Australian Foreign Policy*, 64; Butler, *Grand Strategy*, III, Pt. II, 495; Samuel Milner, *Victory in Papua* (USAWWII; Washington, 1957), 28-29; DM to GCM, Apr. 25, 1942, RG 4, MMBA; Curtin to DM, Apr. 28, 1942; Prime Minister Winston S. Churchill to FDR, Apr. 29, 1942; GCM to DM, Apr. 29, 1942; DM to GCM, May 1, 3, 1942, OPD-EF; Maurice Matloff and Edwin M. Snell, *Strategic Planning for Coalition Warfare, 1941-1942* (USAWWII; Washington, 1953), 96-97.

17. Charles A. Willoughby, "The Initial Mission: Aid to the Philippines" [MS on supply efforts, Dec., 1941-Mar., 1942], 1-12, Willoughby Papers; Brett to Curtin, Mar. 17, 1942, SWPA G-3 Jnls.; Alan S. Watt to Acting SecState Sumner Welles, Mar. 17, 1942, File 740.011PW/2202, RG 59, NA; Leighton and Coakley, *Global Logistics and Strategy*, 166-69; C. Hartley Grattan, *The United States and the Southwest Pacific* (Cambridge, Mass., 1961), 180-87; Grattan, *Southwest Pacific Since 1900*, 165-66.

18. GCM to DM, Apr. 8, 1942, RG 4, MMBA; Milner, *Papua*, 20-22; Matloff and Snell, *Strategic Planning*, 167-69; McNeill, *America, Britain, and Russia*, 156; Rosenman, comp., *Public Papers and Addresses of Roosevelt*, XI, 198-99; Sherwood, *Roosevelt and Hopkins*, II, 595; William D. Leahy, *I Was There: The Personal Story of the Chief of Staff*

to *Presidents Roosevelt and Truman Based on His Notes and Diaries Made at the Time* (New York, 1950), 96.

19. Brett to AGWAR, Mar. 17, 1942, PSF, FDRL; AFPAC, Studies in the History of General Douglas MacArthur's Commands in the Pacific [4 pts., MS covering Apr., 1942–Aug., 1945], Pt. I, The Philippine Campaign and the Papuan Campaign, 15–18, RG 4, MMBA; GCM to DM, Mar. 22, 1942, OPD-EF; H. V. Evatt, *Australia in World Affairs* (Sydney, 1946), 6–8.

20. GCM to DM, Apr. 3, 8, 1942, OPD-EF; GCM to DM, OPD 381 (4-10-42 Sec. 1) SWPA; DM to GCM, Apr. 4, 1942; GCM to DM, Apr. 14, 1942, RG 4, MMBA; Curtin to DM, Apr. 17, 1942, SWPA G-3 Jnls.

21. GCM and King to FDR, Mar. 29, 1942, enclosing SWPA and POA directives, RG 4, MMBA. A JCS memo which was added to MacArthur's directive states:

> The following is the position of the United States Chiefs of Staff:
> (1) With regard to the possible movement of Australian troops out of Australian territory, the following by [the] United States Chiefs of Staff to the President is self-explanatory:
> "Proposals of [the] United States Chiefs of Staff (for operations in the Southwest Pacific Area) made to the President as United States Commander-in-Chief are subject to review by him from the standpoint of higher political considerations and to reference by him to the Pacific War Council in Washington when necessary. The interests of the Nations whose forces or land possessions may be involved in these military operations are further safeguarded by the power each Nation retains to refuse the use of its forces for any project which it considers inadvisable."
> (2) With regard to the right of appeal of the Local Commander to his own Government and freedom of communication between a Local Commander referring to the Government, it was never contemplated by the United States Chiefs of Staff that a Local Commander should be interfered with in any way in communicating with his own Government in any manner he desired. In fact such action is the direct corollary to the principles already approved by the President and enunciated above.
> This communication is explanatory of and should be read in conjunction with the Directive to which it thus becomes a part.

22. Gen. Orders 1, SWPA GHQ, Apr. 18, 1942; Gen. Orders 2, SWPA GHQ, Apr. 19, 1942, SWPA G-3 Jnls.; GCM to DM, Apr. 9, 1942; DM to GCM, June 15, 1942, OPD-EF. A list of subordinate commanders and units of SWPA's land, sea, and air forces as of Apr. 18 is found in DM to GCM, Apr. 20, 1942, OPD-EF.

23. Morton, *Strategy and Command,* 617; DM to TAG, Apr. 22, 1942,

OPD-EF; Louis Morton, *Pacific Command: A Study in Interservice Relations* (Colorado Springs, 1961), 8. Regarding the change in his title, MacArthur told Defense Minister Frederick G. Shedden:

> I can find no precedent anywhere for the actual title of Supreme Commander and its use for general and colloquial designation was not in my opinion intended to be the actual formal title to be assumed by the individual selected to command. General Wavell evidently was also of this opinion and I think the precedent established by him should be followed. There are many other reasons to support this view such as the relatively small size of the command here, the many restrictive influences under which it will operate, the title of Commander-in-Chief held by the Commander of the contiguous area, the general acceptance of the term Commander-in-Chief throughout the years as designating the senior officer commanding, the confusion in the minds of the rank and file if there are three Commanders-in-Chief of the Allied Forces all junior to the actual operational commander, and the belief I have that general public opinion not only in our own countries but emphasized and propagandized in hostile ones will be inclined to think the title to be somewhat tinged with military egotism.

DM to Shedden, Apr. 13, 1942, RG 4, MMBA.
24. Willoughby and Chamberlain, *MacArthur*, 79–80.
25. GCM to DM, Mar. 18, 1942, quoted in Matloff and Snell, *Strategic Planning*, 272; Paul Hasluck, *The Government and the People, 1942–45* (AW39-45; Canberra, 1952), 113–14.
26. Curtin to DM, Apr. 15, 1942, RG 4, MMBA.
27. Wainwright, *Wainwright's Story*, 67; int., H. Johnson, Hill, Carter, Collier, Guyton.
28. A. M. James to FDR, Mar. 17, 1942, OF 4771, FDRL; int., Bluemel; Kenneth S. Davis, *Experience of War: The United States in World War II* (Garden City, 1965), 161.
29. Chunn, ed., *Of Rice and Men*, 196–97. The poem was written by an American soldier under the pseudonym "Aquill Penn."
30. Brougher, "Battle of Bataan," 5.
31. Rosenman, comp., *Public Papers and Addresses of Roosevelt*, XI, 164; FDR press conference, Mar. 20, 1942; *New York Times*, Mar. 21, 29, 1942; Ernest J. King, with Walter M. Whitehill, *Fleet Admiral King: A Naval Record* (New York, 1952), 413; Raymond G. Carroll to Stephen Early, Mar. 31, 1942, OF 4771, FDRL; Ross T. McIntyre, *White House Physician* (New York, 1946), 198–99.
32. Tokyo *Japan Times and Advertiser* (morning ed.), Mar. 19, 1942; L. D. Meo, *Japan's Radio War on Australia, 1941–1945* (Melbourne, 1968), 97–98; Pogue, *Marshall*, II, 253–54; William Flythe to Marvin H. McIntyre, Jan. 26, 1942, OF 4771, FDRL; Memphis *Commercial Ap-*

peal, Mar. 18, 1942; int., Eisenhower; GCM to FDR, Aug. 22, 1944, PSF, FDRL; *Congressional Record,* 77th Cong., 2nd Sess., LXXXVIII, A392, A803, A876–77, 1088, 1724; GCM to Sutherland, Jan. 31, 1942, RG 2, MMBA. After the war Eisenhower told Lt. Gen. Robert L. Eichelberger that he had refused the Medal of Honor after the North African invasion "because he knew of a man who had received one for sitting in a hole in the ground — meaning MacArthur." Jay Luvaas, ed., *Dear Miss Em: General Eichelberger's War in the Pacific, 1942–1945* (Westport, 1972), 76.

33. Sutherland to GCM, Mar. 16, 1942, PSF, FDRL.
34. GCM to FDR, Aug. 22, 1944, PSF, FDRL; CCS to DM, Feb. 14, 1942, CCS 371 Philippines (2-9-42); Pogue, *Marshall,* II, 254.
35. Gen. Order No. 16, War Dept., Apr. 1, 1942, PSF, FDRL. The date of award was given in the order as Mar. 25, 1942.
36. Robert Sherrod, Marginal Notes on MacArthur's *Reminiscences,* 147, Sherrod Papers; GCM to Sutherland, Mar. 25, 1942, RG 2, MMBA; DM to GCM, Mar. 26, 1942, RG 4, MMBA; *New York Times,* Mar. 29, 1942; Hunt, *Untold Story,* 281.
37. William H. Standley, with Arthur A. Ageton, *Admiral Ambassador to Russia* (Chicago, 1955), 97; *New York Times,* Feb. 6, 18, 19, Mar. 2, 16, 18, Apr. 9, 19, 28, 1942; Raleigh, N.C., *News and Observer,* Apr. 22, 1942; Josephus Daniels to DM, Apr. 22, 1942; Rep. Luther A. Johnson to DM, Apr. 2, 1942; Thomas E. Kennedy to DM, Mar. 21, 1942; Lino Padron Rivera to FDR, Mar. 26, 1942, RG 10, MMBA; Francis T. Miller, "General Douglas MacArthur," *Coronet,* XII (July, 1942), 187; Little Rock *Arkansas Gazette,* Mar. 11, 1942.
38. *New York Times,* Mar. 29, Apr. 6, 7, 14, 29, May 1, 1942; William P. Sidley to DM, Mar. 27, 1942; Charles E. Hughes to DM, Apr. 5, 1942; Herbert C. Hoover to DM, Mar. 27, 1942; Charles G. Dawes to DM, Apr. 4, 1942; Alvin Austin to DM, June 16, 1942; DM to Austin, June 18, 1942, RG 10, MMBA; Gen. John J. Pershing to DM, Mar. 27, 1942, John J. Pershing Papers, LC. Pershing, whose relationship to Mac-Arthur had been strained at times after 1918, warmly supported him during World War II. MacArthur, in turn, asked Warren Pershing, the general's son, to be his aide, but the youth preferred to enter the Army as a private. DM to Pershing, Feb. 15, 1942; Pershing to DM, Feb. 16, 1942, Pershing Papers.
39. *New York Times,* Jan. 25, Feb. 24, Mar. 29, Apr. 13, 18, 26, 27, May 26, 1942; Judge Murray Hulbert to Basil O'Connor, Mar. 29, 1942; Stimson to FDR, Mar. 30, 1942, OF 4771, FDRL; Brig. Gen. Albert L. Cox to TAG, Apr. 27, 1942; Gov. Julius P. Heil to DM, June 5, 1942; Emily Hardy to DM, Apr. 5, 1942, RG 10, MMBA; C. A. Dykstra to Maj. Gen. Edwin Watson, Apr. 10, 1942, PPF 4914, FDRL.
40. *New York Times,* Apr. 5, 26, 27, May 11, 1942; V. Y. Dallman to McIntyre, Mar. 6, 1942, OF 4771, FDRL; Frank C. McCutcheon to DM,

May 5, 1942, RG 10, MMBA; "MacArthur Statue Highlights Recent Art Gift," *At Denison* [Denison University alumni periodical], XXXI (Jan., 1971), 1.

41. Col. George W. Cocheu to DM, May 7, 1942; Charles F. Kindt, Jr., to DM, Apr. 15, 1942, RG 10, MMBA; Gertrude Algase to Col. LeGrande A. Diller, Apr. 1, 1942, RG 3, MMBA; int., Willoughby.

42. Robert R. McCormick to DM, Mar. 21, 1942; Mrs. Henry R. Luce to DM, June 9, 1942; Col. Clement H. Wright to DM, Apr. 14, 1942, RG 10, MMBA; Burns, *Roosevelt*, 211; Shadegg, *Clare Boothe Luce*, 136; W. A. Swanberg, *Luce and His Empire* (New York, 1972), 264; *Illustrated London News*, Mar. 7, 1942; New York *Herald Tribune*, Apr. 2, 1942; London *Times*, Apr. 6, 1942; *New York Times*, Apr. 17, 1942; Memphis *Commercial Appeal*, Mar. 18, 1942; Washington *Star*, Dec. 21, 1941; "Destiny's Child," *Time*, XXXVIII (Dec. 29, 1941), 16–17; Paul V. McNutt, "MacArthur: A First-class Fightin' Man," *American Legion*, May, 1942, 6–7; "A Soldier's Soldier," *Newsweek*, XIX (Mar. 9, 1942), 15; "Hero-hungry Nation Goes for MacArthur in Big Way," *Life*, XII (Mar. 30, 1942), 43; "A Pacific Offensive?" *Nation*, CLIV (Mar. 28, 1942), 356.

43. *Congressional Record*, 77th Cong., 2nd Sess., LXXXVIII, A298, A431–32, 684, 756–57, 4857–61; New York Senate Resolution, Jan. 27, 1942; Heber Ladner to DM, Jan. 27, 1942; Gov. Coke Stevenson to DM, Feb. 28, 1942; TAG to Mayor Fiorello H. LaGuardia, Feb. 21, 1942, RG 10, MMBA; Leroy M. Edwards to FDR, Mar. 18, 1942, OF 4771, FDRL; *New York Times*, Apr. 24, 1942.

44. *New York Times*, May 20, 1942; Hadley Cantril, ed., *Public Opinion, 1935–1946* (Princeton, 1951), 428.

45. Cantril, ed., *Public Opinion*, 558. See also Elmo B. Roper, *You and Your Leaders: Their Actions and Your Reactions, 1936–1956* (New York, 1957), 88.

46. "Bring MacArthur Home," *Time*, XXXIX (Feb. 23, 1942), 14; Wendell L. Willkie, "Let Us Do More Proposing Than Opposing," *Vital Speeches of the Day*, VIII (Mar. 1, 1942), 299; McCormick to DM, Mar. 21, 1942; Brig. Gen. Robert E. Wood to DM, Mar. 31, 1942, RG 10, MMBA; int., Turner Catledge, Mar. 25, 1971; *New York Times*, Feb. 23, Mar. 2, Apr. 15, 1942; San Francisco *Examiner*, Mar. 3, 1942; Chicago *Tribune*, Mar. 28, 1942; Albert Ross to FDR, Apr. 14, 1942, OF 4771, FDRL; New York *Daily News*, Apr. 14, 1942.

47. *New York Times*, Feb. 10, 11, Mar. 17, 1942; Rep. Hamilton Fish to DM, Mar. 26, 1942; William H. Rankin to DM, Mar. 29, 1942; Roger Powell to DM, Apr. 7, 1942, RG 10, MMBA; Irving Brant, "The Truth About MacArthur," *New Republic*, CVII (Dec. 28, 1942), 851.

48. Arthur H. Vandenburg, Jr., ed., *The Private Papers of Senator Vandenburg* (Boston, 1952), 76.

49. *Ibid.*, 75–77; H. Bradford Westerfield, *Foreign Policy and Party Poli-*

tics: Pearl Harbor to Korea (New Haven, 1955), 242–43; Brant, "The Truth About MacArthur," 851–53.

50. DM to GCM, Mar. 21, 1942, AG 311.23 (2-4-42) GHQ SWPA; Gen. Orders 44, USAFFE Hq., Mar. 16, 1942, RG 4, MMBA; Chynoweth to author, Aug. 23, 1971.

51. GCM to Wainwright, Mar. 19, 20, 1942, OPD 381 (3-19-42 Sec. 1) Philippines; FDR to CG, USAFFE [Wainwright], Mar. 20, 1942, OPD-EF; DM to GCM, Mar. 21, 24, 1942, AG 311.23 (2-4-42) GHQ SWPA; Pogue, *Marshall*, II, 256–58; Toland, *But Not in Shame*, 279.

52. Int., H. Johnson, Hill; Wainwright to DM, Apr. 30, 1942; DM to GCM, Apr. 22, 1942, RG 4, MMBA; GCM to DM, Apr. 22, 25, 1942, OPD 381 (4-22-42) Australia; Lt. Gen. Joseph T. McNarney to DM, Apr. 16, 1942; GCM to DM, Apr. 1, 1942; GCM to Wainwright, Mar. 18, 1942, OPD-EF; Wainwright to GCM, Apr. 18, 1942, CCS 371 Philippines (2-9-42).

53. USAFFE-USFIP Op. Rpt., Annex XIII, 43–44, 50–54; DM to GCM, Apr. 13, 21, 1942, CCS 371 Philippines (2-9-42); Mellnik, *Philippine Diary*, 97; GCM to DM, Apr. 2, 3, 7, 1942, OPD 381 (4-2-42) Philippines; GCM to DM, Apr. 22, 28, 1942, OPD-EF.

54. Wainwright to TAG, Apr. 4, 5, 6, 1942, OPD 381 (4-4-42) Philippines; Wainwright, *Wainwright's Story*, 80.

55. DM to GCM, Apr. 1, 1942, RG 4, MMBA; GCM to DM, Apr. 4, 1942; DM to Wainwright, Apr. 4, 1942, OPD 381 (4-4-42) Philippines; int., Collier.

56. USAFFE-USFIP Op. Rpt., 61; Wainwright, *Wainwright's Story*, 298–99; Toland, *But Not in Shame*, 298–99.

57. Wainwright to GCM, May 5, 1942; DM to GCM, May 6, 1942, CCS 371 Philippines (2-9-42); DM to Wainwright, Apr. 14, May 3, 1942; Wainwright to DM, May 5, 1942, RG 4, MMBA; Considine, *It's All News to Me*, 276–77; Whan, ed., *A Soldier Speaks*, 119.

58. Brig. Gen. Lewis C. Beebe to Sutherland, May 2, 1942; Sutherland to Beebe, May 3, 1942; Wainwright to DM, May 3, 1942; Wainwright to FDR, May 5, 1942; Lt. Gen. Masaharu Homma to Wainwright, May 7, 1942, RG 4, MMBA; Wainwright to DM, May 3–6, SWPA G-3 Jnls.; Operations Log, USFIP Hq., May 3–7, 1942, Braly Papers; int., Guyton; John Toland, *The Rising Sun: The Decline and Fall of the Japanese Empire, 1936–1945* (2 vols., New York, 1970), I, 387–400; handwritten draft of statement by DM on Corregidor's fall, n.d. [c. May 6, 1942], Douglas MacArthur Papers, LC. Like MacArthur earlier, Wainwright overestimated the enemy's strength, claiming that by early May Homma had 250,000 troops, whereas the real figure was less than a fourth of that number. Wainwright, *Wainwright's Story*, 86.

59. Wainwright to Sharp, May 6, 7, 1942; DM to Sharp, May 6, 11, 1942, RG 4, MMBA; DM to GCM, May 9, 1942, OPD-EF.

60. Sharp to DM, May 10, 1942; Sharp to Chynoweth, May 10, 1942; Sharp

to Col. Albert F. Christie, May 10, 11, 12, 19, 1942; Christie to Sharp,
May 10, 12, 19, 1942, RG 4, MMBA; int. Chynoweth; Brig. Gen. Bradford G. Chynoweth, Report of Visayan Forces — World War II [dated
Dec. 31, 1942], 51–56, Chynoweth Papers; Lt. Gen. Robert L. Eichelberger, Diary, Mar. 23, 1945, Robert L. Eichelberger Papers, Duke University.

61. Int., Willoughby; Stimson Diary, Sept. 8, 1942; GCM to DM, July 31,
1942; DM to GCM, Aug. 1, 1942, RG 4, MMBA; Chandler, ed., *Eisenhower Papers*, I, 278–79; Pogue, *Marshall*, II, 258–59. Truman presented the Medal of Honor to Wainwright in a White House ceremony
in Sept., 1945. The citation stated that the general had "distinguished
himself by intrepid and determined leadership" and "at the repeated
risk of life above and beyond the call of duty in his position." Wainwright, *Wainwright's Story*, 295–96; U.S. Dept. of the Army, *The Medal
of Honor of the United States Army* (Washington, 1948), 272.

On the Death March, see Miller, *Bataan Uncensored*, 211–30; Dyess,
Dyess Story, 68–97; Levering, *Horror Trek*, 62–78; and the best secondary account, Falk, *Bataan: The March of Death*, 143–202. Falk says
that about 650 of 9921 Americans and 5000 to 10,000 of 62,100 Filipinos died on the Death March.

62. Willoughby and Chamberlain, *MacArthur*, 2–3.

63. Morton, *Fall of the Philippines*, 584. See also Rutherford, *Fall of the
Philippines*, 152–53; Sidney L. Mayer, *MacArthur* (New York, 1971),
89–91.

64. Wigmore, *Japanese Thrust*, 90–508; Long, *MacArthur*, 83; Robert R.
Smith, *Triumph in the Philippines* (USAWWII; Washington, 1963), 94.

PART II. *"Papuan Campaign"*

Basic works in Part II that will not be cited in the chapter notes except
when quoted are Craven and Cate, eds., *Plans and Early Operations*,
403–83; idem, *The Pacific: Guadalcanal to Saipan, August 1942 to July
1944* (AAFWWII; Chicago, 1950), 3–128; Dod, *Corps of Engineers*, 107–
224; Robert L. Eichelberger, with Milton Mackaye, *Our Jungle Road to
Tokyo* (New York, 1950), 3–62; George H. Gill, *Royal Australian Navy,
1939–1942* (AW39–45; Canberra, 1957), 573–649; idem, *Royal Australian
Navy, 1942–1945* (AW39–45; Canberra, 1968), 1–249; Douglas Gillison,
Royal Australian Air Force, 1939–1942 (AW39–45; Canberra, 1962), 446–94,
515–678; Hunt, *MacArthur and the War Against Japan*, 78–105; idem,
Untold Story, 282–95; Kenney, *Kenney Reports*, 3–194; Long, *MacArthur*,
97–120; Luvaas, ed., *Dear Miss Em*, 26–66; MacArthur, *Reminiscences*,
152–67; McCarthy, *South-west Pacific Area*; Milner, *Victory in Papua*;
Samuel E. Morison, *Coral Sea, Midway and Submarine Actions, May 1942–*

August 1942 (HUSNOWWII; Boston, 1949), 3–68, 219–30, 245–63; *idem, Breaking the Bismarcks Barrier, 22 July 1942–1 May 1944* (HUSNOWWII; Boston, 1950), 3–50; Morton, *Strategy and Command,* 274–386; Whitney, *MacArthur,* 64–84; Willoughby and Chamberlain, *MacArthur,* 68–100; Willoughby, ed., *MacArthur Reports,* I, 45–99, II, Pt. I, 124–90.

CHAPTER IV. *"Offensive Preparations"*

pages 156–193

1. Adm. Chester W. Nimitz to Rear Adm. Frank J. Fletcher, Apr. 22, 1942; DM to CG, Noumea, Apr. 25, 1942; TAG to DM, Apr. 10, 13, 14, 15, 19, 20, 21, 25, 28, 1942, OPD 381 SWPA; SWPA G-2 message summary, Apr. 28, 29, 1942, SWPA G-3 Jnls.; Col. Charles A. Willoughby to Brig. Gen. Stephen J. Chamberlin, Apr. 21, 1942, Willoughby Papers.

   When questioned after the war on whether Japanese plans in 1942 included an invasion of Australia, Gen. Hideki Tojo commented: "We never had enough troops to do so. We had already far out-stretched our lines of communication . . . We expected to occupy all New Guinea, to maintain Rabaul as a holding base, and to raid northern Australia by air. But actual physical invasion — no, at no time." Gillison, *Royal Australian Air Force,* 524n.

2. Allied Air Forces G-2, Appreciation of the Coral Sea Battle, May 5–8, 1942, SWPA G-3 Jnls.; DM to GCM, May 13, 1942, CCS 371 Philippines (2-9-42); USSBS, *The Fifth Air Force in the War Against Japan* (Washington, 1947), 78; USSBS, *The Campaigns of the Pacific War* (Washington, 1946), 52–57; Samuel E. Morison, *The Two-Ocean War: A Short History of the United States Navy in the Second World War* (Boston, 1963), 143–44.

3. Gill, *Royal Australian Navy, 1942–1945,* 50; Morison, *Coral Sea, Midway,* 39.

4. E. B. Potter and Chester W. Nimitz, eds., *Triumph in the Pacific: The Navy's Struggle Against Japan* (Englewood Cliffs, N.J., 1963), 14–15; Masatake Okumiya and Jiro Horikoshi, with Martin Caidin, *Zero!* (New York, 1957), 95–106; DM to GCM, May 13, 1942, CCS 371 Philippines (2-9-42); Morison, *Coral Sea, Midway,* 63–64; Meo, *Japan's Radio War,* 64; int., Brig. Gen. Robert H. Van Volkenburgh, Aug. 26, 1971; Nimitz to King, May 20, 1942; DM to Nimitz, May 19, 1942, RG 4, MMBA.

5. DM to GCM, May 13, 1942, CCS 371 Philippines (2-9-42); Allied Air Forces G-2, Appreciation of the Coral Sea Battle, May 5–8, 1942, SWPA G-3 Jnls.; int., Edmonds with Sgt. Graf, Edmonds Papers; GCM to DM, May 9, 11, 13, 1942, OPD-EF; Nimitz to King, May 20, 1942, RG 4, MMBA.

6. DM to GCM, May 13, 1942, CCS 371 Philippines (2-9-42).
7. Brig. Gen. Thomas T. Handy to Brig. Gen. Walter B. Smith, May 14, 1942; GCM to DM, May 19, 1942; Joint U.S. Staff Planners Mins., May 20, 23, 1942, CCS 381 POA (5-11-42).
8. Meo, *Japan's Radio War*, 63–65; Tokyo *Japan Times and Advertiser* (morning ed.), May 8, 9, 1942; Capt. Robert H. Alexander (USN) to author, May 29, 1971; Brant, "The Truth about MacArthur," 851; int., F. Johnson; Vice Adm. Ralph E. Davison, Aug. 2, 1971; Elliott Roosevelt, ed., *F.D.R.: His Personal Letters* (4 vols., New York, 1947–50), IV, 1320–21.
9. GCM to DM, Apr. 30, 1942, OPD-EF; DM to GCM, May 1, 1942, RG 4, MMBA.
10. Gill, *Royal Australian Navy, 1942–45*, 54–55; GCM to DM, May 9, 1942, OPD-EF.
11. DM to GCM, May 10, 1942, RG 4, MMBA.
12. DM to GCM, May 15, 1942, RG 4, MMBA; Meo, *Japan's Radio War*, 97–98.
13. Theodore H. White to Sherrod, May 11, 1942, Sherrod Papers; GCM to DM, May 14, 22, 25, 1942; DM to GCM, May 19, 23, 1942, OPD-EF; FDR to GCM, May 6, 1942, CCS 371 Philippines (2-9-42); FDR to DM, May 6, 1942; DM to GCM, May 8, 1942, RG 4, MMBA; Matloff and Snell, *Strategic Planning*, 217–26; Burns, *Roosevelt*, II, 226; Gill, *Royal Australian Navy, 1942–45*, 56–57.
14. Potter and Nimitz, *Triumph in the Pacific*, 18–23; Morison, *Two-Ocean War*, 147–63; DM to Nimitz, June 8, 1942, RG 5, MMBA. In his *Reminiscences*, 159, MacArthur's report of the Midway losses is badly in error.
15. Nelson T. Johnson to Stanley K. Hornbeck, Mar. 18, 1942, in John J. Reed, "American Diplomatic Relations with Australia during the Second World War" (unpublished Ph.D. dissertation, University of Southern California, 1969), 204; *New York Times*, June 13, 14, 15, Aug. 6, 1942; London *Times*, June 15, 1942; Sydney *Daily Telegraph*, June 14, 1942; DM Diary, June 13, 1942.
16. DM Diary, Mar. 28–July 21, 1942; int., Willoughby; Long, *MacArthur*, 88; Ind, *Bataan*, 378–89; DM to AGWAR, Apr. 30, 1942; DM to GCM, June 30, 1942, RG 4, MMBA; Rovere and Schlesinger, *General and President*, 62–63; Huff, *My Fifteen Years*, 73–83; London *Times*, Apr. 27, 1942; *New York Times*, June 18, 22, 1942. For the anniversary of the Soviet entry into World War II, MacArthur issued another paean praising the Red Army's "indomitable stand" and "restless surge westward." He called upon the Allied people to "unite in salute to that great Army and that great Nation which so nobly strives with us for the victory of liberty and freedom." DM to John Rodgers [secy., Australia-Soviet Friendship League], June 4, 1942, RG 10, MMBA.

17. John D. Millett, *The Organization and Role of the Army Service Forces* (USAWWII; Washington, 1954), 52–53; Richard L. Watson, Jr., "Air Action in the Papuan Campaign, 21 July 1942 to 25 January 1943" [MS study, USAAF Hist. Div., 1944], 6; Willoughby and Chamberlain, *MacArthur*, 71–76; U.S. State Dept., *Foreign Relations, 1942*, I, 552–54; Leighton and Coakley, *Global Logistics and Strategy*, 496–503.

18. Elliott R. Thorpe, *East Wind Rain: The Intimate Account of an Intelligence Officer in the Pacific, 1939–49* (Boston, 1969), 91; Gen. Orders 80, War Dept., Sept. 19, 1945, copy enclosed with George F. Qua to author, Nov. 14, 1971; int., Marshall, Fitch, Johns; Maj. Gen. Thomas A. Lane, June 25, 1971; Brig. Gen. Harry Van Wyk, Aug. 28, 1971; Gen. Orders 1, USASOS Hq., July 20, 1942, SWPA G-3 Jnls.; GCM to DM, July 10, 1942, RG 4, MMBA; Joseph Bykofsky and Harold Larson, *The Transportation Corps: Operations Overseas* (USAWWII; Washington, 1957), 428–29. Marshall was succeeded as USASOS commander by Brig. Gen. James L. Frink in Sept., 1943; the former returned to his duties as SWPA deputy CofS.

19. Willoughby and Chamberlain, *MacArthur*, 70; D. P. Mellor, *The Role of Science and Industry* (AW39–45; Canberra, 1958), 212–13, 302; Hasluck, *Government and People*, 236–38, 751–54; Buggy, *Pacific Victory*, 300–02; Stauffer, *Quartermaster Corps*, 102–25.

20. Leighton and Coakley, *Global Logistics and Strategy*, 412–14; Walker, *Australian Economy*, 273–320; Thorpe, *East Wind Rain*, 96–97; int., Frederic S. Marquardt, Sept. 5, 1971.

21. SWPA G-2 Estimate of the Labor Situation in Australia, June 14, 1942, SWPA G-3 Jnls.

22. Int., Willoughby, Van Volkenburgh; Col. Sidney F. Mashbir, Sept. 1, 1971; *Army Times* editors, *Modern American Secret Agents* (New York, 1966), 42–80; Sidney F. Mashbir, *I Was an American Spy* (New York, 1953), 209–77; Eric A. Feldt, *The Coastwatchers* (New York, 1946), 74–77; Ellis M. Zacharias, *Secret Missions: The Story of an Intelligence Officer* (New York, 1946), 291–93; USSBS, *Fifth Air Force*, 82, 85; Honolulu *Star-Bulletin and Advertiser*, Sept. 1, 1968.

23. Int., Willoughby, Mashbir; Allison Ind, *Allied Intelligence Bureau: Our Secret Weapon in the War Against Japan* (New York, 1958), vii–viii, 51–53, 65–242; Willoughby, ed., *MacArthur Reports*, I, 54; Thorpe, *East Wind Rain*, 92–98; Mellor, *Role of Science and Industry*, 546–47; Gavin Long, *The Final Campaigns* (AW39–45; Canberra, 1963), 617–22. The fullest account of SWPA intelligence activities is Charles A. Willoughby, ed., *The Intelligence Series: G-2 USAFFE, SWPA, AFPAC, FEC, SCAP* (18 vols., Tokyo, 1948).

24. DM to GCM, May 1, 1942; GCM to DM, June 3, 1942; DM to Brett, June 10, 1942; Brett to DM, June 11, 1942, RG 4, MMBA; DM to GCM, Apr. 25, 1942, OPD-EF; int., Maj. Gen. James G. Christiansen,

Aug. 4, 1971; AFPAC, Papuan Campaign, 18–25; William F. McCartney, *The Jungleers: A History of the 41st Infantry Division* (Washington, 1948), 22–29; H. W. Blakeley, *The 32d Infantry Division in World War II* (Madison, 1957), 20–32; Gillison, *Royal Australian Air Force,* 541–43.

25. Ulysses Lee, *The Employment of Negro Troops* (USAWWII; Washington, 1966), 600–02; DM to Gen. Thomas Blamey, June 9, 1942; Chamberlin to Sutherland, June 20, 1942; Blamey to Maj. Gen. Basil M. Morris, SWPA G-3 Jnls.; Buggy, *Pacific Victory,* 34–43.

26. Maj. Gen. Robert C. Richardson to DM, July 4, 1942, RG 4, MMBA.

27. GCM to DM, July 30, 1942, RG 4, MMBA; Richardson to DM, Aug. 9, 1942, Robert C. Richardson Papers, Hoover Institution on War, Revolution, and Peace, Stanford University.

28. King to DM, Apr. 17, 1942, RG 4, MMBA; GCM to DM, June 1, 1942, OPD-EF; William Emerson, "Franklin Roosevelt as Commander-in-Chief in World War II," *Military Affairs,* XXII (Winter, 1958), 195; Herbert Feis, *Churchill, Roosevelt, Stalin: The War They Waged and the Peace They Sought* (Princeton, 1957), 41; Arthur Bryant, *The Turn of the Tide: A History of the War Years Based on the Diaries of Field-Marshal Lord Alanbrooke, Chief of the Imperial General Staff* (Garden City, 1957), 312–13.

29. Gill, *Royal Australian Navy, 1942–45,* 126–27; Sherwood, *Roosevelt and Hopkins,* II, 168; GCM to DM, May 11, 1942, OPD-EF; DM to Blamey, June 11, 1942, in McCarthy, *South-west Pacific Area,* 606.

30. DM to GCM, June 8, 1942; GCM to DM, June 10, 1942, OPD-EF; int., Handy, Hull; Clark G. Reynolds, *The Fast Carriers: The Forging of an Air Navy* (New York, 1968), 30–31; Gillison, *Royal Australian Air Force,* 536–38; William Frye, *Marshall: Citizen Soldier* (Indianapolis, 1947), 328–31.

31. Int., Willoughby; AFPAC, Papuan Campaign, 39–41; Tulsa I and II plans, RG 4, MMBA; Robert Sherrod, *History of Marine Corps Aviation in World War II* (Washington, 1952), 69–70; DM to GCM, June 24, 1942, RG 4, MMBA.

32. DM to GCM, June 28, 1942; GCM to DM, June 29, 1942, OPD-EF; GCM to DM, June 27, 1942, RG 4, MMBA; Matloff and Snell, *Strategic Planning,* 258–65; Leighton and Coakley, *Global Logistics and Strategy,* 388–89; John Miller, Jr., *Guadalcanal: The First Offensive* (USAWWII; Washington, 1949), 8–19.

33. JCS to DM, July 2, 1942, RG 4, MMBA; Pogue, *Marshall,* II, 379–81; Oliver A. Gillespie, *The Pacific* (OHNZSWW; Wellington, 1952), 59–65; Kent R. Greenfield, *American Strategy in World War II: A Reconsideration* (Baltimore, 1963), 7; GCM to DM, July 3, 1942; DM to GCM, July 4, 1942, OPD-EF; GCM to DM, July 23, 1942, RG 4, MMBA.

34. Tulsa I and II plans, RG 4, MMBA; int., Van Volkenburgh; Gill, *Royal Australian Navy, 1942–45,* 118–19.
35. Int., Van Volkenburgh; GHQ SWPA G-2 daily communiqués, July 18–23, 1942, RG 407, WNRC (microfilm, MSU); USSBS, *The Allied Campaign Against Rabaul* (Washington, 1946), 20–21. Unless otherwise cited, SWPA and AFPAC communiqués are from RG 407, WNRC.
36. DM to Capt. Dudley W. Knox (USN), Aug. 21, 1942, RG 10, MMBA. Knox, who was a distinguished historian and headed the Navy Department's office of naval records and library, was a life-long friend and admirer of MacArthur's.

CHAPTER V. *"Across the Owen Stanleys"*
pages 194–244
1. E. J. Kahn, Jr., *G. I. Jungle: An American Soldier in Australia and New Guinea* (New York, 1943), 47–50; Buggy, *Pacific Victory,* 33; George H. Johnston, *Pacific Partner* (New York, 1944), 99, 106; Lee and Henschel, *MacArthur,* 165–66; Thorpe, *East Wind Rain,* 91–92.
2. Johnston, *Pacific Partner,* 99–100.
3. DM to GCM, June 18, July 7, 1942; GCM to DM, June 29, July 13, 1942; DM to Brett, July 14, 1942, RG 4, MMBA; int., Kenney, Fitch; Brig. Gen. William L. Ritchie, June 24, 1971; Arnold, *Global Mission,* 331; Kenney, *Kenney Reports,* 27, 28–29, 44–45; Pogue, *Marshall,* II, 376–77; George H. Brett, "The MacArthur I Knew," *True,* Oct., 1947, 26; DM, *Reminiscences,* 157; Long, *MacArthur,* 106; Kenney, *MacArthur,* 9; Lee and Henschel, *MacArthur,* 167.
4. Int., Kenney; SWPA press release, Mar. 10, 1944; DM to Gen. Hoyt S. Vandenberg, Mar. 21, 1949, RG 5, MMBA; USSBS, *Fifth Air Force,* 7–8; Watson, "Air Action in the Papuan Campaign," 6–7, 50–52; Craven and Cate, eds., *Guadalcanal to Saipan,* 99–100; Charles Bateson, *The War with Japan: A Concise History* (East Lansing, 1968), 186–88; Donald M. Goldstein, "Ennis S. Whitehead, Aerospace Commander and Pioneer" (unpublished Ph.D. dissertation, University of Denver, 1970), 88–91; Kenney, *Kenney Reports,* 53.
5. DM and Vice Adm. Robert L. Ghormley to JCS, July 8, 1942, OPD-EF; King to GCM, July 10, 1942; JCS to DM and Ghormley, July 10, 1942, CCS 381 SWPA (7-10-42); Kenney, *Kenney Reports,* 31; Miller, *Guadalcanal,* 8–75; John L. Zimmerman, *The Guadalcanal Campaign* (Washington, 1949), 6–49; Alexander A. Vandegrift, with Robert B. Asprey, *Once a Marine: The Memoirs of General A. A. Vandegrift* (New York, 1946), 104–19; Jeter A. Isely and Philip A. Crowl, *The U.S. Marines and Amphibious War: Its Theory and Its Practice in the Pacific* (Princeton, 1951), 104–05.
6. DM to GCM, Aug. 2, 1942, OPD-EF; DM to GCM [SWPA Op. Rpts.],

July 22–Aug. 20, 1942, SWPA G-3 Jnls.; OPD Summary of Pacific Operations, 1942–1945, 2, MHRC; McCarthy, *South-west Pacific Area,* 141; Bateson, *War with Japan,* 196–200.

7. DM to GCM [SWPA Op. Rpts.], Aug. 21–Sept. 18, 1942; GHQ SWPA G-2 daily communiqués, Sept. 1–18, 1942; Willoughby, ed., *MacArthur Reports,* II, Pt. I, 164.

8. OPD, Pacific Ops., 32–33; Ghormley to Nimitz, Aug. 29, 1942; Adm. V. A. C. Crutchley to author, Aug. 27, 1971; AFPAC, Papuan Campaign, 53–55; SWPA G-2 Weekly Summary, Sept. 1–7, 1942, SWPA G-3 Jnls.; Buggy, *Pacific Victory,* 161–73; John Vader, *New Guinea: The Tide Is Stemmed* (New York, 1971), 48–65; Willoughby, ed., *MacArthur Reports,* I, 70; Bykofsky and Larson, *Transportation Corps,* 485–86; Milner, *Papua,* 88.

9. McCarthy, *South-west Pacific Area,* 174, 176, 186; DM to GCM, Aug. 30, Sept. 12, 1942; Blamey to DM, Sept. 28, 1942, RG 4, MMBA; Herring to author, May 22, 1972; int., Kenney, Fitch; Vader, *New Guinea,* 77; Kenney, *Kenney Reports,* 89–94, 124.

10. Kenney, *Kenney Reports,* 112; Gen. Henry H. Arnold, Diary, Sept. 25–26, 1942, Henry H. Arnold Papers, File 168.65–42, AFHRD. See also Arnold, *Global Mission,* 336–49.

11. Arnold Diary, Sept. 25–Oct. 2, 1942; Gen. Henry H. Arnold to GCM, Oct. 6, 1942, OPD 384 (4-3-42).

12. Leighton and Coakley, *Global Logistics and Strategy,* 383, 388; Matloff and Snell, *Strategic Planning,* 217, 298–306; Feis, *Churchill, Roosevelt, Stalin,* 42–43; Greenfield, *American Strategy,* 71–73, 79–80; Bryant, *Turn of the Tide,* 288–89.

13. DM to GCM, Aug. 8, 1942, RG 4, MMBA.

14. GCM to DM, Aug. 10, 1942, *ibid.*

15. DM to GCM Aug. 11, 1942, *ibid.;* Arnold Diary, Sept. 25, 1942; int., Eisenhower.

16. Hasluck, *Government and People,* 175–93; DM to GCM, Aug. 30, 1942; DM to Curtin, Oct. 6, 1942, RG 4, MMBA.

17. Ghormley to Nimitz, Aug. 17, 1942; King to Nimitz and Ghormley, Aug. 27, 1942; GCM to DM, Aug. 11, 14, 1942; DM to GCM, Sept. 3, 1942, RG 4, MMBA; JCS Mins., Sept. 1, 1942, CCS 381 SWPA (7-10-42); Watson, "Air Action in the Papuan Campaign," 23–24; Miller, *Guadalcanal,* 33–34, 107–08, 137; Hough, *et al., Pearl Harbor to Guadalcanal,* 241; Sherrod, *Marine Corps Aviation,* 71, 85, 99; Isely and Crowl, *U.S. Marines and Amphibious War,* 89–98, 118–19, 155; Samuel B. Griffith, II, *The Battle for Guadalcanal* (Philadelphia, 1963), 110th–11; Andrieu d'Albas, *Death of a Navy: Japanese Naval Action in World War II* (New York, 1957), 161; Gilbert Cant, *America's Navy in World War II* (New York, 1943), 328–29.

18. Miller, *Guadalcanal,* 152, 172–73; U.S. Navy Dept., *Navy Dept. Communiques 1–300,* 111; King to GCM, Oct. 3, 1942, CCS 381 SWPA

(7-10-42); GCM to DM, Oct. 16, 1942; DM to GCM, Oct. 17, 1942; DM to Stimson, Oct. 18, 1942, RG 4, MMBA. Until the arrival of the Army's 164th Inf. Rgt. from Noumea on Oct. 13, some Marines on Guadalcanal had built up considerable resentment against the Army for not helping them. Although neither the Joint Chiefs nor Ghormley expected MacArthur to send troops there, the Marines sometimes blamed him, as the following doggerel indicates:

We asked all the Doggies [Army troops] to come to Tulagi
But General MacArthur said "No."
When asked for his reason —
"It isn't the season.
"Besides you have no U.S.O.!"

Robert Leckie, *Strong Men Armed: The United States Marines Against Japan* (New York, 1962), 80–81.

19. Adm. William D. Leahy to Lewis W. Douglas, Oct. 26, 1942; Douglas to Leahy, Oct. 28, 1942; Combined Military Transportation Committee Mins., Nov. 18, 1942, CCS 381 SWPA (7-10-42); William F. Halsey and Joseph Bryan, III, *Admiral Halsey's Story* (New York, 1947), 108–09; Samuel E. Morison, *The Struggle for Guadalcanal, August 1942–February 1943* (HUSNOWWII; Boston, 1949), 184–85, 286–87; Haugland, *AAF Against Japan*, 133; Sherrod, *Marine Corps Aviation*, 115, 118; Zimmerman, *Guadalcanal Campaign*, 165; U.S. Navy Dept., *Navy Dept. Communiques 1–300*, 130–31; int., F. Johnson; Kramer J. Rohfleisch, "Guadalcanal and the Origins of the Thirteenth Air Force" [MS study, USAAF Hist. Div., 1945], 43–44, 57, AFHRD. In his *Reminiscences*, 161, 163, MacArthur twice refers to "Guadalcanal on Bougainville," which indicates not his ignorance but careless copy editing and proofreading of his manuscript.

20. Bryant, *Turn of the Tide*, 400–01; Stauffer, *Quartermaster Corps*, 84–87, 91–92, 147; Chester Wardlow, *The Transportation Corps: Responsibilities, Organization, and Operations* (Washington, 1951), 284; Millett, *Army Service Forces*, 60; Huston, *Sinews of War*, 543–44; Willoughby and Chamberlain, *MacArthur*, 70.

21. Zimmerman, *Guadalcanal Campaign*, 14–15; Miller, *Guadalcanal*, 43–45; Vandegrift, *Once a Marine*, 114; Hugh J. Casey, ed., *Engineers of the Southwest Pacific* (7 vols., Washington, 1947–59), III, 25, 27.

22. Adm. Thomas C. Kinkaid, Narrative of Operations in World War II [oral transcript, 1961], 11, CUOHRO; DM to GCM, Sept. 16, 1942, OPD-EF; GCM to DM, Oct. 19, 1942, RG 4, MMBA; Rohfleisch, "Guadalcanal," 43–45; Charles A. Lockwood, *Sink 'Em All: Submarine Warfare in the Pacific* (New York, 1951), 47–48; Morton, *Pacific Command*, 14; Halsey and Bryan, *Halsey's Story*, 138–40; DM Diary, Sept. 11, 1942.

23. CCS Mins., Nov. 20, 1942, CCS 381 SWPA (7-10-42); Ghormley to DM,

Aug. 14, 1942; DM to GCM, Aug. 15, 16, 17, 1942; DM to Curtin, Sept. 23, 1942, RG 4, MMBA.

24. Zimmerman, *Guadalcanal Campaign,* 165–67; int., Handy, Hull; Brig. Gen. Frederick P. Munson, July 2, 1971; Morton, *Strategy and Command,* 363.

25. U.S. War Dept., *Papuan Campaign: The Buna-Sanananda Operation (16 November 1942–23 January 1943)* (Washington, 1944), 4–5; AFPAC, Papuan Campaign, 55–62; Kenney, *Kenney Reports,* 101; USSBS, *Fifth Air Force,* 25–27, 85; Morison, *Bismarcks Barrier,* 32.

26. DM Diary, Oct. 2–4, 1942; Kenney, *Kenney Reports,* 105–106; Long, *MacArthur,* 111; Bateson, *War with Japan,* 206. Haugland, who received the Silver Star, bailed out of a crash-bound B-26 and spent several weeks in enemy-infested jungles before being rescued.

27. Kenney, *MacArthur,* 103–04; DM Diary, Nov. 4–6, 1942, and Jan. 9, 1943.

28. DM to GCM, Oct. 16, 1943, OPD-EF; Blakeley, *32d Div.,* 44–46.

29. Woodburn Kirby, *et al., The War Against Japan* (HSWWUKMS; 5 vols., London, 1957–69), II, 286–89; DM to Blamey, Nov. 2, 1942, DM Misc. 201; Johnston, *Pacific Partner,* 103.

30. McCarthy, *South-west Pacific Area,* 290, 299, 307–08, 310; Buggy, *Pacific Victory,* 180–95, 201–02.

31. Vice Adm. Arthur C. Carpender to DM, Nov. 10, 1942, SWPA G-3 Jnls.; Leighton and Coakley, *Global Logistics and Strategy,* 408; Blanch D. Coll, Jean E. Keith, and Herbert H. Rosenthal, *The Corps of Engineers: Troops and Equipment* (USAWWII; Washington, 1958), 384–85; William F. Heavey, *Down Ramp! The Story of the Army Amphibian Engineers* (Washington, 1947), 28; McCarthy, *South-west Pacific Area,* 352. On Oct. 1 Willoughby estimated that there were 5000 Japanese troops on the Kokoda Trail and 1000 at Gona and Buna. SWPA G-2 Monthly Summary, Oct. 1, 1942, RG 3, MMBA.

32. Kahn, *GI Jungle,* 76–133; Blakeley, *32d Div.,* 68–70; Edgar F. Puryear, Jr., *Nineteen Stars* (Washington, 1971), 127.

33. DM to Blamey, Nov. 26, 1942; Blamey to DM, Nov. 27, 1942, SWPA G-3 Jnls.; DM to GCM, Nov. 22, 27, 29, 1942; Vice Adm. William F. Halsey to DM, Nov. 28, 1942, RG 4 MMBA; int., Bulkeley.

34. Int., Kenney; Kenney, *Kenney Reports,* 153.

35. Luvaas, ed., *Dear Miss Em,* 32–33; Kenney, *Kenney Reports,* 157; int., Kenney, Byers; DM Diary, Nov. 30, 1942.

CHAPTER VI. *"Belated Victory"*
pages 245–286
1. Hunt, *MacArthur and the War Against Japan,* 89; Thorpe, *East Wind Rain,* 124; Huff, *My Fifteen Years,* 84.

2. Int., Kenney.
3. Kahn, *GI Jungle,* 66; George H. Johnston, *The Toughest Fighting in the World* (New York, 1943), 176-77; "Hero in New Guinea," *Time,* XL (Nov. 30, 1942), 31; Martin, *GI War,* 260; Johnston, *Pacific Partner,* 95; int., Johns.
4. Int., Kenney.
5. *New York Times,* Oct. 26, 30, Nov. 4, Dec. 5, 1942; New York *Daily News,* Aug. 13, 1942; Ernest K. Lindley, "Why MacArthur Hasn't Led," *Newsweek,* XX (Nov. 9, 1942), 28; Brant, "The Truth About Mac-Arthur," 851-53; Pogue, *Marshall,* II, 394-96; Whan, ed., *A Soldier Speaks,* 123; Maj. Gen. Roy D. Keehn to DM, June 8, 1942; Carlos P. Romulo to DM, July 12, Aug. 18, Oct. 2, 1942; Col. William A. Ganoe to DM, Oct. 28, 1942; William M. Nichols to DM, Oct. 29, 1942, RG 10, MMBA. Col. Sidney Mashbir said that King told him in early Sept., 1942, Roosevelt and Marshall "are not going to permit him [MacArthur] to become the conqueror of the Philippines until the 1944 presidential nomination is closed." Contrary to established notions about King's attitude, Mashbir staunchly maintained that in Navy circles "the hostility toward MacArthur came from a totally different source." Int., Mashbir.
6. Stimson Diary, Oct. 29, 1942.
7. Sydney *Argus,* Oct. 29, 1942.
8. *Ibid.;* Nelson T. Johnson to DM, Nov. 7, 1942, RG 10, MMBA; Maj. Gen. George Van Horn Moseley to DM, Nov. 10, 1942, George Van Horn Moseley Papers, LC; San Francisco *Examiner,* Nov. 5, 1942. See also Maj. Gen. F. Gilbreath to DM, Nov. 6, 1942; John C. O'Laughlin to DM, Nov. 10, 1942; Mrs. R. R. Dewey to DM, Nov. 19, 1942; W. Kirk Deselm to DM, Jan. 11, 1943, RG 10, MMBA.
9. Cantril, ed., *Public Opinion,* 559, 621-22, 624.
10. *Ibid.,* 625.
11. Kahn, *GI Jungle,* 20, 50; McCarthy, *South-west Pacific Area,* 625-26; Martin, *GI War,* 267.
12. DM to Blamey, Feb. 12, 1942, RG 4, MMBA.
13. DM Diary, Dec. 9, 1942; Luvaas, ed., *Dear Miss Em,* 30-31; McCarthy, *South-west Pacific Area,* 627; confidential communications of SWPA officers to author.
14. W. Harrop to Rev. S. W. McKibbin, Oct. 12, 1942; McKibbin to DM, Oct. 13, 1942; Rev. J. H. G. Auld to DM, Oct. 13, 1942; DM to Auld, Oct. 18, 1942, RG 10, MMBA.
15. DM to GCM, Mar. 29, 1942, OPD-EF; Lee, *Employment of Negro Troops,* 431-33.
16. Zimmerman, *Guadalcanal Campaign,* 156; Griffith, *Guadalcanal,* 216; Vandegrift, *Once a Marine,* 205-07; Frank O. Hough and John A. Crown, *The Campaign on New Britain* (Washington, 1952), 21; int.,

Gen. Oliver P. Smith (USMC), Aug. 25, 1971; Lt. Gen. Edward A. Craig (USMC), Sept. 3, 1971; Lt. Gen. Alpha L. Bowser (USMC), Sept. 3, 1971; George McMillan, *The Old Breed: A History of the First Marine Division in World War II* (Washington, 1949), 145–48.

17. Vandegrift, *Once a Marine*, 207–09; DM Diary, Jan. 24, 1942; Isely and Crowl, *U.S. Marines and Amphibious War*, 163, 185.

18. Vandegrift, *Once a Marine*, 209.

19. Luvaas, ed., *Dear Miss Em*, 36, 37; int., Byers; Milner, *Papua*, 209; Blakeley, *32d Div.*, 81, 83.

20. Lt. Gen. Robert L. Eichelberger, Dictations, May 31, June 24, 1957, quoted in Luvaas, ed., *Dear Miss Em*, 38–39.

21. Int., Byers; Maj. Gen. Robert L. Eichelberger to Sutherland, Dec. 3, 1942, SWPA G-3 Jnls.; Eichelberger Diary, Dec. 2, 1942; Blakeley, *32d Div.*, 83–84.

22. Blakeley, *32d Div.*, 84–85; Kenney, *Kenney Reports*, 159; DM to Curtin, Dec. 4, 1942, RG 4, MMBA; Luvaas, ed., *Dear Miss Em*, 51, 70. While working with the Army's historical program at the end of the war, Harding, a former editor of the *Infantry Journal*, showed a high degree of editorial objectivity in working with his historians on the Buna operation and exhibited no bitterness toward Eichelberger or MacArthur. Int., Col. John M. Kemper, July 13, 1971. (Kemper also worked in the Army's historical office at that time.)

23. AFPAC, Papuan Campaign, 77–80; Ralph Honner, "This Is the 39th [Battalion]," in Norman Bartlett, ed., *Australia at Arms* (Canberra, 1962), 220–30; Buggy, *Pacific Victory*, 196–215; Milner, *Papua*, 216, 329; McCarthy, *South-west Pacific Area*, 510; int., Willoughby, Byers, Van Volkenburgh; Herring to author, May 22, 1972.

24. Int., Byers; Eichelberger to Miss Em [his wife], Dec. 5, 1942; Eichelberger to Col. Chauncey L. Fenton, Oct. 20, 1943, Eichelberger Papers; Blakeley, *32d Div.*, 79–114.

25. DM to Eichelberger, Dec. 13, 1942, in Eichelberger, *Jungle Road*, 42–43.

26. Luvaas, ed., *Dear Miss Em*, 46; Eichelberger to Sutherland, Dec. 16, 1942, SWPA G-3 Jnls.

27. DM Diary, Dec. 25–30, 1942; Luvaas, ed., *Dear Miss Em*, 49; Herring to author, May 22, 1972; *New York Times*, Jan. 8, 1943.

28. DM to GCM, Jan. 5, 1943, OPD-EF; Eichelberger, *Jungle Road*, 49; Luvaas, ed., *Dear Miss Em*, 51–52. Milner, *Papua*, 343, 344, states that MacArthur returned to Brisbane on Jan. 8, but MacArthur's office diary entry of Jan. 9 says he departed Moresby at 7:00 A.M. and arrived at Brisbane at 4:00 P.M. that day after a luncheon stop at Townsville.

29. GHQ SWPA communiqué, Jan. 8, 1942, in Willoughby, ed., *MacArthur Reports*, I, 98. In this vol. the communiqué is quoted out of context as if it were issued near the end of the Sanananda operations, which actually terminated on Jan. 22.

30. GHQ SWPA G-2 daily communiqués, Jan. 12–21, 1942; McCartney, *Jungleers*, 31–42; Luvaas, ed., *Dear Miss Em*, 62; Lt. Col. B. G. Baetcke to Chamberlin, July 9, 1943, SWPA G-3 Jnls.; Eichelberger, *Jungle Road*, 57; McCarthy, *South-west Pacific Area*, 533.

31. Vader, *New Guinea*, 92, 96, 103; Blakeley, *32d Div.*, 115–27; McCartney, *Jungleers*, 43–49; Luvaas, ed., *Dear Miss Em*, 63–64.

32. Misc. 201 File of Lt. Gen. Robert L. Eichelberger, CMH; DM to GCM, Feb. 23, 1943, RG 10, MMBA; Luvaas, ed., *Dear Miss Em*, 64, 66. MacArthur's order of the day announcing the DSC citations was issued on Jan. 9, 1943, and closed with these words: "To Almighty God I give thanks for that guidance which has brought us to this success in our great Crusade. His is the honor, the power and the glory forever, Amen." Willoughby, ed., *MacArthur Reports*, I, 99n.

33. Luvaas, ed., *Dear Miss Em*, 65.

34. Secy. of Defense Frederick Shedden, Report of the Dissemination of Information on Operations in the Southwest Pacific Area, Jan. 20, 1943, RG 4, MMBA; Hasluck, *Government and People*, 407–08; Buggy, *Pacific Victory*, 194–95; Eichelberger, *Jungle Road*, 46–47; Rovere and Schlesinger, *General and President*, 74–75; Joseph J. Mathews, *Reporting the Wars* (Minneapolis, 1957), 219–20; Lady Muriel Wootten to author, Jan. 9, 1971.

35. Quoted in Long, *MacArthur*, 119.

36. McCartney, *Jungleers*, 41–42; Milner, *Papua*, 372. On casualty totals, see Milner, *Papua*, 370–74; McCarthy, *South-west Pacific Area*, 531; Miller, *Guadalcanal*, 350.

37. Eichelberger to Samuel Milner, Mar. 8, 1954, Eichelberger Misc. 201.

38. Confidential communication to author.

39. Edward V. Rickenbacker, *Rickenbacker: An Autobiography* (Englewood Cliffs, 1967), 332–33. Rickenbacker delivered to MacArthur an "oral message" from Stimson, which was probably stinging, to judge from his comment: "Though I remember every word of it to this day, I shall not repeat it. Stimson and MacArthur took it with them to the grave, and so shall I."

40. GHQ SWPA press release, Jan. 24, 1943, in Willoughby, ed., *MacArthur Reports*, I, 98.

41. Greenfield, *American Strategy*, 111–12; Watson, "Air Action in the Papuan Campaign," 1–2, 79; USSBS, *Fifth Air Force*, 3–4; USSBS, *Employment of Forces Under the Southwest Pacific Command* (Washington, 1947), 1–2; USSBS, *Summary Report (Pacific War)* (Washington, 1946), 4–6; U.S. State Dept., *Conferences at Washington and Casablanca*, 775–77; Osmar White, *Green Armor* (New York, 1945), 9–27, 212–17.

42. Int., F. Johnson; Blamey to DM, Nov. 19, 1942, RG 4, MMBA; Chamberlin to Vice Adm. Daniel E. Barbey, Sept. 8, 1960, Daniel E. Barbey Papers, NHD; King to GCM, Dec. 23, 1942, OPD-EF; Daniel E. Barbey,

MacArthur's Amphibious Navy: Seventh Amphibious Force Operations, 1943–1945 (Annapolis, 1969), x, 3–10, 20; Stimson and Bundy, *On Active Service,* 506–07.

43. Johnston, *Pacific Partner,* 106.
44. T. Dodson Stamps and Vincent J. Esposito, eds., *A Military History of World War II* (2 vols., West Point, 1953), 352; Pogue, *Marshall,* II, 369; Stimson to DM, Jan. 6, 1943, RG 4, MMBA; Curtin to DM, Jan. 25, 1943, RG 5, MMBA; Herring to author, May, 22, 1972. In recognition of their leadership in the Papuan campaign, King George VI conferred on MacArthur and Blamey the honor of Knight Grand Cross of the Military Division of the Order of the Bath. Eichelberger, Kenney, and Whitehead were made Knight Commanders of this order. In addition, MacArthur received his third DSM from the War Dept.

PART III. *"Cartwheel Operations"*

Basic works in Part III that will not be cited in the chapter notes except when quoted are Barbey, *MacArthur's Amphibious Navy,* 3–167; Craven and Cate, eds., *Guadalcanal to Saipan,* 129–356, 549–74; David Dexter, *New Guinea Offensives* (AW39–45; Canberra, 1961), 1–789; Dod, *Corps of Engineers,* 225–75, 520–69; Eichelberger, *Jungle Road,* 63–99; Gill, *Royal Australian Navy, 1942–45,* 250–397; Hough and Crown, *New Britain;* Hunt, *MacArthur and the War Against Japan,* 106–46; *idem, Untold Story,* 296–325; Kenney, *Kenney Reports,* 197–366; Walter Krueger, *From Down Under to Nippon: The Story of Sixth Army in World War II* (Washington, 1953), 3–55; Long, *MacArthur,* 121–42; Luvaas, ed., *Dear Miss Em,* 66–101; MacArthur, *Reminiscences,* 168–89; John Miller, Jr., *Cartwheel: The Reduction of Rabaul* (USAWWII; Washington, 1959); Morison, *Bismarcks Barrier,* 51–448; Morton, *Strategy and Command,* 364–605; George Odgers, *Air War Against Japan, 1943–45* (AW39–45; Canberra, 1957), 1–334; Whitney, *MacArthur,* 84–110; Willoughby and Chamberlain, *MacArthur,* 100–43, 171–74; Willoughby, ed., *MacArthur Reports,* I, 100–45, II, Pt. I, 190–261.

CHAPTER VII. *"Northward to Huon Gulf"*

pages 289–335
1. SWPA Op. Rpts., Jan. 29–Feb. 6, 1943, SWPA G-3 Jnls.; USSBS, *Employment of Forces,* 16–17; McCarthy, *South-west Pacific Area,* 588; DM, *Reminiscences,* 170.
2. USSBS, *Fifth Air Force,* 57–58; USSBS, *Interrogations,* II, 500; Okumiya and Horikoshi, *Zero,* 172–73; Buggy, *Pacific Victory,* 222–27; Johnston, *Toughest Fighting,* 238–39; William N. Davis, Jr., review of

Craven and Cate, eds., *Guadalcanal to Saipan,* in *American Historical Review,* LVI (Apr., 1951), 622; Davis, *Experience of War,* 379–92.

3. Richard L. Watson, Jr., "The Fifth Air Force in the Huon Peninsula Campaign, January to October 1943" [MS study, USAAF Hist. Div., 1946], 96–101, AFHRD; USSBS, *Campaigns,* 174–75; GHQ SWPA G-2 daily communiqués, Mar. 1–7, 1943; John Creswell, *Sea Warfare, 1939–1945* (Berkeley, 1967), 248; Kirby, *War Against Japan,* II, 375–76; Gillison, *Royal Australian Air Force,* 694; Morison, *Bismarcks Barrier,* 62; Kenney, *Kenney Reports,* 206; DM to Brig. Gen. Ennis C. Whitehead, Mar. 4, 1943, RG 5, MMBA; int., Sherrod with Diller.

4. GHQ SWPA communiqué, Mar. 5, 1943; London *Times,* Mar. 5, 1943; *New York Times,* Mar. 5, 1943. MacArthur's final sentence appears in the newspaper versions, but not in the copy of the communiqué in RG 3, MMBA.

5. Washington *Post,* Apr. 15, 1943; Brig. Gen. Albert C. Wedemeyer to GCM, Apr. 15, 1943, DM File, OPD 201.

6. Washington *Post,* Sept. 4, 1945; Craven and Cate, eds., *Guadalcanal to Saipan,* 146–47; Morison, *Bismarcks Barrier,* 62.

7. Craven and Cate, eds., *Guadalcanal to Saipan,* 148; GCM to DM, Sept. 7, 1943, RG 4, MMBA.

8. DM to GCM, Sept. 7, 1943, RG 4, MMBA.

9. GCM to DM, Sept. 8, 1943; Kenney to Arnold, Sept. 14, 1943, RG 4, MMBA; Robert Payne, *The Marshall Story: A Biography of General George C. Marshall* (New York, 1951), 196.

10. Washington *Post,* Sept. 4, 1945; Davis, review, *American Historical Review,* LVI, 621–22; Goldstein, "Whitehead," 123–38; Rovere and Schlesinger, *General and President,* 78.

11. Brig. Gen. Jarred V. Crabb, Report on the Battle of the Bismarck Sea [dated Dec., 1945], 1, 4, Ennis C. Whitehead Papers, File 168.6008–24, AFHRD. Besides other documents in the Whitehead collection, material in AFHRD relating to the Bismarck Sea controversy can be found in the Fifth Air Force, V Fighter Command, V Bomber Command, GHQ SWPA, USSBS, and ACS/AS Intelligence files.

12. Int., Kenney. In Sept., 1945 Rear Adm. Toshitane Takata, former deputy chief of staff of the Combined Fleet, stated, "The American estimate of the Bismarck Sea battle was too conservative. I think every ship, of more than 30 in the convoy, went to the bottom." Haugland, *AAF Against Japan,* 163.

13. Kenney, *Kenney Reports,* 205; DM, *Reminiscences,* 171; Morison, *Bismarcks Barrier,* 64.

14. GCM to DM, Jan. 11, 1943; Curtin to DM, Feb. 8, 1943, RG 4, MMBA; CCS Mins., Jan. 17, 1943, CCS 381 SWPA (7-10-42); U.S. State Dept., *Conferences at Washington and Casablanca,* 547–49, 555–56, 774–75; John Miller, Jr., "The Casablanca Conference and Pacific Strategy,"

Military Affairs, XIII (Winter, 1949), 209–15; DM Diary, Feb. 19, 1943; Albert C. Wedemeyer, *Wedemeyer Reports!* (New York, 1958), 205–07.

15. JPS to JCS, Feb. 15, 1943, CCS 381 Japan (8-25-42); DM to Nimitz and Halsey, Jan. 13, 1943; DM to GCM, Jan. 27, 1943, RG 4, MMBA; int., Handy; Gen. Albert C. Wedemeyer, July 6, 1971; Morton, *Strategy and Command*, 386; Maurice Matloff, *Strategic Planning for Coalition Warfare, 1943–1944* (USAWWII; Washington, 1959), 88–99.

16. Pacific Military Conference Mins., Mar. 12–13, 1943, CCS 381 (2-28-43) Sec. 1–2; SWPA G-3 Staff Study, Elkton Plan, Mar. 11, 1943, RG 3, MMBA; DM to GCM, Feb. 15, 1943, RG 4, MMBA; int., Handy, Wedemeyer, Hull; Wedemeyer, *Wedemeyer Reports*, 214; Morton, *Strategy and Command*, 391; Leighton and Coakley, *Global Logistics and Strategy*, 694–95; Pogue, *Marshall*, II, 160–66; Kenney, *Kenney Reports*, 215–16. Col. Larry Lehrbas, of SWPA PRO, and an aide each for Sutherland and Kenney accompanied the SWPA delegation to Washington.

17. JPS to JCS, Mar. 16, 1943, CCS 381 (2-28-43) Sec. 2; Adm. Charles M. Cooke to Handy, Mar. 23, 1943, OPD-EF; GCM to DM, Mar. 23, 1943; DM to GCM, Mar. 25, 1943, RG 4, MMBA; Kramer J. Rohfleisch, "The Thirteenth Air Force, March–October 1943" (MS study, USAAF Hist. Div., 1946), 16–18; Leahy, *I Was There*, 152–53.

18. JCS to DM, Mar. 28, 1943, RG 4, MMBA; JCS Mins., Mar. 28, 1943, CCS 381 (2-28-43) Sec. 2; Morton, *Strategy and Command*, 399, 400, 641.

19. Int., Fitch, Van Wyk; Adm. Albert G. Noble, June 24, 1971; Col. René E. Frailé, Aug. 30, 1971; Chamberlin to Barbey, Sept. 8, 1960, Barbey Papers; Robert W. Coakley and Richard M. Leighton, *Global Logistics and Strategy, 1943–1945* (USAWWII; Washington, 1968), 208, 418–20, 435–41, 490–94, 497–500; Roskill, *War at Sea*, II, 413–15; Reynolds, *Fast Carriers*, 69–70; Stauffer, *Quartermaster Corps*, 67; Krueger, *From Down Under*, 3–10; Gen. Orders 1, USAFFE Hq., Feb. 26, 1943; Gen. Orders 1, Sixth Army Hq., Feb. 16, 1943, DM Misc. 201; DM to GCM, Jan. 11, 1943; DM to Curtin, Feb. 8, 1943, RG 4, MMBA; DM Diary, Feb. 8, 1943.

20. Krueger, *From Down Under*, 10. One SWPA officer suggests that Alamo Force was created mainly "to confuse the enemy as to numbers and units." Virgil Ney, *Evolution of a Theater of Operations Headquarters, 1941–1967* (Washington, 1967), 52.

21. Dexter, *New Guinea Offensives*, 222.

22. DM to GCM, July 31, 1943, in Morton, *Strategy and Command*, 408.

23. Luvaas, ed., *Dear Miss Em*, 153, 187. For an excellent discussion of Nimitz's headquarters setup, see Morton, *Strategy and Command*, 481–501.

24. DM Diary, Apr. 15–17, 1943; Halsey and Bryan, *Halsey's Story*, 153–55; Edwin P. Hoyt, *How They Won the War in the Pacific: Nimitz and His Admirals* (New York, 1970), 224–25; DM, *Reminiscences*, 173–74.

25. Halsey and Bryan, *Halsey's Story*, 154–55.
26. King to GCM, May 2, 1943, OPD 381 (Security); GCM to DM, May 3, 1943, CM-OUT 1108, Classified Message Center File, RG 407, NA; DM to GCM, May 5, 16, 27, 1943, RG 4, MMBA. The Elkton III Plan is printed in Morton, *Strategy and Command*, 675–85.
27. CCS Mins., June 15, 1943; King to JCS, June 10, 1943; King to GCM, June 11, 1943; GCM to DM, June 11, 1943, CCS 381 (2-28-43) Sec. 3; DM to GCM, June 12, 20, 24, 1943, RG 4, MMBA; Samuel E. Morison, *Aleutians, Gilberts, and Marshalls, June 1942–April 1944; With an Introduction on Fast Carrier Operations, 1943–1945* (HUSNOWWII; Boston, 1951), 79–84; Philip A. Crowl and Edmund G. Love, *Seizure of the Gilberts and Marshalls* (USAWWII; Washington, 1955), 18–21; Robert D. Heinl and John A. Crown, *The Marshalls: Increasing the Tempo* (Washington, 1954), 5–7; Matloff, *Strategic Planning*, 135–39, 185–93; Basil H. Liddell Hart, *History of the Second World War* (New York, 1970), 498–500.
28. DM to GCM, June 20, 1943, RG 4, MMBA.
29. *Ibid.;* Pogue, *Marshall,* III, 251–53.
30. The Japanese Army-Navy Central Agreement of March 25, 1943, is printed in Willoughby, ed., *MacArthur Reports,* II, Pt. I, 205. Figures on Japanese air strength are from *ibid.,* 207.

   In his *Reminiscences,* 174–75, MacArthur describes in detail the ambush of Yamamoto, frequently using "I" and "we" as if his SWPA intelligence and air personnel were responsible for tracking and downing the admiral's plane. He closes his narrative of the crash thus: "One could almost hear the rising crescendo of sound from the thousands of glistening white skeletons at the bottom of Pearl Harbor."
31. OPD, Pacific Ops., 36–42; Adm. Theodore S. Wilkinson, South Pacific Campaign Through Solomon Islands and Bismarck Archipelago [oral transcript, 1944], 1–5, Theodore S. Wilkinson Papers, NHD; int., Craig; Gen. J. Lawton Collins, Aug. 30, 1967; Halsey to DM, Aug. 30, 1943, SWPA G-3 Jnls.; Joseph E. Zimmer, *The History of the 43d Infantry Division, 1941–45* (Baton Rouge, n.d. [c. 1946]), 21–35; Halsey and Bryan, *Halsey's Story,* 158–50; John N. Rentz, *Marines in the Central Solomons* (Washington, 1952), 60–61, 150–52; Karig, *et al.,* *Battle Report,* III, 206–07. The Central Solomons invasion was code-named Toenails.
32. Int., Bulkeley; Lt. Gen. Walter Krueger, Report of Chronicle [Woodlark-Kiriwina] Operation, Aug. 23, 1943, SWPA G-3 Jnls.; Lido Mayo, *The Ordnance Department: On Beachhead and Battlefront* (USAWWII; Washington, 1968), 255–57; Willoughby, ed., *MacArthur Reports,* I, 121. The Woodlark-Kiriwina operations were code-named Chronicle, and the code designation of the Markham-Huon operations was Postern.
33. Haugland, *AAF Against Japan,* 163–68; GHQ SWPA press release,

Aug. 18, 1943, in Willoughby, ed., *MacArthur Reports*, I, 122; DM to GCM [SWPA Op. Rpts.], Sept. 4–9, 1943, SWPA G-3 Jnls.

34. DM Diary, Sept. 5, 1943; GHQ SWPA press release, Sept. 5, 1943, Willoughby Papers; int., Kenney; Kenney, *MacArthur*, 108; Kenney, *Kenney Reports*, 289, 292; DM, *Reminiscences*, 179; Bateson, *War with Japan*, 256. On Kenney's recommendation, MacArthur was awarded the Air Medal after his flight to Nadzab.

35. SWPA G-2 Daily Summary of Enemy Intelligence, Aug. 29–Sept. 5, 1943, SWPA G-3 Jnls.; Australian Military Forces, *Jungle Warfare with the Australian Army in the South-west Pacific* (Canberra, 1944), 69–80; Frederick Howard, "Minimum Orders," in Bartlett, ed., *Australia at Arms*, 231–39; Buggy, *Pacific Victory*, 228–47. According to Barbey, Kenney claimed that "the amphibious assault at Lae was unnecessary as he could have taken it with some paratroops." Barbey to Fellers, Aug. 19, 1960, Barbey Papers.

36. JCS Mins., June 29, 1943, CCS 381 POA (6-10-43) Sec. 1; GCM to DM, July 21, 1943; DM to GCM, July 23, 1943, RG 4, MMBA; John Miller, Jr., "MacArthur and the Admiralties," in Greenfield, ed., *Command Decisions*, 288–90.

37. Joint War Plans Committee, Report on Specific Operations in the Pacific and Far East, 1943–44, Aug. 5, 1943, CCS 381 Japan (8-25-42) Sec. 6; Matloff, *Strategic Planning*, 193–95; Luvaas, ed., *Dear Miss Em*, 72.

38. Final Report of the Combined Chiefs of Staff to the President and Prime Minister at the Quadrant Conference, 24 August 1943, 9, CCS 381 (10-17-43) Sec. 1.

39. CCS Mins., Aug. 21, 1943, CCS 381 Japan (8-25-42) Sec. 6; Henry I. Shaw, Jr., et al., *Central Pacific Drive* (HUSMCOWWII; Washington, 1966), 231–32; Feis, *Churchill, Roosevelt, Stalin*, 150–51; Churchill, *Second World War*, V, 86–87; Bateson, *War with Japan*, 296–97.

40. Brisbane *Courier-Mail*, Sept. 27, 1943; int., Ritchie.

41. Col. William L. Ritchie to GCM, Sept. 28, 1943, RG 4, MMBA.

42. GCM to DM, Oct. 2, 1943, RG 4, MMBA.

43. Matloff, *Strategic Planning*, 235; DM, *Reminiscences*, 166. In 1954 MacArthur told an Army historian that "the potential value militarily of Rabaul to our arms was to furnish an advance naval base." He claimed that it was he who made the decision to "leave Rabaul 'to die on the vine'" when Kenney reported that his air reconnaissance had shown the harbor at Manus to have excellent facilities and to be less strongly defended. DM's Answers to Morton Questionnaire.

CHAPTER VIII. *"Three-Pronged Offensive"*

pages 336–374

1. New York *Herald Tribune,* Oct. 5, 1943; Dexter, *New Guinea Offensives,* 483; Joint Staff Planners, General Progress Report on Recent Operations and Future Plans in the Pacific, Nov. 25, 1943, CCS 350.05 Pacific (11-25-43); OPD, Pacific Ops., 53–59; AMF, *Jungle Warfare,* 103–10; Buggy, *Pacific Victory,* 248–63.

2. Arnold to DM, Oct. 16, 1943, RG 5, MMBA; DM to Kenney, Nov. 4, 1943, RG 4, MMBA; Gen. H. H. Arnold, Estimate of Enemy Air Situation — Pacific, Nov. 23, 1943, CCS 381 (6-4-43) Sec. 2; Richard L. Watson, Jr., "The Fifth Air Force in the Huon Peninsula Campaign, October 1943 to February 1944" [MS study, USAAF Hist. Div., 1947], 16–17, 154, 197–98; d'Albas, *Death of a Navy,* 266–67; Okumiya and Horikoshi, *Zero,* 223–30; J. M. S. Ross, *The Assault on Rabaul: Operations by the Royal New Zealand Air Force, December 1943–May 1944* (OHNZWW; Wellington, 1949), 3, 31; Crowl and Love, *Gilberts and Marshalls,* 69–70; USSBS, *Allied Campaign Against Rabaul,* 35–37.

3. Halsey and Bryan, *Halsey's Story,* 174–75; King and Whitehill, *King,* 497; Sherrod, *Marine Corps Aviation,* 170; John R. Rentz, *Bougainville and the Northern Solomons* (Washington, 1948), 9–13.

4. OPD, Pacific Ops., 60–65; Rear Adm. Aaron S. Merrill, Comments on Battles Off Empress Augusta Bay and Cape St. George, November 1943 [MS, Naval War College, Jan. 21, 1944], Aaron S. Merrill Papers, University of North Carolina, Chapel Hill; Vice Adm. Theodore S. Wilkinson, Narrative of Palau, Ulithi, Leyte, and Lingayen Experiences [oral transcript, 1945], 6–8, Theodore S. Wilkinson Papers, NHD.

5. Barbey to Chamberlin, Aug. 26, 1960; Chamberlin to Barbey, Sept. 8, 1960, Barbey Papers; Gen. Lemuel C. Shepherd, Jr., to author, June 23, 1971; Vandegrift, *Once a Marine,* 243; Barbey, *MacArthur's Amphibious Navy,* 98, 100; Burke Davis, *Marine! The Life of Lt. Gen. Lewis B. (Chesty) Puller, USMC (Ret.)* (Boston, 1962), 187–88.

6. McMillan, *Old Breed,* 168–70.

7. Kinkaid, Narrative, 7–8; W. N. Swan, *Spearheads of Invasion: An Account of the Seven Major Invasions Carried Out by the Allies in the South-west Pacific Area During the Second World War, as Seen from a Royal Australian Naval Landing Ship Infantry* (Sydney, 1953), 54.

8. Alamo Force Op. Rpts., Dec. 26, 1943–Jan. 4, 1944, SWPA G-3 Jnls.; Swan, *Spearheads,* 48–61; McMillan, *Old Breed,* 159–227; Frank O. Hough, *The Island War: The United States Marine Corps in the Pacific* (Philadelphia, 1947), 148–83; Vandegrift, *Once a Marine,* 245–47; Hough and Crown, *New Britain,* 182.

9. DM to Lt. Gen. Walter Krueger, Dec. 31, 1943, RG 4, MMBA; Miller,

Cartwheel, 294–95; Morison, *Bismarcks Barrier*, 377–78; Brooks E.
Kleber and Dale Birdsall, *The Chemical Warfare Service: Chemicals
in Combat* (USAWWII; Washington, 1966), 549–51.

10. Blakeley, *32d Div.*, 133–47; Krueger to DM, Dec. 28, 1943; DM to
Krueger, Dec. 28, 1943, RG 4, MMBA; Alamo Force Op. Rpts., Jan.
2–10, 1944, SWPA G-3 Jnls.
11. Morton, *Strategy and Command*, 573; OPD, Pacific Ops., 71–73. On the
Gilberts operations, see Crowl and Love, *Gilberts and Marshalls*, 18–
165; James R. Stockman, *The Battle for Tarawa* (Washington, 1947).
12. DM to Wood, Nov. 17, 1943; DM to Moseley, Jan. 5, 1944; DM to Maj.
Gen. George B. Duncan, Mar. 3, 1944, RG 10, MMBA.
13. Matloff, *Strategic Planning*, 396–401, 550–54; Samuel E. Morison, *Strategy and Compromise* (Boston, 1958), 78–82; A. Russell Buchanan, *The
United States and World War II* (2 vols., New York, 1964), I, 277–78.
14. DM to Lt. Gen. Brehon B. Somervell, Aug. 14, 1943, CM-IN 10721.
15. Int., Van Wyk; DM Diary, Sept. 29–Oct. 4, 1943; GCM to DM, Sept. 6,
1943; DM to GCM, Oct. 10, 1943, RG 4, MMBA; Coakley and Leighton, *Global Logistics*, 455–62; Millett, *Army Service Forces*, 75; Stauffer, *Quartermaster Corps*, 149–50; Bykofsky and Larson, *Transportation Corps*, 443–46.
16. DM to GCM, Nov. 15, 1943, RG 4, MMBA; Matloff, *Strategic Planning*, 320–21; Robert R. Palmer, *et al.*, *The Procurement and Training
of Ground Combat Troops* (USAWWII; Washington, 1948), 226–32.
17. Aubrey S. Newman, "Power of Words in Messages and Orders," *Army*,
XXIII (Apr., 1973), 45.
18. Int., F. Johnson, Davison; Adm. Arleigh A. Burke, July 2, 1971; Adm.
Russell S. Berkey, July 9, 1971; Vice Adm. Alvin D. Chandler, June 5,
1971; GCM to DM, Oct. 9, 27, 1943; DM to GCM, Oct. 10, 1943, RG 4,
MMBA; O'Laughlin to DM, Dec. 23, 1943, RG 10, MMBA; Kinkaid,
Narrative, 1–10; DM Diary, Nov. 29, 1943; Sutherland to Chamberlin,
Sept. 2, 1943; Col. Herbert B. Wheeler to Chamberlin, Sept. 3, 1943,
SWPA G-3 Jnls.; U.S. Navy Dept. communiqué, Sept. 29, 1943, in U.S.
Navy Dept., *Navy Department Communiques 301 to 600 and Pacific
Fleet Communiques, March 6, 1943, to May 24, 1945, with Other
Official Statements and Pertinent Press Releases* (Washington, 1945),
77; Morison, *Aleutians, Gilberts, and Marshalls*, 37–38, 66; Hoyt, *How
They Won the War*, 327–31; Frye, *Marshall*, 346–48. Carpender and
MacArthur's relations improved toward the end, and the SWPA commander awarded him the Army Distinguished Service Medal. DM to
GCM, Oct. 28, 1943; DM to King, Nov. 23, 1943, RG 4, MMBA.
19. Int., Rear Adm. Raymond D. Tarbuck, Sept. 4, 1971.
20. DM's Answers to Morton Questionnaire.
21. O'Laughlin to DM, Dec. 23, 1943, RG 10, MMBA; DM Diary, Sept.
9–11, 1943; Sydney *Telegraph*, Aug. 30, Sept. 17, 22, 1943; New York

Herald Tribune, Sept. 22, 1943; Washington *Times-Herald,* Sept. 22, 23, 25, 1943; Pogue, *Marshall,* III, 281–82.

22. London *Daily Mirror,* Sept. 30, 1943.

23. Sulzberger, *Long Row of Candles,* 221; Churchill, *Second World War,* V, 302–04; FDR press conference, Oct. 5, 1943; Sen. H. Styles Bridges to FDR, Oct. 9, 1943; FDR to Bridges, Oct. 25, 1943, OF 4771, FDRL. On Nov. 25, 1943, the *Nippon Times Weekly* (Tokyo) reported gleefully that serious friction existed between MacArthur and Mountbatten. Actually there is no evidence of difficulties between the two commanders.

24. House Resolutions 252–53, Mar. 14, 1944, in *Congressional Record* (House), 78th Cong., 2nd Sess. (1944), 2647–50; Washington *Times-Herald,* Sept. 25, 1943; Stimson and Bundy, *On Active Service,* 452; Millett, *Army Service Forces,* 405–13; Davis, *Experience of War,* 444–45; Pogue, *Marshall,* III, 263–78.

25. A summary of Reno III appears in Morton, *Strategy and Command,* 661–67, 686–92.

26. *Ibid.,* 541; DM to GCM, Oct. 31, 1943, RG 4, MMBA; Matloff, *Strategic Planning,* 312–17; Pogue, *Marshall,* III, 168.

27. JPS, Report to JCS on Specific Operations for the Defeat of Japan, 1944, Nov. 9, 1943, CCS 381 Japan (8-25-42) Sec. 8.

28. Matloff, *Strategic Planning,* 307–87; Pogue, *Marshall,* III, 303–18; Shaw, *et al., Central Pacific Drive,* 233–34. An irate citizen of Vicksburg, Miss., wrote to Roosevelt while he was still in the Middle East, "I would like to know just why General MacArthur has not been included in the conferences relating to the defeat of Japan . . . If we, the people, could have a voice in this thing we would undoubtedly say, 'Let MacArthur plan the mode of attack.' " Mrs. Eva W. Davis to FDR, Dec. 2, 1943, RG 10, MMBA.

29. Wesley F. Craven and James L. Cate, eds., *The Pacific: Matterhorn to Nagasaki, June 1944 to August 1945* (AAFWWII; Chicago, 1953), 35–37; USSBS, *Summary Report (Pacific War),* 29; Watson, "Fifth Air Force, Oct. 1943–Feb. 1944," 57–60.

30. DM to GCM, Jan. 1, 1944, RG 4, MMBA; John Winton, *The Forgotten Fleet: The British Navy in the Pacific, 1944–45* (New York, 1970), 33–37; John Ehrman, *Grand Strategy* (HSWWUKMS; 5 vols. to date, London, 1956–64), V, 431–33; Churchill, *Second World War,* V, 576–81; Hasluck, *Government and People,* 423–45; Burns, *Roosevelt,* 444; Reynolds, *Fast Carriers,* 301–03.

31. Combined Staff Planners Mins., Nov. 28, Dec. 1, 1943, CCS 381 Japan (8-25-42) Sec. 9; Combined Staff Planners, Report to CCS on Overall Plan for the Defeat of Japan, Dec. 2, 1943, in Morton, *Strategy and Command,* 668, 669; Arnold, *Global Mission,* 473; Coakley and Leighton, *Global Logistics,* 294; King and Whitehill, *King,* 532–33.

32. Pogue, *Marshall*, III, 323; DM Diary, Sept. 12–16, 1943; Kenney, *Kenney Reports*, 332–34; King and Whitehill, *King*, 526.
33. Hunt, *Untold Story*, 313–14; DM, *Reminiscences*, 183.
34. Int., Handy.
35. Stimson Diary, Nov. 22, 1944; DM, *Reminiscences*, 184; GCM to DM, Dec. 24, 1943; DM to GCM, Dec. 24, 1943; Handy to DM, Dec. 23, 1943, RG 4, MMBA.
36. Rosenman, comp., *Public Papers and Addresses of Roosevelt*, XII, 556; London *Times*, Dec. 28, 1943.
37. Melbourne *Herald*, Dec. 28, 1943.

CHAPTER IX. *"Climax in the Bismarcks"*

pages 375–402
1. GHQ SWPA G-2 daily communiqués, Dec. 26, 1943–Apr. 26, 1944; AMF, *Jungle Warfare*, 110–29; Dexter, *New Guinea Offensives*, 761, 763; Vader, *New Guinea*, 137–41; Basil Collier, *The War in the Far East, 1941–1945: A Military History* (New York, 1969), 386–87.
2. JCS to DM, Jan. 23, 1944, RG 4, MMBA; OPD, Pacific Ops., 88–93; Halsey and Bryan, *Halsey's Story*, 188; William C. Frierson, *The Admiralties: Operations of the 1st Cavalry Division (29 February–18 May 1944)* (Washington, 1945), 1–4; Heinl and Crown, *Marshalls*, 114–16; USSBS, *The Reduction of Truk* (Washington, 1947), 11–13; Rentz, *Bougainville and the Northern Solomons*, 114–17; Gillespie, *Pacific*, 168–95; Dudley W. Knox, *A History of the United States Navy* (rev. ed., New York, 1948), 549.
3. Miller, "MacArthur and the Admiralties," 291–98; Kenney, *Kenney Reports*, 215, 359, 360; DM, *Reminiscences*, 188; Harris G. Warren, "The Fifth Air Force in the Conquest of the Bismarck Archipelago, November 1943 to March 1944" [MS study, USAAF Hist. Div., 1946], 100–03, AFHRD; Frierson, *Admiralties*, 11–12; Haugland, *AAF Against Japan*, 212–15.
4. DM Diary, Feb. 27–29, 1944; Barbey, *MacArthur's Amphibious Navy*, 153; Krueger, *From Down Under*, 49.
5. Int., Berkey, Faillace, Noble; Dr. Roger O. Egeberg, June 30, 1971; Miller, *Cartwheel*, 326; Frierson, *Admiralties*, 22; Capt. Albert G. Noble, Action Report of Bombardment and Occupation of Momote Airdrome, Los Negros Island, Admiralty Group, on 29 February 1944 [dated Mar. 3, 1944], NHD.
6. Bertram C. Wright, comp., *The First Cavalry Division in World War II* (Tokyo, 1947), 15–70; Brewer Task Force Hq. Diary of the Admiralty Islands Campaign, 29 February–2 April 1944, File 98-TFIB-09, RG 407, WNRC; OPD, Pacific Ops., 94–97; Robert Amory, Jr., and Reuben M.

Waterman, eds., *Surf and Sand: The Saga of the 533d Engineer Boat and Shore Regiment and 1461st Engineer Maintenance Company, 1942–45* (Andover, 1947), 77–93.

7. Noel F. Busch, "MacArthur and His Theater," *Life*, XVI (May 8, 1944), 100–01; *New York Times*, Mar. 1, 1944; Frierson, *Admiralties*, 31; Wright, *1st Cav. Div.*, 18–19; Miller, "MacArthur and the Admiralties," 299–300.

8. Int., Egeberg. Later Swift awarded MacArthur a Bronze Star with Arrowhead for his Los Negros performance. An Australian Army historian commented, "Probably no other Commander-in-Chief would have allowed his staff to recommend him for decorations in this way or would have shown such boyish delight when he received them." Long, *MacArthur*, 140n.

9. Frierson, *Admiralties*, 149; DM to Brig. Gen. William C. Chase, Mar. 5, 1944, RG 5, MMBA; Dod, *Corps of Engineers*, 521–26; Adm. William M. Fechteler, Reminiscences [oral transcript, 1962], 40, CUOHRO; Barbey, *MacArthur's Amphibious Navy*, 157; Millis, ed., *War Reports*, 549; Miller, "MacArthur and the Admiralties," 301–02.

10. DM to GCM, Feb. 2, 26, 27, 1944; GCM to DM, Feb. 28, Mar. 9, 1944, RG 4, MMBA; Nimitz to King, Feb. 23, 1944, CM-IN 16947; Dod, *Corps of Engineers*, 523–25; Reynolds, *Fast Carriers*, 142–43; Pogue, *Marshall*, III, 439–41.

11. Int., F. Johnson; DM Diary, Mar. 3–5, 1944; Halsey and Bryan, *Halsey's Story*, 186–90. James Forrestal, asst. secy. of the Navy, visited MacArthur at Brisbane on Feb. 8, 1944, but, of course, the Manus controversy had not yet erupted.

12. JCS Mins., Mar. 8–12, 1944, CCS 381 Japan (8-25-42) Sec. 9; Leahy, *I Was There*, 228–30; McNeill, *America, Britain, and Russia*, 399–400.

13. GCM to DM, Mar. 2, 1944, RG 4, MMBA; JCS to DM, Mar. 2, 1944, OPD-EF; JCS Mins., Mar. 7–12, 1944, CCS 381 Japan (8-25-42) Sec. 9; Fellers to Barbey, Aug. 3, 1960, Barbey Papers; int., Ritchie, Tarbuck; Joint Strategic Survey Committee, Strategy in the Pacific, Feb. 15, 1944, CCS 381 POA (6-10-43) Sec. 2; Shaw, et al., *Central Pacific Drive*, 234–36; Reynolds, *Fast Carriers*, 116–19; Philip A. Crowl, *Campaign in the Marianas* (USAWWII; Washington, 1960), 14–20; Robert R. Smith, *The Approach to the Philippines* (USAWWII; Washington, 1953), 6–12; King and Whitehill, *King*, 537–40; Leahy, *I Was There*, 250–51; Robert R. Smith, "Luzon versus Formosa," in Greenfield, ed., *Command Decisions*, 463–65; Ehrman, *Grand Strategy*, V, 450–52.

14. JCS to DM and Nimitz, Mar. 12, 1944, OPD-EF.

15. DM to GCM, Mar. 14, 1944; GCM to DM, Mar. 17, 1944, OPD-EF; JCS to DM, Mar. 25, 1944; JCS Mins., Mar. 17, 1944, CCS 381 Japan (11-11-43).

16. DM to GCM, Feb. 23, 1944, CM-IN 16430; Joint War Plans Commit-

tee, Requirements for Pacific–Far East Operations, Feb. 29, 1944; Joint Logistics Plans Committee, Logistical Aspects of Bases and Phases, Pacific Campaign, Feb. 14, 1944, CCS 381 Japan (11-11-43); Matloff, *Strategic Planning*, 456–65; Huston, *Sinews of War*, 435–36; Coakley and Leighton, *Global Logistics*, 406–11.

17. Maj. Gen. Omar T. Pfeiffer, Memoirs [oral transcript, June, 1968], 242, MCHD; int., Davison, Willoughby.
18. Int., Munson, F. Johnson; Robert Sherrod, *On to Westward: War in the Central Pacific* (New York, 1945), 234.
19. Charles A. Lockwood and Hans C. Adamson, *Battles of the Philippine Sea* (New York, 1967), 7.
20. Cato D. Glover, *Command Performance with Guts* (New York, 1969), 44–45; DM Diary, Mar. 21, 25, 1944; int., F. Johnson.
21. Int., Tarbuck.
22. DM Diary, Mar. 26–27, 1944; Kenney, *Kenney Reports*, 377; int., Kenney, Marshall, F. Johnson.
23. Adm. Cato D. Glover to Nimitz, Mar. 2, 1965, in Glover, *Command Performance*, 46.
24. Int., F. Johnson, Davison, Marshall; Reynolds, *Fast Carriers*, 146. Commenting in 1949 on the draft of Leahy's memoirs, MacArthur said that, despite "much rumor-mongering," his wartime relations with Nimitz were conducted "on the warmest plane of cordiality," although "obviously we had professional differences of opinion." DM to Leahy, Dec. 28, 1949, RG 5, MMBA.

CHAPTER X. *"Political Misadventure"*

pages 403–440

1. Eugene H. Roseboom, *A History of Presidential Elections: From George Washington to Richard M. Nixon* (3rd ed., New York, 1970), 480–81; Westerfield, *Foreign Policy and Party Politics*, 242–43; Herman E. Bateman, "The Election of 1944 and Foreign Policy" (unpublished Ph.D. dissertation, Stanford University, 1952), 12–22; Arthur S. Link, *American Epoch: A History of the United States Since the 1890's* (3rd ed., 3 vols., New York, 1967), III, 568; Burns, *Roosevelt*, 498–99.
2. *New York Times*, Apr. 8–9, 1943; London *Times*, Apr. 8, 1943; Charles E. McCord to DM, Apr. 8, 1943; McCormick to DM, Feb. 7, 1944, RG 10, MMBA; Pogue, *Marshall*, III, 177–78; Vandenberg, *Private Papers*, 77–78; C. David Tompkins, *Senator Arthur Vandenberg: The Evolution of a Modern Republican, 1884–1945* (East Lansing, 1970), 232–34.
3. Sen. Arthur Vandenberg to Willoughby, Aug. 17, 1943, in Vandenberg, *Private Papers*, 80.

4. Misc. letters to DM, Aug.–Oct., 1943, RG 10, MMBA; Vandenberg, *Private Papers*, 82.
5. Cantril, ed., *Public Opinion*, 626, 632. For other polls in 1943–44 registering opinions of MacArthur as a possible candidate, all of which showed similar trends, see *ibid.*, 428, 630–31, 633, 634, 635; *New York Times*, May 24, July 14, Sept. 18, 1943; Roper, *You and Your Leaders*, 56–57, 90–91, 100–03, 151–54.
6. *New York Times*, Sept. 19, Nov. 27, 1943, and Feb. 23, 1944; Cantril, ed., *Public Opinion*, 263–64; Roper, *You and Your Leaders*, 152–54; James P. Reilly to DM, Mar. 8, 1943, RG 10, MMBA; J. Woodford Howard, Jr., *Mr. Justice Murphy: A Political Biography* (Princeton, 1968), 274n.
7. Compiled from Cantril, ed., *Public Opinion*, 634; Roper, *You and Your Leaders*, 56, 154.
8. Wood to DM, Nov. 8, 1943; Roy W. Howard to DM, Nov. 13, 1943; Moseley to DM, Dec. 14, 1943; O'Laughlin to DM, Nov. 29, 1943, RG 10, MMBA; Minneapolis *Star Journal*, Dec. 1, 1943. For articles on the activities of MacArthur-for-President organizations, which appeared almost daily, see *New York Times*, Aug., 1943–Apr., 1944.
9. Int., Willoughby; Henry R. Luce to DM, June 8, 1944, RG 10, MMBA; Sherrod Notes; Swanberg, *Luce*, 198–99; Pogue, *Marshall*, III, 177–78; John McCarten, "General MacArthur: Fact and Legend," *American Mercury*, LVIII (Jan., 1944), 7–8, 11.
10. Brisbane *Courier-Mail*, Jan. 21, 1944; Early to FDR, Jan. 24, 1944, MacArthur Folder, PSF; R. J. Marshall to AGWAR, Jan. 26, 1944, RG 4, MMBA; list of MacArthur's citations, honors, and decorations, DM Misc. 201; *New York Times*, Mar. 11, 1944. Robert P. Patterson, under secy. of war, told reporters in Apr., 1943, that the War Dept. did not intend to retire MacArthur when he reached sixty-four: "General MacArthur's services have been of extraordinary value to this country. There is no reason to warrant any opinion that this country will not continue to avail itself of his services." *New York Times*, Apr. 23, 1943.
11. McCarten, "Fact and Legend," 7–18; *New York Times*, Mar. 10, 1944; Brisbane *Courier-Mail*, Mar. 11, 1944.
12. DM to AGWAR, Mar. 11, 1944, RG 4, MMBA. MacArthur would have been outraged if he had known that the only published article about him that was placed in his OPD 201 file was the McCarten essay of Jan., 1944.
13. GCM to DM, Mar. 12, 1944, RG 4, MMBA; *New York Times*, May 6, 1944; "Discussion," *American Mercury*, LVIII (Apr., 1944), 507–08; (May, 1944), 634–35.
14. *Harper's* editors to Early, Apr. 19, 1944, OF 4771. Early had been an admirer of MacArthur's since 1916 when the latter was in charge of

War Department censorship. Another long-time friend of the SWPA commander's on the White House staff was Brig. Gen. Edwin ("Pa") Watson, a presidential aide.

15. "MacArthur and the Censorship," *Harper's Magazine*, CLXXXVIII (May, 1944), 537.

16. *New York Times*, May 4, 6, 1944.

17. The publications on MacArthur in 1942–44 included Francis T. Miller, *General Douglas MacArthur: Fighter for Freedom* (Philadelphia, 1942); Robert Considine, *MacArthur the Magnificent* (Philadelphia, 1942); Frank C. Waldrop, ed., *MacArthur on War: His Military Writings* (New York, 1942); Carlos P. Romulo, *I Saw the Fall of the Philippines* (Garden City, 1942); Powell M. Gulick, *MacArthur of the U.S.A.* (New York, 1942); Howard Hastings, *General Douglas MacArthur in Picture and Story* (New York, 1942); William A. Kelley, *MacArthur: Hero of Destiny* (Greenwich, Conn., 1942); Rainbow Division Veterans Association, *Let Us Remember: [MacArthur's] Address to the Rainbow Division, July 14, 1935* (Maysville, O., 1942); Helen Nicolay, *MacArthur of Bataan* (New York, 1942); Mariano Perla, *MacArthur . . .* (Buenos Aires, 1942); Edward Rice, Jr., *General Douglas MacArthur: Exciting Life Story* (New York, 1942); Castelo de Morais, *MacArthur . . .* (Lisbon, 1943); John Hersey, *Men on Bataan* (New York, 1943); editors, Curtis Publishing Co., *General Douglas MacArthur . . .* (Philadelphia, 1944); Frazier Hunt, *MacArthur and the War Against Japan* (New York, 1944).

18. McCormick to Maj. Philip F. LaFollette, Apr. 9, 1943; Fish to DM, June 5, 1943; Moseley to DM, Dec. 14, 1943; DM to Moseley, Jan. 5, 1944, RG 10, MMBA.

19. Int., Willoughby; Maj. Gen. Courtney Whitney, Aug. 28, 1967; Wood to DM, Nov. 8, 1943; DM to Wood, Nov. 17, 1943; Howard to DM, Nov. 12, 1943, RG 10, MMBA; Vandenberg, *Private Papers*, 79, 81–83.

20. Arthur H. Vandenberg, "Why I Am for MacArthur," *Collier's*, CXIII (Feb. 12, 1944), 14, 48–49.

21. Excerpt from Arthur Hale's Mutual Broadcasting System program, Oct. 16, 1943, OPD 201 File of DM, RG 165, NA; Indianapolis *Star*, Dec. 22, 1943; *New York Times*, Dec. 26, 1943; Melbourne *Herald*, Dec. 28, 1943; Sydney *Morning Herald*, Dec. 26, 1943.

22. DM Diary, Jan. 19, 1944; *New York Times*, Jan. 28, 1944. The editor of the Melbourne *Sun* was still not satisfied and declared on Feb. 7, 1944, "It's easy to appreciate a soldier's disinclination to break his silence every time his name is asked for political ends. But the Supreme Command of the Southwest Pacific is a matter of very real interest to Australians, who would welcome an early declaration to end the ambiguous situation."

23. Kenney, *MacArthur*, 249–50; int., Willoughby; Col. Laurence E.

Bunker, July 12, 1971; Hunt, *Untold Story*, 321; Whitney, *MacArthur*, 516; Maj. Gen. Charles H. Bridges to DM, Aug. 18, 1945, RG 10, MMBA; DM, *Reminiscences*, 184. When Kenney and Sutherland were in Washington in early 1943, they met with Vandenberg and Clare Luce at the latter's apartment where they "talked at length about MacArthur." Vandenberg, *Private Papers*, 77.

24. Huff, *My Fifteen Years*, 89; int., Marshall, Marquardt, Catledge; DM Diary, May 27, 1943; Luvaas, ed., *Dear Miss Em*, 71, 77; Turner Catledge, *My Life and the Times* (New York, 1971), 155–56; Wood to DM, Dec. 29, 1943; Wood to Willoughby, Jan. 6, 1944, RG 10, MMBA.

25. DM Diary, Aug. 25–Sept. 24, 1943; Sen. Ralph O. Brewster to DM, Sept. 25, 1943; Lord Wilson to DM, Sept. 8, 1943, RG 10, MMBA; Eichelberger to DM, Sept. 2, 4, 7, 14, 1943; DM to Eichelberger, Sept. 4, 1943, RG 3, MMBA; Adm. John H. Hoover, Memoirs [oral transcript, 1964], 330–31, CUOHRO; Halsey and Bryan, *Halsey's Story*, 166–67; Joseph P. Lash, *Eleanor and Franklin: The Story of Their Relationship, Based on Eleanor Roosevelt's Private Papers* (New York, 1971), 682–91. Eichelberger commented after Mrs. Roosevelt's departure, "There were so many ways of cutting my throat on this job that I feel I am very lucky to be out of it." Eichelberger to his wife, Sept. 15, 1943, Eichelberger Papers.

26. Wood to DM, Dec. 30, 1943; Wood to Willoughby, Jan. 6, 1943, RG 10, MMBA. See also MacArthur's large private correspondence of 1942–44 in the same record group.

27. Luvaas, ed., *Dear Miss Em*, 90, 100; Eichelberger, *Jungle Road*, 99; DM Diary, Jan. 26, 1944; London *Times*, Jan. 27, 1944; *New York Times*, Jan. 27, 1944. The photograph to which Eichelberger referred is reproduced in Luvaas, ed., *Dear Miss Em*, following p. 148.

28. Charles D. Hilles to Albert White, Nov. 29, 1943; Hilles to O'Laughlin, Dec. 3, 1943; O'Laughlin to DM, Dec. 23, 1943, RG 10, MMBA; *New York Times*, Dec. 10, 1943; Mar. 9, 14, Apr. 16, 21, 1944.

29. John G. Pallange to DM, Feb. 16, 1944, RG 10, MMBA; Vandenberg, *Private Papers*, 83–84; *New York Times*, Mar. 3, 30, Apr. 1, 5, 7, 1944; George H. Meyer, *The Republican Party, 1854–1964* (New York, 1964), 462–63; Herbert Eaton, *Presidential Timber: A History of Nominating Conventions, 1868–1960* (New York, 1964), 393–99.

30. Chicago *Tribune*, Mar. 14, Apr. 10th–12, 1944; *New York Times*, Apr. 16, 1944.

31. *New York Times*, Apr. 13, 1944.

32. Rep. A. L. Miller to DM, Sept. 18, 1943, and Jan. 27, 1944; DM to Miller, Oct. 2, 1943, and Feb. 11, 1944, RG 10, MMBA; *New York Times*, Apr. 14–15, 1944; "The MacArthur Candidacy," *Time*, XLIII (Apr. 24, 1944), 19; Hunt, *Untold Story*, 321–23; John Gunther, *The*

Riddle of MacArthur: Japan, Korea and the Far East (New York, 1950), 58–60.

33. *New York Times,* Apr. 14–15, 1944; Ernest K. Lindley, "MacArthur's Excursion into Politics," *Newsweek,* XXIII (Apr. 24, 1944), 29; Washington *Times-Herald,* Apr. 15, 21, 1944; Isidor F. Stone, "MacArthur's Political Foray," *Nation,* CLVIII (Apr. 22, 1944), 466.
34. Brisbane *Courier-Mail,* Apr. 17, 1944; *New York Times,* Apr. 17, 1944.
35. Vandenberg, *Private Papers,* 84–86; *New York Times,* Apr. 18, 25, 1944; Miller to Ernest K. Lindley, Apr. 19, 1944; Miller to DM, Apr. 22, 1944, RG 10, MMBA.
36. DM, *Reminiscences,* 184–85; *New York Times,* Apr. 30, 1944.
37. *New York Times,* May 1, 5, 1944; London *Times,* May 1, 1944; "Nor Would I Accept It," *Time,* XLIII (May 8, 1944), 15; O'Laughlin to DM, May 5, 1944; Maj. Gen. Perry L. Miles to DM, May 28, 1944; T. Clarence Wilkinson to DM, May 8, 1944, RG 10, MMBA; Vandenberg, *Private Papers,* 84, 85–86; DM, *Reminiscences,* 185; Hunt, *Untold Story,* 320–21; FDR press conference, May 6, 1944; Leahy, *I Was There,* 237.
38. *New York Times,* May 14–June 29, 1944; Eaton, *Presidential Timber,* 399–401; Vandenberg, *Private Papers,* 88–89.

PART IV. *"Advance to the Philippines"*

Basic works in Part IV that will not be cited in the chapter notes except when quoted are Barbey, *MacArthur's Amphibious Navy,* 158–290; M. Hamlin Cannon, *Leyte: The Return to the Philippines* (USAWWII; Washington, 1954); Craven and Cate, eds., *Guadalcanal to Saipan,* 575–670; *idem, Matterhorn to Nagasaki,* 275–412; Dod, *Corps of Engineers,* 527–87; Eichelberger, *Jungle Road,* 100–80; Stanley L. Falk, *Decision at Leyte* (New York, 1966); Gill, *Royal Australian Navy, 1942–45,* 396–574; Hunt, *MacArthur and the War Against Japan,* 147–76; *idem, Untold Story,* 325–56; Kenney, *Kenney Reports,* 369–504; Krueger, *From Down Under,* 56–210; Long, *Final Campaigns,* 1–140; *idem, MacArthur,* 142–63; Luvaas, ed., *Dear Miss Em,* 102–201; MacArthur, *Reminiscences,* 189–238; Samuel E. Morison, *New Guinea and the Marianas, March 1944–August 1944* (HUSNOWWII; Boston, 1953), 45–145; *idem, Leyte, June 1944–January 1945* (HUSNOWWII; Boston, 1948); Odgers, *Air War Against Japan,* 335–90; Smith, *Approach to the Philippines;* Whitney, *MacArthur,* 110–80; Willoughby and Chamberlain, *MacArthur,* 144–70, 174–260; Willoughby, ed., *MacArthur Reports,* I, 145–254, II, Pt. I, 261–363, Pt. II, 365–466.

CHAPTER XI. *"Victories and Complications"*
pages 443–482
1. SWPA G-2, Enemy Order of Battle and Strengths, General Pacific Area, 31 May 1944; Chamberlin to Krueger, Apr. 14, 1944, SWPA G-3 Jnls.; int., Willoughby, Fellers, Ritchie, Lane, F. Johnson, Davison; Barbey to Fellers, July 29, 1960; Fellers to Barbey, Aug. 3, 1960, and Nov. 9, 1965, Barbey Papers; DM, *Reminiscences*, 189; Kirby, *War Against Japan*, III, 417–19. Halsey claimed he first suggested the Hollandia leap to MacArthur at a conference at Brisbane, March 3, 1944, but Fellers disputed this later. Morison, *New Guinea and Marianas*, 10n; Fellers to Barbey, Nov. 17, 1965, Barbey Papers.
2. Adm. Thomas C. Kinkaid, South Pacific, Aleutians, and Seventh Fleet Experiences [oral transcript, Navy Dept., June 21, 1945], 2–9, NHD; int., Davison, Noble; Swan, *Spearheads*, 78–93; Haugland, *AAF Against Japan*, 215–16.
3. Int., Maj. Gen. Chester A. Dahlen, Sept. 8, 1971; Capt. H. A. Spanagel, Report of Bombardments by U.S.S *Nashville* of Hollandia, Seleo Islands, Aitape, and Special Missions in Connection Therewith, 22 April 1944 [dated Apr. 25, 1944], 1–3, NHD; OPD, Pacific Ops., 100–05; Willoughby, ed., *MacArthur Reports*, I, 146n; McCartney, *Jungleers*, 76–87; Harold Riegelman, *Caves of Biak: An American Officer's Experiences in the Southwest Pacific* [1942–45] (New York, 1955), 97–131; Swan, *Spearheads*, 84–85.
4. GHQ SWPA communiqués, Apr. 22–May 2, 1944; Kleber and Birdsell, *Chemical Warfare Service*, 498–99; McCartney, *Jungleers*, 88–92; Amory and Waterman, eds., *Surf and Sand*, 104–24.
5. GHQ SWPA communiqué, Apr. 24, 1944.
6. DM Diary, Apr. 18–24, 1944; McMillan, *Old Breed*, 226–27; int., F. Johnson, Egeberg, Faillace; Spanagel, Report of Bombardments by U.S.S. *Nashville*, 1–3; Eichelberger, *Jungle Road*, 107; Puryear, *Nineteen Stars*, 148; Barbey, *MacArthur's Amphibious Navy*, 172; DM, *Reminiscences*, 191n. When Rupertus paid his last call before leaving SWPA on May 2, 1944, MacArthur awarded him a DSM.
7. Eichelberger, *Jungle Road*, 121–22.
8. Stauffer, *Quartermaster Corps*, 89, 164–65, 175–76; Coakley and Leighton, *Global Logistics*, 465, 469–70, 474.
9. Eichelberger, *Jungle Road*, 113–14.
10. Int., Berkey, Noble, Faillace; OPD, Pacific Ops., 114–19; Barbey, *MacArthur's Amphibious Navy*, 173; McCartney, *Jungleers*, 93–101; William J. Barnard, ed., *The 6th Infantry Division in World War II, 1939–1945* (Washington, 1947), 41–51; 33rd Inf. Div. Hist. Com., *The Golden Cross; A History of the 33d Infantry Division in World War II* (Wash-

ington, 1948), 51–67. Sibert assumed command of Tornado Task Force on June 12, 1944.

11. Odgers, *Air War Against Japan*, 220; DM to Krueger, May 31, 1944; Krueger to DM, May 28, 30, 31, June 1, 1944, SWPA G-3 Jnls.; OPD, Pacific Ops., 110–12; McCartney, *Jungleers*, 102–31; Blakeley, *32d Div.*, 175–77.

12. DM to Krueger, June 5, 14, 16, 1944; Krueger to DM, June 5, 8, 14, 16, 19, 1944, RG 4, MMBA; Eichelberger to his wife, June 16, 1944, Eichelberger Papers; int., Byers, Dahlen; Bateson, *War with Japan*, 312; McCartney, *Jungleers*, 117; Riegelman, *Caves of Biak*, 136–39. Brig. Gen. Ralph W. Coane, the 41st Div. artillery commander, told MacArthur and Krueger that Fuller was "neurotic." Coane to DM, June 29, 1944; Coane to Krueger, June 29, 1944, RG 4, MMBA.

   Fuller had a conference with MacArthur in Brisbane on Aug. 11, 1944, but nothing is known of their talk. That Nov. Fuller was awarded a DSM for his "exceptional ability and sound judgment" in leading the 41st Div., Apr., 1942–June, 1944. DM Diary, Aug. 11, 1944; McCartney, *Jungleers*, 191–92.

13. DM to GCM, May 31, 1944; Krueger to DM, Aug. 1, 1944; Vice Adm. Thomas C. Kinkaid to DM, May 31, June 1, 1944, SWPA G-3 Jnls.; int., Berkey, Noble; Kinkaid, Experiences, 9; Riegelman, *Caves of Biak*, 139–55; USSBS, *Campaigns*, 180–81; Morison, *Two-ocean War*, 320–45.

14. Potter and Nimitz, *Triumph in the Pacific*, 102–03. At Saipan over 3400 Americans died, whereas less than 1700 were killed in MacArthur's operations from Hollandia-Aitape through Morotai, Apr.–Sept., 1944.

15. Krueger to DM, July 2, Aug. 1, 1944, SWPA G-3 Jnls.; DM to Krueger, July 5, 1944, RG 4, MMBA; SWPA G-2 daily communiqués, July 2–10, Aug. 1–3, 1944; OPD, Pacific Ops., 113, 128–30; Barnard, ed., *6th Div.*, 52–59; Haugland, *AAF Against Japan*, 222–24; Charles Pearson, "Picnic at Sansapor," in *Yank* editors, *The Best from Yank, the Army Weekly* (Cleveland, 1945), 147.

16. DM to GCM, Aug. 9, 1944, in Willoughby, ed., *MacArthur Reports*, I, 161.

17. McCarthy, *South-west Pacific Area*, 620; Gill, *Royal Australian Navy, 1942–45*, 223; Ernest L. Woodward, *British Foreign Policy in the Second World War* (HSWWUKS; London, 1962), 376–78; Kenney, *Kenney Reports*, 384; Joint Intelligence Staff, Report on Japanese Strength in the East Indies, May 4, 1944; Joint War Plans Committee, Operations in East Indies, China and Southeastern Asia — Estimate of Vital Natural Resources in East Indies, May 6, 1944, CCS 381 (4-7-44).

18. Hasluck, *Government and People*, 433–37; Long, *Final Campaigns*, 7, 14; Leahy, *I Was There*, 254–55; Kirby, *War Against Japan*, IV, 9.

19. DM to GCM, Aug. 27, 1944, OPD-EF.

20. Churchill, *Second World War*, VI, 165–67.

21. DM to Dr. H. J. van Mook, Dec. 10, 1944, RG 4, MMBA; Cordell Hull, *The Memoirs of Cordell Hull* (2 vols., New York, 1948), II, 1599–1601; U.S. State Dept., *Foreign Relations, 1944*, V, 1195–98, 1286–89.

22. Watt, *Australian Foreign Policy*, 73–77; Mansergh, *British Commonwealth Affairs*, IV, 129–30; Johnston, *Pacific Partner*, 107–13; Grattan, *United States and Southwest Pacific*, 191–200; idem, *Southwest Pacific Since 1900*, 166–75, 182–88; Reed, "Diplomatic Relations with Australia," 261–324; H. V. Evatt, *Foreign Policy of Australia: Speeches* (Sydney, 1945), 102–05; idem, *Australia in World Affairs*, 124–25.

23. Johnston, *Pacific Partner*, 89–94, 104–05; Herring to author, May 22, 1972; int., Willoughby, Marshall, Whitney; DM to Curtin, Feb. 5, 1943; Curtin to DM, Feb. 9, 1943, RG 4, MMBA; DM to Curtin, Aug. 22, 1943, RG 5, MMBA; Blamey to DM, June, 1943, RG 10, MMBA; London *Times*, Mar. 20, 1943; Melbourne *Herald*, Mar. 21, 1944; DM Diary, Mar. 17, 1944; Whan, ed., *Soldier Speaks*, 129–30; Evatt, *Foreign Policy*, 102–03.

24. DM to Curtin, Feb. 13, 1943; Curtin to DM, Aug. 5, 1943; Kenney to DM, Aug. 23, 1943, RG 4, MMBA; Mellor, *Science and Industry*, 318–20, 420–21, 458.

25. Grattan, *Southwest Pacific Since 1900*, 177–79; Stauffer, *Quartermaster Corps*, 99–124; Mellor, *Science and Industry*, 609–10; Long, *Final Campaigns*, 395.

26. DM Diary, Mar. 13, 1943; Allan S. Walker, *The Island Campaigns* (AW39-45, Medical Ser.; Canberra, 1957), 236–38; idem, *Middle East and Far East* (AW39-45, Medical Ser.; Canberra, 1953), 45–47; idem, *Clinical Problems of War* (AW39-45, Medical Ser.; Canberra, 1952), 99, 109–17; idem, *Medical Services of the R.A.N. and R.A.A.F.* . . . (AW39-45, Medical Ser.; Canberra, 1961), 342; DM to AGWAR, June 3, 1944, RG 4, MMBA; DM, *Reminiscences*, 196.

27. Melbourne *Herald*, Mar. 20, 1944; *New York Times*, Mar. 20, 1944; int., Niederpruem.

28. Maj. Gen. Frank H. Berryman to Herring, May 17, 1944, in Dexter, *New Guinea Offensives*, 281; Walker, *Island Campaigns*, 371.

29. Dexter, *New Guinea Offensives*, 283.

30. Air Vice Marshal George Jones to DM, Mar. 24, 1943; Air Vice Marshal William D. Bostock to DM, Mar. 25, 1943; DM to Jones, Mar. 25, 1943, SWPA G-3 Jnls.; Bostock to DM, Feb. 5, 1944, RG 4, MMBA; Gillison, *Royal Australian Air Force*, 593–98; Odgers, *Air War Against Japan*, 436, 439.

31. Hasluck, *Government and People*, 215–20, 340–49, 414–16, 429–31. About 640,000 Australians were serving in the armed services at the peak in June, 1943.

32. DM to Krueger, Apr. 14, 1944, SWPA G-3 Jnls.; Odgers, *Air War Against Japan*, 292; Long, *Final Campaigns*, 23; Hasluck, *Government*

and People, 567–69; Walker, *Island Campaigns*, 300; Kirby, *War Against Japan*, V, 125–26.

CHAPTER XII. *"Approaching the Philippines"*
pages 483–520
1. Willoughby, ed., *MacArthur Reports*, I, 148, 157; Smith, *Approach to the Philippines*, 132; int., Lt. Gen. Joseph C. Hutchison, July 27, 1971; Brig. Gen. John A. Elmore, June 25, 1971; DM to Krueger, Aug. 10, 1944, RG 4, MMBA; OPD, Pacific Ops., 105–07; Blakeley, *32d Div.*, 148–69; Zimmer, *43d Div.*, 42–43.
2. GHQ SWPA G-3 Staff Study, Interlude: Outline Plan for Occupation of Southwest Morotai, July 19, 1944, RG 3, MMBA; 31st Inf. Div., *History of the 31st Infantry Division in Training and Combat, 1940–1945* (Baton Rouge, 1946), 21–24; 33rd Div., *Golden Cross*, 68–85; Blakeley, *32d Div.*, 171–74; OPD, Pacific Ops., 131–34; Kinkaid, *Experiences*, 9–10; int., Hutchison, Elmore, Faillace, Munson.
3. Int., Egeberg; DM Diary, Sept. 9–16, 1944; Brisbane *Courier-Mail*, Sept. 16, 1944; GHQ SWPA press releases, Sept. 15–16, 1944, DMBP.
4. OPD, Pacific Ops., 120–27; New York *Journal-American*, July 17–18, 1944, quoted in Sherrod, *On to Westward*, 90–91; Carl W. Hoffman, *Saipan: The Beginning of the End* (Washington, 1950), 261–62; Isely and Crowl, *U.S. Marines and Amphibious War*, 342–71; Crowl, *Campaign in the Marianas*, 441–47. See also Carl W. Hoffman, *The Seizure of Tinian* (Washington, 1951); O. R. Lodge, *The Recapture of Guam* (Washington, 1954).
5. Vice Adm. Theodore S. Wilkinson, Narrative of Experiences as Commander, Third Amphibious Force, 1944–45 [oral transcript, Navy Dept., Feb. 28, 1945], 1–6, NHD; Potter and Nimitz, *Triumph in the Pacific*, 96–99; Smith, *Approach to the Philippines*, 573; OPD, Pacific Ops., 135–41; Frank O. Hough, *The Assault on Peleliu* (Washington, 1950), 179, 183, 190–91; Vandegrift, *Once a Marine*, 269; DM, *Reminiscences*, 202.
6. Luvaas, ed., *Dear Miss Em*, 114–15; int., Kenney, Willoughby, Marshall, Munson, Mashbir, Faillace.
7. Kenney, *MacArthur*, 92–93.
8. *Ibid.*, 93–95; Thorpe, *East Wind Rain*, 124; Frederic S. Marquardt, "The MacArthur Story," Chicago *Sun-Times*, July 10, 1950; William J. Dunn, "MacArthur's Mansion and Other Myths," *Army*, XXIII (Mar., 1973), 39–40; DM Diary, Sept. 11–Oct. 26, 1944; Manila *Star Reporter*, June 8, 1945.
9. Huff, *My Fifteen Years*, 95.
10. Goldstein, "Whitehead," 188, 190; USSBS, *The Thirteenth Air Force*

in the War Against Japan (Washington, 1946), 10–11; Charles W. Boggs, Jr., *Marine Aviation in the Philippines* (Washington, 1951), 1–3; Craven and Cate, eds., *Guadalcanal to Saipan*, 646.

11. Int., Lt. Gen. Earl W. Barnes, July 1, 1971; Goldstein, "Whitehead," 192–96, 212–15; USSBS, *Fifth Air Force*, 31–34; Benjamin E. Lippincott, *From Fiji Through the Philippines with the Thirteenth Air Force* (New York, 1948), 193; Sherrod, *Marine Corps Aviation*, 268–69.

12. Charles A. Lindbergh, *The Wartime Journals of Charles A. Lindbergh* (New York, 1970), 870–913; Kenney, *Kenney Reports*, 412; USSBS, *Fifth Air Force*, 70th–71, 105; Haugland, *AAF Against Japan*, 228–30; Don Congdon, ed., *Combat: The War with Japan* (New York, 1962), 217–33. MacArthur and Kenney tried to borrow some B-29's from the new XX Bomber Command in the Marianas to use against Balikpapan, but the Joint Chiefs rejected the request.

13. DM to GCM, May 11, 1944, RG 4, MMBA; Gen. Orders 3, Eighth Army Hq., Sept. 7, 1944, Eichelberger Papers; Eichelberger, Army Day Speech, June 7, 1948, Eighth Army File, RG 407, WNRC; Luvaas, ed., *Dear Miss Em*, 140, 149; Eichelberger, *Jungle Road*, 157; int., Willoughby. At Hollandia on Apr. 22, 1944, MacArthur told Eichelberger in an indirect manner that he would head the next army created in the SWPA theater. Eichelberger to his wife, June 25, 1944, Eichelberger Papers.

14. Casey, ed., *Engineers of the Southwest Pacific*, II, 158–60; Willoughby, ed., *MacArthur Reports*, I, 181.

15. 33rd Div., *Golden Cross*, 41, 43.

16. Bykofsky and Larson, *Transportation Corps*, 443–46; Coakley and Leighton, *Global Logistics*, 469–70.

17. Int., Van Wyk, Johns; Wardlow, *Transportation Corps*, 291–95; GCM to DM, Sept. 2, 1944; DM to GCM, Sept. 2, 1944, RG 4, MMBA; Joint Logistics Plans Committee Mins., June 30–Nov. 19, 1944; Brig. Gen. W. A. Wood, Jr., to Secretariat, Joint Logistics Committee, July 28, 1944; Joint Military Transportation Committee, Report on Availability of Resources for Pacific Operations, Sept. 30, 1944, CCS 381 Japan (11-11-43) Sec. 4.

18. DM to Halsey, June 1, 1944, SWPA G-3 Jnls.; GCM to DM, June 10, 1944, OPD-EF; GCM to DM, Oct. 30, 1944, CM-OUT 114386; GCM to DM, Nov. 4, 1944, CM-OUT 116070; Coakley and Leighton, *Global Logistics*, 560–70, 813–15; Bykofsky and Larson, *Transportation Corps*, 523.

19. Karl L. Rankin, Report on the Philippines, Nov. 25, 1943, in U.S. State Dept., *Foreign Relations, 1943*, III, 1108–17; D. G. E. Hall, *A History of South-East Asia* (3rd ed., New York, 1968), 778–79; Steinberg, *Philippine Collaboration*, 71–99, 106–08.

20. USAFFE G-2, Report on Who's Who in the Philippines, Principally in

the Puppet Government [dated Sept. 25, 1944], RG 16, MMBA; Kami-mura Shimichi, "Touring the South with Prime Minister Tojo," Tokyo *Nippon Times Weekly*, XVI (Oct. 28, 1943), 6–9; "Joint Declaration Adopted by the Assembly of Great East Asiatic Nations," *ibid.* (Nov. 11, 1943), 3; José P. Laurel, "Our Destiny Is in Our Hands," *ibid.*, 40–41; "The General Assembly of Greater East-Asiatic Newspapers," *ibid.* (Nov. 25, 1943), 1–2; Friend, *Between Two Empires*, 211–45.

21. Rankin, Report, Nov. 25, 1943.

22. Wright, "To Hell — and Back," 64–65.

23. Int., Mendoza; Maj. Gen. Charles A. Willoughby, "Brief History of the Philippine Guerrillas to October 1944" [dated Oct. 6, 1944], RG 16, MMBA; Russell W. Volckmann, *We Remained: Three Years Behind the Enemy Lines in the Philippines* (New York, 1954), 174–220; *Army Times* editors, *Secret Agents*, 42–54; Jan Valtin, *Children of Yesterday* (New York, 1946), 282; James, ed., *South to Bataan, North to Mukden*, 37–38. Among the most detailed American sources on the Philippine guerrilla movement are those in the Courtney Whitney Papers, RG 16, MMBA, and the *Intelligence Series* ed. by Willoughby, especially Vol. I, *The Guerrilla Resistance Movement in the Philippines,* and Vol. II, *Intelligence Activities in the Philippines: Japanese Occupation.* See also Charles A. Willoughby, comp., *The Guerrilla Resistance Movement in the Philippines* (New York, 1972).

24. Cannon, *Leyte,* 17; Ind, *Allied Intelligence Bureau,* 196.

25. Quezon to DM, May 2, 1943; DM to AGWAR, Aug. 31, 1943; DM to Quezon, Oct. 10, 1943, RG 4, MMBA; Maj. Allison Ind to Willoughby, May 5, 1943, RG 16, MMBA; SWPA G-2 daily Philippine message sheets, Jan., 1943–Dec., 1944, SWPA G-3 Jnls.; int., Willoughby, Marquardt; Ind, *Allied Intelligence Bureau,* 146–74, 209; George R. Thompson and Dixie R. Harris, *The Signal Corps: The Outcome (Mid-1943 Through 1945)* (USAWWII; Washington, 1966), 273.

26. Int., Whitney, Willoughby; Joseph R. Hayden, Summary of Talks with President Quezon, Mar. 4–22, 1944, RG 4, MMBA; DM to TAG, June 13, 1949, RG 5, MMBA; Col. Courtney Whitney to Sutherland, May 27, June 1, July 9, 15, 1943, RG 16, MMBA.

27. Int., Fellers, Mashbir, Marquardt; Maj. Faubion Bowers, July 8, 1971; Brig. Gen. William J. Donovan to DM, Apr. 26, 1943; DM to AGWAR, Nov. 4, 1943, RG 4 MMBA; DM to TAG, June 7, 1946, RG 5, MMBA; Robert E. Sherwood to Elmer Davis, Aug. 31, 1943, CCS 385 Philippines (1-1-43); *New York Times*, Dec. 9, 1943; Mashbir, *American Spy*, 21–23; Corey Ford, *Donovan of OSS* (Boston, 1970), 252–54.

28. Int., H. Johnson, Wright, Bluemel, Collier, Guyton; Sgt. Calvin R. Graef, Reminiscences of "Hell Ship" Voyage, 1944 [oral transcript, Oct. 1, 1971], DMBP; William M. Taylor, Jr., "Hell Ships: Voyages of Japanese Prison Ships, 1942–1945" (unpublished M.A. thesis, Miss. State University, 1972); Wainwright, *Wainwright's Story*, 225.

29. William E. Brougher, Diary, Aug. 1, 1943, in James, ed., *South to Bataan, North to Mukden,* 83.
30. GCM to DM, Feb. 23, Oct. 7, 1943; DM to GCM, Feb. 25, July 28, 1943, RG 4, MMBA; Sydney *Daily Mirror,* Feb. 1, 1944; Dyess, *Dyess Story,* 9–13, 16–19; Mellnik, *Philippine Diary,* 279–81; Falk, *Bataan,* 206.
31. Lt. Col. J. R. McMicking to Col. Manuel Nieto, July 22, 1944, RG 4, MMBA; Frederic S. Marquardt, "Osmena and Quezon," Manila *Philippines Free Press,* Dec. 15, 1962; Romulo, *I Walked with Heroes,* 228; Steinberg, *Philippine Collaboration,* 102–03; Friend, *Between Two Empires,* 229–31.
32. DM to AGWAR, Oct. 29, 1943, RG 4, MMBA; Friend, *Between Two Empires,* 235–36, 250; Quezon, *Good Fight,* vii–ix. See also MacArthur-Quezon correspondence, 1942–44, in RG 4, MMBA.
33. DM to Quezon, Sept. 27, Oct. 10, 1943; DM to GCM, Aug. 6, Oct. 10, Nov. 2, 1943, RG 4, MMBA; Hayden, Summary of Talks with Quezon, Mar., 1944; Milton W. Meyer, *A Diplomatic History of the Philippine Republic* (Honolulu, 1965), 4–16; George E. Taylor, *The Philippines and the United States: Problems of Partnership* (New York, 1964), 108–09. Quezon signed the Declaration by the United Nations in June, 1942, thereby pledging the Philippine government-in-exile to subscribe to, among other things, the principles of the Atlantic Charter. U.S. State Dept., *Foreign Relations, 1942,* I, 906–08.
34. DM to Quezon, Sept. 27, 1943, RG 4, MMBA.
35. Gen. Orders 62, War Dept., Aug. 2, 1944; press release by Stimson, Aug. 1, 1944, AG 091.11 Philippine Commonwealth (8-2-44); *New York Times,* Aug. 2–3, 1944; Pres. Sergio Osmeña to DM, Aug. 2, 10, 1944; DM to Osmeña, Aug. 11, 1944, RG 4, MMBA.
36. U.S. State Dept., *Foreign Relations, 1942,* I, 909–10; *ibid., 1943,* III, 1099; GCM to DM, Mar. 16, 1944; DM to GCM, Mar. 17, 1944, RG 4, MMBA; Eyre, *Roosevelt-MacArthur Conflict,* 121–46; Steinberg, *Philippine Collaboration,* 103–06; Garel A. Grunder and William E. Livezey, *The Philippines and the United States* (Norman, 1951), 244–45; James, *Years of MacArthur,* I, 536; DM Diary, Sept. 7, 21, 1944.
37. Cannon, *Leyte,* 199; U.S. State Dept., *Foreign Relations, 1944,* V. 1299–30.
38. DM to Maj. Gen. John Hildring, Sept. 2, 1944, RG 4, MMBA.
39. Steinberg, *Philippine Collaboration,* 105–06, 108–12; Friend, *Between Two Empires,* 247–51; Taylor, *Philippines and U.S.,* 116–17.

CHAPTER XIII. *"Decision and Attack"*

pages 521–565
1. CCS Mins., June 11, 1944; Joint Staff Planners Mins., May 12, 17, 24, June 7, 1944, CCS 381 (5-3-55); JCS to Maj. Gen. John R. Deane, July

5, 1944, CCS 381 Japan (10-4-43) Sec. 2; Smith, "Luzon versus Formosa," 461–66; Matloff, *Strategic Planning*, 479–81; Ehrman, *Grand Strategy*, VI, 203–06; JCS to DM and Nimitz, June 12, 1944, OPD-EF.

2. DM to GCM, June 18, 1944, OPD-EF.

3. Int., Handy, Hull, Munson, Ritchie; Kinkaid, *Narrative*, 368; Smith, "Luzon versus Formosa," 466–69; Pogue, *Marshall*, III, 443–44; Halsey and Bryan, *Halsey's Story*, 194–95; Leahy, *I Was There*, 259.

4. King and Whitehill, *King*, 566–68; Burns, *Roosevelt*, 488–90; *New York Times*, Aug. 31, 1944; Luvaas, ed., *Dear Miss Em*, 155.

5. Int., Fellers; DM Diary, July 26–27, 1944; Diller to DM, July 11, 1944, RG 10, MMBA; Leahy, *I Was There*, 249–50; DM, *Reminiscences*, 196; Hunt, *Untold Story*, 331.

6. Samuel I. Rosenman, *Working with Roosevelt* (New York, 1952), 456–57.

7. Hunt, *Untold Story*, 332, 333; Leahy, *I Was There*, 250; Pogue, *Marshall*, III, 452; DM, *Reminiscences*, 198–99; Luvaas, ed., *Dear Miss Em*, 155, 156. Because no records were kept of the Pearl Harbor conference, and the surviving personal accounts are incomplete and contradictory on the order of events, the exact sequence of activities is impossible to reconstruct definitively.

8. Lockwood, *Sink 'Em All*, 201–02; Whitney, *MacArthur*, 123; Lockwood and Adamson, *Philippine Sea*, 130–31; DM, *Reminiscences*, 197, 198; Cannon, *Leyte*, 5; Leahy, *I Was There*, 250–51.

9. Luvaas, ed., *Dear Miss Em*, 155–56; Hunt, *Untold Story*, 333; DM, *Reminiscences*, 199; DM Diary, July 28–30, 1944; Leahy, *I Was There*, 252; Lockood, *Sink 'Em All*, 202; FDR to his wife, July 29, 1944, in Roosevelt, ed., *F.D.R.: His Personal Letters*, IV, 1527.

10. Matloff, *Strategic Planning*, 484; Luvaas, ed., *Dear Miss Em*, 155, 156; Willoughby and Chamberlain, *MacArthur*, 233, 234; Lee and Henschel, *MacArthur*, 172; FDR press conference, July 29, 1944; Rosenman, comp., *Public Papers and Addresses of Roosevelt*, XIII, 220; FDR to DM, Aug. 9, Sept. 15, 1944; DM to FDR, Aug. 26, 1944, PPF 4914. The preceding two FDR-to-DM letters are quoted in DM, *Reminiscences*, 199–200, with some minor but odd deletions unmarked by ellipsis points.

11. Sherwood, *Roosevelt and Hopkins*, II, 440–41; Matloff, *Strategic Planning*, 482. For interpretations which maintain that a firm decision regarding the Philippines was made at Pearl Harbor, see Whitney, *MacArthur*, 125; Willoughby and Chamberlain, *MacArthur*, 236; Lee and Henschel, *MacArthur*, 170–71; Gunther, *Riddle of MacArthur*, 9–10; Eichelberger, *Jungle Road*, 165–66.

12. Smith, *Triumph in the Philippines*, 8.

13. *Ibid.*, 8–10; Coakley and Leighton, *Global Logistics*, 406–14; Ehrman, *Grand Strategy*, VI, 206–08; Morison, *Leyte*, 12.

14. Int., Willoughby, Ritchie; Kinkaid, Experiences, 10; Halsey and Bryan, *Halsey's Story*, 198–201; King and Whitehill, *King*, 571–72; Arnold, *Global Mission*, 527–28; Theodore Taylor, *The Magnificent Mitscher* (New York, 1954), 250; Sherman, *Combat Command*, 270–71; Kenney, *Kenney Reports*, 432; DM to JCS, Sept. 15, 1944, CM-IN 17744.

15. Int., Ritchie; Smith, *Triumph in the Philippines*, 11–15; Matloff, *Strategic Planning*, 484–87; DM Diary, Aug. 6–7, 1944. Those attending the Brisbane conference of Aug. 6–7, 1944, were MacArthur, Sutherland, Kenney, and Marshall of GHQ SWPA; Lt. Gen. Barney M. Giles, Arnold's CofS; Maj. Gen. John E. Hull, theater group chief, OPD; Maj. Gen. Clayton L. Bissell, War Dept. G-2; Maj. Gen. Wilhelm D. Styer, Somervell's deputy; Maj. Gen. Frank O. D. Hunter, commander of First Air Force; Brig. Gen. Otto L. Nelson, McNarney's executive officer; and Col. William L. Ritchie, SWPA section chief, OPD.

16. Coakley and Leighton, *Global Logistics*, 412–16, 571; Smith, *Triumph in the Philippines*, 15–17; Reynolds, *Fast Carriers*, 248–49.

17. Cannon, *Leyte*, 11; Morison, *Leyte*, 63; DM, *Reminiscences*, 212.

18. SWPA G-3 Staff Study, Operation King Two, 4th ed., Sept. 19, 1944, RG 3, MMBA; Morison, *Leyte*, 58, 113.

19. Kinkaid, Narrative, 294–95.

20. Adapted from table in Willoughby, ed., *MacArthur Reports*, I, 183n.

21. Int., Gen. Clyde D. Eddleman, June 29, 1971; Cannon, *Leyte*, 36, 51; Morison, *Two-Ocean War*, 421–24; Stauffer, *Quartermaster Corps*, 247–77; R. Ernest Dupuy and Trevor N. Dupuy, *The Encyclopedia of Military History: From 3500 B.C. to the Present* (New York, 1970), 1178.

22. U.S. Navy Dept., *Navy Dept. Communiques 301 to 600*, 250; Halsey and Bryan, *Halsey's Story*, 207–08.

23. Rear Adm. Arthur D. Struble, Narrative of Philippine Operations, 1944–45, as Commander of Group Two, Seventh Amphibious Force [oral transcript, Navy Dept., Aug. 18, 1945], 1–2, NHD; DM Diary, Oct. 14–19, 1944; Capt. C. E. Coney, Report of U.S.S. *Nashville*'s Participation in Amphibious Operations at Leyte Gulf, P.I., Oct. 16–25, 1944 [dated Oct. 26, 1944], 1–3, NHD; Swan, *Spearheads*, 125–61; Smith, ed., *Navy in World War II*, 834–38; Morison, *Two-Ocean War*, 433–34.

24. DM, *Reminiscences*, 214–15.

25. Int., Noble, Struble, Eddleman, Dahlen; Maj. Gen. Roscoe B. Woodruff, Sept. 8, 1971; SWPA G-3 Op. Rpts., Oct. 19–20, 1944, SWPA G-3 Jnls.; Kinkaid, Experiences, 11; Maj. Gen. Roscoe B. Woodruff, "Leyte: Historical Report of the 24th Infantry Division Landing Team, 20 October 1944–25 December 1944," 1–11, in possession of Gen. Woodruff (photocopy, DMBP); Wright, *1st Cav. Div.*, 71–80; Orlando

Davidson, *et al.*, *The Deadeyes: The Story of the 96th Infantry Division* (Washington, 1947), 19–21. MacArthur allegedly chose to call the Leyte target day "A-day" rather than the usual "D-day" because, since June 6, 1944, the latter term had become virtually synonymous in the public mind with Eisenhower's invasion of Normandy.

26. Int., Kenney, Fellers, Egeberg, Faillace, Marquardt; Dunn, "MacArthur's Mansions and Other Myths," 41–43; Marquardt, "MacArthur Story"; "MacArthur Returns and Returns," *Life*, LXXII (Feb. 18, 1972), 24–25, and letters to editor, *ibid.* (Mar. 10, 31, 1972); Coney, *Nashville* Report, 1–3; DM Diary, Oct. 20, 1944; Falk, *Leyte*, 101–03; Kenney, *Kenney Reports*, 448; Lockwood and Adamson, *Philippine Sea*, 157–58; "Battle for the Philippines," *Fortune*, XXXI (June, 1945), 157–58.

27. Valtin, *Children of Yesterday*, 32–33.

28. Dunn, "MacArthur's Mansions and Other Myths," 42; Leyte addresses by DM, Osmeña, and Romulo, DM Misc. 201; Osmeña to DM, Oct. 20, 1944, RG 4, MMBA; "Battle for the Philippines," 158; Romulo, *I Walked with Heroes*, 235–36; Thompson and Harris, *Signal Corps*, 278–79; Eyre, *Roosevelt-MacArthur Conflict*, 209–12.

29. Int., Kenney, Fellers, Mashbir, Egeberg, Marquardt; DM Diary, Sept. 29, 1944; Kenney, *MacArthur*, 95, 96; Roger O. Egeberg, "General Douglas MacArthur," *Transactions of the American Clinical and Climatological Association*, LXXVIII (1966), 167; S. S. Stratton, "Tiger of Malaya," *U.S. Naval Institute Proceedings*, LXXX (Feb., 1954), 141.

30. DM Diary, Oct. 21–22, 1944; Egeberg, "MacArthur," 141; Kenney, *Kenney Reports*, 450; Osmeña to DM, Oct. 21, 1944; DM to Osmeña, Oct. 21, 1944; FDR to DM, Oct. 21, 1944, RG 4, MMBA; Churchill to DM, Oct. 22, 1944, RG 5, MMBA. For other congratulatory messages to MacArthur on his return to Leyte, see RG 4 and RG 5, MMBA. The ceremony in which Osmeña awarded the Medal of Valor to MacArthur took place at Malacañan Palace, Manila, on Mar. 10, 1945.

31. Barbey, *MacArthur's Amphibious Navy*, 250, 251; DM Diary, Oct. 23, 1944; int., Tarbuck, Kenney; Falk, *Leyte*, 110–11; London *Times*, Oct. 24, 1944; Carlos P. Romulo, *I See the Philippines Rise* (Garden City, 1946), 127–29.

32. DM Diary, Oct. 24–26, 1944; Morison, *Leyte*, 138.

33. Published accounts of the battle for Leyte Gulf are numerous, and three of them are outstanding: Morison, *Leyte*, 159–332; C. Vann Woodward, *The Battle for Leyte Gulf* (New York, 1947); James A. Field, *The Japanese at Leyte Gulf: The Shō Operation* (Princeton, 1947). In his memoirs MacArthur devotes 26 pp. to the ground, air, and sea operations of the Leyte campaign, of which 11 pp. are on the naval battle of Oct. 23–26, 1944. See DM, *Reminiscences*, 211–37.

About two months before the battle for Leyte Gulf, Tarbuck "did some intensive intelligence work" and figured out the probable locations of the main components of the Combined Fleet. By plotting factors of speed and distance in circles from those bases, he found that the locus, or common intersection of the circles, was Leyte Gulf. He even predicted accurately the Japanese movements through San Bernardino and Surigao straits, as well as the composition of the attack forces. Willoughby and Chamberlin, however, discounted Tarbuck's study and apparently did not deem it worthy of passing on to Kinkaid and his commanders. Int., Tarbuck, Mashbir.

34. Cannon, *Leyte*, 92; Woodward, *Leyte Gulf*, 229–31, 235; Kenney, *MacArthur*, 170; DM to Halsey, Oct. 29, 1944; DM to Nimitz, Oct. 29, 1944, RG 4, MMBA; DM, *Reminiscences*, 230.

CHAPTER XIV. *"From Leyte to Mindoro"*
pages 566–610

1. USAAF, *Mission Accomplished: Interrogations of Japanese Industrial, Military, and Civil Leaders of World War II* (Washington, 1946), 22; USSBS, *Campaigns*, 287; USSBS, *Employment of Forces*, 43–45; USSBS, *Fifth Air Force*, 61–63; Cannon, *Leyte*, 94; Falk, *Leyte*, 107–08; Saburo Hayashi, *Kōgun: The Japanese Army in the Pacific War*, trans. Alvin D. Coox (Quantico, 1959), 121–25; Willoughby, ed., *MacArthur Reports*, I, 226.

2. DM Diary, Nov. 6–10, 1944; Falk, *Leyte*, 218–20; Boggs, *Marine Aviation*, 24–46; Halsey and Bryan, *Halsey's Story*, 231–33; Reynolds, *Fast Carriers*, 286–88; Sherman, *Combat Command*, 316; Morison, *Leyte*, 355; Sherrod, *Marine Corps Aviation*, 260–61, 272, 275–76, 286; Smith, ed., *Marine Corps*, 694–96.

3. USSBS, *Fifth Air Force*, 35, 105–06; Goldstein, "Whitehead," 199–237; Haugland, *AAF Against Japan*, 231–42; DM Diary, Dec. 12, 1944; *New York Times*, Dec. 13, 1944; Craven and Cate, eds., *Matterhorn to Nagasaki*, 385; Sixth Army, Report of Operations: Leyte, 20 October–25 December 1944, 83–84, Sixth Army Records, File 106-0.3, RG 407, WNRC.

4. Sixth Army, Leyte Op. Rpt., 37–39; 24th Div., Leyte Op. Rpt., 12–38; OPD, Pacific Ops., 142–43; Davidson, *et al., Deadeyes*, 21–23, 37–41; Kleber and Birdsell, *Chemical Warfare Service*, 576.

5. DM Diary, Nov. 8, 12, 1944; Falk, Leyte, 258, 259; Maj. Gen. Roscoe B. Woodruff, "World War II [Experiences]," 58–59, in possession of Gen. Woodruff (photocopy, DMBP); int., Woodruff; Valtin, *Children of Yesterday*, 167–87, 206, 215–16; 24th Div., Leyte Op. Rpt., 39–72; Luvaas, ed., *Dear Miss Em*, 247; Blakeley, *32d Div.*, 178–201.

6. Sixth Army G-3 Op. Rpts., Nov. 1–Dec. 15, 1944, SWPA G-3 Jnls.; John M. Finn, "Shoestring Ridge," *Infantry Journal*, LVII (Sept.,

1945), 47; Cannon, *Leyte*, 293; Falk, *Leyte*, 288–89; Toland, *Rising Sun*, II, 715–45; int., Struble; Kinkaid, Narrative, 374; Max Myers, *Ours to Hold It High: The History of the 77th Infantry Division in World War II* (Washington, 1947), 139–59; GHQ SWPA communiqué, Dec. 8, 1944.

7. Brig. Gen. Bonner F. Fellers, Report on Philippine Civil Affairs [c. Nov. 10, 1944], 1–2, RG 10, MMBA; William Chickering to David Hulburd, Nov. 4, 1944, Sherrod Papers; U.S. State Dept., *Foreign Relations, 1944*, V, 1305–09; Eyre, *MacArthur-Roosevelt Conflict*, 147–48; DM, *Reminiscences*, 235.

8. Fellers, Philippine Civil Affairs, 1–2.

9. Thorpe, *East Wind Rain*, 151–52; Friend, *Between Two Empires*, 247–49; JCS to DM, Nov. 9, 1944, CCS 383.21 Philippines (10-4-44); Osmeña to FDR, Nov. 9, 1944, Map Room File, FDRL.

10. Int., Kenney, Marshall, Fellers, Fitch, Faillace, Egeberg, Marquardt; Kenney, *Kenney Reports*, 453.

11. Sgt. Vincent L. Powers, "Reprints: Stories from GHQ Advance Echelon, Leyte-Luzon" [mimeographed, Manila, 1945], 14–15, Official File, Harry S. Truman Papers, HSTL.

12. *Ibid.*, 7–10; int., Fitch, Munson, Faillace, Egeberg, Catledge, Marquardt; Luvaas, ed., *Dear Miss Em*, 170; Frederic S. Marquardt, "A Sentimental Journey," Phoenix *Arizona Republic*, June 3, 1971; *idem*, "The MacArthur Story," Manila *Times*, July 26, 1950; Catledge, *My Life and the Times*, 155.

13. Int., Byers.

14. Int., Willoughby, Catledge; Eichelberger to DM, Nov. 2, 1944, RG 10, MMBA; Catledge, *My Life and the Times*, 155–56; Walter Millis, ed., *The Forrestal Diaries* (New York, 1951), 17–18; DM Diary, Oct. 26, 1944–Jan. 4, 1945; *New York Times*, Dec. 15, 1944.

15. Edward M. Flanagan, Jr., *The Angels: A History of the 11th Airborne Division, 1943–1946* (Washington, 1948), 62–63.

16. Int., Marshall, Egeberg; Thanksgiving Day Menu of Commander-in-Chief's Mess, GHQ Tacloban, Nov. 23, 1944, RG 10, MMBA; DM Diary, Nov. 23, Dec. 24–25, 1944; Powers, "Reprints," 15; Huff, *My Fifteen Years*, 86–88, 95.

17. Int., Willoughby, Egeberg; O'Laughlin to DM, Sept. 1, 1944, RG 10, MMBA; Stimson and SecNavy James V. Forrestal to FDR, Dec. 13, 1944, PPF 4914; DM Diary, Dec. 16, 26, 1944; DM to FDR, Dec. 16, 1944, RG 5, MMBA; *New York Times*, Dec. 16, 27, 1944; TAG to DM, Apr. 13, 1946, RG 4, MMBA; Leahy, *I Was There*, 282. MacArthur's date of rank as general had earlier been adjusted to Sept. 16, 1936; his five-star date of rank was Dec. 18, 1944. Halsey and Bradley attained five-star rank in Dec., 1945, and Sept., 1950, respectively. Pershing alone had the title of "General of the Armies."

18. Cannon, *Leyte*, 244.
19. DM Diary, Oct. 26, 1944–Jan. 3, 1945; Fellers, Philippine Civil Affairs, 1.
20. Luvaas, ed., *Dear Miss Em*, 176–77.
21. Int., Kenney, Willoughby, F. Johnson, Fitch; Maj. Gen. Frank H. Britton, July 28, 1971; Kenney, *MacArthur*, 64–65.
22. Egeberg, "MacArthur," 165.
23. Int., Britton, Munson, Mashbir; Kinkaid, Experiences, 4.
24. Int., Byers.
25. Int., Marshall; confidential communications of former GHQ SWPA officers to author; Manila *Free Philippines*, May 14, 1945; Luvaas, ed., *Dear Miss Em*, 216; Mattie E. Treadwell, *The Women's Army Corps* (USAWWII; Washington, 1954), 410–14, 416, 418, 422–23, 453–59, 472.
26. Treadwell, *Women's Army Corps*, 414.
27. Statement by DM to WAC Col. Boyce, Oct. 14, 1945, in *ibid.*, 423.
28. Luvaas, ed., *Dear Miss Em*, 179; confidential communications of former GHQ SWPA officers to author.
29. Willoughby, ed., *MacArthur Reports*, II, Pt. II, 432; Myers, *Ours to Hold It High*, 160–211; Hayashi, *Kōgun*, 126–29; Flanagan, *Angels*, 30–66.
30. Int., Eddleman, Byers; Lt. Gen. Joseph M. Swing, Aug. 26, 1971; OPD, Pacific Ops., 146–47; Morison, *Leyte*, 394; Flanagan, *Angels*, 65. The sources differ greatly on the strength and losses of the Thirty-fifth Army on Leyte.
31. Eichelberger, *Jungle Road*, 181–82. In mid-Jan., 1945, units of the 7th Div. landed on the Camotes Islands, southwest of Ormoc Bay, which were secured in a few days against light opposition except on Poro, where intense but brief fighting occurred.
32. DM Diary, Nov. 6–8, 1944; DM to GCM, Nov. 30, 1944, CM-IN 29666; SWPA G-3 Staff Study, Mike I Operation, 2nd ed., Oct. 7, 1944, RG 3, MMBA; Reynolds, *Fast Carriers*, 285–95.
33. Kinkaid, Narrative, 380–81.
34. Int., Noble.
35. Catledge, *My Life and the Times*, 155.
36. Int., Catledge.
37. SWPA G-3 Staff Study, Love III Operation, 2nd ed., Sept. 28, 1944, RG 3, MMBA; Rear Adm. Forrest P. Sherman, press conference, Jan. 8, 1945, NHD; J. J. Clark, with Clark G. Reynolds, *Carrier Admiral* (New York, 1967), 206.
38. Int., Struble, Noble, Woodruff; Rear Adm. Arthur D. Struble, Philippine Campaign [oral transcript, Navy Dept., Aug. 18, 1945], 3–4, NHD; Woodruff, "World War II," 62–63; USSBS, *Fifth Air Force*, 35–36; Haugland, *AAF Against Japan*, 242–45; Halsey and Bryan, *Halsey's Story*, 234–43; Smith, *Triumph in the Philippines*, 52–53; Statement of

Lt. Col. Yorio Ishikawa, n.d. [c. Oct., 1945], in Willoughby, ed., *Mac-Arthur Reports,* I, 254.

PART V. *"The Last Campaigns"*

Basic works in Part V that will not be cited in the chapter notes except when quoted are Barbey, *MacArthur's Amphibious Navy,* 291–320; Craven and Cate, eds., *Matterhorn to Nagasaki,* 413–504; Dod, *Corps of Engineers,* 587–683; Eichelberger, *Jungle Road,* 181–267; Gill, *Royal Australian Navy, 1942–45,* 575–717; Hunt, *Untold Story,* 356–406; Kenney, *Kenney Reports,* 507–79; Krueger, *From Down Under,* 211–344; Long, *Final Campaigns,* 141–636; *idem, MacArthur,* 163–81; Luvaas, ed., *Dear Miss Em,* 202–310; MacArthur, *Reminiscences,* 238–80; Samuel E. Morison, *The Liberation of the Philippines: Luzon, Mindanao, the Visayas, 1944–45* (HUSNOWWII; Boston, 1959); Odgers, *Air War Against Japan,* 391–499; Smith, *Triumph in the Philippines,* 18–42, 54–721; Whitney, *MacArthur,* 181–226; Willoughby and Chamberlain, *MacArthur,* 260–99; Willoughby, ed., *MacArthur Reports,* I, 254–467; II, Pt. II, 467–771.

CHAPTER XV. *"Familiar Grounds"*

pages 613–669

1. SWPA G-3 Staff Studies, Mike I, Mike IV, and Mike VII, RG 3, MMBA; Smith, *Triumph in the Philippines,* 30.
2. Adapted from table in Willoughby, ed., *MacArthur Reports,* I, 254n.
3. Int., Berkey, Davison, Struble, Noble.
4. Powers, "Reprints," 15–17. "January 3–4" has been substituted for "January 4th" in the quotation for the sake of accuracy since Mac-Arthur departed on the day of January 4.

   In his *Reminiscences,* 239, MacArthur borrows heavily and without acknowledgment from the first two paragraphs of the portion of Powers' story quoted herein.
5. DM to Churchill, Jan. 7, 1945, RG 4, MMBA; Kinkaid, Experiences, 14–15; Vice Adm. Jesse B. Oldendorf, Lingayen Gulf Operation [oral transcript, Navy Dept., Feb. 20, 1945], 1–5, NHD; int., Berkey, Davison; Swan, *Spearheads,* 180–216; Capt. W. M. Downes, Report of U.S.S. *Boise's* Operations Incident to Amphibious Assault and Landings on Luzon Island, P.I., 1 January 1945 to 31 January 1945, Inclusive [dated Feb. 5, 1945], 1–3, NHD; Okumiya and Horikoshi, *Zero,* 247–50; Rikihie Inoguchi and Tadashi Nakajima, with Roger Pineau, *The Divine Wind: Japan's Kamikaze Force in World War II* (Annapolis, 1958), 222; USSBS, *Campaigns,* 188–89; DM, *Reminiscences,* 240; Barbey, *MacArthur's Amphibious Navy,* 298.

6. Int., Marshall, Fellers, Egeberg, Faillace; Kinkaid, Narrative, 395; Amory and Waterman, eds., *Surf and Sand*, 125–60; Barnard, ed., *6th Div.*, 60–71; Zimmer, *43d Div.*, 44–47; Heavey, *Down Ramp*, 6–7; Stanley A. Frankel, *The 37th Infantry Division in World War II* (Washington, 1948), 221–31; 40th Inf. Div. Hist. Com., *40th Infantry Division: The Years of World War II, 7 December 1941–7 April 1946* (Baton Rouge, 1947), 109–10; "MacArthur Returns and Returns," 24–25; GHQ SWPA communiqué, Jan. 10, 1945; 33rd Div., *Golden Cross*, 87–93.

7. Int., Eddleman, Byers; DM to Krueger, Jan. 17, 1945, RG 4, MMBA; DM Diary, Jan. 13, 25, 1945; Stanley L. Falk, *Liberation of the Philippines* (New York, 1971), 96–97; Zimmer, *43d Div.*, 48–41; Barnard, ed., *6th Div.*, 72–89; Luvaas, ed., *Dear Miss Em*, 207, 214, 225.

8. Hayashi, *Kōgun*, 129–30; OPD, Pacific Ops., 16–20; A. Frank Reel, *The Case of General Yamashita* (Chicago, 1949), 20–24.

9. Int., Eddleman, Byers; Stauffer, *Quartermaster Corps*, 156, 280–81; 33rd Div., *Golden Cross*, 86–113; Barnard, ed., *6th Div.*, 89–98; Zimmer, *43d Div.*, 62–65; 40th Div., *40th Div.*, 110–18; Frankel, *37th Div.*, 232–42; Riegelman, *Caves of Biak*, 205–30; DM, *Reminiscences*, 244.

10. Kinkaid, Narrative, 393–95; Morison, *Liberation of the Philippines*, 178; Millis, ed., *Forrestal Diaries*, 26; Smith and Finch, *Coral and Brass*, 247–48; Whitman S. Bartley, *Iwo Jima: Amphibious Epic* (Washington, 1954), 41. Also in late Jan., 1945, MacArthur received orders from the War Dept. to release seventy cargo ships, which were scheduled to carry supplies and munitions to Vladivostok for the Red Army. He said, "I protested violently . . . No heed was given my warnings." He claimed that he challenged the shipment of aid to the Soviets at that late date in the war, but, as will be discussed later, Forrestal and others in early 1945 found him eager to get the Soviet Union into the war against Japan. DM, *Reminiscences*, 244.

11. Int., Swing, Byers, Eddleman; Brig. Gen. William C. Dunckel to Eichelberger, Mar. 3, 1945, Eichelberger Papers; Wright, *1st Cav. Div.*, 125–28; Flanagan, *Angels*, 67–80, 123; Frankel, *37th Div.*, 242–50.

12. Smith, *Triumph in the Philippines*, 240; Kenney, *MacArthur*, 98; Willoughby, ed., *MacArthur Reports*, II, Pt. II, 494.

13. Frankel, *37th Div.*, 251–58; Wright, *1st Cav. Div.*, 129–32; Flanagan, *Angels*, 81–84.

14. GHQ SWPA communiqué, Feb. 6, 1945. For messages of early Feb., 1945, offering congratulations to MacArthur on his capture of Manila, see RG 3, 4, and 10, MMBA. Many American and Allied newspapers also interpreted his communiqué of Feb. 6 as proclaiming the fall of the city.

15. DM Diary, Feb. 7, 1945.

16. DM, *Reminiscences*, 247, 248; int., Chabot.

17. Int., Swing, Faillace, Marquardt; Luvaas, ed., *Dear Miss Em*, 216; Frankel, *37th Div.*, 259–96; Flanagan, *Angels*, 85–92; Wright, *1st Cav. Div.*, 132–33.
18. The Rev. John F. Hurley to the Rev. Giovanni Montini, Mar. 1, 1945; Romulo to DM, Mar. 20, 1945, RG 10, MMBA; SWPA G-2, Report on the Destruction of Manila and Japanese Atrocities, February 1945, RG 16, MMBA; U.S. Senate, Committee on Military Affairs, *Sack of Manila* (Washington, 1945); David Bergamini, *Japan's Imperial Conspiracy: How Emperor Hirohito Led Japan into War Against the West* (New York, 1971), 1051–52; Reel, *Yamashita*, 101–03, 112–17, 152–54; GHQ SWPA communiqué, Mar. 3, 1945; Flanagan, *Angels*, 93–98.
19. DM to Krueger, Feb. 16, 1945, RG 4, MMBA. See also Krueger to DM, Feb. 16, 1945, *ibid.*
20. Frankel, *37th Div.*, 295–96; Wright, *1st Cav. Div.* 133–34.
21. Int., Swing, Elmore, Egeberg; DM Diary, Feb. 19, 23, 27, 1945; DM, *Reminiscences*, 247; Whitney, *MacArthur*, 364. A ridiculous rumor later started that MacArthur had refused to allow the artillery to fire on the Manila Hotel in order to protect his personal property and his supposed investment in the hotel. Marquardt, "MacArthur Story."
22. Manila *Free Philippines*, Feb. 28, 1945; DM, *Reminiscences*, 251–52.
23. DM Diary, Feb. 27, 1945; DM, *Reminiscences*, 252; Whitney, *MacArthur*, 364.
24. Int., Dahlen, Elmore; 34th Inf. Rgt., "Dragon's Teeth: Operation M-7 (Western Luzon), Jan.–Feb. 1945," in possession of Gen. Dahlen (photocopy, DMBP); Valtin, *Children of Yesterday*, 313–32; Smith, *Triumph in the Philippines*, 329.
25. DM Diary, Feb. 16, 1945; int., Egeberg, Elmore.
26. Egeberg, "MacArthur," 168.
27. Int., Elmore, Berkey; Struble, Narrative, 5–7; USSBS, *Fifth Air Force*, 68–70; Belote and Belote, *Corregidor*, 204–48; Harold Templeman, *The Return to Corregidor* (New York, 1945), 1–67. On Feb. 25, 1945, Hurley, now ambassador to China, and Gen. Albert C. Wedemeyer, who had replaced Stilwell as CBI commander, visited the SWPA chief at Hacienda Luisita. They had come by way of Tacloban where Maj. Gen. Norman Kirk, the Army's surgeon general, had been waiting two days for GHQ permission to fly to Luzon. GHQ rejected his request for unknown reasons, and, according to Wedemeyer, Kirk "was very much put out" over the seeming rebuff. A friend of MacArthur's in Washington said that a month later Kirk and certain Pentagon individuals were still upset about his refusal to see the surgeon general. Int., Wedemeyer; Brig. Gen. Paul I. Robinson, Aug. 3, 1971; DM Diary, Feb. 25, 1945; Wedemeyer, *Wedemeyer Reports*, 338–39, 341; Col. James E. Cassidy to DM, Mar. 28, 1945, RG 10, MMBA.
28. DM Diary, Mar. 2, 1945; int., Egeberg, Faillace; Templeman, *Return to Corregidor*, 20–21.

29. Whan, ed., *A Soldier Speaks,* 136.
30. Luvaas, ed., *Dear Miss Em,* 230, 231; Brig. Gen. Crawford F. Sams, "Medic" [MS memoirs, 1955], 334–37, in possession of Gen. Sams (photocopy, DMBP); int., Robinson, Egeberg; Amb. U. Alexis Johnson, June 24, 1971; Brig. Gen. Crawford F. Sams, Aug. 25, 1971; Casey, ed., *Engineers,* VI, 361–62; Stauffer, *Quartermaster Corps,* 91.
31. Int., Egeberg.
32. Powers, "Reprints," 31; DM Diary, Mar. 15, 1945; Manila *Free Philippines,* Mar. 16, 1945; *New York Times,* Mar. 25, 1945.
33. Powers, "Reprints," 33–34.
34. Maj. Gen. Innis P. Swift, to DM, Jan. 31, 1945; Lt. Col. William T. Holladay to Maj. Gen. Robert S. Beightler, Feb. 15, 1945; DM to Mrs. DM, Feb. 16, 1945; Roy Beard to DM, Feb. 17, 1945, RG 3, MMBA; DM Diary, Apr. 27, 1945; Fellers to Barbey, Mar. 22, 1967, Barbey Papers; testimony of Thomas W. Poole, Nov. 7, 1945, in USAFWESPAC, U.S. vs. Gen. Tomoyuki Yamashita: Transcript of Public Trial, 1945, XI, 1421, War Crimes Office Files, RG 153, NA.
35. Int., Kenney.
36. Mrs. DM to Maj. Gen. Clovis E. Byers, Dec. 23, 1944, Clovis E. Byers Papers, Hoover Inst. See also Byers to Mrs. DM, Dec. 21, 1944, *ibid.*
37. Mrs. DM to DM, Jan. 26, 1945, RG 3, MMBA.
38. DM to Mrs. DM, Feb. 18, 1945, *ibid.*
39. Int., Egeberg, Fellers; Bernard P. Chitty, May 26, 1971; DM Diary, Mar. 6, 1945; Herbert Asbury and Frank Gervasi, "MacArthur: Story of a Great American Soldier," *Collier's,* CXVII (July 21, 1945), 30; *New York Times,* Mar. 8, 1945.
40. Huff, *My Fifteen Years,* 99–100; Mrs. DM to Mrs. William E. Brougher, Apr. 3, 1945, Brougher Papers; Maj. Gen. Clayton Bissell to Mrs. DM, July 6, 1945; Lt. Col. E. T. Thompson to Mrs. DM, May 15, 1945, RG 10, MMBA; int., various officers who were at GHQ Manila, 1945.
41. DM Diary, Mar. 6–Aug. 28, 1945; Huff, *My Fifteen Years,* 101–02; Washington *Daily News,* Apr. 8, 1964.
42. Whitney, *MacArthur,* 547. MacArthur wrote the piece, entitled "A Father's Prayer," sometime during the war years, but the exact date has not been established.
43. Int., Egeberg.
44. Barbey, *MacArthur's Amphibious Navy,* 232.
45. Philip LaFollette, *Adventure in Politics: The Memoirs of Philip LaFollette,* ed. Donald Young (New York, 1970), 268–69.
46. Kenney, *MacArthur,* 244.
47. GHQ SWPA, Roster of Officers, 1 June 1945, RG 3, MMBA; Eichelberger to his wife, Jan. 10, 1945, Eichelberger Papers; DM to AGWAR, Feb. 18, 1945, RG 4, MMBA. The generalizations on personality and staff represent an effort to synthesize the opinions expressed to the author in over 110 interviews with wartime colleagues of the general.

CHAPTER XVI. *"Expanding Operations and Responsibilities"*
pages 670–730

1. DM to Krueger, Feb. 5, 1945, RG 4, MMBA; OPD, Pacific Ops., 159–62; Woodruff, "World War II," 63–67; Flanagan, *Angels*, 99–129; Francis D. Cronin, *Under the Southern Cross: The Saga of the American Division* (Washington, 1951), 246–64.

2. Zimmer, *43d Div.*, 66–75; Smith, *Triumph in the Philippines*, 389.

3. DM to Krueger, Apr. 19, 1945, RG 4, MMBA.

4. Krueger to DM, Apr. 21, 1945; DM to Krueger, Apr. 22, 1945, *ibid.;* DM Diary, Apr. 27, 1945.

5. Zimmer, *43d Div.*, 76–82; Craven and Cate, eds., *Matterhorn to Nagasaki*, 436; Goldstein, "Whitehead," 260–64.

6. 33rd Div., *Golden Cross*, 94–282; Frankel, *37th Div.*, 304–18.

7. Blakeley, *32d Div.*, 202–54, 274; Luvaas, ed., *Dear Miss Em*, 176.

8. Frankel, *37th Div.*, 325–28; Manila *Free Philippines*, May 24, 1945; Smith, *Triumph in the Philippines*, 539.

9. Volckmann, *We Remained*, 204–12; DM, *Reminiscences*, 241.

10. Blakeley, *32d Div.*, 254–75; 33rd Div., *Golden Cross*, 283–327; Frankel, *37th Div.*, 329–52.

11. Fellers to DM, Mar. 29, 1945, RG 3, MMBA; 33rd Div., *Golden Cross*, 335; DM Diary, Apr. 18, 1945; Manila *Free Philippines*, Apr. 18, 1945; Romulo, *I Walked with Heroes*, 215; Hernando J. Abaya, *Betrayal in the Philippines* (New York, 1945), 59–60, 98–99. Aguinaldo, the old Filipino who had led the insurrection at the turn of the century, collaborated with the Japanese, but MacArthur, says Marquardt, "issued orders that he should not be bothered in any way." Marquardt to author, June 28, 1972. See also Emilio Aguinaldo to DM, Mar. 3, 1945, RG 10, MMBA; Aguinaldo to Harry Storin, Jr., Mar. 12, 1945, DMBP.

12. Friend, *Between Two Empires*, 249–55; Abaya, *Betrayal*, 91–92, 203–04; DM, *Reminiscences*, 237; Dale Pontius, "MacArthur and the Filipinos," *Asia and the Americas*, XLVI (Oct., 1946), 437–40; Grunder and Livezey, *Philippines and U.S.*, 255–56.

13. Manila *Daily News*, Aug. 26, 1945, quoted in Abaya, *Betrayal*, 99; Eyre, *Roosevelt-MacArthur Conflict*, 176–93; Bernstein, *Philippine Story*, 204–07. In 1947 Abaya stated that MacArthur "owns shares of stock in several Soriano mines, including the Acoje Chromite Co., the Antamok Goldfields, and others." Abaya, *Betrayal*, 172n. Unfortunately no evidence was found to substantiate or refute his assertion.

14. M. H. Jacaban to Secy. of Interior Harold L. Ickes, Apr. 9, 1945, Records of the Office of the Philippine High Commissioner, RG 126, NA; DM to GCM, May 9, 1945, RG 4, MMBA; *New York Times*, Jan. 22, 1945; U.S. State Dept., *Foreign Relations, 1945*, VI, 1213–15; Ma-

nila *Free Philippines,* Apr. 5, 13, 1945; George Woodbridge, comp., *UNRRA: The History of the United Nations Relief and Rehabilitation Administration* (3 vols., New York, 1950), II, 454–57; Bernstein, *Philippine Story,* 219–21.

15. Osmeña to FDR, Feb. 6, 28, Mar. 12, 1945, Map Room File, FDRL; Pres. Harry S. Truman to DM, Aug. 26, 1945, RG 9, MMBA; Sen. Carl Hayden to DM, June 28, 1945; George E. Ijams to Thomas J. Kehoe, July 4, 1945, RG 10, MMBA; GCM to DM, May 2, 1945; DM to GCM, May 2, 1945, RG 4, MMBA; DM Diary, May 23–26, July 21, 1945; *New York Times,* May 10, 24, July 8, 20, 1945; Thorpe, *East Wind Rain,* 161–64; Friend, *Between Two Empires,* 250–53; Eyre, *Roosevelt-MacArthur Conflict,* 151–59, 213–18; Buss, "Philippines," 55–56; Harry S. Truman, *Memoirs* (2 vols., Garden City, 1955–56), I, 275–77; confidential communication to the author.

16. José C. Zulueta to DM, Apr. 16, 1945; Rep. Enrique B. Magalona to DM, Aug. 23, 1945; Philippine Congress, Joint Resolution No. 2, June 9, 1945, RG 10, MMBA; Reel, *Yamashita,* 6–7; Grunder and Livezey, *Philippines and U.S.,* 246–47. In Joint Resolution No. 1 on June 9, 1945, the Philippine Congress expressed the Filipino people's gratitude to the United States for their liberation and declared that the islands' entire manpower and other resources would be at America's disposal in prosecuting the war against Japan to the end.

17. Philippine Congress, Joint Resolution No. 3, June 9, 1945, RG 10, MMBA. The honorary degree of Doctor of Laws was conferred upon MacArthur *(in absentia)* by the University of Queensland, Brisbane, in Apr., 1945, and by the University of Santo Tomas, Manila, in Aug., 1945.

18. DM Diary, June 9, 1945; Manuel Roxas, Introduction of Gen. MacArthur to the Philippine Congress, July 9, 1945, RG 10, MMBA.

19. DM, Address Before the Philippine Congress, July 9, 1945, RG 10, MMBA.

20. U.S. State Dept., *Foreign Relations, 1945,* VI, 1195–1202, 1231–35; Truman to Attorney Gen. T. C. Clark, Oct. 25, 1945, AG 093 Philippines (10-25-45); *New York Times,* Aug. 24, 1945; Thorpe, *East Wind Rain,* 162–63; Steinberg, *Philippine Collaboration,* 122–33, 172–76; Buss, "Philippines," 56–59.

21. Bernstein, *Philippine Story,* 204–05.

22. Blamey, Appreciation [Report] on Operations of the AMF in New Guinea, New Britain and the Solomon Islands, May 18, 1945, in Long, *Final Campaigns,* 609–10.

23. Buggy, *Pacific Victory,* 276–83; OPD, Pacific Ops., 11, 68–70, 84, 108–09; Bateson, *War with Japan,* 381–82; Vader, *New Guinea,* 147–55; Kirby, et al., *War Against Japan,* V, 132–34; Walker, *Island Campaigns,* 332–33; Long, *Final Campaigns,* 269.

24. S. E. Benson, *The Story of the 42 Aust. Inf. Bn.*, 157–58, quoted in Long, *Final Campaigns*, 238.

25. Hasluck, *Government and People*, 569–76; Brisbane *Courier-Mail*, Sept. 7, 1944; Melbourne *Herald*, Mar. 17, 1945; Kirby, *et al.*, *War Against Japan*, V, 134; Long, *MacArthur*, 118.

26. The messages of Apr. 21 and 23, 1945, are quoted in Acting Prime Min. Joseph B. Chifley to DM, Apr. 30, 1945, RG 4, MMBA.

27. GCM to DM, Mar. 2, 1945, RG 4, MMBA; Coakley and Leighton, *Global Logistics*, 574.

28. Blamey to Shedden, Feb. 19, 1945, in Long, *Final Campaigns*, 43–44.

29. Curtin to DM, Feb. 27, 1945, RG 4, MMBA.

30. DM to Curtin, Mar. 5, 1945, *ibid.*

31. SWPA G-3 Staff Studies, Oboe I–VI, Mar.–Apr., 1945, RG 3, MMBA; Eichelberger Diary, Mar. 3, Apr. 9, 28, 1945; DM Diary, Mar. 13–14, May 4–5, 1945; Leahy, *I Was There*, 438; Long, *Final Campaigns*, 50; Hasluck, *Government and People*, 558–60, 577–82.

32. DM Diary, Mar. 10, 1945; Sherwood, *Roosevelt and Hopkins*, II, 525–26; int., Handy, Hull, Ritchie; Cline, *Washington Command Post*, 307–08; Morris Janowitz, *The Professional Soldier: A Social and Political Portrait* (Glencoe, 1960), 291–302.

33. Luvaas, ed., *Dear Miss Em*, 99, 190, 251, 292.

34. DM to AGWAR, Jan. 27, 1945, RG 4, MMBA; Gen. Dwight D. Eisenhower to GCM, Sept. 25, 1944, in Joseph P. Hobbs, ed., *Dear General: Eisenhower's Wartime Letters to Marshall* (Baltimore, 1971), 207.

35. *New York Times*, Feb. 19, 1932; int., Mashbir; Robert G. Albion and Robert H. Connery, *Forrestal and the Navy* (New York, 1962), 260–61; Demetrios Caraley, *The Politics of Military Unification: A Study of Conflict and the Policy Process* (New York, 1966), 92; Vincent Davis, *Postwar Defense Policy and the U.S. Navy, 1943–1946* (Chapel Hill, 1966), 140–42; Paul Hammond, *Organizing for Defense: The American Military Establishment in the Twentieth Century* (Princeton, 1961), 162–64; Walter Millis, *Arms and the State: Civil-Military Elements in National Policy* (New York, 1958), 146–47.

36. Coakley and Leighton, *Global Logistics*, 579–80; Morton, *Pacific Command*, 25–26.

37. T. B. O'Steen to Sen. Claude Pepper, Feb. 13, 1945, RG 3, MMBA; O'Laughlin to DM, Sept. 1, 1944; John Coggeshall to Gov. Thomas E. Dewey, Sept. 14, 1944; Wood to DM, Oct. 13, 1944, and May 6, 1945, RG 10, MMBA; "Destination Tokyo," *Newsweek*, XXIV (Feb. 19, 1945), 33.

38. DM to GCM, Dec. 17, 1944, RG 4, MMBA.

39. JCS to DM and Nimitz, Apr. 5, 6, 1945, *ibid.*; Leahy, *I Was There*, 238; Frye, *Marshall*, 364; Kenney, *Kenney Reports*, 533; Reynolds, *Fast Carriers*, 363–64; Coakley and Leighton, *Global Logistics*, 580–82;

Benis M. Frank and Henry I. Shaw, Jr., *Victory and Occupation* (HUSMCOWWII; Washington, 1968), 400–02; Ney, *Theater of Operations Headquarters*, 52–53. In his *Reminiscences*, 258, MacArthur expressed great sorrow over the death of Curtin, yet he strangely omitted any mention of the passing of his greatest benefactor during the years 1933–45, Roosevelt.

40. Coakley and Leighton, *Global Logistics*, 583, 607–08; Kenney, *Kenney Reports*, 537; Millis, ed., *Forrestal Diaries*, 45–46.
41. Willoughby, ed., *MacArthur Reports*, I, 368.
42. Coakley and Leighton, *Global Logistics*, 576–77, 591–93, 600–10, 619–20; Huston, *Sinews of War*, 557–59; Wardlow, *Transportation Corps*, 174–76; Millett, *Army Service Forces*, 88–89; U.S. State Dept., *The Conference of Berlin (The Potsdam Conference), 1945* (FRUSDP; 2 vols., Washington, 1960), I, 823; DM Diary, May 15–16, Aug. 1, 1945.
43. Arnold Diary, June 17, 1945. See also Arnold's summary remarks on his visit to Manila in *Global Mission*, 568–71.

CHAPTER XVII. *"South to Borneo, North to Tokyo"*
pages 731–792

1. Int., Smith, Bowser, Craig; Millis, ed., *Forrestal Diaries*, 26; Bartley, *Iwo Jima*, 41; Smith, *Coral and Brass*, 247–48; OPD, Pacific Ops., 179–81; Hoyt, *How They Won the War in the Pacific*, 492–93; Sherrod, *Marine Corps Aviation*, 382–83; Frank and Shaw, *Victory and Occupation*, 84; Goldstein, "Whitehead," 275–88.
2. Int., Christiansen.
3. Tokyo *Nippon Times*, Aug. 7, 10, 1945; Sherrod, *On to Westward*, 236; GHQ AFPAC communiqué, Aug. 5, 1945.
4. Int., Woodruff, Munson; DM Diary, May 26, June 18, 1945; Manila *Free Philippines*, June 9, 1945; Barbara W. Tuchman, *Stilwell and the American Experience in China, 1911–45* (New York, 1971), 518–21; Luvaas, ed., *Dear Miss Em*, 278, 286–87.
5. GCM to DM, June 19, 1945, RG 4, MMBA.
6. DM to GCM, June 19, 1945, *ibid.*
7. GCM to DM, June 20, 21, 1945; DM to Gen. Joseph W. Stilwell, June 20, 1945; Maj. Gen. Alexander D. Surles to DM, June 23, 1945, *ibid.*; Baltimore *Sun*, June 23, 1945.
8. Surles to DM, June 29, 1945, RG 4, MMBA; Luvaas, ed., *Dear Miss Em*, 237; GCM to DM, Aug. 3, 1945; DM to GCM, Aug. 3, 1945, RG 9, MMBA.
9. Potter and Nimitz, *Triumph in the Pacific*, 163; Morison, *Liberation of the Philippines*, 214; Kirby, *et al.*, *War Against Japan*, V, 126–27; Falk, *Liberation of the Philippines*, 133; SWPA G-3 Staff Studies, Victor I–V, Feb.–Apr., 1945, RG 3, MMBA.

10. Morison, *Liberation of the Philippines,* 214.
11. Smith, *Triumph in the Philippines,* 584–85.
12. McCartney, *Jungleers,* 132–57; Haugland, *AAF Against Japan,* 253–55; OPD, Pacific Ops., 163–67, 201–21; Boggs, *Marine Aviation,* 108–25.
13. Struble, Philippine Campaign, 7–9; 40th Div., *40th Div.,* 119–24.
14. Cronin, *Southern Cross,* 309–54; 40th Div., *40th Div.,* 125–38.
15. Int., Berkey, Britton; OPD, Pacific Ops., 168–69; Bruce Jacobs, "The Jungle Fighters: The Story of the Americal Division," *Saga,* July, 1947, 91–92; Cronin, *Southern Cross,* 265–308.
16. Int., Struble, Noble, Woodruff, Dahlen, Hutchison; Woodruff, "World War II," 67–84; Amory and Waterman, eds., *Surf and Sand,* 161–204; Eichelberger, *Jungle Road,* 224; McCartney, *Jungleers,* 158–66; Valtin, *Children of Yesterday,* 370–87.
17. GHQ AFPAC communiqué, July 5, 1945.
18. DM to Eichelberger, Apr. 21, 1945, RG 5, MMBA.
19. Luvaas, ed., *Dear Miss Em,* 248.
20. OPD, Pacific Ops., 175–78; Swan, *Spearheads,* 234–52; Buggy, *Pacific Victory,* 284–89; USSBS, *Thirteenth Air Force,* 15–16; Kirby, *et al., War Against Japan,* V, 134–36; Roskill, *War at Sea,* III, Pt. II, 358–59; Haugland, *AAF Against Japan,* 255–57; Vader, *New Guinea,* 156; Mayer, *MacArthur,* 143–44; Joe G. Taylor, "Close Air Support in the War Against Japan" [MS study, USAF Hist. Div., 1955], 326–36.
21. Chifley to DM, May 9, 10, 1945; DM to Chifley, May 10, 1945; Chifley, Statement to the Australian Parliament, May 10, 1945, RG 4, MMBA; Melbourne *Herald,* May 9, 1945; Sydney *Morning Herald,* May 9, 1945.
22. Chifley to DM, May 18, 20, 1945, and DM to Chifley, May 20, 1945, quoted in Long, *Final Campaigns,* 388–89.
23. Buggy, *Pacific Victory,* 389–98; Bateson, *War with Japan,* 382–84; OPD, Pacific Ops., 172–74; Roskill, *War at Sea,* III, Pt. II, 359–62; Kirby, *et al., War Against Japan,* V, 136–37.
24. Long, *Final Campaigns,* 547.
25. *Ibid.;* Luvaas, ed., *Dear Miss Em,* 260; Willoughby and Chamberlain, *MacArthur,* 275.
26. The description of MacArthur's trip, June 3–15, 1945, is based on int., Kenney, Woodruff, Fellers, Hutchison, Faillace, Egeberg; DM Diary, June 3–15, 1945; Fellers to Barbey, Nov. 2, 1966, Barbey Papers; Manila *Free Philippines,* June 15, 1945; London *Times,* June 12, 1945; Eichelberger, *Jungle Road,* 238–45; Kenney, *Kenney Reports,* 550–56; Whitney, *MacArthur,* 196–97; Cronin, *Southern Cross,* 384; McCartney, *Jungleers,* 1.
27. Woodruff, "World War II," 79.
28. Other than Barbey's description cited in the following note, details of MacArthur's trip, June 27–July 3, 1945, can be found in int., Kenney, Fellers, Faillace, Egeberg; DM Diary, June 27–July 3, 1945; Fellers to

Barbey, Nov. 2, 1966, Barbey Papers; Kenney, *Kenney Reports*, 561–62; Gill, *Royal Australian Navy, 1942–45*, 652, 654; Manila *Free Philippines*, July 4, 1945.

29. Barbey, *MacArthur's Amphibious Navy*, 319–20.
30. DM, *Reminiscences*, 261, 262; *New York Times*, Apr. 6, Oct. 21, 1955.
31. GCM to FDR, Jan. 23, 1945, CCS 381 Japan (10-4-43) Sec. 6; DM Diary, Feb. 24, 28, 1945; Washington *Post*, Mar. 25, Oct. 20, 1955; *New York Times*, Oct. 21, 1955; Millis, ed., *Forrestal Diaries*, 30–32; Sherwood, *Roosevelt and Hopkins*, II, 512; John L. Snell, ed., *The Meaning of Yalta: Big Three Diplomacy and the New Balance of Power* (Baton Rouge, 1956), 153–54, 201–02; Athan G. Theoharis, *The Yalta Myths: An Issue in U.S. Politics, 1945–1955* (Columbia, Mo., 1970), 204–06; Leahy, *I Was There*, 318–19; Herbert Feis, *The Atomic Bomb and the End of World War II* (rev. ed., Princeton, 1966), 6–7, 8–9, 13–14; Louis Morton, "Soviet Intervention in the War with Japan," *Foreign Affairs*, XL (July, 1962), 658; Greenfield, *American Strategy*, 21–22. MacArthur's office diary cites the meetings with Lincoln and Forrestal but not the one with Freeman.
32. Coakley and Leighton, *Global Logistics*, 563–64, 568, 578, 584–88, 591–95, 609–11, 617–18; U.S. State Dept., *Conference of Berlin*, I, 903–10, 929–31, II, 1239, 1313–18, 1336–41, 1462–71; USSBS, *Fifth Air Force*, 37–38; King and Whitehill, *King*, 598, 605, 610–11; Frank and Shaw, *Victory and Occupation*, 402–03; Leahy, *I Was There*, 385; Leslie R. Groves, *Now It Can Be Told: The Story of the Manhattan Project* (New York, 1962), 263–64; GCM to DM, Apr. 12, 1945, RG 4, MMBA.
33. DM to GCM, Apr. 20, 1945, RG 4, MMBA.
34. GHQ AFPAC G-3 Staff Study, Olympic: Operations in Southern Kyushu, 2nd ed., May 28, 1945, RG 4, MMBA; Sams, "Medic," 330–37; John A. Kraft, Jr., "The Battle [Olympic and Coronet plans]," *V.F.W. Magazine*, Sept., 1945, 34–37.
35. GHQ AFPAC G-3 Staff Study, Coronet, 2nd ed., Aug. 15, 1945, RG 4, MMBA; Joint Intelligence Committee, Report on Japanese Capabilities Post-Coronet, June 9, 1945, CCS 381 POA (4-21-45); Willoughby, ed., *MacArthur Reports*, I, 423; Ehrman, *Grand Strategy*, VI, 268–71; Stanley W. Dzuiban, *Military Relations Between the United States and Canada, 1939–1945* (USAWWII; Washington, 1959), 269; New Zealand Dept. of Internal Affairs, War History Branch, *Documents Relating to New Zealand's Participation in the Second World War* (OHNZSWW; 3 vols., Wellington, 1949–63), III, 496.
36. Samuel E. Morison, *Victory in the Pacific, 1945* (HUSNOWWII; Boston, 1960), 353–55; Willoughby, ed., *MacArthur Reports*, I, Supplement, 1–12; Willoughby and Chamberlain, *MacArthur*, 289.
37. U.S. State Dept., *The Axis in Defeat: A Collection of Documents on*

American Policy Toward Germany and Japan (Washington, 1945), 27–33; Morison, *Victory in the Pacific,* 336–53; Feis, *Atomic Bomb,* 66–149; Truman, *Memoirs,* I, 427–33; Albion and Connery, *Forrestal,* 178–79; Mashbir, *American Spy,* 354–68; USSBS, *The Effects of Strategic Bombing on Japanese Morale* (Washington, 1947), 149–50; Robert J. C. Butow, *Japan's Decision to Surrender* (Stanford, 1954), 142–250; Toshikazu Kase, *Journey to the Missouri,* ed. David N. Rowe (New Haven, 1950), 240–58.

38. James J. Halsema to author, Nov. 16, 1970.

39. Int., Willoughby, Mashbir; Col. Virgil Ney, July 6, 1971; Manila *Free Philippines,* Aug. 12, 1945; DM Diary, Aug. 7, 1945; Considine, *It's All News to Me,* 342–43; Feis, *Atomic Bomb,* 99–100; Gar Alperovitz, *Atomic Diplomacy: Hiroshima and Potsdam; The Use of the Atomic Bomb and the American Confrontation with Soviet Power* (New York, 1967), 239.

40. Truman, *Memoirs,* I, 438–45; U.S. State Dept., *Foreign Relations, 1945,* V. 634–35; Woodward, *British Foreign Policy,* 572.

41. Directive to the Supreme Commander for the Allied Powers, Aug. 15, 1945, RG 5, MMBA. See also GCM to DM, Aug. 15, 16, 1945, RG 9, MMBA.

42. DM to Truman, Aug. 15, 1945, RG 9, MMBA. For the many congratulatory messages MacArthur received upon his SCAP appointment, see RG 5 and RG 9, MMBA.

43. Int., Marshall, Mashbir; GCM to DM, Aug. 13, 1945, RG 9, MMBA; SCAP, Documents Presented at Manila, P.I., 19 and 20 August 1945 to Japanese Representatives . . . RG 5, MMBA; Mashbir, *American Spy,* 278–310; Cline, *Washington Command Post,* 350; Bergamini, *Japan's Imperial Conspiracy,* 124–26. See misc. messages between MacArthur and the Japanese government, Aug. 15–29, 1945, RG 9, MMBA.

44. GHQ AFPAC G-3, Monthly Summary of Ops., Sept., 1945, RG 4, MMBA; Edward J. Smith to author, Sept. 27, Oct. 12, Nov. 8, 1971, enclosing excerpts of notes of Maj. Gen. William H. Gill and photocopies of Gill's correspondence with Yamashita, Aug. 27–31, 1945; U.S. State Dept., *Foreign Relations, 1945,* VI, 670–71, 1037–39, VII, 495–98; Blakeley, *32d Div.,* 266–75; Roskill, *War at Sea,* III, Pt. II, 382–84; Kirby, et al., *War Against Japan,* V, 236; Samuel E. Morison, *Supplement and General Index* (HUSNOWWII; Boston, 1962), 3–6; Bergamini, *Japan's Imperial Conspiracy,* 1047.

45. Japanese Government to DM, Aug. 17, 24, 28, 31, 1945, RG 9, MMBA; Lt. Gen. Kuzma N. Derevyanko to Mrs. DM, Aug. 30, 1945, RG 10, MMBA; Amb. John R. Deane to DM, Aug. 23, 26, 29, 1945; GCM to DM, Aug. 17, 1945; DM to GCM, Aug. 18, 1945, CCS 381 Japan (10-4-43) Sec. 9; U.S. State Dept., *Conference of Berlin,* I, 223–24, II, 408, 412–13; DM Diary, Aug. 26, 1945; *New York Times,* Aug. 27,

1945; McNeill, *America, Britain, and Russia,* 640–44; Wardlow, *Transportation Corps,* 297–98; Haugland, *AAF Against Japan,* 489–94; John R. Deane, *The Strange Alliance: The Story of Our Efforts at Wartime Co-operation with Russia* (New York, 1947), 272–85.

46. DM to GCM, Apr. 7, May 16, 30, 1945, RG 4, MMBA; Joint Civil Affairs Committee, Report on Responsibility for Military Government in Japan, Apr. 29, 1945, CCS 383.21 Japan (3-13-45) Sec. 1; U.S. State Dept., *Axis in Defeat,* 107–14; Hugh Borton, *American Presurrender Planning for Postwar Japan* (New York, 1967), 1–37; Bergamini, *Japan's Imperial Conspiracy,* 128–31; Sherwood, *Roosevelt and Hopkins,* II, 526; Feis, *Atomic Bomb,* 160–63.

47. Sutherland to Col. Charles T. Tench, Aug. 21, 1945, RG 5, MMBA; Tench to DM, Aug. 28, 1945, RG 9, MMBA; int., Swing, Britton, Sams, Munson, Elmore, Fellers, Egeberg, Mashbir, Bowers, Faillace; Flanagan, *Angels,* 153–54; Mashbir, *American Spy,* 311–13; Sherman, *Combat Command,* 377–78; Halsey and Bryan, *Halsey's Story,* 274–81; Toland, *Rising Sun,* II, 1069–71; William Craig, *The Fall of Japan* (New York, 1967), 285–95.

48. Eichelberger, *Jungle Road,* 262–63; Whitney, *MacArthur,* 215.

49. Int., Swing, Britton, Mashbir; Yoshio Kodama, *I Was Defeated,* trans. Taro Fukuda (Tokyo, 1949), 186–88.

50. Int., Wedemeyer, Whitney, Mashbir; Stimson to DM, Aug. 21, 1945; DM to Stimson, Aug. 21, 1945, RG 9, MMBA; James, ed., *South to Bataan, North to Mukden,* 186–87; Whitney, *MacArthur,* 216–17.

51. Int., Fellers, Mashbir, Faillace; Mashbir, *American Spy,* 320–34; Kase, *Journey,* 4–9; Halsey and Bryan, *Halsey's Story,* 281–82; War Diary of U.S.S. *Buchanan,* 1–3 Sept., 1945, 1, NHD; Sherman, *Combat Command,* 379–82.

52. Willoughby, ed., *MacArthur Reports,* I, 455.

53. U.S. State Dept., *Axis in Defeat,* 33–37; Tokyo *Nippon Times,* Sept. 3, 1945; Mashbir, *American Spy,* 324–26; Kase, *Journey,* 9–10; Halsey and Bryan, *Halsey's Story,* 282–84; Tuchman, *Stilwell,* 522; Winton, *Forgotten Fleet,* 352–54; U.S. National Archives, *Public Papers of the Presidents of the United States: Harry S. Truman; Containing the Public Messages, Speeches, and Statements of the President, April 12 to December 31, 1945* (Washington, 1961), 254–57. The number of carrier aircraft involved in the fly-over on Sept. 2, 1945, was actually about 450.

Kenney said MacArthur used six pens to write his signature, later giving them to Wainwright, Percival, Mrs. MacArthur, and the archives of the U.S. military and naval academies, and retaining one himself.

54. DM, *Reminiscences,* 275–76.

INDEX

Index

Abaya, Hernando J., 892
Abcede, Lt. Col. Salvador, 745
Abra Valley, Luzon, 688
Abucay, Luzon, 52, 55, 67, 649, 802
"Abucay Withdrawal" (Lee), 67
Abuyog, Leyte, 573
Acoje Chromite Company, Luzon, 892
Adachi, Lt. Gen. Hatazo, 238, 328, 337, 376, 443-44, 447-48, 483-85, 705
A-day, Leyte, 552-54, 558-59, 570, 573, 592, 884
Adelaide, Australia, 107-9, 114, 179, 797
Admiralty Islands, 330-31, 334, 346, 364, 481; ops., 377-87; Manus dispute, 387-91, 722
Advance New Guinea Force, 210
Adversario, Sgt. Domingo, 73
Africa, 50, 761
Afua, Neth. New Guinea, 485
Agno River, 26, 39, 41, 622-23
Agoo, Luzon, 683
A-Gō Operation, 457, 461-62
Aguinaldo, Emilio, 92, 892
Agusan Valley, Mindanao, 748
Ah Cheu, 74-75, 100, 102, 245, 660, 663, 840
Aircraft, Northern Solomons (AIRNORSOLS), 497
Air Medal, 864
Aitape, N.E. New Guinea, 355, 360, 457, 615, 702; ops., 444-45, 447, 449, 453, 455, 483-86, 490; DM visits, 453, 800
Akers, Ensign A. B., 840

Akin, Maj. Gen. Spencer B., 80, 100, 101, 122, 444, 554, 668, 796, 840
Alamo Force, 312-13, 343, 346, 499, 711, 862. See also U.S. Army: Sixth Army
Alamogordo, N.M., 772
Alaska, 222
Albany, N.Y., 403
Aleutian Islands, 167, 211, 216, 222, 305, 358. See also Alaska; Attu; Kiska
Alexishafen, N.E. New Guinea, 376, 449, 483, 490
Algeria, 214
Alice Springs, Australia, 107-8, 797
Allen, Maj. Gen. Arthur S., 229, 236-37
Allen, Frederick Lewis, 416, 417
Allied Air Forces (SWPA): under Brett, 121, 156-66, 179-80, 197-98; under Kenney, 198-201, 211, 218, 223, 225-26, 281-82, 292-303, 311-14, 320-21, 324-25, 337, 339, 495, 546. See also U.S. Army Air Forces: Fifth Air Force, Thirteenth Air Force; Royal Australian Air Force
Allied Central Bureau (SWPA), 177
Allied Geographical Section (SWPA), 178, 224
Allied Intelligence Bureau (SWPA), 178, 508-9
Allied Land Forces (SWPA), 121, 253-57, 312-13, 499, 711. See also Australian Army; U.S. Army: Sixth Army, Eighth Army
Allied Munitions Assignments Board, 469